A
Rhetoric
Case Book

Francis Connolly

FORDHAM UNIVERSITY

HARCOURT,
BRACE
AND COMPANY
New York

Contents

Contents: Selections

iv

PART TWO
Arrangement and Style in the Whole Composition

SECTION XII   DESCRIPTION

SECTION XIII   NARRATION

Contents: Selections   ix

A Note to the Instructor

The purpose of this book is to provide the beginning student with principles, models, and exercises that will help him learn how to communicate his ideas effectively. It assumes that the average student is able to master the methods of rhetorical analysis, arrangement, and style, and that this mastery is most effectively achieved and developed by combining the study of principles and the analysis of models with the extensive practice of original composition.

The plan selected to accomplish this purpose is this:

1. To begin each section with a brief, clear statement and definition of rhetorical principles, and thus to prepare the student for the discovery of these principles in the examples that follow;
2. To analyze the examples or cases and to derive the rhetorical principle or principles that each example contains;
3. To provide the student with a graduated series of intensive exercises in rhetorical analysis and in original composition, based upon examples or cases.

Behind this plan, however, are certain convictions on the art of rhetoric. Rhetoric, as Genung remarks, does not exist by itself. It is the art of writing or speaking clearly, interestingly, and effectively. It involves the use of language and therefore is directly related to grammar or the rules of language. Since it is essentially concerned with statement and demonstration, it is clearly connected with logic, or the rules of thought. Insofar as rhetoric deals with human communications—and human communications are never wholly impersonal—it frequently strays into the area of poetry. Who among us cannot find in Churchill, in H. S. Commager, in Newman, in Parkman, even in the colder lucidities of Barbara Ward, flares of imagination and emotion which light up rather than darken their communication to the human intelligence?

Neither does rhetoric ignore psychology or the social habits of the body of readers a writer addresses. Indeed, many of the great teachers of rhetoric, Aristotle among them, devote great attention to the analysis of the emotions, prejudices, and ignorance of the audience. The new science of semantics, explained in Section VI, is largely concerned with the psychological and social attitudes of readers and writers alike. Ethics too crosses the art of rhetoric, for the character of a writer, evidenced in his honesty of purpose, his fairness to his opponents, his humility in the face of his own limitations, his magnanimous toleration of small or mean or ignorant attacks in the interest of a common good, are sometimes more convincing than the technical mastery of arguments. Indeed, as Longinus nobly asserted, and as others have continued to observe throughout the centuries, great writing is the utterance of great souls.

Writing then has clear connections with grammar, logic, poetry, psychology, sociology, ethics; let us add, with all the arts and sciences. The greater the person and the more he knows, the better his capacity as a writer, and our great writers all compel us to share their appetite for the immense variety of human interests. Nothing is alien to the writer.

Nevertheless, rhetoric, despite its multiple connections with all the arts and sciences, has its own special province. It is not a vagrant art begging for shelter in the mansions of philosophy or the halls of history. It rightfully possesses the title of science because it has discovered and organized its own body of principles without, one must add, degenerating into a pedantic or mechanical accuracy. It is more obviously an art because writers have constantly engaged in the practice of speaking and writing excellently. If this is not immediately evident, consider the armies of correct grammarians, expert logicians, trained historical scholars, eminent social scientists, and even edifying divines who write badly or certainly less effectively than becomes their genuine knowledge or lofty purpose. No one will suppose that these writers of a tired jargon fail simply through lack of imagination alone, or lack of vision, or of the poetic spark. Some poets have written dull, awkward, and incoherent prose. Knowing a subject, even oneself, and knowing the best way to express the subject in effective prose are separate but related skills. Knowing a subject is a matter of observation and reflection; knowing how to express oneself well requires in addition a faculty of making or doing, a command of the medium of language in which observations and reflections may be set forth for the common understanding of human society. If you have nothing to say the command of rhetoric will not cover your ignorance. But if you have something to say, however humble it may be, the command of rhetoric will enable you to express it.

Very probably there were many master mariners who knew seamanship as well as, or better than, Joseph Conrad. One doesn't doubt that some of them might have excelled Conrad in a Board of Trade examination in navigation. But it is most unlikely that they could have written their own versions of life at sea. For their knowledge did not contain the habitual knowledge of the artist, the knowing how to express his knowledge, which is the command of rhetoric.

METHOD

As we have mentioned above, the plan of this book centers on the *cases, examples.* To keep the student aware of the relevance of these examples and their logical interconnection, each group of examples is preceded by a brief statement of the rhetorical principle it illustrates. Each section (i.e., chapter) begins with relatively brief and simple examples. The comment and analysis that follow each example are graduated in intensity. Throughout the earlier sections they stress diction, definition, sentence structure, and paragraph development. Simple outlining is introduced in Section III. Beginning with the review exercises after Section VII, the comment and analysis stress the combining of the various forms of analysis in the whole composition.

Repetition and review are essential features of this text. Thus there are exercises in diction, sentence style, and paragraph analysis in Section XV as well as in Section II. Furthermore, the basic methods of analysis, developed separately in Part One, are re-examined in Part Two. Similarly, the principles of arrangement and style developed in Section VIII appear throughout Sections IX-XV. In like fashion, exposition, treated as a form of discourse in Sections IX and X, is reconsidered in its relation to argument, persuasion, and the other forms of discourse treated in later sections. So too, the outline, explained briefly in Section III, is employed extensively in Part Two. This emphasis on repetition rests on the belief that progress in composition is less a matter of learning new and unusual techniques than it is a matter of intensifying one's knowledge of basic principles.

The rhetorical terminology throughout is uniform but not rigid. The editor has occasionally used alternative phrases, such as deductive reasoning for syllogism, not only to avoid using an expression better explained in another place but also to encourage some flexibility in the student's attitude toward his subject. For this reason, too, numerous samples of the informal summary, as well as the formal topical, sentence, and paragraph outlines, will be found in this text.

The editor is acutely aware that some rhetoricians once garroted rhetoric with irrelevant theory. Hence the logical elements, especially those pertaining to formal reasoning, have been made practical for the beginning student. This book attempts to explore only those theoretical points that are immediately derived from the examples. For this reason certain traditional devices (conjugates, for instance) no longer employed by good modern writers, certain grace notes associated with a lingering taste for elegant variation, have been largely omitted. Other traditional preoccupations of rhetoricians, like the procedures of legal and deliberative oratory, have been sacrificed with mere mention in the interests of subject matter more within the range of the beginning student.

Because this book relies so heavily on the explication of the examples, or cases, much of its value depends on the use of the exercises in analysis and composition. The explanation of the many texts is contained in the introductions to each section, in the outlines, the comment, and the brief parenthetical remarks placed among the exercises themselves. But the full discovery of the principles and the development of the habits these principles engender depend on the full use of the exercises. Here it is the instructor who must decide how much or how little he will demand, whether to pursue fully the rules of a scientific induction or to probe a fallacy to its original deviation from logical method or to wring still another meaning from a metaphor.

Hence this book, like all textbooks, is a collaborative effort in which the editor, like the producer of a play, selects and arranges the material and provides as much help as he can to the director and the actors. But the instructor and the students will interpret the drama, rehearse their parts, and present the action according to their own good judgment. The final performance is theirs alone. This idea of collaboration, which involves a profound sense of dependence on his colleagues, the editor has kept firmly before him.

HANDBOOK REFERENCES

For those who wish to use a supplementary handbook with A RHETORIC CASE BOOK, there have been provided throughout the text specific references to the current editions of five leading handbooks of English: *Writing and Thinking,* Fifth Edition, by Norman Foerster,

J. M. Steadman, Jr., and James B. McMillan (Houghton Mifflin, 1952); *Harbrace College Handbook,* Third Edition, by John C. Hodges (Harcourt, Brace, 1951); *The Macmillan Handbook of English,* Revised Edition, by John M. Kierzek (The Macmillan Company, 1947); *Writer's Guide and Index to English,* Revised Edition, by Porter G. Perrin (Scott, Foresman, 1950); and *The Harper Handbook of College Composition* by George S. Wykoff and Harry Shaw (Harper, 1952).

The footnote references to these handbooks are listed alphabetically by authors. Numbers in italics refer to sections; numbers in roman type refer to pages.

ACKNOWLEDGMENTS

For the predominant method this book contains, namely its dependence on cases or examples, the author is indebted to the whole fellowship of rhetoricians and linguists, from Aristotle to C. C. Fries. He is particularly indebted to Professor Francis P. Donnelly (Fordham) to whom he dedicates this book in gratitude for his scholarly books on rhetoric, for the skill of his teaching, for the graciousness of his conversation.

Among other persons who have helped in various ways to make this book more useful to the student, the author wishes to thank Professors G. J. Cronin, W. F. Lynch, and Joseph O'Neill. The author is grateful to Mr. Avery Dulles for reading the sections on logic and to Dr. William O'Connor for reading the material pertaining to science. He acknowledges a special debt of gratitude to Mary K. Connolly, Jean Colmcillson, and Consilia Buxum Collis for their intensive testing of every precept and exercise this book contains.

F. C.

PART ONE

The Subject,
and the Basic Methods of Analysis

SECTION
I

Preliminaries: The Four Elements of Rhetoric

WHAT RHETORIC IS

Rhetoric is simply the art of writing well. Rhetoric points out and illustrates the rules for presenting ideas in clear, vigorous, and interesting prose. It tells us, and shows us, how a writer can communicate his thoughts and impressions effectively to a reader. The study of rhetoric leads us step by step from the initial problem of delimiting a subject to the final problem of expressing that subject in an appropriate style.

WHAT YOU ALREADY KNOW ABOUT RHETORIC

Clearly, then, you as a student already know a good deal about rhetoric. For one thing, you know that the three qualities of effective style are clarity, vigor, and interest. Ever since you entered high school these three basic rules of style have in one way or another been kept before you.

Stretch your memory back to your first class in high school English. You were writing a short theme on baseball, the subject you knew best at the time. You wanted to say that Bob Feller hurried his pitch to Hodges because Reese, on third base, threatened to steal home with the tying run. But you wanted to be impressive, and so you searched out a new word in the dictionary and you wrote, "Bob Feller accelerated the next pitch, fearing Reese would pilfer home."

1

Only later, after you had had occasion to discuss the theme with your teacher, did you discover that "accelerated" is neither *exact* nor *idiomatic;* nor had you in this sentence made *clear* whether you were referring to the speed of the pitch itself or to the speed with which Feller delivered the pitch. Moreover, you learned that "fearing," as used here, is a misplaced modifier, that the sentence is not fully coherent, that "pilfer" is jargon.

On other occasions you learned that in some contexts a general word like *walked* is less appropriate than a specific word like *staggered* or that certain expressions like "cold as ice" and "hot as fire" are hackneyed.

Thus you learned from a curriculum spiced with rhetoric that there were higher degrees of accuracy in words and expressions than mere grammatical correctness. Think back to those times, and you will discover that there is indeed a good deal that you already know about rhetoric.

Do you remember these rules for good *sentences?*

On Clearness. To achieve clarity make your sentences unified and coherent. A sentence is unified when all its parts contribute to a single main idea or impression.

Place words together in their logical relationship. Use parallel structure and maintain a consistent point of view to assure coherence.

On Vigor or Emphasis. Use concrete, specific words rather than general expressions.

For vividness use figurative or imaginative language.

Use idiomatic expressions rather than bookish or literary language to give your writing the tang of speech.

Emphasize important ideas by placing them prominently in the sentence. Use balanced sentences to make a contrast effective.

On Interest. Pay attention to the sound structure of your sentences. A good sentence should have rhythm and melody.

Do you remember, too, these rules for the *paragraph?*

On Clearness. Make your paragraph clear by relating each sentence to the topic sentence, i.e., the sentence that expresses the central thought. Link the sentences within the paragraph by repeating key words, by using transitions, by using parallel structure. Avoid an unnecessary shift in point of view.

On Vigor. Make your paragraph striking by placing important ideas at the beginning or at the end of the paragraph, by spending more time on the main idea than on the subordinate ideas, by using a climactic order whenever possible.

On Interest. Sentences should be varied in length and structure to avoid dullness.

Include as many illustrative details as possible.

Certainly you have seen these rules before.* They are the fundamental, age-old rhetorical rules for sentences and paragraphs. You will be reminded of them again and again because these same rules apply to the study of the whole composition, with which we are particularly concerned in this book.

Our study of the whole composition will embrace four steps:

1. The selection of a subject
2. The analysis of a subject and the selection of a central theme
3. The arrangement of this analyzed material in the best order
4. The expression of thoughts in the best possible language

THE FIRST ELEMENT OF RHETORIC: THE SELECTION OF A SUBJECT

Your first task as a writer is the selection of a *subject*. The subject is *what you write about*.

At first glance, therefore, the subject hardly seems to deserve discussion. You will say that there is no difficulty about the subject; the subject is assigned. The teacher lists a topic or a group of topics and then tells you how to write about one of them. Last year, for instance, you had to write a theme on Columbus. You were told to explain why he was important to you. You were told—

But it is already clear that the term *subject* as used in this chapter may have a different meaning from the one you have attached to it. As used above, the word *subject* refers to a general topic, an area of investigation, a whole continent, so to speak. But what we mean by subject is a special phase of that general topic, not the continent but a smaller area, a section of the general topic that can be fully explored.

A general topic therefore is not the same as a subject in our restricted sense of the term. Thus, for example, the term "Columbus," understood in all its possible meanings and references, is a general topic,

* If you need a more detailed review of these rules consult your handbook: Foerster, pp. 3-71; Hodges, *23-31;* Kierzek, pp. 31-112; Perrin, pp. 169-302; Wykoff, *51-80.* (As is explained in the Note to the Instructor [pp. xiii-xiv] references are made to five leading handbooks. Italicized numbers refer to *sections,* roman numbers to pages.)

an area of investigation, a whole continent. To explain everything about the term "Columbus" would require many volumes. Now Columbus, understood in this broad sense, was not really the *subject* of your composition. In your composition you didn't include everything that is known about Columbus. You wrote about his importance to you. More than likely you wrote about one aspect, or phase, of Columbus—his discovery of America, perhaps. This small segment of the total meaning of Columbus was your *real subject*. Columbus, understood in the broad sense, was the *general* topic; Columbus, narrowed down to the discoverer of America, was *your* subject.

There are several important reasons for driving home the distinction between the general topic or area of investigation (which we have compared to a continent) and the *real subject*, or the special phase of the general topic (which we have compared to a specific spot that you are going to explore intensively). One reason is that any writer must write about what he knows. You are not expected to know everything about large topics. To know all there is to know about Columbus is a lifetime job for a specialist. But you can write honestly and effectively about the phase of Columbus that you know intimately, or that you can learn about with reasonable effort.

A second reason for distinguishing between a general topic or area of investigation and the real subject is this: a subject, as opposed to a general topic, must be specifically adapted to the needs of an *occasion* and to the writer's *purpose*.

Occasion

By *occasion* we mean the context, or the set of circumstances, that governs your choice of a subject. Thus, for example, the specific *audience* you address is one circumstance that affects your choice of a subject. "Columbus, the Discoverer of America" is an appropriate subject for a high school audience; it would be a trite subject in an historical journal read by advanced students. Another circumstance affecting your choice of subject is the requisite *length* of your composition. A good subject for a 3000-word term paper on Columbus is not necessarily a good subject for a 500-word weekly composition. The student will find the adjustment of the subject to the length of the composition one of his great and continuing problems. Still other circumstances affecting a choice of subject are the availability of research material and the relevance of the subject to some particular event, such as a national holiday, an election, or a political crisis.

Purpose

By *purpose* we mean the writer's intention expressed in the questions: What is it I want to say about the subject? Do I want to state the principal facts about Columbus; that is, do I want to inform my audience in an exposition? Do I wish to convince them by argument? Do I wish to persuade or describe or narrate? Thus, purpose is equivalent to the writer's choice of one of the forms of discourse—exposition, argument, persuasion, description, or narration.

Hitherto you may have taken both *occasion* and *purpose* for granted. They were what we call "stock" occasions and "stock" purposes. Thus, the occasion was a class assignment. The audience was your teacher or your classmates. The length of your assignment was carefully prescribed. The topics assigned were restricted to your own immediate experiences. The purpose was stated in the assignment, as, for example, *explain* in about 300 words the results of Columbus' first voyage, or, *narrate* the principal events of Columbus' second voyage. Thus subject, occasion, and purpose were all presented at once, and your problem was solved for you in advance. You proceeded then to give some evidence of your ability to write correct prose. As a result, you may have been led to assume that at no time do subject, occasion, and purpose need investigation.

But in your present study you will find the opposite to be true. Here the topics will still be assigned and the occasion and the purpose indicated in the assignment. But you will also be asked to select your subjects in the light of specific rather than "stock" occasions and purposes. Thus you will be introduced gradually to realistic writing situations. In these situations you will not write merely to test your skill in the use of language. You will attempt rather to explain your subject for a *definite* purpose and a *definite* occasion.

Let us illustrate what this realistic writing situation means by showing how several writers in the light of specific occasions and clearly defined purposes have narrowed down the general topic, Columbus, to precise subjects.

The First Case. Recently a college president was asked to deliver the principal address before a society of Italian-Americans at a Columbus Day dinner. The speech, he was told, should not exceed forty minutes. He learned from the chairman on arrangements that in the last two years the principal speakers, both politicians, had mentioned Columbus merely in passing to ingratiate themselves with Italian voters, but had developed political topics at length. The college president then decided he could safely talk on the general topic, "Columbus."

But what phase of the topic should he consider? What aspect of Columbus was most appropriate to the *occasion?* Not a learned discussion of moot points in Columbus' biography, or a comparison between the interpretations offered by Columbus' two great biographers, Samuel Eliot Morison and Salvador de Madariaga. Such subjects would be of interest only to scholars. Nor would emphasis on Columbus' contribution to the Spanish empire be of great concern to Italian-Americans.

Clearly, this occasion permitted several *purposes:* the speaker could *narrate* the Columbus story in a popular and entertaining way; he could *argue* that Columbus was the most important of the explorers; he could *explain* how Columbus was a symbol of the Italian contribution to American culture. He chose the third purpose as most suitable to the occasion.

His occasion and purpose defined, he then searched for the precise aspects of the general topic, Columbus, that were best suited to the purpose and occasion. After considerable thought he decided that the precise aspects of Columbus' life that suited his purpose and the occasion were:

a. Columbus' scientific vision
b. His religious faith

The speaker then recognized that these traits of Columbus' character could be adapted to his Italian-American audience because both of these traits were an inheritance from the Italy of the Renaissance period. Thus, the *real subject* became "Columbus, a Man of Scientific Vision and of Religious Faith." This subject was suitable to the occasion—Columbus Day, a commemorative dinner, an audience of Italian-Americans. It was also suitable to the writer's purpose, that is, his intention to explain how Columbus was a symbol of the Italian contribution to American life.

Hence in our first case the writer proceeded from occasion to topic to purpose to subject. Notice how the selection of the subject was closely linked to the other two elements, occasion and purpose.

The Second Case. Mr. X, an authority on Columbus, was asked to prepare an expository article of about 3000 words for the Columbus Day issue of a popular weekly magazine. The only stipulation of the editor was that, "It should have some bearing on Columbus." In effect, then, the editor defined the author's topic (Columbus) and purpose (to explain). Upon investigation Mr. X found out that the average reader of the magazine was a woman, a college graduate, married, and a housewife. These circumstances, taken together with the purpose and the topic, suggested a subject to Mr. X, namely the story of Queen Isabella's donation of her jewels. Obviously, Mr. X thought, this romantic subject would interest women readers.

Then he remembered that the average reader was a college graduate. For a college graduate the old story of Isabella's gift to Columbus would be trite.

Mr. X respected facts. Hence he did not choose to embroider the old legend. He therefore discarded the story of the jewels.

Keeping his audience in mind, he next explored the idea of Columbus as a father. He narrowed this down to Columbus, the father, seen through the eyes of his sons. But this aspect of Columbus was still without focus. Precisely how did Columbus appear to his sons, Diego and Ferdinand Columbus? Mr. X then reviewed Don Ferdinand's memoirs about his father and concluded that Columbus appeared to his son as a stern but loving parent. The subject finally chosen was "Columbus, a Stern but Loving Father."

Thus the general topic "Columbus" was narrowed down to a specific subject that fitted the occasion and the purpose. Notice that the difference between the subject in Case 1 and Case 2 was dictated by the occasion and the purpose.

Notice that in Case 1 the writer proceeded from occasion to topic to purpose to subject. In Case 2, however, the writer proceeded from topic and purpose to occasion to subject.

The Third Case. Mr. Y, a college student, discovered S. E. Morison's biography of Columbus, *The Admiral of the Ocean Sea,* on a required reading list. The book excited him. Its rich and varied detail about the voyages, its sympathetic analysis of Columbus' character, and its emotional sweep aroused in him an admiration for the author's subject. Shortly after reading the book, Mr. Y decided to enter the public speaking contest at his college. The rules of the contest were: Speakers were to talk for fifteen minutes on a subject of general interest. The judges were to estimate the speech composition by asking, "What did the speaker intend to say? How well did he say it? Was it worth saying?"

Mr. Y thus had a well-defined occasion. He also had a general topic, Columbus. His real job was to define his purpose. What should he do?

Explain? Argue? Describe? Narrate? The topic provided material for all forms of discourse. His source, Morison's *The Admiral of the Ocean Sea,* provided leads in all these directions. Mr. Y studied the rules of the contest and found some light in the third query. Was it worth saying?

What was the most important thing to say about Columbus? The basis of Mr. Y's own admiration for Columbus was the Great Navigator's perseverance. Time and again Columbus was disappointed. For years his theories were rejected. Eventually his ideas were proved right. His mission in life succeeded even though he suffered neglect and misfortune. Certainly Columbus' perseverance was worth talking about.

Later Mr. Y found out that all his rivals had selected topics of contemporary interest, such as the Korean War, world peace, and political reform. An instructor advised him to bring his subject up to date by pointing out the relevance of Columbus to the present day. Mr. Y wrestled with his problem and finally decided on this phase of his subject: "Columbus' Perseverance, a Model for the Leaders of the United Nations." He perceived a similarity between the fifteenth-century prejudice against Columbus' ideas and the twentieth-century prejudice against world unity. This suggested the possibility of arguing that, just as Columbus succeeded in discovering the New World by perseverance, so the supporters of the United Nations might also succeed in establishing one world by perseverance.

Thus Mr. Y, also, found in the general topic, "Columbus," a specific subject in line with his purpose and occasion. He proceeded, however, from topic to occasion to purpose to subject.

Thus we may present the various procedures in the three cases in this diagram:

Case 1 → From occasion → to topic → to purpose → to subject
Case 2 → From topic and purpose → to occasion → to subject
Case 3 → From topic → to occasion → to purpose → to subject

SUMMARY

A subject is that phase of a general topic that is most suitable to an occasion and a purpose. An occasion is the set of circumstances that affect the composition, that is, the time, the place, the audience, and the extent of the composition. The purpose is the writer's choice of one of the five main types of discourse (exposition, argument, persuasion, description, and narration) to express his subject.

Exercises

1. Mention three aspects of the following general topics that might serve as the subject of a 500-word factual article of interest to your fellow students.

   Example: *General topic:* Conserving natural resources
            Subjects: Scientists in national defense
                   Flood control in the Missouri Valley
                   Irrigation in the Imperial Valley

   a. Study
   b. Good reading
   c. Recreation
   d. Social life
   e. Self-improvement
   f. Observation of nature
   g. Politics
   h. Sports
   i. Journalism
   j. Prejudice

2. Imagine an occasion suitable for a short exposition of about 500 words on each of the following specific subjects.

   Example: *Subject:* The Emancipation Proclamation
           Suitable occasion: A newspaper editorial on Lincoln's Birthday

   a. Making beet sugar
   b. The hibernation of bears
   c. Weighing anchor
   d. The working of a helicopter
   e. George Washington's generalship
   f. Hitler's death
   g. Romeo and Juliet
   h. A contrast between England and America
   i. Weekend guests
   j. Will Rogers

3. What specific subjects would be appropriate for each of the following purposes?

   Example: *Purpose:* To condemn totalitarianism
           Subject: The technique of the Big Lie

   a. To prove that reading is worthwhile
   b. To show the value of thrift
   c. To demonstrate the comforts of modern life
   d. To praise Abraham Lincoln's greatness
   e. To condemn racism
   f. To praise virtue
   g. To reform politics
   h. To abolish capital punishment

   i. To show the significance of the Civil War in American life

   j. To illustrate the high cost of living

4. What particular aspect of the general topic "Farming" would interest each of the following groups?

   a. Farmers   d. Real estate investors

   b. Economists   e. Painters

   c. Vacationers

5. What particular phase of the topic "American Indian" might interest each of the following groups:

   a. The adult movie-goer   c. The historian

   b. The social worker   d. The European

THE SECOND ELEMENT OF RHETORIC: ANALYZING A SUBJECT AND FINDING A THEME

We have discovered that the selection of the subject is the first step in the art of effective writing. Once the subject is selected, the student comes to the second step in composition, the analysis of the subject and the selection of a theme. Before he begins the actual task of composition the writer must know what his subject actually means, that is, *the main point to be developed,* the theme that unites the composition as the topic sentence unites the paragraph. But the central theme should not be chosen at random. It should be selected only after a careful *analysis* of the subject.

True, the preliminary study of the general topic in the light of the occasion and the purpose not only discovers the subject. As we have seen above, such a study sometimes hints at a possible theme. Thus the college president found his subject, "Columbus, a Man of Scientific Vision and of Religious Faith." He also found, in the idea of Columbus as a symbol of the Italian contribution to American culture, a possible theme for development.

Just as, in constructing a sentence, the student must choose the predicate for his subject, so in writing a whole composition he must choose the main point of his subject that he will predicate throughout. The central theme, then, is the predicate of the subject of the whole composition.

But only after his own ideas are fully clarified and he realizes the possibilities of his subject is the student in a position to decide with certainty what the central theme should be.

What Is Analysis? Analysis is the application of logic to the understanding of a subject under investigation. To analyze a subject logically is to know, as clearly and fully as possible,

1. What the subject means
2. What its causes and effects are, and
3. In certain cases, how the subject works

We fulfill these requirements of logical analysis when we

1. Define the subject
2. Classify and divide it
3. Give examples of it
4. Compare and contrast it with other subjects in the same class
5. Explain why it exists and what effects it creates (causal analysis)
6. Understand how it works (process analysis)

Each of these six methods of analysis is considered separately and at length in Sections II-VII of this book; combinations of these methods of analysis are treated in Sections VIII-XI. Here our principal aim is to show how an outline analysis of a subject by these methods helps the writer to select a suitable theme. Such an analysis will reveal many possible themes. The task of the student is to select that theme which is most appropriate to his purpose and occasion.

We shall also show that in using logical analysis to locate a central theme a writer necessarily discovers the means of *developing* the theme at the same time. A central theme, by definition, is what we predicate of the subject, *the main point to be developed*. Thus, if we discover the main point to be developed under the heading of causal analysis or process analysis or comparison and contrast, it follows that the theme may be developed by causal analysis or process analysis or comparison and contrast. The same logic that helps us to investigate a subject *before composition* applies also to the expression of our ideas on the subject in the actual composition itself. The analysis of the subject before composition is merely the logical preparation for its verbal expression.

Below we shall show how a theme that is discovered by examining a subject in the light of the various methods of analysis may be developed by that same method of analysis. This development will be indicated in parentheses.

Later, in Sections II-VII, as you master each of these methods of analysis, one by one, you will be shown in more detail how each method may help to develop a central theme or a subordinate theme in your composition.

Note: The six methods of analysis have three closely related uses: (1) They help you to analyze a subject and discover a central theme *before writing.* (2) They suggest methods of developing the theme in the *actual composition.* (3) They are also the means of analyzing the writings of others.

The Use of Analysis in Finding a Central Theme and a Method of Development. To show how the analysis of a subject by the six basic methods helps you to select a central theme, let us start with a topic such as "Universities," which is frequently treated in freshman composition during the first semester. The subject derived from this topic is "A Freshman Looks at Midwestern University." The occasion is a written composition of 500 words for class discussion. The purpose is to explain (exposition) one outstanding impression of Midwestern University. (You may choose to substitute your own university for Midwestern in the title.)

At first glance you may find this a bewildering subject. How are you to pick the one important theme; that is, what will you predicate of your subject throughout?

Be logical. Analyze your subject. Find out what are all the logical possibilities of the subject before selecting the central theme and the supporting ideas.

First, you may <u>*define*</u> the subject, Midwestern University. One definition of Midwestern is that it is an institution "devoted to advanced study, professional training, research, and the education of leaders." (R. M. HUTCHINS) Note that each element of this definition, namely *advanced study, professional training, research,* and *the education of leaders,* may also be defined. You may also explore other definitions by prominent educators. Thus from analysis by definition a student may derive themes such as the following:

1. Midwestern University is devoted to advanced study. (Develop by defining advanced study at Midwestern.)
2. Midwestern University educates leaders. (Develop by defining leaders.)

3. Midwestern University fosters research in its chemistry department. (Develop by defining research in the chemistry department.)

Second, the student may *classify or divide* the subject. Midwestern may be classified with other institutions of learning and with organizations such as research foundations, learned societies, academies of arts and letters. It may be divided into its component parts. Thus, the university considered as a group of men and women consists of administrative staff, faculty, student body, and custodial staff. Considered as a collection of schools, the university consists of the college of arts and science, the graduate school, the school of commerce, and so on. Each of these schools may be subdivided according to principal areas of study. Thus the college of liberal arts may be broken down into three main divisions: the humanities (philosophy, language, literature), the natural sciences (chemistry, biology, physics), and the social sciences (history, economics, sociology). Subdivision may be carried still further, as in the division of history into ancient history, medieval history, modern history; or as in the division of chemistry into organic and inorganic chemistry. Thus, from analysis by classification and division a student may derive themes like the following:

1. Midwestern University consists of many different schools and colleges. (Develop by dividing schools and colleges.)
2. Midwestern University offers a complete course in the humanities. (Develop by classifying or dividing the humanities.)
3. Midwestern University consists of several other groups besides the student body. (Develop by classifying and dividing the other groups at Midwestern, namely the faculty, administrative staff, and custodial staff.)

A *third* method of analysis is *exemplification*. Here the student may investigate specific examples of Midwestern's educational activity, such as the creative writing program, a project in atomic research, the university's record in providing leadership in cooperation with government and industry. Other illustrations of Midwestern's activity are the training in journalism provided by the school papers and magazines, and personal development of the students through dramatics, debating, and sports. Thus from analysis by exemplification a student may derive themes like the following:

1. Midwestern University sponsors a creative writing program. (Develop by giving specific details of the creative writing program.)
2. Midwestern University provides leadership in the field of government. (Develop by giving specific examples of faculty personnel or alumni who have headed government agencies.)
3. Midwestern University offers opportunity for personal growth in its sports program. (Develop by giving specific examples of athletes who have obviously *benefited* by sports.)

A *fourth* method of analysis is comparison and contrast. Here one finds many additional suggestions for a possible theme. Midwestern University may be compared with Harvard and Yale, Oxford and Cambridge, Ohio and Michigan with reference to academic quality, prestige, accomplishment. Furthermore, the standards of education at Midwestern may be compared with the standards of education set by educators like John Henry Newman, Sir Richard Livingstone, R. M. Hutchins, or James B. Conant. Or the student may contrast Midwestern students to students at eastern universities or European universities. Thus from analysis by comparison and contrast a student may derive themes like the following:

1. Midwestern University offers a more extended course in agriculture than X college. (Develop by comparing the courses given or by contrasting the length of the respective courses.)
2. Midwestern University is not so strict in its academic discipline as R. M. Hutchins demands. (Develop by comparing the standards at Midwestern with those stated by Mr. Hutchins. See Section XI of this book.)
3. Midwestern University's informality is in sharp contrast with the formality of European universities like Paris or Berlin. (Develop by contrasting the classroom manners of Midwestern students and European students, as reported in magazines.)

A *fifth* method of analysis is causal analysis. The student may ask what immediate reasons led to the formation of Midwestern University and what the effects of the university have been. Causal analysis inquires into the combination of factors that gave rise to the university, that is, the benefactors, the teachers and scholars, the educational needs of the time, the influence of religion, philosophy, and economics,

and the social pressures of the local community. By causal analysis the student may also trace the effects of Midwestern on American society. Through this method of analysis he seeks answers to such questions as, "Has Midwestern raised the educational standards of the state? Has Midwestern produced eminent writers, doctors, teachers, and citizens? Are Midwestern alumni happier and better-adjusted men because of their attendance at the University? Does Midwestern seek to form the educated man or does it intend merely to impart information? Does Midwestern help a man to analyze ideas, to think for himself, to discriminate among values?" Thus from causal analysis a student may derive themes like the following:

1. Midwestern University was founded to give free education to citizens of the state of Centralia. (Develop by enumerating the purposes of the founders.)
2. Midwestern University has produced eminent men. (Develop by enumerating the men whose success may be traced to Midwestern's influence.)
3. Midwestern University has raised the educational standards of the state. (Develop by tracing the effect of Midwestern policies on teaching in grammar schools, high schools, and so on.)

The *sixth* method of analysis is *process analysis*. Process analysis is concerned with how the university functions. Some sense of Midwestern University's functioning may be seen in the program of courses, the schedules of classes, seminars, university lectures, the methods of teaching, examining, and correcting. A process analysis might trace a typical day, week, month, or semester of an average Midwestern student or professor or of an average Midwestern class. Or the writer might attempt to trace the mental growth of a student from his freshman through his senior year by studying the change in some of his basic attitudes toward society and culture. Thus from process analysis a student may derive themes like the following:

1. Midwestern University encourages a student to feel at home. (Develop by tracing the life of a student through one semester.)
2. Midwestern University has an efficient method of registration. (Develop by tracing the steps in the registration process.)
3. Midwestern University has a well-integrated physical training program. (Develop by showing how the physical training program works for the average student.)

Here, indeed, is God's plenty. The freshman with a subject in search of a central theme now has a multitude of themes to choose from. Some themes, such as those suggested under causal analysis, he will reject because they may require more research than he has time for or more maturity of judgment than he may presently possess. But he is now in a position to choose intelligently the central theme that—given his subject, his purpose, and his occasion—he can develop with most success.

Note that in the above discussion we have been concerned with a short composition in which the central theme is developed by only one method of analysis. However, it must be understood that in many compositions, especially longer ones, the central theme is not simple (to employ the grammatical terminology used in describing a sentence), but compound or complex. That is, there may be two or more equal or coordinate themes, or there may be one principal theme and one or more subordinate but allied themes. For example, a longer composition on the subject, "A Freshman Looks at Midwestern University," might be outlined as follows:

1. Midwestern University offers a complete course in the humanities. (Develop by division.)
2. Midwestern University offers a course in the humanities that is superior to that offered in other universities. (Develop by comparison and contrast.)
3. Midwestern University offers a course in the humanities that is conducted by seminars. (Develop by process analysis.)

or

1. Midwestern University is an eminent educational institution. (Develop by classification—central theme.)
   a. Midwestern University has produced eminent men. (Develop by causal analysis—subordinate theme.)
   b. Midwestern University compares favorably with the best universities of the country. (Develop by comparison and contrast—subordinate theme.)

Thus the student may combine several methods of developing his theme if he so desires. There is no rule that restricts him to use a single method of analysis. Analysis is a tool, not a tyrant; a preparation for writing, not an endless labyrinth of ideas. It serves its purpose when it provides the writer with the logical understanding of the materials of his composition.

Exercises

1. Which theme derived by a *definition* of the subject, "A Freshman Looks at Midwestern University," would you select for an expository composition of 500 words? Give reasons for your choice.
2. Which theme derived by *classifying and dividing* the subject, "A Freshman Looks at Midwestern University," seems too extensive for development within 500 words? Explain your answer.
3. In your opinion which theme derived by *exemplification* of the subject, "A Freshman Looks at Midwestern University," would be most appealing for a classroom discussion? Give reasons for your choice.
4. Suggest three themes of your own derived from analysis of the subject, "A Freshman Looks at Midwestern University," by *comparison and contrast*.
5. Which theme derived by *causal analysis* of the subject, "A Freshman Looks at Midwestern University," would require considerable research before writing? Which theme could you develop from your own observation and experience? Explain your answers.
6. Suggest three themes of your own derived from a *process analysis* of the subject, "A Freshman Looks at Midwestern University."
7. Below are listed some topics from which subjects for a short expository essay of 500 words may be derived. Select a subject for each topic. Analyze each subject according to the outline contained in this section. Then write a sentence expressing the central theme you consider most appropriate for each of the subjects.

    Example: *Topic:* An American city
            Subject: Chicago
            Central theme: Chicago is the industrial heart of Mid-America

a. Poetry	f. On giving lessons
b. Jobs	g. Going to college
c. School spirit	h. Advertising
d. Examinations	i. Lawns
e. Local political bosses	j. Trapping

8. Below are listed some sentences that state a central theme for an expository essay. Indicate one or more appropriate methods (definition, classification and division, exemplification, comparison and contrast, causal analysis, process analysis) of developing these theme sentences.

    Example: The game warden enjoyed camping out in the forest. Contrast to living in town.

    a. Education is essential in modern life.
    b. Railroad travel has certain advantages over air travel.

c. Whenever I hear the word *hatred*, I think of three men who symbolize hatred for me.

d. The soldier, the policeman, and the letter carrier have much in common.

e. The foreigner will get a clear view of American diversity if he tries to picture this country as a group of regions.

f. Building a garage is a task that the average man can do for himself.

g. If you ignore your classmates your social life is determined in advance.

h. Professors are divided into three essential types.

i. To distinguish between means and ends is the first mark of an intelligent man.

THE THIRD ELEMENT OF RHETORIC: ARRANGEMENT

Analysis of the subject provides a theme and logical methods of developing that theme. But analysis does not determine the order in which the central theme will be introduced, developed, and concluded. In extended compositions, where many methods of analysis and many combinations of these methods are employed, a principle of order must determine which idea comes first. This is the function of the third element of rhetoric, arrangement.

Arrangement, then, is the most effective organization of *the whole composition.* This means that the whole composition, not merely the individual parts, will have

1. An effective physical structure, that is, an appropriate beginning, middle, and end

2. An effective logical structure, that is, unity and coherence of thought

3. An effective rhetorical structure, that is, an order that will hold the interest and stir the feelings of the reader

This we shall consider in Section VIII, after we have completed the study of the six basic methods of analysis.

THE FOURTH ELEMENT OF RHETORIC: STYLE

Style is the effective expression of our ideas in *language*. It is concerned with the qualities of clarity, vigor, and interest in the use of words, in the construction of sentences and paragraphs, in the articulation of the whole composition. Style is the final thinking out into language, the arranging of our words to correspond to the arrangement of our ideas. We shall be concerned with this aspect of style throughout the book. But style as an expression of the writer's personality will be considered in Section XV.

We now turn to a detailed study of the six basic methods of analysis: definition, classification and division, exemplification, comparison and contrast, causal analysis, process. As we have noted above, these methods of analysis have three uses:

1. To discover the central theme
2. To suggest methods of developing the theme in the actual composition
3. To analyze the writings of others

We have already explained the first use in detail and the second use in a preliminary fashion. We shall now proceed to a full explanation of the second and third uses of analysis.

The primary purpose in analyzing the selections, or examples, that follow is to provide the student with concrete illustrations of the practical use of analysis as an aid to original composition.

A. Define a term by distinguishing between the denotation and connotation of words. Support your distinction by specific examples.

LEWIS HANKE: *What Is Propaganda?*

B. Define an abstract term by familiar examples and simple expressions.

GUSTAVE WEIGEL: *Definition of Meaning*

C. Define a complex term by distinguishing all its important meanings. Support your distinctions by examples.

1 HERBERT L. SAMUEL: *On Chance*
2 ARNOLD J. TOYNBEE: *Civilization*

D. Define a series of terms by distinguishing the meaning of each term.

1 ETIENNE GILSON:
Dogmatism and Tolerance
2 SIR RICHARD LIVINGSTONE:
A Complete Human Being
3 SAMUEL ELIOT MORISON:
What Is Good Writing?

E. Define personal perceptions or subjective emotions by pointing directly at the thing the term means to you.

1 LEARNED HAND: *The Spirit of Liberty*
2 SIR ARTHUR QUILLER-COUCH:
What Is Literature?

F. Define a subject not generally known by developing both elements, that is, both class and member.

LEWIS MUMFORD: *Jefferson as Architect*

SECTION II

Definition

G. Define a well-known general subject by enumerating the salient characteristics of the class to which the subject belongs.

CLIFTON FADIMAN: *The Decline of Attention*

H. For greater clarity and emphasis, especially at the end of a spoken discourse, repeat the definition in various ways.

JOHN HENRY NEWMAN:
. What Is a University?

I. For dramatic effect, define the subject by stating what it is not.

1 WILLIAM FAULKNER: *The True Writer*
2 SAMUEL TAYLOR COLERIDGE:
The High Road of Life

J. When you dispute the meaning of a word or idea, define your opponent's view as well as your own.

ANTHONY STANDEN: *What Is Science?*

General Exercises

JAMES ANTHONY FROUDE: *What Is History?*

STRICT LOGICAL DEFINITION

Definition is a logical method of analysis which places the subject that is to be defined in a general class (genus) and differentiates it from all other members of that class. For example, a logical definition of rhetoric might be: Rhetoric is the art (genus) of effective writing (different from the arts of painting, music). Another logical definition might be: Exposition is a form of discourse (genus) which primarily aims to explain (different from the aims of persuasion or pure description). A third logical definition might be: Biology is a science (genus) which is concerned with living organisms (different from geology and physics).

These logical definitions are accurate and comprehensive. They state exactly what the subject is. But, while they go beyond the merely verbal definitions supplied by many shorter dictionaries, they are not sufficiently extensive or meaningful to supply the information the average reader needs. They do not provide a wholly satisfactory answer to the question, "What is it?"

RHETORICAL DEFINITION

For the purpose of rhetoric, a strictly logical definition may not suffice. A rhetorically effective definition may be needed, that is, a definition which is full, clear, interesting, and appropriate to a particular subject and occasion. Thus, for example, in defining liberty with reference to the emancipation of the American slaves, Lincoln did not give a strictly logical definition, such as, "Liberty is the free exercise of the right to dispose of one's own person under law." Rather, he said informally but effectively:

> The shepherd drives the wolf from the sheep's throat for which the sheep thanks the shepherd as it is liberated. Now the wolf denounces him as the destroyer of liberty. The sheep and the wolves are not agreed upon a definition of the word *liberty*.

And precisely the same difference prevails today among us human creatures and all professing to love liberty. Hence we behold the process by which thousands are passing from under the yoke of bondage, hailed by some as the advancing of liberty and bewailed by others as the destruction of all liberty.

Recently the people have been doing something to define liberty, and thanks to them the wolf's dictionary has been repudiated.

Lincoln's definition implies clearly what is meant by the logical definition cited above—liberty is the free exercise of the right to dispose of one's own person under law. In addition it is full, clear, interesting, and apt for the occasion. In short, it is a rhetorically effective definition.

HOW TO MAKE A DEFINITION EFFECTIVE

A definition is effective when a term, that is, the word or expression signifying the subject to be defined, is understood precisely as the author intends it. A good definition not only prevents misunderstanding; it also helps to explain the subject and aims to achieve the writer's purpose. Below are listed ten ways of using definitions effectively in a variety of realistic situations. Each of these ways is illustrated in the examples given in this section.

A. One means of effective definition is the careful distinction between the denotation and connotation of words. The denotation of a word is what the word actually means. Thus liberty actually means a state of freedom. The connotation of a word is what the word suggests or implies in a given context. Liberty, as Lincoln pointed out, connotes different things to different men. Another specimen of definition using connotation appears in Example A of this section.

B. Closely related to the distinction between denotation and connotation of words is the second method of definition, namely the illustration of abstract terms. Abstractions like liberty, democracy, politics, philosophy are often matters of great dispute, even among educated men. You can avoid misunderstanding if you define abstract ideas by giving concrete examples. Thus, in defining *meaning,* Gustave Weigel gives a familiar example of television. Furthermore, he reduces the abstract expression—*meaning* is the grasp of the knowable element of a reality—to the simpler expression—

meaning is the answer to the eternal questions what and why. (See Example B.)

C. Many important terms are not only abstract; they are also complex; that is, they contain a variety of meanings. Thus words like *chance* or *civilization* need to be distinguished as well as illustrated, as we shall see in the examples by Viscount Samuel and Arnold Toynbee. (See Examples C1, C2.)

D. Just as some single terms are complex and require distinction, so too other sets of terms are necessarily defined in a series. For example, each of the three elements of an effective style—clarity, vigor, and interest—has some bearing on the others. Vigor is impossible without clarity; clarity in part depends on interest. These terms must therefore be defined in a series. Etienne Gilson, Sir Richard Livingstone, and Samuel Eliot Morison define three closely related terms in Examples D1, D2, D3.

E. Perhaps the most frequent source of misunderstanding between writer and reader occurs when the writer uses terms that express his personal perceptions or emotions. Therefore, such a subject as "My Favorite Poem," while it may be defined in logical terms, is best identified by pointing directly at the poem itself or by relating your own experience of the poem. Thus, for example, Learned Hand defines the spirit of liberty by pointing to his own experience of the spirit of liberty. (See Example E1.) Sir Arthur Quiller-Couch, in defining the mystery of poetic experience, identifies his own experience of poetry by citing a series of quotations. (See Example E2.)

F. Another use of definition to avoid misunderstanding is suggested by Lewis Mumford in his "Jefferson as Architect." Here Mr. Mumford logically defines his subject, Thomas Jefferson as architect, by placing Jefferson's work at the University of Virginia (member) in the class of excellent architecture. For the average reader both elements of this logical definition, namely architecture and Jefferson's work as an architect, need development. Mumford's example illustrates the importance of elaborating both elements of a definition of a subject that is not generally known.

G. When the subject to be defined is general and well known, such as newspapers or magazines, it is frequently more effective to enumerate the salient characteristics of the whole class than merely to offer one or two specific examples. In some situations specific examples may center attention unduly on the individual differences (species) rather than on the common characteristics (genus). One may avoid this source of misunderstanding, then, by developing the qualities of the class, as Clifton Fadiman illustrates in "The Decline of Attention," Example G.

H. In an extended discourse, especially a spoken discourse, it is always possible that a definition, although clearly stated at the beginning, may be forgotten or confused by the time the writer reaches his conclusion. This difficulty may be avoided by repeating the definition in various ways throughout the discourse and especially at the end. Repeating definitions not only promotes clarity; it also helps to insure emphasis. This we shall see illustrated in J. H. Newman's "What Is a University?" in Example H.

I. Frequently a subject is more clearly defined to certain audiences by showing what it is not. Thus, for instance, good writing is often defined by contrast with bad writing, and a virtuous man might be defined by contrast with a man of vice. This means of developing a definition is employed by William Faulkner and Samuel Taylor Coleridge to make their meaning dramatic and vivid. (See Examples I1, I2.)

J. Definition is an essential method of analysis in argument or dispute. Often the basic point at issue is the meaning of a term. In such a situation much misunderstanding may be avoided if the writer explains his own meaning of the subject, and his opponent's meaning as well. This is illustrated in Anthony Standen's "What Is Science?" in Example J.

Note: The examples in this section are all relatively brief illustrations of the use of definition. Complete definitions of important ideas, such as liberty, education, and law, require extended analysis in which the method of definition is combined with other methods to be studied hereafter. Several examples of fully developed definitions may be found in the following essays: "The Method of Scientific Investigation" by T. H. Huxley, Section VII; "The Meaning of America in the World Today" by Charles Malik, Section VIII; and "Faith for Freedom" by Barbara Ward, Section X. Other essays in this book which make considerable use of definition are those by James Bryce and R. M. Hutchins, Section XI; and Hilaire Belloc, Section XV.

a. Define a term by distinguishing between the denotation and connotation of words. Support your distinction by specific examples.

What Is Propaganda?

BY LEWIS HANKE

The word "propaganda" has ugly connotations today. It makes us think of the serried ranks of "official" documents purporting to show that someone else was responsible for starting the first World War, and it is made the equivalent of the grand mendacities originating in Moscow every night. "Propaganda" in this sense uses the smear technique which has come to be a despicable device known to all of us. In Maryland, it is alleged that the simple device of placing ex-Senator Millard Tydings' photograph in juxtaposition to one of a known communist and then distributing the faked picture as a campaign document had such an effect on the voters that the man whose press agent was responsible for this creation is now sitting in the Senate of the United States instead of Tydings.

Las Casas * was a propagandist in the earlier and more honest usage of the term, when it meant, as the dictionary puts it, an "effort directed systematically toward the gaining of public support for an opinion or a course of action." In this sense propaganda may be and has been

* [Bartolome de Las Casas (1474-1566) was a famous preacher, writer, and reforming bishop. He is best known as a defender of the natives against exploitation by the Spanish conquerors of Central and South America.—EDITOR.]

used for religious, political, cultural, and social ends, and such diverse institutions as the United States Chamber of Commerce, the Anti-Saloon league, the Carnegie Endowment for International Peace, and the American Council of Learned Societies all employ propaganda. The alteration of private or public conduct, the *Columbia Encyclopedia* tells us, has usually been the result of propaganda. Certainly the effort of some Spaniards to protect the Indians of the New World and to incorporate them into a western, Christian civilization would have been a much more feeble movement if Las Casas had not arisen to speak on their behalf in such declamatory tones that Spaniards simply had to listen to this powerful and skillful propagandist.

Comment

Note here how, in the first paragraph, Mr. Hanke defines the *connotative* sense of the word *propaganda,* and then gives several examples of its use in this connotative sense. In the second paragraph he defines the *denotative* meaning of propaganda and gives examples of its use in this sense of the term. Thus by distinguishing between the two senses of the term he makes his own meaning clear. He intends to treat Las Casas as a propagandist in "the earlier and more honest usage of the term." No one can honestly misunderstand him.

Analysis and Composition

1. Consult your dictionary for the etymological meaning of *propaganda.* (Etymology refers to the derivation of a word. In most dictionaries the derivation is shown in brackets.) To what extent does the definition of *propaganda* quoted in paragraph 2 agree with the etymological definition?

2. Consult your dictionary for the etymological definition of each of the following words used in the example above:

mendacities	political	incorporate
photograph	cultural	civilization
juxtaposition	employ	declamatory
distribute	alteration	
religious	conduct	

3. Write out a logical definition (genus and species) for each of the following terms:

civilization   politics
culture   religion

4. In a manner similar to the selection above, develop in two short paragraphs the connotative and denotative definitions of one or more of the following words. Support your definitions by several examples.

oligarchy   left wing   politics
sophomore   rhetorician   cavalier
impersonator   devil's advocate   inquisitor
candidate   detail

---

b. Define an abstract term by familiar examples and simple expressions.

Definition of Meaning

BY GUSTAVE WEIGEL

We must define the word "meaning." This term is treacherous, because it seems so obvious but when we try to explain its import, we feel quite inadequate. It is like the word "time." For as St. Augustine said, if you do not ask me what it means, I know; but if you ask me, I do not.

Meaning is a correlative to understanding. Now understanding can be opposed to mere experience. We have all experienced a television apparatus, for we have seen the pictures that are produced by such a machine. However, we do not understand it. We cannot make one,

DEFINITION OF MEANING: from "The Meaning of the Moment" by Gustave Weigel in *Cross Currents*, volume ii, no. 3.

nor can we grasp the theories involved in the organization of the mechanism. When we understand the inner workings and the theory, we have grasped the meaning. When we experience, we only establish contact with an object. The man who made the plans for the first television obviously never saw one, but he understood a television set, and because he understood, he could make one. To understand I must grasp the knowable element of a reality. This element makes the reality luminous to the thinker. Because of such a grasp he can answer the child's question "what" and "why."

Let it suffice to say that meaning is the answer to the question "what" and "why." The child is so dedicated to these two words that he annoys his elders by using them *ad nauseam,* but the child in this matter shows itself to be human. Our difficulties with the "New Art" arise because we do not know what it means, and we feel hopelessly confused by some of the spokesmen of the new movement who tell us that it does not mean anything. We cannot tolerate that reply, because we spontaneously believe that all things must have meaning. If the thing is static or statically considered we ask "what is it" and if the thing is in flux, we ask "why is it moving?" Meaning therefore is the answer to the eternal questions "what" and "why."

Comment

It should be noted at once that this is a preliminary definition of *meaning,* that is, an explanation of how the author intends to use the term in his essay. A full definition would require a very extended essay.

This definition, while brief, is nevertheless remarkably acute. In paragraph 1 the author classifies the subject to be defined (meaning) as a treacherous term. Then he compares *meaning* to a similarly difficult term, *time.* His next step (¶2) is to connect *meaning* with the simpler term *understanding. Understanding* is then defined in contrast to *experience.* This contrast is developed in the example of the television set. *Understanding* is then logically defined as the "grasp [of] the knowable [that is, the mentally comprehensible] element of a reality." The effect of *understanding* is clarity in the thinker's own mind. This clarity in turn permits him to answer the child's questions "what" and "why."

The definition has proceeded as follows: meaning = understanding; understanding = mental comprehension; mental comprehension = ability to answer the questions what and why.

In the third paragraph the author applies his definition of meaning as the ability to answer the questions what and why to the problem of the "New Art." What and why are distinguished from each other in the next to last sentence. The definition of meaning is repeated in the last sentence.

The student is not expected to grasp all the implications of this definition. What he should study intensively is the author's ability to make one of the most difficult abstractions reasonably clear to the intelligent reader by using examples and familiar expressions.

Analysis and Composition

1. After consulting your dictionary, explain the meaning of each of the following words as they are used in the example above:

correlative   contact   spontaneously
experience   luminous   static
theories   *ad nauseam*   flux
mechanism

2. Judging by the vocabulary and tone, what kind of audience is the author addressing?

3. Is the final definition of *meaning* oversimple? Why, or why not?

4. In three short paragraphs define one or more of the following terms. Be sure to give examples for all abstract terms. Aim to be understood by the average newspaper reader.

airplane   grammar   topic sentence
a military tank   popularity   elegance
civil rights   humor
opinion   elevator

C. Define a complex term by distinguishing all its important meanings. Support your distinctions by examples.

1. On Chance

BY HERBERT L. SAMUEL

1 The word Chance has always been in common use to denote whatever happens fortuitously, without known cause; we therefore accept Chance unquestioningly, as being a real agency acting in the universe. Professor Born, writing on the natural philosophy of Cause and Chance, does not start with any definition of the word, or stay to examine whether it denotes anything that is factual, in the sense that the events which it is supposed to govern are factual. Apparently he considers that common usage is sufficient. But when we come to investigate the matter more closely we shall find that it is far from sufficient.

2 Let us take one or two examples. Go to the very temple of Chance, a gambling casino, and look at the roulette table. A horizontal wheel, divided into numbered compartments, is set revolving by the croupier, and he launches a ball into it in the opposite direction; when the wheel comes to rest and the ball drops into one of the

ON CHANCE: from *Essay in Physics,* copyright, 1952, by Herbert L. Samuel. Reprinted by permission of Harcourt, Brace and Company, Inc., and of Messrs. Basil Blackwell, publishers, Oxford, England.

compartments, that number wins. The results are, for us, pure chance, in the sense that there is no possibility of our predicting them. Yet, as a matter of fact, the difference of the result in each case depends upon two factors that are strictly causal—the velocity of the wheel when it is set revolving and the velocity of the ball when it is thrown in. And each of these depends upon the degree of effort on the part of the croupier in moving his arm. It would be possible to devise a machine which would start the roulette revolving and throw in the ball; and if the machine were nicely adjusted, and all interference by air currents or otherwise excluded, the same number could be made to win every time.* But the croupier's arm not being a machine, neither he nor any-one else can gauge the amount of force that is being exerted on any particular occasion. Once the movements of the arm have been made, the result will follow with certainty. The causes are there. The ele-ment we term Chance consists merely in the impossibility of our ascer-taining and measuring those causes.

3 Or we might hear in the railway carriage, going up to town in the morning, someone say this: "My elderly neighbor had a most un-fortunate accident yesterday. He happened not to put on his spectacles, and when he went out did not see a piece of orange peel which chanced to be on the path just outside his gate: he slipped and broke his leg. It was sheer bad luck, the sort of accident that might happen to anyone." But if we were to re-state the incident omitting the tenden-tious words "unfortunate . . . accident . . . happened . . . chanced . . . bad luck," we might reach a different conclusion. Two sets of prior events were involved: someone walking along the footway eating an orange had dropped a piece of peel just outside that gate, and a short-sighted man living in the house had forgotten to put on his glasses before going out. From the combination of those two sets of causes the result followed. It could have been foreseen. In fact someone might well make the comment that, if careless people drop orange peel on the pavement and short-sighted people neglect to put on their spectacles, injuries are bound to occur sooner or later.

4 Considered subjectively, as from the individual concerned, all such

* A machine has in fact been made, for use in cricket practice, which will deliver a ball again and again uniformly; speed, pitch, and break are changeable and regulated be-forehand. Photographs of the machine were given in *The Illustrated London News,* of October 22, 1949.

LEVELS

ERS ASSOC

EETING

7:30 P.M.

ptember 27,

IN HOPE. MC

to the meeting.

scuss and prese

events may be regarded as the result of "luck," of pure chance. Considered mathematically, the chances of their occurring can be calculated, according to the rules of probability, on the basis of past experience. Considered in themselves, as part of the operations of the universe, each event is unique, the consequence of a particular combination of prior events which has occurred in that place, at that moment, once for all.

Comment

Viscount Samuel first questions the definition that chance is "whatever happens fortuitously, without known cause." After examining two instances of chance, the roulette wheel and the accident, he concludes that the word *chance* has three distinct explanations: a subjective explanation, a mathematical explanation, and a more universal explanation (see ¶4). Note that the word *chance* is not only an abstract term but a complex term as well. Each of the three meanings is equally valid in different situations.

Analysis and Composition

1. Give an etymological definition (derivation from original source) of the following words:

    fortuitously   casino   tendentious
    agency   croupier   combination
    universe   velocity   subjectively
    investigate   excluded

    Does Viscount Samuel use these words in an etymological sense in the selection above?

2. Viscount Samuel distinguishes three possible meanings in the word *chance*. Consult your dictionary and determine whether there are other possible meanings.

3. Distinguish between two possible meanings of the following words:

    civilization   culture   refinement
    authority   rebellion

    Give at least one example of each meaning you distinguish.

4. Write three short paragraphs on one or more of the following terms. Define by distinguishing two or three meanings of the word. Give examples to support each distinction.

democracy	duty	contempt
victory	dominion	divorce
hope	end	condition
aggression		

2. Civilization

BY ARNOLD J. TOYNBEE

[1]In human terms, how are we to describe the Greek civilization, or our own Western civilization, or any other of the ten or twenty civilizations which we can count up on our fingers? [2]In human terms, I should say that each of these civilizations is, while in action, a distinctive attempt at a single great common human enterprise, or, when it is seen in retrospect, after the action is over, it is a distinctive instance of a single great common human experience. [3]This enterprise or experience is an effort to perform an act of creation. [4]In each of these civilizations, mankind, I think, is trying to rise above mere humanity—above primitive humanity, that is—towards some higher kind of spiritual life. [5]One cannot depict the goal because it has never been reached—or, rather, I should say that it has never been reached by any human society. [6]It has, perhaps, been reached by individual men and women. [7]At least, I can think of certain saints and sages who seem to me, in their personal lives, to have reached the goal, at least in so far as I myself am able to conceive what the goal may be like. [8]But if there have been a few transfigured men and women, there has never been such a thing as a civilized society. [9]Civilization, as we know it, is a movement and not a condition, a voyage and not a harbour. [10]No known civilization has ever reached the goal of civilization yet. [11]There has never been a communion of saints on earth. [12]In the least uncivilized society at its least uncivilized moment, the vast majority of its members have remained very near indeed to the primitive human level. [13]And no society has ever been secure of holding such ground as it has

managed to gain in its spiritual advance. ¹⁴All the civilizations that we know of, including the Greek, have already broken down and gone to pieces with the single possible exception of our own Western civilization—and no child of this civilization who has been born into our generation can easily imagine that our own society is immune from the danger of suffering the common fate.

Comment

Toynbee's central idea here is that civilization may be seen either in action or in retrospect (S2). Civilization in action is seen as an act of creation, as an aspiration to spiritual life that is never reached save by exceptional individuals, as a movement, as a voyage. The other meaning of civilization is based on retrospect. In retrospect no civilization has ever achieved its goal; it is always breaking down and going to pieces. Both meanings of civilization are true, but the second meaning is stressed towards the end of the paragraph.

Analysis and Composition

1. Define the following words as they are used in the above selection:

   distinctive (S2)   primitive humanity (S4)   condition (S9)
   retrospect (S2)   transfigured (S8)   immune (S14)
   creation (S3)   movement (S9)

2. What is your understanding of Toynbee's distinction between civilization and the goal of civilization in sentence 10?
3. The word *civilization* is used eleven times in fourteen sentences. Is this word used in exactly the same sense each time? Give reasons for your answer.
4. Explain in your own words what Toynbee says in sentence 12. Supply specific examples to support the meaning of the sentence.
5. Write a paragraph distinguishing at least two meanings of one of the following terms:

   American culture   modern living   men of distinction

d. Define a series of terms by distinguishing the meaning of each term.

---

1. Dogmatism and Tolerance

BY ETIENNE GILSON

I beg leave to begin by defining some of the terms I am going to use, or, rather, to define the sense in which I am going to use them.

I will call "totalitarian" any form of political society that sets no moral limits on the powers of the State. Such societies are well defined by Mussolini's formula: "Nothing outside of the State, above the State, against the State; everything to the State, for the State, in the State."

I will call "democratic" any nontotalitarian form of political society. A democratic society does not deny the authority of the State as representative of the body politic and enforcing laws in view of the common good, but it recognizes the presence, in human beings, of something that is outside of the State, above the State, and which it may become necessary to protect against the encroachments of the State. As an instance of such things, I would cite truth.

I will call "dogmatism" the philosophical attitude of those who maintain that some propositions are not merely probable, or practically certain, but unconditionally true, provided only we agree on the meaning of their terms and are able to understand them. As instances of such propositions, I would quote: Even a wealthy man stands in need of friends (ARISTOTLE); Peace is the tranquillity which attends order (AUGUSTINE); Every action has goodness insofar as it has being, whereas it is lacking in goodness insofar as it is lacking in something that is due to its fullness of being (THOMAS AQUINAS); Human beings must not be used as means, but respected as ends (KANT). Personally, I hold all these propositions as absolutely true, but I am not saying that they are either self-evident or incontrovertible; my only point is that I will call dogmatism the philosophical attitude of anyone who recognizes the unconditional truth of any such propositions.

Comment

These three paragraphs constitute the introduction to an address, the central idea of which is that *dogmatism* as the author understands it is anti-totalitarian. Gilson here defines three terms—*totalitarianism, democracy,* and *dogmatism*. Each term is important to an understanding of the central idea of the address. Furthermore, each of the three terms defined helps to explain the other terms. Thus, democracy is partly defined as an opposite of totalitarianism. Dogmatism, in so far as it maintains that some propositions are unconditionally true, by implication limits the moral authority of the totalitarian state, and by implication accepts the democratic belief that there are rights outside the authority of the state. Note also how two of the three definitions in the series are supported by quotations, and the third, democracy, by an instance of democratic recognition of rights beyond the state.

Analysis and Composition

1. Decide whether the author's definition of totalitarianism is a logical definition. Does Mussolini's formula constitute a logical definition? Give reasons for your answer.
2. Test the accuracy of the author's definition of democracy by applying his sense of the term to the United States, Great Britain, or France.
3. Distinguish between the denotation and the various connotations of the term *dogmatism*.
4. Given the subject, "Democracy, Its Authority and Freedom," construct a preliminary definition of each term.
5. Write out a logical definition of the following words:

| tranquillity | order | goodness |
| means | ends | propositions |

2. A Complete Human Being

BY SIR RICHARD LIVINGSTONE

[1]And what is a complete human being? [2]Again I shall take the Greek answer to this question. [3]Human beings have bodies, minds, and characters. [4]Each of these is capable of what the Greeks called "virtue" . . . or what we might call "excellence." [5]The virtue or excellence of the body is health and fitness and strength, the firm and sensitive hand, the clear eye; the excellence of the mind is to know and to understand and to think, to have some idea of what the world is and what man has done and has been and can be; the excellence of the character lies in the great virtues. [6]This trinity of body, mind, and character is man; man's aim, besides earning his living, is to make the most of all three, to have as good a mind, body, and character as possible; and a liberal education, a free man's education, is to help him to this; not because a sound body, mind, and character help to success, or even because they help to happiness, but because they are good things in themselves, and because what is good is worthwhile, simply because it is good. [7]So we get that clear and important distinction between technical education which aims at earning a living or making money or at some narrowly practical skill, and the free man's education which aims at producing as perfect and complete a human being as may be.

Comment

In this paragraph man's aim or end is defined as excellence in body, mind, and character (Ss1-5). Then liberal education is defined as the means to achieve this end (Ss6-7). Sentence 6 involves a neat piece of deductive reasoning (reasoning from the general to the particular). Whatever helps a man to have as good a body, mind, and character as possible is good for its own sake. But liberal education helps a man to have as good a body, mind, and character as possible. Therefore a liberal education is good for its own sake.

Analysis and Composition

1. Decide whether education, <u>the complete man</u>, or human excellence is the main subject defined in this paragraph.
2. Could any of the subjects mentioned in Exercise 1 be defined properly without defining the other terms in the series? Give reasons for your answer. *defined, not understood*
3. How are the three subjects linked in sentences 6 and 7? *General to particular*
4. Could the author have been clearer by defining each of the three elements in separate paragraphs, as Gilson does in Example D1 above? Give reasons for your answer. *Possibly - but would have destroyed unity*
5. Write a paragraph using definition in answer to the following questions:
   a. What is a technical education?
   b. What is a liberal education?
   c. What is character formation?
   d. What is happiness?

3. What Is Good Writing?

BY SAMUEL ELIOT MORISON

Now, the purpose of a quick, warm synthesis between research, thinking, and writing is to attain the three prime qualities of historical composition—clarity, vigor, and objectivity. You must think about your facts, analyze your material, and decide exactly what you mean before you can write it so that the average reader will understand. Do not fall into the fallacy of supposing that "facts speak for themselves." Most of the facts that you excavate from the archives, like all relics of past human activity, are dumb things; it is for you to make them speak by proper selection, arrangement, and emphasis. Dump your entire collection of facts on paper, and the result will be unreadable if not incomprehensible.

So, too, with vigor. If your whole paragraph or chapter is but a hypothesis, say so at the beginning, but do not bore and confuse the reader with numerous "buts," "excepts," "perhaps," "howevers," and "possiblys." Use direct rather than indirect statements, the active rather than the passive voice, and make every sentence and paragraph an

WHAT IS GOOD WRITING? from *History as a Literary Art* by Samuel Eliot Morison. Old South Leaflets, series ii, no. 1.

organic whole. Above all, if you are writing historical narrative, make it move. Do not take time out in the middle of a political or military campaign to introduce special developments or literary trends, as Mc-Master did to the confusion of his readers. Place those admittedly important matters in a chapter or chapters by themselves so that your reader's attention will not be lost by constant interruption.

That brings us to the third essential quality—objectivity. Keep the reader constantly in mind. You are not writing history for yourself or for the professors who (you may imagine) know more about it than you do. Assume that you are writing for intelligent people who know nothing about your particular subject but whom you wish to convince of its interest and significance. I once asked the late Senator Beveridge why his *Life of John Marshall,* despite its great length and scholarly apparatus, was so popular. He replied, "The trouble with you professors of history is that you write for each other. I write for people almost completely ignorant of American history, as I was when I began my research."

Comment

Note here how the three qualities of good historical writing are linked together in the first sentence of this selection. As in the two previous examples, each definition in the series depends upon its predecessor. Thus the advice to be vigorous is intimately tied up with clarity, as is suggested in the last two sentences of the second paragraph. So too the third quality, objectivity, bears a direct relationship to the first element in the series, clarity. The student may note in passing how the first paragraph in this selection confirms the ideas presented in Section I of this book. When Mr. Morison urges you to "think about your facts, analyze your material, and decide exactly what you mean" before you write, he is stressing the second element of rhetoric, that is, analysis of the subject and choice of a central theme. Note too that the third essential quality of historical writing, objectivity, is related to the quality of interest as well as to clarity.

Analysis and Composition

1. Write original sentences using the following words correctly:

   synthesis   fallacy   apparatus
   objective   incomprehensible   subjective

2. Do the qualities of clarity, vigor, and objectivity logically define historical composition? Give reasons for your answer.
3. Using this selection as a model, develop one or more of the following definitions:
   a. A happy man is one who has all he needs, will have it forever, and will never tire of it.
   b. A good runner has speed, endurance, and competitive spirit.
   c. The ideal house is well planned, contains good materials, and is conveniently located.

---

e. Define personal perceptions or subjective emotions by pointing directly at the thing the term means to you.

---

1. The Spirit of Liberty

BY LEARNED HAND

What then is the spirit of liberty? I cannot define it; I can only tell you my own faith. The spirit of liberty is the spirit which is not too sure that it is right; the spirit of liberty is the spirit which seeks to understand the minds of other men and women; the spirit of liberty

THE SPIRIT OF LIBERTY: reprinted from *The Spirit of Liberty* by Learned Hand, by permission of Alfred A. Knopf, Inc. Copyright 1952 by Alfred A. Knopf, Inc.

is the spirit which weighs their interests alongside its own without bias; the spirit of liberty remembers that not even a sparrow falls to earth unheeded; the spirit of liberty is the spirit of Him who, near two thousand years ago, taught mankind that lesson it has never learned, but has never quite forgotten: that there may be a kingdom where the least shall be heard and considered side by side with the greatest.

Comment

Note here that no effort is made to offer a logical definition. Judge Hand merely offers his own experience or sense of the spirit of liberty. This paragraph is unusual for its repetition of the subject and for its consistent parallel structure.*

Analysis and Composition

1. Find as many definitions as you can for the following words:

spirit   understanding

faith   bias

2. In a manner similar to Example E1 above write a short paragraph in answer to one of the following questions:
   a. What is the spirit of America?
   b. What is school spirit?
   c. What is integrity?
   d. What is a gentleman?

* See handbooks: Foerster, pp. 17-23; Hodges, 26; Kierzek, 56; Perrin, pp. 282-83; Wykoff, 74.

2. What Is Literature?

BY SIR ARTHUR QUILLER-COUCH

Definitions, formulae (some would add, creeds) have their use in any society in that they restrain the ordinary unintellectual man from making himself a public nuisance with his private opinions. But they go a very little way in helping the man who has a real sense of prose or verse. In other words, they are good discipline for some thyrsus bearers, but the initiated have little use for them. As Thomas à Kempis "would rather feel compunction than understand the definition thereof," so the initiated man will say of the "Grand Style," for example—"Why define it for me?" When Viola says simply:

> I am all the daughters of my father's house,
> And all the brothers too,

or Macbeth demands of the Doctor:

> Canst thou not minister to a mind diseased,
> Pluck from the memory a rooted sorrow . . . ?

or Hamlet greets Ophelia, reading her Book of Hours, with

> Nymph, in thy orisons
> Be all my sins remembered!

or when Milton tells of his dead friend how

> Together both, ere the high lawns appear'd
> Under the opening eyelids of the morn,
> We drove afield,

or describes the battalions of Heaven:

> On, they move
> Indissolubly firm; nor obvious hill,
> Nor strait'ning vale, nor wood, nor stream divides
> Their perfect ranks,

or when Gray exalts the great commonplace;

WHAT IS LITERATURE? taken from *On the Art of Writing* by Sir Arthur Quiller-Couch. Reprinted by permission of G. P. Putnam's Sons, publishers.

The boast of heraldry, the pomp of power,
And all that beauty, all that wealth e'er gave,
Awaits alike th' inevitable hour.
The paths of glory lead but to the grave,

or when Keats casually drops us such a line as

The journey homeward to habitual self,

or, to come down to our own times and to a living poet, when I open
on a page of William Watson and read:

O ancient streams, O far descended woods,
Full of the fluttering of melodious souls! . . .

"why then (will say the initiated one), why worry me with any definition of the Grand Style in English, when here, and here, and again
here—in all these lines, simple or intense or exquisite or solemn—I
recognize and feel the *thing?*"

Indeed, Sir, the long and the short of the argument lie just here.
Literature is not an abstract Science, to which exact definitions can be
applied. It is an Art rather, the success of which depends on personal
persuasiveness, on the author's skill to give as on ours to receive.

Comment

In his concluding paragraph Sir Arthur Quiller-Couch defines literature
as an art which depends on the author's skill and persuasion, and the
reader's skill in understanding. The more effective definition, however,
occurs in the preceding paragraph, where he identifies literature in the
"grand style" by a series of quotations. This method of developing a subject depends upon the writer's good sense and good judgment. When you
define by pointing directly at the thing that the term means to you, you
must be sure that the thing is unmistakable. Thus from the eight quotations listed in the Example E2 above the discerning reader should be able
to recognize and feel the grand style of poetry.

Analysis and Composition

1. Explain your impression of the grand style defined by Quiller-Couch in a paragraph of 200 words.
2. Define the following words and use them in an original sentence:

   Prescribed forms, rules or models   *refined, delicate*

formulae	orisons	exquisite
thyrsus bearers	casually	abstract *to steal or run away.*

   staff entwined with ivy at festivals of Bacchus   *by chance*   *apart from concrete or material*

3. Write out a formal definition of friendship and then point directly to personal experiences that identify the subject defined.
4. List some impressions which might be used to define one or more of the following terms:

beauty	charm	graciousness
urbanity	mental cruelty	misery
glory	fury	well-being

---

f.   **Define a subject not generally known by developing both elements, that is, both class and member.**

Jefferson as Architect

BY LEWIS MUMFORD

The University of Virginia was the marvelous embodiment of three great architectural essentials. The first was a well-conceived and well-translated program, based upon a fresh conception of the functions of a modern university. A good building serves as the physical and symbolic setting for a scheme of life: to build well, the first step is to understand the purposes, the motives, the habits, and the desires of those who are to be housed. Architecture, if it is to be anything better than scene painting, must be evolved from the inside out; and the architect must therefore begin, not with the land or the structure, but with the needs that the land or the structure are finally to satisfy. Unlike modern millionaires, who so often put up collegiate buildings for the pleasure of seeing their names on the façades, and who imagine that the more money they spend, the more highly their names will be edified, Jefferson began with certain definite convictions about the needs of students and scholars. Hence a certain modesty and economy of detail; hence a respect for human proportions. Although Jefferson spent freely when the need arose—I have told how he imported stone-cutters from Italy to carve the capitals—there was no splurging in these buildings, if one perhaps excepts the unfortunate library. Jefferson had a carefully thought-out program; and he carried it through.

The second great architectural essential is that individual buildings should never be conceived as isolated units; they should always be conceived and executed as parts of the whole. Buildings exist in a landscape, in a village, or in a city; they are parts of a natural or an urban setting; they are elements in a whole. The individual unit must always be conceived and modified in terms of the whole. This cannot be done by architects who have their nose on the draughting board, and who, in their own conceit, have no regard for the principle of neighborliness and no interest in the surrounding works of nature or man.

A certain discipline, a certain restraint, even a certain sacrifice of private tastes and preferences is necessary if an individual is going to develop a positive character: people who do what they like, when and how they like, are not merely a nuisance to their neighbors, but they turn out to be weak characters, to boot. It is the same in architecture. The beauty of the University of Virginia buildings that Jefferson designed does not lie in any single detail; it does not lie in any single building; it does not even lie in any single row: it derives from the order and purpose that underlies the whole and creates a harmony, practical and esthetic, between its various parts. That is a lesson which the architects and builders largely forgot in the two generations that followed Jefferson's death. To pick up that tradition and reinstate it has been one of the main tasks of our own time, and it is one that is still only imperfectly performed.

The third great quality that Jefferson showed was his ability to modify details to meet a special situation, while holding to a rigorous and consistent plan. This is a quality that has special meaning for us today; for we are too often the helpless victims of the very mechanical order we have created. Now Jefferson was as much enamored as our most machine-minded contemporaries of regularity, of mathematical proportions, of mechanical accuracy; and his readiness to make departures from such order, when necessity arose, is one of the proofs of his mastership. Geometry satisfies a deep desire of the human mind: the desire for order, certainty, regularity, for form and stability in a world of flux. When this order is embodied in building, it satisfies the mind that man is for the moment on top and in control of the situation. But that victory of order always has its dangers, as the Greeks, who so well mastered geometry, were aware: the danger is that it may flout human needs, as completely as Procrustes did when he chopped off human legs in order to make his guests fit the beds they were to sleep in. Life without order is chaotic; but order without life is the end of everything, and eventually the end of order, too, since the purpose of order in building is to sustain human life. In the University of Virginia, Jefferson struck a balance between formal order and vital order, between the logic of building and the logic of life.

Comment

Note how each of Mumford's four paragraphs *develops* one essential element of good architecture (class) and some proof that Jefferson's work at the University of Virginia possessed that element, that is, is a member of that class. Thus the deductive reasoning in paragraph 1 is: One trait of good architecture is a carefully thought-out program. Jefferson's work at the University of Virginia had a carefully thought-out program. Therefore Jefferson's work at the University of Virginia possessed one trait of good architecture. This elaboration of both the class and member is necessary. The class, good architecture, is not widely known. Nor is Jefferson's ability as an architect clearly recognized.

Analysis and Composition

1. What is the reasoning in paragraphs 2 and 4? (See comment above for sample of reasoning.)
2. What is the reasoning of the passage as a whole?
3. Does this passage contain a sufficiently complete definition of good architecture?
4. Is there sufficient proof that Jefferson was a good architect?
5. Give logical definitions of each of the following terms used in Example F above:

architecture	façade	harmony	geometry
symbol	proportion	tradition	certainty
college	beauty	plan	

6. Develop one of the following subjects by explaining both elements of the definition:
   a. Robert E. Lee as a general
   b. Shakespeare as a playwright
   c. Franklin D. Roosevelt as a President

9. Define a well-known general subject by enumerating the salient characteristics of the class to which the subject belongs.

The Decline of Attention

BY CLIFTON FADIMAN

The magazines that really talk to the heart of our country are . . . the digest, the pulps, the picture magazine, the weekly news catalogues, the smooth-paper monthly mammoths. These vary widely in

THE DECLINE OF ATTENTION: from "The Decline of Attention" by Clifton Fadiman. By permission of *The Saturday Review*.

literary finish and "sophistication"—but they have in common this: they make no rigorous demand on the faculty of attention.

Some of the obvious characteristics of this journalism are: brevity, superficiality, simplification, the emphasis on timeliness (with its corollary, the conscious neglect or unconscious ignorance of the past), planned nonliterary English, the avoidance of abstract ideas, the compartmentalization of life (this compartmentalization, as in the news magazine, is the verbal analogue of mass production's division of labor), the emphasis on "personalities" as well as the avoidance of *personality*, the exploitation of the "column" as against the discursive essay, the preference of the wisecrack to wit, the featuring of headlines (here, as elsewhere, modern journalism reveals its kinship, quite proper and natural, with advertising), the often remarkable ingenuity displayed in "packaging," an almost religious veneration for the "fact" (to be "well informed" is our substitute for the capacity to reflect), the rapid alternation of appeals (known as "balance," or something for everybody), and the careful exploitation of certain not highly cerebral interests, mainly in the areas of vicarious sex, criminality, violence, "inspiration," gadget-worship, and the idolization of contemporary gods, such as cinema stars, sports heroes, and clean-faced high-school girl graduates.

In general, a successful, technically admirable attempt is made to *attract* the attention without actually *engaging* it; to entertain rather than challenge, or, to use the editor's quite legitimate phrase, to be "readable"—that is, to present material which can be read easily and forgotten quickly.

Comment

In paragraph 1 Mr. Fadiman defines his subject—the magazines that speak to the heart of America—by assigning them to a class (genus) of reading that does not demand vigorous attention. This class is identified in paragraph 2 by sixteen characteristics. Notice that Mr. Fadiman does not mention specific magazines (species); neither does he cite actual examples of the characteristics listed in paragraph 2. He assumes that all his readers (the essay appeared originally in *The Saturday Review of Literature*) know the magazines to which he refers and are aware of the characteristics he mentions. Thus he avoids arguments that might follow from the use of specific examples. The author emphasizes the class rather than the species, the common element rather than the differentiating element. This type of definition is not so frequently employed as the methods represented in the previous examples. But, in certain situations, it may be used with devastating effect, as Mr. Fadiman demonstrates.

Analysis and Composition

1. Give the meaning of the following words as they are used in Mr. Fadiman's context:

simplification	"packaging"	"inspiration"
compartmentalization	exploitation	clean-faced
analogue	cerebral	technically admirable
discursive essay	vicarious	

2. Would you prefer the author to identify his general subject—the large-circulation magazines—by citing specific examples? Give reasons for your answer.

3. Do you find all the characteristics listed in paragraph 2 obvious characteristics of journalism? If not, criticize Mr. Fadiman's use of the word *obvious*.

4. Decide whether the development of two or three characteristics of large-circulation magazines would have had a greater effect than the heaping together of sixteen characteristics.

5. Paragraph 2 consists of only one sentence containing 180 words, five parentheses, seven words with quotations marks, one italicization. Can you justify the length and punctuation of this sentence for one or more of the following reasons?

   a. The author wishes to call attention, by ironic overstatement, to the excessive brevity, superficiality, and simplification of the articles in mass-circulation magazines.

   b. He aims to overwhelm the reader by a multitude of reasons.

   c. He is writing for a literary audience that has no difficulty in understanding him.

6. Is paragraph 3 an adequate summation of paragraph 2?

7. Decide whether the central theme expressed in paragraph 1, that these magazines "make no rigorous demand on the faculty of attention," is the same as the statement given in paragraph 3, that these magazines "present material which can be read easily and forgotten quickly."

8. Develop several of the following general subjects by enumerating the characteristics of the class to which they belong in the manner of Example G above:

generals	senators	umpires
deans	professors	athletic coaches
spies	FBI men	railway conductors

principles: Climax   proportion
Suspense   structure
End position

h.

For greater clarity and emphasis, especially at the end of a spoken discourse, repeat the definition in various ways.

What Is a University?

BY JOHN HENRY NEWMAN

A University is a place of concourse, whither students come from every quarter for every kind of knowledge. You cannot have the best of every kind everywhere; you must go to some great city or emporium for it. There you have all the choicest productions of nature and art all together, which you find each in its own separate place elsewhere. All the riches of the land, and of the earth, are carried up thither; there are the best markets, and there the best workmen. It is the centre of trade, the supreme court of fashion, the umpire of rival talents, and the standard of things rare and precious. It is the place for seeing galleries of first-rate pictures, and for hearing wonderful voices and performers of transcendent skill. It is the place for great preachers, great orators, great nobles, great statesmen. In the nature of things, greatness and unity go together; excellence implies a centre. And such, for the third or fourth time, is a University; I hope I do not weary out the reader by repeating it. It is the place to which a thousand schools make contributions; in which the intellect may safely range and speculate, sure to find its equal in some antagonist activity, and its judge in the tribunal of truth. It is a place where inquiry is pushed forward, and discoveries verified and perfected, and rashness rendered innocuous, and error exposed, by the collision of mind with mind, and knowledge with knowledge. It is the place where the professor becomes eloquent, and is a missionary and a preacher, displaying his science in its most complete and most winning form, pouring it forth with the zeal of enthusiasm, and lighting up his own love of it in the breasts of his hearers. It is the place where the catechist makes good his ground as he goes, treading in the truth day by day into the ready memory, and wedging and tightening it into the expanding reason. It is a place which wins the admiration of the young by its celebrity, kindles the affections of the middle-aged by its beauty, and rivets the fidelity of the old by its associations. It is a seat of wisdom, a light of the world, a minister of the faith, an Alma Mater of the rising generation. . . .

Comment

This paragraph summarizes Newman's views on the meaning of a university. It is especially notable for its repetition of two key words. *University,* the subject defined, together with its synonyms and pronouns, is used eight times. *Place,* the genus or class to which the university belongs, together with its synonyms and pronouns, is used more than eight times. Some dozen or more characteristics that differentiate the university from other places, characteristics that may be summed up under the heading *intellectual activity,* occur throughout. The repetition of the key ideas, that is, *university, place, intellectual activity,* is matched by the repetition of parallel structure in the sentences:

> "It is a place where inquiry is pushed forward"
> "It is the place where the professor becomes eloquent"
> "It is the place where the catechist makes good his ground"

Note too the parallel structure of the participial phrases:

> "displaying his science"
> "pouring it forth"
> "lighting up his own love"
> "treading in the truth"
> "wedging and tightening it"

The definition is emphatic as well as clear. In addition to the force achieved by repetition there is a gradual intensification of the feeling of admiration for the university. The last two lines rise to a definite climax in "a minister of the faith, an Alma Mater of the rising generation."

Analysis and Composition

1. Give two definitions for each of the following words:

    concourse   speculate   Alma Mater
    talents   catechist

2. Does this passage contain a logical definition? Explain your answer.
3. Develop by methods similar to those used by Newman one or more of the following subjects:
    a. What is a high school?
    b. What is a political convention?
    c. What is public opinion?
    d. What is character?
    e. What is a good reputation?

I.   For dramatic effect, define the subject by stating what it is not.

---

1. The True Writer

BY WILLIAM FAULKNER

The young man or woman writing today has forgotten the problems of the human heart in conflict with itself which alone can make good writing because only that is worth writing about, worth the agony and the sweat.

He must learn them again. He must teach himself that the basest of all things is to be afraid; and, teaching himself that, forget it forever,

THE TRUE WRITER: from Nobel Prize speech of William Faulkner. By permission of *The Saturday Review*.

leaving no room in his workshop for anything but the old verities and truths of the heart, the old universal truths lacking which any story is ephemeral and doomed—love and honor and pity and pride and compassion and sacrifice. Until he does so he labors under a curse. He writes not of love but of lust, of defeats in which nobody loses anything of value, of victories without hope and worst of all without pity or compassion. His griefs grieve on no universal bones, leaving no scars. He writes not of the heart but of the glands.

Comment

Here Faulkner defines the true writer by saying what he is (Ss1-3) and what he is not (Ss4 to the end). The contrast in the last four sentences makes his definition more forceful.

Analysis and Composition

1. How do the emotional connotations of the following phrases help to make this definition effective?
   a. "The agony and the sweat"
   b. "Old verities and truths of the heart"
   c. "Not of love but of lust"
2. Show how the following opposites help to define the subject of this passage:

       old—new
       permanent—ephemeral
       mind—body
       hope—despair

3. In a paragraph of 50 words develop three of the following subjects by showing what the subject is not:

   a. Devotion to duty   e. Prudence
   b. Anticommunism   f. True patriotism
   c. Tolerance   g. Good manners
   d. Caution   h. A cultivated accent

2. The High Road of Life

BY SAMUEL TAYLOR COLERIDGE

[1]Shakespeare's plays . . . keep at all times to the high road of life. [2]Shakespeare has no innocent adulteries, no interesting incests, no virtuous vice;—he never renders that amiable which religion and reason alike teach us to detest, or clothes impurity in the garb of virtue, like Beaumont and Fletcher. [3]Shakespeare's fathers are roused by ingratitude, his husbands stung by unfaithfulness; in him, in short, the affections are wounded in those points in which all may, nay, must, feel. [4]Let the morality of Shakespeare be contrasted with that of the writers of his own, or the succeeding, age, or of those of the present day, who boast their superiority in this respect. [5]No one can dispute that the result of such a comparison is altogether in favour of Shakespeare; even the letters of women of high rank in his age were often coarser than his writings. [6]If he occasionally disgusts a keen sense of delicacy, he never injures the mind; he neither excites, nor flatters, passion, in order to degrade the subject of it; he does not use the faulty thing for a faulty purpose, nor carries on warfare against virtue, by causing wickedness to appear as no wickedness, through the medium of a morbid sympathy with the unfortunate. [7]In Shakespeare vice never walks as in twilight; nothing is purposely out of its place;—he inverts not the order of nature and propriety,—does not make every magistrate a drunkard or glutton, nor every poor man meek, humane, and temperate; he has no benevolent butchers, nor any sentimental rat-catchers.

Comment

Coleridge defines Shakespeare's superior morality (the high road of life) partly by contrasting it with the morality of other writers (Ss2-4) but chiefly by showing what Shakespeare does not do (Ss5-8). Thus by the use of negatives Coleridge defines what he means by keeping "to the high road of life" (S1). This passage serves to remind us that definition frequently borrows other methods of development, such as contrast.

Analysis and Composition

1. Name the positive qualities imputed to Shakespeare by negatives in this paragraph.
2. Consult your handbook for the meaning of "the exact word." *   Show how the following words exactly serve Coleridge's purpose:

roused	delicacy	benevolent
stung	morbid	sentimental
disgusts		

3. "Innocent adulteries," "interesting incests," "virtuous vices" are all absurd or paradoxical phrases. Point out other paradoxes in this passage. How do these paradoxes contribute to the central thought?
4. What emotional effect is created in this passage? What details contribute to this effect?
5. Use negatives to define one or more of the following subjects. Choose details that will arouse some feeling in your reader.
   a. The neutral Swiss
   b. The racial bias of Nazi Germany
   c. The humanitarianism of Charles Dickens
   d. The busy life of a big city
   e. The peace propaganda of the communists
   f. The emotional effect of a great poem
   g. The sentimentality of popular songs
   h. The luxury of traveling first class
   i. Lincoln's patience with subordinates
   j. A good teacher's power of illustration
6. Reread examples II E1 and II H. Then determine how the terms *liberty* and *university* may be defined negatively.
7. In a paragraph of 200 words write a negative definition of a university or of the spirit of liberty.

---

* See handbooks: Foerster, *58*; Hodges, *20*; Kierzek, *36*; Perrin, pp. 326-28; Wykoff, *89a-b*.

J.

When you dispute the meaning of a word or idea, define your opponent's view as well as your own.

What Is Science?

BY ANTHONY STANDEN

1 What exactly is this "Science" that is so highly regarded? Buckets of ink have been used up in defining it, but the simplest way is to say, "Science is any knowledge that is arrived at by the Scientific Method" —and then to define the scientific method. Many more buckets of ink have been used in explaining this method, but its essentials can be described rather easily, as a series of definite steps, roughly as follows. The first step is observation. Usually what is observed is the result of a deliberately contrived experiment (but not necessarily, for astronomy is a science, and it is impossible to do any experiments with the stars). A number of observations are collected, and then the scientist goes into a huddle with himself and forms a hypothesis, that is, a suggested explanation, of some sort or other, of the facts that have been observed. A hypothesis is, if you like, a sort of guess. In the next step the scientist says, "*If* my hypothesis is true, then when I do such and such an experiment, so and so ought to happen." The final step is to do the appropriate experiment, and see if the hypothesis is substantiated. If the result of the experiment is different from what was expected, the hypothesis is rejected at once—it's wrong. If the experiment agrees, the hypothesis is accepted tentatively. As further experiments are done,

perhaps by other scientists, the hypothesis is continually put to the test of experiment, and if it survives a large number of experiments, and can explain them all, it is promoted to a "theory." A theory is simply a well-tested hypothesis, but there is no sharp dividing line. Even the very best of theories may turn out to be wrong, for tomorrow an experiment may be done that flatly contradicts it. Scientists suppose that they always remember this faint shadow of doubt that hangs over all their theories, but in practice, as we shall see later, they often forget it.

2 Besides these essentials of the scientific method, there are some other qualities usually associated with science, and that are connoted if not denoted by the word. One of these is accuracy in observation, which quite clearly is necessary. Quantitative measurement is also very highly stressed. Even more highly regarded is the absence of bias, or freedom from prejudice, that scientists think they enjoy. In the higher realms of science it really is uncommonly difficult to be properly impartial when comparing two theories, your own and somebody else's, or to be sure, in making a hypothesis, to give the other fellow's results just as much weight as your own. Most scientists do this remarkably fairly and well, in their own specialized fields, though whether they can practice this virtue outside their own little duck ponds is much more questionable; at any rate they pat themselves hard on the back for doing it at all. But they reserve the greatest praise for their own objectivity. It is continually stressed, in all scientific training, that subjective feelings must not enter. The scientist records the result of an experiment in terms of observations, usually readings of instruments; he pays no attention to whether he likes it or not. The objects in front of him are what he is talking about, not his own subjective feelings about them. He must record a result that contradicts his theory just as objectively as one that agrees with it. According to what some scientists say, one could almost define science as pure concentrated essence of objectivity. And this explains why science is, for some people, devoid of appeal, and why it leaves out much that is of interest to everybody, for we are all of us, as human beings but not as scientists, tremendously interested in our own subjective feelings.

3 Another belief firmly held by all scientists, even the quieter ones, is that they define their terms accurately, and express themselves with a praiseworthy precision which everybody should imitate. It is hard to see how they can keep up this belief, seeing that all of them spend quite a lot of time in reading what is written by other scientists, and that clear expression is as rare among scientists as it is anywhere else.

The answer to this puzzle can only be that scientists are no better readers than anybody else, and don't know clear writing when they see it. At any rate they spend a great deal of trouble in framing definitions for their words. Sometimes the definitions actually say what the words mean, sometimes they don't. But they are impressed with the advantages of this procedure, and they teach words, supposing that in so doing they are teaching science. They will have you call the mammals the "Mammalia," or the backboned animals "Vertebrata." They will teach you that a spider is not an insect, that a whale is not a fish, or sometimes, by a crazy mismanagement of words in the name of science, that a shark is not a fish (because it is not a bony fish). They will teach you that the Latin name of an animal or a plant is the "scientific" name, as if one knew anything about science simply through knowing Latin names, although the whole Linnaean system of names, they will freely admit, is in an appalling mess. They will teach you that "work" is "force times distance" instead of being anything you do that is disagreeable and that you get paid for. In the realm of higher abstractions they will teach you powerful phrases like "electronic resonance" and "emergent evolution": they will define these in tight phrases which convey a meaning only to those who already understand it, and if you can produce, in an examination, the correct defining words, then you pass the test. And all this has as much, and no more, to do with real science as knowing the names of the pieces and the squares on a chessboard has to do with being able to play chess.

4 The dreadful cocksureness that is characteristic of scientists in bulk is not only quite foreign to the spirit of true science, it is not even justified by a superficial view. It is of course quite possible to write the history of science as one long crescendo, whose ultimate glorious achievement is the present—and what wonderful people we must be. It is always given in this way, in teaching, as part of a little introduction which is a pep talk for the particular science being dealt with. The Greeks were very clever people, the introduction will go, and they thought of many ingenious theories, but they were lazy, and did not do experiments with their hands. Their foremost philosopher was Aristotle, and it is now the fashion to say that he was not altogether too bad, but the medievals were bad who believed things on Authority, the authority of Aristotle. Modern Science began with Galileo and Newton, and has run steadily ahead ever since, with a great acceleration of progress in the last fifty years, with radioactivity, the discovery

of X rays, Einstein, Bohr, the structure of the atom, Oppenheimer, the Manhattan Project and the Atomic Energy Commission (leaving out the Un-American Activities Committee). But the same story can be told with a humiliating reverse English on it: if the climax and pinnacle of science is our knowledge of the atom *now,* then what was known ten years ago must have been decidedly imperfect, for science has made great strides since then. What was known twenty years ago was even more imperfect, and the science of fifty years ago hardly worth knowing. Using a little imagination, we can ask what will become of the science of today, some twenty or thirty years from now? Unless the rate of scientific advance shows a notable slacking off (and there are no signs of this) our best knowledge of today will become decidedly frowsy.

Comment

Mr. Standen is not defining science as it is in itself. Rather he is criticizing science as it is regarded by those who claim that all knowledge is "scientific" knowledge. Therefore the definition he gives is that of his opponents. His own definition appears elsewhere in the book from which this passage is taken.

Analysis and Composition

1. Decide whether the definition of science in paragraph 1 is a logical definition.
2. Show how science is defined by connotation in paragraph 2.
3. The author criticizes the accuracy and precision of some scientific terms in paragraph 3. What standards of "real science" are implied in the last sentence of this paragraph?
4. How does the author's ridicule of "the dreadful cocksureness that is characteristic of scientists in bulk" support his own implied standard of real science?
5. Criticize in two or three written paragraphs some false definition of one or more of the following terms:
   a. Success in life
   b. Social adjustment
   c. The spirit of compromise
   Be sure to define the view you wish to criticize before advancing your own.

GENERAL EXERCISES

1. Write a brief definition of one or more of the terms listed below according to this outline:
   a. The derivation of the word
   b. Its principal uses in the past
   c. Its genus or class and specific difference
   d. Variety of application today

culture	tyranny	state
slander	finality	informer
hypocrisy	love	wisdom
governor	devotion	action

2. After analyzing the following statements about literature, write a short definition of each of the italicized words. Be sure to define the word in the context of the sentence.

   Sample: Rhetoric is *skill* in the use of words. Skill is the ability to do something well as the result of knowledge and practice. Skill in the use of words means the ability to use words to communicate ideas to a given audience.

   a. In all good writing the source and fountain is *wisdom.*—HORACE
   b. No other test can be applied to literature than *length of duration* and *continuance of esteem.*—SAMUEL JOHNSON
   c. The great *end* of all art is to make an *impression* on the *imagination* and the *feeling.*—REYNOLDS
   d. Gusto in art is power or passion *defining* any object.—HAZLITT
   e. The poetry of words is the *rhythmical* creation of *Beauty.*—POE
   f. *Activity* in *serenity* is the motto of classical literature.—SAINTE-BEUVE
   g. Literature is the *meeting-ground* of two *souls.*—CHARLES DU BOS

3. Correct the possible obscurities in one or more of the following false statements by a precise definition of the italicized terms. Then rewrite the sentence to make the meaning unmistakable.

   Sample: The majority is always *right.* The primary meaning of *right* as an adjective is, according to *The American College Dictionary,* "in accordance with what is just or good." Obviously, according to this definition the majority is not always right, since majorities have been known to make bad political decisions, as in the German vote for Hitler. A more accurate statement is: The opinion of the majority, which represents the agreement of the greater number of a group of people, should not be discounted without good reason.

a. Society is made up of *classes,* not *individuals.*
b. Urban life is more *civilized* than country life.
c. A *moral* man is always *right.*
d. We can never be *sure* of *anything.*
e. He doesn't believe in law; he is a *law* unto himself.
f. An infallible consequence of allowing youth too much *liberty* is the abuse of liberty.
g. To *vote* for a minority candidate is to throw your vote away.
h. War is a biological necessity of *human nature.*

4. Write out definitions of the italicized word or words in each group listed below. In your definition show the connection of the italicized word with other words in the same group.
   a. *High school,* grammar school, college, trade school, professional school
   b. *Culture,* civilization, good manners, artistic ability, sensitivity
   c. *County government,* city government, state government, federal government
   d. *River,* estuary, lagoon, bay, lake
   e. *Rain,* hail, sleet, snow, frozen rain
   f. *Verb,* noun, pronoun, adjective, adverb
   g. *Compound-complex sentence,* simple sentence, complex sentence, compound sentence
   h. *Comma,* period, colon, semicolon
   i. *War,* insurrection, banditry, piracy, police action

5. In a short composition of 500 words consisting of an introductory paragraph, three paragraphs of development, and a concluding paragraph, evaluate Froude's definition of history in the light of the following occasions:
   a. As the introduction to a high school textbook
   b. As an appendix of a college textbook
   c. As a personal statement
   d. As a part of an essay for fellow historians

What Is History?

BY JAMES ANTHONY FROUDE

History is the account of the actions of men; and in "actions" are comprehended the thoughts, opinions, motives, impulses of the actors and of the circumstances in which their work was executed. The actions without motives are nothing, for they may be interpreted in many ways, and can only be understood in their causes. If *Hamlet* or *Lear* was exact to outward fact—were they and their fellow-actors on the stage exactly such as Shakespeare describes them—and if they did the acts which he assigns to them, that was perfect history, and what we call history is only valuable as it approaches to that pattern. To say that the character of real men cannot be thus completely known, that their inner nature is beyond our reach, that the dramatic portraiture of things is only possible to poetry, is to say that history ought not to be written, for the inner nature of the persons of whom it speaks is the essential thing about them; and, in fact, the historian assumes that he does know it, for his work without it is pointless and colourless. And yet to penetrate really into the hearts and souls of men, to give each his due, to represent him as he appeared at his best to himself, and not to his enemies, to sympathise in the collision of principles with each party in turn, to feel as they felt, to think as they thought, and to reproduce the various beliefs, the acquirements, the intellectual atmosphere of another age, is a task which requires gifts as great or greater than those of the greatest dramatists, for all is required which is required of the dramatist, with the obligation to truth of ascertained fact besides. It is for this reason that historical works of the highest order are so scanty. The faculty itself, the imaginative and reproductive insight, is among the rarest of human qualities. The moral determination to use it for purposes of truth only is rarer still—nay, it is but in particular ages of the world that such work can be produced at all. The historians of genius themselves, too, are creatures of their own times and it is only at periods when men of intellect have "swallowed formulas," when conventional and established ways of thinking have ceased to satisfy, that, if they are serious and conscientious, they are able "to sympathise with opposite sides."

6. Decide on the most appropriate method (A-J in the introduction to this section) of defining each of the following subjects. Give reasons for your answer.
   a. Language, literature, and a college education
   b. What is advertising?
   c. Nationalism
   d. My idea of enjoyment
   e. John Dewey's contribution to educational theory
   f. The Russian idea of warmongering
   g. Characteristics of Grade B movies
   h. Atomic fission
   i. The ideal political condidate
7. Develop by definition, in a paragraph of 300 words, one of the subjects listed in Exercise 6.
8. Which of the following statements are logical definitions? Explain your answer.

Sample: Rhetoric is the art of expression. This is not a logical definition. The genus, art, is correctly stated, but the species, expression, does not differentiate rhetoric from other arts of expression such as painting and music.

a. A conservative is a man who votes for Senator Taft. He has money in the bank, and he hates to pay taxes.
b. A poet is a man who writes poems.
c. Man is the only animal capable of laughter.
d. A battleship is a naval vessel heavier than cruisers but not so heavy as the largest aircraft carriers.
e. A radical is a man who carries out his basic principles to their ultimate limits.
f. California is a land of ease and opportunity.
g. A radical is a man who roots out abuses.
h. The function of a state university is to prepare the future citizen for efficient social service.
i. [The educated man is one] who has been so trained in youth that his body is the ready servant of his will and it does with ease and pleasure all the work that, as a mechanism, it is capable of; whose intellect is a clear, cold logic engine, with all its parts of equal strength and in smooth working order; ready, like a steam engine, to be turned to any kind of work, and spin the gossamers as well as forge the anchors of the mind; whose mind is stored with the knowledge of the great fundamental truths of nature and of the laws of her operations; one who, no stunted ascetic, is full of life and fire, but whose passions are trained to come to heel by a vigorous will, the servant of a tender conscience; who has learned to love all beauty, whether of nature or of art, to hate all vileness, and to respect others as himself.—T. H. HUXLEY

9. Examine the following list of general topics. After analyzing each topic in the light of the given occasion, derive an appropriate *subject* and a *central theme* that may be developed chiefly by definition. Assume that your *purpose* is an expository discourse.

Sample: *General topic:* Political factions
      Occasion: A 300-word letter to a newspaper deploring factionalism
      Subject: The Dixiecrats
      Central theme: The Dixiecrats have confused national issues with local politics

General Topic	*Occasion*
The whaling industry in New England	A 1000-word essay for a prize contest commemorating the centenary of the whaling industry in New England
Southern industry	A 200-word reply to a statement made in a magazine that the South is wholly agricultural
Vacation resorts	A 500-word explanation for a Chamber of Commerce folder explaining the recreation facilities of a Florida beach community
The United States Constitution	A 400-word answer to an examination question, "What is the United States Constitution?"
Flag Day	A 300-word definition for an American Legion prize essay contest
Our gravest problem	A 500-word definition of the most important political or social problem for consideration on the "Youth Wants to Know" television program
True success	A 300-word definition of the kind of man you want to become in twenty years for a round-table discussion with your vocational guidance counselor
Police action	A 300-word definition requested by your instructor in government after a class discussion on the meaning of war
Internal waterways	A term paper of 1500 words defining the influence of rivers and canals on American growth.

10. As directed by your instructor, write an essay on one of the topics listed in Exercise 9.

A. State clearly the common element on which the classification or division depends.

    1 AVERY O. CRAVEN AND WALTER JOHNSON:
            The Cycle of American History

    2 JOSEPH ADDISON: *What Is a Pedant?*

    3 E. F. CALDIN:
            *Science: Its Material and Mental
                          Influence*

B. Make the classification or division as complete as necessary.

    1 MARSTON BATES:
            Characteristics of the Tropics

    2 PHILIP GRAHAM: *Showboats*

    3 PETER FLEMING: *My Brazilian Expedition*

C. Make the classification and division apt and purposeful.

    1 PLATO: *Apology*

    2 RUSSELL LYNES: *On Weekend Guests*

    3 PHILIP RAHV: *Paleface and Redskin*

General Exercises

    VERNON LOUIS PARRINGTON:
                        Puritan and Yankee

**SECTION
III**

Classification and Division

CLASSIFICATION and division are means of logical analysis closely related to definition. Analysis by definition resolves a subject into its component parts, by stating

    a. The class or whole to which a subject belongs. (This class, if it is a logical whole, may be called *genus*. See explanation of logical whole later in this introduction.)

    b. The difference or distinguishing element, whereby the subject is set apart from the remainder of the class.

Thus to define is partly to generalize or classify, and partly to specify or divide.

Analysis by *classification* examines one arm of a definition—the genus or class—in greater detail. To classify is to determine the whole of which the subject is a part.

Analysis by *division* examines the other arm of definition—the distinguishing element—in greater detail. To divide is to determine the parts of which the subject is a whole.

CLASSIFICATION

By definition, the subject, New York, is a sovereign state (part) of the United States (whole or class).

By classification, we may analyze the class (United States) of the subject (New York). Or, we may discover other classes to which the subject belongs. Thus New York may be classified not only as a sovereign state of the United States. It may also be classified according to various other principles or bases of classification. For example:

Subject	Classification	Basis of Classification
(Part of a Whole)	(Whole of Which the Subject is Part)	(Why the Subject Belongs in the Class)
New York	Middle Atlantic state	Regional status of New York
	One of original thirteen states	History
	One of most important states	Wealth and population
	Maritime state	Ports and harbors on Atlantic and Great Lakes

Thus, by helping us to know the various classes (or wholes) of which New York is a part, classification assists us to understand and to develop our subject.

DIVISION

In analysis by division we regard the same subject as a whole which is composed of parts. Thus the subject, New York, considered as a whole, may be broken down into parts, as for example,

Subject	Division	Basis of Division
(A Whole)	(Parts that Constitute the Subject)	(Why the Parts Are Grouped Together)
New York	Counties, cities, towns, and villages	Political organization
	Urban, suburban, and rural areas	Concentration of population
	Wealthy, middle-class, or lower-income areas	Average financial income of its citizens
	Industrial, farming, commercial areas	Principal occupation of the inhabitants

Further subdivisions are also possible, as, for example, the division of farming areas into sections devoted to dairy farming, truck gardening, orchards, viticulture, and so on. Thus division, by helping us to know the parts which constitute our subject (the whole), is also a helpful means of analysis.

CLASSIFICATION AND DIVISION IN SIMPLE ANALYSIS

At this stage of our study classification and division may be considered as parts of the same process of analysis because the study of the subject as a part of a whole (classification) and the study of the same subject as a smaller whole divisible into parts (division) are as closely related to each other as up is to down. Classification is an upward movement, the grouping of the subject in a class or genus. Division is a downward movement, the partition of the subject into lesser wholes or into individual parts. In many instances division is merely classification in reverse. Both classification and division use the same rules, and they serve the same end, which is to make a subject understandable.

CLASSIFICATION AND DIVISION IN REASONING

However, there is a theoretical distinction between classification and division that becomes more important when these two methods are extended from simple analysis of the subject to proving, or reasoning about, some phase of the subject. Thus when we reason from the particular to the general (classification) we use the process called induction. When we reason from the general to the particular (division) we use the process called deduction.

A scientific induction establishes the identity of a class by examining and grouping the particulars together by virtue of a common element. A scientific deduction establishes the truth of the particulars by proving that they belong to a class whose identity has been established. Often a deductive argument is possible only after the identity of the class has been established by a previous induction.

For example, three boys—Smith, Brown and Jones—are presented to us for placement in high school Latin. We know nothing about their previous studies, and therefore we give them an examination which shows that all three have mastered elementary Latin. On this evidence, we group them in a class which we call Intermediate Latin I by virtue of a principle of classification—a qualifying examination. The class having been established by an induction, we may now argue from the general to the particular. If someone asks whether Smith knows any Latin we can answer, "Yes. He's in Intermediate Latin I."

The full statement of our deductive reasoning is this: Anyone who is a member of Intermediate Latin I has indicated a knowledge of elementary Latin by passing a qualifying examination. But Smith is a member of Intermediate Latin I. Therefore Smith has indicated a knowledge of elementary Latin.

(Induction is also discussed in connection with Mark Twain's essay in Section IV. A full discussion of deduction and induction appears in T. H. Huxley's essay and in the accompanying analysis in Section VII, and throughout Section XI.)

THE RULES FOR CLASSIFICATION AND DIVISION

In this section we are concerned with classification and division as closely related methods of simple analysis rather than as deductive and inductive reasoning. Considered in this limited way, the rules for classification and division may be stated thus:

Make your classification and division clear, that is, state clearly the common element on which the classification or division depends.

Make your classification and division as complete as necessary.

Make your classification and division apt and purposeful.

(Note: All good classifications and divisions are at once clear, complete, apt, and purposeful. However, in the course of our study throughout this section we shall concentrate on one rule at a time. In the longer examples (D2, D3) we shall consider the three rules together.)

A. *The First Rule: State clearly the common element on which the classification or division depends.* This means that you must determine what is the *basis* or reason for your classification or division. By basis or principle we mean the common element or characteristic by virtue of which various parts are grouped in a whole, or by virtue of which a whole is divided into its various parts. You have seen this rule illustrated above in the classifications and divisions of the subject New York.

 1. The classification and division of a *physical whole*. A *physical* whole is a *quantitative* unit whose parts may be measured. Thus New York, considered as land, population, or buildings, is a physical whole. So too an automobile, a house, a continent

are physical units or wholes. We may classify and divide physical wholes in several conventional ways, such as:

a. *Time order,* as in the division of events according to when they occurred

b. *Place, or space order,* as in the division of North America into Alaska, Canada, the United States, Mexico, the several Central American republics, and nearby islands

c. *Mechanical order,* as in the division of the parts of a machine in accordance with their function

2. The classification and division of a *logical whole.* Many subjects must be classified or divided, not by the order of time or place or by some other physical measurement but by virtue of logical qualities, that is, of common characteristics perceived by the mind. In this connection it is most important to understand that a *logical* unit or whole and a *physical* unit or whole cannot be classified and divided in the same way.

A *logical* whole is a mental reality. Thus the concepts of *patriotism, love, habeas corpus* are logical wholes. The particular parts of these wholes are grouped in a class by virtue of a common element perceived by the mind. These parts are not necessarily related in the order of time or space. Patriotism occurs in Greece as well as in Mexico; love may be found in ancient times as well as in modern times. Neither can the parts of a logical whole be measured. The logical whole and its parts are *ideas,* not so many pounds of facts, not so many parts of a machine.

Adlai Stevenson understood this distinction when he wrote, "When an American says he loves his country he means not only that he loves the New England hills, the prairies glistening in the sun, or the wide rising plains, the mountains and the seas [the physical whole]. He means that he loves an inner air, an inner light in which freedom lives and in which a man can draw the breath of self-respect" [the logical whole].

A book will serve as a useful example. *Physically* a book consists of so many pages of print. The physical book is made of paper, thread, printed ink, glue, boards, and cloth. It may be measured and weighed. *Logically* a book is a body of ideas which may be classed as a novel, a biography, a drama, or some other logical whole.

To summarize: A classification or division, then, is clear when it states and follows a definite principle of classification or division. This you will see in Example A1, in which Craven and Johnson divide American history according to chronological order. In Example A2 Addison classifies pedants by showing that all pedants, of which his specimens stand as representatives, possess the common characteristic of not knowing how to think outside their own specialty. In Example A3 E. F. Caldin explains the role of science in the modern world by dividing science according to its material and mental effects upon civilization.

Overlapping and cross-division. A clear principle of classification and division will prevent two common errors, namely overlapping and cross-division. *Overlapping* occurs when one class includes another class in the same listing, as, for example, this division of the subject, "Eastern Seaboard of the United States":

a. New England
b. New York
c. The Middle Atlantic states
d. The Southern Atlantic states

Here, New York is not a coordinate of the other divisions. It should be included under the Middle Atlantic states.

Cross-division occurs when a subject is divided by two or more methods of division. For example, to divide New York into counties, industrial areas, and seaports would be to employ three separate methods of division (see outline at beginning of this section) and thus to cross-divide. However cross-division should not be confused with the practice of classifying and dividing a subject in the same passage. Many introductory paragraphs, such as Example A1, state a physical division and then assign each of these divisions to one or more logical classes. In such instances the same subject is considered in two different senses, in one sense as a physical whole and in the other sense as a logical whole. Thus, for example, New York may be considered as one physical unit of the United States, or as a species of the United States considered as a logical whole.

B. *The Second Rule: Make the classification or division as complete as necessary*. A classification or division is complete when the parts taken together equal the whole. It is possible, for instance, to have a clear method of division, and yet to have an *incomplete* division. Thus, for example, if you were to divide Europe on the basis of its political boundaries, and then to list only France, Italy, and Germany, the method of your division would be clear but the actual division would be incomplete. Spain, Greece, Belgium, and other nations should be included.

Completeness is not merely a matter of numbers. If a class consists of only two members, a simple division is exhaustive. If on the other hand a class consists of ten members, then a division including nine is incomplete.

The nature and extent of the subject (the whole) determines the correct number of its parts. Thus, for example, Marston Bates divides the tropics into four natural regions in Example B1; Mr. Graham divides showboats into four basic divisions and several subdivisions in Example B2; Mr. Fleming in Example B3 classifies his subject, the people who advised him, into eleven categories. In each example the nature and extent of the subject determine the number of the parts.

C. *The Third Rule: Make the classification or division apt and purposeful.* You must not forget that, as a writer, you do not classify and divide merely for the sake of displaying special knowledge of a subject. Such would be the pedant's game that Joseph Addison ridicules in Example A2 and that Shakespeare immortalized in Polonius' long-winded catalogue of the drama in *Hamlet* (Act II, Scene 2, lines 415-21).

The writer should choose the classification and division that is *apt,* i.e., suitable to his subject and his occasion, and *purposeful.* Thus, Plato in Example C1 uses a simple either/or division, apt for his subject and occasion. The dilemma he presents is also helpful in achieving his purpose, namely in winning our assent to the argument that death is a benefit. On the other hand, Russell Lynes in C2 divides and subdivides his subject, weekend guests, into thirteen parts—an arrangement justified by his particular subject and occasion and in line with his purpose. In Example C3 Philip Rahv classifies American authors under two headings, paleface and redskin, in the light of his purpose and occasion.

Let us note once again that good classifications and divisions are clear, complete, apt, and purposeful at the same time.

a. State clearly the common element on which the classification or division depends.

1. The Cycle of American History

BY AVERY O. CRAVEN
AND WALTER JOHNSON

The history of the American people may be divided roughly into three periods. The first is the colonial period, in which different European groups, with differing cultural patterns, were adjusting themselves to one another and to the American environment and, thereby, evolving a new people and a new nation. The second is the national period, in which the young United States of America turned its back on Europe, marched steadily westward across the American continent, and transformed it, region by region, from a simple wilderness into a land of farms and towns and complex social-industrial institutions. Connections with the outside world were reduced to a minimum, and Americans, engaged in American tasks, sharpened and modified their own national characteristics, both personal and institutional, and emerged before the world as a powerful nation with positive interests and values uniquely its own. The third period is the one in which we find ourselves, at the present time, an integral part of the larger world. We are back where we started. The days of isolation are over. Just before the dawn of the twentieth century the United States found itself, half reluctantly, again facing outward. American goods and American capital had already invaded other lands; interests and values

THE CYCLE OF AMERICAN HISTORY: from *The United States: Experiment in Democracy,* by Avery O. Craven and Walter Johnson. Reprinted by permission of Ginn and Company, publishers.

had forced a war with Spain and bequeathed us a colonial empire; and then the blunt fact of world interdependence pushed us into two great European wars. The cycle was thus completed, but the attitudes and assumptions inherited from the two earlier periods of American life, and their need of readjustment, have left much of mental confusion and much of uncertainty. We often appear to be a people whose bodies are in one age and whose minds are in an earlier one. The great task of adjustment still plagues the American people.

Comment

This is an example of division and classification, not of cross-division, as we observed in the introduction to this section. The subject—the history of the American people considered as a physical whole—is divided into three chronological periods, the colonial, national, and modern. Here the principle of division is time order. But note too that all of the periods are grouped together, that is, classified, under a logical whole, the pattern of history, by virtue of one common characteristic, namely the "great task of adjustment."

Analysis and Composition

1. Find as many synonyms as you can for the word *adjust.* Then determine where the authors have used these synonyms for *adjust* throughout the paragraph. (You should find at least six equivalents.)
2. Point out the transitional sentences and expressions in this passage.*
3. Criticize the exactness † of the following words and expressions in the context of the passage:

   cultural patterns   positive interests   attitudes and assumptions
   American environment   integral part

4. Find adequate principles of division for the following topic sentences:

   Sample: *Topic sentence:* Immigrants help America.

Division	Principle of Division
A. By making us more aware of foreign languages and literatures	Contribution to cultural life

* See handbooks: Foerster, *89*; Hodges, *31b*; Kierzek, *60*; Perrin, pp. 193-94; Wykoff, *72.*

† See handbooks: Foerster, *58*; Hodges, *20*; Kierzek, *36*; Perrin, pp. 326-28; Wykoff. *89a-b.*

B. By introducing their special skill in
   music and other fine arts
C. By providing fresh attitudes on social
   and intellectual problems

Topic Sentences:

a. American literature may be divided into four (or five) periods.
b. There are two (or three) types of internationalist.
c. The chief characteristic of the American is his mobility.

5. Write a paragraph not exceeding 300 words on one of the topic sentences listed in Exercise 4.

2. What Is a Pedant?

BY JOSEPH ADDISON

A man who has been brought up among books, and is able to talk of nothing else, is a very indifferent companion, and what we call a pedant. But, methinks, we should enlarge the title, and give it to everyone that does not know how to think out of his profession and particular way of life.

What is a greater pedant than a mere man of the town? Bar him the playhouses, a catalogue of the reigning beauties, and an account of a few fashionable distempers that have befallen him, and you strike him dumb. How many a pretty gentleman's knowledge lies all within the verge of the court? He will tell you the names of the principal favorites, repeat the shrewd sayings of a man of quality, whisper an intrigue that is not yet blown upon by common fame; or, if the sphere of his observations is a little larger than ordinary, will perhaps enter into all the incidents, turns, and revolutions in a game of ombre. When he has gone thus far he has shown you the whole circle of his accomplishments, his parts are drained, and he is disabled from any farther conversation. What are these but rank pedants? And yet these are the men who value themselves most on their exemption from the pedantry of colleges.

I might here mention the military pedant, who always talks in a camp, and is storming towns, making lodgments, and fighting battles from one end of the year to the other. Everything he speaks smells of gunpowder; if you take away his artillery from him, he has not a word to say for himself. I might likewise mention the law pedant, that is perpetually putting cases, repeating the transactions of Westminster Hall, wrangling with you upon the most indifferent circumstances of life, and not to be convinced of the distance of a place, or of the most trivial point in conversation, but by dint of argument. The state pedant is wrapped up in news and lost in politics. If you mention either of the kings of Spain or Poland, he talks very notably; but if you go out of the *Gazette* you drop him. In short, a mere courtier, a mere soldier, a mere scholar, a mere anything, is an insipid pedantic character, and equally ridiculous.

Of all the species of pedants which I have mentioned, the book pedant is much the most supportable; he has at least an exercised understanding and a head which is full though confused, so that a man who converses with him may often receive from him hints of things that are worth knowing, and what he may possibly turn to his own advantage, though they are of little use to the owner. The worse kind of pedants among learned men are such as are naturally endued with a very small share of common sense, and have read a great number of books without taste or distinction.

The truth of it is, learning, like traveling and all other methods of improvement, as it finishes good sense, so it makes a silly man ten thousand times more insufferable by supplying variety of matter to his impertinence, and giving him an opportunity of abounding in absurdities.

Comment

"A mere courtier, a mere soldier, a mere scholar" are members of the class, pedant. They are grouped in this class because they all have one common characteristic, namely they cannot think beyond the narrow limits of their own profession or way of life.

Analysis and Composition

1. Consult the *Oxford English Dictionary* to find the eighteenth-century usage of the following terms used in Example A2:

distempers	man of quality	rank
pretty	parts	indifferent

2. In your opinion does Addison justify his statement that we should enlarge the meaning of the word *pedant*? Give reasons for your answer.

3. In a manner similar to Addison's, write a paragraph of 300 words on one of the following titles:
   a. What Is a Snob?
   b. What Is a Bookworm?
   c. What Is a Politician?
   d. What Is an Efficiency Expert?
   e. What Is a Low-Brow?
   f. What Is a Social Lion?

3. Science: Its Material and Mental Influence

BY E. F. CALDIN

1 [1]While many writers, and among them not a few men of science, are convinced that we live at a crisis in Western civilization, opinions are divided about the nature of the crisis and the role which science has to play in helping to resolve it. [2]According to some, science will be responsible for our ruin, because it has given mankind the power to destroy itself. [3]According to others, science will work our salvation, because it is only another name for reason, and if we drop our outworn modes of thought we can use it to build a new metaphysic, a new ethic, and a new religion. [4]According to others again, science can put an end to want, and if we abolish want we shall abolish also hatred, envy, and avarice; therefore we need science for both the physical and the moral health of society.

2 [1]Such diagnoses, crude as they are in their identification of science with technology and in their estimate of its capabilities, contain at least this much truth. [2]Western civilization has been immensely affected both mentally and materially by forces that claim their origin from the advance of science since the time of Galileo. [3]On the one hand, industry has based itself on specialized technical knowledge, which in turn relies upon science. [4]Industrialization has vastly altered the machinery of living, the material background of life; it has brought about great changes in transport, communications, health services, and entertainment, for instance, in the last hundred years, and there is no reason to think that we have reached the end of these changes. [5]Technical invention has besides devised means by which a relatively small band of men can exterminate whole populations. [6]Such techniques could not be devised without a scientific understanding of nature. [7]Science and

SCIENCE: ITS MATERIAL AND MENTAL INFLUENCE: from *The Wind and the Rain*, V (Spring, 1949), used with the permission of the editor, Neville Braybrooke.

scientists have thus become of great importance to industrial societies, though indirectly and at one remove, via technology. [8]On the other hand, the success of science in interpreting nature has struck very forcibly the imagination of Western man, especially since the work of man like Darwin, Freud, and Pavlov began to extend it to living things and even mental life. [9]At a time when philosophers and theologians have fallen into disrepute with the general public, the successes of science in its own field are so impressive that many have been led to suppose that all thought would benefit by the same approach—that it is only a matter of time before science will settle finally the great questions that men have always asked about life. [10]Because of these two influences—one material, the other mental—many people regard science not only as the cure for want and pain, but as the method of thought *par excellence,* the one great source of truth.

Comment

In paragraph 1 opinions on science are divided according to several estimates of the role, or function, of science in the present crisis in Western civilization. In paragraph 2 the influence of science is divided according to its effect on material and mental life. In both paragraphs the logical division is clearly marked by the grammatical arrangement. Thus in paragraph 1 the three opinions on science are prefaced by "according to"; in paragraph 2 the phrase "On the one hand" (S3) introduces the influence of science on material life; "On the other hand" (S8) introduces the influence of science on mental life. Sentence 10 sums up the influence of science on many people today.

These two paragraphs are the beginning of an essay that demonstrates the necessity of harmonizing scientific knowledge with other kinds of knowledge to help solve the crisis in Western civilization.

Analysis and Composition

1. In a short paragraph develop by definition (see Section II) each of the following terms as they are used in this example.

science	diagnoses	mental
metaphysic	industrialization	material
ethic	technology	*par excellence*

2. In two short paragraphs develop one of the following subjects. Support each member of the division by examples.

Subject	Principle of Division	Division
The role of the automobile	According to its influence	1. On industrial life 2. On social life
The value of a college education	According to its influence	1. On personal happiness 2. On social welfare
The importance of television	According to its influence	1. On public opinion 2. On public taste

---

b. Make the classification or division as complete as necessary.

---

1. Characteristics of the Tropics

BY MARSTON BATES

From the beginning the process of discovery and exploration has had a profound effect on the peoples "discovered" and the regions "explored." The tropical regions that we see today have everywhere been modified to a greater or lesser extent by the migrations of European peoples and by the expansion of Western civilization, so that it is very difficult to put together a picture of these lands as they must have appeared before Columbus blundered into the West Indies or da Gama found his way around the Cape of Good Hope. Yet, without this picture, how are we to judge how much of the present is due to this explosion of western Europe, and how much to the characteristics of the tropical regions themselves?

CHARACTERISTICS OF THE TROPICS: reprinted from *Where Winter Never Comes* by Marston Bates; copyright 1952 by Marston Bates; used by permission of the publishers, Charles Scribner's Sons.

Each tropical region has reacted to the European contact in a distinct and characteristic way. In America, the local civilizations tumbled on contact with the Europeans, like so many houses of cards; and in some places, like the West Indies, even the people themselves disappeared. A new sort of culture, that of Latin America, was built on the wreck of these peoples and civilizations. At first the new civilization was purely colonial, but gradually it assumed an independent character under the influence of local conditions and with the gradual resurgence of indigenous cultural elements like those of the art of Mexico.

In Asia, the local civilizations at first maintained both cultural and political independence, resisting the brutal arrogance of the first European "discoverers," though yielding to the temptations of trade. But the Europeans gradually gained political dominance over most of tropical Asia through a series of bloody maneuvers among themselves and the various regional sovereignties; the story of the Portuguese, the Spaniards, the English, the Dutch and, last of all, the French and the Germans, in this region, is long, complicated and disgraceful. Cultural resistance has been stronger, however, than political resistance, and the regional civilizations have maintained a sort of continuity despite the European onslaughts. Christianity, for instance, which is generally considered to be the most important European cultural export, has made little progress, though the region has been swept by other proselytizing religions like Buddhism and Mohammedanism.

In Africa, the tropical people, at the time of European contact, had not developed any indigenous civilization. Nevertheless, they showed a surprising cultural and physical resistance—not melting away like the American Indians. I suspect that this difference was partly a matter of disease. The Europeans brought a whole lot of new diseases to America, which helped greatly in finishing off the Indians; in Africa, however, local diseases like yellow fever, malaria, sleeping sickness, and so forth, managed frequently to finish off the Europeans who tried to live in the place. In the end, the Europeans decided that "the climate was unhealthy," and restricted their African enterprises to exploitive forays by administrators and traders. These might have a disruptive enough effect on local cultural patterns, but they could not result in the development of a totally new pattern like that which has emerged in Latin America.

In Australia, to complete this tour, the local people melted away before the Europeans, as did the American Indians of the West Indies and of the United States, leaving an empty space in which a transplant of European culture could be established. The Australian situation is most closely comparable with that of the United States; and it is also essentially a Temperate Zone culture, though with a large tropical extension in Queensland. This Queensland area is of particular interest to any student of the tropics because it provides a unique opportunity to study the effect of a tropical environment on an English culture and European population.

Comment

Mr. Bates' principle of division is *the characteristic way in which the tropical regions have reacted to European contact.* The tropical region (class) is divided into specific tropical areas in America, Asia, Africa, and Australia—all the continents save Europe are included. Europe of course has no tropical area.

Analysis and Composition

1. In a few sentences describe the original (or etymological) meaning of each of the following words:

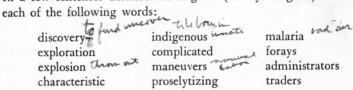

    discovery   indigenous   malaria

    exploration   complicated   forays

    explosion   maneuvers   administrators

    characteristic   proselytizing   traders

2. List *complete* divisions for each of the italicized words.

    Sample: The *satellite states* conform to Russia's foreign policy.
             Division of satellite states: Poland, Hungary, Czechoslovakia, Rumania, Bulgaria, China.

    a. All the *departments of the federal government* have suffered cuts in appropriation.
    b. Each of the *agencies of communication* covered the convention.
    c. Civilian Defense provides leadership for all *areas of the city.*
    d. The library has stored its books *according to subject.*

e. The five floors of the hospital contain virtually *all the facilities required for good medical practice.*

f. A typical state university campus contains *a variety of buildings.*

g. The citizens of a university community consist of *various groups.*

h. The nations of South America signalized their sovereignty by developing *beautiful and stately capitals.*

3. Write a short composition based on one of the divisions developed in answer to Exercise 2. Use one paragraph for an introduction, one for each division, and one for a conclusion.

4. For oral discussion, bring to class three examples of good division found in a textbook you are currently using.

2. Showboats

BY PHILIP GRAHAM

1 In the palmiest days of the business the large boats carried from twenty-five to thirty-five people, about equally divided between stage entertainment, including music, and other duties, such as running the boat and cooking. The smaller boats were family affairs with a few pick-ups added.

2 Salaries were low, especially for actors. While the engineer would be drawing $60 per week and the cook $40, the villain would be getting $12, the fetching little ingénue perhaps as much as $15, and a competent team, usually man and wife or sisters, as much as $20. These salaries represented clear money, however, for food and room were furnished, with no hotel bills, no tips, no traveling expenses of any kind. Very little wardrobe was needed. Furthermore, landings afforded slight opportunity for spending money—no night clubs, no attractive stores, no social life. Many a seasoned trouper, in debt for years, has been amazed at his accumulated savings at the end of his first showboat cruise.

3 Actors were on a showboat for an infinite variety of reasons. Some, with or without talent, were the owner's children, and from babyhood had been fitted into convenient niches in the programs. Some were tired professionals from the bright lights, some were dancers, acrobats, and magicians from sideshows and carnivals, seeking rest and relaxa-

SHOWBOATS: from *Showboats: The History of an American Institution* by Philip Graham. Copyright, University of Texas Press.

tion for one season. Some were "ham actors," dragged in by that alluring advertisement run in the *Billboard* every spring, men and women as restless as migratory birds. A few were country boys and girls lured by the glamor of the stage and the freedom of the river. . . .

4 Every showboat cast was sure to include certain typical characters that came to be associated with the business. The little ingénue, pretty, innocent, and big-eyed, plays the female leads. Between acts she is the singing soubrette, clasping a big bouquet of roses, artificial unless it happens to be rose season, as she sings songs that she perhaps only half understands. . . .

5 The villain is likely to be the best-natured person on the boat, a little voluble both on and off stage. Because of his experience and maturity, he is often chosen by the members of the cast as their director. . . .

6 The leading man of the cast, sometimes called the juvenile lead, is somewhat like a bridegroom, necessary but not much talked about. . . . He is likely to be young and handsome, as meticulous in his dress as funds will permit, and he combs his hair back in a full pompadour. If single, he usually thinks he is in love with the little ingénue, who plays opposite him in the melodrama. . . .

7 The comedian is seldom a jolly person, for it is his business to make others laugh, and he works hard at his job. He need not be comically ugly, but he is almost sure to have that big nose, those prominent cheek bones, that narrow-eyed sad expression that make the perfect setting for clown's paint. . . . [He] is aware of the heavy cargo of sentiment and tradition that his boat is carrying, and he therefore confines his fun to the borderline of propriety, and adjusts it nicely to the relief of the strained emotions of melodrama. Naturally the audience is more grateful to him than is the cast.

Comment

Mr. Graham's exposition of showboats in mid-nineteenth century America is developed by a series of four divisions. The first paragraph divides the subject, *showboats,* on the basis of the size of the crew and company. The division in the second paragraph is according to the salaries paid to the company. The third paragraph divides the acting company with respect to the motives of the individual actors. Paragraphs 4-7 divide the cast according to the principal characters. The four divisions are orderly in themselves; that is, each has a definite basis of division. There is no overlapping. Moreover, the separate divisions are all united in the larger class of showboat. The division is complete, since the sum of the parts equals the whole. Note that a complete division does not necessarily mean a *completely developed* division. In this selection each of the divisions might have been developed at much greater length. However, the present development is ample for a short essay.

Analysis and Composition

1. Are the following divisions clear and complete? Test for clarity by determining the basis for the division. Test for completeness by determining whether the sum of the parts equals the whole. Correct the division when necessary.
   a. Subject: A small midwestern farm
      1. Its size and the number of people on it
      2. Yearly income
      3. The motives of the typical farmer
      4. The farmer's activities in spring, summer, fall, and winter
   b. Subject: National parks
      1. Principal parks and their location
      2. Scenic qualities
      3. Recreational facilities
      4. Educational advantages
   c. Subject: Washington, D.C.
      1. Its size, population, and location
      2. Principal government buildings and monuments
      3. Universities and private institutions
      4. Private homes and gardens
   d. Subject: Modern travel
      1. The airplane
      2. Railroads
      3. Automobiles
      4. Ships
      5. Hiking
   e. Subject: Vacation retreats
      1. The hotel
      2. The boardinghouse
      3. The motel
      4. Lodgings
      5. Cottages
2. Each of the informal divisions listed below has one or more of the following faults:

  a. It has no clear principle of division
  b. The division overlaps
  c. The division is incomplete
Locate the fault and construct a good division.

  a. Subject: Good reading

1. Books of travel	3. Robinson Crusoe
2. Essays	4. Magazines

  b. Subject: The United States Army

1. Commissioned officers	4. Privates
2. Noncommissioned officers	5. Civilians
3. Educational advantages	

  c. Subject: Baseball

1. Infield	4. Umpires
2. Outfield	5. The ball park
3. Pitchers and catchers	

  d. Subject: *Oliver Twist*

1. The author	4. The style
2. The background	5. The climax
3. The material	

  e. Subject: Camping out

1. Selecting a site	4. Cooking
2. Pitching a tent	5. Cleaning up
3. Lighting a fire	6. Packing a horse

3. Write a short expository essay of about 400 words on one of the subjects listed in Exercises 1 and 2 above. Be sure to use a correct division.

3. My Brazilian Expedition

BY PETER FLEMING

I kept as quiet as I reasonably could, for it is unpleasant to be regarded as either a lunatic or a hero when you know perfectly well that you are merely going to take an exceptionally long holiday. All the same, it was amusing and instructive to watch people's reactions.

There were the Prudent, who said: "This is an extraordinarily foolish thing to do." There were the Wise, who said: "This is an extraordinarily foolish thing to do; but at least you will know better next time." There were the Very Wise, who said: "This is a foolish thing to do, but not nearly so foolish as it sounds." There were the Romantic, who appeared to believe that if everyone did this sort of

MY BRAZILIAN EXPEDITION: reprinted from *Brazilian Adventure* by Peter Fleming; copyright 1933 by Charles Scribner's Sons; used by permission of the publishers.

thing all the time the world's troubles would soon be over. There were the Envious, who thanked God they were not coming; and there were the other sort, who said with varying degrees of insincerity that they would give anything to come. There were the Correct, who asked me if I knew any of the people at the Embassy. There were the Practical, who spoke at length of inoculations and calibres. There were the people whose geography was not their strong point, and who either offered me letters of introduction to their cousins in Buenos Aires or supposed that I would find a good many Aztec ruins. There were the Apprehensive, who asked me if I had made my will. There were the Men Who Had Done a Certain Amount of That Sort of Thing in Their Time, You Know, and these imparted to me elaborate stratagems for getting the better of ants and told me that monkeys made excellent eating, and so for that matter did lizards, and parrots; they all tasted rather like chicken.

Comment

The principle that determined Mr. Fleming's eleven divisions is the characteristic reaction of various people in response to the announcement of his journey. All these reactions are said to be "amusing and instructive"—a classification certainly warranted by the particular statements. Furthermore, the classification is complete insofar as the sum of the parts equals the whole, that is, the number of Mr. Fleming's acquaintances who provided amusing or instructive reactions.

Analysis and Composition

1. The unity of Example B3 stems from the movement of each sentence towards the central thought: "It was amusing and instructive to watch people's reactions." The coherence of the passage is established by the parallelism of the "There were the . . . who" construction which precedes each of the eleven divisions. What devices does the author use to gain emphasis? How does he avoid monotony? *
2. Show how Mr. Fleming's subject could be divided according to other principles of division, such as the age or sex of the people who comment on the adventure.

* For means of emphasis, see Foerster, pp. 24-31, 75-80; Hodges, 29; Kierzek, 61-66; Perrin, pp. 287-95; Wykoff, 79; for ways of achieving variety, see Foerster, pp. 39-42, 81; Hodges, 30; Kierzek, 67; Perrin, pp. 278-83; Wykoff, 80.

3. Examine the following topic sentences with a view to developing them in a manner similar to Example B3. (Sample: It was interesting to hear my friends comment on the election. There were the jubilant, the indifferent, and the depressed. . . .)
   a. Inflation upset the whole nation.
   b. The audience responded in various ways to the speaker's humor.
   c. The reactions of the various teams in the Olympic games gave us interesting clues to national temperament.
   d. You can tell what kind of man you are dealing with by watching the way he spends his money.
   e. The evidence of a good teacher is a student's development in later life.
4. Write a short composition developing one of the topic sentences listed in Exercise 3 above. Make your division include three or more parts.

C. Make the classification and division apt and purposeful.

1. Apology

BY PLATO

Let us reflect in another way, and we shall see that there is great reason to hope that death is a good; for one of two things—either death is a state of nothingness and utter unconsciousness, or, as men say, there is a change and migration of the soul from this world to another.

Now, if you suppose that there is no consciousness, but a sleep like the sleep of him who is undisturbed even by dreams, death will be an unspeakable gain. For if a person were to select the night in which his sleep was undisturbed even by dreams, and were to compare with this the other days and nights of his life, and then were to tell us how many days and nights he had passed in the course of his life better and more pleasantly than this one, I think that any man, I will not say a private man, but even the great king, will not find many such days or nights, when compared with the others. Now, if death be of such a nature, I say that to die is gain; for eternity is then only a single night.

But if death is the journey to another place, and there, as men say, all the dead abide, what good, O my friends and judges, can be greater than this? If, indeed, when the pilgrim arrives in the world below, he is delivered from the professors of justice in this world, and finds the true judges who are said to give judgment there, Minos and Rhadamanthus and Aeacus and Triptolemus,* and other sons of God who were righteous in their own life, that pilgrimage will be worth making. What would not a man give if he might converse with Orpheus and Musaeus and Hesiod and Homer? Nay, if this be true, let me die again and again. I myself, too, shall have a wonderful interest in there meeting and conversing with Palamedes, and Ajax the son of Telamon, and any other ancient hero who has suffered death through an unjust judgment; and there will be no small pleasure, as I think, in comparing my own sufferings with theirs. Above all, I shall then be able to continue my search into true and false knowledge; as in this world, so also in the next; and I shall find out who is wise, and who pretends to be wise, and is not. What would not a man give, O judges, to be able to examine the leader of the great Trojan expedition; or Odysseus or Sisyphus, or numberless others, men and women too! What infinite delight would there be in conversing with them and asking them questions! In another world they do not put a man to death for asking questions: assuredly not. For besides being happier than we are, they will be immortal, if what is said is true.

Wherefore, O judges, be of good cheer about death, and know of a certainty, that no evil can happen to a good man, either in life or after death. He and his are not neglected by the gods; nor has my own approaching end happened by mere chance. But I see clearly that the time had arrived when it was better for me to die and be released from trouble; wherefore the oracle gave no sign. For which reason, also, I am not angry with my condemners, or with my accusers; they have done me no harm, although they did not mean to do me any good; and for this I may gently blame them.

Still, I have a favour to ask of them. When my sons are grown up, I would ask you, O my friends, to punish them; and I would have

---

* See glossary of proper names below.

you trouble them, as I have troubled you, if they seem to care about riches, or anything, more than about virtue; or if they pretend to be something when they are really nothing,—then reprove them, as I have reproved you, for not caring about that for which they ought to care, and thinking that they are something when they are really nothing. And if you do this, both I and my sons will have received justice at your hands.

The hour of departure has arrived, and we go our ways—I to die, and you to live. Which is better God only knows.

Glossary of Proper Names

Minos	Mythical king of Crete, son of Zeus, a judge in Tartarus, the realm of the dead
Rhadamanthus	Brother of Minos, also a judge in the lower world
Aeacus	Mythical king of Aegina, grandfather of Ajax and Achilles; after his death a judge in the lower world
Triptolemus	Mythical king of Eleusis and Metaneira, founder of agriculture; also a judge in the lower world
Orpheus	Mythical minstrel of Thrace
Musaeus	Mythical Greek poet
Hesiod	The oldest Greek poet after Homer
Homer	The oldest of the Greek poets; author of the *Iliad* and *Odyssey*
Palamedes	A Greek hero of the Trojan War
Odysseus	A Greek hero, principal figure in the *Odyssey*
Sisyphus	A king of Corinth, condemned in hell to roll uphill a stone which constantly fell back

Comment

The principle of this division is expressed in the form of a dilemma, that is, a simple disjunction or division in which each alternative concludes in the speaker's favor. Plato divides his subject, death, into two categories: it is either a state of nothingness or a state in which the soul lives in another world. The completeness of this division may be shown by the impossibility of finding a third alternative. In establishing each of his two divisions, Plato simultaneously achieves his purpose, that is, the conviction that death is a good. This linking of classification or division with purpose is essential to effective writing. We do not divide for division's sake. We divide in the light of our purpose.

Analysis and Composition

1. Given the following purposes, divide your subject into two categories, each of which, when proved, will establish your purpose.

   Sample: *Purpose:* To convince students that study must be classed as a benefit.

   Division: Study is either a benefit to you or a benefit to the society of which you are a part. In either case study is a benefit.

   a. Purpose: To persuade parents to take an interest in their children's education.

   b. Purpose: To convince people that bull fighting should be stopped.

   c. Purpose: To convince Frenchmen that dueling should not be tolerated.

   d. Purpose: To explain why it is a citizen's duty to vote.

2. Show how each of the following purposes requires a different division of the same subject. Answer by constructing a brief outline for each purpose.

   Subject: A farm

   a. Purpose: To show why a farm is a good financial investment at this time.

   b. Purpose: To explain the normal operation of a farm.

   c. Purpose: To refute the opinion that farm life is necessarily lonely.

   d. Purpose: To describe the natural beauty of a farm in the spring.

   e. Purpose: To express the satisfaction of a farmer at the end of a harvest.

   f. Purpose: To contrast a farm boy's day with that of a boy in a large city.

3. Write a composition of approximately 400 words on one of the subjects analyzed by division in Exercises 1 or 2 above.

2. On Weekend Guests

BY RUSSELL LYNES

1 What makes a good guest is a subtle complex of personality, manners, and delicacy of feeling, coupled with one's own state of forbear-

ON WEEKEND GUESTS: from *Guests* by Russell Lynes. Copyright, 1951, by Harper and Brothers.

ance at the moment when the guest appears. There are friends one can always depend on, but they are likely to be old friends for whom no amount of trouble is a burden and whose awareness of one's short-comings is equaled by their readiness to accept them.

2 But not all guests can be old friends; they are merely the certain islands of calm and delight in a summer filled with potential catas-trophe. Let us consider those other guests, most of whom we have invited in overexpansive moments to share our hospitality.

II

3 The standard weekend guests are a couple, but there the standard stops and the variations set in. We cannot discuss all of the variations, but let us take a few common ones and face up to this problem now that summer is well under way and it is too late to do anything about it.

4 Age makes less difference in guests than you would think; it is "habit patterns" (as the psychologists call the ruts of behavior) that are important to consider in dealing with guests. If, for example, you have invited what seemed to you on urban acquaintance a lively, active couple, you may as well resign yourself to their spending most of the weekend asleep. Being lively in the city is an extremely enervating business, and your couple will make up for it over the weekend. There is no use leaving the lawnmower conspicuously displayed; these are not the kind of people who are going to volunteer to push it. The chances are that they will arrive late for dinner on Friday, completely equipped for tennis, golf, and swimming, and it will take the whole family to stow them and their tack in the guest room. By nine o'clock one of them will say: "Oh, this country air. I can hardly keep my eyes open." And by nine-thirty they'll both be asleep upstairs.

5 On Saturday morning it becomes obvious that these active urban types are country sluggards. They emerge dressed like manikins from a resort shop—the man in slacks and loafers and plaid shirt and his wife in shorts and sandals and halter—in the clothes, in other words, that people who spend much time in the country haven't time for—and they wear dark glasses. If you are sensible, you have been up for a good while yourself and got the lawn mowed (your guests love to lie in bed and listen to the reassuring whir of a lawnmower) and had your breakfast. You have made a list of the things you want to do without regard to what your friends want to do. If they feel like it

they'll patter along when you go to town to shop; if they don't, they are perfectly happy sitting in reclining chairs, their faces lifted like platters to the sun.

6 You need not worry about all the sports equipment they brought with them. That was a gesture. They won't begin to bustle until late afternoon when it is cocktail time. Then they will replace their shorts with something longer, and emerge after they have used up all the hot water, ready to use up all the gin.

7 The chances of what may then happen are about equally divided; they may drink so fast and furiously (they feel so full of health from a day in the sun) that they will again be ready for bed by nine-thirty. If this happens, Sunday's performance will echo Saturday's. If, however, they decide to make an evening of it, they won't appear until just before lunch on Sunday, by which time you can have had at least a half a day to yourself. The rest of the day you may as well throw away.

8 By contrast, let us look at a quite different sort of couple from the city. It would be risking too much to say that the opposite type, the kind of couple who reflect the cares and the harrying tempo of urban life and have a peaked air about them, are invariably the active ones over a weekend in the country, but there is some truth in it. They are likely to arrive somewhat bedraggled, usually by train, with the hot sooty look of people emerging from a couple of hours on a local in which the air conditioning has broken down. The first breath of clear country air brightens their gray faces; they stand on the platform and look around them as though refreshing their memories of what a tree looks like. They have a small suitcase each and carry no athletic equipment. If everything about the landscape enchants them as you drive them home, you should be warned that you are in for an active two days.

9 This sort of couple has a good deal in common with puppies. You throw out any kind of suggestion, and they scamper after it and bring it back and drop it at your feet. Everything is grist for their mill, but they have forgotten to bring the mill. If you suggest tennis, they'd just love tennis, but, of course, they have no rackets and no sneakers, and after you have ransacked the house and tried your own, your wife's, and your children's sneakers on them and have concluded that you are in for a game of patball, they settle down to beat the pants off you with rackets that you have long since given up as warped and worthless.

10 You can save up the lawn for this type. One will surely cut it for you while the other weeds the flowers, or they may work in shifts. You will have difficulty keeping them out of the kitchen, if you are the sort who thinks of the kitchen as your private sanctum, because they will insist on helping with the dishes. The only real trouble you will encounter arises if you are so misguided as to leave them to their own devices to entertain themselves. Their puppy eyes will look at you as though you ought to be throwing a ball for them. You even have to suggest to them that it is time to go to bed. When you put them on the train on Sunday evening, you will notice that for all the healthful paces through which they have put you and themselves, they will have that same gray and harried look they had when they arrived.

11 These two kinds of couples are, of course, merely composites of many other species. But what of the couples who do not seem to make pairs and who go their separate ways? And what of those couples of which you like one member and can't abide the other? For our purposes they have to be considered as individuals. There are those who think that the state of being a guest relieves them of all responsibility and those who consider guesthood a perpetual challenge. In either case the extremes are difficult to cope with.

III

12 The range of individual guests is, of course, endless, and perforce we must confine ourselves to those whose eccentricities have some chance of seeming to be part of larger and more universally recognized patterns. You can make your own synthesis (nobody is anybody these days who doesn't at least try to make a synthesis) and match them as you please.

13 Some guests want to be left alone, and some say they want to ("Don't bother about me. Just go about your business. I'll find plenty to do.") and are miserable if they are.

14 The first of these lone wolves can be the pleasantest of all guests if they are resourceful, can take care of themselves happily, and at the same time pervade your household with the warm feeling that they enjoy just being in it. At their best they don't mind being interrupted in their own pursuits if there is some activity in which you want them

to join. At their worst they make you feel that all they want out of you is a bed and three meals a day and a chance to ignore you. These are the men and women who come for the weekend to get away from people (including you) and to have a little quiet. They think they have discharged all of their responsibilities if they bring a box of chocolates that they have bought in the railroad station. They are so well able to take care of themselves that they make you feel as though you were in their employ.

15 A guest of the second type (who really does not want to be left alone but protests that he does) offers an acute problem of tact. He appears at breakfast with a small stack of books, a magazine, and some writing paper, bright-eyed and presumably equipped for the day. He quickly sets the books aside and takes your morning paper. (The sort of person who has a number of books from which to choose is rarely a reader. He is always looking for a chance to find time to sit down with a good book, but curiously he never seems to find it. He won't find it over the weekend either.) After his third cup of coffee, you may get back the paper, and your friend will wander off to find a place to read one of the books. In half an hour or less he'll be hovering around again. "Too nice a day to sit and read," he'll say, and that is your signal to quit whatever you are doing and invent something to keep him busy. His resources and imagination were exhausted by picking out which books in your library he would fondle.

16 If this type stretches your tact, then you should be especially warned of the guest who makes an elaborate show of being tactful about you. He acts as though he knows that he is too much trouble and that everything you do for him is a great nuisance. He is constantly leaping out of his chair to perform some little service for you or for your wife, to get out the ice, to find the children's ball in the bushes, or to fetch the wood for the fireplace, all of which would be ingratiating if it weren't done half-apologetically. You soon find yourself wanting to tell him to sit down and relax, but instead you respond with an elaborate display of tact on your own part. He is wearisome because he is so hard to live up to.

17 Even so he is preferable to the intentionally tactless guest who thinks that to make light of your shortcomings as a host is a demonstration of easy fellowship and poise. He laughs at the way you lay a fire, and insists on taking your effort apart and stacking the kindling

in his way. He reminds you that the leaky faucet in the bathroom could be fixed with a five-cent washer and fifteen minutes' work, and that you have put the wrong kind of composition shingles on your house; he could have got a much better brand for you wholesale at half the price you paid. He follows you wherever you go all weekend long; he stands in the kitchen door while you are getting drinks or a meal. If you play golf with him he tells you how to correct your slice, and if he sees you chopping wood he will observe that you are lucky you haven't cut your leg off long since, handling an axe the way you do. When he is not telling you how you ought to live, his conversation is almost entirely about the remarkable place at which he spent last weekend, with friends who did everything in such style. He is unaware that the walls of most country places are excellent conductors of sound, and you have no respite from him for some time after he has presumably gone to bed. If he is married, you can listen to him telling his wife that you would have a nice little place if you only knew how to take care of it.

18 Even the careless guest is preferable to the tactless type, though he too offers some minor aggravations. He strews the place with his belongings, he breaks a blade of the lawnmower on a rock anyone ought to be able to see, and he invariably is inspired to take a dip in the lake or river or ocean just as you are about to produce lunch or supper. When he does ultimately appear to be fed he will have deposited his wet bathing suit over the back of a piece of upholstered furniture. There is no malice in his soul, though, and it is possible to love him.

19 It is impossible, on the other hand, to love the belligerently indolent guest who frustrates all attempts to make his visit pleasant or interesting. That is not to say that a host should force entertainment on anyone who doesn't want it, for a good host knows when to put enticements in his guest's way and when not to. But the belligerently indolent guest has a gift for making it quite obvious to his host that he expects to be entertained, yet displays a distinct distaste for any diversion that may be suggested to him. This is a common characteristic in children, and in adults it is, I believe, an indication of retarded maturity. I have often seen adults behave like a child I know who continually asks, "What'll I do now?" When a suggestion is made to him he has a pat reply. "Would you like to go swimming?" you ask him, and the reply is invariably, "Not particularly." "Well then," you say,

trying again, "how would you like to play catch?" "Not particularly," he says, and so it goes. When such guests, children or adults, do finally submit themselves to some plan you have suggested, they give you the uncomfortable sensation that they wish you had been bright enough to invent something really entertaining.

20 If this kind of guest is tiring because he is a constant challenge to your ingenuity, the opposite type, the ebullient guest, who sets out to give his host and hostess a rousing good time, takes the least planning and is the most exhausting. He arrives full of ideas, of projects for excursions, of resolve to get you out and give you some real exercise, and unless you want to be rude to him (which is necessary in extreme cases) it is best just to put yourself in his hands.

21 There are a number of common manifestations of the ebullient guest, each requiring a special defensive operation and its own system of logistics. I happen to have a house in the Berkshires. These gentle hills were at one time (especially in the environs of Stockbridge and Lenox) remarkable for the size and extravagance of the summer estates which graced their slopes. There is a legend in the Berkshires that a young man who was at Yale just before the turn of the century sent his mother a telegram in which he said, "Bringing some '97 friends for weekend," and his mother wired back, "Terribly sorry have room for only seventy-six." Most of the big estates are now hotels, or schools, or church institutions, and the Berkshires have become a hotbed of summer culture. We have music festivals at Tanglewood that rival Salzburg and Glyndebourne in fame. We have dance festivals at a place called Jacob's Pillow, and we have enough summer theaters to give several platoons of Broadway stars their annual breath of fresh air. We used to frequent these places; in fact months before the music festival our friends could be seen conspicuously angling for invitations. We finally grew tired of running a lodging house for our music- and dance-minded acquaintances, and we ourselves took to angling for invitations elsewhere during that part of the summer. It was the ebullient guests who wanted to be sure that we got our dosage of culture who finally drove us to take umbrage.

22 Umbrage is one way to cope with the ebullient. Another way is to lend your guest the family car, and if necessary your wife, and let them go on an excursion of their own making. A third method is to buy two tickets to the festival or the dance or the theater and say that they are all you could get (which could easily be true) and insist that

the guests use them. This is both a generous gesture and assurance of a few hours' respite.

23 There is one kind of ebullience, however, which I have frequently encountered and have never been able to discover an answer to. It is found in a single guest or in a couple who seem to know a great many more people in the vicinity to which you have invited them than you do. The minute they get in the house they start calling up their friends. By the end of fifteen minutes they have invited themselves and you to one house for lunch, another for drinks, and have possibly even got you committed to appear at the Saturday night country club dance. You may, on the other hand, find yourself giving a cocktail party for a lot of people you scarcely know and have been successfully avoiding for years. Short of cutting the telephone wires before your guests arrive, I know of no way to keep their socially manic behavior in control.

Comment

The purpose of this essay is to explain humorously the American institution of weekend guests. According to Mr. Lynes, most weekend guests have one common characteristic: they irritate their hosts. This large class of weekend guests is divided into smaller classes—into couples (active and passive) and individuals (the lone wolf and the afraid to be alone; the excessively tactful and the tactless; the careless, the indolent, and the ebullient). Each of these smaller classes is then characterized by a special trait. Thus the essay is mainly developed by means of classification and division. This is evident in the following topical outline:

Guests
    A. Pleasant (¶1)
    B. Unpleasant (¶2-3)
       1. Couples (¶4-11)
          a. Active (¶4-7)
          b. Passive (¶8-11)
       2. Individuals (¶12-23)
          a. Lone wolf (¶13-14)
          b. Lonesome (¶15)
          c. Tactful (¶16)
          d. Tactless (¶17)
          e. Careless (¶18)
          f. Indolent (¶19)
          g. Ebullient (¶20-23)

Analysis and Composition

1. Construct a sentence outline of the essay "On Weekend Guests." A suggested method is to write complete sentences based on the topical outline above and to supply the necessary connectives.*

   Sample: A. Weekend guests may be divided into the pleasant and the unpleasant.
   1. A pleasant guest is one who has good manners.
   2. An unpleasant guest is one who is a potential catastrophe.

2. Mr. Lynes's division was dictated by his humorous purpose. Other purposes would require other divisions. Write out divisions of the subject, "Weekend Guests," appropriate to the following purposes:
   a. For the wives of businessmen who must entertain the executives of a company
   b. For bachelors entertaining a group of sportsmen
   c. For an alumni secretary planning a homecoming
   d. For a foreign student who does not understand American customs
   e. For the instruction of untrained domestic servants
3. Write a composition of approximately 500 words based on the outline of one of the purposes listed in Exercise 2.

3. Paleface and Redskin

BY PHILIP RAHV

1 Viewed historically, American writers appear to group themselves around two polar types. Paleface and redskin I should like to call the two, and despite occasional efforts at reconciliation no love is lost between them.

2 Consider the immense contrast between the drawing-room fictions of Henry James and the open air poems of Walt Whitman. Compare Melville's decades of loneliness, his tragic failure, with Mark Twain's boisterous career and dubious success. At one pole there is the litera-

---

* See handbooks: Foerster, *36b*; Hodges, *32c*; Kierzek, p. 145; Perrin, pp. 671-72; Wykoff, *36*.

ture of the lowlife world of the frontier and of the big cities; at the other the thin, solemn, semi-clerical culture of Boston and Concord. The fact is that the creative mind in America is fragmented and one-sided. For the process of polarization has produced a dichotomy between experience and consciousness—a dissociation between energy and sensibility, between conduct and theories of conduct, between life conceived as an opportunity and life conceived as a discipline.

3 The differences between the two types define themselves in every sphere. Thus while the redskin glories in his Americanism, to the paleface it is a source of endless ambiguities. Sociologically they can be distinguished as patrician vs. plebeian, and in their esthetic ideals one is drawn to allegory and to the distillations of symbolism, whereas the other inclines to a gross, riotous naturalism. The paleface is a "highbrow," though his mentality—as in the case of Hawthorne and James—is often of the kind that excludes and repels general ideas; he is at the same time both something more and something less than an intellectual in the European sense. And the redskin deserves the epithet "lowbrow" not because he is badly educated—which he might or might not be—but because his reactions are primarily emotional, spontaneous, and lacking in personal culture. The paleface continually hankers after religious norms, tending toward a refined estrangement from reality. The redskin, on the other hand, accepts his environment, at times to the degree of fusion with it, even when rebelling against one or another of its manifestations. At his highest level the paleface moves in an exquisite moral atmosphere; at his lowest he is genteel, snobbish, and pedantic. In giving expression to the vitality and to the aspirations of the people, the redskin is at his best; but at his worst he is a vulgar anti-intellectual, combining aggression with conformity and reverting to the crudest forms of frontier psychology.

4 James and Whitman, who as contemporaries felt little more than contempt for each other, are the purest examples of this dissociation.* In reviewing *Drum Taps* in 1865 the young James told off the grand plebeian innovator, advising him to stop declaiming and go sit in the corner of a rhyme and meter school, while the innovator, snorting at the novelist of scruples and moral delicacy, said "Feathers!" Now this mutual repulsion between the two major figures in American literature would be less important if it were mainly personal or esthetic in

---

* According to Edith Wharton, James changed his mind about Whitman late in life. But this can be regarded as a private fact of the Jamesian sensibility, for in public he said not a word in favor of Whitman.

reference. But the point is that it has a profoundly national and social-historical character.

5 James and Whitman form a kind of fatal antipodes. To this, in part, can be traced the curious fact about them that, though each has become the object of a special cult, neither is quite secure in his reputation. For most of the critics and historians who make much of Whitman disparage James or ignore him altogether, and vice versa. Evidently the high valuation of the one is so incongruous with the high valuation of the other that criticism is chronically forced to choose between them—which makes for a breach in the literary tradition without parallel in any European country. The aristocrat Tolstoy and the tramp Gorky found that they held certain values and ideas in common, whereas James and Whitman, who between them dominate American writing of the nineteenth century, cannot abide with one another. And theirs is no unique or isolated instance.

6 The national literature suffers from the ills of a split personality. The typical American writer has so far shown himself incapable of escaping the blight of one-sidedness: of achieving that mature control which permits the balance of impulse with sensitiveness, of natural power with philosophical depth. For the dissociation of mind from experience has resulted in truncated works of art, works that tend to be either naive and ungraded, often flat reproductions of life, or else products of cultivation that remain abstract because they fall short on evidence drawn from the sensuous and material world. Hence it is only through intensively exploiting their very limitations, through submitting themselves to a process of creative yet cruel self-exaggeration, that a few artists have succeeded in warding off the failure that threatened them. And the later novels of Henry James are a case in point.

7 The palefaces dominated literature throughout the nineteenth century, but in the twentieth they have been overthrown by the redskins. Once the continent had been mastered, with the plebeian bourgeoisie coming into complete possession of the national wealth, and puritanism had worn itself out, degenerating into mere respectability, it became objectively possible and socially permissible to satisfy that desire for experience and personal emancipation which heretofore had been systematically frustrated. The era of economic accumulation had ended and the era of consummation had arrived. To enjoy life now became one of the functions of progress—a function for which the palefaces were temperamentally disqualified. This gave Mencken his opportunity to emerge as the ideologue of enjoyment. Novelists like Dreiser,

Anderson, and Lewis—and, in fact, most of the writers of the period of "experiment and liberation"—rose against conventions that society itself was beginning to abandon. They helped to "liquidate" the lag between the enormous riches of the nation and its morality of abstention. The neo-humanists were among the last of the breed of palefaces, and they perished in the quixotic attempt to re-establish the old values. Eliot forsook his native land, while the few palefaces who managed to survive at home took to the academic or else to the "higher" and relatively unpopular forms of writing. But the novelists, who control the main highway of literature, were, and still are, nearly all redskins to the wigwam born.

8 At present the redskins are in command of the literary situation, and the literary life in America has seldom been so deficient in intellectual power. The political interests introduced in the nineteen-thirties have not only strengthened their hold but have also brought out their worst tendencies; for the effect of the popular political creeds of our time has been to increase their habitual hostility to ideas, sanctioning the relaxation of standards and justifying the urge to come to terms with semi-literate audiences.

9 The redskin writer in America is a purely indigenous phenomenon, the true-blue offspring of the western hemisphere, the juvenile in principle and for the good of the soul. He is a self-made writer in the same way as Henry Ford is a self-made millionaire. On the one hand he is a crass materialist, a greedy consumer of experience, and on the other a sentimentalist, a half-baked mystic listening to inward voices and watching for signs and portents. Think of Dreiser, Lewis, Anderson, Wolfe, Sandburg, Caldwell, Steinbeck, Farrell, Saroyan: all writers of genuine and some even of admirable accomplishments, whose faults, however, are not so much literary as faults of raw life itself. Unable to relate himself in any significant manner to the cultural heritage, the redskin writer is always on his own; and since his personality resists growth and change, he must constantly repeat himself. His work is ridden by compulsions that depress the literary tradition, because they are compulsions of a kind that put a strain on literature, that literature more often than not can neither assimilate nor sublimate. He is the passive instead of the active agent of the *Zeitgeist,** he lives off it rather than through it, so that when his particular gifts happen to coincide with the mood of the times he seems modern and contemporary, but once the mood has passed he is in danger of being

* The spirit of the times.

quickly discarded. Lacking the qualities of surprise and renewal, already Dreiser and Anderson, for example, have a "period" air about them that makes a re-reading of their work something of a critical chore; and one suspects that Hemingway, that perennial boy-man, is more accurately understood as a descendant of Natty Bumppo, the hero of Fenimore Cooper's Leatherstocking tales, than as the portentously disillusioned character his legend makes him out to be.

10 As for the paleface, in compensation for backward cultural conditions and a lost religious ethic, he has developed a supreme talent for refinement, just as the Jew, in compensation for adverse social conditions and a lost national independence, has developed a supreme talent for cleverness. (In this connection it is pertinent to recall T. S. Eliot's remark about Boston society, which he described as "quite refined, but refined beyond the point of civilization.") Now this peculiar excess of refinement is to be deplored in an imaginative writer, for it weakens his capacity to cope with experience and induces in him a fetishistic attitude toward tradition; nor is this species of refinement to be equated with the refinement of artists like Proust or Mann, as in them it is not an element contradicting an open and bold confrontation of reality. Yet the paleface, being above all a conscious individual, was frequently able to transcend or to deviate sharply from the norms of his group, and he is to be credited with most of the rigors and charms of the classic American books. While it is true, as John Jay Chapman put it, that his culture is "secondary and tertiary" and that between him and the sky "float the Constitution of the United States and the traditions and forms of English literature"—nevertheless, there exists the poetry of Emily Dickinson, there is *The Scarlet Letter,* there is *Moby Dick,* and there are not a few incomparable narratives by Henry James.

11 At this point there is no necessity to enter into a discussion of the historical and social causes that account for the disunity of the American creative mind. In various contexts a number of critics have disclosed and evaluated the forces that have worked on this mind and shaped it to their uses. The sole question that seems relevant is whether history will make whole again what it has rent asunder. Will James and Whitman ever be reconciled, will they finally discover and act upon each other? Only history can give a definite reply to this question. In the meantime, however, there are available the resources of effort and of understanding, resources which even those who believe in the strict determination of the cultural object need not spurn.

Comment

The purpose of this essay is to show that the classification of American authors into paleface and redskin points to a similar fragmentation of American cultural life. Thus the author's classification is directly related to his purpose. The principle of classification is the basic philosophy of life of the authors; the difference between the two classes appears in the sphere of (a) sociology, (b) esthetic ideals, and (c) moral ideals (see ¶3). The following table may help to explain Mr. Rahv's essay.

Class: Paleface	*Class: Redskin*
Characteristics	
Patrician	Plebeian
Tendency to allegory and symbols	Riotous naturalism
Highbrow (cultured)	Lowbrow (uncultured)
Idealistic	Accepts his environment
Moral delicacy	Amoral vitality
Intellectual and abstract	Juvenile and factual
Specific Examples	
Hawthorne	Whitman
Henry James	Mark Twain
T. S. Eliot	Dreiser
Melville	Lewis
Emily Dickinson	Wolfe
	Sandburg
	Hemingway

Analysis and Composition

1. Find denotative definitions of the following words:

polar   ambiguities   ideologue

dubious   symbolism   Zeitgeist

dichotomy   antipodes   sublimate

dissociation   truncated   portentously

2. Give the connotative meaning of the following words:

semi-clerical   patrician   plebeian

fetishistic   bourgeoisie

3. Attempt to find additional characteristics for each of the two classifications. List additional authors in each category.

4. Is there a third class of American author, neither paleface nor redskin? If so, who are the members of this class? If a third class exists, is Mr. Rahv's classification complete?

5. Granted that Mr. Rahv has not cited every possible author in each of the two classes he is discussing, does he cite a *sufficient* number of them to justify his classification? (An acceptable meaning of sufficient number is a *fair sampling* of a class, sufficient to establish the probable identity of the class.)

6. Paragraph 9 lists a number of redskin authors as examples of materialism, of greed for experience, and of sentimentality and half-baked thinking. Should Mr. Rahv give detailed evidence of the presence of these qualities in the authors cited? Has he a right to assume the knowledge of such evidence on the part of his readers? Under what circumstances would detailed evidence be necessary?

7. List some basic characteristics of each of the following classes:

the snob	the idler	the man of action
the good citizen	the servile man	the indifferent student
the ideal professor	the awkward guest	the lady's man
the working mother	the nervous public speaker	

8. Write a brief composition on one or more of the topics listed in Exercise 7.

9. Write a brief composition in which you contrast opposite types, such as the idler and the worker. Consult Exercise 7 for topics.

10. Test the following divisions of the subject, "College Students," for clarity and completeness. Then draw up your own outline on the same subject.

   A. Classification according to the motives for attending college
      1. Students attend college for three principal reasons—fun, love of learning, financial success.
      2. Those who attend college for fun join social clubs, attend games, take easy courses, avoid the serious-minded.
      3. Those who attend college for love of learning demand good teaching, read widely, select courses for their intrinsic value, master the fundamental disciplines.
      4. Those who attend college to make money prefer a degree they can sell, ignore the humanities, consider a good grade more important than knowledge.

   B. Classification according to basic temperaments
      1. At bottom all college students are mixtures of four types: they are either bright or dull, and they are either energetic or lazy.

2. The bright and energetic need only to direct their studies wisely.
3. The bright and lazy should concentrate on character building.
4. The dull and energetic should limit their ambitions.
5. The dull and lazy should withdraw.

11. Write a short essay based on the outline constructed in Exercise 10.

GENERAL EXERCISES

1. Work out an outline based on classification or division for a brief expository composition on one or more of the following subjects:

Scholastic requirements	Extracurricular activities
A day well spent	My father's job
Our neighborhood	My sister's friends
Ways of taking it easy	Characters I admire
Varieties of television actors	Types of policemen

2. Write a short composition (about 500 words) based on the outline constructed according to Exercise 1.

3. The following outline contains several faults of division (see introduction to this section). Reconstruct the outline so that the division is clear, complete, and related to the purpose.

Purpose: To explain to citizens that juvenile delinquency is a public problem.

Central theme: The juvenile delinquent is a problem to the public as well as to his family.

A. The juvenile delinquent is a public expense.
   1. Extra police must be assigned.
   2. The courts become crowded.
   3. He holds back his class at school.
   4. He is a nuisance to his parents.
B. The juvenile delinquent is an expense to his parents.
   1. They must bail him out.
   2. He does not earn extra money by paper routes.
   3. He is careless about family property.
   4. He steals and breaks things, for which the parents must pay.
C. The juvenile delinquent is a bad example to others.
   1. He tempts others to follow him.
   2. He annoys the teachers and policemen.

3. He shames his family.
4. He becomes unfit to serve his country.
4. Correct the following divisions according to the principle of division specified. Complete the outline when necessary.
A. Subject: The history of Western civilization
  Principle of division: Time order
  1. The debt to Greece and Rome
  2. The Renaissance
  3. The Middle Ages
  4. The French and Russian Revolutions
  5. The contemporary world
  6. The continuity of history
B. Subject: The life of Dickens
  Principle of division: Time order
  1. Dickens' parents
  2. His boyhood
  3. The state of English literature
  4. Dickens' character
  5. The youth of Dickens
  6. Dickens as an illustrator
  7. Dickens' sentimentality and realism
  8. The art of the novels
  9. Dickens' courtship and marriage
  10. Dickens and America
C. Subject: The Atlantic coastline
  Principle of division: Space order
  1. General characteristics of the Atlantic coastline
  2. Maine and Florida
  3. Cape Cod and the North Carolina islands
D. Subject: Washington's army at Valley Forge
  Principle of division: The misery of the soldiers
  1. The sick
  2. The wounded
  3. The homesick
  4. The Hessians and other foreigners
  5. The waverers
  6. The hungry
  7. The impatient
  8. The officers
  9. The privates
E. Subject: Fishing
  Principle of division: The kinds of tackle used in fishing
  1. Dropping a line
  2. Rod fishing
  3. Seining
  4. Spear fishing
  5. Live bait
  6. Artificial flies
  7. Trawling
  8. On-shore fishing

5. The following passage represents a series of rough notes on the subject "Poetry." First add notes of your own. Then select and rearrange these miscellaneous observations in an orderly outline with three main headings.

a. A poem says something, but in a way different from prose.

b. It has rhythm—a recurrent stress—like the words of a song.

c. It often rhymes.

d. Poetry is easy to remember.

e. Poetry is hard to define because it includes Shakespeare's plays and a short lyric by Robert Burns.

f. There is a mysterious magic in some of Keats's poems.

g. How does humor get into poetry? There are many ridiculous poems like W. S. Gilbert's ballads.

h. At bottom a poem has a truth, not just cleverness of expression.

i. The truth in poetry makes you excited.

j. Is the magic in poetry another name for imagination?

k. Some words sing by themselves apart from meaning—phrases like "summer afternoon," "cellar door," "the murmurous haunt of bees on summer eves"; "Row us out to Desenzano, to the Sirmione row"; "Absent thee from felicity awhile."

l. A poem is much more intense than prose, as a great actor is more intense than a schoolgirl reciting *Hiawatha*.

6. Determine which of the following statements contain obscure or incomplete classifications and divisions. State reasons for your opinion.

a. A recent poll showed that a good marriage depends on three factors—health, wealth, and stealth.

b. Jones saw two films last week. Both confirmed his impression that the motion picture industry is under the influence of a malign power attempting to destroy the American mind.

c. Popular songs consist of rhumbas, sambas, waltzes, foxtrots, bebop, and jazz.

d. Smith perjured himself on at least one occasion; he can never be trusted.

e. We may divide all literature into poetry and prose.

f. There are four basic emotions—love and hate, hope and fear.

g. Radio newscasters are either reporters, commentators, editorialists, or plain quacks.

h. For the purpose of our survey we may divide all buildings into useful and monumental, into modern or obsolete, and into esthetic or ugly.

i. The basic norm of job classification is the requirement of the work, not the skill of the worker.

   j. Modern American magazines are classed as comics, pulps, slicks, pix, middle-brow monthlies, high-brow quarterlies, and altitudinous annuals that no one reads.

7. Analyze the paragraph below by answering the following questions:
   a. Is the principle of division clear? Is there any overlapping or cross-division?
   b. Is the division complete? Prove your answer.
   c. What purpose does the division serve?

Puritan and Yankee

BY VERNON LOUIS PARRINGTON

Common report has long made out Puritan New England to have been the native seat and germinal source of such ideals and institutions as have come to be regarded as traditionally American. Any critical study of the American mind, therefore, may conveniently seek its beginnings in the colonies clustered about Massachusetts Bay, and will inquire into the causes of the pronounced singularity of temper and purpose that marked off the New England settlements from those to the south, creating a distinctive New England character, and disciplining it for later conquests that were to set a stamp on American life. The course of its somewhat singular development would seem from the first to have been determined by an interweaving of idealism and economics—by the substantial body of thought and customs and institutions brought from the old home, slowly modified by new ways of life developing under the silent pressure of a freer environment. Of these new ways, the first in creative influence was probably the freehold tenure of landholdings, put in effect at the beginning and retained unmodified for generations; and the second was the development of a mercantile spirit that resulted from the sterility of the Massachusetts soil, which encouraged the ambitious to seek wealth in more profitable ways than tilling barren acres. From these sources emerged the two chief classes of New England: the yeomanry, a body of democratic freeholders who constituted the rank and file of the people, and the gentry, a group of capable merchants who dominated the commonwealth from early days to the rise of industrialism. And it was the interweaving of the aims and purposes of these acquisitive yeomen and gentry—harmonious for the most part on the surface, yet driving in different directions—with the ideal of a theocracy and the inhibitions of Puritan dogma, that constitutes the pattern of life to be dealt with here. The Puritan and the Yankee were the two halves of the New England whole, and to overlook or underestimate the contributions of either to the common life is grossly to misinterpret the spirit and character of primitive New England.

8. Below you will find a list of topics and a suggested principle of classification or division. Find a suitable purpose and central theme. Then outline the development of an expository theme (600 words) by classification or division.

Topic	*Principle of Classification or Division*
Parks	Extent of recreational facilities
Restaurants	Quality of food
Breeds of horses	Speed
Newspapers	Political affiliation
Teachers	Degree of friendliness
Coeds	Neatness of appearance
Campus diversions	Degree of amusement
Slick magazines	Type of story
Automobiles	Social prestige
Suburbs	Social rank
Jobs	Ease or difficulty
Essays	Readability
Feminine movie stars	Acting ability
College clubs or fraternities	Democratic spirit
Churches	Architectural pattern
Sports	Number of participants
Hunting	Seasons
Bores	Reasons for boring
Alumni	Attitude on football
Parents	Attitude towards their children's friends
Colleges	Scholastic discipline
Sisters or brothers	Critical attitude
Book reviews	Fairness in reporting the book
Selective Service Boards	Degree of courtesy
Librarians	Willingness to help the student

9. Write an expository composition of about 600 words on one of the topics listed in Exercise 8.

A. Whenever possible, use an example that is immediate and direct.

1. J. B. PRIESTLEY: *Romantic Recognition*
2. BERGEN EVANS:
   On the Intelligence of Dogs

B. Make an example vivid by using realistic detail: say who, when, where, how.

1. ELWYN BROOKS WHITE: *Book Learning*
2. FRANKLIN P. ADAMS: *Quirks*

C. Whenever, as with a complex idea, the connection between example and idea is not immediately evident, make certain to establish a valid connection.

1. HERBERT L. SAMUEL: *On Cause*
2. LEWIS MUMFORD:
   Contemplation and Action
3. C. S. LEWIS:
   The Law of Right and Wrong

D. In establishing proof by example, provide for each step in the argument (1) a group of apt examples (2) of sufficient number to support the conclusion.

MARK TWAIN:
Fenimore Cooper's Literary Offenses

General Exercises

T. HARRY WILLIAMS: *Grant as a General*

SECTION IV

Example

EXEMPLIFICATION is a method of analyzing a general subject by citing one or more of its members. Thus an example of the general subject (class) skyscraper is the Empire State Building; an example of frontiersman is Daniel Boone; an example of lyric poetry is Keats's "Ode to a Nightingale."

The student who has just completed Sections II and III will have no difficulty in seeing that example is intimately related to definition and to classification and division. Thus examples are frequently combined with definition, as in II A, where Lewis Hanke cites the example of a senatorial campaign as an instance of the use of false propaganda, and in II D3, where S. E. Morison cites the example of Senator Beveridge's biography of John Marshall to illustrate the genus good historical writing.

Examples are also frequently combined with classification and division. Thus Plato in III C1 cites a number of individuals as examples of pleasant companions in the world after death. Similarly, Philip Rahv (III C3) cites the example of Henry James to illustrate the class paleface and the example of Walt Whitman to illustrate the class redskin. Some form of exemplification occurs in all the selections in Sections II and III, as the comments and analyses point out.

While exemplification *as a method of analysis* has been illustrated in the two previous sections, it deserves more extended study *as a means of development*. For it is one thing to cite examples of a class and quite another thing to cite the most effective examples and to develop those examples in the most effective way. On the surface, nothing seems easier than giving an example. "A good writer, such as

Shakespeare," slips glibly from tongue or pen. Shakespeare is undoubtedly the greatest writer in the English language and his work may be used to illustrate many principles of good writing. But merely to say, "A good writer, such as Shakespeare," is meaningless unless the example is developed fully to meet the needs of purpose and occasion. An example, in short, should be immediate (that is, directly related to the idea it illustrates), vivid, coherent, cogent. Just any example won't do.

The derivation of the term *example* helps us to understand more fully the requirements of effective exemplification.

THE DERIVATION OF "EXAMPLE"

The English word *example* is derived, through French, from the Latin word *exemplum,* itself a shortened form of *exempulum. Exempulum,* in turn, is a noun derived from the verb *eximo,* which means "to take out," or "to take away from." The noun denotes "something chosen from a number of the same kind." By connotation *exemplum* came to mean something chosen from a number of the same kind because of the excellence of that thing as a representative of the class. Thus the abbreviation "e.g." (*exempli gratia,* "for example") was used, and still is used, as a label for an outstanding instance, example, or proof that unmistakably explains the class to which it belongs. So clear was the meaning of *exemplum* that it was borrowed to give a name to one of the principal literary types of the Middle Ages and the Renaissance, the exemplary tale, or *exemplum*—a short narrative that pointed up a general truth—the extension into narrative of the rhetorical *exemplum.*

Thus the derivation of the word example emphasizes the four important elements of good exemplification: immediacy, vividness, coherence, and cogency. In short, the useful example is not merely a member of a class; it is an effective illustration of that class.

A. THE FIRST PRINCIPLE OF EXEMPLIFICATION

The first principle applies to immediacy, and may be stated thus: *Whenever possible, use an example that is immediate and direct.*

A direct or immediate example illustrates an idea with a minimum of general explanation. A direct or immediate example is specific, concrete, exact, and therefore memorable. Many proverbs illustrate this first rule. Thus, "People who live in glass houses shouldn't throw stones" is a concrete example of the general truth that we should be careful about condemning another's fault. The example literally speaks for itself. So also is the genus hypocrisy exemplified by the man who saw the mote in another's eye and missed the beam in his own. The Good Samaritan stands as a direct and immediate example of brotherly love.

All good writers strive to present general observations within the compass of a short example. Thus, Dickens, speaking through Mr. Jingle, writes of the sagacity of dogs and of romantic love in *Pickwick Papers*:

> Ah! you should keep dogs—fine animals—sagacious creatures—dog of my own once—Pointer—surprising instinct—out shooting one day— entering enclosure—whistled—dog stopped—whistled again—Ponto—no go; stock still—called him—Ponto, Ponto wouldn't move—dog trans- fixed—staring at a board—looked up, saw an inscription—"Gamekeeper has orders to shoot all dogs found in this enclosure"—wouldn't pass it— wonderful dog—valuable dog that—very.

Note here how the general idea, the sagacity of dogs, is illustrated with a minimum of comment. So too the idea of romantic love is di- rectly presented in the next example:

> Conquests! Thousands. Don Bolaro Fizzgig—Grandee—only daughter —Donna Christina—splendid creature—loved me to distraction—jealous father—high-souled daughter—handsome Englishman—Donna Christina in despair—prussic acid—stomach pump in my portmanteau—operation performed—old Bolaro in ecstasies—consent to our union—join hands and floods of tears—romantic story—very.

Examples of equal directness appear in the short essays by J. B. Priestley, A1, and Bergen Evans, A2, in this section.

B. THE SECOND PRINCIPLE OF EXEMPLIFICATION

The second principle applies to vividness, and may be stated thus: *Make an example vivid by using realistic detail; say who, when, where, how.*

Often the writer can draw upon familiar examples known to his audience either by experience or by reading. Thus Dickens did not need to "explain" the examples cited above. Thus Priestley in A1 needs only to mention the names Prometheus and Eugenie because he has a right to assume that both these figures are well known to most readers. Prometheus, the hero who stole fire from Olympus, is the eternal romantic symbol of human aspiration; Eugenie, Empress of France, dictator of fashion and taste, is a recognized symbol of feminine beauty and refinement.

But, in most instances, a writer must present his examples fully. He cannot assume that the reader will supply the details out of a common fund of information. Hence the need to name names, places, times, circumstances. And even when the examples are direct and immediate, these realistic details add a note of vividness that appeals to the imagination. How effective this appeal is you will discover in E. B. White's "Book Learning" (IV B1) and in F. P. Adams' "Quirks" (IV B2).

C. THE THIRD PRINCIPLE OF EXEMPLIFICATION

The first two principles of exemplification will help you make your examples clear and vivid. The third and fourth principles have to do with two different problems, coherence and cogency.

The third principle applies to coherence, and may be stated thus: *Whenever, as with a complex idea, the connection between example and idea is not immediately evident, make certain to establish a valid connection.*

There are times when the coherence of the example and the idea is not immediately evident. Thus in explaining the full meaning of cause, Viscount Samuel in IV C1 cannot assume that his example, the accident, will speak for itself. Cause is too complex an idea to be directly explained in a simple illustration. Hence Samuel ties in the example with his idea of cause, and thus distinguishes among the several possible interpretations of the example.

So too Lewis Mumford (IV C2), in explaining the interconnection of contemplation and intelligent action, establishes a valid link between his example—the weekly exercise—and the point he wishes to make. Without such a connection the example might be understood in several different applications.

In IV C3, C. S. Lewis also establishes clearly the connection between his examples of typical quarrels and his general idea, the law of right and wrong. If only the first paragraph of Lewis' essay were read, the point of his examples would be difficult to discover. But in paragraph 2 the author makes plain his purpose: the examples do not merely illustrate the fact that men quarrel; they illustrate rather that various standards of conduct are at the bottom of the quarrels. Then in paragraph 3 Lewis shows how these various standards are related to a universal law of right and wrong. Thus the examples are clearly linked to the idea.

D. THE FOURTH PRINCIPLE OF EXEMPLIFICATION

The fourth principle applies to cogency, and may be stated thus: *In establishing proof by example, provide for each step in the argument (1) a group of apt examples (2) of sufficient number to support the conclusion.*

We have touched upon this principle in the introduction to Section III under the heading "Classification and Division in Reasoning." There we pointed out that in reasoning from the parts (examples) to the whole (genus) in order to establish or prove a general truth we use the process known as induction. Hence, in an argument by induction we group together appropriate examples in sufficient number to justify a general conclusion.

In Example IV D Mark Twain shows by three specific examples (paragraphs 10-13) that Cooper's *The Deerslayer* is not accurate in some of its observations. These examples (the size of the stream, the dimensions of the ark, the five Indians) are apt in that they set forth ludicrous inconsistencies which betray an inaccurate sense of observation. Obviously an induction based on three out of a score of possible examples is not complete. But the number is *sufficient* for an intelligent reader to estimate the probability or improbability of Mark Twain's opinion. Three apt examples, especially if they are typical of many others, are usually enough to support a conclusion in nontechnical argument.

The three examples mentioned above support the first step in Mark Twain's argument—that Cooper revealed an inaccurate sense of observation in *The Deerslayer*. Two other groups of examples attempt to prove that Cooper (1) lacked inventive power and (2) used language inexactly. These three steps lead to Twain's final opinion, namely that Cooper's *Deerslayer* is not a work of art in any sense.

Note: The student who wishes to study the methods of reasoning in greater detail at this time may turn to VII C.

---

a. Whenever possible, use an example that is immediate and direct.

---

1. Romantic Recognition

BY J. B. PRIESTLEY

Romantic recognition. Two examples will do. When we were flying from Erivan, the capital of Armenia, to Sukhum, on the Black Sea, a Soviet scientist, who spoke English, tapped me on the shoulder and then pointed to a fearsome rock face, an immeasurable slab bound in the iron of eternal winter. "That," he announced, "is where Prometheus was chained." And then all my secret terror—for a journey among the mountains of the Caucasus in a Russian plane is to my unheroic soul an ordeal—gave way for a moment to wonder and delight, as if an illuminated fountain had shot up in the dark. And then, years earlier, in the autumn of 1914, when we were on a route march in Surrey, I happened to be keeping step with the company commander, an intelligent Regular lent to us for a month or two. We were passing a little old woman who was watching us from an open carriage, drawn up near the entrance to a mansion. "Do you know who that is?" the captain asked; and of course I didn't. "It's the Empress Eugenie," he told me; and young and loutish as I was in those days, nevertheless there flared about me then, most delightfully, all the splendor and idiocy of the Second Empire, and I knew that we, every man Jack of us, were in history, and knew it once and for all.

Comment

Prometheus, one of the most famous figures in Greek mythology, stole fire from the gods and taught men the various arts. For this Zeus caused him to be chained to a rock where a vulture gnawed at his liver. An eternal symbol of the creative spirit, Prometheus was immortalized by Aeschylus, the Greek poet, and by Shelley in his "Prometheus Unbound."

The Empress Eugenie (1826-1920) was the famous wife of Napoleon III and still is remembered as a symbol of elegance, romantic charm, and feminine beauty.

Priestley clarifies the term *romantic recognition* by two examples. These two examples unmistakably point to his general idea. They tell us, without a verbal definition, that romantic recognition is the sudden understanding, accompanied by wonder and delight, of a truth long known but imperfectly realized.

Note: It is the usual practice of most writers to describe a class such as romantic recognition in a sentence or two before proceeding to the specific examples. However, in this passage Priestley rightly allows the examples to convey the meaning. (See also the comment on Priestley in the introduction to this section.)

Analysis and Composition

1. List some original examples of romantic recognition.
2. Discover two or more examples which will illustrate the following subjects:

a. Puppy love	i. Lost chances
b. Hero worship	j. Right decisions
c. Abuse of power	k. The eager student
d. Filial admiration	l. The persecuting boss
e. Perfect consent	m. Enjoying holidays
f. Calculated insult	n. Awesome scenes
g. Justifiable anger	o. Ludicrous happenings
h. Desperate remedies	on solemn occasions

3. Write a short composition on one or more of the subjects listed in Exercise 2.
4. Examine the italicized words in the following topic sentences carefully.*

* See handbooks: Foerster, pp. 43-44, *37d*; Hodges, *31a*; Kierzek, pp. 69-70, *68*; Perrin, pp. 185-87; Wykoff, *53*.

Then select two examples which will serve as illustrations of these italicized words.

Sample: *Topic:* The power of the state is illustrated by *two of its agencies.* *Examples:* The police and the army.

  a. The *American community* has been affected by the growth of the chain store.
  b. The *influence of culture* does not respect national boundaries.
  c. The *aftermath of war* may be seen even in the sheltered precincts of the home.
  d. Today *the small business man* is the last survivor of the early pioneer.
  e. The essence of nationality is a *common family instinct.*
  f. American democracy grew *from experience* as well as from books.
  g. There is *nothing friendlier* than a candidate for public office.
5. Write one or more paragraphs based on the topic sentences listed in Exercise 4. Use examples.
6. Reread Dickens' paragraph on romantic love in the introduction to this section. Rewrite this paragraph in complete, connected sentences.

2. On the Intelligence of Dogs

BY BERGEN EVANS

1 Merely to list popular misconceptions about four-footed animals would fill a volume. Nothing has caught man's attention more forcibly than those living creatures which, from the beginning of time, he has perceived to resemble himself. But the confused impressions of them that he has accumulated speak ill of his ability to accept the evidence of his senses.

2 Familiarity seems to breed no contempt for fiction. Those animals that have been most observed are the subjects of the most delusions. One would think, for instance, that dogs would be the least mysterious of all quadrupeds; whereas there are probably more old wives' tales about dogs than about all other animals put together. Perhaps the acuteness of their sense of smell has something to do with it. Man's consciousness is predominantly visual—"seeing is believing," we say—and few people are able to imagine what an olfactory consciousness might

ON THE INTELLIGENCE OF DOGS: reprinted from *The Natural History of Nonsense* by Bergen Evans, by permission of Alfred A. Knopf, Inc. Copyright 1946 by Bergen Evans.

be like. Virginia Woolf tried it in *Flush,* but less gifted people find it easier to talk about "mysterious instincts."

3 And how they do talk! It is almost impossible to pass an evening in a group of ordinary, middle-class, well-to-do people without hearing some instance of a dog's supernatural powers; and the least expression of doubt or the slightest attempt at cross-examination is sure to provoke a great deal of warmth. Dogs are sacred in our culture and nothing about them is more sacred than their ability to foretell the future, to warn of impending calamities, and to sense "instinctively" the death of a master or mistress who may chance at that moment to be far away.

4 Dog stories flow through the news in a never-ending stream. One day we read that a cocker spaniel, sent home from the Pacific by an aviation machinist's mate, "intuitively" recognized his master's wife. The next day there is an edifying account of a Seeing Eye dog which at a concert sat through *God Save the King* "with quiet dignity" but "arose on all fours and stood with the rest of the audience" when *The Star-Spangled Banner* was sung.

5 In nothing is the clairvoyance of dogs more frequently manifested than in their ability to read character, particularly to perceive hidden villainy. Thus while the dull humans in *Little Dorrit* are deceived by the suavity of Rigaud, the little dog knows him "instinctively" for what he is and, despite punishment by his gullible master, persists in his warning attacks until the villain is unmasked. Nor are such performances confined to literature. A Chicago housewife wrote in triumphant indignation to the salvage office of the WPB to say that her bulldog's growling had warned her that their wastepaper collector was dishonest. She had ignored the faithful creature's warning, however, only to find, after the collector had gone, that she had been short-changed four cents. The WPB promised to make up the deficiency.

6 Dogs are able to detect even temporary changes in character. Albert Payson Terhune tells us that a favorite dog of his "would get up quietly after my second or third drink and leave the room." The devoted beast, Mr. Terhune adds, "seems to note and resent a subtle change in me."

7 So established, in fact, is this mystic analytic power of dogs that it has never been explained why banks waste money on expensive alarm systems when a dog stationed at the door could at once give notice not only of robbers but of forgers, embezzlers, dealers in shady securities—and strange examiners. Perhaps bank presidents do not want their employees to know when they have had one too many at lunch. . . .

Comment

Mr. Evans offers five examples of the alleged intelligence of dogs. These examples refer directly to the theme of the essay, popular misconceptions about dogs, which is presented in the first sentence and is repeated throughout the passage in such words as "confused impressions," "delusions," "old wives' tales," and similar expressions. But even without these explanatory aids the meaning of the examples is unmistakable.

Note here that Mr. Evans comments on the examples by clearly manifesting his own attitude towards the stories about dogs' intelligence. "Dogs are sacred in our culture," he remarks ironically. "Intuitively" is put in quotes to suggest the author's skepticism. The fifth and sixth paragraphs are laced with ridicule. The author's ironical tone is emphasized by the satire in the first sentence of paragraph 7, especially in the phrase "mystic analytic power." Thus not only do the examples point immediately to the mistaken belief in the intelligence of dogs, but the tone—that is, the author's reaction towards the subject he is explaining—also indicates a humorous contempt for popular superstitions.

Analysis and Composition

1. Explain the meaning of the following words as they are used in the passage above:

> delusions   clairvoyance   mystic
> olfactory   gullible

2. Which of the following statements do you find the most accurate expression of the idea Mr. Evans is illustrating? Give reasons for your answer.
   a. Dogs are not really intelligent.
   b. Men are very unintelligent when they discuss the intelligence of dogs.
   c. Dogs are sacred in our culture.
   d. The mistaken belief that dogs are intelligent is evident in ordinary conversation and in newspaper reports.
   e. Popular belief in the intelligence of dogs dwells on the dogs' intuition, clairvoyance, and mystic analytic powers.
3. Write out in 100 words or less your own statement of Mr. Evans' general idea.
4. Reread Dickens' paragraph on the sagacity of dogs in the introduction to this section. By analysis of the tone, determine whether Dickens meant this example to be understood seriously.

5. Find three or more examples to illustrate each of the following main ideas. Make these examples as direct as possible.
   a. The American movie-goer has horses on the brain.
   b. Sheep are more stupid than they appear.
   c. One of the grossest fictions abroad today is that every American boy wants to become the President of the United States.
   d. The essence of a good compromise is the recognition that variety is not contradiction, that we do not need to choose between black and white.
   e. In the popular conception an educated man is hopelessly confused with the man who has a superficial knowledge of facts.
   f. To hear New Yorkers talk about the country west of the Hudson is a lesson in bad geography.
   g. Popular American idols are usually athletes, actors, or warriors.
   h. The most enduring of all superstitions is the belief in the printed word.
   i. Every man has a secret belief in the infallibility of his own taste.
6. Write a short composition on one or more of the topics listed in Exercise 5. Make sure your examples refer directly and unequivocally to the main idea.

---

b. Make an example vivid by using realistic detail: say who, when, where, how.

---

1. Book Learning

BY ELWYN BROOKS WHITE

Farmers are interested in science, in modern methods, and in theory, but they are not easily thrown off balance and they maintain a healthy suspicion of book learning and of the shenanigans of biologists, chem-

BOOK LEARNING: from *One Man's Meat* by E. B. White, published by Harper and Brothers. Copyright, 1942, by E. B. White.

ists, geneticists, and other late-rising students of farm practice and management. They are, I think, impressed by education, but they have seen too many examples of the helplessness and the impracticability of educated persons to be either envious or easily budged from their position.

I was looking at a neighbor's hens with him one time when he said something which expressed the feeling farmers have about colleges and books. He was complaining about the shape of the henhouse, but he wanted me to understand that it was all his own fault it had turned out badly. "I got the plan for it out of a book, fool-fashion," he said. And he gazed around at his surroundings in gentle disgust, with a half-humorous, half-disappointed look, as one might look back at any sort of youthful folly.

Scientific agriculture, however sound in principle, often seems strangely unrelated to, and unaware of, the vital, gruelling job of making a living by farming. Farmers sense this quality in it as they study their bulletins, just as a poor man senses in a rich man an incomprehension of his own problems. The farmer of today knows, for example, that manure loses some of its value when exposed to the weather; but he also knows how soon the sun goes down on all of us, and if there is a window handy at the cow's stern he pitches the dressing out into the yard and kisses the nitrogen good-by. There is usually not time in one man's lifetime to do different. The farmer knows that early-cut hay is better feed than hay which has been left standing through the hot dry days of late July. He hasn't worked out the vitamin losses, but he knows just by looking at the grass that some of the good has gone out of it. But he knows also that to make hay he needs settled weather—better weather than you usually get in June.

I've always tried to cut my hay reasonably early, but this year I wasn't able to get a team until the middle of July. It turned out to be just as well. June was a miserable month of rains and fog mulls. The people who stuck to their theories and cut their hay in spite of the weather, took a beating. A few extremists, fearful of losing a single vitamin, mowed in June, choosing a day when the sun came out for a few minutes. Their hay lay in the wet fields and rotted day after day.

The weather was unprecedented—weeks of damp and rain and fog. Everybody talked about it. One day during that spell I was holding forth to a practical farmer on the subject of hay. Full of book learning,

I was explaining (rather too glibly) the advantages of cutting hay in June. I described in detail the vitamin loss incurred by letting hay stand in the field after it has matured, and how much greater the feed value was per unit weight in early-cut hay, even though the quantity might be slightly less. The farmer was a quiet man, with big hands for curling round a scythe handle. He listened attentively. My words swirled around his head like summer flies. Finally, when I had exhausted my little store of learning and paused for a moment, he ventured a reply.

"The time to cut hay," he said firmly, "is in hayin' time."

Comment

Mr. White's purpose here is to illustrate the practical farmer's attitude towards the advice of agricultural scientists. In general, the farmer believes the scientist's advice is sound in principle but impractical. Mr. White illustrates this general idea by giving the farmer's annoyance at impractical suggestions on building a hen house, conserving fertilizer, and the time for haying. The force of these examples depends in great part upon the realistic background, the mixture of narrative and description, and the clearly defined attitude of the writer.

Analysis and Composition

1. How does Mr. White establish his own attitude towards his subject by the use of the following words and expressions?

book learning	gentle disgust
shenanigans	vitamin loss

2. Show how the farmer's two statements sum up the main point of the essay.
3. Find a realistic situation similar to the one used in "Book Learning" that will illustrate one or more of the following titles:
   a. The views of a mother of six on a book on child care
   b. A poor man's thoughts upon being told to take a vacation
   c. A master sergeant's opinion of a new lieutenant's lecture on drill
   d. The City Art Commission and the Committee on the Budget
   e. Advertising claims and public expectations
   f. A student's attitude towards a lengthy reading assignment

g. An automobile driver's reflections on traffic rules

h. A fat man's reaction to a strict diet

i. A small boy considering the inconsistencies of the advice to be seen but not heard.

4. Write a composition of 300 to 500 words on one of the titles listed in Exercise 3. Use examples.

2. Quirks

BY FRANKLIN P. ADAMS

This is the true story of the heroes and the heroines who have confided to me some of their prodigalities and penuries.

Take me, who never questioned any of my four children's expensive traits, like clothes and books, and private schools and colleges. I am a conspicuous turner-out of electric lights, on which I might save 16 cents a year. Incidentally, candor forces the admission that those schools and colleges paid off, for two of my boys are now self-supporting.

Take my wife, a comparatively easy job. She is a return-postcard saver. When we get a return postcard, she uses it, scratches out the return address, and sends it to someone else. This saves, she says, about $1.50 a year. She is a great one to save dresses, have them cleaned at the Eagle place in Hartford, and first thing I know, I get a Bill Rendered, $59.50. "What is this for?" I ask gently. "I had your bathrobe cleaned, and some dresses." Over each of many boxes from the same place, when opened, she says, "Why I ever had that old dress cleaned, I do not know." So she either hives it away or sends it abroad, costing also a tidy sum for postage.

A friend of mine lives in the New York nineties. He is seventy-three. For years when a package has come to the house, he has carefully untied it instead of cutting it, and has saved countless miles of more string than anybody can possibly use. Yet he thinks nothing of taking a cab six days a week, going either to Gramercy Park or the Salmagundi Club, at 47 Fifth Avenue.

I know a prodigal hostess. There is usually a guest or two. They are always importuned to stay a week, though they may have come there for a day or two. She, and the cook, set a marvelous and expensive table.

QUIRKS: reprinted by permission of the author and *The Atlantic Monthly*.

It must cost at least $10 a day for each guest. They are asked to stay a week or more because she hates to spend money for sheets and pillow cases to be laundered for another guest.

I know a man who always hangs back and lets the other man pay the subway fare, but will let a friend have $500 with no hope of getting it back. I know another man who would take you to dinner, and who is careless about money. Yet, no matter what the fare is, hungry or not, he will not leave anything on the plate. "Often I don't like it," he confessed, "but I hate to see food wasted."

A friend of mine, John McNulty, has a closet full of fine shoes. I never have been there when he hasn't been shining them and polishing them, instead of going next door and having them done. This I can understand, for he thinks so much of his footgear that he won't trust them to an ordinary bootblack. What am I talking about? I do the same thing myself.

To this day, I won't eat bread. As a boy, if I didn't eat bread, I wasn't allowed to have meat and potatoes, or a dessert. So I ate bread, and said that if I ever had anything to say, I'd never eat bread. This bread famine has been going on for more than forty years.

There is another penury that I—and many others—loathe. We get letters, almost form letters, saying the English teacher has assigned her, or him, to write an article about you. And will you please write a thousand words or so about how you get your inspiration, when you do your best work, and anything else about yourself. You are supposed to write the piece for nothing, of course. In the rare times when postage is furnished, I quote Dr. Samuel Johnson, who said, "No one but a blockhead ever wrote except for money."

I know a motion picture star who makes untold money a year, who came east from Hollywood with a great hole in his coat. A soft touch for anybody, "I hate to buy a new coat," he said. I know a really wealthy man who telephones his spinster sister, from New York to California, but has one of those three-minute egg glass timepieces in the telephone booth so that he won't talk more than three minutes.

Again my wife: she doesn't have to make a dateline, such as I have had to on newspapers and on the radio; yet she writes her letters on the train, loathing to waste that hour reading or looking at the Connecticut countryside. I tell her something or other, some big news. "How do you know that?" she asks. "I read it in your paper," I reply.

"Do you think that all I have to do is read the paper every day?" But she wastes time, according to me, telephoning for hours.

There are many of us who would rather buy a new type machine than change the ribbon on a good machine. After all, we say, ribbons don't grow on trees.

Comment

"Quirks" contains eleven illustrations of the prodigalities and penuries of Mr. Adams, his friends, and his acquaintances. Notice how the author uses realistic detail. In each example the person is identified by name or by some characteristic. A place is clearly stated or implied. The precise details of prodigality or penury are given. Dialogue also contributes to the realistic flavor. Note how all these examples, except the eighth, are direct and immediate as well as vivid. The reader does not need the convenient sign-posting of the first and last paragraphs to infer that these examples illustrate quirks of prodigality and penury. The examples speak for themselves.

Analysis and Composition

1. Imagine three or more realistically detailed examples to illustrate the following subjects:
   a. Idiosyncrasies in spelling and pronunciation.
   b. Quirks of dress—women's hats and shoes.
   c. My private superstitions.
   d. Men's haircuts and women's hairdos.
   e. On tipping inefficient waiters.
   f. Allergies towards human beings.
   g. Unorthodox methods of travel.
   h. Sick grandmothers, or some notable excuses.
   i. They were embarrassed, too.
2. Write a short essay of not more than 500 words on one of the subjects listed in Exercise 1. Strive to make the examples speak for themselves.

C.

Whenever, as with a complex idea, the connection between example and idea is not immediately evident, make certain to establish a valid connection.

1. On Cause

BY HERBERT L. SAMUEL

1 There is nothing mysterious or mystic in causation. It is merely the statement of a matter of fact—that a particular combination is followed by a particular effect. If we wish for a symbolic notation it would not be that "A is followed by B," but that "events $a, b, c, d \cdots$ in combination are followed by an event x." And we name $a, b, c, d \cdots$ and not $m, n, o, p \cdots$, precisely for the reason that these are antecedent events such as have already produced x, and therefore, exactly repeated, will produce another x again. The conclusion is implicit in the premises.

2 In the practical affairs of life we are accustomed to pick out one or two among the events which are closely antecedent to the one under consideration, because these are conspicuous or unexpected; the rest of the situation is accepted as given and normal, and therefore needing no investigation. This is natural, and sufficient for the purposes in view; but the habit is liable to mislead us when we come to examine the philosophy of causation.

3 [1]Let us consider an illustration. [2]We read that an inquest has been held on a man who had been killed by an explosion of gas in his house; the evidence showed that there had been a gas leakage one night in the

ON CAUSE: from *Essay in Physics*, copyright, 1952, by Herbert L. Samuel. Reprinted by permission of Harcourt, Brace and Company, Inc., and of Messrs. Basil Blackwell, publishers, Oxford, England.

basement, and that he had gone to look for it with a lighted candle. [3]Accordingly the Coroner's Court has returned a verdict that that had been the cause of the death, by misadventure. [4]For legal and other practical purposes that would be sufficient. [5]But if we were to analyse the matter more closely we should find that although the death was due to the explosion and the explosion to the man's own action, both the explosion and the action were the consequences of a whole con-catenation of previous events. [6]For instance, the man did not know, or had forgotten, that it is dangerous to look for a gas leak with a naked light; he happened to have at hand a candle and not an electric torch; a leak had occurred owing to faulty plumbing, or to a tap not having been properly turned off; his house was lighted by gas and not by elec-tricity;—and more remotely, the domestic use of a gas liable to explode had been introduced in the nineteenth century; coal measures existed geologically; also that this man had been born, and was alive at that time and present at that spot. [7]Few of these circumstances were rele-vant for the purposes of the Coroner's Court, and it would have been absurd to have taken them into account; yet all of them came into the causal complex, because, if any one of them had been absent, that ex-plosion would not have happened and that man would not have been killed.

Comment

A careful reading of this passage reveals the importance of establishing a valid connection between the example and the idea. Note that the main idea illustrated is the "causal complex" as distinguished from the everyday notion of cause. Hence the illustration provides us with an example which explains that distinction. On the one hand, the coroner picks out the one or two events that are necessary for a legal verdict; on the other hand, the philosopher takes into account the whole concatenation of previous events. Thus the illustration matches the distinction made in the first two para-graphs. Samuel makes the connection between the example and the idea particularly evident in sentences 4, 5, and 7 of paragraph 3.

Analysis and Composition

1. Consult an unabridged dictionary for the meaning of the following terms:

mystic	inquest	concatenation
causation	misadventure	electric
antecedent	consequences	liable

2. Discover some effective illustrations of the idea of cause other than that offered by Samuel. (Sample subjects: the causes of your city or town, your university, an automobile.)

3. Decide whether the following statement of the group of causes that produced a car is sufficiently complete, or incomplete in one or more essential factors and hence unreliable. The producers of the latest-model Packard are: the designer of the car; the workers in the factory; the tools; the designer of the tools; materials in the car; the designers and suppliers of the materials; the models which preceded the present model; the tradition of handicraft in which the workers were trained.

4. In the light of your decision about Exercise 3 would you accept the following statement as a satisfactory description of the cause of the hypothetical car? The latest model of the Packard is the product of its engineers and their assistants. Give reasons for your answer.

5. Develop apt examples of the italicized words in the following statements:
   a. *Individual decisions* are still important in the conduct of modern war.
   b. *Primitive peoples* survive in the modern world.
   c. *Fear of failure* is worse than failure itself.
   d. Great progress has been made in the *discovery of new drugs*.
   e. We choose our friends by a *combination of sortilege and instinct*.

6. Write a paragraph developing one or more of the topics listed in Exercise 5. Be sure to make plain the connection between the example and the idea it illustrates.

2. Contemplation and Action

BY LEWIS MUMFORD

1 In my class on the nature of personality at Stanford University, I once asked my students, as part of a weekly exercise, to make a plan for the way in which they intended to spend a whole day; and then, when the day was over, to set down what they actually did hour by hour and compare it with their original program. That proved a useful exercise: for each student was surprised to find how easily his firmest intentions had been diverted by a little succession of outside pres-

sures and stimuli over which he had exercised no control. This was not the miscarriage of Napoleon's set plans of battle, a matter through which Tolstoy sardonically illustrated the opposition between reason and calculation and the unexpectedness of life itself, since battles too easily get out of hand through forces too complex for human control. No: in the case of the students it was a demonstration, quite typical of our whole culture, of how the infirmity of our inner convictions and intentions, indeed our profound lack of self-respect, makes us the easy prey of chance stimuli, which exercise undue authority merely because they come from the outside.

2 Today external arresting sensations take the place of rational meanings as in advertising: external stimuli replace inner purposes; and so we drift, from moment to moment, from hour to hour, indeed from one end of a lifetime to another, without ever regaining the initiative or making an active bid for freedom. Since we do not discipline and direct our dreams we submit to nightmares: lacking an inner life, we lack an outer life that is worth having, too; for it is only by their coeval development and their constant interpenetration that life itself can flourish.

3 The moral should be plain: if, as Gregory the Great said, he who would hold the fortress of contemplation must first train in the camp of action, the reverse, for our times, is even more essential: he who would sally forth with a new plan of action must first withdraw to the innermost recesses of contemplation, on whose walls, when he becomes accustomed to the solitude and the darkness, a new vision of life will appear: not the objective after-image of the world he has left, but the subjective fore-image of the world he will return to and re-make.

Comment

The main idea of this passage is the interconnection of contemplation and intelligent action. This idea is stated conclusively in paragraph 3. The example illustrating the idea occurs in paragraph 1, where Mumford explains the weekly exercise given to his students at Stanford. Note how inevitably this example is pointed to a general truth, namely that outside pressures and stimuli overcome an original plan based on reason and calculation. Thus the example is linked with the main point of the passage—the need for the constant interpenetration of contemplation and action.

Note too the effective use of metaphor in paragraph 3, where contemplation is compared to a fortress.

Analysis and Composition

1. In what sense does Mumford use the following terms:

sardonically	rational meanings	coeval
convictions	stimuli	contemplation
intentions	freedom	after-image
sensations	discipline	fore-image

2. After a careful rereading of the passage, explain how the example of the student exercise in paragraph 1 is or is not a clear demonstration of the infirmity of inner conviction or intentions.

3. Perform the experiment suggested in the first paragraph of the passage above by writing your own plan on how you will spend tomorrow. Then, in a short composition of approximately 500 words, compare your actual day with the planned day.

4. Determine whether the following examples illustrate a belief in Mumford's theory that a good plan of action depends upon thought:
   a. The practice of granting a sabbatical year to scholars teaching at universities
   b. The summer recess for all students
   c. The Princeton Institute for Advanced Studies
   d. The theory of the creative pause particularly evident in the lives of Tennyson and Milton. (Both poets were silent for approximately ten years after their first publications.)
   e. The rotation policy of the armed forces
   f. Dr. Johnson's periodic retreats from society
   g. A walk in the woods before an examination
   h. The annual inventory of a business organization
   i. The sales conference

5. Test the validity of the following general statements, taken or adapted from the passage above, by supplying two or more effective examples.

   Sample: *Statement:* Today external arresting sensations take the place of rational meanings, as in advertising.
   Examples: A bathing beauty advertising a lawnmower; an athlete advertising a cereal.

   a. Our inner convictions are an easy prey to chance stimuli, such as the suggestions of friends.
   b. We rarely make an active bid for freedom from the conventions of hospitality.
   c. We cannot have a good outer life without a good inner life.

d. Most people are the slaves of the telephone.

e. Our time is not our own.

6. In a composition of 300 words develop by use of examples one of the statements listed in Exercise 5.

3. The Law of Right and Wrong

BY C. S. LEWIS

1 Every one has heard people quarrelling. Sometimes it sounds funny and sometimes it sounds merely unpleasant; but however it sounds, I believe we can learn something very important from listening to the kind of things they say. They say things like this: "That's my seat. I was there first"—"Leave him alone, he isn't doing you any harm"—"Why should you shove in first?"—"Give me a bit of your orange, I gave you a bit of mine"—"How'd you like it if anyone did the same to you?"—"Come on, you promised." People say things like that every day, educated people as well as uneducated, and children as well as grown-ups.

2 Now what interests me about all these remarks is that the man who makes them isn't just saying that the other man's behaviour doesn't happen to please him. He is appealing to some kind of standard of behaviour which he expects the other man to know about. And the other man very seldom replies, "To hell with your standard." Nearly always he tries to make out that what he has been doing doesn't really go against the standard, or that if it does, there is some special excuse. He pretends there is some special reason in this particular case why the person who took the seat first should not keep it, or that things were quite different when he was given the bit of orange, or that something has turned up which lets him off keeping his promise. It looks, in fact, very much as if both parties had in mind some kind of Law or Rule of fair play or decent behaviour or morality or whatever you like to call it, about which they really agreed. And they have. If they hadn't, they might, of course, fight like animals, but they couldn't *quarrel* in the human sense of the word. Quarrelling means trying to show that the other man's in the wrong. And there'd be no sense in trying to do that unless you and he had some sort of agreement as to what Right

THE LAW OF RIGHT AND WRONG: from C. S. Lewis, *The Case for Christianity,* New York, 1943. Used with the permission of The Macmillan Company, New York, and Geoffrey Bles, Ltd., London.

and Wrong are; just as there'd be no sense in saying that a footballer had committed a foul unless there was some agreement about the rules of football.

3 Now this Law or Rule about Right and Wrong used to be called the Law of Nature. Nowadays, when we talk of the "laws of nature" we usually mean things like gravitation, or heredity, or the laws of chemistry. But when the older thinkers called the Law of Right and Wrong the Law of Nature, they really meant the Law of *Human* Nature. The idea was that, just as falling stones are governed by the law of gravitation and chemicals by chemical laws, so the creature called man also had *his* law—with this great difference, that the stone couldn't choose whether it obeyed the law of gravitation or not, but a man could choose either to obey the Law of Human Nature or to disobey it. They called it Law of Nature because they thought that every one knew it by nature and didn't need to be taught it. They didn't mean, of course, that you mightn't find an odd individual here and there who didn't know it, just as you find a few people who are colour-blind or have no ear for a tune. But taking the race as a whole, they thought that the human idea of Decent Behaviour was obvious to everyone. And I believe they were right. If they weren't, then all the things we say about this war are nonsense. What is the sense in saying the enemy are in the wrong unless Right is a real thing which the Germans at bottom know as well as we do and ought to practise? If they had no notion of what we mean by right, then, though we might still have to fight them, we could no more blame them for that than for the colour of their hair.

Comment

Paragraph 1 offers six brief illustrations of quarreling by reporting snatches of dialogue. In each quarrel someone says that the other fellow is wrong.

Paragraph 2 then shows that in each quarrel the speaker assumes that the other fellow is wrong because of an implicit standard of right and wrong. This implicit standard of right and wrong is shown to be a general assumption in all dispute.

Paragraph 3 identifies this standard of right and wrong with the universal law of human nature. This law is further defined and illustrated by a reference to World War II.

Analysis and Composition

1. Define each of the following terms as they are used by C. S. Lewis:

   behavior   rule   nature
   standard   gravitation
   law   heredity

2. The remarks cited in paragraph 1 are all said to imply some kind of standard of behavior. What standard is implied in each? Give reasons for your answer.

3. You can test particular judgments and opinions by discovering the general standard which they imply. You can find the general standard by extending the qualities of the particular example to all members of the class. Thus:

Particular Judgment	*Implied General Standard*
Gray is a good actor because he is versatile.	*All* good actors are versatile.
Smith is a valuable halfback because he can punt as well as run and pass.	All valuable halfbacks can punt as well as run and pass.
Ernie Pyle is an example of a good journalist because his words are simple and his sentences are short.	All good journalists use simple words and short sentences.
The Desert of Love is a film masterpiece because it is uninhibited.	All film masterpieces are uninhibited.

   Test the following particular judgments and opinions by discovering the general standard (or assumption) they imply.

   a. You can't blame a child for being aggressive because the fault lies with his parents, his home conditions, and his general environment.
   b. You've got to admire Roscoe because he keeps fit and works like a beaver.
   c. The advantages of attending State University are overwhelming. It has a student union. You'll meet men who will eventually be on top. The faculty is first rate, too.
   d. You can't quit the Democratic party now. It would be taken as a repudiation of all the social gains made by the New Deal.
   e. The Union Club is very conservative. No one talks to you without an invitation.
   f. The company must get rid of Olsen. He's too interested in his own good and in other people's failures.
   g. I expect you to give my views as much attention as I give yours.

h. Do not interfere with a child's natural growth by telling him what to read or think.

i. I prefer Smith because he admits that he doesn't know all the answers.

j. The New York *Bugle* cannot be trusted because its editors are unprincipled in their selection of the facts they print, inaccurate in their report of these facts, and erroneous in their interpretation of them.

k. I distrust Murray's news items about France because he doesn't speak French and he knows no French history.

l. If you do not support this appropriation bill, which provides for the conduct of the war, you are a traitor to your country.

4. In several paragraphs develop three examples that will illustrate *one* of the following ideas. Be sure to relate your example to the main idea.

a. The essentials of a good movie
b. Industrial progress
c. Tolerance
d. *Noblesse oblige*
e. Humor

f. Loyalty
g. Good writing
h. Effective definition
i. Bad acting
j. Bad manners

---

d. In establishing proof by example, provide for each step in the argument (1) a group of apt examples (2) of sufficient number to support the conclusion.

Fenimore Cooper's Literary Offenses

BY MARK TWAIN

The Pathfinder and *The Deerslayer* stand at the head of Cooper's novels as artistic creations. There are others of his works which contain parts as perfect as are to be found in these, and scenes even more thrilling. Not one can be compared with either of them as a finished whole.

The defects in both of these tales are comparatively slight. They were pure works of art.—PROF. LOUNSBURY.

The five tales reveal an extraordinary fulness of invention.
. . . One of the very greatest characters in fiction, Natty Bumppo. . . .
The craft of the woodsman, the tricks of the trapper, all the delicate
art of the forest, were familiar to Cooper from his youth up.—Prof.
Brander Matthews.

Cooper is the greatest artist in the domain of romantic fiction yet produced by America.—Wilkie Collins.

1 It seems to me that it was far from right for the Professor of
English in Yale, the Professor of English Literature in Columbia, and
Wilkie Collins to deliver opinions on Cooper's literature without having read some of it. It would have been much more decorous to keep
silent and let persons talk who have read Cooper.

2 Cooper's art has some defects. In one place in *Deerslayer,* and in
the restricted space of two-thirds of a page, Cooper has scored 114 offenses against literary art out of a possible 115. It breaks the record.

3 There are nineteen rules governing literary art in the domain of
romantic fiction—some say twenty-two. In *Deerslayer* Cooper violated
eighteen of them. These eighteen require:

4] 1. That a tale shall accomplish something and arrive somewhere.
But the *Deerslayer* tale accomplishes nothing and arrives in the air.

2. They require that the episodes of a tale shall be necessary parts
of the tale and shall help to develop it. But as the *Deerslayer* tale is not
a tale, and accomplishes nothing and arrives nowhere, the episodes
have no rightful place in the work, since there was nothing for them
to develop.

3. They require that the personages in a tale shall be alive, except
in the case of corpses, and that always the reader shall be able to tell
the corpses from the others. But this detail has often been overlooked
in the *Deerslayer* tale.

4. They require that the personages in a tale, both dead and alive,
shall exhibit a sufficient excuse for being there. But this detail also has
been overlooked in the *Deerslayer* tale.

5. They require that when the personages of a tale deal in conversation, the talk shall sound like human talk, and be talk such as
human beings would be likely to talk in the given circumstances, and
have a discoverable meaning, also a discoverable purpose, and a show
of relevancy, and remain in the neighborhood of the subject in hand,
and be interesting to the reader, and help out the tale, and stop when
the people cannot think of anything more to say. But this requirement

has been ignored from the beginning of the *Deerslayer* tale to the end of it.

6. They require that when the author describes the character of a personage in his tale, the conduct and conversation of that personage shall justify said description. But this law gets little or no attention in the *Deerslayer* tale, as Natty Bumppo's case will amply prove.

7. They require that when a personage talks like an illustrated, gilt-edged, tree-calf, hand-tooled, seven-dollar *Friendship's Offering* in the beginning of a paragraph, he shall not talk like a Negro minstrel in the end of it. But this rule is flung down and danced upon in the *Deerslayer* tale.

8. They require that crass stupidities shall not be played upon the reader as the "craft of the woodsman, the delicate art of the forest," by either the author or the people in the tale. But this rule is persistently violated in the *Deerslayer* tale.

9. They require that the personages of a tale shall confine themselves to possibilities and let miracles alone; or, if they venture a miracle, the author must so plausibly set it forth as to make it look possible and reasonable. But these rules are not respected in the *Deerslayer* tale.

10. They require that the author shall make the reader feel a deep interest in the personages of his tale and in their fate; and that he shall make the reader love the good people in the tale and hate the bad ones. But the reader of the *Deerslayer* tale dislikes the good people in it, is indifferent to the others, and wishes they would all get drowned together.

11. They require that the characters in a tale shall be so clearly defined that the reader can tell beforehand what each will do in a given emergency. But in the *Deerslayer* tale this rule is vacated.

5] In addition to these large rules there are some little ones. These require that the author shall

12. *Say* what he is proposing to say, not merely come near it.

13. Use the right word, not its second cousin.

14. Eschew surplusage.

15. Not omit necessary detail.

16. Avoid slovenliness of form.

17. Use good grammar.

18. Employ a simple and straightforward style.

6] Even these seven are coldly and persistently violated in the *Deerslayer* tale.

7 Cooper's gift in the way of invention was not a rich endowment; but such as it was he liked to work it, he was pleased with the effects, and indeed he did some quite sweet things with it. In his little box of stage properties he kept six or eight cunning devices, tricks, artifices for his savages and woodsmen to deceive and circumvent each other with, and he was never so happy as when he was working these innocent things and seeing them go. A favorite one was to make a moccasined person tread in the tracks of the moccasined enemy, and thus hide his own trail. Cooper wore out barrels and barrels of moccasins in working that trick. Another stage property that he pulled out of his box pretty frequently was his broken twig. He prized his broken twig above all the rest of his effects, and worked it the hardest. It is a restful chapter in any book of his when somebody doesn't step on a dry twig and alarm all the reds and whites for two hundred yards around. Every time a Cooper person is in peril, and absolute silence is worth four dollars a minute, he is sure to step on a dry twig. There may be a hundred handier things to step on, but that wouldn't satisfy Cooper. Cooper requires him to turn out and find a dry twig; and if he can't do it, go and borrow one. In fact, the Leatherstocking Series ought to have been called the Broken Twig Series.

8 I am sorry there is not room to put in a few dozen instances of the delicate art of the forest, as practised by Natty Bumppo and some of the other Cooperian experts. Perhaps we may venture two or three samples. Cooper was a sailor—a naval officer; yet he gravely tells us how a vessel, driving towards a lee shore in a gale, is steered for a particular spot by her skipper because he knows of an *undertow* there which will hold her back against the gale and save her. For just pure woodcraft, or sailorcraft, or whatever it is, isn't that neat? For several years Cooper was daily in the society of artillery, and he ought to have noticed that when a cannon-ball strikes the ground it either buries itself or skips a hundred feet or so; skips again a hundred feet or so— and so on, till it finally gets tired and rolls. Now in one place he loses some "females"—as he always calls women—in the edge of a wood near a plain at night in a fog, on purpose to give Bumppo a chance to show off the delicate art of the forest before the reader. These mislaid people are hunting for a fort. They hear a cannon-blast, and a cannon-ball presently comes rolling into the wood and stops at their feet. To

the females this suggests nothing. The case is very different with the admirable Bumppo. I wish I may never know peace again if he doesn't strike out promptly and *follow the track* of that cannon-ball across the plain through the dense fog and find the fort. Isn't it a daisy? If Cooper had any real knowledge of Nature's ways of doing things, he had a most delicate art in concealing the fact. For instance: one of his acute Indian experts, Chingachgook (pronounced Chicago, I think), has lost the trail of a person he is tracking through the forest. Apparently that trail is hopelessly lost. Neither you nor I could ever have guessed out the way to find it. It was very different with Chicago. Chicago was not stumped for long. He turned a running stream out of its course, and there, in the slush in its old bed, were that person's moccasin-tracks. The current did not wash them away, as it would have done in all other like cases—no, even the eternal laws of Nature have to vacate when Cooper wants to put up a delicate job of woodcraft on the reader.

9 We must be a little wary when Brander Matthews tells us that Cooper's books "reveal an extraordinary fulness of invention." As a rule, I am quite willing to accept Brander Matthews' literary judgments and applaud his lucid and graceful phrasing of them; but that particular statement needs to be taken with a few tons of salt. Bless your heart, Cooper hadn't any more invention than a horse; and I don't mean a high-class horse, either; I mean a clotheshorse. It would be very difficult to find a really clever "situation" in Cooper's books, and still more difficult to find one of any kind which he has failed to render absurd by his handling of it. Look at the episodes of "the caves": and at the celebrated scuffle between Maqua and those others on the tableland a few days later; and at Hurry Harry's queer water-transit from the castle to the ark; and at Deerslayer's half-hour with his first corpse; and at the quarrel between Hurry Harry and Deerslayer later; and at—but choose for yourself; you can't go amiss.

10 If Cooper had been an observer, his inventive faculty would have worked better; not more interestingly, but more rationally, more plausibly. Cooper's proudest creations in the way of "situations" suffer noticeably from the absence of the observer's protecting gift. Cooper's eye was splendidly inaccurate. Cooper seldom saw anything correctly. He saw nearly all things as through a glass eye, darkly. Of course a man who cannot see the commonest little everyday matters accurately is working at a disadvantage when he is constructing a "situation." In

the *Deerslayer* tale Cooper has a stream which is fifty feet wide where it flows out of a lake; it presently narrows to twenty as it meanders along for no given reason, and yet when a stream acts like that it ought to be required to explain itself. Fourteen pages later the width of the brook's outlet from the lake has suddenly shrunk thirty feet and become "the narrowest part of the stream." This shrinkage is not accounted for. The stream has bends in it, a sure indication that it has alluvial banks and cuts them; yet these bends are only thirty and fifty feet long. If Cooper had been a nice and punctilious observer he would have noticed that the bends were oftener nine hundred feet long than short of it.

11 Cooper made the exit of that stream fifty feet wide, in the first place, for no particular reason; in the second place, he narrowed it to less than twenty to accommodate some Indians. He bends a "sapling" to the form of an arch over this narrow passage, and conceals six Indians in its foliage. They are "laying" for a settler's scow or ark which is coming up the stream on its way to the lake; it is being hauled against the stiff current by a rope whose stationary end is anchored in the lake; its rate of progress cannot be more than a mile an hour. Cooper describes the ark, but pretty obscurely. In the matter of dimensions "it was little more than a modern canal-boat." Let us guess, then, that it was about one hundred and forty feet long. It was of "greater breadth than common." Let us guess, then, that it was about sixteen feet wide. This leviathan had been prowling down bends which were but a third as long as itself, and scraping between banks where it had only two feet of space to spare on each side. We cannot too much admire this miracle. A low-roofed log dwelling occupies "two-thirds of the ark's length"—a dwelling ninety feet long and sixteen feet wide, let us say—a kind of vestibule train. The dwelling has two rooms— each forty-five feet long and sixteen feet wide, let us guess. One of them is the bedroom of the Hutter girls, Judith and Hetty; the other is the parlor in the daytime, at night it is papa's bedchamber. The ark is arriving at the stream's exit now, whose width has been reduced to less than twenty feet to accommodate the Indians—say to eighteen. There is a foot to spare on each side of the boat. Did the Indians notice that there was going to be a tight squeeze there? Did they notice that they could make money by climbing down out of that arched sapling and just stepping aboard when the ark scraped by? No; other Indians would have noticed these things, but Cooper's

Indians never notice anything. Cooper thinks they are marvelous creatures for noticing, but he was almost always in error about his Indians. There was seldom a sane one among them.

12 The ark is one hundred and forty feet long; the dwelling is ninety feet long. The idea of the Indians is to drop softly and secretly from the arched sapling to the dwelling as the ark creeps along under it at the rate of a mile an hour, and butcher the family. It will take the ark a minute and a half to pass under. It will take the ninety foot dwelling a minute to pass under. Now, then, what did the six Indians do? It would take you thirty years to guess, and even then you would have to give it up, I believe. Therefore I will tell you what the Indians did. Their chief, a person of quite extraordinary intellect for a Cooper Indian, warily watched the canalboat as it squeezed along under him, and when he had got his calculations fined down to exactly the right shade, as he judged, he let go and dropped. And *missed the house!* He missed the house and landed in the stern of the scow. It was not much of a fall, yet it knocked him silly. He lay there unconscious. If the house had been ninety-seven feet long he would have made the trip. The fault was Cooper's not his. The error lay in the construction of the house. Cooper was no architect.

13 There still remained in the roost five Indians. The boat has passed under and is now out of their reach. Let me explain what the five did— you would not be able to reason it out for yourself. No. 1 jumped for the boat, but fell in the water astern of it. Then No. 2 jumped for the boat, but fell in the water still farther astern of it. Then No. 3 jumped for the boat, and fell a good way astern of it. Then No. 4 jumped for the boat, and fell in the water *away* astern. Then even No. 5 made a jump for the boat—for he was a Cooper Indian. In the matter of intellect, the difference between a Cooper Indian and the Indian that stands in front of the cigar shop is not spacious. The scow episode is really a sublime burst of invention; but it does not thrill, because the inaccuracy of the details throws a sort of air of fictitiousness and general improbability over it. This comes of Cooper's inadequacy as an observer.

14 The conversations in the Cooper books have a curious sound in our modern ears. To believe that such talk really ever came out of people's mouths would be to believe that there was a time when time was of no value to a person who thought he had something to say; when it was the custom to spread a two-minute remark out to ten;

when a man's mouth was a rolling mill, and busied itself all day long in turning four-foot pigs of thought into thirty-foot bars of conversational railroad iron by attenuation; when subjects were seldom faithfully stuck to, but the talk wandered all around and arrived nowhere; when conversations consisted mainly of irrelevancies, with here and there a relevancy, a relevancy with an embarrassed look, as not being able to explain how it got there.

15 Cooper was certainly not a master in the construction of dialog. Inaccurate observation defeated him here as it defeated him in so many other enterprises of his. He even failed to notice that the man who talks corrupt English six days in the week must and will talk it on the seventh, and can't help himself. In the *Deerslayer* story he lets Deerslayer talk the showiest kind of book talk sometimes, and at other times the basest of base dialects. For instance, when some one asks him if he has a sweetheart, and if so, where she abides, this is his majestic answer: "She's in the forest—hanging from the boughs of the trees, in a soft rain—in the dew on the open grass—the clouds that float about in the blue heavens—the birds that sing in the woods—the sweet springs where I slake my thirst—and in all the other glorious gifts that come from God's Providence!"

16 And he preceded that, a little before, with this: "It consarns me as all things that touches a fri'nd consarns a fri'nd."

17 And this is another of his remarks: "If I was Injin born, now, I might tell of this, or carry in the scalp and boast of the expl'ite afore the whole tribe; or if my inimy had only been a bear!"—and so on.

18 We cannot imagine such a thing as a veteran Scotch commander-in-chief comporting himself in the field like a windy melodramatic actor, but Cooper could. On one occasion Alice and Cora were being chased by the French through a fog in the neighborhood of their father's fort:

"*Point de quartier aux coquins!*" cried an eager pursuer, who seemed to direct the operations of the enemy.

"Stand firm and be ready, my gallant 60ths!" suddenly exclaimed a voice above them; "wait to see the enemy; fire low, and sweep the glacis."

"Father! father!" exclaimed a piercing cry from out the mist; "it is I! Alice! thy own Elsie! spare, O! save your daughters!"

"Hold!" shouted the former speaker, in the awful tones of parental agony, the sound reaching even to the woods, and rolling back in solemn echo. " 'Tis she! God has restored me my children! Throw open the sally-port; to the field, 6oths, to the field; pull not a trigger, lest ye kill my lambs! Drive off these dogs of France with your steel."

19 Cooper's word sense was singularly dull. When a person has a poor ear for music he will flat and sharp right along without knowing it. He keeps near the tune, but it is *not* the tune. When a person has a poor ear for words, the result is a literary flatting and sharping; you perceive what he is intending to say, but you also perceive that he doesn't *say* it. This is Cooper. He was not a word musician. His ear was satisfied with the *approximate* word. I will furnish some circumstantial evidence in support of this charge. My instances are gathered from half a dozen pages of the tale called *Deerslayer*. He uses "verbal" for "oral"; "precision" for "facility"; "phenomena" for "marvels"; "necessary" for "predetermined"; "unsophisticated" for "primitive"; "preparation" for "expectancy"; "rebuked" for "subdued"; "dependent on" for "resulting from"; "fact" for "condition"; "fact" for "conjecture"; "precaution" for "caution"; "explain" for "determine"; "mortified" for "disappointed"; "meretricious" for "factitious"; "materially" for "considerably"; "decreasing" for "deepening"; "increasing" for "disappearing"; "embedded" for "enclosed"; "treacherous" for "hostile"; "stood" for "stooped"; "softened" for "replaced"; "rejoined" for "remarked"; "situation" for "condition"; "different" for "differing"; "insensible" for "unsentient"; "brevity" for "celerity"; "distrusted" for "suspicious"; "mental imbecility" for "imbecility"; "eyes" for "sight"; "counteracting" for "opposing"; "funeral obsequies" for "obsequies."

20 There have been daring people in the world who claimed that Cooper could write English, but they are all dead now—all dead but Lounsbury. I don't remember that Lounsbury makes the claim in so many words, still he makes it, for he says that *Deerslayer* is a "pure work of art." Pure, in that connection means faultless—faultless in all details—and language is a detail. If Mr. Lounsbury had only compared Cooper's English with the English which he writes himself—but it is plain that he didn't; and so it is likely that he imagines until this day that Cooper's is as clean and compact as his own. Now I feel sure, deep down in my heart, that Cooper wrote about the poorest English that exists in our language, and that the English of *Deerslayer* is the very worst that even Cooper ever wrote.

21 I may be mistaken, but it does seem to me that *Deerslayer* is not a work of art in any sense; it does seem to me that it is destitute

of every detail that goes to the making of a work of art; in truth, it seems to me that *Deerslayer* is just simply a literary *delirium tremens*.

Comment

An analysis of Mark Twain's case against James Fenimore Cooper may be stated as follows:

Central theme: Cooper's *Deerslayer* is not a work of art in any sense.
Argument:
A. A work of art in the field of romantic fiction should possess power of invention, accurate observation, and judicious use of language (¶1-6). (Note: This statement represents the serious sense of the argument. Twain actually cites humorously eighteen rules of good fiction and indulges in a long and amusing exposition of Cooper's literary status.)
B. Cooper's *Deerslayer* shows a lack of inventive power (¶7-9) (developed by examples).
C. Cooper's *Deerslayer* shows a lack of accurate observation (¶10-13) (developed by examples).
D. Cooper's *Deerslayer* shows a lack of judgment in handling language:
   1. In dialogue (¶14-18) (developed by examples)
   2. In word sense (¶19)
   3. In usage (¶20)
E. Therefore Cooper's *Deerslayer* is not a work of art in any sense (¶21).

Notice that in each step of his argument, B, C, and D, Mark Twain has found apt examples and provides them in sufficient number to establish his conclusion. The conclusion, needless to say, is a probable opinion, not an absolute truth. A more detailed study of Mark Twain's use of examples as proof will be developed in the following questions for analysis. The study of examples as a method of inductive reasoning has already been mentioned in the introduction to Section III. (Induction will be explained in detail in Sections VII and XI.)

Analysis and Composition

1. Determine whether Mark Twain's statement of his central theme in the last paragraph is fundamentally serious or a purely humorous exaggeration, or a mixture of the serious and the comic. Give reasons for your answer.
2. Paragraphs 3-6 cite eighteen characteristics of the class romantic fiction. While this multiple division serves the purpose of humor, it is not or-

derly (see Section III). Determine a single principle of division and group these eighteen divisions under three main headings. Avoid overlapping.

3. Paragraphs 7-9 offer numerous examples of Cooper's *lack of invention*. Twain does not give a formal definition of invention, but his examples point unmistakably to his meaning. Judging from the examples, write a paragraph explaining what you think invention meant to Twain.

4. Paragraphs 10-13 give examples of Cooper's failure as an *observer*. Examine each of the following examples of Cooper's faulty observation with a view to determining whether it results in a serious loss of credibility or a forgivable inconsistency.
   a. The size of the stream (¶10)
   b. The dimensions of the ark (¶11)
   c. The episode of the five Indians (¶13)

5. Has Mark Twain given a sufficient number of examples to prove that Cooper lacked the power of observation? Give reasons for your answer.

6. Decide whether accurate observation is necessary in a work of romantic fiction. If not, is Mark Twain's objection to Cooper's faulty observation irrelevant?

7. Paragraphs 14-18 give examples of Cooper's *faulty dialogue*. Are there a sufficient number of these examples to justify the classification of the whole book as "faulty" in dialogue? If not, how many examples do you think are necessary in order to justify such a classification? Explain your answer.

8. Paragraph 19 offers examples of Cooper's *faulty word sense*. Judge for yourself the accuracy of Mark Twain's evidence by studying the denotation and connotation of the words listed in paragraph 19. Summarize your judgment in a paragraph agreeing or disagreeing with Mark Twain's conclusion.

9. Paragraph 20 appears to attack Cooper's handling of sentences and paragraphs. It offers no illustrations. In your opinion does this paragraph begin a new division, or does it sum up the two previous divisions, namely, word sense and dialogue?

10. Paragraph 21 states the central theme—*The Deerslayer* is not a work of art in any sense. Do the specific illustrations contained in paragraphs 3-19 justify this general assertion? Note particularly the phrases "in any sense" and "it does seem to me."

11. Exercises 2-9 were designed to help you trace the line of inductive reasoning (from particular to general) in Mark Twain's essay. Twain used specific examples to prove that Cooper's *Deerslayer* lacked invention, observation, good dialogue, and word sense. These lacks (and lack of good English in general) argue to a lack of art. Now reread the outline given under *Comment* and determine whether sentence A fairly

represents the serious side of Mark Twain's argument. Give reasons for your answer.

12. In one sense Mark Twain's essay is a refutation of the statements which are quoted at the beginning of his paper. After rereading these quotations, and paragraphs 1 and 21, comment in a paragraph on the accuracy of each of the following observations:
   a. Mark Twain answers Lounsbury, Matthews, and Collins indirectly by substantially proving views opposite to their own.
   b. Mark Twain's essay contains a direct answer to each point raised by the three authors.
   c. Mark Twain makes Professors Lounsbury and Matthews look silly, but he hasn't touched the issue raised by Wilkie Collins, for, when Collins wrote in the middle of the nineteenth century, Cooper *was* the greatest of our romantic writers of fiction.
   d. Mark Twain's attack on Cooper is bias masquerading as humor.
   e. Mark Twain's uncultivated mind is here revealed in all its horrifying literalness.
   f. Mark Twain let the air out of the inflated literary reputation of a fourth-rate writer who earned his fame by default.

13. According to the following outline, write a brief review of a short piece of fiction assigned by your instructor.
   a. State the principal literary qualities of the story.
   b. Give several examples of each of these qualities.
   c. Determine whether these qualities show inventive power, accuracy of observation, and a judicious use of language. For additional criteria of good fiction consult Mark Twain's rules of literary art (¶4-5).

GENERAL EXERCISES

A

The following passage on General Grant contains various methods of analysis, some of which you have not yet studied. But one of the chief methods is that of exemplification. You will understand this clearly if you answer the following questions as *fully* as you can. Answer by précis or paraphrase, as your instructor directs.

1. What specific examples support the general observation that "at first sight, most people were not impressed by him [Grant]; many found him a comic figure" (¶1)?
2. What examples does Mr. Williams use to illustrate Grant's "ideal training experience for the job of general in chief" (¶2)?

3. List the specific examples of lessons in strategy Grant learned by experience (¶3).
4. What specific examples of Grant's achievements justify classifying him as the greatest general of the Civil War (¶4)?
5. Wherein did the staffs of Lee and Grant differ, and how did that difference illustrate the disparate outlooks of the commanders, and thus prove Grant's superiority (¶6)?

Grant as a General

BY T. HARRY WILLIAMS

1 Grant was forty-two years old in 1864. He was five feet eight in height and weighed about one hundred thirty-five pounds. His eyes were dark gray, his hair and short full beard were chestnut brown. His left eye was a little lower than the other, and he had a wart on his right cheek. His frame was slightly stooped. There was little magnetism in his appearance and personality. He never inspired troops to frenzies of applause or affection, as did McClellan and Burnside. At first sight, most people were not impressed by him; many found him a comic figure. A sensitive observer who first saw Grant soon after he came to Washington said the General was an extraordinary person but did not look it. Young Charles Francis Adams, Jr., of a family not given to uttering praise lightly, wrote his father in London that Grant could pass for a dumpy, slouchy little subaltern who was fond of smoking. But he knew how to manage men quietly, Adams added, and he possessed exquisite judgment. In a penetrating evaluation, Adams said that in a crisis all would instinctively lean on Grant. Another keen student of human nature, Colonel Theodore Lyman of Meade's staff, saw immediately past Grant's exterior to the real man. He noted that Grant's face had three expressions: deep thought, extreme determination, and great simplicity and calmness. Summing Grant up, Lyman said that the General looked as if he had determined to butt his head through a brick wall and was about to do it.

2 Grant's war service before 1864 had been an ideal training experience for the job of general in chief. He was a better war director because he had come up the hard and long way. He had started as a small unit commander and then had gone on to bigger commands as he had proved on the field that he could handle larger responsibilities. He learned self-confidence from his successes and patience and determination from his failures. His experience with small commands was fortunate for Grant. It taught him the importance of looking after such things as ammunition supplies and means of transportation—the prosaic vital things that can make or

GRANT AS A GENERAL: reprinted from *Lincoln and His Generals* by T. Harry Williams, by permission of Alfred A. Knopf, Inc. Copyright, 1952, by Alfred A. Knopf, Inc.

break an army. Most valuable of all, he first encountered the problems of army administration on a small scale and mastered one set before he met another and more complex one. He learned administration from the regimental level up, which was a better way than if he had suddenly been placed in charge of a huge army as McClellan had been.

3 At the beginning of the war, Grant knew as much about the theory and history of war as the average West Point graduate and regular army officer, which was not very much. He did not, after the conflict started, study the higher art of war from books, but he studied it closely from the events he witnessed and experienced. At Henry and Donelson, he saw the moral value of being on the offensive, and he learned at Shiloh the danger of neglecting the principle of precaution. In nearly all of his early operations, he demonstrated that he understood one of the most important of all strategic principles, that of making the destruction of the enemy army his primary objective. Grant absorbed some of his knowledge of war from other officers, and on many occasions used the brains of others, which is what a great general should do. As Sherman well expressed it, Grant possessed "in an eminent degree that peculiar and high attribute of using various men to produce a common result. . . ." His brilliant victories at Vicksburg and Chattanooga were partly the result of his own developing strategic powers and partly of his ability to use the powers of his subordinates to accomplish his purpose. When he became general in chief, Grant was about as perfectly trained and formed for the post as any general could be.

4 Grant was, judged by modern standards, the greatest general of the Civil War. He was head and shoulders above any general on either side as an over-all strategist, as a master of what in later wars would be called global strategy. His Operation Crusher plan, the product of a mind which had received little formal instruction in the higher art of war, would have done credit to the most finished student of a series of modern staff and command schools. He was a brilliant theater strategist, as evidenced by the Vicksburg campaign, which was a classic field and siege operation. He was a better than average tactician, although like even the best generals of both sides he did not appreciate the destruction that the increasing firepower of modern armies could visit on troops advancing across open spaces.

5 Lee is usually ranked as the greatest Civil War general, but this evaluation has been made without placing Lee and Grant in the perspective of military developments since the war. Lee was interested hardly at all in "global" strategy, and what few suggestions he did make to his government about operations in other theaters than his own indicate that he had little aptitude for grand planning. As a theater strategist, Lee often demonstrated more brilliance and apparent originality than Grant, but his most audacious plans were as much the product of the Confederacy's inferior

military position as his own fine mind. In war, the weaker side has to improvise brilliantly. It must strike quickly, daringly, and include a dangerous element of risk in its plans. Had Lee been a Northern general with Northern resources behind him, he would have improvised less and seemed less bold. Had Grant been a Southern general, he would have fought as Lee did.

6 Fundamentally Grant was superior to Lee because in a modern total war he had a modern mind, and Lee did not. Lee looked to the past in war as the Confederacy did in spirit. The staffs of the two men illustrate their outlook. It would not be accurate to say that Lee's general staff were glorified clerks, but the statement would not be too wide of the mark. Certainly his staff was not, in the modern sense, a planning staff, which was why Lee was often a tired general. He performed labors that no general can do in a big modern army—work that should have fallen to his staff, but that Lee did because it was traditional for the commanding general to do it in older armies. Most of Lee's staff officers were lieutenant colonels. Some of the men on Gran't general staff, as well as the staffs of other Northern generals, were major and brigadier generals, officers who were capable of leading corps. Grant's staff was an organization of experts in the various phases of strategic planning. The modernity of Grant's mind was most apparent in his grasp of the concept that war was becoming total and that the destruction of the enemy's economic resources was as effective and legitimate a form of warfare as the destruction of his armies. What was realism to Grant was barbarism to Lee. Lee thought of war in the old way as a conflict between armies and refused to view it for what it had become—a struggle between societies. To him, economic war was needless cruelty to civilians. Lee was the last of the great old-fashioned generals, Grant the first of the great moderns.

B

Develop by means of examples one or more of the following themes in a composition of 500 words. Use the means of exemplification (A-D) that is most appropriate in each case.

1. "Patriotism means putting country before self."—ADLAI STEVENSON
2. "Patriotism is the last refuge of scoundrels."—DR. JOHNSON
3. Laws are never good substitutes for good habits.
4. World War II witnessed the rise of several great military leaders.
5. Poets and peasants have something in common; poets and pedants are utterly unlike.
6. Western movies have four main characters: a hero with a heart of gold, a heroine as white as snow, a villain as dark as hell, and a good-natured comic.
7. You can count great major-league catchers on the fingers of one hand.

8. The chief molders of public opinion are orators, writers, and teachers.

9. One observes on all sides a great demand for practical education.

10. Several large towns became great cities as a result of World War II.

C

The following passages contain one or more violations of the four principles of exemplification developed in this section. Pick out the fault (or faults). Rewrite the passage correctly.

1. Romance. Soft murmurous voices whisper of exotic experiences. I am carried away from humdrum realities.

2. You ask for an example of an egghead. One of these intellectual fellows visited here last summer. He rented a place up the hill and spent all his time discussing. He never took advantage of the facilities for enjoyment. He kept on discussing things with anyone who passed by. (This example clearly violates principle B. The example fails to state who, when, where, how. The example might read: "You ask for an example of the egghead. A professor named Smith visited Northfield last summer. He rented the Miller cottage on Butternut Hill Road and spent his time talking national politics and world affairs with his weekend guests or Jenkins, the mail carrier, or Rev. Parsons, or Jethro Slemp, the manager of the supermarket. He never fished the lake or climbed Bear Hill or pitched horseshoes down at the firehouse. Once he held up Betsy Adams, our schoolteacher, an hour talking by his gate.")

3. One example of the naturalistic writer is John Steinbeck. Another is James T. Farrell. Theodore Dreiser is a third example of the naturalistic writer.

4. Socialistic practices, such as group medicine, are gradually working their way into American life.

5. In 1898 the United States declared war on Spain. In 1910 United States troops invaded Mexico. In 1917 the United States attacked Germany. Within thirty years the United States was involved in World War II. All these facts point to one conclusion: the United States has consistently promoted war.

6. The Dean spoke at the assembly. He talked about student life in general. He mentioned the various buildings on the campus and explained their use. He gave the names of some assistant deans who are assigned to help students, told us where we could find them if we needed their help, and urged us to try hard.

7. My roommate's composition was very good. He criticized illiberal attitudes and set forth a liberal point of view on his subject.

8. A romantic is one who sees the world through rose-colored glasses. He paints things as he would like to see them, not as they are. He selects

pleasing incidents and suppresses those that are unpleasant. There are many writers of this kind today.

9. On the other hand, look at my opponent's record. He never served in the armed forces. He does not belong to the American Legion. Instead, he is a known member of the League to Support the Fulbright Scholarships Abroad. I say he has never been interested in your problems and mine.

10. It was only through science that America became great. This is proved by the many inventions of the nineteenth and twentieth century. It is only through education that science has increased. This we see in the many colleges and universities where science is taught. It is only through progressive legislation that education is fostered. We have only to look back to the days before we had such legislation to see how true this is. Science, education, progressive legislation—these are the three necessities of modern life.

A. Establish the precise point of likeness or difference on which the comparison or contrast is based.

SECTION V

B. In attacking a false comparison prove that there is an essential difference between the two terms of the comparison.

C. Supply whatever historical background is necessary to make a comparison or a contrast understandable.

D. Use comparison and contrast in combination with other methods of analysis for interest and emphasis.

General Exercises

Comparison and Contrast

IN COMPARISON we analyze a subject by discovering the *likeness* between two or more things in the same class; in contrast we analyze a subject by discovering the *differences* between two or more things in the same class. The word *class* reminds us that comparison and contrast stem directly from the methods of logical analysis studied previously in Sections II, III, and IV.

Thus in definition we examined a subject in relation to its class and to its difference from other members of the class. In classification we were concerned with the class as a whole. In division and example we were concerned with the members of the class. Now, in comparison and contrast we shall consider the relation between two or more members in the same class. The following dialogue will illustrate this connection.

"Who was Plato?" someone says, asking for a *definition.*

"He was a Greek philosopher of the fourth century, B.C."

"Was he any good?" This is a request for *classification.*

"Probably the very best. He started the world thinking. He asked all the important questions and he even answered one or two."

"What did he do?" The questioner wants an *example.*

"Well, he wrote the *Dialogues, The Republic,* and other books. He taught Aristotle. He developed the doctrine of universal ideas. . . ." (By citing several *examples* the speaker has given a brief *division* of Plato's life work.)

"Well, then, how does he *compare* with modern philosophers?"

"Well, there are *some* points in common, but many more differences between them. The *contrasts* outnumber the *comparisons.*"

Thus it is not long before we reach comparison and contrast. Indeed, most of us started our search for knowledge by making comparisons—between the Yankees and the Giants, between Ann and Mary, between this teacher and that. And we'll never cease comparing the value of good books, the prices of clothing, the relative merits of our neighbors.

The comparative process, then, helps us to know a subject by analyzing the likeness or difference between one object and other objects in the same class. Thus the basic elements in a comparison are:

    a. The terms of the comparison, or the various objects compared
    b. The points of likeness or difference between the objects compared

The first two of the four principles of comparison and contrast that we shall discuss in this section are derived from the foregoing analysis of the logic of this method. The first principle applies to logical exactness; the second applies to false comparisons.

A. THE FIRST PRINCIPLE OF COMPARISON AND CONTRAST

The first principle of comparison and contrast applies to logical exactness, and may be stated thus: *Establish the precise point (or points) of likeness or difference on which the comparison or contrast is based.*

Obviously two members of the same class—two students, John Smith and James Black; two poets, Tennyson and Browning; two scientists, Darwin and Huxley—have much in common and may be compared in many respects. One helps to explain the other, particularly when one term of the comparison is less familiar than the other. But in the analysis of a particular subject only one or a very few of the points of likeness (or difference) may be relevant. If the reader is not to be confused by the many likenesses between the terms of the comparison, he must know precisely on what point or points the comparison is being made. Hence the basic principle of all comparison and contrast is to establish clearly the point of the comparison and contrast. This principle is demonstrated in Examples A1, A2, and A3, and in General Exercise B.

B. THE SECOND PRINCIPLE OF COMPARISON AND CONTRAST

The second principle of comparison and contrast applies to false comparisons, and may be stated thus: *In attacking a false comparison prove that there is an essential difference between the two terms of the comparison.* A false comparison asserts a likeness where no likeness exists, or where the likeness is only partial. An old adage, "All comparisons limp," sums up the tendency towards false comparison. We must be on guard against this tendency, especially in argument. This principle we shall examine in Examples B1 and B2 and in the General Exercises C and D.

Thus far we have been concerned with the strict or logical use of comparison and contrast, in the positive sense in the first principle and in the negative sense in the second principle. However, there are important rhetorical uses of comparison and contrast that the historian and the poet constantly bring before us.

C. THE THIRD PRINCIPLE OF COMPARISON AND CONTRAST

The historian reminds us that the terms of the comparison are often historical realities that must be fully developed. Thus in an essay with the theme, "Hitler is a twentieth-century Attila," some historical explanation of Attila is necessary for the average reader. So too a comparison between America's past and Europe's past, or between two figures like Hamilton and Jefferson, requires the support of considerable factual analysis.

Hence we realize that in historical writing an effective comparison or contrast must be not only logically exact but also adequate in its development. Thus the third principle of comparison and contrast is: *Supply whatever historical background is necessary to make a comparison or a contrast understandable.* We shall explore this principle in connection with Learned Hand's study of Jefferson and Hamilton (C1), Aldous Huxley's extended comparison and contrast of Europe and America (C2), and in General Exercise B.

D. THE FOURTH PRINCIPLE OF COMPARISON AND CONTRAST

The poet reminds us that comparison and contrast may be used as imaginative devices to create and maintain interest. Because it is usually a comparison between two things in different classes (things which have some point of likeness or difference but cannot be strictly compared), the poet's metaphor is rarely if ever a strict comparison. Hence, when the poet hunts out the hidden resemblance between a dove and white hands, a scorpion's sting and a diseased conscience, a solitary star and man's loneliness, he is not attempting to draw an exact parallel but a resemblance which rhetoricians call a *similitude*.

But even though the poetic metaphor is only a resemblance, it helps the reader to catch at certain suggestive meanings. The similitude appeals to the imagination and often, as in Examples D1 and D2, to the emotions.

Hence our fourth principle of comparison and contrast applies to the use of this method as an imaginative device, and may be stated thus: *Use comparison and contrast in combination with other methods of analysis for interest and emphasis.*

Note: Two additional selections appear in the General Exercises of this section. These exercises review some of the principles of Sections II-IV, as well as the principles of this section. Note also: An extended argument from comparison is called analogy. See Section XI.

a. Establish the precise point of likeness or difference on which the comparison or contrast is based.

1. You Can't Hurry in Brazil

BY PETER FLEMING

Delay in Brazil is a climate. You live in it. You can't get away from it. There is nothing to be done about it. It should, I think, be a source of pride to the Brazilians that they possess a national characteristic which it is absolutely impossible to ignore. No other people can make this boast. The English are a race of shopkeepers; but it is possible to

YOU CAN'T HURRY IN BRAZIL: reprinted from *Brazilian Adventure* by Peter Fleming; copyright 1933 by Charles Scribner's Sons; used by permission of the publishers.

live in England without being seriously inconvenienced by the process of barter which rages round you. A tendency on the part of the traveller to melancholy or extravagance need not be curbed among the gay and thrifty French. Self-revelation may be practised among the inscrutable Chinese, and generosity among the Scots. You don't have to be a bigamist to go to Turkey, and a coward can find contentment in plucky little Belgium. But a man in a hurry will be miserable in Brazil.

Comment

Here Mr. Fleming clarifies what he means by delay in Brazil. He describes it as a climate, as inevitable, as impossible to ignore. His repetitions suggest that you can't imagine what it is, really, unless you have been there. He assumes that his readers (Mr. Fleming wrote primarily for English readers) haven't been to Brazil but that they know something about the national characteristics of neighboring countries and of several other lands. Hence he explains the inevitability of delay in Brazil by contrasting it with the national characteristics of other countries that would be better known to Englishmen. The exact point of the contrast between the unfamiliar idea, the Brazilian characteristic of delay, and the familiar ideas, the national traits of England, France, and the other nations is this: the foreigner may ignore all the various national traits except that of Brazil. Only incidentally does Fleming contrast the various national characteristics of merchant-mindedness, gaiety, thrift, and so on, with the Brazilian characteristic of delay.

Analysis and Composition

1. List several legitimate points of *likeness* between each of the following terms.

    Sample: *Terms:* United States and Canada
    Points of likeness: Democratic government, membership in United Nations, colonial origin

    a. Brazil and Argentina
    b. Maine and California
    c. Baseball and track
    d. Grant and Lee
    e. Spanish and English as international languages
    f. A singer and a violin
    g. Physical effort and moral effort

h. Human life and the sea
i. Cats and kings
j. A novel and a play

2. State one or more legitimate points of *difference* between each of the terms listed in Exercise 1.
3. Name two specific terms which may be compared with reference to each of the following ideas (points of comparison).

Sample: *Point of comparison:* Speed
        Terms of comparison: Sound and light
Second sample: *Point of comparison:* Educational eminence
        Terms of comparison: Yale and Harvard

a. Quality of lightness
b. Business efficiency
c. Intelligence
d. Imaginative power
e. Isolationism
f. Good construction
g. The wise use of power
h. Heartlessness
i. Justice

4. Complete the following sentences by supplying the missing terms of the comparison.
   a. In exhilarating climate Switzerland excels _____.
   b. A paragraph is a fuller expression of an idea than a _____ or a _____.
   c. If we admire the Washington monument how much more ought we to admire _____ and _____.
   d. As a sample of pure Gothic architecture Notre Dame of Paris is inferior to _____ and _____.
   e. Shakespeare's *Othello* is superior to his _____ in plot construction.
5. In a paragraph of 300 words develop one or more of the comparisons discovered in your answers to Exercise 1.
6. In a paragraph of 300 words develop one or more of the contrasts discovered in your answers to Exercise 2.

2. The Jungle and the Sea

BY MARSTON BATES

There are, as a matter of fact, many *analogies between* tropical forests and tropical seas. *In both,* the naturalist is always conscious of the

THE JUNGLE AND THE SEA: reprinted from *Where Winter Never Comes* by Marston Bates; copyright 1952 by Marston Bates; used by permission of the publishers, Charles Scribner's Sons.

third dimension, height or depth. We walk at the bottom of the forest and float on the top of the sea, and to explore this third dimension we have to use a deal of ingenuity in climbing or diving. But *in both,* the conditions of life gradually change from the bottom to the top in ways that are *curiously parallel,* resulting in a zoning by depth.

The zoning depends on the *same basic factor in both cases*—light. The light that strikes the surface of the sea diminishes rapidly with depth, so that the ocean floor is a region of perpetual darkness. *Similarly,* the light is cut by the dense foliage of the tropical forest. The forest floor region is not eternally dark, but the light is dim enough to exercise a selective influence on the kind of plants that can grow there.

The basic industry of photosynthesis is thus largely restricted to the canopy zone of the forest or to the surface region of the sea, and the organisms that live below depend in the long run on materials that drop down from above. The surface of the sea is inhabited by incredible millions of microscopic animals and plants, and there is a sort of constant rain of corpses of these organisms into the depths below, to serve as food supply for the bottom dwellers. *Similarly,* the inhabitants of the floor zone of the forest depend on the constant supply of dead leaves, of fallen fruits, flowers, branches and trunks, or on materials found in the soil.

The zoning of life in the sea is possible because of the density of water, which enables organisms to keep at whatever depth they prefer. Most organisms have just about the same density as sea water, so that swimming and floating are easy. Floating in the air, though, is *a different thing,* achieved only by very tiny organisms or by special arrangements like those of certain spiders that drift with long strands of silk. Flying, *in contrast with swimming,* is much *harder* work, so that no animal is able to live its whole life flying the way marine animals may live, always swimming or drifting with the current. The zoning in the forest depends on the trees, which form its basic structure, and getting to the top is a matter of climbing.

Comment

Mr. Bates here compares and contrasts two aspects of tropical nature. The points of the comparison between the tropical forest and the tropical sea are (*a*) height or depth and (*b*) their common dependence on light. The one point of contrast is the different density of water and air. Hence fewer forest animals than marine animals can reach the zone of light. Mr. Bates's pattern of comparison and contrast is artfully threaded together by connective words and expressions. Note that the italicized words in the passage help to connect the two terms compared and contrasted.

Analysis and Composition

1. A correct understanding of this passage requires a clear definition of several scientific terms. Consult an unabridged dictionary for the meaning of the following expressions:

   photosynthesis *light to manufacture food for plants*   microscopic animals

   organisms   density *weight @ unit volume*

2. This passage is notable for its orderly development of topic sentences. Pick out the topic sentence of each paragraph and show how each of the other sentences in the paragraph is an extension of the thought expressed in the topic sentence.*

3. List several points of likeness and unlikeness between six of the following pairs of subjects:
   a. A lecture and a discussion
   b. A paleface and a redskin
   c. A poet and a pedant
   d. Liberal education and technical education
   e. Amateur baseball and professional baseball
   f. Your father and your mother
   g. Dwight Eisenhower and Harry Truman
   h. A jet plane and a gasoline-engine plane
   i. Book learning and practical learning
   j. Two of your friends

4. Write a short composition of about 500 words on one or more of the above topics.

3. Joan and David

BY THOMAS DE QUINCEY

What is to be thought of *her?* What is to be thought of the poor shepherd girl from the hills and forests of Lorraine, that—like David,

---

* See handbooks: Foerster, pp. 43-44, *37d*; Hodges, *31a*; Kierzek, pp. 69-70, *68*; Perrin, pp. 185-87; Wykoff, *53*.

the Hebrew shepherd boy from the hills and forests of Judea—rose suddenly out of the quiet, out of the safety, out of the religious inspiration, rooted in deep pastoral solitudes, to a station in the van of armies, and to the more perilous station at the right hand of kings? The Hebrew boy inaugurated his patriotic mission by an *act,* by a victorious *act,* such as no man could deny. But so did the girl of Lorraine, if we read her story as it was read by those who saw her nearest. Adverse armies bore witness to the boy as no pretender; but so they did to the gentle girl. Judged by the voices of all who saw them *from a station of good will,* both were found true and loyal to any promises involved in their first acts.

Enemies it was that made the difference between their subsequent fortunes. The boy rose to a splendor and a noonday prosperity, both personal and public, that rang through the records of his people and became a byword among his posterity for a thousand years, until the sceptre was departing from Judah. The poor, forsaken girl, on the contrary, drank not herself from the cup of rest which she had secured for France. She never sang together with the songs that rose in her native Domrémy as echoes to the departing steps of invaders. She mingled not in the festal dances at Vaucouleurs which celebrated in rapture the redemption of France. No! for her voice was then silent; her feet were dust. Pure, innocent, noble-hearted girl! This was amongst the strongest pledges for *thy* truth, that never once—no, not for a moment of weakness—didst thou revel in the vision of coronets and honor from man.

Comment

De Quincey first establishes precisely the points of likeness between Joan of Arc and King David. They were both pious shepherds who suddenly rose from solitude to lead armies and free their respective nations. But there are points of contrast between them. David survived to become an honored king and prophet; Joan reaped no earthly reward. By comparing St. Joan with King David, De Quincey shows that his subject deserves our highest admiration. By contrasting their fortunes, he elicits our pity for Joan. This emotional passage is the introduction to a celebrated essay in defense of Joan of Arc against attacks by Michelet, a nineteenth-century French historian.

Analysis and Composition

1. How does the parallel structure * in this passage aid in establishing coherence?
2. De Quincey calls Joan a "poor shepherd girl," a "gentle girl," a "poor, forsaken girl," a "pure, innocent, noble-hearted girl." What other words or expressions arouse compassion or admiration for Joan?
3. De Quincey is especially noted for the splendid rhythm and euphony of his sentences.† Note particularly sentence 2 in paragraph 2. The rhythm here may be indicated in part by this arrangement:

>   /   /   /   /
> The boy rose to a splendor and a noonday prosperity,
>
>   /   /
> both personal and public,
>
>   /   /   /
> that rang through the records of his people
>
>   /   /   /
> and became a byword among his posterity
>
>   /   /
> for a thousand years,
>
>   /   /   /
> until the sceptre was departing from Judah.

Note too the euphonious alliterations of *p*, *r*, and *s* sounds: *ro*se, *spl*endor, *pros*pe*r*ity, *p*e*rs*onal, *sc*e*pt*re, *p*o*st*erity.

In a similar manner indicate the rhythm and euphony in three other sentences of this passage.

3. Attempt to arouse sympathy for one of the following historical characters by developing an appropriate comparison and contrast:

a. Mary Queen of Scots	f. Thomas More
b. Barbara Fritchie	g. The garrison at Corregidor
c. Abraham Lincoln	h. Robert E. Lee
d. Nathan Hale	i. U. S. Grant
e. Woodrow Wilson	j. The Marines at Iwo Jima

* See handbooks: Foerster, pp. 17-23; *86*; Hodges, *26*; Kierzek, pp. 59-62, *56*; Perrin, pp. 282-83; Wykoff, *74*.

† See handbooks: Foerster, *63*; Hodges, *30f*; Kierzek, pp. 62-66; Perrin, pp. 295-96; Wykoff, *98*.

b.
In attacking a false comparison prove that there is an essential difference between the two terms of the comparison.

1. American Policy and North Africa

·BY THE EDITORS OF *Time*

The French say one stumbling block [to the settlement of nationalistic uprisings in their North African colonies] is encouragement given to Arab ambitions by anticolonial sentiment in the United States. What makes the colonial problem in North Africa different is the presence of nearly 2,000,000 French settlers, many of them born in North Africa, which they regard as their home. Americans on the scene frequently accuse the settlers of being more narrow, repressive and intransigent than the French government. Marshal Alphonse Juin, commander of the NATO ground forces in Europe, was born at Bone in Algeria. Last week Juin (onetime Resident-General of Morocco, 1947-51) strongly attacked the U.S.'s wavering attitude. "There was nothing to get excited about so long as our opponents were only the Arab bloc, bound together by Moslem solidarity, and the U.S.S.R. with her satellites . . . but today we are seriously threatened with the possibility of seeing the U.S. join this group. . . . This fact is very grave for it wounds us sentimentally and strikes at our idea of what should be the international solidarity to which we have already made such heavy contributions."

When an American tells a Frenchman that the U.S. once fought a war to throw off a colonial power, the Frenchman is apt to reply that the Americans have oversimplified their own history. The Indians were the true local population of America and they were pretty well exterminated by the colonists, say the French. In other words, colonialism in U.S. history involves three elements, not two: the natives (the Indians), the European colonists (George Washington), and the parent government (George III). When the Americans instinctively and sentimentally rush to the side of the Arabs in North Africa, they are mindful of the American Revolution, and think they are siding with George Washington. They actually should be thinking, say the French, of their own Indian wars, and should realize that they are siding with Sitting Bull, while committed by a military alliance to General Custer. The American dilemma: What happens if the Sioux go seriously on the warpath and Custer decides to make a last stand? America's great military bases in North Africa are in Indian territory.

Comment

In this passage from *Time*, the American view of French colonial policy in North Africa is stated as a comparison: The Americans compare their position in relation to Great Britain at the time of the Revolution with that of the Arab nationalists in the French colonies who wish to throw off French rule. The French attempt to refute this comparison by pointing out that there were three elements in the American colonial situation and that the Americans are considering only two of these elements in their comparison. The point of the French argument then is: The American situation in colonial times is essentially different from the present French colonial situation in North Africa.

Analysis

1. State in your own words the United States' point of view in reference to the French North African colonies.
2. What is the point of likeness between the North African Arabs and the colonial Americans? What is the point of difference?
3. Decide whether the French argument that the American comparison is false is an effective answer to the American point of view. Give reasons for your opinion.
4. Is the comparison of the Arabs with the Sioux Indians an exact comparison? Give reasons for your answer.

2. On Reforming the Supreme Court

BY THOMAS WOODLOCK

Not a few people seem to be confused in their thinking concerning the controversy over the Supreme Court by the appeal to the analogy of Great Britain. Parliament in Britain has unlimited power to legislate without interference from the courts. Why should not Congress do the same? It may be helpful to repeat the fundamental distinction between Great Britain's system and our own. Simple as it is, many do not seem to appreciate its force.

It rests upon one fact, namely, that we have a written organic law from which Congress derives its powers, while Britain has none. Our Constitution not merely confers certain powers on Congress, but also lays upon it certain restrictions. It says in terms that it may do certain things and may not do certain other things. It may do only the things the Constitution permits. It may not do certain other things, because it has not been granted the power to do them, although it is not in terms prohibited from doing them; it must not do certain things, because they are specifically prohibited. It is the creature and the subject of the organic law of the nation—the federal Constitution.

The British Parliament, by a long evolution expressed in a series of statutes over several centuries, is the supreme legislative authority in the land. These statutes, up to and including the law which emasculated the House of Lords, are the British equivalent of our organic law, and behind them the House of Commons is absolute in its powers. What, then, is the "British Constitution" of which so much is heard from time to time?

The easiest way to describe it is to say that it consists of anything that the British voters may happen to approve at a general election, fought upon a controverted question of public policy. The House of Commons could tomorrow pass a bill abolishing the British monarchy. The House of Lords could reject the bill. The premier could force the king to dissolve Parliament and an election would follow. If the voters returned a majority supporting the premier, the Commons could repass the bill, the House of Lords would be compelled to approve it and the

ON REFORMING THE SUPREME COURT: from *Thinking It Over* by Thomas Woodlock. The Declan X. McMullen Company, Inc., New York, N. Y.

king would have to give the royal assent of his own deposition. That, in substance, is the British Constitution and that is the way it works.

The British courts deal with the statutes of the land in precisely the same way as our Supreme Court deals with the Constitution. Their task is to interpret and define these laws as our Supreme Court's task is to interpret and define the Constitution. The House of Lords, through its law lords, is the highest court in the land. In both cases the judicial function is the same, for it is the fundamental function of the judiciary according to its very nature. Because of that nature, the judiciary must be free from all interference or control. This is an axiom in Great Britain, and it should be an axiom in this country, for the fundamental liberties of the citizen are absolutely dependent upon its observance. The slightest tampering with the freedom of the courts in the performance of their natural function, either by the legislative or executive power, would be instantly rejected in Great Britain, as it ought to be here.

As a consequence of the British system, any Parliamentary election may be equivalent to a national convention amending the Constitution. In the last thirty years more than one election has so functioned. It is necessary to note that the last great constitutional change, the act stripping the House of Lords of practically all its *legislative* powers, was passed under a threat that, if the peers did not consent to their own sterilization, the King would "pack" the upper House with enough peers to swamp the recalcitrants. There is no analogy here with proposals to "pack" the Court. The question was one wholly in the *legislative* order, and did not in any way touch the *judicial* function. The operation was wholly within the powers of the people. Nor did it touch the judicial power of the Lords. Moreover, the act was merely the final stage of a long evolution—at least a century—in which the upper House had become gradually more yielding to the popular will as expressed by the Commons. Had it not been exceptionally obstinate in opposition to Mr. Asquith's liberal measures, the act might not have been proposed.

Comment

Mr. Woodlock here attacks the false comparison implied in popular thinking about the famous Supreme Court controversy of some years ago. This thinking ran as follows: If the British Parliament can legislate without interference from the courts, the United States Congress, which is the American equivalent of the Parliament, should be able to do the same. Mr. Woodlock argues against this comparison by saying, in effect: The United States has a written Constitution that in a sense defines Congress, while Britain has no written constitution at all but only a series of statutes and precedents. Therefore, the two terms (the United States Congress and the British Parliament) are not really comparable. In accordance with the United States Constitution, the laws made by the United States Congress are subject to review by the federal courts; in the United States a law may be declared to be in conflict with the Constitution—it is "unconstitutional"; but in Britain any such ruling is clearly impossible, since no separate, written constitution exists.

Analysis and Composition

1. Define the following words and expressions used in the Example above:

controversy	restrictions	judiciary
analogy	emasculated	axiom
organic law	deposition	recalcitrants

2. In several paragraphs refute one of the following comparisons by showing important ways in which the two terms of the comparison differ. The important points in the comparison are italicized.

   a. If we could do without an income tax *during the first 140 years of our history,* we can do so *in the next 140 years.*

   b. A strict code of discipline works *in the Army;* hence it should be enforced *in student life.*

   c. *The United States Congress* is like *a town meeting* on a national scale.

   d. *An American election* may be compared to *a popularity contest.*

   e. The *struggle for success in life* is like a *football game.*

   f. *Public-opinion polls* are truer indexes of democratic feeling than the *opinions expressed in Congress.*

   g. Since America grew into a great nation *by avoiding foreign entanglements in the past,* it can remain a great nation *by avoiding foreign entanglements in the future.*

C. Supply whatever historical background is necessary to make a comparison or a contrast understandable.

1. Jefferson and Hamilton

BY LEARNED HAND

1 The political notions of the time were divided into two contrasting groups which it has been the custom to associate with the great names of Jefferson and Hamilton. It is easy to associate Jefferson's ideas with those of Rousseau, from whom on the outside they seem to have been drawn. This, as I understand it, is wrong, but he had drunk deeply at the springs of Physiocracy,* and in any event he believed in the basic virtue of mankind, once set free from artificial restraints. He found his ideal in a community of independent families, each intrenched in its farm, self-subsistent, independent, needing no regulation, and tolerant of little interference, especially from government. Those who invoke his name today must be shocked at his scorn of the mob of mechanics and artisans, whose turbulence and separation from some particular plot of earth unfitted them in his eyes for sharing in the Good Life. A nation in which information, or what passes as such, can be instantaneously sent from one end to the other, in which the craving for conformity demands uniformity in belief, which for that reason wears the same clothes, reads the same print and follows

---

* A school of political economy which regarded land as the basis of wealth and taxation.

JEFFERSON AND HAMILTON: reprinted from *The Spirit of Liberty* by Learned Hand, by permission of Alfred A. Knopf, Inc. Copyright 1952 by Alfred A. Knopf, Inc.

the same fashions, amusements and conventions, would have seemed to him scurvy and sordid. He would have found little in the America of today to justify that Utopia of which he had dreamed.

2 The extraordinary richness of his own nature, his omnivorant interest in all the activities of man, no doubt colored his picture of a life on the land; yet it also enabled him to transmute into a rosy ideal the dumb aspirations of his people, and so they looked to him for their leadership for a quarter of a century after his accession to power, and if we count Jackson as his dubious disciple, for that much longer. Clearly there was something in his outlook which responded to the needs of those among whom he lived.

3 Hamilton was a horse of another color, always an exotic, succeeding in his statecraft only because of the disorders which immediately followed the Revolution; whose genius needed the cloak of Washington beneath which his real work was hid for near a century. He was no Utopian; he did not believe in the perfectibility of human nature. Government was a combination of those interests in the community which collectively would be irresistible; a combination resting upon self-interest. When he secured the passage of the Constitution, it was by means of such a combination: the landed class, the manufacturers, and the public creditors. In the doubtful contest for ratification, as Beard has shown, it was these votes which eventually won, and it was under the aegis of Washington that he managed to carry on for those critical eight years. With the constant movement of the frontier westward, the underlying, but less articulate, aspirations of a rural people finally asserted themselves.

4 The animosity between the two men was well founded and inevitable. They represented, and we are right still to take them as our most shining examples of, two theories of human society: that which demands external control, and that which insists upon the opportunity for personal expression. Jefferson's victory seemed to him to be the sanction of all that the Revolution had implied; the liberation of a free people from the domination of greed and corruption, opening vistas of human felicity not theretofore known on earth. For its fuller expression he was willing, forced by a sad necessity, to sacrifice his constitutional scruples and forever compromise his party by the acquisition of Louisiana. To Hamilton, Jefferson's accession was the beginning of the end, the last step in a plunge towards anarchy. The squalid

political quarrel for the domination of the rump of Federalism which ended in his death, had for him a deeper significance than the leadership in a party then apparently writhing to dissolution. The Eighteenth Brumaire was five years past, and though the Coronation [of Napoleon] at Notre Dame was still some months away, recent events already foreshadowed it. In the final breakdown of that Jacobinism which he and his associates thought certain and early, the need would arise for some transatlantic Bonaparte to gather the shreds of society, and build a state upon surer foundations than that weak instrument in which at heart he had never really believed. To prevent Federalism, the sacred chalice, from passing into the obscene hands of a turncoat and a traitor [Burr]'was worth the chance that cost him his life.

5 Each man would have said that he was the champion of liberty, and each would have been right. To one the essential condition of any tolerable life was the free expression of the individual, the power to lead his life on his own terms, to enjoy the fruits of his industry, to garner the harvest of his hands and brain, without subtraction by a horde of office-holders, locusts who laid waste the land and spread the venal doctrine of their right to eat what others had sown, the blight, the virus, of a society of honest men, enjoying the earth which God, at least in this blessed country, had patently spread out for their satisfaction. The other saw in all this no more than the maunderings of a toxic dream. What was the assurance of man's capacity to deal with his own fate? Was it not clear that virtue and intelligence among the sons of Adam was as rare as physical prowess, indeed much rarer? Liberty could not rest upon anarchy; it was conditioned upon an ordered society, in which power should rest where power should be, with the wise and the good, who could be at least presumptively ascertained as those who in the battle of life had already given some signs of capacity. It was an empty phantom to assume some automatic regulation by which without plan and direction public affairs manage themselves. The concerns of a great people are not all individual; they have collective interests without which their life can scarcely rise above that of savages, each shifting for himself, without comfort, security, or the leisure which alone makes existence endurable. Jacobins might bawl of liberty, but really they meant no more than the tyranny of their own domination over the mob.

Comment

Judge Hand contrasts Hamilton and Jefferson in their fundamental theories of human society. Both men are seen to be true champions of liberty, each according to his own lights. The gist of this contrast is stated in paragraph 5. But, wisely, the historical background is fully developed in the four preceding paragraphs, where the author deals first with Jefferson (¶1-2) and then with Hamilton (¶3) before treating both of them together (¶4-5). Thus we are prepared to understand the full sense of the contrast. Note too that the earlier paragraphs not only supply facts about Jefferson and Hamilton, but they also allude to certain general historical influences on the two men, such as physiocracy and the French Revolution.

Analysis and Composition

1. In an unabridged dictionary find definitions of the following terms:

   mechanics   omnivorant   Brumaire
   artisans   transmute   Jacobinism
   turbulence   perfectibility   maunderings
   Utopia   rump   toxic

2. State in your own words the basic ideas in paragraphs 1 and 2.
3. Show how Judge Hand uses definition in paragraphs 1 and 3.
4. How does the author support the topic sentence of paragraph 4, which is, "The animosity between the two men was well founded and inevitable"?
5. In paragraph 4 there is a comparison between American politics and French Revolutionary politics. What is the point or basis of this comparison? Is the comparison exact? Give reasons for your answer.
6. In paragraph 5 Judge Hand states the contrast between the Jeffersonian and Hamiltonian concepts of liberty. Show how this statement has been drawn from the historical exposition in the previous paragraphs.
7. In a composition of 400 words develop some aspect of one of the following topics by comparison and contrast. Be sure to supply whatever historical background is needed to make your subject clear to the average reader of a daily newspaper.
   a. Theodore Roosevelt and Franklin D. Roosevelt
   b. Small-town life fifty years ago and today
   c. Transportation in colonial days and today
   d. Lee and Grant
   e. Al Smith and Herbert Hoover
   f. Queen Elizabeth and Mary Queen of Scots
   g. The *Monitor* and the *Merrimac*

2. America and Europe
Yesterday's Influence on Today

BY ALDOUS HUXLEY

1 A study of the effect of the Past on the Present. Strange things (it may seem a paradox, but it is nevertheless the truth) are easier to understand than those we know too well. The nearer, the more everyday and familiar an event is, the greater the difficulty we find in comprehending it or even realizing that it *is* an event—that it actually takes place. Habit causes us to react automatically to the things which surround us. Confronted by the unknown, we are forced to think; hence our passionate dislike of unfamiliar things; but in the face of the known, we are hardly better than machines. When we live habitually, we function with the greatest practical efficiency, the least possible waste of energy; but we are scarcely more aware of the world in which we are living and acting than the automobile is aware of the landscape through which it is being driven. For the conscious, thinking part of us, habit abolishes the environment by making it too familiar. We must make a great mental effort if we would analyze and comprehend the things we take for granted. The people who do not take for granted, who are not content merely to live in the familiar world, but want to understand it too, are called philosophers and men of science. They are not numerous. Most of us are content to live in our immediate surroundings as fishes live in water, taking it for granted that our particular mode of existence is the only possible mode, and so completely familiar with the element which we inhabit, that we are not conscious of its nature and hardly, even, of its bare existence.

2 To travel is to change one's element. Passing from a liquid into a windy world, the most unscientifically minded of fish is suddenly enabled to criticize and comprehend the water which, as an inhabitant, it had ignored. And the traveler discovers in foreign countries many obvious facts about his own—facts which he had overlooked while at home, because they were too close to him. Thus, it was while journeying in India that I came to understand the inward nature of our European civilization. Talking with Orientals whose mentality was prescientific, I realized, as never before, the significance of that scientific

AMERICA AND EUROPE: reprinted by permission of Mr. Huxley.

outlook which has become the world-view of the contemporary West. And it was in America—in the country which, for all practical purposes, has no history—that I discovered the importance to us Europeans of our past and the extent to which (though we may be quite unaware of it) it influences our thoughts and actions in the present.

3 In externals, life on one side of the Atlantic looks very much like life on the other. Western Europe is as completely and intensively industrialized as America. Huge populations of propertyless wage earners inhabit the cities of each continent. In both, business is the principal occupation of the better educated classes, and the great industrialists and financiers wield almost, if not quite, as much political power in England, France and Germany as they do in the United States. True, there is one important difference. America, being a very large and opulent continent inhabited by a relatively very small population, is much richer than Europe; there is still, in America, more than enough to go round. Europe, on the other hand, is overcrowded, as America will begin to be some hundred years hence when the present population has doubled or trebled itself. Prosperity creates self-satisfaction and optimism; and contemporary America is as full of these spiritual commodities as was middle-class England in the palmy days of her industrial supremacy, between 1840 and 1900. But though the level of prosperity is lower in Europe than in America, the courses of European wealth, such as it is, are the same as those of American wealth, and the externals of life in the great industrial and commercial centers of both continents are very similar. And yet, in spite of this external similarity, Europe and America remain profoundly foreign to one another. The European's outlook, his standards, his point of view are, in many important respects, quite unlike the American's. So much so, that an Englishman will often find it easier to understand the mentality of an Austrian or a Frenchman than that of an American. The American, it is true, speaks his language; but the Frenchman and the Austrian are Europeans and, inhabiting the same continent, share the Englishman's historical background. Their views about man and things will be closer to his than those of the American, who comes from a country that has not known the Middle Ages. St. Francis of Assisi and the Holy Roman Empire, Scholastic Philosophy, the Guilds, the Feudal System seem remote enough. Nevertheless they continue to exercise their influence on modern Europe. A visit to America makes one realize how great that influence is, how profoundly our contemporary

ideas about many of the most important aspects of social life are modified by the past. I propose in this article to give one or two of the most striking examples of the way in which history has conditioned the European point of view, making it different from the American.

4 Business being the main activity of the educated classes in both continents, one would expect the attitude toward it to be the same in Europe as in America. And yet, for purely historical reasons, it is not. In America it is true to say business is accepted wholeheartedly as an end in itself, to which the highest activities of the best men can be worthily devoted. I have read pronouncements by American clergymen who affirmed, in so many words, that "Business is Religion." And it has become a commonplace of the modern American sermon, newspaper article and advertisement that the businessman is doing service of the highest kind. "Service" is the modern American businessman's favorite word. It was also one of the favorite words of the Founder of Christianity and of his most remarkable medieval disciple, St. Francis of Assisi. But the same word does not always mean the same thing. When we demand the precise signification of the eminently Christian word "service," as used by successful businessmen, we find that it means roughly this: Selling the public what it wants (or what it can be persuaded by means of advertising to imagine it wants) in an efficient way and with the maximum profit compatible with legal standards of honesty. Would Christ or St. Francis have defined it in the same way? One wonders. In any case, that is the definition of "service" current in business circles. The word hallows the thing. The aura of service shines round the American businessman like a halo.

5 In Europe the businessman finds it more difficult to persuade his fellows that his is a noble existence of perpetual service and he himself the highest of human types. For Europe is still haunted, in spite of all the changes of the last seven hundred years by the ghost of the medieval tradition. In the eyes of the medieval church, avarice, or the love of money, was one of the deadly sins. Nor was the church satisfied with deploring abstractly and on principle the activities of those who tried to get rich quick. Religious condemnation was reflected in legal practice by a host of enactments limiting and controlling the activities of financiers, manufacturers, and middlemen. Interest, when it was permitted at all, might not exceed a certain moderate rate;

speculative profits were regarded as illegal; monopolists were prosecuted on earth as well as condemned to eternal torments in another world; the man who made a "corner" in necessary commodities was not only damned, but fined also and imprisoned. The medieval state, which was for all practical purposes a manifestation of the medieval church, thought it a part of its duty to curb men's lust for money, just as it curbed and regulated their sexual instincts and their passions of violence and revenge.

6 By the beginning of the eighteenth century the churches had ceased to regard economics as a province of human activity in which they were entitled to interfere. But their previous protests against avarice remained on record, and the tradition that they had once interfered in economic matters still lingered, even though they interfered no longer. States shortly followed the example of the churches and left their subjects to settle their economic problems among themselves—with what appalling results any student of the early history of industrialism is familiar. The political economists of the new generation did not condemn the lust for money, as their religiously minded predecessors had done, and instead of trying to control and regulate it, demanded that it should be allowed to express itself freely, without interference by religion or law. For the economist, avarice is simply the motive power that works the economic machine, in precisely the same way that water is the motive power that works the mill. The faster the mill wheel turns, the better. If the flow of water is interfered with, the wheel will turn more slowly. Therefore there must be no interference. The modern state accepts this conception with but few modifications, interfering only to prevent the weak from being too brutally exploited by avaricious employers and the consuming public from being too unconscionably swindled by avaricious producers and middlemen. It continues, like its medieval predecessor, to condemn the intemperate manifestations of sexuality and rage, but leaves the avaricious man almost entirely free to satisfy his lust for money and even rewards him, when successful and rich, with honors and political power.

7 This state of things holds good on both sides of the Atlantic. But whereas it would be true to say that, in America, the attitude of the economists and of the state is substantially the attitude of the public at large, in Europe, on the contrary, public opinion is not quite so wholeheartedly convinced of the moral excellence of business and

businessmen. The influence of the Middle Ages still faintly persists in the Old World. It is now exactly seven hundred years since St. Francis of Assisi sang the praises of the Lady Poverty and devoted himself to her service. But something of his spirit survives even today, so that industrialism and business, though triumphant in fact, do not in Europe receive the homage to which their predominance seems to entitle them. They rule the external world, but not men's minds. Poverty, particularly if it is poverty for the sake of some idea, is still rather respectable in Europe and the enriched businessman is not looked up to as the highest type of citizen. Indeed, the aristocratic tradition unites itself with the religious tradition of the Middle Ages and causes him actually to be disparaged and looked down upon, even while he is envied and obeyed. Of the aristocratic tradition I shall have more to say later. Meanwhile, I should like to point out another result of the medieval ethico-religious tradition. Europe is notoriously far more tolerant of the class of ideas labeled "socialistic" than is America, where they are looked upon with horror, as positively criminal. The rich European businessman probably objects to socialism quite as strongly as does his brother on the opposite side of the Atlantic; but public opinion at large is not so violently opposed to it as it is in America. Indeed, the ideas of socialism seem familiar and almost obvious to minds on which the religious teaching of the Middle Ages still exerts a certain influence. Politically, medieval Europe was a collection of despotisms, large and small. But its economic system, based on the assumption that the love of money is a sin which must be repressed and controlled like any other undesirable natural proclivity, bore a close resemblance to modern state socialism. Human beings are only frightened by the things they do not know. Obscurely and almost unconsciously, the European is familiar with the ideas of socialism, because they are to a great extent implicit in the religious beliefs (still predominantly medieval) with which he has been brought up. The American public, cut off from the Middle Ages and unfamiliar with these ideas, finds them stupid, wicked and worthy of violent suppression.

8 Another heritage from the Middle Ages—a heritage which conditions the modern European outlook and makes it different from the American—is the tradition of aristocracy. Hereditary aristocracies have ceased in almost all European countries to possess special privileges and exercise special political powers. In England, it is true, the Second

Chamber still consists of hereditary peers. Certain political theorists object to these legislators, whose only qualification to be law-givers is that they happen to have been born with a title. Theoretically, they may be objectionable: but I cannot see that they do their business any worse than an assembly consisting of an equal number of men chosen at random, as a jury, would do it. And as a democrat, I for one would always prefer the present House of Lords to any specially elected or nominated assembly of financiers, industrialists, retired colonial governors, superannuated experts in various branches of applied science and so forth, whose training and habits of mind would tend to make them far more meddlesome and tyrannous than the sporting country gentlemen who form the majority of the English Second Chamber today. But that is by the way. The English aristocracy still possesses political power, but vastly less than it did; and its special privileges have long since been abolished. It is no longer an oppressive ruling class. The same applies to other parts of Europe. In all countries the hereditary aristocracy is only the ghost of what it was. And yet its influence on contemporary social life and on current ideas is still important. How important, a European only realizes when he has visited a country which has not known the Middle Ages and where the idea of hereditary aristocracy is not only foreign but even traditionally odious.

9 In a country where there is no hereditary aristocracy the leaders of society are the rich. This is not the case in countries where aristocracy survives as a social and political institution or even as a mere tradition. Wealth, it is true, can almost always force its way into an aristocratic clique; but in no circumstances is it equivalent to aristocracy. Wealth as such does not carry, in an aristocratic country, the prestige which belongs to it in a society founded on a different principle. Money, in an aristocratically organized society, can command and control men's actions (as it does in other societies), but not their thoughts; one cannot buy the respect which an ancient name evokes in the minds of those who have been brought up in the aristocratic tradition, nor its romantic glamour. The enriched businessman may buy his way into the exclusive world of hereditary aristocracy; but he will be secretly, or even openly, looked down upon by those whose company he frequents. Commerce was regarded as degrading in the Middle Ages; an aristocrat did not buy and sell. The tradition dies hard.

10 Snobbery for snobbery, there is not much to choose between a snobbery whose object is the titled and a snobbery which adores the

very rich. They are equally comic. But snobbery is not the only fruit of traditional aristocracy. It has other by-products of a much more interesting nature. The most important of these by-products is the more or less complete indifference to public opinion which characterizes the members of a hereditary aristocracy. It is obvious that, if you are born with a certain acknowledged social superiority, which is independent of material circumstances (for a poor aristocrat is still an aristocrat) and of which nothing can deprive you, you need not feel preoccupied about public opinion. "What will the neighbors say?" You do not care two pins what they say. What they say can do nothing to damage your position, which you hold by something approaching a divine right. This indifference to public opinion is the cause, among those who feel it, of a good deal of stupid and uncontrolled behavior. Liberty easily turns to license; it takes a strong man to be free with dignity. Rich and foolish young men who happen to be hereditary aristocrats probably behave worse, on the average, than rich and foolish young men whose fathers were manufacturers or bankers. If the aristocratic indifference to public opinion resulted only in this, it would hardly be worth talking about. But not all aristocrats are foolish. A strong and intelligent man who feels himself to be above public opinion will not behave badly; he will behave independently, doing what he thinks right and rational, regardless of the prejudices of the crowd. Among the European aristocracies there is always to be found a good supply of unyielding independent characters, whose eccentricity, fostered by their sense of superiority, can sometimes attain almost to the pitch of madness.

11 In our too completely standardized world a leavening of strong minded eccentrics is a most desirable thing; the tradition of hereditary aristocracy produces them almost automatically. The eccentric aristocrat does good by his example. Careless of public opinion himself, he gives to eccentricity a certain respectability which it cannot possess in countries where public opinion rules every class of society, even the richest, and where all departures from the average are looked on with grave suspicion. Moreover, aristocracies have always been the patrons of the arts and letters, even to a certain extent of the sciences. To play with new ideas has been one of the traditional sports, along with hunting and love-making, of the more intelligent of European aristocrats. They have protected otherwise defenseless innovators coming from the lower strata of society and have shielded them with their prestige and

power from the rage of the ignorant and therefore conservative mob, to which all novelty, every attempt to change established prejudices, is abhorrent. Personal liberty—the liberty of every man to act and think, within reasonable limits, as he likes—is undoubtedly greater in Europe than in America, where "liberty" means the liberty of the majority to impose its will on the minority and to make compulsory by law and, still more, by the force of public opinion, a general uniformity of habits, customs and beliefs. Legal and nonlegal interference in the private lives of individuals has gone to extraordinary lengths in America! In many parts of the United States unfamiliar, and therefore unpopular, ideas are persecuted with violence. People who hold unpopular beliefs and whose habits of life are different from those of the majority enjoy in Europe a degree of freedom which would never be accorded them in most of the states of America. This freedom is largely due, I believe, to the influence of the surviving hereditary aristocracies, to whom the idea of personal liberty is sacred and who therefore do their best to protect, not only their own, but even other people's freedom to think and behave as they like.

Comment

Essentially this comparison and contrast of Europe and America depends on history, as the following summary indicates:

I. Europe and America are similar in many ways. But Europe has a different attitude toward business and personal liberty. The root of the difference is Europe's history and America's lack of history.
II. Europe's attitude toward business stems from the ethical and religious ideals of the Middle Ages, whereas America's attitude stems from the rationalized avarice of the industrial revolution.
III. Europe's attitude toward personal liberty stems from an aristocratic contempt for public opinion, whereas America's attitude toward personal liberty is based on the sanctity of majority opinion.

In general, then, the major emphasis is on differences (contrast) rather than similarities (comparison) between Europe and America. These differences tend to prove two closely interwoven themes:

a. That Europe is more mature than America in its attitude toward business and personal liberty.
b. That European maturity is traceable to two historical traditions rooted in Europe's medieval past.

Analysis and Composition

1. Determine whether the following arguments, properly developed, would refute one or both of Mr. Huxley's themes:
   a. There is more substantial social justice in America than in Europe.
   b. Personal liberty has not been a marked characteristic of the fascist regimes of Germany and Italy or the communism of central Europe.
   c. The aristocratic tradition has been publicly repudiated by England, France, and Italy in favor of a democracy more closely allied to American ideals.
   d. Mr. Huxley is inconsistent. He praises Europe and lives in California by his own choice.
   e. The core of American liberals has always opposed the tyranny of the majority on questions of civil rights and personal taste.
2. Comment on the following statements in connection with the essay as a whole:
   a. Mr. Huxley's essay is not sufficiently specific in its comparisons. It is intelligent without being informed.
   b. Mr. Huxley's essay succeeds in defining the most attractive features of Europe in comparison with the least attractive features of America.
   c. There's no use talking down history. What happened happened. Mr. Huxley isn't arguing. He's merely stating facts.
3. What reason does Mr. Huxley give to support his assertion that "strange things . . . are easier to understand than those we know too well" (¶1)?
4. Why was it easier for Mr. Huxley to discover the importance of the European past by a visit to America rather than by remaining in Europe (¶2)?
5. Paragraph 3 explains why Europe and America remain profoundly foreign to one another in spite of certain external similarities. What similarities and what differences are mentioned in this paragraph?
6. Paragraph 4 emphasizes the different meanings given to the word *service* by Europeans and Americans. Mr. Huxley acquired his sense of the American use of the word by reading and conversation. Do you agree that the American businessman means by service what Mr. Huxley says he means? Give some evidence for your opinion by citing contemporary sermons, newspaper articles, or advertisements.
7. Paragraphs 5 and 6 represent a contrast between the medieval contempt for avarice and the modern admiration of it. Test the validity of this contrast by finding specific examples which oppose Huxley's statement that the modern state "leaves the avaricious man almost entirely free

to satisfy his lust for money and even rewards him, when successful and rich, with honors and political power."

8. Analyze in detail the comparison between avarice and the water in the mill pond in paragraph 6.

9. Determine from the context of paragraph 7 what Aldous Huxley means by socialism. In your opinion does he confuse the social ideals of Christianity with modern political and economic socialism? (An acceptable definition of modern socialism is: A politico-economic system based on the common ownership of the means of production and the exchange of wealth.)

10. Do you agree that "in a country where there is no hereditary aristocracy the leaders of society are the rich" (¶9)? Give reasons for your answer.

11. Explain in detail Huxley's comparison between the effect of money in an aristocratic and in a nonaristocratic society. Does Huxley establish the common point of difference between the two societies? Does he attempt to indicate the degree of the difference between them?

12. Is the first sentence in paragraph 11 effectively supported by the details that follow?

13. Classify the sentences in paragraph 7 according to the following principles: *

   a. The kind of sentence (example: sentence 1, simple; sentence 2, compound)
   b. Sentence unity achieved by good subordination
   c. Sentence unity achieved by parallelism and balance
   d. Sentence variety achieved by different kinds of sentences
   e. Sentence variety achieved by different sentence beginnings (adverbs, phrases, clauses, etc.)
   f. Sentence emphasis achieved by periodic development

14. Classify the sentences in paragraphs 4, 5, and 6 according to the principles listed in Exercise 13.

* See handbooks:

a. Foerster, pp. 7-11; Hodges, *1e*, 2; Kierzek, pp. 40-43; Perrin, pp. 247-59; Wykoff, *4a*.

b. Foerster, pp. 7-17; Hodges, *24*; Kierzek, *47*; Perrin, pp. 257-59; Wykoff, *77*.

c. Foerster, pp. 17-33, *77, 86*; Hodges, *26*; Kierzek, pp. 59-62, *56*; Perrin, pp. 282-83; Wykoff, *77*.

d and e. Foerster, pp. 39-42, *81*; Hodges, *30*; Kierzek, pp. 53-59, *67*; Perrin, pp. 278-83; Wykoff, *80*.

f. Foerster, *75*; Hodges, *29b*; Kierzek, *61*; Perrin, pp. 280-82; Wykoff, *79d*.

d. Use comparison and contrast in combination with other methods of analysis for interest and emphasis.

1. On Slavery

BY ABRAHAM LINCOLN

[¹If I saw a venomous snake crawling in the road, any man would say I might seize the nearest stick and kill it; but if I found that snake in bed with my children, that would be another question. ²I might hurt the children more than the snake, and it might bite them. ³Much more, if I found it in bed with my neighbor's children, and I had bound myself by a solemn compact not to meddle with his children under any circumstances, it would become me to let that particular mode of getting rid of the gentleman alone.] ⁴But if there was a bed newly made up, to which the children were to be taken, and it was proposed to take a batch of young snakes and put them there with them, I take it no man would say there was any question how I ought to decide. ⁵That is just the case. ⁶The new territories are the newly made bed to which our children are to go, and it lies with the nation to say whether they shall have snakes mixed up with them or not. ⁷It does not seem as if there could be much hesitation what our policy should be.

Comment

Lincoln's similitude comparing slavery with a snake is extremely effective. It is familiar, yet startling. Not an argument in itself, it nevertheless has the force of argument. Thus from this short paragraph one receives the

ɔN SLAVERY: speech at New Haven, Conn., March 6, 1860.

following impressions: Slavery is like a snake and therefore repulsive. To permit slavery in the new territories is the same as putting a batch of snakes in children's beds. Slavery is a snake that will poison our freedom. The cogency of this similitude strengthens Lincoln's main arguments in the speech from which this paragraph was taken.

Analysis and Composition

1. Sentence 5 reads, "That is just the case." Lincoln means here that there is a parity between the situation described in sentence 4 and the situation described in sentence 6.
   a. In what sense are the cases exactly the same?
   b. In what sense do they differ?
   c. Estimate the cogency of this comparison.
2. Describe the effect Lincoln creates by comparing slavery to a batch of snakes and comparing freedom to children.
3. Develop one or more of the following comparisons in a paragraph of 300 words. Be sure to say what you want the reader to decide about the subject.
   a. Communism compared to an underground mine
   b. The Red Cross compared to a lifeline
   c. Education compared to cultivating a garden
   d. The home compared to a small kingdom
   e. The United Nations compared to a permanent truce tent

2. Protagoras

BY PLATO

I said: I wonder whether you know what you are doing?

And what am I doing?

You are going to commit your soul to the care of a man whom you call a Sophist. And yet I hardly think that you know what a Sophist is; and if not, then you do not even know to whom you are committing your soul and whether the thing to which you commit yourself be good or evil.

I certainly think that I do know, he replied.

Then tell me, what do you imagine that he is?

I take him to be one who knows wise things, he replied, as his name implies. . . .

And what is that which the Sophist knows and makes his disciples know?

Indeed, he said, I cannot tell.

Then I proceeded to say: Well, but are you aware of the danger which you are incurring? If you were going to commit your body to some one, who might do good or harm to it, would you not carefully consider and ask the opinion of your friends and kindred, and deliberate many days as to whether you should give him the care of your body? But when the soul is in question, which you hold to be of far more value than the body, and upon the good or evil of which depends the well-being of your all,—about this you never consulted either with your father or with your brother or with any one of us who are your companions. But no sooner does this foreigner appear, than you instantly commit your soul to his keeping. In the evening, as you say, you hear of him, and in the morning you go to him, never deliberating or taking the opinion of anyone as to whether you ought to entrust yourself to him or not;—you have quite made up your mind that you will at all hazards be a pupil of Protagoras, and are prepared to expend all the property of yourself and of your friends in carrying out at any price this determination, although, as you admit, you do not know him, and have never spoken with him: and you call him a Sophist, but are manifestly ignorant of what a Sophist is; and yet you are going to commit yourself to his keeping.

When he heard me say this, he replied: No other inference, Socrates, can be drawn from your words.

I proceeded: Is not a Sophist, Hippocrates, one who deals wholesale or retail in the food of the soul? To me that appears to be his nature.

And what, Socrates, is the food of the soul?

Surely, I said, knowledge is the food of the soul; and we must take care, my friend, that the Sophist does not deceive us when he praises what he sells, like the dealers wholesale or retail who sell the food of the body; for they praise indiscriminately all their goods, without knowing what are really beneficial or hurtful: neither do their customers know, with the exception of any trainer or physician who may happen to buy of them. In like manner those who carry about the wares of knowledge, and make the round of the cities, and sell or retail them to any customer who is in want of them, praise them all alike; though I should not wonder, O my friend, if many of them were really ignorant of their effect upon the soul; and their customers equally ignorant, unless he who buys of them happens to be a physician of the soul. If, therefore, you have understanding of what is good and evil, you may safely buy knowledge of Protagoras or of any one; but if not, then, O my friend, pause, and do not hazard your dearest interests at a game of chance. For there is far greater peril in buying knowledge than in buying meat and drink: the one you purchase of the wholesale or retail dealer, and carry them away in other vessels, and before you receive them into the body as food, you may deposit them at home and call in any experienced friend who knows what is good to be eaten or drunken, and what not, and how much, and when; and then the danger of purchasing them is not so great. But you cannot buy the wares of knowledge and carry them away in another vessel; when you have paid for them you must receive them into the soul and go your way, either greatly harmed or greatly benefited; and therefore we should deliberate and take counsel with our elders; for we are still young—too young to determine such a matter. And now let us go, as we were intending, and hear Protagoras; and when we have heard what he has to say, we may take counsel of others; for not only is Protagoras at the house of Callias, but there is Hippias of Elis, and, if I am not mistaken, Prodicus of Ceos, and several other wise men.

Comment

In showing why we must deliberate and take counsel before submitting ourselves to someone's teaching, Plato's spokesman, Socrates, uses several interesting similitudes. One is the comparison between knowledge and food. Closely associated with this comparison is the likeness between the sophists, "thought merchants," and the food dealers. Neither of these two similitudes is a strict comparison. Nevertheless, both serve admirably to make the writer's purpose clear and interesting.

Analysis and Composition

1. Summarize the reasoning employed in this passage. Then, in a paragraph of 300 words, show how the comparisons mentioned above assist in making the reasoning effective.
2. Write a comment of not more than 50 words agreeing or disagreeing with the following statements:

a. Socrates leads his pupil from the familiar example to the unfamiliar one.
b. Plato seems to make knowledge and food exact equivalents.
c. Plato's comparisons here assume that man has a spiritual soul.
d. Plato appears to counsel undue docility in youth.

3. In a manner similar to that of Example D2, use a similitude in the course of developing one of the following subjects. Note that the italicized word or words in each theme suggest the similitude.
   a. A good teacher is a *physician* of the mind.
   b. A poor student is like *a refractory colt.*
   c. The sentences in a good composition are like *a well-drilled team.*
   d. A poor composition is as disorderly as *a mob of women* in a bargain basement.

GENERAL EXERCISES

A

Pick out the comparisons and contrasts in Examples I1 and I2 in Section II; in Examples B1, C2, and C3 in Section III, and in Examples C1 and C2 and General Exercise A in Section IV.

B

Two Kinds of German Immigrant

BY PAUL HORGAN

"Wahrheit und Dichtung"
("Truth of fact and truth of poetry")

Scattered across the landscape are the vestiges of other Germanic occupations of the last century. These survive in the names of business houses, in the oddly European flavor of residences of a certain type in older parts of cottonwoody towns, and in an occasional old man with a cosmopolitan point of view, who will talk with you first about world affairs, and after that about the lamb crop.

Two types of Germans came with the immigrant discovery of Southwestern empire.

TWO KINDS OF GERMAN IMMIGRANT: reprinted from *Figures in a Landscape* by Paul Horgan with the permission of the publisher, Harper and Brothers, and the author.

One was the young Jew, vivid in his imagination at the commercial challenge of a world where commerce—*Wahrheit,* as he understood it— was unknown, and markets had only local enterprise, and coins changed hands only when the wagons drew into the plaza of the town and stood under the cottonwoods while the traders exchanged overpriced goods and sometimes more precious news. The young German Jew would be appalled at the cost of and the risk of turning barter into commerce; but there was only one way, and that was to struggle with the country itself. He joined the Chihuahua-Santa Fe trading expeditions, traveling up and down the Rio Grande valley, through hardship and terror, winning with his native timidity a physical success in the pioneer spirit. Many like him founded great fortunes. His history was that of one man against an immense empire that impassively offered a myriad defeats and deaths. In Santa Fe he married a Spanish girl, set up a *gemütlich* establishment, raised a large family, sent for his brothers to come from Germany and manage branches of his mercantile house, and became a powerful man. He resisted the shabby tyrannies of many a Mexican governor. He was free at last to recreate his racial and national patterns in a wild country; his ideals had warmth and vitality; and in a new society, achievement counted for more than race itself. In the Latin he found a satisfying sympathy for his capacity of joy in emotion. He came, in time, to love all the very tokens of peril through which he survived. To his Jewish name was added the courtesy style of *Don.* He succeeded both in the terms of life he brought with him, and those he found here in this landscape.

He was the man of the practical world, at liberty to apply his commercial genius and produce victory from unlikely circumstances.

The other German was the lyric idealist, who saw life as *Dichtung* and preferred it so. For him, too, victory was waiting; for his aim was not riches above all else, but liberty; and if in the new land liberty could be achieved in the nostalgic trappings of the old country, where liberty was unknown, then here, too, was triumph in terms of both the old life and the new. To a German of the nineteenth century—and that is to say a capitalized Romantic—the American frontier was the last, the newest, the best home of romance. Possibly he was the only man in the landscape who knew *at the time* that here was romance itself and that the toil, the danger, and the chance of the frontier were poetry in birth.

Whatever the difference between these two German characters, they had one great virtue in common, and that was an energetic belief in what they wanted to do. Indeed, they might be called geographical fanatics, to whom questions of taste, propriety, or the future's opinion never occurred. Such questions are usually the luxuries of the heirs of those men who grappled with the plains and the mountains. The critical faculty can be based only

on the sacrifices of others. It will always have its own comfort in the illusion of classical repose, and it will find foolish the extravagances of the
Schilleresque German of the nineteenth century. But it will miss the alliance
between life and imagination which in many forms created that hybrid style
which still gives us evidence, in our day, of what ways of life men strove
to keep intact by them in the wilderness.

1. Analyze the above passage by Paul Horgan according to this outline:
   a. Pick out the theme.
   b. Pick out two definitions (see Section II).
   c. State the classification and division (see Section III).
   d. Pick out two examples (see Section IV).
   e. Point out the precise points of likeness and difference between the
      merchant and the poet.
2. In a manner similar to that illustrated by Mr. Horgan develop a comparison and contrast between two members of one of the following
   classes:
   a. Italian (or German, Irish, or Polish) immigrants
   b. College professors
   c. Football players
   d. Retired businessmen
   e. Movie-goers
   f. War heroes

C

1. Reread the rules of a good comparison in the introduction to this section. Then analyze the following arguments from comparison to determine in what sense they may be true and in what sense they may be
   false.
   a. The decline of the Roman Empire was the result of a general decay
      in morals, widespread divorce and licentiousness, a contempt for
      human life. We see the same signs in America today. America is
      going the way of the Roman Empire.
   b. The Russian threat today is exactly like that of Genghis Khan. Primi-
      tive, bloodthirsty, fearless, the Russians regard the West as an effete
      civilization ready to be plundered. What happened in Genghis Khan's
      time is happening today.
   c. All great advances of the human race have been accompanied by
      great change. One generation must die so that another may live.
      Rome conquered Greece and gave way to Christianity. Christianity
      in turn gave way to modern science. Now the time has come for
      science to give way to world government by free-thinking men.
   d. The ideal intellectual is completely free of emotional bias. He is in-
      deed a thinking machine, cold, accurate, precise.

e. The reformers, both moral and esthetic, who attack the lurid magazines and pocket books, are missing the point. Publishing is a business. It gives value for the dollar received. Moreover, an attack on the pulp magazines and pocket books is not only an attack on private enterprise but on democracy itself. People want these books. And what the people want the publisher must give.

f. We have taught the world how to use modern science. There is no reason why we can't teach it Americanism. If we package our product right they'll buy. Even Russia will buy.

g. A governor of a state is by definition the pilot of a ship. He must keep to his course and never change. It is not for him to invent new theories of seamanship, new vessels, new rules for the crew. He has his orders. Let him obey them.

h. It is absurd to talk of labor sharing in management. Do apprentice seamen tell admirals how to fight a war? Should a brainless girl typist give tips to a trained executive?

i. I say the heads of our government ought to be in jail. Here is my reason. If I borrowed money, and then borrowed more to pay the first debt, and then made a third loan to pay the second, and continued borrowing, I'd land in jail. That's what happened to Ponzi and Livermore and all the other financial racketeers. But that's just what the government does all the time. It keeps borrowing from Peter to pay Paul. Now the heads of the government are responsible for this criminal borrowing. They ought to be sent to jail.

j. I see no difference between the average political campaign and slander. I have heard people call a candidate for high office an idiot, a money grabber, and a secret conniver with the Red underground. None of it was true. Isn't that slander? And if it is I don't know why we tolerate such campaigns as examples of free speech.

2. Write a rebuttal of one or more of the *faulty* comparisons listed in Exercise C1. Be careful to state the important differences between all the factors that are compared.

D

The selection below attempts to show that there is a great difference between the college graduate of the 1950's and the college graduate of the 1920's and 1930's. The difference is said to be due to historical change. As a result of history the new generation of college students (*a*) is more aware of complexity, (*b*) has a keener sense of responsibility, and (*c*) feels it belongs to the human race. Despite its brilliance, this essay appears to lack historical background. The present generation of college students—one term of the comparison—is adequately presented. But the other term of the comparison—the college generation of earlier days—is not explained. You will be asked to estimate this criticism and to answer other questions after a careful reading of the essay.

The Present Generation of College Students

BY THORNTON WILDER

1 I have been an intermittent teacher all my life and when, as this year, I return to a university community, I find myself continually drawing comparisons, not comparisons between institutions but comparisons between something far more striking and instructive, comparisons between attitudes, tacit assumptions, the thought-world of students that I have known throughout the decades of my teachings; attitudes that we held in 1917, 1918, 1919, and 1920, attitudes that my students in the University of Chicago held in the '30s, and the attitudes which I see in the students around me this year. What a difference! What a difference!

2 Now the students today have been told sufficiently that they are living in an age which has variously been called by Professor Toynbee, Mr. Auden, and others, the Age of Upheaval and the Age of Anxiety. And indeed it seems so to the seniors whom we graduated this morning, who were 12 years old at the time of the attack on Pearl Harbor. They have spent their lives then in our view in stormy or in threatening weather. They never knew, as we who were born about the turn of the century, they never knew that evenly running world to which one of our Presidents gave the name of Normalcy.

3 When I go about my occupation of drawing comparisons, I become aware that those who live in troubled weather build or discover resources that we in 1920 felt no need to call upon. Like species among the order of the animal kingdom, they develop adaptations. These resources, of course, are not of their manufacture but they find what they need from the currents of thought and literature that are about us all, and it is how they assimilate it that is interesting to us. I am talking about tacit assumptions of which these students are often not aware. But what they are aware of is that many of the concepts to which we older persons clung are to them irrelevant, irrelevant and irritating.

4 The twentieth century is shifting its foundations and it is altering its emphases with striking rapidity. The scientists and the poets and the writers have described this new mentality which is moving into place. The man on the street is beginning to be aware of it. But to teach the young today is to put one's self in the way of learning from the superior student the

THE PRESENT GENERATION OF COLLEGE STUDENTS: part of an address delivered at the annual meeting of the Harvard Alumni Association on May 21, 1951. It is reprinted here by special permission of the *Harvard Alumni Bulletin* and Mr. Wilder.

new description of man in his relations. And that is what supports and sustains those who have only known troubled weather.

5 I teach literature. I teach the consecrated classics but I am attentive also to the masters of modern literature and if I were not so my students would have waked me up to them. About five years ago a professor who was a friend of mine in a university far from here once said to me, "You know, when a student in my classes has written a brilliant paper on the *Scarlet Letter* or on *Tom Jones,* I invite him into my office to compliment him and to make his acquaintance, and we talk for a while. Often, too often, the young man or woman on leaving my office turns and says to me, 'Well, Professor X, of course, we like these books we read for you, but what we are really interested in is T. S. Eliot, James Joyce, Franz Kafka, Gertrude Stein, Ezra Pound.'"

6 And the professor said to me, "Now, what's the matter? I spent my life studying great literature. These books are purportedly in the English language, yet I cannot read five pages of them with any pleasure, to say nothing of intelligibility. I have no choice but to think that my most gifted students are either hypocrites, imitative snobs, or else barbarians who don't know beauty and clarity when they see it."

7. Well, that is the gulf between the generations and it is up to us to be very attentive to it. Now, freshmen and sophomores stop me on the street and visit me in my room to ask me about these very writers. And that shows us that these writers are fulfilling a profound need for those who live in stormy weather. And I find three tacit assumptions within their work that are reflected in the best young twentieth-century minds, assumptions that we could not have grasped in 1920. First, the young person today in the light of science sees himself not as one of many hundred thousands, not as one of many millions, but as one of billions. Secondly, there is a whole new tacit assumption in relation to responsibility. And, thirdly, there is a new realization that the things that separate men from one another are less important than the things that they have in common.

1. Write an answer of not less than a paragraph to each of the following questions on Mr. Wilder's essay.
    a. Why are comparisons of the "attitudes, tacit assumptions, the thought-world of students" more striking and instructive than the comparisons between institutions (¶1)?
    b. Comment on the aptness of the comparison between our times and stormy weather (¶2, 3, 4).
    c. Comment on the force of the comparison between the new attitudes of college students and adaptations in the animal kingdom (¶3).

d. Show how "tacit assumptions and basic attitudes," first used in paragraph 1, is repeated in paragraph 3 in a clearer context.

e. What other key expressions, like stormy weather, are repeated in the first four paragraphs? throughout the whole essay?

f. Is the example of Professor X and his gifted student (¶5-6) a clear illustration of the basic attitude of the new generation of student?

g. In your opinion is Mr. Wilder's assumption (¶7) that freshmen and sophomores are interested in Kafka, Stein, and Pound correct? Give reasons for your answer.

h. In a sense this essay develops only one side of the comparison—the student of today. Mr. Wilder assumes that his audience, members of the Harvard alumni, have first-hand knowledge of the college men of the twenties. Others without this first-hand knowledge must infer what Mr. Wilder means from the other term of the comparison. Does this lack of historical development make this paper unintelligible? Give reasons for your answer.

E

1. Write a brief comparison on one or more of the following subjects. Develop both terms of the comparison unless one of the terms is very well known to a general reader.

   a. Characterization in a modern talking picture and a silent film
   b. A student before and after attending high school
   c. Fashions in dress, pre-war, war, post-war
   d. A farm community before and after the invention of the automobile
   e. What a difference between the freshman and the sophomore!
   f. My high school classmate before and after I went away to college
   g. The ocean in calm and the ocean in storm
   h. A tornado strikes a sleepy town
   i. Hitler's army before and after D day in Normandy

2. Study the following subjects carefully. Pick out the one you know best. Draw up a preliminary informal outline and then write a composition of approximately 500 words combining comparison and contrast with other methods of development.

   a. Dormitories and fraternity houses.
   b. Whales and submarines.
   c. Liberal arts or business administration.
   d. It is better to have loved and lost.
   e. Slanging it,—humor lower than the pun.
   f. No man makes progress without a rival.
   g. The best is the enemy of the good.

h. A mediocre ideal is contemptible; mediocre achievement is better than most men ever attain.

i. Knowing why we study and knowing how to study are equally necessary.

j. My room at home and my room at college.

3. Check your completed composition with your preliminary outline. Have you departed from your original outline? If so, write a new outline which conforms to the complete composition.*

* See handbooks: Hodges, *32d-i*; Kierzek, *10h*; Perrin, p. 738; Wykoff, *45a-c*.

A. Make evident the interconnection of cause and effect.

1 HENRY BAMFORD PARKES:
  How the Revolution Changed America
2 GEORGE ORWELL: *The Sporting Spirit*
3 SAMUEL ELIOT MORISON:
  The Art of Writing History
4 ARNOLD BENNETT:
  Why a Classic Is a Classic

B. Discriminate between cause and effect and mere occasion and condition.

HENRY BAMFORD PARKES: .
  Why Men Came to America

C. Explain causes that are obscure or difficult by analysis of their effects; explain effects by analysis of an existing and operating cause.

1 C. E. MONTAGUE: *The Last Question of All*
2 WINSTON S. CHURCHILL:
  We Must Not Despair

General Exercises

HUGH R. WALPOLE:
  The Usefulness of Semantics

SECTION VI

Cause and Effect

CAUSAL analysis is a logical method of investigating a subject in relation to the elements that produced it (cause) and in relation to the elements that the subject itself will produce (effect). Thus cause answers the question, "Why did this happen?" Effect answers the question, "What will this do?"

Let us say at once that causal analysis, taken in its full meaning, is a difficult form of analysis. As Viscount Samuel pointed out in Example IV C1, the total cause of any event is a vast combination of elements stretching far back in time. The total cause, as his example of the accident made clear, is a complex of personal and physical factors that can be grasped only in a general way. Thus, for example, when we attempt to discover the causes of the Korean War we find that many incidents and influences combined to bring it about. There were, for instance, on the personal side, the plans of the North Korean communist leaders and their allies, and the South Koreans' will to resist. The influence of world communism played an important part. The political, economic, and social status of Korea, its relation to the United Nations—all these more or less impersonal elements are partial reasons for the war. The past history of Korea as a Japanese dependency had some bearing on the war; so did the decision to establish Russian and American zones of influence. Nor is the attempt to predict the total complex of the results of the Korean War any easier than the discovery of the causes. Some effects are clearly evident. Men have died, women and children have starved, the land has been ravaged, animosities have been inflamed. But no one can trace all the effects of the war into the future. Other events will surely occur that may change the flow of effects stemming from that conflict.

But here we are not concerned with the total cause of events on so grand a scale. Our business is the practical one of inquiring into the connection between *A* and *B,* between the fall and the broken leg, between the faulty wire and the burned house, between the painter and the picture, between the author and the book he produces. In other words, we are considering a cause as something that is the *positive, necessary,* and *immediate* reason for the existence of something else. Conversely, we are regarding an effect as the *positive, necessary,* and *immediate* result of the operation of a cause. Cause and effect are necessarily related. A cause necessarily produces its effect; an effect necessarily supposes and contains its cause. Hence they must be studied together.

THE THREE ELEMENTS OF CAUSAL ANALYSIS

Let us examine and illustrate the three important elements of causal analysis.

A Cause Is Positive. By positive we mean that the cause translates itself, that is, conveys itself into the effect. Hence we say a cause *produces* or determines an effect. Thus a poet translates his ideas into a poem, and a carpenter translates wood into a desk. The poet's ideas as causes carry over essentially into the poem; the wood, as a cause, is translated into the desk. Influences without this positive character are not true causes. For example, a condition of the poet's writing the poem is a place to write. But the place to write is not translated essentially into the work. A carpenter needs a workbench. But the workbench is not translated into the desk.

A Cause Is Necessary. By necessary we mean that the cause inevitably produces its effect. In other words, when a cause operates, the effect is always present. When the effect is present, the cause is present, too. Thus, when two parts of hydrogen and one part of oxygen are combined, we must have water; when we have water, we must have a combination of hydrogen and oxygen. If we fire a bullet into a human body, a wound must result; if there is a bullet wound in a human body, there is an inevitable cause, the firing of the bullet.

A Cause Is Immediate. By immediate we mean that the cause is *directly* connected with the effect, and does not operate through a second cause. Thus, for example, the immediate cause of a painter's breaking his leg is a fall from a ladder. (A remote cause was the painter's acceptance of a contract to paint a house. The ultimate cause was the painter's need to make a living, which caused him to agree to paint the house.)

When we understand cause as the positive, necessary, and immediate reason for the existence of something else, and effect as the positive, necessary, and immediate result of the operation of a cause, we have at hand a ready means of analyzing a subject.

CAUSAL ANALYSIS DISTINGUISHED FROM ANALYSIS OF CIRCUMSTANCES

Causal analysis should be distinguished from another method of analysis that superficially resembles it, namely analysis of circumstances. Although this method of analysis is included in the next section (VII), it is necessary to explain some phases of it here.

Analysis of circumstances is a logical method of investigating a subject by studying the conditions of time, place, person, thing, manner, and degree that are normally associated with the subject. These circumstances or conditions stand in *immediate* relation to the subject. But, unlike cause and effect, they do not exercise a positive or necessary influence on the subject, nor are these circumstances themselves the effects of the subject.

Nevertheless, there are times when circumstances may resemble causes. For instance, many circumstances normally precede or follow each other, and are for this reason called *antecedents and consequents*. Thus, for example, the ringing of a bell (antecedent) normally precedes the beginning of class (consequent). The bell does not actually cause a class to begin. The cause of class beginning is the combined decision of teachers and students. The bell merely signalizes the beginning of class. It is not the positive, necessary, and immediate cause. If the teachers and students decided to ignore the bell, the only consequent would be sound of the bell. Yet antecedents and consequents are often confused with cause and effects because writers and students fall into the habit of thinking that if *B* follows *A* in the order of time, then *A* is the cause of *B*. (This is the *post hoc ergo propter hoc* fallacy—"after this therefore because of this.")

Furthermore, causal analysis is often confused with a second type of circumstance, that is, with *necessary conditions*. Necessary conditions are circumstances that of themselves are not causes or effects but are required for the operation of a cause. Thus, light is a necessary condition of sight. Light of itself can never produce sight, the actual cause of which is the operation of the eye. But without light a man with excellent vision cannot see. So too paper, or a similar substance, is a necessary condition for a written composition.

Frequently mere *occasions,* that is, circumstances that are favorable to the operation of a cause, are mistakenly called causes. Thus we hear it said that, "He studies because he has a quiet room," or "He emigrated because of economic pressure." A quiet room is conducive to study, but the true cause is the student's own resolve. So too economic pressure, as H. B. Parkes shows in Example B, is a circumstance favorable to emigration but is not the true cause. If economic pressure causes emigration then it must follow, according to the definition of cause above, that wherever there is economic pressure emigration will always result.

PRINCIPLES OF CAUSAL ANALYSIS

The three principles of causal analysis are implicit in the definitions we have stated above. The first of these principles applies to the positive, necessary, and immediate connection of cause and effect, and may be stated as follows: *Make evident the interconnection of cause and effect.* This principle we shall examine in Examples A1, A2, A3, A4 and in General Exercises A and B.

The second principle applies to the distinction between causal analysis and circumstantial analysis, which are sometimes confused. This principle may be stated as follows: *Discriminate between cause and effect and mere occasion and condition.* This rule we shall examine in Example B and in General Exercises C and D.

The third principle applies to situations wherein, for various reasons, it is necessary or convenient (a) to explain a cause by analysis of its existing effect, or (b) to explain an effect by analysis of an existing, that is, an operating, cause.

Such situations occur frequently. Thus there are times when a cause may only be known through its effect. The 1952 election is a case in point. We know the cause of President Eisenhower's victory, that is, the electoral decision of some 33,000,000 voters, only through the effect, the election itself. Similarly, we know electricity as a cause only through its effects.

Another illustration of the discovery of a cause in the analysis of the effect occurs in Example C1. Here C. E. Montague begins to describe the cause of literary excitement. But this cause is obscure, since it resides in the genius of an individual author expressing itself in the medium of language. At best one can know only that such a cause exists and operates. There is no "presentable explanation" for the mystery of literary genius. Hence Mr. Montague searches for the cause in the *effect*. A close analysis of a genuine effect always discovers the essential qualities of the cause, because an effect necessarily contains its cause.

The reverse process, that is, the discovery of an effect by analysis of the cause, occurs frequently in *deliberative* reasoning, that is, in reasoning about something to be done in the future. Thus a Congressman or Senator will argue that the passage of a law (cause) will have a beneficial *effect* in the future by an analysis of the proposed law. His argument might follow a pattern like this.

"This immigration bill is sponsored by able Senators and Representatives; it is based on the traditional American principle of offering refuge to men and women who are oppressed; it provides for their assimilation into American society without disturbing the rights of American citizens; it is intended to build up American manpower and at the same time to furnish proof to the world at large that America is a generous and unselfish nation."

The legislator is arguing causally. His logical position is that the immigration bill as a cause contains the wisdom of its able sponsors, high principles, prudent provisions, and a noble purpose. Hence if the bill is put into *operation* these qualities in the cause will be translated into the effect. Therefore America will benefit by the passage of the immigration bill.

In Example C2 Winston S. Churchill uses a similar argument from causal analysis with great skill. This selection from his address on "The Twentieth Century, Its Promise and Realization" calls upon the free world not to despair in the face of unprincipled use of scientific power by enemies of freedom. He argues that man's nature (the cause) is so constituted that he will never yield (effect) to enslavement. Man's spiritual nature is thus an existing and operating cause; hence the effect, liberty, is predictable. As long as man exists he will always struggle to be free.

The principle that explains these two types of causal analysis may be stated as follows: *Explain causes that are obscure or difficult by analysis of their effects; explain effects by analysis of an existing and operating cause.*

Note: Most writers do not use the above principles of causal analysis in a rigid way, except in highly technical arguments which are governed by the strict rules of logic. Thus you will not find in the following examples mathematically precise demonstrations of causal analysis but rather a free use of the principles in the light of the author's subject, purpose, and occasion.

a. Make evident the interconnection of cause and effect.

1. How the Revolution Changed America

BY HENRY BAMFORD PARKES

The chief achievements of the Revolution, apart from the winning of independence from Great Britain, were to be found in the new state constitutions adopted during the war. The general trend was toward agrarian democracy, though this went much further in some states than in others. In general, the franchise was widely extended, so that most farmers acquired the right to vote; and the western regions were given fair representation in the legislatures. The transfer of power from the seaboard aristocracies to the small farmers was symbolized by the movement inland of a number of the state capitals.* The democratic groups believed in a system of outright and direct majority rule, in which almost all powers should be given to a unicameral legislature subject to re-election at frequent intervals. Their

---

* State capitals were moved inland during the revolutionary period in Virginia, North Carolina, South Carolina, and Georgia, and soon afterwards in New York and Pennsylvania. Attempts to move the capitals of Massachusetts and Maryland were unsuccessful.

HOW THE REVOLUTION CHANGED AMERICA: reprinted from *The American Experience* by Henry Bamford Parkes, by permission of Alfred A. Knopf, Inc. Copyright 1947 by Henry Bamford Parkes.

ideas were realized most completely in the new constitution of Pennsylvania, drafted by a convention in which Franklin was the presiding officer, and bitterly opposed not only by Loyalists but also by merchants, such as Robert Morris, who supported independence. At the other extreme were the constitutions of Massachusetts, Virginia, and South Carolina, in which the wealthy classes were able to retain a considerable measure of control. After the adoption of these new constitutions, men of a new type were elected to political office even in those states which had remained most conservative. Rural lawyers with small-farmer affiliations, like Patrick Henry in Virginia and George Clinton in New York, sat in the chairs from which the royal governors of Great Britain had been expelled.

Equally important were the economic reforms of the Revolution. The state legislatures came into possession both of the estates of the big Loyalist landowning families and of the public lands that had formerly belonged to the crown. These were broken into small farms and either sold or distributed in the form of bounties to soldiers. Unfortunately, speculators were able to take advantage of this legislation, but the intention was to democratize more fully the ownership of property. The same objective was sought by the abolition in almost all the states of the laws of primogeniture and entail; the purpose was to hasten the rapid subdivision of those big estates which remained and to make it impossible for any landed aristocracy to perpetuate itself in America. Such measures indicated a conscious intention of extending the "general happy mediocrity" of American society. At the same time another European survival—the privileged position of the Anglican Church—was abolished; except in New England, church and state were separated and religious freedom established.

Comment

The remote cause here is the American Revolution. The direct and immediate causes are the new state constitutions which tended towards agrarian democracy. The positive, necessary, and immediate effects of the state constitutions are the extended franchise, fairer representation, more direct elections. The practical economic effects of the Revolution (by way of the state legislatures) are the distribution of large estates, abolition of primogeniture and entail, and the abolition of a state-supported church. Note that the new type of official elected to office after the adoption of the new state constitutions is not a direct result of these constitutions. The new constitutions simply provided the conditions favorable to the election of such officials.

Analysis and Composition

1. Define

agrarian democracy	entail
unicameral legislature	happy mediocrity
primogeniture	

In what sense are these expressions the key ideas in the passage?

2. The idea of cause and effect is essentially tied in with *change*. In other words, the cause, as a positive, necessary, and immediate influence, *changes* something into something else. Note the words in this example expressing change: achievements, the new state constitutions, general trend. Find five or more other expressions that signify change in this passage.

3. Develop one or more of the following statements by explaining causes or effects:
   a. The Marshall Plan was of immediate assistance to European nations.
   b. The results of the Point Four Program are not generally known.
   c. The Missouri Valley Authority has developed a huge project for flood control, irrigation, and electrical development.
   d. John's personal career proceeded according to his plan.
   e. The achievements of the Good Neighbor policy are many.
   f. The influence of progressive education may be seen in the curriculum.
   g. The arrangement of the book as revealed in the table of contents is the effect of the author's careful planning.
   h. The reaction of the regiment in battle attested to its lack of training.

2. The Sporting Spirit

BY GEORGE ORWELL

1 Now that the brief visit of the Dynamo football team * has come to an end, it is possible to say publicly what many thinking people

* The Moscow Dynamos, a Russian football team, toured Britain in the autumn of 1945, playing against leading clubs.

THE SPORTING SPIRIT: from *Shooting an Elephant and Other Essays* by George Orwell, copyright, 1945, 1946, 1949, 1950, by Sonia Brownell Orwell. Reprinted by permission of Harcourt, Brace and Company, Inc., and of Martin, Secker and Warburg, Ltd., London.

were saying privately before the Dynamos ever arrived. That is, that sport is an unfailing cause of ill-will, and that if such a visit as this had any effect at all on Anglo-Soviet relations, it could only be to make them slightly worse than before.

2 Even the newspapers have been unable to conceal the fact that at least two of the four matches played led to much bad feeling. At the Arsenal match, I am told by someone who was there, a British and a Russian player came to blows and the crowd booed the referee. The Glasgow match, someone else informs me, was simply a free-for-all from the start. And then there was the controversy, typical of our nationalistic age, about the composition of the Arsenal team. Was it really an all-England team, as claimed by the Russians, or merely a league team, as claimed by the British? And did the Dynamos end their tour abruptly in order to avoid playing an all-England team? As usual, everyone answers these questions according to his political predilections. No doubt the controversy will continue to echo for years in the footnotes of history books. Meanwhile the result of the Dynamos' tour, in so far as it has had any result, will have been to create fresh animosity on both sides.

3 And how could it be otherwise? I am always amazed when I hear people saying that sport creates goodwill between the nations, and that if only the common peoples of the world could meet one another at football or cricket, they would have no inclination to meet on the battlefield. Even if one didn't know from concrete examples (the 1936 Olympic games, for instance) that international sporting contests lead to orgies of hatred, one could deduce it from general principles.

4 Nearly all the sports practised nowadays are competitive. You play to win, and the game has little meaning unless you do your utmost to win. On the village green, where you pick up sides and no feeling of local patriotism is involved, it is possible to play simply for the fun and exercise: but as soon as the question of prestige arises, as soon as you feel that you and some larger unit will be disgraced if you lose, the most savage combative instincts are aroused. Anyone who has played even in a school football match knows this. At the international level, sport is frankly mimic warfare. But the significant thing is not the behavior of the players but the attitude of the spectators: and, behind the spectators, of the nations who work themselves into furies over these absurd contests, and seriously believe—at any rate

for short periods—that running, jumping, and kicking a ball are tests of national virtue. . . .

Comment

Here Orwell argues (1) that the international football matches between the Soviet Dynamos and the four English teams were a cause of fresh animosity on both sides, and (2) that hatred, as an effect, is inherent in international sports as practiced nowadays. International sports, he adds in paragraph 4, are a "question of prestige, . . . mimic warfare, . . . tests of national virtue" and hence can arouse only savage and combative instincts.

Analysis and Composition

1. Decide whether Mr. Orwell establishes the interconnection between the international football match as a cause and hatred as an effect.
2. In paragraph 4 Orwell modifies his subject, sports, by the expression "practised nowadays." Determine whether this qualifying phrase, and similar phrases throughout the paragraph, are meant to set forth certain special *conditions* that affect the operation of the cause in this particular instance. In forming your answer consider the popularity in America of such foreign sports figures as Paavo Nurmi, Fred Perry, Henri Cochet, and the Australian Davis Cup team, and the popularity in Latin America of American baseball players and boxers.
3. Note that Orwell refers primarily to international sports. Although it would be wrong to extend his argument to all sports, he does suggest that school football matches sometimes arouse the most savage combative instincts. Do you agree with him or not? Give reasons for your answer.
4. Write a brief outline according to causal analysis of one or more of the following subjects:
   a. A college football team may detract from the chief aims of a college education.
   b. Any organized athletics will excite the gambling instinct.
   c. The effects of a sound athletic policy are to produce a sound body fit to serve a sound mind.
   d. A national sport such as baseball is an agent of national unity.
   e. Of their very nature sports help us to release our aggressive instincts in a civilized way.
5. Write a short essay based on causal analysis of one of the subjects listed in Exercise 4.

3. The Art of Writing History

BY SAMUEL ELIOT MORISON

1 Exploring American history has been a very absorbing and exciting business now for three quarters of a century. Thousands of graduate students have produced thousands of monographs on every aspect of the history of the Americas. But the American reading public for the most part is blissfully ignorant of this vast output. When John Citizen feels the urge to read history, he goes to the novels of Kenneth Roberts or Margaret Mitchell, not to the histories of Professor this or Doctor that. Why?

2 Because American historians, in their eagerness to present facts and their laudable anxiety to tell the truth, have neglected the literary aspects of their craft. They have forgotten that there is an art of writing history.

3 Even the earliest colonial historians like William Bradford and Robert Beverly knew that; they put conscious art into their narratives. And the historians of our classical period, Prescott and Motley, Irving and Bancroft, Parkman and Fiske, were great literary craftsmen. Their many-volumed works sold in sufficient quantities to give them handsome returns; even today they are widely read. But the first generation of seminar-trained historians, educated in Germany or by teachers trained there, imagined that history would tell itself, provided one were honest, thorough, and painstaking. Some of them went so far as to regard history as pure science and to assert that writers thereof had no more business trying to be "literary" than did writers of statistical reports or performers of scientific experiments. Professors warned their pupils (quite unnecessarily) against "fine writing," and endeavored to protect their innocence from the seductive charm of Washington Irving or the masculine glamor of Macaulay. And in this flight of history from literature the public got left behind. American history became a bore to the reader and a drug on the market; even historians with something to say and the talent for saying it (Henry Adams, for instance) could not sell their books. The most popular American histories of the period 1890-1905 were those of John Fiske, a philosopher who had no historical training, but wrote with life and movement.

THE ART OF WRITING HISTORY: from *History as a Literary Art* by Samuel Eliot Morison. Old South Leaflets, series ii. no. 1.

4 Theodore Roosevelt in his presidential address before the American Historical Association in 1912 made a ringing plea to the young historian to do better:

> He must ever remember that while the worst offense of which he can be guilty is to write vividly and inaccurately, yet that unless he writes vividly he cannot write truthfully; for no amount of dull, painstaking detail will sum up the whole truth unless the genius is there to paint the truth.

5 And although American historians cannot hope as Theodore Roosevelt did to "watch the nearing chariots of the champions," or look forward to the day when "for us the war-horns of King Olaf shall wail across the flood, and the harps sound high at festivals in forgotten halls," we may indeed "show how the land which the pioneers won slowly and with incredible hardship was filled in two generations by the overflow from the countries of western and central Europe." We may describe the race, class, and religious conflicts that immigration has engendered, and trace the rise of the labor movement with a literary art that compels people to read about it. You do not need chariots and horsemen, harps and war-horns to make history interesting.

6 Theodore Roosevelt's trumpet call fell largely on deaf ears, at least in the academic historical profession. A whole generation has passed without producing any really great works on American history. Plenty of good books, valuable books, and new interpretations and explorations of the past; but none with fire in the eye, none to make a young man want to fight for his country in war or live to make it a better country in peace. There has been a sort of chain reaction of dullness. Professors who have risen to positions of eminence by writing dull, solid, valuable monographs that nobody reads outside the profession, teach graduate students to write dull, solid, valuable monographs like theirs; the road to academic security is that of writing dull, solid, valuable monographs. And so the young men who have a gift for good writing either leave the historical field for something more exciting, or write more dull, solid, valuable monographs. The few professional historians who have had a popular following or appeal during the last thirty years are either men like Allan Nevins who were trained in some juicier profession like journalism, or men and women like the Beards who had the sense to break loose young from academic trammels.

7 In the meantime, the American public has become so sated by dull history textbooks in school and college that it won't read history unless disguised as something else under a title such as *The Flowering of*

Florida, The Epic of the East, or *The Growth of the American Republic.* Or, more often, they get what history they want from historical novels.

8 Now I submit, this is a very bad situation. The tremendous plowing up of the past by well-trained scholars is all to the good, so far as it goes. Scholars know more about America's past than ever; they are opening new furrows and finding new artifacts, from aboriginal arrowheads to early 20th-century corset stays. But they are heaping up the pay dirt for others. Journalists, novelists, and free-lance writers are the ones that extract the gold; and they deserve every ounce they get because they are the ones who know how to write histories that people care to read. What I want to see is a few more Ph.D.'s in history winning book-of-the-month adoptions and reaping the harvest of dividends. They can do it, too, if they will only use the same industry at presenting history as they do in compiling it.

9 Mind you, I intend no disparagement of historians who choose to devote their entire energies to teaching. Great teachers do far more good to the cause of history than mediocre writers. Such men, for instance, as the late H. Morse Stephens who stopped writing (which he never liked) as soon as he obtained a chair in this country, and the late Edwin F. Gay, who never began writing, inspired thousands of young men and initiated scores of valuable books. Thank God for these gifted teachers, I say; universities should seek out, encourage, and promote them far more than they do. My remarks are addressed to young men who have the urge to write history, and wish to write it effectively.

10 There are no special rules for writing history; any good manual of rhetoric or teacher of composition will supply the rules for writing English. But what terrible stuff passes for English in Ph.D. dissertations, monographs, and articles in the historical reviews! Long, involved sentences that one has to read two or three times in order to grasp the meaning; poverty in vocabulary, ineptness of expression, weakness in paragraph structure, constant misuse of words and, of late, the introduction of pseudo-scientific and psychological jargon. There is no fundamental cure for this except better teaching of English in our schools and by all teachers, *whatever their other subjects.* If historical writing is infinitely better in France than in America, and far better in the British Isles than in America, it is because every French and British teacher of history drills his pupils in their mother tongue, requiring a constant stream of essays and reports, and criticizing written

work not only as history but as literature. The American university teacher who gives honor grades to students who have not yet learned to write English, for industrious compilations of facts or feats of memory, is wanting in professional pride or competency.

11 Of course what we should all like to attain in writing history is style.

"The sense for style," says Whitehead " . . . is an aesthetic sense, based on admiration for the direct attainment of a foreseen end, simply and without waste. Style in art, style in literature, style in science, style in logic, style in practical execution, have fundamentally the same aesthetic qualities, namely attainment and restraint. The love of a subject in itself and for itself, where it is not the sleepy pleasure of pacing a mental quarter-deck, is the love of style as manifested in that study."

"Style, in its finest sense, is the last acquirement of the educated mind; it is also the most useful. It pervades the whole being. . . . Style is the ultimate morality of mind."

12 Unfortunately, there is no royal road to style. It cannot be attained by mere industry; it can never be achieved through imitation, although it may be promoted by example. Reading the greatest literary artists among historians will help; but do not forget that what was acceptable style in 1850 might seem turgid today. We can still read Macaulay with admiration and pleasure, we can still learn paragraph structure and other things from Macaulay, but anyone who tried to imitate Macaulay today would be a pompous ass.

13 Just as Voltaire's ideal curé advises his flock not to worry about going to Heaven, but to do right and probably by God's grace they will get there; so the writer of history had better not work consciously to develop a style but concentrate on day-by-day improvement in craftsmanship. Then perhaps he may find some day that his industry, which left readers cold, is carried to a large popular audience by something that the critics call style.

Comment

Professor Morison begins with the statement of an effect—the American reading public does not read the work of professional historians (¶1). This effect he characterizes as bad, because history should be read not only by professional historians but by the general public as well (¶1, repeated in ¶7 and 8).

What is the cause of this effect? It is the neglect by the professional historians of the art of writing in their desire to be accurate and scientific (central theme, ¶2).

How does Morison prove the connection between the effect and the cause?

First, he contrasts the classic historians, who were literary craftsmen as well as scientists, with the later school of pure research scholars (¶3).

Second, he redefines the purpose of history (¶4 and 5) as an art in which vividness is as important as accuracy.

Third, he traces the bad effects of the scientific school of historians on young scholars (¶6-8).

Fourth (¶9), he distinguishes between the teacher and the writer and thus limits his subject to the historical writer.

Fifth, he traces (¶10) the cause of bad historical writing to the faulty teaching of English in the schools by teachers of all subjects.

Sixth, he pleads for the study of good style, which he again defines and explains (¶11-13).

In short, Morison *has shown* that a writer with a bad style necessarily produces bad historical writing just as a writer with a good style (style in Whitehead's phrase is the love of subject in itself and for itself) produces good historical writing.

There are many distinctive qualities in Professor Morison's essay, such as his short introduction to the topic (¶1), his effective statement of the central theme (¶2), his use of authorities, and his vigorous language. (He also combines contrast and definition with his causal analysis.) But the outstanding characteristic of the essay is the cogency of the causal analysis, that is, the interconnection of cause and effect. This is evident in the details of Morison's proof as well as in the larger outline which is given above. For instance in paragraph 3 he asserts that "Prescott and Motley, Irving and Bancroft, Parkman and Fiske were great literary craftsmen." The effect of their conscious art, he immediately points out, was their success in their day and in our own time. Later in the same paragraph, when he wishes to show the effect of scientific history, he points ironically to the absence of readers. The infallible test of good writing, he implies, is its power to hold an audience. The ultimate effect of bad writing is to drive an audience away.

Analysis and Composition

1. Consult a biographical dictionary or other reference books and then identify the following:

Kenneth Roberts	William H. Prescott
Margaret Mitchell	John L. Motley
William Bradford	Francis Parkman
Robert Beverly	John Fiske

2. Define in a few sentences each of the following words:

monograph	artifacts	jargon
classical	aboriginal	turgid
seminar	disparagement	curé
engendered	dissertations	

3. What is the effect of putting conscious craft into writing (¶3)? What is the effect of regarding history as pure science?

4. In paragraph 6 Mr. Morison speaks of "a chain reaction of dullness." Do the sentences following this statement constitute causal analysis? Give reasons for your answer.

5. In paragraph 10 what is said to be the cause of good writing? Compare this statement with Examples II D3, and IV D.

6. After a careful reading of paragraphs 11-13 construct your own definition of style. Give three examples of good style drawn from the selections that appear in the earlier sections of this book.

7. Write a brief essay, in accordance with the outline given below, on one of the following subjects. Choose the subject with which you are most familiar.

a. Why adults read comics
b. Why an educated man should know music
c. Why we don't take advantage of public lectures
d. The effects of a world history course
e. The value of joining a student society

Outline

A. *Introduction:* State your subject and theme clearly, interestingly, and challengingly, as the subject and theme are stated in Morison's essay.

B. *History of the question:* Write several paragraphs providing the factual background necessary to understand your theme.

C. *Proof of the theme:* Show clearly by causal analysis the reason why your theme is correct.

D. *Summary and conclusion:* Restate your central theme and principal arguments in a single paragraph.

4. Why a Classic Is a Classic

BY ARNOLD BENNETT

1 The large majority of our fellow citizens care as much about literature as they care about airplanes or the program of the legislature.

WHY A CLASSIC IS A CLASSIC: from *Literary Taste and How to Form It* by Arnold Bennett. Copyright 1927 by Doubleday and Company, Inc. By permission of Doubleday and Company, The Owners of the Copyright, and Messrs. Jonathan Cape Ltd.

They do not ignore it; they are not quite indifferent to it. But their interest in it is faint and perfunctory; or, if their interest happens to be violent, it is spasmodic. Ask the two hundred thousand persons whose enthusiasm made the vogue of a popular novel ten years ago what they think of that novel now, and you will gather that they have utterly forgotten it, and that they would no more dream of reading it again than of reading Bishop Stubbs's *Select Charters*. Probably if they did read it again they would not enjoy it—not because the said novel is a whit worse now than it was ten years ago; not because their taste has improved—but because they have not had sufficient practice to be able to rely on their taste as a means of permanent pleasure. They simply don't know from one day to the next what will please them.

2 In the face of this one may ask: Why does the great and universal fame of classical authors continue? The answer is that the fame of classical authors is entirely independent of the majority. Do you suppose that if the fame of Shakespeare depended on the man in the street it would survive a fortnight? The fame of classical authors is originally made, and it is maintained, by a passionate few. Even when a first-class author has enjoyed immense success during his lifetime, the majority have never appreciated him so sincerely as they have appreciated second-rate men. He has always been reënforced by the ardor of the passionate few. And in the case of an author who has emerged into glory after his death, the happy sequel has been due solely to the obstinate perseverance of the few. They could not leave him alone; they would not. They kept on savoring him, and talking about him, and buying him, and they generally behaved with such eager zeal, and they were so authoritative and sure of themselves, that at last the majority grew accustomed to the sound of his name and placidly agreed to the proposition that he was a genius; the majority did not care very much either way.

3 And it is by the passionate few that the renown of genius is kept alive from one generation to another. These few are always at work. They are always rediscovering genius. Their curiosity and enthusiasm are exhaustless, so that there is little chance of genius being ignored. And, moreover, they are always working either for or against the verdicts of the majority. The majority can make a reputation, but it is too careless to maintain it. If, by accident, the passionate few agree with the majority in a particular instance, they will frequently remind the majority that such and such a reputation has been made, and the

majority will idly concur: "Ah, yes. By the way, we must not forget that such and such a reputation exists." Without that persistent memory-jogging the reputation would quickly fall into the oblivion which is death. The passionate few only have their way by reason of the fact that they are genuinely interested in literature, that literature matters to them. They conquer by their obstinacy alone, by their eternal repetition of the same statements. Do you suppose they could prove to the man in the street that Shakespeare was a great artist? The said man would not even understand the terms they employed. But when he is told ten thousand times, and generation after generation, that Shakespeare was a great artist, the said man believes—not by reason, but by faith. And he, too, repeats that Shakespeare was a great artist, and he buys the complete works of Shakespeare and puts them on his shelves, and he goes to see the marvelous stage effects which accompany *King Lear* or *Hamlet,* and comes back religiously convinced that Shakespeare was a great artist. All because the passionate few could not keep their admiration of Shakespeare to themselves. This is not cynicism; but truth. And it is important that those who wish to form their literary taste should grasp it.

4 What causes the passionate few to make such a fuss about literature? There can be only one reply. They find a keen and lasting pleasure in literature. They enjoy literature as some men enjoy beer. The recurrence of this pleasure naturally keeps their interest in literature very much alive. They are forever making new researches, forever practicing on themselves. They learn to understand themselves. They learn to know what they want. Their taste becomes surer and surer as their experience lengthens. They do not enjoy today what will seem tedious to them tomorrow. When they find a book tedious, no amount of popular clatter will persuade them that it is pleasurable; and when they find it pleasurable no chill silence of the street crowds will affect their conviction that the book is good and permanent. They have faith in themselves. What are the qualities in a book which give keen and lasting pleasure to the passionate few? This is a question so difficult that it has never yet been completely answered. You may talk lightly about truth, insight, knowledge, wisdom, humor, and beauty. But these comfortable words do not really carry you very far, for each of them has to be defined, especially the first and last. It is all very well for Keats in his airy manner to assert that beauty is truth, truth beauty, and that that is all he knows or needs to know. I, for one, need to know a lot more. And I never shall know. Nobody, not even Hazlitt

or Sainte-Beuve, has ever finally explained why he thought a book beautiful. I take the first fine lines that come to hand—

> The woods of Arcady are dead,
> And over is their antique joy—

and I say that those lines are beautiful because they give me pleasure. But why? No answer! I only know that the passionate few will broadly agree with me in deriving this mysterious pleasure from these lines. I am only convinced that the liveliness of our pleasure in those and many other lines by the same author will ultimately cause the majority to believe, by faith, that W. B. Yeats is a genius. The one reassuring aspect of the literary affair is that the passionate few are passionate about the same things. A continuance of interest does, in actual practice, lead ultimately to the same judgments. There is only the difference in width of interest. Some of the passionate few lack catholicity, or, rather, the whole of their interest is confined to one narrow channel; they have none left over. These men help specially to vitalize the reputations of the narrower geniuses such as Crashaw. But their active predilections never contradict the general verdict of the passionate few; rather they reënforce it.

5 A classic is a work which gives pleasure to the minority which is intensely and permanently interested in literature. It lives on because the minority, eager to renew the sensation of pleasure, is eternally curious and is therefore engaged in an eternal process of rediscovery. A classic does not survive for any ethical reason. It does not survive because it conforms to certain canons, or because neglect would not kill it. It survives because it is a source of pleasure, and because the passionate few can no more neglect it than a bee can neglect a flower. The passionate few do not read "the right things" because they are right. That is to put the cart before the horse. "The right things" are the right things solely because the passionate few *like* reading them. Hence—and I now arrive at my point—the one primary essential to literary taste is a hot interest in literature. If you have that, all the rest will come. It matters nothing that at present you fail to find pleasure in certain classics. The driving impulse of your interest will force you to acquire experience, and experience will teach you the use of the means of pleasure. You do not know the secret ways of yourself; that is all. A continuance of interest must inevitably bring you to the keenest joys. But, of course, experience may be acquired judiciously or injudiciously, just as Putney may be reached *via* Walham Green or *via* St. Petersburg.

Comment

The active causes that determine which books shall be called classics are not the majority (¶1) but the passionate few (¶2). The passionate few are continually preserving or restoring classics (¶3), i.e., operating as causes of an effect. Their principal motive, the reason why the passionate few act as causes, is a keen and lasting pleasure in literature (¶4). This motive is a permanent interest (¶5) because it is part of the nature of the passionate few, and will always produce its effect, that is, the preservation or restoration of the classics.

Analysis and Composition

1. Define the following words as they are used in the essay above:

      indifferent   classical   catholicity
      perfunctory   savoring   predilections
      spasmodic   enthusiasm   canons
      pleasure

2. In paragraphs 3-5 Bennett attempts to show that the passionate few are the positive, necessary, and immediate causes of the survival and restoration of the classics. How does he establish the interconnection between the passionate few (as cause) and the survival and restoration of the classics (as effect)?

3. In paragraph 4 how does Bennett explain the variety of taste among the passionate few? Does his explanation contradict the element of necessity in the cause-effect relationship by suggesting that sometimes the cause operates one way, sometimes another? Give reasons for your answer.

4. Compare Arnold Bennett's description of the effect of a literary classic (¶5) with Quiller-Couch's description of the effect of poetry in Example II E2. In what sense are these effects the same? in what sense different?

5. Consider carefully the following objections to Mr. Bennett's statements. State reasons for agreeing or disagreeing with these objections.

   a. Most educated people *do* know what pleases them. They express their opinions by reading or refusing to read. However, it is true that the majority of readers, as opposed to the passionate few, cannot express their reasons for enthusiasm.

   b. It is not the passionate few, but Dr. Johnson's common reader, who determines a classic. The passionate few are the advocates, the ordinary educated reader is the judge.

   c. The "passionate few" who keep the renown of genius alive from generation to generation are most likely schoolteachers and publishers.

   d. To define a classic as that "which gives pleasure to the minority which is intensely and permanently interested in literature" (i.e., the passionate few) and to define the passionate few as those who are intensely and permanently interested in the classics is to argue in a circle. Bennett says in effect that *A* is true because of *B, B* is true because of *A*.

   e. Bennett reduces literature to an unarguable matter of taste.

6. Use several causal arguments, together with other means of development, to develop one of the following subjects:

   a. Why rural New England remains beautiful

   b. Why Detroit is the automobile center of America

   c. Why Conrad (or another writer) is considered a great writer

   d. Why a college is a college

   e. Why Columbus discovered America

   f. Why students go to college

   g. Why the United Nations holds a great hope for peace

   h. Why Eisenhower was elected

   i. Why America is a world leader among nations

b. Discriminate between cause and effect and mere occasion and condition.

Why Men Came to America

BY HENRY BAMFORD PARKES

1 The impulse of migration may be described, negatively, as an impulse of escape. The American fled from a Europe where he could

WHY MEN CAME TO AMERICA: reprinted from *The American Experience* by Henry Bamford Parkes, by permission of Alfred A. Knopf, Inc. Copyright 1947 by Henry Bamford Parkes.

find no satisfying fulfillment of his energies and was confronted by conflicts and dilemmas that had no easy solution. The groups who came to all parts of the New World were, in general, those who were most acutely discontented with their status in European society and who had the least hope of being able to improve it. The Hispanic colonies were settled mainly by impoverished members of the lower nobility and by adventurers from the lower classes. Unable to achieve aristocratic status at home, they hoped to win riches, land, and glory for themselves in America. Most of the early immigrants to the United States came from the petty bourgeoisie in the English cities or from the yeoman farmers; a few were motivated primarily by the desire to put into practice novel religious or political ideas, but the majority expected to improve their economic condition. The later migration from the other European countries into both North and South America was similar in character, including some religious and political refugees, but consisting mainly of ambitious younger sons of the bourgeoisie and of oppressed and land-hungry peasants from Ireland, Germany, Scandinavia, Italy, and the Austrian and Russian empires. All sought in the New World an environment where they could act more freely, without being restricted by traditional forms of authority and discipline or by a scarcity of land and natural resources.

2 Of the various factors that caused men to come to America, the economic was no doubt the most important. Throughout the period of the migrations, there was no free land in Europe; natural resources were limited; and the population was always in danger of increasing faster than the means of subsistence. Migration always occurred chiefly from areas of Europe where agriculture was still the chief occupation and where (owing to the growth of big estates or to genuine over-crowding) the demand for land was in excess of the supply. This was true of Spain in the sixteenth century, of England in the early seventeenth, and of Ireland, Germany, Scandinavia, Italy, and the Slavic countries of the east in the nineteenth.

3 An almost equally influential stimulus to migration was the European class system. This was, in fact, perhaps the chief cause of European economic privation, since the big estates of the aristocracy diminished the supply of land available for the peasants. Before the discovery of America, European society had been molded by feudalism into a tightly knit organic structure in which every individual, from the king at the top to the humblest peasant at the bottom, was expected to know

his place and to perform the duties appropriate to it. These class differences had originated with the barbarian invasions during the fall of the Roman Empire, or even earlier, and for a thousand years they had been a deeply rooted part of the European consciousness. Ambitious and enterprising members of the middle and lower classes could sometimes improve their position, either individually or in groups, but the battle against aristocratic privilege was always difficult, and never reached a conclusion. For such persons the opening of the New World beyond the Atlantic promised an easier escape from frustration and the sense of inferiority.

4 Privation and inequality weighed upon all underprivileged persons in Europe, but did not cause all of them to come to America. Human behavior is conditioned by economic and social factors in the sense that these establish the problems to be solved, but it is not determined by them: how particular individuals choose to act in a given situation depends upon deeper, more intangible, and more mysterious forces. Confronted by the same difficulties, some individuals preferred to submit to them or to continue struggling with them, while others, generally the more restless and adventurous, decided to come to the New World. Thus the settlement of America was a selective process that attracted those members of the European middle and lower classes who had the appropriate bent and disposition; it appealed not necessarily to the ablest or the strongest, but usually to the most enterprising. In a sense it may be said that America was from the beginning a state of mind and not merely a place.

Comment

Mr. Parkes's exposition of the reasons why (cause and accompanying conditions) men came to America (effect) involves a clear discrimination between causal analysis and the analysis of occasions and conditions. These reasons are stated in order as

   a. The psychological factor, or the impulse to escape (¶1)
   b. Economic factors (¶2)
   c. The social factor, that is, the European class system (¶3)
   d. The factor of personal decision (¶4)

Note that Mr. Parkes states clearly in paragraph 4 that it was not the first three factors that operated as a strict cause (although he has loosely described them as causes in accordance with contemporary usage). Thus he says, "Human behavior is *conditioned* by economic and social factors in the sense that these establish the problems to be solved, but it is not *determined* by them: how particular individuals *choose to act* [the real cause] in a given situation depends upon deeper . . . forces."

Mr. Parkes is saying in essence that a cause is positively, necessarily, and immediately related to its effect. Hence such alleged "causes" as the psychological, economic, and social factors described in the first three paragraphs are not true causes. They are not true causes because they do not positively produce or determine the effect. If psychological, economic, and social factors, whether alone or in combination, were true causes, then two things would follow:

> a. Whenever these factors were present, everyone would emigrate, or
> b. Whenever these factors were not present, no one would emigrate.

But as Parkes points out above this is not true. "Confronted by the same difficulties, some individuals preferred to submit to them or to continue struggling with them, while others . . . *decided* to come to the New World." (It is also true that many who were not oppressed psychologically, economically, or socially came to America.)

In short, the true cause of migration is the decision to act; the various psychological, economic, and social factors are only the occasions and conditions which assist in the operation of the cause.

Analysis and Composition

1. Define the following expressions:

impulse	environment	factors
dilemmas	stimulus	intangible
status	privation	selective process
petty bourgeoisie	feudalism	

2. Paragraph 1 is developed by a division of the class, American immigrant. Reread the introduction to Section III and then write a short outline of this division.

3. In paragraph 3 Parkes states that the European class system "was, in fact, . . . the chief cause of European economic privation." Does he show the interconnection of cause and effect here? Give reasons for your answer.

4. The concluding sentence of paragraph 4 sums up the passage by stating that America was "a state of mind and not merely a place." Is this state-

ment a classification of America as a logical whole and a physical whole? Do not frame your answer before rereading the introduction to Section III.

5. Analyze the following situation to determine which was the cause and which were the conditions or occasions of Mr. Smith's death: One afternoon John Smith's doctor told him that he had heart disease and that he should avoid shock. The doctor was in error, as he had confused Smith's medical record with that of a namesake. Alarmed, Smith decided to ride home in a taxi rather than in a crowded bus. The taxi driver, who had neglected to test his brakes, bumped into a parked car. Smith became excited. He hastily paid the driver and began to walk across the street. In his confusion he did not notice a bus swinging around the corner. The bus driver, assuming Smith had seen him, failed to apply his brakes in time. The bus struck Smith and killed him.

6. The guidance officer of State University listed the following factors as explanations of James Jones's difficulties in freshman year. Which factors are causes, which conditions or occasions?
   a. Failure to plan his study hours
   b. Excessive interest in social activities
   c. An antagonistic roommate
   d. Indifference of his parents to educational progress
   e. Dislike of the required course in mathematics
   f. Unexcused absences from classes
   g. A limited understanding of the purposes of the college course he is taking
   h. Worry about the draft
   i. A series of heavy colds
   j. Fear of failure

7. In your study of American history you may have discovered a character named Pedro de Silva. Nothing is known of de Silva until he appears in the Wyoming territory in the 1880's. From that time on his name is mentioned frequently in frontier documents. A court record refers to him as an expert interpreter of French, Spanish, and German. The library of the Wyoming Historical Society contains his 50,000-word history of the Crow Indians, written in flawless English and showing a master's knowledge of Indian life. A well-founded oral tradition describes de Silva as a tall, courteous man, somewhat reserved, but extremely anxious to help his neighbors. He derived his livelihood from breeding and selling horses. When he died there was an unusual display of bereavement throughout the whole territory.

Regard these facts as effects and consequences of unknown causes and antecedents in de Silva's previous history. Although you cannot name these causes and antecedents exactly, what can you infer about their essential nature from the facts stated above? Frame your answer in a short essay entitled "De Silva's Background Reconstructed."

8. Write a short essay on one of the following subjects, or on a similar subject of interest to you. When necessary, discriminate between the real cause and other relevant factors.

a. Why I came to college
b. Why the Korean War happened
c. Why I admire the Lincoln Memorial
d. Why I prefer to live in _____
e. Why some authority is necessary in a free country

C. Explain causes that are obscure or difficult by analysis of their effects; explain effects by analysis of an existing and operating cause.

---

1. The Last Question of All

BY C. E. MONTAGUE

I

All lines of thought about literature lead to one ultimate question. It lies at the end of more roads than Rome ever did. Why are we moved as strongly and as strangely as we are by certain simple groupings of a few ordinary words?

Bacon says that the nature of things is best seen in the smallest possible quantities of them. Take, then, some unit or atom of beautiful

THE LAST QUESTION OF ALL: reprinted from *A Writer's Notes on His Trade* by C. E. Montague, by permission of Chatto and Windus, publishers, London, and the estate of C. E. Montague.

writing—a line of verse or a sentence of prose that has stirred you
uncommonly. It may be Falstaff's "We have heard the chimes at midnight"; or

> the tide of pomp
> That beats upon the high shore of this world.

Or

> visited all night by troops of stars,

in Coleridge's "Hymn Before Sunrise." How comes it that these special sequences of quite common words can take hold of you with a
high hand, filling your mind and thrilling it with a poignant ecstasy,
a delicious disquiet, akin to the restlessness and the raptures of lovers?
When I was an idle boy going to school and discovered the lines, out
of Scott,

> Yet the lark's shrill fife may come
> At the day-break from the fallow,
> And the bittern sound his drum,
> Booming from the sedgy shallow,

they made me so drunk with delight that I had to walk up and down
empty compartments of trains, saying them over and over again, as
incapable as a bluebottle either of sitting quiet or ceasing to hum.
The adult Stevenson would seem to have been bitten by much of the
same gadfly when first he read certain verses of Meredith's "Love in
the Valley":

> Lovely are the curves of the white owl sweeping
> Wavy in the dusk lit by one large star.

He told Mr. Yeats how he went about whooping the heavenly stuff to
the Dryads of the Riviera, "waking with it all the echoes of the hills
about Hyères." Everybody must know the sensation. But how to account for it?

2

Of course you can easily go a small part of the way towards a full
explanation. In the Meredith lines, for example, certain contributory
lures and graces are obvious—the engaging "Sing a song o' sixpence"
melody, the play that is made with a few picked consonants, winged
and liquidly gliding, and the winning way the second line is retarded
at its close by the three stressed monosyllables, like a well-mannered
horse pulled up by a well-mannered rider. The Scott passage, too, has

its taking devices of craftsmanship. There is the deftly managed consonantal chord of *bdf* pervading it to its advantage. There is the drumlike beat of its main vowels and the reedy hiss of the successive sibilants to help evoke the picture in the two last lines.

Such devices are not to be sniffed at. They help. They are like jewels and lace skilfully worn by a beautiful woman. But these are not the intrinsic and ultimate beauty of their wearer. The Venus of Melos had none; and some of the most lovely sentences ever written are almost as bare of any applied ornament, anything we can detach and define. The critical analyst has to throw up his hands, almost at once, when he tries to precipitate with his acids the charm of

> Brightness falls from the air;
> Queens have died young and fair;
> Dust hath closed Helen's eye,

or of

> She walks in beauty, like the night
> Of cloudless climes and starry skies.

The context, of course, counts for something: every gem is the better for a fine setting. But no gem of the first water is made by its setting. These small splinters of perfection in the art of letters would still bewitch us if they had no context at all. As if to prove as much, Shakespeare struck off one of them—

> Childe Roland to the dark tower came—

and left it contextless, to haunt the minds of poets like one of the isolated granules of beauty surviving from the Greek anthology. For it, too, has the essential gem-like quality—a kind of dazzling unreason, as it may seem at first sight—a power of taking you captive without giving you any materials for a presentable explanation of your surrender.

3

If we cannot say why we capitulate thus, we may at least try to fix and describe the sensations that visit us while the charm is at work.

For one thing, we are deeply excited. We are shaken or lifted out of our ordinary state of consciousness. Many of our faculties are, for the moment, enhanced. We feel keener perceptions coming into action within us. We are given the use of more than our normal stock of penetrative sympathy: we feel that we can enter into people's feelings and understand the quality of their lives better than ever before.

Another effect of the drug is that, while it is acting strongly, the whole adventure of mankind upon the earth gains, in our sight, a new momentousness, precariousness, and beauty. The new and higher scale of power in ourselves seems to be challenged by an equal increase in the size of the objects on which it is exercised. Living becomes a grander affair than we had ever thought.

A third effect on the mind is a powerful sense—authentic or illusory— of being in the presence of extraordinary possibilities. You feel as if new doors of understanding and delight were beginning to open around you. Some sort of mysterious liberation or empowerment seems to be approaching. You are assured, in an unaccountable way, that wonderful enlightenments, still unreceived, are on their way to you, like new stars that are nearing the point in space at which they will come within range of our sight.

4

These sensations may not be defined or measured as closely as doctors measure a patient's temperature, his pulse, and his blood pressure. And yet they are worth describing, if only because you will find that you are also describing something else by the way. The nearer you get to saying just what you feel, when under the spell of great writing, the nearer are you, too, to defining the state of mind and heart in which great things are written.

Comment

Outline (*numbers correspond to numbered sections in essay*)

1. We are moved strongly and strangely by simple groupings of ordinary words such as the lines quoted from
   a. Shakespeare
   b. Coleridge
   c. Scott
   d. Meredith
2. The reason for our emotion is only partly explained by
   a. Exquisite sound
   b. Context
3. We cannot explain exactly the mysterious cause of our emotional response to literature, but we may describe its effects as

a. Deep excitement or penetrative sympathy
b. An increased scale of imaginative power
c. An extraordinary sense of liberation

4. From these characteristic effects we may come to understand the essential characteristics of the cause, that is, the mind and heart of the writer.

Thus Montague describes the mysterious cause of literary excitement by an analysis of effects.

Analysis and Composition

1. Define each of the following expressions:

poignant ecstasy	presentable explanation
delicious disquiet	capitulate thus
Dryads of the Riviera	enhanced
consonantal chord	penetrative sympathy
intrinsic and ultimate beauty	momentousness
precipitate with his acids	precariousness
isolated granules of beauty	empowerment

2. Montague's metaphors here are splendid auxiliaries to his causal analysis. (See Section V, introduction and D1 and 2 comment for the use of metaphors as an aid to argument.) Show how the following metaphors and similes contribute to the exposition of effects by making these effects more vivid and emphatic:

a. "As incapable as a bluebottle either of sitting quiet or ceasing to hum"
b. "Whooping the heavenly stuff"
c. "Winged and liquidly gliding"
d. "Like a well-mannered horse pulled up by a well-mannered rider"
e. "The drum-like beats . . . and the reedy hiss"
f. "Like jewels and lace skilfully worn by a beautiful woman"
g. "These small splinters of perfection"
h. Literature as a "drug"
i. "New doors of understanding and delight"
j. "As doctors measure a patient's temperature, his pulse and his blood pressure"

3. List some characteristic effects of experiences like
a. Listening to music
b. Observing great painting
c. Notre Dame Cathedral at midnight on Christmas
d. The Grand Canyon at sunset

4. Write a short composition describing the characteristic effects of one of the subjects developed in answer to Exercise 3.

2. We Must Not Despair

BY WINSTON S. CHURCHILL

1 One of the questions which you are debating here is defined as "the failure of social and political institutions to keep pace with material and technical change." Scientists should never underrate the deep-seated qualities of human nature and how, repressed in one direction, it will certainly break out in another. The *genus homo*—if I may display my Latin, I have some—not much—the *genus homo* is a tough creature who has travelled here by a very long road. His nature has been shaped and his virtues ingrained by many millions of years of struggle, fear, and pain, and his spirit has, from the earliest dawn of history, shown itself upon occasion capable of mounting to the sublime, far above material conditions or mortal terrors. He still remains, man still remains, as Pope described him two hundred years ago:

> Placed on this isthmus of a middle state,
> A being darkly wise, and rudely great . . .
> Created half to rise and half to fall,
> Great lord of all things, yet a prey to all;
> Sole judge of truth, in endless error hurled,
> The glory, jest, and riddle of the world.

2 In his introductory address, Dr. Burchard, the Dean of Humanities, spoke with awe of "an approaching scientific ability to control men's thoughts with precision." I shall be very content, personally, if my task in this world is done before that happens. Laws just or unjust may govern men's actions. Tyrannies may restrain or regulate their words. The machinery of propaganda may pack their minds with falsehood and deny them truth for many generations of time. But the soul of man thus held in a trance or frozen in a long night can be awakened by a spark coming from God knows where, and in a moment the whole structure of lies and oppression is on trial for its life. Peoples in bondage need never despair. Let them hope and trust in the genius of mankind. Science, no doubt, if sufficiently perverted, could exterminate us all, but it is not in the power of material forces, at present

WE MUST NOT DESPAIR: from "The Twentieth Century, Its Promise and Realization" by Winston S. Churchill. Published in *Mid-Century* (John E. Burchard, editor) by the Technology Press of Massachusetts Institute of Technology, and John Wiley & Sons, Inc., New York. Reprinted by permission of the publishers.

or in any period which the youngest here tonight need take into practical account, to alter permanently the main elements in human nature
and restrict the infinite variety of forms in which the soul and genius
of the human race can and will express itself.

3 How right you are, Dr. Compton, in this great institution of technical study and achievement, to keep a Dean of Humanities and give
him so commanding a part to play in your discussions! No technical
knowledge can outweigh knowledge of the humanities in the gaining
of which philosophy and history walk hand in hand. Our inheritance
of well-founded slowly conceived codes of honor, morals, and manners,
the passionate convictions which so many hundreds of millions share
together of the principles of freedom and justice, are far more precious
to us than anything which scientific discoveries could bestow. Those
whose minds are attracted or compelled to rigid and symmetrical
systems of government should remember that logic, like science, must
be the servant and not the master of man. Human beings and human
societies are not structures that are built or machines that are forged.
They are plants that grow and must be tended as such. Life is a test
and this world a place of trial. Always the problems, or it may be the
same problem, will be presented to every generation in different forms.
The problems of victory may even be more baffling than those of defeat.
However much the conditions change, the supreme question is how we
live and grow and bloom and die, and how far each human life conforms to standards which are not wholly related to space or time.

Comment

Churchill here argues that scientists should never underrate the deep-
seated qualities of human nature. The *genus homo* (mankind) as a cause
will necessarily reject tyranny (effect). Note how, in paragraph 1, Churchill
defines the *genus homo* as tough, enduring, and capable of mounting to
the sublime. In paragraph 2 he shows that *genus homo* as a cause will
always result in the exercise of liberty. In paragraph 3 he further defines the genus man in terms of humanistic knowledge, in contrast to mere
technical knowlege and rigid systems of logic. The third paragraph reinforces the argument by adding to our knowledge of the cause, the *genus
homo*. Thus mankind is seen not only as tough, enduring, and capable of
mounting to the sublime, but also as the inheritor of codes of honor, morals,
and manners, and as passionately convinced of the value of liberty and
justice.

Analysis and Composition

1. Define each of the following expressions as they are used in the context of the selection:

nature	technical knowledge
sublime	symmetrical systems of government
material conditions	conditions
genius of mankind	standards

2. Show how the quotation from Alexander Pope (*Essay on Man,* Epistle 2, 11-12; 15-18) in paragraph 1 helps you to understand what the *genus homo* is.

3. In paragraph 2 Churchill states the effect that results from the nature of mankind—that man can always react against the structure of lies and oppression. But he also implies other effects, such as the permanence of the main elements of human nature, one of which is the love of liberty. State one additional effect implied in paragraphs 2 and 3.

4. The effectiveness of Churchillian prose depends on several elements, one of which is the use of figurative language such as personification and metaphor. Churchill employs personification, that is, the endowment of things or ideas with personal qualities, when he says, "Tyrannies may restrain or regulate. . . ." "Science . . . could exterminate us all. . . ." "Logic . . . must be the servant and not the master of man." Churchill uses metaphor, that is, an implied comparison between two things of a different class, when he says, "The machinery of propaganda may pack their minds. . . . But the soul of man thus held in a trance or frozen in a long night can be awakened by a spark. . . . Human beings . . . are not structures . . . or machines. . . . They are plants that grow. . . ." Show how these figures of speech create an emotional and imaginative impression in line with Churchill's purpose.

5. Churchill is noted for his effective sentence structure. Analyze the sentences in paragraph 2 according to the following directions:
   a. Point out several examples of effective parallel structure.*
   b. Point out three examples of effective subordination.†
   c. Point out the various types of sentences used: simple, complex, compound.
   d. Point out one periodic sentence and one sentence arranged in the order of climax.

---

* See handbooks: Foerster, *86*; Hodges, *26*; Kierzek, *56*; Perrin, pp. 282-83; Wykoff, *74.*

† See handbooks: Foerster, *69*; Hodges, *24*; Kierzek, *47*; Perrin, pp. 257-59; Wykoff, *77.*

6. Write a paragraph developing one of the following subjects. Discover the effects by an analysis of the italicized cause or causes.

   a. The effects of *an unbalanced education*.
   b. What will *the draft* do to our reserve of scientific specialists?
   c. Will *a bad diet* destroy the energies of the human race?
   d. Do *bigoted parents* have bigoted offspring?
   e. A *merely technological society* cannot cope with the complex problems of modern society.
   f. Depend upon it, *mothers* will always take care of their children.
   g. A *self-seeking politician* will not serve the best interests of his country.
   h. An *insensitive person* cannot write a poem.

GENERAL EXERCISES

A

The Usefulness of Semantics

BY HUGH R. WALPOLE

1 In the past few years, semantics has caught the interest of the general public. And the general public shows a sound instinct. Semantics [the study of the meaning of words] is a very practical business. The common-sense aspect of it renders it as appealing to the man in the street as to the scholar. Whatever his trade, any serious reader may expect the study of semantics to profit him in three ways.

2 *He will understand better what he hears and reads.*

3 The average man cannot grasp what he hears. Massive psychological evidence in support of this contention would only confirm what our worldly-wise knowledge of scandal and rumor and propaganda tells us already. Considering the famous Martian broadcast incident alone, we would be justified in concluding that we are not perfectly equipped to interpret the evidence of our ears. That involuntary hoax was startlingly effective. Every quarter of an hour, the invasion was halted while an announcer told the audience that this was only a play. A twiddle of the dial either way would immediately have put the listener in auditory contact with more pacific performers, including Messrs. Bergen and McCarthy. At the end of the play, the audience was again reassured by Mr. Orson Welles himself: "If your doorbell rings and nobody's there, that was no Martian—

THE USEFULNESS OF SEMANTICS: reprinted from *Semantics* by Hugh R. Walpole. By permission of W. W. Norton & Company, Inc. Copyright 1941 by Hugh R. Walpole.

it's Hallowe'en!" Yet, immediately afterwards, thousands of people were pouring forth along the roads and streets of New Jersey with wet cloths over their faces. A professor took his torch and geologist's hammer and journeyed out in search of meteorites.

4 Less spectacular samples of serious misunderstanding happen every day. A recent breakdown in communication took place among a learned committee whose very task it was to diagnose such breakdowns. The committee was listening to the reading of a report. In a certain phrase came the word "di-śent," which I must give in its phonetic spelling. When the whole thing had been read, a certain member of the committee said that this word had puzzled him. "When you spoke of 'our common di-śent from the tyrannies of Europe,'" he asked, "was that word d-e-s-c-e-n-t or d-i-s-s-e-n-t?" They found the place, and the whole committee went into committee over the word. But they could not agree which it should be, either from the look of the word on paper or from its meaning in its context.

5 We are no better at understanding what we read. "Retarded children" have a strong representation in the primary grades of our schools. Our educational curricula are cluttered with courses in "remedial reading." Nor do these measures for curing the misinterpretators seem very successful, for similar disabilities are found in every high school and every university. This is no place to go into detailed evidence, but the reader who consults the published works of E. G. Biaggini, William Gray, and I. A. Richards will be convinced that befuddled reading goes on on a grand scale in the colleges and universities of Australia, the United States, and England.

6 Semantics, which shows why words are coined and how they function, is a remedy. The thoughtful educator should give it a chance, whether he is concerned to improve himself or to teach his classes to read better.

7 *He will talk and write more effectively.*

8 Misinterpretation is only half the fault of the listener. Semantics will help speakers and writers to see why misunderstanding occurs. Familiarity with the nature of the symbol-situation should teach the speaker the difference between speech and verbosity. His study of Fictions will show him how to use simpler language when it is appropriate; and practice with the Theory of Definition will increase his skill in communicating his thoughts to a particular audience. He will be better able to convince and persuade when he understands the workings of Metaphor, and when he realizes the different jobs an utterance can do.

9 *He will think more accurately.*

10 This is most important of all. Now, more than ever, men need to foster and strengthen their own powers of keen and unflurried thought. They need greater powers; and they stand in danger of losing such powers as they have. Countries are at war in all five continents. Aggressive leaders, directing totally organized forces, are trying to kill the possibility of ordinary men ever being men again.

11 And today a world at peace would still be a world in danger. Our minds have not kept pace with the almost inconceivable changes in our physical means of transport and communication. Less than fifty years has seen the birth of the Diesel engine, the airplane, moving pictures, wireless telegraphy, radio, telephotography, and television. The earth shrinks rapidly under our feet. A period of time which a century ago would have been consumed while the Londoner was traveling to Bath is now sufficient to take the New Yorker to Moscow. And we no longer have to go to a place in order to hear it—to see it, even. Soon everyone will have the possibility of almost instantaneous communication with everyone else on earth. Two thousand million pairs of ears and eyes, ripe to be swayed; and the forces that want to sway them will not bother to pause every fifteen minutes to warn their audience not to take them literally.

12 The time will come when educators will co-operate in the task of arming their peoples against the dangers of misreading and half-hearing. That, perhaps, must wait for the suppression of those riding masters who sweat to be conquerors. In the meantime the individual will try to clarify his own thoughts, to "cultivate his own garden." Semantics will help him to think more accurately because, by showing how words and thoughts are connected, it helps one to draw the line between verbal and mental problems. He will be less *dependent* on words, better able to concentrate on thoughts, whatever their verbal clothing.

Mr. Walpole here proposes to show that the study of semantics (cause) will help the serious reader in three ways (effects):

   a. By helping him to understand better what he hears and reads
   b. By helping him to talk and write more effectively
   c. By helping him to think more accurately

Read this passage carefully and then answer the following questions:

1. According to Mr. Walpole, what good effects will the study of semantics produce? To what extent are these good effects the result of the *positive* influence of semantics as a cause?
2. How does the author show that there is a *necessary* connection between semantics as a cause and better understanding, talking, writing, and thinking?
3. Cite several instances in which the author shows that semantics is an *immediate* cause of an effect.
4. Decide whether this passage is a convincing demonstration of causal analysis. In forming your decision remember that the writer may substantially live up to the rules of causal analysis without rigidly adhering to them.

5. Semantics is the science of the meaning of words. The meaning of a word is determined by many factors, chief among which are

a. The etymology, or derivation, of the word

b. The past use of the word (see Section II A)

c. The context in which the word is used (see II A, C, D)

d. The intention of the writer (see II J)

e. The response of the reader (see handbooks) *

Thus it is not always easy to determine what people mean when they say X is a *liberal,* or Y a *conservative,* or Z a *radical.* The words may be used denotatively or connotatively. They may refer to political realities or they may not. They may be used to praise or to blame.

Determine how each of the following words may stand for three different meanings by examining them in terms of the five factors stated above. Then use the three meanings of each word in three original sentences.

agnostic	skeptic	mystic
realism	romanticism	idealism
chivalry	feudalism	medieval
scientific	religious	rationalistic
taboo		

6. A word is an innocent neutral in the struggle to clarify ideas. It is the writer's abuse of words that causes us to say, "This word is inexact." Words may be abused

a. When a writer does not know precisely what he wants to say

b. When he knows what he wants to say but attaches his private meaning to the conventional meaning of words

c. When he deliberately uses words to deceive

What other reasons can you find for the abuse of words?

B

Analyze one topic from each of the following groups by listing causes and effects:

1. Why we study: English, history, mathematics, foreign languages, social sciences.

2. Why we read: newspapers, magazines, poetry, fiction.

3. Why we admire: saints, scholars, scientists, heroes.

4. Why we seek: education, property, reputation.

5. Why we hope: to travel, to have leisure, to own an island.

6. Why we are impressed by: the Eiffel Tower, London Bridge, St. Peter's in Rome.

* Foerster, *57*; Hodges, *1, 20a*; Kierzek, *36a*; Perrin, pp. 322-24; Wykoff, *92c*.

7. Why we fought: the Civil War, World War I, World War II, the Korean War.
8. Why we hate: tyranny, cowardice, disloyalty.
9. Why we laugh at: clowns, fuddy-duddies, pretenders.
10. Why we obey: parents, policemen, professors.

C

List one or more *conditions* necessary for the activity of the following causes:

1. Launching a ship
2. Studying for an examination
3. Playing football
4. Holding a lawn tennis tournament
5. Using a public library
6. Training a hound dog
7. Conversing with a foreigner
8. Giving a radio address
9. Buying a house
10. Voting in the regular elections

D

First review the distinctions between cause and effect and conditions, occasions, and antecedents in the introduction to this section and in the comment on Example B. Then determine which of the following statements confuse causes and conditions or occasions. Give reasons for your answers.

1. Charles I was a most unsuccessful king because he was beheaded by his people.
2. Immediately after the election of F. D. Roosevelt we went to war. This shows that Roosevelt wanted war.
3. "After drinking two quarts of Vitex I began to feel better. I owe my present good health to your splendid medicine."
4. War is always caused by the have-nots' envy of the haves.
5. If you mix olive oil and vinegar you will have a simple French dressing.
6. Ghost towns were the result of two factors: the exhaustion of the mines and the lack of families in the population. The population of the old mining towns did not reproduce itself because there were no women.
7. The phenomenal growth of San Francisco in the 1860's was due to three factors: first, its excellent harbor; second, its bracing climate; third, an excellent municipal government which wiped out crime, protected new industries, and encouraged the immigration of substantial citizens.

8. The results of American democratic government were a free and independent citizenry, the encouragement of Yankee ingenuity, a disregard for the trappings of authority, a demand for education.

9. The bad effects of the Korean War are a heavy loss of men and matériel. The good effects are the repulse of communist aggression, the destruction of a large part of the enemy's war potential, and the winning of time to prepare for the future.

10. Science has changed our life by providing rapid means of transport and communication, by improving public health, and by providing new forms of work.

E

Determine which of the following statements is best developed by proceeding from cause to effect; which by proceeding from effect to cause. Give reasons for your answer.

1. The probability of the Allied success in the Normandy invasion could be judged by the extent of their preparation and the nature of their plans.

2. Today we sow the seeds of tomorrow.

3. The story of the Mongol race is shrouded in mystery, but we know what they were like from their conquests in China, Russia, and eastern Europe.

4. Many students do not know what science is, but they see in television, radio, aviation, medicine, and industry what science does.

5. We know nothing about the blind poet Homer except what we read in his *Iliad* and *Odyssey*.

6. Shakespeare's biography is his collected works.

7. Australia is the land of the future.

8. The political reforms and the advanced social legislation in the 1930's were evidences of the changing attitude of the American voter.

9. The student of history is not concerned with predicting the future. He is concerned with a past event or a present reality. He wants to know what was done, how it was done, who did it, and why they did it.

10. We may safely leave the future of our state in the hands of the Whig party. Their leaders are all men of integrity, as the names of Burke, Fox, and Townshend testify. The principles upon which the party is founded are based on liberty under law. The party's specific programs for reform include a reduction of taxes and an extension of the voting franchise.

F

Using causal analysis, write an essay of approximately 1000 words on one of the topics listed in General Exercise B.

SECTION VII

Process Analysis

IN PROCESS analysis, as we have mentioned in Section I, we investigate a subject by noting how it functions or how it happens. Thus process analysis differs from the other methods of analysis. It is not directly concerned with *what* the subject *is* (definition, classification and division, example), or with what it is *like* or *unlike* (comparison and contrast), or with *why* it is and what it *can do* (cause and effect). Process aims chiefly to explain the *way* a subject *came about* or the way it *functions*.

Essentially, then, a process analysis will be concerned with a history of events or a sequence of operations. These events or operations may be divided into three classes:

History, which deals with the record of man's experience.
Nature, which deals with the principles of the natural sciences, such as biology, physics, chemistry, and so on.
Logic, which deals with the rules of thought.

The first class aims to recite events in a certain order, the second to describe the operations of nature, the third to explain the principles of correct thinking.

Let us explain each of these types of process analysis and discover the principle appropriate to each class.

THE METHOD OF ANALYZING AN HISTORICAL PROCESS

Certain subjects, such as those that attempt to show how something came about, necessarily involve historical explanation. Thus to understand the subject "How New York City Became a Metropolis" the writer is obliged to deal with a sequence of events in time. His analysis will be chiefly *circumstantial*.

He may begin with New York just before the opening of the Erie Canal and trace the growth of the city step by step, in *time* from the 1800's to the present, in *place* from lower Manhattan to the outlying boroughs, in *persons* from a population of under a hundred thousand to a population of almost eight million, in *objects* from a few hundred buildings and a few miles of paved streets to thousands of buildings and hundreds of miles of pavement. Other *circumstances* that would engage his attention would be the *manner* of life, the way New Yorkers earned their living and used their leisure.

Such a study of the circumstances of New York's growth is distinct from definition, classification, causal analysis, and the other methods of analysis previously studied. True, in the course of a process analysis there may be occasional references to the other methods of analysis. But process is not *directly* concerned with them. Process concentrates on how the subject came about.

Let us take another example of this kind of process analysis. Recently a student chose to write an expository essay on "The Seeing-Eye Dog." The student decided that he could best achieve his purpose, not by defining or classifying his subject or by tracing causal relationships, but by simply stating the most important circumstances in the process of selecting and training a seeing-eye dog. Thus his preliminary outline read as follows:

A. The selection of seeing-eye dogs
    1. The arrival at the school of a new batch of dogs, chiefly German shepherds, collies, retrievers
    2. The physical examination of the dogs
    3. The psychological testing of the dogs for undesirable traits such as fear, excitability, and so on
B. The training of the dogs
    1. General training in obedience to commands
        a. The system of rewards and punishments
        b. Training in response to given signals
    2. Accustoming the dog to harness
    3. Teaching the dog to adjust his pace to that of the blind
    4. Teaching the dog not to obey a command which would endanger his master

As in the first example, this outline is developed according to process analysis, namely by the enumeration of details or circumstances related in a definite time order.

Hence the appropriate principle for this type of process is: *Make an historical process clear by indicating the principal stages in the sequence of events.*

This type of process is illustrated in the essays by Richard Henry Dana, A1, and Charles Beard, A2.

THE METHOD OF ANALYZING A NATURAL PROCESS

But process is not only concerned with history. The record of nature, as it appears in biology, chemistry, physics, and other natural sciences, is also studied effectively in process analysis.

In reporting on his observations or experiments in the various natural sciences, the student will be called upon constantly to explain his subject by process analysis. Here, however, he must not only set forth the sequence of events or the stages of his experiment, but he must also account for the biological, chemical, or physical changes that occur during the process. Note how in the following student outline both these rules are observed; the sequence is clear, and the changes are explained in terms of the following laws: (a) Extremely high temperatures change the composition of matter; thus heating changes liquid to vapor and, contrariwise, (b) cooling a vapor results in a liquid.

How Gasoline Is Made from Crude Oil

Theme: Making gasoline involves two steps: (a) the production of kerosene from crude oil and (b) the production of gasoline from kerosene. Both these steps illustrate the effect of heat on the physical states and the chemical composition of matter.

A. Kerosene is derived from crude oil
   1. By heating crude oil to vaporize the light kerosene fraction
   2. By condensing this fraction to form liquid kerosene
B. Gasoline is derived from kerosene
   1. By vaporizing kerosene
   2. By subjecting this vapor to extremely high temperatures, **thus** forming gasoline vapor
   3. By condensing this vapor to liquid gasoline

Hence the appropriate principle for this type of process is: *Make a natural process clear (a) by explaining the sequence of an operation and (b) by explaining the natural law which is the principle of the operation.*

We shall see the application of this principle in Alan Devoe's study of the biological phenomenon of hibernation in B1 and in Frederick Graham's explanation of the physical law of flight with reference to the helicopter in B2.

THE METHOD OF ANALYZING A LOGICAL PROCESS

The third type of process is not concerned with the external events of history or with the operations of nature but with logical method itself. Process analysis of this kind investigates the method of reasoning employed in writing or speaking. It examines the definitions, classifications and divisions, examples, comparisons and contrasts, causal analysis, and process itself to determine how these methods of analysis work. It is thought about thought, the mind contemplating its own operations.

Such an analysis necessarily rests on first principles, and may be stated thus: *Make a thought process clear by showing how it conforms to the essential rules of reasoning, namely deduction and induction.*

We shall see this principle in operation in Example C, "The Method of Scientific Investigation" by Thomas Henry Huxley.

Note: For examples of extended process analysis see the following essays in Section X: "The Industrial Revolution in Great Britain," "Faith for Freedom," and "The Dime Novel Heroine"; and "The Retort Circumstantial" and "Save Europe by Uniting Europe" in Section XI.

a. Make an historical process clear by indicating the principal stages in the sequence of events.

1. My First Day's Duty

BY RICHARD HENRY DANA

1 This was my first day's duty on board the ship, and though a sailor's life is a sailor's life, wherever it may be, yet I found everything very different here from the customs of the brig *Pilgrim*. After all hands were called, at daybreak, three minutes and a half were allowed for every man to dress and come on deck, and, if any were longer than that, they were sure to be overhauled by the mate, who was always on deck, and making himself heard all over the ship. The head pump was then rigged, and the decks washed down by the second and third mates, the chief mate walking the quarter-deck and keeping a general supervision, but not deigning to touch a bucket or a brush. Inside and out, fore and aft, upper deck and between-decks steerage and forecastle, rail, bulwarks, and waterways, were washed, scrubbed, and scraped with brooms and canvas, and the decks were wet and sanded all over, and then holystoned. The holystone is a large, soft stone, smooth on the bottom, with long ropes attached to each end, by which the crew keep it sliding fore and aft, over the wet, sanded decks. Smaller hand stones, which the sailors call "prayer books," are used to scrub in among the crevices and narrow places, where the large holystone will not go. An hour or two we were kept at this work, when the head pump was manned and all the sand washed off the decks and sides.

2 Then came swabs and squilgees; and, after the decks were dry, each one went to his particular morning job. There were five boats belonging to the ship—launch, pinnace, jollyboat, quarter-boat, and

gig—each of which had a coxswain, who had charge of it, and was answerable for the order and cleanness of it. The rest of the cleaning was divided among the crew; one having the brass and composition work about the capstan; another the bell, which was of brass, and kept as bright as a gilt button; a third, the harness cask; another, the manrope stanchions; others, the steps of the forecastle and hatchways, which were hauled up and holystoned. Each of these jobs must be finished before breakfast; and, in the meantime, the rest of the crew filled the scuttlebutt, and the cook scraped his kids (wooden tubs out of which the sailors eat) and polished the hoops, and placed them before the galley, to await inspection.

3 When the decks were dry, the lord paramount made his appearance on the quarter-deck, and took a few turns, when eight bells were struck, and all hands went to breakfast. Half an hour was allowed for breakfast, when all hands were called again; the kids, pots, bread bags, etc., stowed away; and, this morning, preparations were made for getting under weigh. We paid out on the chain by which we swung, hove in on the other, catted the anchor, and hove short on the first. This work was done in shorter time than was usual on board the brig; for, though everything was more than twice as large and heavy, the catblock being as much as a man could lift, and the chain as large as three of the *Pilgrim's,* yet there was a plenty of room to move about in, more discipline and system, more men, and more good will.

4 Everyone seemed ambitious to do his best: officers and men knew their duty, and all went well. As soon as she was hove short, the mate, on the forecastle, gave the order to loose the sails, and, in an instant, everyone sprung into the rigging, up the shrouds, and out on the yards, scrambling by one another—the first up the best fellow—cast off the yardarm gaskets and bunt gaskets, and one man remained on each yard, holding the bunt jigger with a turn round the tye, all ready to let go, while the rest laid down to man the sheets and halyards. The mate then hailed the yards—"All ready forward?"—"All ready the crossjack yards?" etc.; and, "Aye, aye, sir!" being returned from each, the word was given to let go; and in the twinkling of an eye the ship, which had shown nothing but her bare yards, was covered with her loose canvas, from the royal mastheads to the decks.

5 Everyone then laid down, except one man in each top to overhaul the rigging, and the topsails were hoisted and sheeted home, all three yards going to the masthead at once, the larboard watch hoisting the fore, the starboard watch the main, and five light hands (of whom I

was one), picked from the two watches, the mizzen. The yards were then trimmed, the anchor weighed, the catblock hooked on, the fall stretched out, manned by "all hands and the cook," and the anchor brought to the head with "cheerily men!" in full chorus. The ship being now under weigh, the light sails were set, one after another, and she was under full sail before she had passed the sandy point.

Comment

Dana here recites the events of his first day aboard a new ship. Note how the process analysis follows a definite time sequence, from daybreak to mid-morning. This essay also explains the standard procedure for setting sail. The order of events is as follows:

A. All hands on deck
B. Cleaning ship
    1. Washing down of decks by second and third mates
    2. Washing, scrubbing, and sanding of remainder of ship by crew
    3. Cleaning of the five small boats by the coxswains
    4. Polishing of brightwork by crew
    5. Cleaning of galley
C. Breakfast
D. Preparations for getting under weigh
    1. Paying out the chain of one anchor
    2. Catting the second anchor
    3. Heaving short on the first anchor
    4. Casting off the gaskets
    5. Laying down to man the sheets and halyards and loosing sails
    6. Setting the topsails and trimming the yards
    7. Weighing anchor and bringing it to the head
E. Ship under weigh

Note how this process analysis includes circumstances of time, person, place, object, and degree which supply concrete and vivid detail.

Analysis and Composition

1. Consult an unabridged dictionary for the meaning of the following terms:

    launch   catting the anchor
    pinnace   heaving short on the anchor

jollyboat	casting off yardarm gaskets and bunt
quarter-boat	gaskets
gig	manning the sheets and halyards
paying out on the chain	trimming the yards

2. Show how the identification of the objects and operations listed in Exercise 1 helps to complete your idea of the whole action.

3. In approximately 500 words develop by process analysis one of the following subjects:
   a. How a plane gets off the ground
   b. The standard operating procedure for landing a passenger plane
   c. How to land a salmon
   d. My first day's duty as a camp counselor
   e. Spring training begins
   f. Orientation week for freshmen
   g. My mother organizes spring cleaning
   h. How to get a book from the library
   i. How to practice golf
   j. My first class in public speaking
   k. How to prepare for an examination
   l. How to avoid congested traffic

2. How the Common Law Developed

BY CHARLES A. BEARD

The first great source of American jurisprudence is the English common law.* Its characteristic feature consists in the fact that its rules are not to be found in a code enacted by the legislature, as is generally the case on the continent of Europe, but in decisions of the courts spread over several centuries. The law is thus built up and developed by judicial rulings. To discover the principle that governs in any particular question, an attorney practicing in a jurisdiction where the common law prevails must find out what has been previously determined by the courts and be guided by their decisions.

---

* Louisiana, whose law is derived from the continental system, is an exception. There are some southwestern states which are not regarded as common law states.

HOW THE COMMON LAW DEVELOPED: from Charles A. Beard, *American Government and Politics*. Copyright 1939 (eighth edition) by The Macmillan Company and used with their permission.

Origins

The common law began its development in medieval England. When a case came before the royal justices in the Middle Ages they tried to ascertain the prevailing custom bearing on the subject and decide the question in accordance with it. Theoretically they did not make the law, but merely formulated the practices of the community into legal rules and gave them an official sanction. As a matter of fact they did make the law, for they interpreted the customs and had the power to select some and discard others, especially if there was a conflict. When another case involving the same point was brought before the judges, they generally followed the rule laid down in the decision of the first case. If however it was thought that the original finding was incorrect or that conditions had changed, they would override the previous decision and work out a new doctrine. Thus flexibility was always possible—one of the best features of the common law. In this way a body of precedents was built up and a set of legal doctrines developed. When an entirely novel case came up, some "general principle" of the common law was evoked in its determination.

Equity

As the common law developed, it gradually became more and more crystallized and less pliant. The judges tended to be technical, and any litigant whose case did not fall within certain well-defined classes was liable to be denied the relief really due him. In numerous instances in which obvious injustice was done there was no remedy at law.

These deficiencies of the common law were countered by the development of a new body of jurisprudence along with it—a system known as *equity*. It was customary for a person who felt that he had been wronged and could obtain no remedy at law to petition the king or the king's chancellor for special consideration. The granting of this favor was at first considered an executive act and purely a matter of grace, but gradually the chancery evolved into a regular court with its own body of equity principles, which were much more elastic and far less technical than the ordinary law. Equity therefore gave relief when none could be had at law; and in many instances where the legal remedy was inadequate it accorded the satisfaction that was really demanded by the plain justice of the situation.

For example, the only redress granted at law for wrongs done to persons or property is money damages, but equity goes much farther and will command a person to do something which is for the benefit of the plaintiff. Thus, in some kinds of contracts, a court of equity will compel the party in default actually to perform his part of the agreement on pain of imprisonment. Again, equity will command a person, by an order called an "injunction," to refrain from doing something which is injurious and unjust to the plaintiff.

English Law Carried to America

The English systems of law and equity just sketched were brought to America. When the colonies cast off allegiance to Great Britain, some of the state constitutions provided that the common law should continue in force; but without such a provision, it was binding in American courts and is applied today in so far as it has not been modified by legislation. Very few commonwealths, however, have retained the system of separate chancery courts. Generally the same court administers both law and equity, and the term "common law" has come to include both law in its technical sense and equity.

State Variations

Although the common law as administered in the various states constitutes a single system of jurisprudence, it has undergone modification in the different jurisdictions. Thus, for instance, on many points the "common law" of Massachusetts and New York will be found to differ. In each state the interpretation which is binding is made by its court of last resort; and as different courts will hold varying views on what is or ought to be the law on a particular topic, the rules applied in different commonwealths will vary. But the courts of each state by no means disregard the decisions of sister states. While the latter are not considered as authoritative as the precedents of the state in which the case is tried, they are treated as advisory statements of the law and have great moral weight, particularly in matters which have not been passed on in that jurisdiction.

Comment

Beard makes the historical development of the common law clear by defining his subject and then tracing it through successive stages of development.

Definition: The common law is a system of jurisprudence which derives its principles from precedents set up by previous decisions, rather than by the enactments of the legislature.

Stage 1. The common law began in medieval England when justices decided cases according to prevailing custom.

Stage 2. Deficiencies in the common law resulted in the development of equity.

Stage 3. The common law and the rules of equity were carried over from England to the American colonies.

Stage 4 (the present). After achieving their independence, the new states modified the common law and the rules of equity in the light of their own experience.

Analysis and Composition

1. Write out a complete logical definition of each of the following terms:

jurisprudence	custom	redress
common law	community	contracts
code	litigant	commonwealth
principle	equity	precedents
jurisdiction	chancery	

2. In your own words show how the rules of equity were a natural historical outgrowth from problems inherent in the common law.
3. How did the American commonwealths modify English common law and equity?
4. Indicate the beginning and the principal stages in the *development* of one or more of the following historical processes. (The student may profitably consult a history text or an encyclopedia.) *
   a. From restricted suffrage to universal suffrage in the United States
   b. How the Labor party developed in England
   c. The rise of the Dixiecrats

* See handbooks: Foerster, *38*; Hodges, *33b1-3*; Kierzek, pp. 172-86; Perrin, pp. 369-77; Wykoff, *48*.

    d. How group medicine developed

    e. Baseball, from its beginnings

    f. Home rule for Ireland

    g. How the unions became a factor in national politics

    h. The growth of a city

    i. How air transport developed

5. Indicate the historical high point and the principal stages in the *decline* of one or more of the following historical processes:

    a. The decline of the Roman Empire (or the Spanish, French, or English Empires)

    b. Water traffic on the Mississippi

    c. The horse in transportation

    d. The Chautauqua circuit

    e. The camp meeting

    f. Splendor in masculine dress

    g. Home entertainment

    h. Formal manners

    i. Fourth of July celebrations

6. Write a composition of about 500 words based on your analysis of one of the topics listed in Exercise 4 or 5.

7. Historical development is often expressed in terms of analogies with human growth or mechanical change. Thus we speak of the growth of a nation in terms of its birth, infancy, youth, maturity, and old age, or we explain a process of political change in terms of action and reaction. Use these analogies, or a more appropriate analogy of your own choice, to explain one or more of the following processes:

    a. How the movies lost out

    b. How the French radicals became conservative

    c. How monarchy disappeared

    d. How I grew to like poetry

    e. How American isolationists became internationalists

    f. How the Puritans became Yankees

    g. How the Klan revived

    h. How professional football started

    i. How wrestling got its black eye

    j. How our population shifted from farm to city

8. Write a composition of 500 words on one of the topics in Exercise 7. Use process analysis.

b. Make a natural process clear (1) by explaining the sequence of an operation and (2) by explaining the natural law which is the principle of the operation.

1. The Hibernation of the Woodchuck

BY ALAN DEVOE

1 The woodchuck's hibernation usually starts about the middle of September. For weeks he has been foraging with increased appetite among the clover blossoms and has grown heavy and slow-moving. Now, with the coming of mid-September, apples and corn and yarrow tops have become less plentiful, and the nights are cool. The woodchuck moves with slower gait, and emerges less and less frequently for feeding trips. Layers of fat have accumulated around his chest and shoulders, and there is thick fat in the axils of his legs. He has extended his summer burrow to a length of nearly thirty feet, and has fashioned a deep nest-chamber at the end of it, far below the level of the frost. He has carried in, usually, a little hay. He is ready for the Long Sleep.

2 When the temperature of the September days falls below 50 degrees or so, the woodchuck becomes too drowsy to come forth from his burrow in the chilly dusk to forage. He remains in the deep nest-chamber, lethargic, hardly moving. Gradually, with the passing of hours or days, his coarse-furred body curls into a semicircle, like a foetus, nose-tip touching tail. The small legs are tucked in, the hand-

THE HIBERNATION OF THE WOODCHUCK: from *Lives Around Us,* copyright 1942 by Alan Devoe; a Creative Age Press book. Farrar, Straus and Young, Publishers.

like clawed forefeet folded. The woodchuck has become a compact ball. Presently the temperature of his body begins to fall.

3 In normal life the woodchuck's temperature, though fluctuant, averages about 97 degrees. Now, as he lies tight-curled in a ball with the winter sleep stealing over him, this body heat drops ten degrees, twenty degrees, thirty. Finally, by the time the snow is on the ground and the woodchuck's winter dormancy has become complete, his temperature is only 38 or 40. With the falling of the body heat there is a slowing of his heartbeat and his respiration. In normal life he breathes thirty or forty times each minute; when he is excited, as many as a hundred times. Now he breathes slower and slower—ten times a minute, five times a minute, once a minute, and at last only ten or twelve times in an hour. His heartbeat is a twentieth of normal. He has entered fully into the oblivion of hibernation.

4 The Long Sleep lasts, on an average, about six months. For half a year the woodchuck remains unmoving, hardly breathing. His pituitary gland is inactive; his blood is so sluggishly circulated that there is an unequal distribution in the chilled body; his sensory awareness has wholly ceased. It is almost true to say that he has altered from a warm-blooded to a cold-blooded animal.

5 Then, in the middle of March, he wakes. The waking is not a slow and gradual thing, as was the drifting into sleep, but takes place quickly, often in an hour. The body temperature ascends to normal, or rather higher for a while; glandular functions instantly resume; the respiration quickens and steadies at a normal rate. The woodchuck has become himself again, save only that he is a little thinner, and is ready at once to fare forth into the pale spring sunlight and look for grass and berries.

6 Such is the performance each fall and winter, with varying detail, of bats and worms and bears, and a hundred other kinds of creature. It is a marvel less spectacular than the migration flight of hummingbirds or the flash of shooting stars, but it is not much less remarkable.

Comment

Mr. Devoe observes three stages in the hibernation of the woodchuck: Stage 1. The period of preparation, intensified during the first half of September (¶1)

Stage 2. The long sleep or hibernation from late September until March (¶2-4)

Stage 3. The reawakening in mid-March (¶5)

Each stage is clearly marked by time sequence, and by the biological condition of the woodchuck during each of the three periods. The biological principle explained is the adaptation of a life pattern to climate and food supply.

Analysis and Composition

1. Define:

hibernation	lethargic	respiration
foraging	fluctuant	pituitary
axils	dormancy	

2. What are the characteristics of the woodchuck during each of the three stages of hibernation?

3. List the periods or stages of one of the following states or activities:

human sleep	digestion	the hiving of bees
circulation of the blood	nutrition	the migration of wild
the foraging of ants for	osmosis	geese
food	ocean currents	from caterpillar to but-
photosynthesis in plants	breathing	terfly

4. Compose an outline for a composition that uses the method of process. List the details of each stage of the process you have selected to answer Exercise 3. Be sure to correlate the natural law which is the principle of the operation with the process.

5. Write a brief composition using process and following the outline constructed for Exercise 4 above.

2. The Helicopter

BY FREDERICK GRAHAM

1 It is in the very nature of the helicopter that its great versatility is found. To begin with, the helicopter is the fulfillment of one of man's earliest and most fantastic dreams. The dream of flying—not just like

THE HELICOPTER: reprinted from the New York *Times Magazine* of August 17, 1952, by permission of the author and the publisher.

a bird—but of flying as nothing else flies or has ever flown. To be able to fly straight up and straight down—to fly forward or back or sidewise, or to hover over one spot till the fuel supply is exhausted.

2 To see how the helicopter can do things that are not possible for the conventional fixed-wing plane, let us first examine how a conventional plane "works." It works by its shape—by the shape of its wing, which deflects air when the plane is in motion. That is possible because air has density and resistance. It reacts to force. The wing is curved and set at an angle to catch the air and push it down; the air, resisting, pushes against the under surface of the wing, giving it some of its lift. At the same time the curved upper surface of the wing exerts suction, tending to create a lack of air at the top of the wing. The air, again resisting, sucks back, and this gives the wing about twice as much lift as the air pressure below the wing. This is what takes place when the wing is pulled forward by propellers or pushed forward by jet blasts. Without the motion the wing has no lift.

3 Now the helicopter combines in its whirling rotor blades—which are merely long, thin wings—both the function of the conventional wing, which is lift, and the function of the propeller, which is thrust. As the blades whirl around the top of the helicopter fuselage the air passes over and under them, giving enough lift to hoist the plane up. By changing the angle of pitch of the whirling rotors, the pilot gives the plane direction. If he tilts the blades forward, the plane goes ahead; if he hauls them back, the craft flies backward. By tilting them to one side or the other he moves to his right or left, and when the angle of pitch is flattened the craft hovers over one spot. This tilting is accomplished by the most important part of the helicopter's moving mechanism—called the rotor head—which is mounted at or near the top of the drive shaft from the power plant.

4 The advantages of the helicopter are fairly high forward speeds—say, 100 plus miles an hour today, with perhaps double that speed forecast for the future—and low speeds which may be slowed to no speed at all as the craft hovers. It does not have to maintain high forward speed to keep aloft and for that reason can nose its way through heavy weather at one mile an hour. That speed makes collision with ground objects less likely and less dangerous than with fixed-wing planes. Another advantage of the "windmill" is that it needs little space for take-off and landing.

5 To offset the advantages are some present disadvantages, although none of them is critical or insurmountable. There may be some question

of safety in the hands of pilots not thoroughly familiar with the helicopter's peculiarities. For one thing, the helicopter cannot fly in strong winds with the same stability—meaning assurance of steady, dependable wing-lift—of the heavy, fixed-wing plane. It will never be as fast as the speediest fixed-wing plane. It cannot fly high enough—say, 18,000 to 20,000 feet—to go over rough, turbulent weather. Certainly, it is not at this stage of development a plane for the average family. Helicopter designers say, however, that most of these disadvantages will some day be overcome.

Comment

Paragraph 1 gives a simple definition of the helicopter. The two principles which explain how the helicopter works are:

1. Lift, or the force of the air against the surface of the rotor blades (¶2)
2. Thrust, or the force of the whirling rotor blades (¶3)

Lift is first explained in terms of the conventional fixed-wing plane, and then in relation to the helicopter. The helicopter's rotor blades perform the function of the conventional wing, lift, *and* of the conventional propeller, thrust. The principle of operation explained, the author then turns in S2, ¶3, to the actual process of helicopter flight. Paragraphs 4 and 5 comment on the advantages and disadvantages of the helicopter in the light of its performance.

Analysis and Composition

1. Define fully the following technical terms:

helicopter	fuselage
density and resistance of air	angle of pitch
lift	rotor head
rotor blades	power plant
thrust	

2. Draw up an outline for one of the following subjects. Be sure you understand the principle of operation.
   a. How a gasoline engine works
   b. How a hydraulic brake works

    c. How a sewing machine operates
    d. How to lay brick
    e. How to install a fencepost
    f. How a lightning rod operates
    g. How a dress is designed
    h. The essentials of radar
    i. Automatic transmission in automobiles
    j. How a slot machine works

3. Write a composition, based on process, on the subject you outlined in answer to Exercise 2.

C. Make a thought process clear by showing how it conforms to the essential rules of reasoning, namely deduction and induction.

The Method of Scientific Investigation

BY THOMAS HENRY HUXLEY

1 The method of scientific investigation is nothing but the expression of the necessary mode of working of the human mind. It is simply the mode at which all phenomena are reasoned about, rendered precise and exact. There is no more difference, but there is just the same kind of difference, between the mental operations of a man of science and those of an ordinary person, as there is between the operations and methods of a baker or of a butcher weighing out his goods in common scales, and the operation of a chemist in performing a difficult and complex analysis by means of his balance and finely graduated weights. It is not that the action of the scales in the one case, and the balance in the other, differ in the principles of their construction or manner of working; but the beam of one is set on an infinitely finer axis than

the other, and of course turns by the addition of a much smaller weight.

2 You will understand this better, perhaps, if I give you some familiar example. You have all heard it repeated, I dare say, that men of science work by means of induction and deduction, and that by the help of these operations, they, in a sort of sense, wring from Nature certain other things, which are called natural laws, and causes, and that out of these, by some cunning skill of their own, they build up hypotheses and theories. And it is imagined by many, that the operations of the common mind can be by no means compared with these processes, and that they have to be acquired by a sort of special apprenticeship to the craft. To hear all these large words, you would think that the mind of a man of science must be constituted differently from that of his fellow men; but if you will not be frightened by terms, you will discover that you are quite wrong, and that all these terrible apparatus are being used by yourselves every day and every hour of your lives.

3 There is a well-known incident in one of Molière's plays, where the author makes the hero express unbounded delight on being told that he has been talking prose during the whole of his life. In the same way, I trust that you will take comfort, and be delighted with yourselves, on the discovery that you have been acting on the principles of inductive and deductive philosophy during the same period. Probably there is not one here who has not in the course of the day had occasion to set in motion a complex train of reasoning, of the very same kind, though differing of course in degree, as that which a scientific man goes through in tracing the causes of natural phenomena.

4 A very trivial circumstance will serve to exemplify this. Suppose you go into a fruiterer's shop, wanting an apple—you take one up, and, on biting, you find it is sour; you look at it, and see that it is hard, and green. You take up another one and that too is hard, green, and sour. The shop man offers you a third; but, before biting it, you examine it, and find that it is hard and green, and you immediately say that you will not have it, as it must be sour, like those that you have already tried.

5 Nothing can be more simple than that, you think; but if you will take the trouble to analyse and trace out into its logical elements what has been done by the mind, you will be greatly surprised. In the first place, you have performed the operation of induction. You found, that, in two experiences, hardness and greenness in apples went together

with sourness. It was so in the first case, and it was confirmed by the second. True, it is a very small basis, but still it is enough to make an induction from; you generalize the facts, and you expect to find sourness in apples where you get hardness and greenness. You found upon that a general law, that all hard and green apples are sour; and that, so far as it goes, is a perfect induction. Well, having got your natural law in this way, when you are offered another apple which you find is hard and green, you say, "All hard and green apples are sour; this apple is hard and green, therefore this apple is sour." That train of reasoning is what logicians call a syllogism, and has all its various parts and terms—its major premise, its minor premise, and its conclusion. And, by the help of further reasoning, which, if drawn out, would have to be exhibited in two or three other syllogisms, you arrive at your final determination. "I will not have that apple." So that, you see, you have, in the first place, established a law by induction, and upon that you have founded a deduction, and reasoned out the special conclusion of the particular case. Well now, suppose, having got your law, that at some time afterwards, you are discussing the qualities of apples with a friend: you will say to him, "It is a very curious thing—but I find that all hard and green apples are sour!" Your friend says to you, "But how do you know that?" You at once reply, "Oh, because I have tried them over and over again, and have always found them to be so." Well, if we were talking science instead of common sense, we should call that an experimental verification. And, if still opposed, you go further, and say, "I have heard from the people in Somersetshire and Devonshire, where a large number of apples are grown, that they have observed the same thing. It is also found to be the case in Normandy, and in North America. In short, I find it to be the universal experience of mankind wherever attention has been directed to the subject." Whereupon your friend, unless he is a very unreasonable man, agrees with you, and is convinced that you are quite right in the conclusion you have drawn. He believes, although perhaps he does not know he believes it, that the more extensive verifications are—that the more frequently experiments have been made, and results of the same kind arrived at—that the more varied the conditions under which the same results are attained, the more certain is the ultimate conclusion, and he disputes the question no further. He sees that the experiment has been tried under all sorts of conditions, as to time, place, and people, with the same result; and he says with you, therefore, that the law you have laid down must be a good one, and he must believe it.

6 In science we do the same thing;—the philosopher exercises precisely the same faculties, though in a much more delicate manner. In scientific inquiry it becomes a matter of duty to expose a supposed law to every possible kind of verification, and to take care, moreover, that this is done intentionally, and not left to a mere accident, as in the case of the apples. And in science, as in common life, our confidence in a law is in exact proportion to the absence of variation in the result of our experimental verifications. For instance, if you let go your grasp of an article you may have in your hand, it will immediately fall to the ground. That is a very common verification of one of the best established laws of nature—that of gravitation. The method by which men of science establish the existence of that law is exactly the same as that by which we have established the trivial proposition about the sourness of hard and green apples. But we believe it in such an extensive, thorough, and unhesitating manner because the universal experience of mankind verifies it, and we can verify it ourselves at any time; and that is the strongest possible foundation on which any natural law can rest.

Comment

Huxley here explains carefully, in a series of closely knit expository paragraphs, the logical processes of deduction and induction.

Scientific investigation is merely the finer expression of ordinary principles of analysis used by everyone in the day-to-day conduct of life (¶1).

Thus induction and deduction are merely technical names for everyday habits of thought (¶2).

Just as Molière's character was delighted to find out that he spoke prose, so the average man should be delighted to hear that he uses induction and deduction every day (¶3).

A familiar example of *induction* is the conclusion, from a few tastes, that hard, green apples are sour; a familiar example of *deduction* is the decision not to buy the untasted hard, green apples because they are sour (¶4-5).

The principles of induction and deduction inherent in these familiar examples are based on logic (¶5) and also apply to scientific investigation (¶6).

A careful reading of this passage, together with a review of the remarks on deduction and induction in Sections III and IV, will lead the student to the following inferences about deductive and inductive reasoning:

Ten Principles of Deduction and Induction

a. In rhetoric the inductive process consists in the development of a general statement from several specific examples.

b. A scientific induction is characterized by a more exact and more complete experimental verification than is necessary or desirable in ordinary exposition or argument.

c. In rhetoric the inductive process is similar to the process of classifying. This is true because when we discover that a number of particular things (such as hard, green apples) have a characteristic quality in common (such as sourness) we are classifying those things according to that quality. (See page 69.)

d. From Huxley's example in paragraph 5 we may infer that a syllogism is the *complete* external form of the deductive argument.

e. Analysis of Huxley's syllogism (¶5) reveals that, essentially, the syllogism consists of two propositions (premises) so connected that a third proposition (conclusion) necessarily follows. In other words, the conclusion is inherent in the premises.

f. In a syllogism the major premise validly asserts a quality characteristic of a general class; the minor premise validly asserts that a species or individual is a member of that general class; the conclusion asserts that the species or individual possesses the characteristic of the class of which it is a member. In other words, what is true of a class is true of a member of the class.

g. The connection between the major and minor propositions (or premises) of a syllogism is exactly expressed by the following formulas:

$$A = B \quad B = C \quad A = C$$

h. A valid syllogistic process involves no more and no less than three propositions and no more and no less than three terms, as expressed in the formula $A = B$; $B = C$; $A = C$.

i. In the formula $A = B$; $B = C$; $A = C$ the connecting link (or middle term) B must be used in exactly the same sense in both the major premise and the minor premise. Otherwise, instead of three factors, A, B, and C, we would have four factors, and the syllogistic process would be invalid. We would in effect be saying $A = B^1$; $B^2 = C$. There is no conclusion inherent in these premises, because B^1 and B^2 are separate terms.

j. In rhetoric we do not use the complete form of the syllogism, but rather an abbreviated form called the *enthymeme*. In the enthymeme we state the conclusion and the major or the minor premise. We omit one premise because it is clearly implied. Hence, in rhetoric, we do not say:

A law which relieves the taxpayer of an unjust burden should be passed.
But this law relieves the taxpayer of an unjust burden.
Therefore this law should be passed.

Rather we say:

Pass this law because it will relieve the taxpayer of an unjust burden.

or:

Pass this law because a law which relieves the taxpayer of an unjust burden should be passed.

Analysis and Composition

1. Consult an unabridged dictionary and the handbooks * for definitions of

induction	premise	enthymeme
syllogism	deduction	proposition

2. The ten statements listed in the comment above contain the basic principles of deductive and inductive reasoning. Prepare for a classroom discussion of these statements by proposing objections to each of them.

3. The last seven statements (*d* to *j*) listed in the comment above concern the syllogism. If you have analyzed and discussed these statements thoroughly you should be able to discover the flaws in a faulty syllogism or enthymeme, as, for example, in the following three instances:

a. Animals cannot think.
   But men are animals.
   Therefore men cannot think.

This is a false process of reasoning because the middle term "animal" is used in two different senses (see statement *i* above). In the major proposition the middle term refers to all animals, while in the minor proposition it refers to rational animals. The principle stated in *f* is also violated because the major premise is not valid.

b. All geniuses are mad.
   But Shakespeare is a genius.
   Therefore Shakespeare is mad.

This is false reasoning because the major premise asserts that madness is a quality of the general class "genius" (see statement *f* above). Madness is a quality of some geniuses, but not necessarily of all geniuses.

* Foerster, *99*; Wykoff, pp. 12-18.

  c. To refute a false enthymeme, first expand it to its full syllogistic form:
   He is a marine; therefore he is tough.
   The implied major premise is: All marines are tough.
   Thus the complete syllogism reads:
>   All marines are tough.
>   But he is a marine.
>   Therefore he is tough.

   The major premise is of doubtful validity (see statement *f* above).
4. Pick out the flaws in the following syllogisms and enthymemes by referring to the appropriate rule listed in the comment.
   a. The white race is civilized.
    The Vikings were members of the white race.
    Therefore the Vikings were civilized. (Consult *i* above.)
   b. He studied the classics in youth and hence was a man of conservative
    tastes. (Consult *f* and *i* above.)
   c. He is a Negro, and therefore a descendant of slaves. (Consult *f* and *i*.)
   d. We ought to do what is expedient.
    But compromise is expedient.
    But justice is the most expedient of all qualities of a true statesman.
    Hence a true statesman will always do what is expedient. (Consult
    e and *h* above.)
   e. Economic well-being is a sign of high civilization.
    But the Swedes are economically superior to the English.
    Therefore the Swedes are more civilized than the English. (Consult
    e and *h*.)
   f. England is traditionally conservative.
    But the British Labor party is anticonservative.
    Therefore the British Labor party is anti-English. (Consult *f*, *h*,
    and *i*.)
   g. Opposites cancel each other out.
    Science and poetry are opposites.
    Therefore you can be a scientist or a poet but not both. (Consult *f*
    and *h*.)
   h. There is no power higher than the human conscience, and so I will
    do exactly as I please. (Consult *h* and *j*.)
   i. There is no such thing as deduction because all reasoning is based
    on facts. (Consult *e*, *f*, and *i*.)
5. State in syllogistic form the basic reasoning in each example in Section
   VI.
6. Write a short composition explaining the deductive or inductive method
   of thought used in one or more of the selections in Section VI.

GENERAL EXERCISES

A

Write a composition of approximately 500 words, using the method of historical process. Be sure to arrange your events in a series of stages.

Suggested Topics

The Korean War
The kitchen stove—from Grandmother's time to today
The Pilgrim turkey—from farm to table
How an assembly line works
How to register for voting
How a suburb develops
How a championship team is organized
How the Community Chest helps a community
How UNESCO started

B

Below is reproduced a process analysis of the mechanical clock by A. L. Kroeber. Note that the principle of operation is the regulated transmission of power; that the stages of the process are (a) power, (b) transmission of power, and (c) regulation of power. Note also that Kroeber blends his exposition of mechanical process with historical process. (See especially the second sentence, paragraph 1.) After a careful reading decide whether this process analysis of the mechanical clock is sufficiently clear for the average reader. Give reasons for your answer.

The Mechanical Clock

BY A. L. KROEBER

1 The essential parts of a mechanical clock or watch are: first, the power, now usually a coiled spring, originally a weight descending from a pulley, as in our cuckoo clocks; second, a series of meshed wheels, at least three in number but usually more, which transmit the power and successively slow the motion, and the last of which carries and turns the hour hand (minute and second hands are later additions); and third, the escapement,

THE MECHANICAL CLOCK: from *Anthropology* by A. L. Kroeber, copyright, 1923, 1948, by Harcourt, Brace and Company, Inc.

which finally slows and regulates the clock's motion to the needed tempo. Each of these three systems, respectively concerned with power, transmission, and regulation, which together make up a mechanical timepiece, has its own history and cultural significance.

2 As to power, it was almost inevitable that this should at first be supplied by falling weights: both on the analogy of falling water or sand, and because the pulley had been familiar in Europe and the Near East since the time of the ancients. The first mechanical clocks were set high, in palace or church towers, serving as they did a whole city. Here their weights had plenty of the needed drop; and there would be an attendant to come around daily and crank back up the great load that was necessitated by the crudeness with which the rest of the mechanism operated. Thus the clock completed by de Vick in Paris in 1370 was driven by a quarter-ton weight that descended thirty-two feet daily. The weight for the strike mechanism was almost three times as heavy. In mills, where power is unfolded, the development has been downward from modest to larger and larger machinery. In clocks, the development has been downward from tower to table and wrist-band size.

3 The transmission, which dilutes the power into slow motion, is the most constant feature of mechanical clocks. It consists today, as it did in the beginning, of a series of cogged gears, the greater wheels engaging small pinions on the axles of the other large wheels. The question arises why this principle, which was perfectly well known in antiquity, was so late as the Middle Ages in being applied to clocks. One reason is the imperfection of mesh in gears made by carpenter's or blacksmith's manipulation, an imperfection that has already been recognized as a factor in the slow development of power mills. A second reason is that the ancients, though they perfectly well understood the principle of the cogwheel, were not accustomed to operate with it. It took, as we have seen, centuries for the vertical water wheel to triumph over the horizontal, largely because it required a single mesh to convert from its vertical motion to the horizontal motion of the millstones. The longest "chain" of transmission recorded from antiquity is a cyclometer—a sort of speedometer to record distance traveled by a cart or wagon—which consisted of five wheels and four screw pinions. The problem was one of converting wheel revolutions into recorded miles; power was provided by the harnessed beasts, and the question of speed was not considered. Even at that, this "hodometer" seems to have been only an occasional luxury gadget, something like the "south-pointing" chariot devices of ancient China. When the most comprehensive application of a mechanical principle is in a toy or sport, it is evident that the principle is not yet firmly rooted in the associated utility techniques, or has already been largely displaced in them.

4 The first clock escapements, large and heavy, were of the type called "foliot balance and verge escape." This means that the saw teeth of the third and last wheel alternately engaged and pushed aside projections on the verge rod, turning this part-way back and forth. Across the verge rod, and swinging with it, was a bar weighted at the ends, the foliot balance, which slowed and more or less regulated the escape movement. In fact, it swung with momentum enough not only to recoil the wheel at each check, but each time actually to raise a little the quarter-ton driving weight at the other end of the transmission. Instead of a steady tick-tock, the sound of such a mechanism must have been a slow whirrrr-bang—almost more like a small pile-driver than like a modern clock.

1. State (a) the principle of operation, (b) the essential parts, and (c) the order of operation of each of the following mechanisms:

A mechanical bell	A bicycle
A monkey wrench	A transformer
A water faucet	A shotgun

2. Write a brief composition using process on one of the topics listed in the above exercise.

3. Write a composition based on some scientific observation or experiment in chemistry, biology, or physics, or in any other area of science that you have studied. In preparing your composition be sure to include the following points:
   a. The purpose of the observation or experiment
   b. The various stages of the observation or experiment
   c. The relationship of each stage to the previous stage and the one following
   d. The conclusions you may draw from the observation or experiment

C

Write a composition of approximately 800 words analyzing the inductive and deductive reasoning in one of the following examples:

a. II D3, Samuel Eliot Morison
b. II F, Lewis Mumford
c. III C3, Philip Rahv
d. IV D, Mark Twain
e. V C2, Aldous Huxley

REVIEW EXERCISES
FOR SECTIONS I-VII

Use the various methods of analysis alone or in combination according to the requirements of your purpose and occasion.

In Sections I-VII we have considered the first two elements of rhetoric, namely the determination of a subject in the light of occasion and purpose (Section I) and the six methods of analyzing a subject—definition, classification and division, examples, comparison and contrast, causal analysis, and process analysis (Sections II-VII). Our purpose in studying these six methods of analysis was to understand how to derive the central theme, and how to develop the theme according to each of the several methods.

However, in most extended compositions, the various methods of analysis are not used singly. Just as the builder of a house uses the separate skills of the stonemason, bricklayer, carpenter, plasterer, painter, and plumber to accomplish his purpose, so too the writer of a composition combines the separate methods of analysis to develop his central theme.

When the writer has decided on his central theme in the light of his purpose and occasion, he will normally locate, at the same time, a principal method of development. But he is not restricted to this method of development. Thus, for example, if a writer decides upon the central theme—The immediate causes of the Korean War may be traced to the activity of the North Korean communists—his main line of development will obviously be causal analysis. But he may also use specific examples to illustrate the activity of the Korean communists, or he may use an historical process to show how the Korean War developed.

Under no circumstances should the student regard the separate methods of analysis as mutually exclusive. The use of definition does not exclude the use of classification and division; a causal development does not exclude the effective use of process. Rather the student should learn how to use any or all of these methods in whatever combination is most effective to achieve his purpose.

A

1. The main method of development used in Examples III C2 and C3 ("On Weekend Guests" by Russell Lynes and "Paleface and Redskin" by Philip Rahv) is classification and division. Show how both writers also employ comparison, contrast, and examples. List any additional method of analysis you can find.

2. The main method of development used in Example IV D ("Fenimore Cooper's Literary Offenses" by Mark Twain) is exemplification. Show how Mark Twain also employs definition, classification, and division.

3. One method of development used by T. Harry Williams in the example cited in Section IV, General Exercise A, is exemplification. Show how he also uses process and comparison and contrast.

4. The main method of development used by Learned Hand in Example V C1 is comparison and contrast. Show how Judge Hand also employs definition and process.

5. The main method of development used by Aldous Huxley in Example V C2 is comparison and contrast. Show how Mr. Huxley also uses process, causal analysis, and definition.

6. The main method of development used by Samuel Eliot Morison in Example VI A3 is causal analysis. Show how Mr. Morison also employs process and examples.

7. The main method of development used in Example VII C is process. Show how Thomas Henry Huxley also employs definition and classification and division.

8. The main method of development used by A. L. Kroeber in General Exercise B, Section VII, is process. Show how Kroeber also uses definition and division.

B

1. After reviewing Section II, select the one of the ten ways of effective definition that would be most useful in each of the following cases. Give reasons for your answer.

> Sample: To define a *liberal*. Most useful way: II A, that is, to distinguish between the denotation and connotation of the word. The reason for the choice of this method is that the word *liberal* has many connotations today. Some of these connotations are: anti-conservative, free-thinker, social reformer, supporter of the Fair Deal, defender of civil rights.

   a. To define the subject *comics* for an audience of adolescents.
   b. To define *democracy* in the concluding paragraph of a speech on democracy in action.
   c. To define the *ideal college man* in an introduction to a long composition on the ideals of American education.
   d. To define *loyalty* in a manner to excite contempt for its opposite.
   e. To define the *title of a composition* on "Reading, Writing, and Conversation—Essential Elements in the Life of a College Man."
2. Write a brief composition on one of the subjects listed above. Use definition and one other method of development.

C

Reread the introduction to Section III and the outlines and analysis of Examples C2 and C3. Then complete the following exercises as directed.

1. Suggest a reasonable principle according to which you could divide your working day at college. In accordance with that principle, write an outline for an expository essay of 500 words. Then complete the composition.
2. State the division in one chapter of a textbook you are currently using. In a short composition show whether or not the division is clear, complete, and appropriate. Point out any other kinds of analysis that you find in the chapter.

D

Reread Section IV. Then complete the following exercises as directed.

1. In a short paragraph supply several direct or immediate examples for each of the following subjects:

a typical Yankee	a time waster
maternal vigilance	bad taste in conversation
small talk	undue humility
silly euphemisms	

2. In a short paragraph supply realistic details that will help develop one or more of the following sentences:
   a. The greatness of a leader depends upon two powers: the power to understand popular desires and the power to disregard those desires for the good of the people.
   b. Civil liberty is an abstraction until someone tries to take it away from you.
   c. My favorite walk takes me past several diverting shop windows.
   d. I have never entered an automobile race, but I know what it must be like after yesterday's trip on the express highway.
   e. My three aunts, all undisputed queens of their respective kitchens, fought for supremacy in planning the family Christmas dinner.

E

Reread Section V. Then complete the following exercises as directed.

1. In your own words define a strict comparison.
2. List several points of likeness and difference between each of the following pairs:
   a. Military service and civil service
   b. The study of English in high school and the study of English in college
   c. The study of the humanities and the study of science
   d. Tom Sawyer and Huckleberry Finn
   e. General Eisenhower and General MacArthur
3. Show how each of the following pairs are *not* comparable in at least one important respect.

   Sample: A sedan and a truck. They cannot be compared on the basis of comfort, for the truck is not designed for comfort.

   a. The executive arm of the American government and the executive arm of the British or French government
   b. A novel and a play
   c. A play and a movie
   d. A freshman and a senior
   e. A state university and a private university
4. In your own words define a similitude.
5. Show how each of the following similitudes may help to arouse imagination or emotional reactions:
   a. A man's career compared to the role of an actor in a play
   b. A president of a corporation compared to the captain of a football team
   c. The process of justice compared to a scale

    d. A disorderly life compared to an unweeded garden
    e. A thoughtless argument compared to a reckless cavalry charge

F

Reread Section VI. Then complete the following exercises as directed.

1. List at least one positive, necessary, and immediate effect for each of the following causes or groups of causes:
    a. The application of a torch to dry wood
    b. The explosion of an atom bomb over a city
    c. The teaching of communist principles to schoolchildren
    d. The government's decision to enforce income tax laws
    e. The passage of a bill to allow unrestricted immigration to the United States
2. The following passage contains a combination of causes, occasions, and conditions that attempt to explain the disastrous football season at Mid western University. After a careful reading decide which elements are strict causes and which are merely conditions or occasions.

More Virility at Midwestern

Midwestern University has just completed the most catastrophic foot ball season in its history. After early victories against Aberdeen Norma and Kenaca State, Midwestern was defeated on successive Saturdays by Centralia, South Central, Northwestern, and Mercantile. True, the fates did not smile upon Midwestern. The Mercantile game was played in a mish-mash of snow and mud, and, as the A.P. report indicated, the offi ciating in the Centralia game was the worst ever witnessed in modern college football.

But there are other reasons that explain this disastrous season. Dean Hawkins' decision to suspend Blackie Giddons and Jack (the Ripper) McGirk for their prankish raid on the sorority houses deprived the team of its two great all-America backs. Coach Homer Grimes's announce ment of his switch to Ohio State destroyed the team's morale.

In addition, Midwestern's rivals were supremely strong this season. Centralia, led by Joe (Zippy) Zazlewski, surpassed all Conference record in forward passing. Cletus Cash, Bud Muzarski, Tipper Devlin, and the rest of the Mercantile line lowered the iron curtain on all their opponent this fall. Northwestern as usual had a smart and aggressive team. Even South Central, inspired by its great scat back, Leo Pasqualerino, rose to heroic heights in its traditional game with Midwestern.

Even so, there are those of us on the Midwestern *Daily Bugle* who fee that the big cause for the team's collapse was the lack of *school spirit*

Midwestern students have gone soft. Since the fad for dirty white shoes, blue blazers, and eastern-style crew haircuts invaded the campus, student morale has disappeared. What Midwestern needs is a return to the days of hobnail boots, blue jeans, sweat shirts, *and* virility.

G

Reread Section VII. Then complete the following exercises as directed.

1. Read one chapter in a history textbook used in your school. Show how historical process is made clear by outlining the sequence of events in the chapter you have selected.
2. Consult a science textbook, or appropriate reference in your library, for materials to explain one of the natural processes listed below. Then write a 500-word process analysis on the subject you have chosen.
   a. A typhoon
   b. Tides
   c. Raising wheat
   d. The migration of salmon or some other species of fish
   e. Rain
3. Show how Example II D3 exemplifies the principles of logical process.

H

Prepare an expository theme of about 1000 words in the following manner.

1. Select a topic. Some topics are listed below. Others may be found in the General Exercises, I through VII.
2. Collect all the information you can on the general topic. Use your college library.
3. Sort out your information on the topic under one of the six basic methods of analysis. (You may find a review of the paradigm on "Midwestern University" in Section I helpful.)
4. Select the precise phase of the general topic you think most important and state your central theme.
5. Prepare a formal outline developing your central theme. (References: handbooks * and Example III C2.) In your outline include as many methods of development as are helpful to support your theme. For instance, if you are writing on the theme "Freedom is the main problem of our time," definition would be an appropriate method of development. But in defining freedom as the main problem you might decide to cite some specific examples of freedom and to contrast the free world

* Foerster, pp. 77-80, *36*; Hodges, *32b-i, 33c*; Kierzek, pp. 143-50; Perrin, pp. 670-75; Wykoff, *36, 50c.*

and the totalitarian world. Do not feel compelled to use all methods of development. Combine various methods in the manner of those writers you have studied in answering Review Exercise A above.

6. Write the first draft of your composition.
7. Check your first draft by asking the following questions:
   a. Have I stated the central theme clearly and shown the relevance of all the parts of my composition to the central theme?
   b. Is my method of development clear? When I have changed from one method of development to another, have I marked the change by a clear transitional sentence or paragraph?
   c. Are my paragraphs clear, that is, centered on one aspect of my theme? Does each paragraph contribute directly to the exposition of the central theme?
   d. Are my sentences clear, that is, centered on the main point in each paragraph? Does each sentence contribute to the central idea of the paragraph? *
   e. Is my diction as exact, as vigorous, and as interesting as I can make it? †
   f. Are my spelling and punctuation correct? ‡
8. Write the finished draft of your composition in the manuscript form specified by your instructor. Note in the margin the methods of development you have employed in your essay.

Suggested Topics

1. The 1952 presidential election campaign
2. The committee system in Congress
3. The war in Indo-China
4. Labor leadership
5. The UN General Assembly
6. Churchill as an orator
7. The Metropolitan Opera
8. The caste system in India
9. The uses of aluminum
10. Men's hats
11. Varieties of insurance
12. Falconry
13. Headache remedies
14. New designs in automobiles
15. Types of fountain pens
16. The uses of plastics
17. Hazing
18. Ways of making wire
19. Microfilms
20. A standard filing system
21. Radar in maritime navigation
22. Frozen foods
23. Sleeping bags
24. Musical styles

* See handbooks: Foerster, pp. 43-49, *37d*; Hodges, *31a*; Kierzek, pp. 69-70, 68; Perrin, pp. 185-87; Wykoff, *53*.
† See handbooks: Foerster, *58, 59, 60*; Hodges, *20*; Kierzek, *36a-40*; Perrin, pp. 318-30; Wykoff, *89, 92-94*.
‡ See handbooks: Foerster, *17-28, 41-49b*; Hodges, *12-17, 18*; Kierzek, *19-27, 28-34*; Perrin, pp. 132-54, 156-68; Wykoff, *16-25, 81*.

PART TWO

Arrangement and Style
in the Whole Composition

SECTION VIII

The Whole Composition

THUS far our study of the art of rhetoric has proceeded as follows:

1. We have learned how to select a subject in the light of our occasion and purpose (Section I).
2. We have learned how to analyze our subject, to discover our central theme, and to develop that theme by one or more of the several methods studied in Sections II-VII.

We are now ready to turn to the third element of rhetoric—arrangement.

Arrangement is the effective organization of our ideas about a subject in a whole composition. Analysis discovers many possible ways of developing a subject, and thus permits us to choose the main ideas that will best serve our central theme, our occasion, and purpose. Arrangement is the order in which these main (or key) ideas may be most effectively presented. By the effective arrangement of the main (or key) ideas we have selected to develop our central theme we ensure unity, coherence, and emphasis in the structure of our composition.

THE THREE PRINCIPLES OF EFFECTIVE ARRANGEMENT

Unity in a composition means that all the various elements of the composition bear directly on the central theme. In practice this unity is secured by a proper introduction of the central theme, adequate development of the central theme, and a conclusion that evolves logically from the development of the central theme. Thus the age-old

273

rhetorical maxim that all compositions must have a beginning, a middle, and an end is not a counsel of perfection but a statement of the basic principle of logical unity. The introduction states the subject to be explained or argued. At times the central theme is clearly set forth in this statement and the method of development indicated; however, the central theme is often not explicitly stated but implied throughout the whole discourse. The development supplies the explanation of, or the evidence to prove, the central theme. The conclusion sums up the explanation or evidence offered throughout the development and draws whatever inference the explanation or evidence allows.*

Coherence in composition means that the various elements of the composition are not only related to the central theme (unity) but are linked together. Thus a coherent composition will follow a logical order of development in which the relation of one part with another will be made apparent to the reader. In practice, coherence is secured by clear-cut divisions, by transitional words, sentences, and paragraphs, and by partial and final summaries.†

Emphasis in composition means that the various elements of a composition are arranged in an order best calculated to excite the readers' interest and feeling. In practice, emphasis is secured by repetition of key words and expressions, climactic order (that is, an order of ascending importance or interest), and by an intensified style, such as that achieved by exclamations, rhetorical questions, and figures of speech. ‡ (Note: These three elements—unity, coherence, and emphasis—are related not only to arrangement but also to style, as we shall point out later in this section.)

Many of the examples studied in Sections II-VII are sufficiently extended—notably III C2, "On Weekend Guests" by Russell Lynes; III C3, "Paleface and Redskin" by Philip Rahv; IV D, "Fenimore Cooper's Literary Offenses" by Mark Twain; and V C2, "America and Europe" by Aldous Huxley—to warrant re-examination from the point of view of arrangement. But for a fresh example, let us turn to Charles Malik's "The Meaning of America in the World Today." Here we shall see how the principles of unity, coherence, and emphasis are exemplified in an extended composition.

---

* See handbooks: Foerster, pp. 77-86; Kierzek, pp. 158-60; Perrin, p. 802; Wykoff, *40*.
† See handbooks: Foerster, p. 67, *37e*; Hodges, *31b*; Kierzek, pp. 92-103; Perrin, pp. 192-95; Wykoff, *41*.
‡ See handbooks: Foerster, pp. 24-31, 75-80; Hodges, 29; Kierzek, *61, 62, 64*; Perrin, pp. 540-41; Wykoff, 92.

Summary of "The Meaning of America in the World Today"

Occasion: University commencement address.
Subject: The meaning of America in the world today.
Purpose: Exposition.
Central theme (implied throughout): America's meaning to the world may be seen by analyzing American freedom, independence, democracy, technology, and action.

Beginning

¶1: The world situation has raised many important issues.

¶2: One of the most important is the meaning of America and her destiny in the world.

¶3: The world studies America because the world's fate is linked with America's fate.

Development

¶4: America means freedom.

¶5: But freedom is a means, not the final end of life.

¶6: The world cries for the full realization of a free life.

¶7: America means independence.

¶8: But independence may not meet the demand for peace, may not be possible, is no more necessary than interdependence, does not satisfy the craving for fellowship.

¶9: American independence must be explained abroad and merged with interdependence.

¶10: America means democracy.

¶11: But democracy is a formal structure which fosters political values and not necessarily other values. It is not the only or the greatest thing for which men hunger.

¶12: Democracy and freedom and independence, while great in themselves, are not completely satisfactory. (¶12 is a partial summary of ¶4-11.)

¶13: America means technology.

¶14: But technology may be an enemy of the spirit.

¶15: What the world abroad needs is not technology but the creative spirit that made American technology possible.

¶16: America means action.

¶17: But the world abroad asks the purpose of American activity.

¶18: Action must be balanced by thought and wisdom.

End

¶19: Summary: The total meaning of America is a positive wisdom that issues forth in freedom, independence, democracy, technology, action.

¶20: The world hopes America's values will be merged with other points of view without loss of integrity.

The Meaning of America in the World Today

BY CHARLES MALIK*

1 Those of us who face the future—those of us who have a future to face—must resign ourselves to wrestling with great issues all our lives. The rising East, the Slavic world, Marxist communism, the mighty social ferment, and the ordeals of Europe are tremendous questions which—so far as we can now pierce the unknown—we are going to live with for a very long time to come. We are all plunged into a world not of our own choosing, in which our existence is riddled through and through by these issues. And he who today seeks escape from the East, or from Russia, or from Europe, or from the din of the masses, into some kind of a placid and protected existence outside this world of danger and trouble, is literally seeking the impossible.

2 There is another issue that is just as great as these. In fact, there are some who consider it even greater. That is the issue of America: her destiny and her meaning to the rest of the world.

3 When people abroad wonder about United States policy and intentions, when they inquire into how the mind of America is likely to develop, they are simply evincing a deep concern for their own fate. In one important sense, there are no more independent fates: we all sink or swim together.

* Mr. Malik is the Minister from Lebanon to the United States and chairman of the UN Human Rights Commission. This article is adapted from a commencement address which he delivered at the University of Notre Dame.

THE MEANING OF AMERICA IN THE WORLD TODAY: reprinted here with the permission of the author and of *The Commonweal*, where it appeared in the issue of August 1, 1952.

4 America means *freedom:* no arbitrary compulsion from outside, the autonomous determination of idea and act from within. This is a great message, particularly since there is a real contest between freedom and slavery throughout the world, and because in many instances the frontiers of freedom, both geographical and intellectual, have had to recede. For years to come, the gospel of free self-determination will be one of the most potent weapons in the war of ideas, and nothing looms so clearly and decisively on the horizon of statesmanship as the sincere attempt at helping to liberate peoples and cultures from communist bondage.

5 But freedom is not the end of human life. After a man becomes free, the question remains: what should he strive after, what and whom can he believe, what may he hope for, what must he be? For it is possible to be "free" and yet to miss the end of life altogether.

6 The crying need therefore is for a deeper, a more grounded and more responsible, elaboration of the content of the free life. One must be honest with the enslaved peoples—whether enslaved politically or spiritually—in telling them that freedom is not the end but the beginning of a life of effort and development whose general character can nevertheless be traced in advance. Freedom is the immediate goal, but the distant lure is nothing short of the full realization of all that properly belongs to man.

7 America means *independence:* that people need not be ruled by aliens, that diverse cultures can develop each according to its own inner genius. This is a great message, instilling hope and self-confidence in the heart of the weak and helpless, especially at a time when mighty new forces, both material and spiritual, are threatening the independence of peoples from every side.

8 But, first of all, independence may not mean peace, unless to start with, it is founded upon principles of peace; for the independent units may either fall out with one another or combine against the rest of the world. Secondly, what if certain peoples or cultures cannot be really independent? Thirdly, in our amazingly contracted world the need is as much for a declaration of interdependence as for one of independence. And fourthly, people crave as much for fellowship as for being alone, and the urge toward community and love is no less real and good than any impulse to individualism.

9 Because there has been some misunderstanding abroad of the content of American independence, it seems necessary to elucidate pre-

cisely how an act of independence in the eighteenth century was radically different from a similar act in the twentieth, and to make it as clear as possible that political independence is one thing, and independence in the realm of culture and spirit is entirely another. So long as there is objective, given, cumulative truth, we cannot be spiritually independent of one another. If oceans and poles can, for a time, physically separate America from the Old World, the intellectual and spiritual roots of this land all go back to Europe and the Mediterranean. And the supreme question today is precisely to rediscover, reaffirm, and re-establish this great spiritual community extending in time for thousands of years.

10 America means *democracy:* that the citizens of the commonwealth themselves elect and dismiss their own rulers, and that the laws have no respect for persons, precisely by respecting equally the inherent humanity of all persons. This is a great message, stressing as it does the dignity of the individual, affirming the primacy of the people, providing a mechanism for the avoidance of tyranny, bracketing all people under the beneficent protection of the law.

11 But even the most perfect design of government is but a formal structure within which men may seek fullness of being. Nor is it certain that if the entire world were democratized, wars would cease. What if two peoples, each fully democratic in its form of government, keep on fundamentally hating each other or coveting each other's goods? Democracy is a great thing, but it is neither the only nor the greatest thing for which man hungers. And there are peoples who, preferring to develop other values than the political, are not much bothered by who rules them, provided they are sufficiently cared for, loved, protected.

12 America can be justly proud of what its democracy has been able to achieve. The rest of the world, however, thirsts for something infinitely deeper than freedom, democracy, and independence; and when it inquires into the American message, it wonders how America is going to blossom in these deeper things.

13 America means *technology:* the reasoned exploitation of the resources of nature for the benefit of man. This is indeed a great contribution, considering the millions and millions of people throughout the world who are helpless before the forces of nature, and for whom a slight improvement in technique will mean a more abundant life

14 But technology may be bought at a high price: the attenuation of the spirit. The inordinate concentration upon material and economic conditions inevitably leads to the blurring of the original sources of the spirit; sources that are utterly independent of all things material. A man who spends all his life exploring and controlling nature may end by thinking of other human beings as things to be controlled. Nor is a technologically perfect world necessarily a good one; for it may still be full of hatred and fear and lust.

15 In the positive American tradition there are deeper things than technology. There are adventure and self-confidence; there is the zest of discovery and the joy of creation; there is mutual helpfulness and self-giving; there is an implicit trust in reason and discussion; and there is a committing of oneself to the Providence of God. It is these things that made technology possible in the first place. If I were an American, I would be justly proud of the infinite techniques that my civilization has created, but I would nevertheless seek first to understand and love the original creative spirit itself, in its joy and in its unity.

16 America means *action:* a premium upon practical objective realization, the passage of idea into fact. This is a wonderful message, considering how much there is still to be done for the betterment of man's lot, and considering that whole cultures have been arrested precisely because either they could not discriminate between fantasy and fact or because their ideas remained eternal abstraction. Boldness to decide, to act, to bring deliberation to an end—nothing can be more wonderful than this.

17 But it is evident that action itself must have an end. Nor can we pass restlessly from action to action if we are to remain human. Action pursued for its own sake leads inevitably to the worship of power; and power corrupts. Thus where and how to rest—that is the question. The old world stands to learn infinitely from the active American life; but now and then it asks itself the question: where does it all lead to?

18 The real justification is not action, nor the accumulation of material things, but the creation of supreme human character made perfect through suffering; and such character—mellowed, wise, deep, understanding, loving—is impossible without rest in truth and God. Nothing is more needful than to balance action by thought and wisdom, movement by being and by the pause that scans the eternal.

19 Freedom, independence, democracy, technology, action—these things belong to the wisdom of America; a real and positive wisdom. The rest of the world must understand that this is part of the total meaning hailing them from this side. It is a much-needed tonic, a fresh breeze of hope.

20 These things would have had a freer course of development if America had not had to come out into the world. As America assumes greater and greater responsibilities and becomes more and more entangled abroad, it is inevitable that her values will be pondered, weighed, questioned. She will find herself limited by other valuations and other points of view. Asia, Africa, the Middle East, the Slavic world, Europe, Latin America—all these cultures also have their own words to utter. And the great question for America is how to listen to all these words, how to merge cooperatively and harmoniously with all these cultures, without either losing heart or compromising her own soul.

UNITY IN "THE MEANING OF AMERICA IN THE WORLD TODAY"

The first three paragraphs of this essay * introduce Malik's central theme—What does America (defined later in her characteristic qualities of freedom, independence, democracy, technology, and action) mean to the world? The American issue is shown to be important not only to Americans but to the whole world, whose fate hinges largely on what America chooses to do. America's destiny and the world's destiny are interdependent.

The introduction therefore announces that the aim of this exposition is (1) to define the meaning of America and (2) to define the attitude of the world towards the meaning of America. Thus the reader is led to expect a series of contrasted definitions.

This is precisely what happens in the development (¶4-18). America's meaning is defined by five predominant American characteristics (¶4, 7, 10, 13, and 16). Then the attitude of the non-American world with reference to each of these five key ideas is explained (¶5, 8, 11,

---

* By *essay* we mean here any brief prose composition that aims to communicate the author's ideas and impressions. Essays are normally classified as (1) formal or informal and (2) as expository, argumentative, persuasive, and so on, depending upon the principal aim of the writer. The essay is further defined and classified in Section XV.

14, and 17). (By key ideas we mean the main ideas set forth in developing the central theme. These ideas are frequently equivalent to the main divisions of a composition.)

Finally, each key idea is expanded and redefined in the light of the contrast (¶6, 9, 12, 15, and 18).

The conclusion draws the necessary inference from the development of the central theme by showing (1) that the total meaning of America to the world at large is the positive wisdom that underlies all the American characteristics and (2) that the American values, analyzed throughout the essay, must be merged cooperatively and harmoniously with the values of other cultures.

Hence the unity of the essay is established (1) by relating the separate parts to the central theme (the parts taken together form the central theme), and (2) by arranging these parts in a proper beginning, middle, and end. Note that the chief method of analysis used throughout is definition combined with contrast. Note also the observance of the law of proportion.* Each of the five key ideas is developed in three paragraphs of almost equal length and of similar pattern: America means . . . ; but the world feels . . . ; the need therefore is . . .

COHERENCE IN "THE MEANING OF AMERICA IN THE WORLD TODAY"

Each of the five characteristic ideas that explain the meaning of America is connected (1) by coordinate arrangement in an exactly parallel division and (2) by frequent and unmistakable transitional words and expressions.

The coordinate arrangement is evidenced by the sequence of groups of three paragraphs, as we have noted above. The transitional words and expressions appear in the paragraph arrangement. Each of the five groups of paragraphs devoted to the key ideas is arranged in a similar pattern. Thus in the first group the topic sentence in the opening paragraph (¶4) is "America means freedom. . . ." In paragraph 5 the contrast is set up by the transitional sentence, "But freedom is not the end of human life." In paragraph 6 the connection between the two preceding paragraphs is established by the conjunction "therefore," and by the comparative adjectives "deeper" and "more grounded."

---

* See handbooks: Foerster, pp. 82-84; Kierzek, p. 160; Wykoff, *37, 57.*

Note too the repetition of the key idea, freedom, and its synonyms.* Repetition is also used here to achieve emphasis.

The same method prevails in each of the other groups of paragraphs. Note the opening sentences in the three paragraphs on independence.

¶7: America means independence. . . .

¶8: But, first of all, independence may not mean . . .

¶9: Because . . . it seems necessary. . . .

Independence is defined and explained in paragraph 7. The transitional conjunction "but," setting up a contrast, begins paragraph 8. The clause at the beginning of paragraph 9 announces a transition and leads us to the expanded view of independence as seen in the light of interdependence.

So too in the paragraphs on action we see the pattern repeated: America means action . . . ; but it is evident that action . . . ; the real justification is not action. . . .

Coherence is also achieved by the partial summary contained in paragraph 12, and by the complete summary in paragraph 19.

EMPHASIS IN "THE MEANING OF AMERICA IN THE
  WORLD TODAY"

Emphasis is achieved in this essay (1) by the repetition of key words and phrases, (2) by a repetition of the pattern of definition, contrast, and expanded definition, and (3) by a climactic order within the several parts and within the whole composition.

The repetition of the important words and phrases is particularly striking. The subject, America's meaning, is stated in a variety of ways: as "the issue of America" (¶2), as "United States policy" and "the mind of America" (¶3). The opening sentences in paragraphs 4, 7, 10, 12, 13, 15, 16, 19, 20 all repeat the subject.

Freedom with its synonyms is used ten times in paragraphs 4-6, and is repeated in paragraphs 12 and 19.

Independence, in its various forms, is used ten times in paragraphs 7-9, and is also repeated in paragraphs 12 and 19.

Democracy is used five times in paragraphs 10-12, and is repeated in paragraph 19.

* See handbooks: Foerster, pp. 29-33; Hodges, *29e*; *31b3*; Kierzek, *62*; Perrin, pp. 289-92; Wykoff, *44d*.

Technology is used five times in paragraphs 13-15, and is repeated in paragraph 19.

Action is used seven times in paragraphs 16-18, and is repeated in paragraph 19.

The repetition of the pattern, that is, three paragraphs on each of the key ideas, adds emphasis. This device of statement, opposite statement, and resolution not only permits the reader to grasp complicated ideas quickly; it also challenges attention by suggesting a dialogue between America on the one hand and the rest of the world on the other.

Emphasis is also achieved by the climactic order within the parts of the composition, and within the whole composition.

The climax within each of the five groups of paragraphs is the result of the challenge stated above. Thus, for example, Mr. Malik defines American democracy in paragraph 10 as a great message. But in paragraph 11 he reminds us that it is neither the only nor the greatest thing for which man hungers. Mr. Malik's audience is interested in what the greatest thing may be. It waits for a revelation in the next paragraph.

As with each of the parts, so with the whole composition. The key ideas are presented in an order of increasing importance and interest. Mr. Malik's conclusion (¶19-20) is not only the logical end of his thought; it is also its emotional peak. Throughout his essay he has suggested that each characteristic trait of American culture, considered singly, or without reference to a real and positive wisdom, does not impress the outside world (or many Americans, for that matter). Freedom is attractive, but it may be abused. Independence is good, but it may hide isolationism. Democracy is a great message, but it does not always prevent war or promote happiness. One side of American technology, he suggests, may be mere gadget-mindedness, and some of our activity may be an attempt to escape from thinking. Certainly Europe and the East have made much of our supposed lack of wisdom. Mr. Malik's last point therefore is a recognition of an emotional as well as a logical issue. In tracing all our achievements to a positive, underlying wisdom Mr. Malik is at once concluding his dialogue between America and the world at large and is stirring the noble hopes and ambitions of all his readers. Hence when he concludes that America's meaning is a real and positive wisdom, a much-needed tonic, a fresh breeze of hope, he has reached both the logical end and the emotional climax at the same time.

Thus we see how unity, coherence, and emphasis, the three principles of good arrangement, operate in a contemporary essay. We shall study these principles throughout Sections IX-XI in a great variety of expositions, arguments, and persuasions. The principles are always the same, but the application differs, depending on the subject, the purpose, and the occasion. Note: Normally these principles will be shown in outline following the essays.

GENERAL EXERCISES ON ARRANGEMENT

1. Make an outline for each of the following essays similar to that of "The Meaning of America in the World Today," found earlier in this section:

    Section III, "Paleface and Redskin" by Philip Rahv
    "On Weekend Guests" by Russell Lynes
    Section IV, "Fenimore Cooper's Literary Offenses" by Mark Twain
    "Grant as a General" by T. Harry Williams
    Section V, "America and Europe" by Aldous Huxley

2. Criticize one or more of the essays outlined in answer to Exercise 1 by answering the following questions:
    a. Does the beginning or introductory section state the subject? Is the central theme stated or implied?
    b. Is there a clear division of the key ideas?
    c. Do all these key ideas bear directly on the central theme? What other means are used to attain unity?
    d. Are these key ideas fully developed? What means of development are used?
    e. Is the transition from one key idea to another clearly established? How is this done? What other means are used to achieve coherence?
    f. Study the topic sentences * of the paragraphs in the body or development of the essays you have outlined. Is each of these topic sentences related to one of the key ideas? If so, show how. If not, determine whether the paragraph is essential to the essay.
    g. Does the arrangement of the key ideas of the essay help to achieve emphasis? Give reasons for your answer.
    h. Does the concluding section repeat the central theme and purpose? If not, decide whether a conclusion is necessary. Give reasons for your answer.

3. Suppose you are asked to give an inspirational talk to a group of new servicemen on the qualities of a good soldier. Your key ideas are:

---

* See handbooks: Foerster, pp. 43-44, *37d*; Hodges, *31a*; Kierzek, pp. 69-70, *68*; Perrin, pp. 185-87; Wykoff, *53*.

a. Good health   d. Courage
b. Obedience   e. Initiative
c. Loyalty
In what order would you introduce these key ideas? Explain the reasons for your order.

4. Select three key ideas for each of the following subjects. Determine the order in which you wish to present these ideas.
   a. The politician   d. Innocence by association
   b. Popularity on the campus   e. The meaning of friendship
   c. Guilt by association
5. Analyze the key ideas in one of the subjects listed above to determine the most helpful method of development according to the means of analysis studied in Sections II-VII.
6. Write a short essay with a clear beginning, middle, and end on one of the subjects analyzed in Exercise 5.

STYLE: THE FINAL STEP IN ARRANGEMENT

The first element in rhetoric is the selection of a subject; the second, the analysis of the subject; the third, the arrangement of the ideas the writer has discovered about the subject. The fourth element, style, is the effective expression of ideas through the choice of right words (diction), through the right arrangement of words in a sentence, through right arrangement of sentences in larger units of composition. Thus style is the final thinking out of our ideas into language.

The qualities of a good style parallel those of good arrangement. Style is linked to arrangement as closely as the foliage of a tree is to its trunk and branches. Style completes the plan or arrangement of ideas, just as leaves complete the function of a tree. A good style will necessarily promote the unity and coherence of the thought to be expressed, and will therefore be *clear;* a good style will necessarily emphasize the main ideas and will therefore be *vigorous;* a good style will be as fresh and vivid as possible and will therefore be *interesting.*

Clarity, vigor, and interest are closely related qualities. These qualities, as we have explained in the comment on Example II D3, "What Is Good Writing?" by S. E. Morison, are often found in the same selection. Thus when Milton wrote as a concluding line of the sonnet "On His Blindness," "They also serve who only stand and wait," he stated *clearly* his attitude on his own blindness. He stated his thought *vigorously,* that is, with an emotional effect particularly noticeable in the climactic last word. Furthermore, he stated the thought *interest-*

ingly, by the use of a slow, solemn, stately rhythm. Thus the sentence is at once clear, vigorous, and interesting.

In some kinds of writing, however, such as scientific prose (see VII, General Exercise), clarity alone suffices. But it is virtually impossible to have vigor and interest without clarity.

Style then, in the sense we have defined it in this section, is best studied

 1. As the extension of arrangement
 2. As the exemplification of the qualities of clearness, vigor, and interest in the use of language

We shall now study how the style—in words, in sentences, and in paragraphs—is the final expression of thought in "Perennial Adolescence" by Bernard Iddings Bell. (Note: Style, considered as the expression of the writer's personality, will be treated in Section XV.)

The Arrangement of "Perennial Adolescence"

Occasion: An appeal to mature Americans in criticism of the perennial adolescence of American society.

Subject: Perennial adolescence.

Purpose: Exposition and persuasion. To explain what perennial adolescence is and to persuade mature Americans to oppose perennial adolescence.

Central theme: American society, symbolized by the Aldrich family, must be rescued from a perennial adolescence that consists in the sterile quest for money, comfort, power, and pseudo-learning. This theme is implied throughout and stated explicitly at the end of the introduction, in paragraphs 9 and 10, and is repeated in paragraphs 24, 28, and 29.

I. Introduction (¶1-10)
 A. In the past humorists have often been pungent analysts of American life (¶1).
 B. Clifford Goldsmith, the creator of the Aldrich family, is such an analyst (¶2).
 C. The Aldrich family is typical of the perennial adolescence of American society (¶3-8).
  1. Henry Aldrich, the teen-age son, is an extreme example of the adolescent American boy (¶3).

2. His sister Mary is his feminine counterpart (¶3).
3. Mr. and Mrs. Aldrich are more tragicomic in their adolescence than their children (¶4-6).
4. Mr. and Mrs. Aldrich have never been taught how to think and hence cannot understand the problems of the contemporary age (¶7-8).

  D. Mr. and Mrs. Aldrich should be shown that they are mentally and morally adrift (¶9).

  E. Mr. and Mrs. Aldrich's adolescence stems from the four aims held up to American society: money, pleasure, power, and erudition (¶10).

II. Development (¶11-27)

  A. The four aims of American society are the sterile quests for
    1. Money (¶11-14)
    2. Comfort (¶15-18)
    3. Power (¶19-21)
    4. Pseudo-learning (¶22-23)

  B. The Aldriches must be rescued from the false aims of riches, comforts, amusements, pedantic preciosity, and bragging strut (¶24).

  C. The true aims are
    1. Creative work (¶25-26)
    2. Love (¶27)

III. Conclusion (¶28-29) (inferences drawn from the ideas presented in the development)

  A. If the Aldriches are not rescued from adolescence we abandon our country to infantilism (¶28).

  B. We may save the Aldriches by courageous criticism (¶29).

Perennial Adolescence

BY BERNARD IDDINGS BELL

1 The late Albert Jay Nock used to remark that the most acute observers of the cultural pattern in America have been not social scientists, educators, clergymen, jurists, philosophers, but humorists. A strong case may be made out for this opinion. One can gain a good

PERENNIAL ADOLESCENCE: from *Crisis in Education*, by Bernard Iddings Bell, and copyright, 1949, by the McGraw-Hill Book Company.

deal of pertinent information not to be found elsewhere about eighteenth-century New England, for example, from perusing the *Johnnycake Papers* and about colonial New York from Irving's *Knickerbocker's History*. The Civil War period and what preceded it and its immediate aftermath are illuminated by the comment of James Russell Lowell and even more by that of Artemus Ward. For the true significance of the eighteen-seventies and -eighties one may not omit a careful reading of Mark Twain. The turn of the century is most cannily interpreted by George Ade, by Bert Leston Taylor, most of all by Finley Peter Dunne, who for many years spilled a weekly column of pungent social analysis from the lips of Mr. Dooley, philosopher of Archey Road. The age of normalcy is revealed by the gentle irony of Booth Tarkington.

2 In our day we can add another name to the honorable roll of jesters sufficiently percipient to illuminate the passing scene. Like his predecessors, this wag is looked on by contemporaries as little more than a designer of drolleries; posterity may deem him more significant, as it gains from his productions a key to the understanding of that bewildering generation of Americans which lived and moved and for the most part made a mess of things in the nineteen-forties. His name is Clifford Goldsmith. He writes a program called *The Aldrich Family* and weekly on the radio has for years delighted with it a large and applauding public.

3 ¹His Henry Aldrich is a teen-age lad, presented as the "typical American boy." ²Henry is almost indecently adolescent. ³He never grows a day older. ⁴Even Penrod seems sophisticated beside him. ⁵Henry is undisciplined, self-assertive, bewildered by life. ⁶Educationally he is the victim of a high school system which underestimates him. ⁷He has acquired no facility in arriving at judgments social or artistic, and he is apparently without religion of any kind. ⁸His time is spent chiefly in futile, pathetic, and undeniably laughable misadventures in the art of living. ⁹He is the creature of circumstance and moved about like a pawn by crowd opinion; his chief endeavor is to find out what are the mores and then to obey them; he is afraid above all things else to think for himself, to go against convention or in any way to criticize it. ¹⁰What a different boy this is from Tom Sawyer or Huck Finn! ¹¹His sister Mary is his feminine counterpart, so without purpose and so truculent as to make Miss Alcott's Meg, Jo, Beth, and Amy seem by comparison vital girls, daring, creative, vastly desirable to have about the house.

4 More tragicomic still are the father and mother of this pair. Mr. and Mrs. Aldrich are as conformist as Henry and Mary, as given to clichés, as vague in self-direction, as incompetent to discriminate, as essentially irreligious. They too are adolescents, middle-aged adolescents, neither children any more nor able to grow up.

5 If these Aldriches are the representative American family they are recognized to be by the multitudes who listen in to this weekly exhibition of incompetency in living, and there is small reason to doubt it, only a miracle can save America from debacle. Such people are unequipped to create or to manage an effective nation, as unable to do that as they are to run their individual lives and face the challenges of home and neighborhood. Politically, they are sure to be easy dupes of any plausible demagogue who comes along with a slogan and a hillbilly band or its urban equivalent. They are not free men and women but base mechanicals. These four people and their neighbors are at once the products and the patrons of mass management, of a functionalized social structure, of a standardized press and radio, of slick magazines and book clubs, of vocationalized education, of pressure salesmanship. The glass held up by Mr. Goldsmith is a mirror in which we can see in epitome the America which once bred and reared daring dreamers, imaginative lovers, creative nonconformists, citizens who grew up, now become a homeland of perennial adolescents.

6 A discerning man, this Clifford Goldsmith! One may hope that transcripts of his broadcasts are being preserved for posterity in the Library of Congress; in the twenty-second century the social historian will find them valuable. They will help to explain why it was that, back in the middle nineteen-hundreds, the most powerful nation on earth was also the most fumbling and ineffective. They will make compassionate the understanding that Americans of our time had lived so long in adolescent terms that, when they were called upon for leadership in a world crisis which demanded mature and wise decisions, they proved incompetent to make those decisions.

7 Mr. and Mrs. Aldrich are too untrained in the art of thinking to understand the cause of the world's present misery and of the unanticipated fumbling of their own country in the post-war handling of its problems, foreign and domestic. They cannot understand why, in spite of material advantages beyond the dreams of man in former ages, they remain somehow so unhappy, so insecure, so restless. They are not what they are by intention. They are counters moved about by social forces which either blindly operate or are venally manipulated.

They are what they are because no one has encouraged them, much less helped them, to bring their native intelligence, which is considerable, to bear upon the problem of ends and means in their own lives, in the life of the nation, in the life of the world in which America is a necessary coöperator.

8 The churches, from which instruction and example in mature living would, it might be thought, have been forthcoming, have gone in more and more for sociability, sentimentality, ceremonial without significance, and unctuous utterance of pseudo-ethical trivialities. The schools have taught them to cheer, and if need be die for, "my country, right or wrong," and that it is man's primary duty to get on in the world and keep up with the Joneses.

9 Mr. and Mrs. Aldrich are not too greatly to be blamed for rudimentary moral judgments; they are to be pitied and, if possible, rescued. They do at least begin to know that the world is all adrift; it may be, if we set ourselves to the task, that we can convince them it is they themselves who have slipped their moorings. But who is at work on this salvage?

10 It might be well to take a brief look at the ends which are in fact being aimed at in this country. There are four of these; they are the very same life objectives which all inexperienced adolescents are apt to think supremely worth while. Two of them—the quest for money and the quest for pleasure—are the goals which increasingly, for a half century at least, have determined the cultural pattern in this country. The other two—the quest for power and the quest for erudition—are purposes equally inadequate, but to the pursuit of them more than a few are already turning as they find themselves increasingly bored by what has become the American way of life.

11 The Aldrichian civilization has been based largely upon an assumption that the great, significant, happy man is he who is able to acquire a super-abundance of possessions; who lives in a house or flat larger and more ornate than he and his family need for reasonable comfort; who has a motorcar without good reason, or two of them when only one is needed, or three or four when two would do; who has more clothes than he can wear out and whose wife dresses with conspicuous expenditure; who has everything his heart desires and money can buy, and cash in the bank wherewith to purchase more of the same. How great a triumph to lift oneself to such a state of being! Since this is assumed to be the target at which an individual should

aim, it follows that this is the social goal toward which national policies must be directed. A rich America is a great America!

12 [1]Such a concept of nobility may appeal, usually does appeal, to the verdant adolescent, but it looks more than a little absurd in the light of a mature experience. [2]One meets many a man who has great wealth and yet to God, his fellows, himself, is manifestly worth nothing. [3]One meets other men who are as rich as these pitiable fellows but who to God, their fellows, themselves, are worth so much that when one thinks of them one pays them the compliment of forgetting their money altogether. [4]One comes to know women so simple, so good, so lovable, as to be indispensable to all who meet them, but who never had a penny, have not now, never will have.

13 A study of history backs up one's experience. Those who in any generation have risen above the ruck of humanity to a place where they are honored as the great ones of the past have almost never had money. There have been a few rich people who are remembered; but examination of their records shows that they are significant not because of their wealth but much more often in spite of it. Not a single outstanding teacher of moral wisdom has failed to warn that riches tend to isolate their owners, make them petty, vulnerable, a little ridiculous. Scarcely a social historian has failed to point out that the land fares ill where wealth accumulates and men decay.

14 Mr. and Mrs. Aldrich may have a faint memory of having heard something of this sort of thing when they were children; Henry and Mary have probably never had it called to their attention. Certainly the family is not likely to be reminded of it by contemporary books or magazines or newspapers, by the radio or the movies, by the billboards, by popular conversation, by the schools; even when they go to church, which is rarely, they seldom get a hint in the sermons that for the country, for their family, for themselves individually, abundance is far more dangerous than poverty. They go their teen-age way, admiring the rich man, aiming to become rich themselves, sure that with wealth comes happiness, certain that for America to fulfill its destiny it is necessary above all else that our physical standard of existence shall be lifted to ever more exalted heights.

15 It is likely to seem to Americans even more obvious, indeed unquestionable, that the great, significant, happy human being is the one who can have the best time, who can the most competently amuse himself. Most of the world's moralists have agreed that this is indeed a better answer to life's problem than the first one. Omar the Persian,

underneath his tree with his book and his bottle and his lady friend, is obviously more commendable than Poor Richard, saving pennies all the week and gloating over his deposit book Saturday night.

16 When the usual American is charged with having a greedy, grasping soul he indignantly denies it, and with some justice. The usual American is concerned not so much with wealth *per se* as with what may be purchased therewith, a life full of entertainment. He is willing to spend money for fun. He buys books by the hundred thousands and magazines by the millions, and some of them he even reads, but mostly for distraction. He prefers either who-done-its or eroticism. He sits rapt while on the screen are entrancingly unfolded before his eyes the adventures of glamorous women and two-fisted men. He pays high prices for seats in the stadium to applaud the gladiators. He buys hard liquor by the case. No man, he thinks, can with justice call him penny-pinching. What more can be asked for in the way of munificence than such prodigal expenditure for purchasable joys?

17 Omar knew better than that. The *Rubáiyát* is a bewailing of the folly of all life, including that life which, despairing of better things, takes refuge in pleasure; if there is no answer but pleasure, there is no answer at all. This is a very different thing from saying that pleasure is the answer. Omar knew, as did that other cynic who wrote the book called Ecclesiastes, that pleasure palls, that the time soon comes when no matter how much of it one possesses, or how exciting, it no longer entertains, no longer distracts from an essential tragedy.

18 A playboy of twenty may be fun to gaze upon, even when we are moved to disapproval; but Heaven deliver us from having to look upon, much worse to be, playboys of forty-five. How hard they work at enjoying themselves and how little they get, and less and less, in return for their labor! The last stage in a search for entertainment as the *summum bonum* is that sense of being fed up which characterizes most Americans of middle age and older. They are restless, without inner security. A happy man has no need to be amused.

19 When men or nations get tired of dodging fundamental questions in a multitude of distractions, they turn to a search for something else that will, so they suppose, give them the sense of significance which they lack and know they lack. This does not necessarily mean, however, that in sophistication they learn wisdom. If they remain adolescent in their approach to life, they are frequently tempted to seek meaning for themselves and for their nation in terms of coercive power. They develop a Messianic complex. They seek to live other

people's lives for them, ostensibly for the good of those other people but really for the sake of their own desired fulfillment. They set out to attain greatness in terms of a supposedly superior understanding irresistibly imposed upon the less percipient. They are bitten by the germ of *Herrenvolkismus*.

20 Precisely to the degree that Mr. and Mrs. Aldrich, and even more their children, begin to get fed up with senseless accumulation of goods and a wearisome round of purchased amusements, they tend to become easy victims of a quite mad belief that America, which is themselves writ large, is called upon to impose its cultural pattern upon the lesser breeds without the Law. It is America which must solve the world-wide Jewish problem, and in the doing of it cover up its own failures in reconciling creeds and colors. It is America which must teach Europe and Asia how to govern themselves, and in the doing of it forget gross misgovernment in Memphis and Chicago and Jersey City and a thousand other boss-ridden communities, as well as the inability to face necessary issues that results from a two-party system in which neither party has unity of convictions and between which there are almost never clear-cut issues. We who cannot solve our own riddles must decide the issues facing humanity at large. We whose hearts are restless with discontent must bring peace to the world. And woe be to the cynic who doubts our competence so to act in the grand manner!

21 Who that observes with trained eye the current scene in America can fail to perceive how increasingly ready our people are to take refuge from the ignobility of greed and the boredom of pleasure in pursuit of power, disguised as fulfillment of a romantic destiny but in reality the escapist device of a disappointed folk?

22 [1]Less socially significant because only a few are competent to follow it, but nevertheless deleterious, is the way of those among us who seek to arrive at significance by pursuing erudition for its own sake, pure scholarship, learning divorced from life. [2]Nothing is more sterile. [3]Man should seek to know in order to live, not to live that he may know. [4]In our institutions of higher learning one finds with the passing years more and more departmentalized pedants hiding in the holes of research, seeking to run away from embarrassing questions, afraid of philosophy and scared to death of religion. [5]It involves no disparagement of contemporary scholarship, no lack of affection for scholars of the moment, to recognize that many of them go in for learning as an escape device which they use to avoid facing what life is all about.

⁶With us Americans the more delightsome Ivory Towers are academic rather than ecclesiastical.

23 There is no real danger here for Henry and Mary (they seem to be too stupid even for the pursuit of pedantry), but there is danger for a number of their young friends, who are moved to seek significance by this sort of intellectual evasion.

24 We need to be rescued from teen-age pursuit of riches, comforts, amusements, pedantic preciosity, bragging strut. There is something vastly better to live for than these, as mature people have always known.

25 Man exists to do creatively, as craftsmanlike as may be, all things that must be done: great things like government or mothering or the healing of minds and bodies; small things like making beds or hoeing corn or driving a truck; things in the public eye like making speeches or unleashing atomic energy or making peace; obscure things like selling groceries or running a bus or teaching school. He finds inner peace who works at whatever is in front of him not for the pay he gets or for what he can buy with that pay, not for applause or gratitude, but for sheer joy in creativity. There is a vast number of tasks to be performed, most of them not romantic. They may be done in one of two ways: just to get them over with as quickly and as painlessly as possible, in which case they become a monotonous burden hard to bear; or each as beautifully as possible, in which case life is good to the taste.

26 Our fathers knew the joy that lies in craftsmanship: they did not advocate it; they took it for granted. We have forgotten it, overlooked it. Craftsmanship is not practiced, taught, or praised. That is why we are restless, unreliable, combative, caught in a web of doubt and dismay. No salmagundi made of things, amusements, lust for power, can assuage our gnawing hunger to create. There will be no recovery of serenity, no mutual patience sufficient for fraternity, until we learn ourselves and teach our children that unless human beings become creative artists they remain petulant children, dangerous, predatory.

27 Our fathers also knew, but few of their progeny seem aware of it, that every man is made, and this is the highest art of all, to give to other men understanding, tolerance, clemency, not with design to get from those others any *quid pro quo,* not even to get from them understanding or clemency or tolerance, but just because this is the kind of thing that man can do and must, most humbly. Man was made to be a lover—not necessarily beloved but a lover. To be artist and lover, this is the destined end of man.

28 If Mr. and Mrs. Aldrich and Henry and Mary cannot be persuaded of the truth of this which the moralists and the religions all teach and to know which is the mark of maturity, if they persist in adolescence, are those of us who are adult tamely to acquiesce and conform? Have we indeed sunk to that most juvenile form of juvenility, the juvenility of grown-up people afraid to smack the children down when they seek to ride roughshod over parents and teachers? We dare not abdicate and make of these United States an autonomous nursery. If we do, we abandon our country to an infantilism which renders it rudderless in a stormy era in which shrewd judgment and serene sureness are required of any nation that would avoid enslavement.

29 In spite of the public school system and a vocationalized higher education, in spite of churches singing nursery rhymes instead of chanting credos, in spite of Hollywood and the radio chains and the newspapers, in spite of everything, it is still entirely possible that the Aldriches—possibly not Mr. and Mrs., who are pretty far gone in fatuity, but Henry and Mary and their children—may grow up. But that will happen only if those who *have* grown up use courage and a clear, strong voice.

UNITY IN "PERENNIAL ADOLESCENCE"

In order to establish the link between arrangement and style, let us briefly examine the arrangement of "Perennial Adolescence."

In the first ten paragraphs Dr. Bell gives the background essential to the proper understanding of his central theme. To do this he establishes the typical characteristics of the Aldrich family by means of division (Section III). He also shows that the Aldrich family is a typical representative of American society and therefore stands as an example of the whole class (Section IV). His central theme is clearly stated in the introduction and is repeated at the end of the development and in the conclusion.

The development itself is a causal analysis of the reasons for the perennial adolescence of the Aldrich family and of American society, of which they are a typical example. In the course of this development (¶10-24) the sterile quest for money, comfort, power, and pseudo-learning is shown to be the positive, immediate, and necessary reason for the state of perennial adolescence. Paragraphs 25-27 state the causes for maturity, namely creative work and love.

In his conclusion Dr. Bell points out the disastrous effects of perennial adolescence and calls upon mature Americans to work for the correction of the defects of American society by courageous criticism. Hence the unity of the essay is established (1) by careful preparation of the central theme, (2) by logical development of the central theme, chiefly by causal analysis supported by examples, and (3) by drawing the necessary conclusions from the development of the central theme.

COHERENCE IN "PERENNIAL ADOLESCENCE"

The coherence of the main section of this essay is established (1) by the coordinated organization of the four causes of perennial adolescence, and (2) by the interconnection of each of these causes, as shown in sentence 1 of paragraph 19 and in paragraph 21 (see outline, II A). The logical order of development is made apparent to the reader by the causal sequence followed throughout the development, by the partial summary in paragraph 24, and by the final summary in paragraphs 28 and 29. The coherence of the smaller units will be studied in the style analysis that follows.

EMPHASIS IN "PERENNIAL ADOLESCENCE"

Emphasis is attained in this essay (1) by the repetition of key words and phrases and (2) by the climactic order of arrangement. Thus adolescence with its various synonyms is mentioned in virtually every paragraph of the essay. The climactic order of arrangement is indicated by the growing seriousness of the argument: the comic aspects of adolescence are set forth in the introduction; the tone becomes increasingly serious throughout the development; the conclusion is extremely vigorous. Indeed, the final two paragraphs, with their direct emotional appeal to mature Americans, reach a majestic climax, ending on the words "use courage and a clear, strong voice."

A third method of achieving emphasis, by the use of a style intensified through such devices as irony, exclamations, rhetorical questions, and figures of speech, will be taken up in the style analysis that follows.

STYLE ANALYSIS OF "PERENNIAL ADOLESCENCE"

In analyzing the style of "Perennial Adolescence" we shall first consider words, then sentences, and finally paragraphs.

Diction, or Style in Words *

A word is *clear* when it expresses an idea or impression exactly.

A word is *vigorous* when it creates a strong emotional impression.

A word is *interesting* when it is a fresh or vivid expression of an idea or an impression.

Dr. Bell's diction, that is, his choice of words to express his idea, is clear, vigorous, interesting, and closely related to the arrangement of his essay.

CLARITY IN WORDS

Note, for example, the exactness of the following italicized expressions—in the context of the sentence from which they are taken, and in the context of the purpose and central theme of the essay.

1. "A weekly column of *pungent* social analysis" (¶1). *Pungent* is derived from the Latin word meaning "to prick." Finley Peter Dunne's humor was frequently biting.
2. "This *wag* is looked on by contemporaries as . . . a designer of *drolleries*" (¶2). *Wag* refers to a humorist, and *drolleries* to mere jesting. Dr. Bell uses the italicized words in a denotative sense. But there are in addition connotative meanings of an ironical nature. He wants the reader to understand that Mr. Goldsmith's contemporaries have missed the point of the radio writer's analysis of the cultural scene.
3. "Even Penrod seems *sophisticated* beside him" (¶3). Here *sophisticated* means experienced or worldly-wise, which expresses perfectly the comparative immaturity of Henry Aldrich. Penrod is a fictional symbol of boyish unsophistication.
4. "Henry is almost *indecently* adolescent" (¶3). Note here that *indecently* refers, not to immodesty, but to the standards that are fitting to the class of adolescents.

* See handbooks: Foerster, pp. 293-348 (*50-66*); Hodges, *19-22*; Kierzek, *36a*, *39-44*. *75*; Perrin, pp. 303-62; Wykoff, pp. 402-03, *82-98*.

5. "More *tragicomic* still are the father and mother of this pair" (¶4). *Tragicomic* refers to a situation which blends tragic and comic elements. The parents' immaturity is more tragic because of their age and responsibility, more comic because it defeats the usual expectation that older people have learned some sense.

Exercises on Clarity

Review denotation and connotation in II A. Then show how Dr. Bell has made exact use of the following words both denotatively and connotatively in the context of his essay.

¶1: cultural pattern, pertinent, perusing, aftermath, illuminated, cannily interpreted, philosopher

¶2: predecessors, posterity

¶3: truculent, desirable

¶5: representative, multitudes, plausible demagogue, base mechanicals, functionalized, vocationalized, epitome, nonconformists

¶7: unanticipated, intention, counters, venally manipulated, coöperator

¶8: sociability, sentimentality, pseudo-ethical

¶9: rudimentary

¶16: *per se,* munificence

¶18: *summum bonum*

¶19: Messianic complex, *Herrenvolkismus*

¶26: salmagundi

¶27: *quid pro quo*

¶28: acquiesce, infantilism

¶29: credos, fatuity

VIGOR IN WORDS

Note the emotional impressions created by the following italicized expressions in the context of the sentence, the paragraph, and the central theme of the essay.

1. "That bewildering generation of Americans that lived and moved and for the most part *made a mess of things*" (¶2). *Made a mess of things* is in sharp contrast with the lofty connotations of the preceding phrases and thus arouses disgust.

2. "Educationally he is the *victim* of a high school system which underestimates him" (¶3). The word *victim* arouses pity for Henry Aldrich, anger for the system.

3. "America . . . now become a *homeland* of perennial adolescents" (¶5). The ironical use of *homeland* arouses resentment for the decline of American culture.
4. "The most powerful nation on earth was also the most *fumbling* and ineffective" (¶6). *Fumbling* here suggests a shameful weakness in a powerful nation.
5. "*Unctuous* utterance of *pseudo-ethical* trivialities" (¶8). *Unctuous* arouses contempt, *pseudo-ethical* disgust, or even anger.

Exercises on Vigor

What emotional impressions are suggested by each of the following words or phrases in their special contexts? Give reasons for your answer.

¶11: How great a triumph
¶12: verdant adolescent
¶14: exalted heights
¶15: gloating over his deposit book
¶16: applaud the gladiators

INTEREST IN WORDS

Note the freshness, the vividness, or the unusual image-making quality of the italicized expressions in the context of the sentences from which they are taken.

1. "Finley Peter Dunne, who for many years *spilled* a weekly column" (¶1). Contrast this word with the less vivid *wrote*.
2. "The multitudes who listen in to this weekly *exhibition of incompetency in living*" (¶5). Contrast this phrase with *middle-class living*.
3. "Dupes of any plausible demagogue who comes along with a slogan and a hillbilly band or its *urban equivalent*" (¶5). What does *urban equivalent* suggest in this context?
4. "One finds . . . more and more departmentalized pedants *hiding in the holes of research*" (¶22). Contrast this phrase with *following overspecialized activities*.
5. "We need to be rescued from . . . *bragging strut*" (¶24). *Bragging strut* is hyperbole, that is, exaggeration for the sake of rhetorical effect. Strut is swagger; bragging is conceited talk or gesture. Compare this phrase with *boastfulness*.

Exercise on Interest

In paragraphs 20-29 pick out five phrases that you find particularly fresh or vivid. Give reasons for your choice.

Sentence Style *

An effective sentence depends in great part upon the right choice of words. It also depends on the satisfactory arrangement of the various elements of the sentence in a structure that is clear, vigorous, and interesting.

SENTENCE CLARITY

A sentence is clear when all the parts contribute to the main idea. We attain *clarity* mainly by the proper use of

    1. Subordination
    2. Parallelism
    3. Connectives

"Perennial Adolescence" is noteworthy for the logical construction of its paragraphs. See particularly the following examples:

    1. Clarity achieved by subordination: †
    "We *who cannot solve our own riddles* must decide the issues facing humanity at large" (¶20).
    2. Clarity achieved by parallel structure (parallel structure places coordinate ideas in grammatically coordinate phrases and clauses: ‡)
    "Man exists to do creatively, as craftsmanlike as may be, all things that must be done:
    great things like government or mothering or the healing of
                      minds and bodies;
    small things like making beds or hoeing corn or driving a truck;

---

* See handbooks: Foerster, pp. 95-99; Hodges, pp. 463-64; Kierzek, pp. 37-45; Perrin, pp. 247-52, 257-64; Wykoff, 4, *4a*, pp. 348-49.

† See handbooks: Foerster, pp. 7-14, *69, 79*; Hodges, *24*; Kierzek, *47*; Perrin, pp. 257-59, 781-82; Wykoff, pp. 49-51, *77*.

‡ See handbooks: Foerster, pp. 17-20, *86*; Hodges, *26*; Kierzek, pp. 59-62, *56*; Perrin, pp. 282-83; Wykoff, *74*.

things in the public eye like making speeches or unleashing
atomic energy or making peace;
obscure things like selling groceries or running a bus or teaching school" (¶25).
3. Clarity achieved by connectives: *
"He finds inner peace who works at whatever is in front of him
not for the pay he gets
or for what he can buy with that pay,
not for applause or gratitude,
but for sheer joy in creativity" (¶25).

Exercises on Clarity

1. Pick out five sentences in the selection that exemplify good subordination.
2. Pick out five examples of parallel structure in paragraphs 20-26.
3. Underline the connectives in paragraph 14.

SENTENCE VIGOR

A sentence is vigorous when its parts are arranged so that the main
idea or impression is asserted in the strongest possible way. We attain
vigor mainly by

1. Using periodic sentences
2. Using balanced construction
3. Arranging ideas in the order of climax †
4. Placing key words in the most emphatic way ‡

"Perennial Adolescence" achieves vigor

1. By the use of periodic sentences ‡ (a periodic sentence withholds its meaning until the end and thus creates suspense):
"In spite of the public school system and a vocationalized higher
education, in spite of churches singing nursery rhymes instead
of chanting credos, in spite of Hollywood and the radio chains
and the newspapers, in spite of everything, it is still entirely
possible that the Aldriches—possibly not Mr. and Mrs., who are

* See handbooks: Foerster, pp. 13-14, *89*; Hodges, *26b*; Kierzek, pp. 34-35; Perrin,
pp. 501-04; Wykoff, p. 46, *14*.
† Foerster, pp. 24-25, *76*; Hodges, *29b-c*; Kierzek, *64*; Perrin, p. 473; Wykoff, *79e*.
‡ See handbooks: Foerster, pp. 27-28, *75*; Hodges, *29b*; Kierzek, p. 450; Perrin, pp.
280-82; Wykoff, *79d*.

pretty far gone in fatuity, but Henry and Mary and their children—may grow up" (¶29).

Note here the force of the final idea—growing up—created by suspense.

2. By the use of balanced construction * (a balanced sentence uses a similar grammatical construction to express contrasted ideas):
"Man should seek to know in order to live, not to live that he may know" (¶22).

3. By the use of climactic order † (a climactic arrangement is an order of increasing force):
"In our institutions of higher learning one finds with the passing years more and more departmentalized pedants hiding in the holes of research, seeking to run away from embarrassing questions, afraid of philosophy and scared to death of religion" (¶22).
Note here the increasing force of "hiding," "seeking to run," "afraid," and "scared to death."

4. By placing key words in an emphatic position: ‡
"No *salmagundi* made of things, amusements, lust for power, can assuage our growing hunger to *create*" (¶26).
Note emphatic position of *salmagundi* and *create*—the two key ideas—at the beginning and end of the sentence.

Exercises on Vigor

1. Pick out two sentences that illustrate each of the following: periodic structure, balance, climactic order.
2. Pick out three sentences where key words are used at the beginning or end. Show how their position increases the vigor of the sentence.

SENTENCE INTEREST

A sentence is interesting when it is fresh or vivid in its arrangement. We achieve *interest* mainly by

1. Using questions, exclamations, and figures of speech, such as metaphor, hyperbole and alliteration

* See handbooks: Foerster, pp. 28-29, 77; Hodges, *29g*; Kierzek, *63*; Perrin, p. 283; Wykoff, pp. 54, 117-18.

† See handbooks: Foerster, pp. 24-25, 76; Hodges, *29b-c*; Kierzek, *64*; Perrin, p. 473; Wykoff, *79e*.

‡ Foerster, pp. 25-27, 82; Hodges, *29a*; Kierzek, *61*; Perrin, pp. 293-95.

2. Varying the cadence or rhythm of a sentence
3. Varying the length and kind of sentences in a paragraph (see the analysis of paragraph style, and its subdivision, paragraph interest, later in this chapter)

Note in "Perennial Adolescence" that

1. Interest is achieved by

a. Questions:

"What more can be asked for in the way of munificence than such prodigal expenditure for purchasable joys?" (¶16)
Note that this ironical question comes after seven almost unvaried sentences.

b. Exclamations:

"And woe be to the cynic who doubts our competence so to act in the grand manner!" (¶20)
This exclamation, following two balanced sentences, forestalls monotony.

c. Metaphors:

"They do at least begin to know that the world is all adrift; it may be, if we set ourselves to the task, that we can convince them it is they themselves who have slipped their moorings. But who is at work on this salvage?" (¶9)
Note here (1) the implied comparison (metaphor) between the mental and moral confusion of the Aldriches and a ship that has lost its moorings, and (2) a second related comparison, implied in the question, between a salvage party and the mature Americans who attack perennial adolescence. Both these comparisons tend to arouse the imagination to the peril of the Aldriches.

2. Interest, as well as vigor, is achieved by varying the cadence or rhythm of a sentence.

Sentence 2 in paragraph 28 is an effective rhetorical question, a fine example of balance, but, above all, an outstanding model of effective cadence. Note how the rhythm, indicated by / for stressed, ⌣ for unstressed syllables, and ∥ for pause, is varied by increasing the number of stressed syllables in the last line where the harsh metaphor "ride roughshod" is at once the logical heart of the sentence and its emotional climax. Also note the alliteration.

Have we indeed sunk
to that most juvenile form of juvenility, //
the juvenility of grown-up people afraid
to smack the children down // when they seek
to ride roughshod over parents and teachers?

Exercises on Interest

1. In order to show how the interrogative sentence (¶21) promotes interest
   a. State the same idea in declarative form, and
   b. Compare the effect of the two sentences.
2. What is the effect of the exclamations used in paragraphs 6 and 11?
3. Pick out a metaphor or simile, not mentioned above, that helps to promote interest.
4. Analyze, in the manner described above, the rhythm of sentence 1, paragraph 29; of sentence 2, paragraph 15; of sentence 1, paragraph 5. How does the variation of cadence contribute to the interest and vigor of the sentence?

Paragraph Style *

A paragraph is a unit of a larger composition. It consists of a group of sentences that are related to some one aspect of the central theme. A good paragraph is composed of clear, vigorous, and interesting words and sentences. In addition, there are certain rules of clarity, vigor, and interest that apply especially to the paragraph.

PARAGRAPH CLARITY

A paragraph is *clear* when each sentence contributes to the central thought. (The central thought is either implied or expressed in a topic sentence.) Clarity also demands coherence, that is, an orderly flow of sentences marked by repetition of key ideas.

Paragraph 3 of "Perennial Adolescence" is a good example of clarity in paragraph structure. This paragraph explains the adolescent character of the Aldrich family and thus helps to introduce the central theme (see outline, I C, pp. 286-87).

* Foerster, pp. 43-68, 229-32; Hodges, *31*; Kierzek, pp. 463-73; Perrin, pp. 191-202; Wykoff, pp. 307-47.

Topic sentence: "Henry Aldrich (a 'typical American boy') is almost indecently adolescent" (Ss 1 and 2).

This central thought is clearly developed. Each sentence contributes to the central thought by justifying the classification (Section III) of Henry as a perennial adolescent. Thus Henry is a perennial adolescent because:

He never grows up (S3).

He is even more adolescent than Penrod, a national symbol of unsophistication (S4).

He is undisciplined, self-assertive, and bewildered (S5).

He is educationally deficient (S6).

He cannot discriminate in matters of society, art, or religion (S7).

He misspends his time (S8).

He is a creature of circumstance (S9).

He lacks the initiative and common sense of Tom Sawyer and Huck Finn (S10).

He is as purposeless and truculent as his sister Mary, his feminine counterpart (S11).

Note too how the key word, Henry Aldrich, is repeated throughout. Henry occurs in every sentence as the subject, as a term of comparison, or by reference of pronouns. Altogether, Henry occurs fourteen times in eleven sentences. It is impossible therefore to misunderstand the author's meaning.

Exercises on Clarity

1. Show how paragraphs 6, 10, 14, and 18 are directly related to the central theme.
2. In order to show the clarity of paragraphs 6, 10, 14, and 18
   a. State the central thought of each
   b. Show how each sentence contributes to the central thought
   c. Point out the repetition of the key ideas

PARAGRAPH VIGOR

A paragraph is *vigorous* when we stress the central thought by

1. Placing key words in an emphatic position
2. Using parallel and balanced construction
3. Using climactic order

Paragraph 12 of "Perennial Adolescence," which shows how the quest for money is sterile is a good example of vigor in paragraph structure.

Topic: Such a concept of nobility [based on wealth] does not appeal to mature experience.

1. *Emphatic position of key idea,* money. In sentence 3 "money" is placed emphatically near the end; in sentence 4 a "penny" occurs near the end and is the object unstated, but understood, of the concluding verb.

2. Note the *parallel construction* of sentences 2, 3, and 4: "One meets. . . . One meets. . . . One comes to know. . . ." Each of the sentences is also balanced; that is, it contains a similar grammatical construction to express contrasted ideas.

3. Observe the *climactic order* of the examples in sentences 2, 3, and 4. The first man has money and is worth nothing; the second man is worth while, despite his money; the poor woman has no money but is the most lovable. Note too the climactic arrangement of the words in the last sentence: (1) so simple, (2) so good, (3) so lovable; (1) who never had a penny, (2) have not now, (3) never will have.

Exercise on Vigor

Following the method set forth in the comment above, examine paragraphs 11, 13, 15, 16, and 19 and show how the author achieves vigor in each.

PARAGRAPH INTEREST

A paragraph is *interesting* when the sentences are combined with pleasing effect by:

1. Varying the length of the sentences
2. Varying the kind of sentences
3. Varying the beginnings of sentences

Paragraph 22 of "Perennial Adolescence" is a good example of interesting paragraph structure.

a. Note the variety in the length of the sentences. Sentence 1, 41 words; sentence 2, 4 words; sentence 3, 16 words; sentence 4, 39 words; sentence 5, 41 words; sentence 6, 13 words.

b. Note the variety in the kind of sentence: simple sentences, 2, 4, and 6; complex sentences, 1, 3, and 5.

c. Note the variety in the beginnings of the sentences. Sentences 1, 4, and 6 begin with phrases; sentences 2 and 3 with the subject noun; sentence 5 with a subject pronoun. Sentence 5 is a fine example of parallelism; note the participial phrases (hiding, seeking, afraid, scared to death).

Exercise on Interest

Following the method set forth in the comment above, examine paragraphs 20, 26, and 28 and show how the author achieves interest in each.

GENERAL EXERCISES ON STYLE

Analyze the style of the examples cited below as directed. Use the style analysis of "Perennial Adolescence" as a model, unless instructed otherwise by your teacher. In estimating the style of the various writers regard their audience as being of the same maturity as the audience of Dr. Bell.

1. Analyze Example II H, "What Is a University?" by J. H. Newman, for the quality of clarity in its diction.
2. Analyze Example II I2, "The High Road of Life" by S. T. Coleridge, for the quality of vigor in its diction.
3. Analyze Example VI C1, "The Last Question of All" by C. E. Montague, for the quality of interest in its diction.
4. Analyze Example II B, "Definition of Meaning" by Gustave Weigel, for the quality of clearness in its sentences.
5. Analyze Example V A3, "Joan and David" by Thomas De Quincey, for the quality of vigor in its sentences.
6. Analyze Example II D3, "What Is Good Writing?" by Samuel Eliot Morison, for the quality of interest in its sentences.
7. Analyze Example II C1, "On Chance" by Herbert L. Samuel, for the quality of clearness in paragraph structure.
8. Analyze Example VI C2, "We Must Not Despair" by Winston Churchill, for the quality of vigor in its paragraph structure.
9. Analyze Example VI A4, "Why a Classic Is a Classic" by Arnold Bennett, for the quality of interest in its paragraph structure.
10. Write an exposition of approximately 800 words on one or more of the topics listed below:

a. A comparison between the diction of George Orwell (Example VI A2) and C. E. Montague (Example VI C1) from the point of view of interest.

b. A comparison between the sentence structure of Arnold Toynbee (Example II C2) and of Learned Hand (Example V C1) from the point of view of clarity.

c. A comparison between the paragraphs of Aldous Huxley (Example V C2) and of Mark Twain (Example IV D) from the point of view of clarity.

d. A comparison between the sentences of Lewis Mumford (Example II F) and Joseph Addison (Example III A2) from the point of view of interest.

e. A comparison between the paragraphs of Charles Malik and Bernard Iddings Bell (this section) from the point of view of clarity and vigor.

11. In your opinion which examples in Sections II-VIII are the best illustrations of a clear style? Give reasons for your answer.

12. In your opinion which examples in Sections II-VIII are the best illustrations of a vigorous style? Give reasons for your answer.

13. In your opinion which examples in Sections II-VIII are the best illustrations of an interesting style? Give reasons for your answer.

14. In your opinion which examples in Sections II-VIII best illustrate the combination of clarity, vigor, and interest? In arriving at your opinion be sure to weigh the relative difficulties of the subject and purpose.

15. Write an exposition of about 1000 words on the topic, "Cultivating a Style in English Composition." You may find it helpful to reread the following examples:

II D3, "What Is Good Writing?"
II E2, "What Is Literature?"
II I1, "The True Writer"
IV D, "Fenimore Cooper's Literary Offenses"
VI A3, "The Art of Writing History"
VI C1, "The Last Question of All"

A. Choose for your character sketch a person with definite traits. Make these traits illustrate some important idea.

ANNE O'HARE MC CORMICK:
The Mayor of Florence

B. Let the subject of a character exposition explain himself by his own words and by his own actions.

ALISTAIR COOKE: *Will Rogers*

C. Make the various characteristics of your subject serve to present one *predominant* impression.

GEORGE DANGERFIELD: *John Quincy Adams*

D. Account for any major change in the order of arrangement (1) by announcing the change and (2) by explaining briefly the necessity for the change.

DOUGLAS SOUTHALL FREEMAN:
Robert E. Lee: The Pattern of a Life

General Exercises

Exposition of Character

IN SECTIONS I-VIII we have made a preliminary study of the four elements of rhetoric:

1. Subject, occasion, and purpose
2. Analysis of the subject
3. Arrangement
4. Style

From this study we have derived principles that apply to all forms of discourse: exposition, argument, persuasion, description, and narration. The application of these principles differs in each particular form of discourse, however, because each form has its own special purpose.

Exposition aims to explain a subject; argument aims to win assent to a belief held by the writer; persuasion aims to stimulate the reader to some kind of action; description aims to present qualities perceived by the senses; and narration aims to recount the movement of events.

WHY WE STUDY EXPOSITION FIRST

We study exposition first because:

1. It is in itself the most common form of discourse.
2. It is linked to other forms of discourse, which are usually found in combination with exposition, and thus prepares the ground for further study.
3. It permits us to observe clearly the various uses of the methods of analysis alone and in combination.

That exposition is the most common form of discourse is evident from its *definition* and from the student's own experience. As that form of discourse in which we aim to explain a subject, exposition is the means of communicating our ideas about people, of interpreting historical events and social problems, of clarifying political opinions, of examining evidence in a particular field of study—in short, of explaining anything that can be explained.

Its general importance and the frequency of its use may also be determined by the student's own experience in analyzing the material in the eight previous sections of this book. Fifty-four of the sixty-odd examples already studied are predominantly expository. These examples range from the exposition of ideas about man and society to the explanation of simple occurrences, from brief clarifications of the meaning of terms to extended expositions of logical method, from short studies of typical Americans to elaborate definitions of the American character. Exposition plays an equally predominant role in the student's reading and writing on other subjects, such as history or economics, where he is asked to explain much more often than he is asked to argue, to persuade, to describe, or to narrate.

Secondly, exposition is linked to other forms of discourse. Just as the various methods of analysis—definition, classification, exemplification, and so on—are rarely used in their pure form but are combined with other methods of analysis (see Review Exercises after Section VII), so too the several forms of discourse are normally combined. To argue, one must first explain the issues under dispute and the background of the question. To persuade, one must first explain why the proposed action is reasonable. To narrate, one must clarify the meaning of the action. Even description can hardly be maintained beyond a few pages without the support of exposition. Thus exposition plays an important role in all the other forms of discourse; furthermore, exposition frequently includes these other forms of discourse in its own development.

In studying exposition, therefore, we shall anticipate some of the problems that will be taken up later. (Note: A summary of the relations between exposition, argument, and persuasion appears in the introduction to Section XI.)

The third reason for studying exposition before the other forms of discourse is that it permits us to observe more clearly the use of the various methods of analysis alone and in combination. Many arguments and persuasions are bound by certain rules or conventions of debate, and are frequently addressed to readers who have at least some basic knowledge of, or interest in, the issues under dispute. But exposition, of its nature an attempt to clarify, is usually less demanding of the reader. It is, moreover, considerably simpler in its approach to the subject. Hence an exposition is much more likely to follow an explicit method of development than the other forms of discourse.

TYPES OF EXPOSITION

There are two principal types of exposition: exposition of character and exposition of facts and ideas.

Both types are alike in that they make common use of the principles of good arrangement. Both types attempt to explain; both types analyze a subject to determine a central theme; both express the central theme by using the various means of development; both employ the principles of effective style.

The two types differ, however, in the application of these principles to particular subjects and occasions. Each problem in exposition raises its own peculiar difficulties. Thus, for example, an exposition of an idea, such as Samuel's explanation "On Chance," II C1, usually stresses definition, a method of development that might have no place in an exposition of character traits such as F. P. Adams' "Quirks," IV B2. The exposition of historical events, such as Henry Bamford Parkes's "Why Men Came to America," VI B, leans heavily on causal development or process development. The exposition of character, on the other hand, is more readily developed by examples and comparison and contrast.

Each type of exposition, then, has its characteristic problems. Moreover, even within the separate types of exposition, we may observe certain variations in the use of the principles of arrangement and style. Let us investigate here some of the special problems of character exposition. We shall consider the exposition of facts and ideas in Section X.

Note: Character exposition is frequently absorbed in the exposition of facts and ideas. Often it is studied as a subordinate division of the second and larger class of exposition. We consider it first because it involves less complex subject matter and thus forms a more convenient introduction to the study of exposition.

Exposition of Character

Exposition of character is one of the most useful varieties of expository writing. It aims to explain what a man really exemplifies, how he acts and thinks, what the main motives of his life are, how he affects the world about him, and how he compares with other men of the same generation, class, or profession. Character exposition is as entertaining as it is useful. We have already observed this in Russell Lynes's analysis "On Weekend Guests," III C2.

But there is no infallible method of writing good character sketches or short biographies. The general formula, as always, is: Apply your principles wisely.

In this section you will find four examples of character exposition: a study of a contemporary mayor of Florence by Anne O'Hare McCormick; of Will Rogers by Alistaii Cooke; of President John Quincy Adams by George Dangerfield; of Robert E. Lee by Douglas S. Freeman. Each of these essays is a splendid example of effective combination of the basic principles of analysis, of good arrangement, and of brilliant style; but the analysis, the arrangement, and the style of each is different. One reason for this variety is that each of the subjects—the mayor of Florence, Will Rogers, John Quincy Adams, Robert E. Lee—presents a different problem to the writer. Much is known about one man, little or nothing about another. Each subject exhibits a different predominant trait, which demands a different style of exposition. For example, the life of Robert E. Lee provided Mr. Freeman with ample opportunity for a formal, eulogistic style, an opportunity obviously denied to Alistair Cooke by the character and occupations of Will Rogers. Thus the subject of the exposition, as well as the attitude of the writer, determines the arrangement and style.

Furthermore, the special intention of the writer may affect the exposition. For instance, Mrs. McCormick aims to illustrate an important idea by means of a short character sketch of her subject. Mr. Cooke, on the other hand, is less concerned with illustrating an idea; his aim rather is to create an imaginative impression of a singularly interesting person. Mr. Dangerfield treats John Quincy Adams with the austere objectivity of a historian, while Douglas S. Freeman obviously intends to hold up Robert E. Lee as a man to venerate and admire. Each of these authors has selected his material and developed it in a manner appropriate to the subject and his purpose, as the outlines, commentary, and analytical exercises will point out. All the general principles of good arrangement and style are present, but in different ways and in different proportions.

Special Problems of Character Exposition

Study of the four essays in this section will reveal that, although each essay applies all the relevant principles of analysis, arrangement, and style wisely, each is a notable example of the successful solution of one of the special problems of character exposition. These special problems are:

1. What type of subject is best suited for character exposition?
2. What is the best way to reveal a character in an exposition?
3. How can the writer explain a complex character without making his own writing complicated?
4. How can the writer combine several orders of arrangement or several methods of analysis without loss of unity and coherence?

Anne O'Hare McCormick solves the first problem effectively by selecting as a subject *a person with definite traits.* No one is interested in a character who is trivial, featureless, drab. A writer should choose a character with strong traits, traits *that express a living idea.* A real personality is not a bundle of physical accidents. He stands by himself and he stands for something; he exists and he is meaningful. A good example of such a person is the subject of Mrs. McCormick's "Mayor of Florence."

The second problem is solved effectively by Alistair Cooke, who makes his subject, Will Rogers, *explain himself by his own words and by his own actions.* The reader can judge a character more accurately by seeing what he does and hearing him speak than by listening to the writer's interpretation of the character. While interpretation is essential to direct the reader to the significance of what is said and done, it is always the handmaiden of the objective fact. At bottom, interpretation merely analyzes what a man has done and what he has said.

George Dangerfield's essay illustrates a method of solving the third problem. His subject, John Quincy Adams, was a man of diverse traits, a complex personality who can hardly be explained without some interpretation. Yet Mr. Dangerfield unifies his essay by *relating the various characteristics of his subject to one predominant impression.*

The final problem is, of course, the most difficult. It applies to longer biographical essays where the author is required to arrange his material according to two equally important methods of analysis.

Douglas S. Freeman in his essay on Robert E. Lee was obliged by the nature of his subject to develop two main traits of Lee's character —Lee's simplicity and spirituality. The first trait, developed chiefly by process analysis, was most appropriately presented in a time order. But, since the development of the second trait required definition and examples, which are methods of analysis that are not conveniently presented in a time order, Freeman was forced to abandon the chronological pattern established in the early part of the essay. Yet he took care to introduce the second arrangement by a careful transition, which explained the shift in order and thereby avoided confusion.

Thus Douglas S. Freeman solved the fourth special problem of character exposition. His solution may be stated: If your purpose and subject require you to use more than one arrangement, you should *account for any major change in the order of arrangement* (a) *by announcing the change and* (b) *by explaining briefly the necessity for the change.*

---

a.   Choose for your character sketch a person with definite traits. Make these traits illustrate some important idea.

The Mayor of Florence

BY ANNE O'HARE MC CORMICK

1 Florence is one of many Italian cities which ousted their Communist administrations in last spring's municipal elections. In its long

THE MAYOR OF FLORENCE: reprinted from the New York *Times* of December 12, 1951, by permission of the author and the publisher.

and turbulent history this capital of the Renaissance has always been a kind of city-state, as jealous of its independence as of its unrivaled art treasures. Many wars have been fought in the shadow of Giotto's tower, from the battles of Guelphs * and Ghibellines † to the clashes between Fascists and anti-Fascists at the beginning and end of the Mussolini era. The fortresslike Palazzo Vecchio has been the seat of regimes without number. For months on end an American military governor sat in the splendid old room, the Sala Clemente, which was occupied for four years by a Communist Mayor and is now presided over by a Christian Democrat.

2 The process of change continues, a tide beating against stones that until now it has not submerged, but in recent years perhaps no transition has been more strikingly personified than in the contrast between Mayor Mario Fabiani, the Communist, and his successor, Giorgio La Pira.

3 Fabiani is described as a sincere and idealistic Communist. The Florentines did not grumble more than usual under his administration because he did not try to make drastic changes in their way of life. When a man becomes Mayor of Florence, they say, even a man tied to Moscow and the party line, the tradition of the city takes hold of him. That he is now President of the Provincial Council signifies that his following and the appeal of communism are still strong in the Florence district. In all of Tuscany, in fact, though it is a country of prosperous farms and vineyards, the Communists polled a heavy vote last summer.

4 Nevertheless the city itself demonstrated that it had had enough of communism by defeating Fabiani and electing by a majority of nearly 6000 a man who did not seek the office and who must be one of the most unusual figures that have risen to the surface in the evolution of post-war Italy.

5 La Pira is a modest little man of 47 who looks like an eager boy. Most of his life was spent as professor of Roman law at the University of Florence. His only experience in politics was a term as representative of his party in the Chamber of Deputies and as Under Secretary of Labor in De Gasperi's cabinet. He is a deep student of social problems, not in books but in the back streets and tenements of Florence.

* Guelphs, the popular party.
† Ghibellines, the aristocrat party.

6 The new Mayor is called "Il Santo"—The Saint—by some of his followers because of his ascetic habits and his devotion to the poor. He has slept in night refuges to share the lot of the homeless and has been known to give away his coat to a shivering beggar. Every Sunday morning he serves a hot breakfast to all who ask for it in two of the city churches. "Most Communists around here are not ideologists but just hungry human beings," he declares. "The best way to fight communism is to feed them and give them work."

7 A pair of yellow canaries singing in a cage in a deep window embrasure strikes an odder note in La Pira's magnificent medieval office than the little wooden crucifix standing on his enormous desk. The birds and the cross, his manner of life and the fact that he was born in Assisi lead Florentines to say that their Sindaco* is trying to emulate St. Francis. La Pira smiles and shakes his head at this suggestion. The gentleness and love of St. Francis are sorely needed in our angry age, he remarks, but the fighting spirit of St. Dominic is also necessary to carry on "the Christian revolution." It is quite evident that La Pira has dedicated himself to "the Christian revolution," which he defines as a battle to restore the dignity of the human being.

8 It is too soon to judge his administration, but he attacks his problems with vigor and enthusiasm. Certainly he has initiated more changes than his predecessor. Under Communist rule the aristocratic tradition of the Palazzo Vecchio was strictly maintained, but under La Pira the courtyards are the refuge of hoboes expecting a handout from the Mayor, who gives practically all his salary to the poor.

9 As Mayor, La Pira has a simple four-point program. It is to provide more housing, increase employment, give public assistance to the needy, and encourage the arts. The last point he considers as important as the others. "A city like Florence cannot live without music, art, and beauty," he says.

10 Maybe the pattern of administration will not alter much under the new regime. The Florentines complain that they cannot run their own affairs because too many local decisions are made in Rome. There is the bitter question of the Ponte Santa Trinita, for instance. The counterpart funds for the reconstruction are available, but nothing is done because Florence wants its favorite bridge rebuilt on the old foundations, as it was, and Rome has the last word and it is "No."

* Sindaco, mayor.

The same controversy partly explains why great gaps left by mines on both sides of the Ponte Vecchio still disfigure the banks of the Arno.

11 But the change of administration shows that when the Communists lose the key posts the whole emphasis and outlook are different. Mayor La Pira believes that Communist rule is finished in Florence, but that depends on what his party and others can do to overcome promises with performance. The point of interest in this case is that the shift of emphasis is toward the people irrespective of party.

Comment

Mrs. McCormick's essay is an excellent illustration of analysis and arrangement.

Let us first study her method of analysis.

Her subject is Giorgio La Pira, the mayor of Florence. The precise aspect of the subject which she chooses to discuss is that *Mayor La Pira is a striking personification of change* (central theme) from communist rule to Christian democracy. In accordance with this purpose Mrs. McCormick has analyzed each phase of her theme to be sure her readers understand what she means. First she discusses change in general by offering a brief *process analysis* (Section VII) of Florentine history (¶1). In paragraph 2 she states her thesis and begins to establish it by setting forth a *contrast* (Section V) between the old mayor and the new. The old mayor, Fabiani, is then *described* (analysis by definition, Section II) not for his own sake but as a personification of the thing changed (¶3). The fourth paragraph shows the transition from the old mayor to the new. In paragraph 5 Mayor La Pira's past is set forth in a brief *process exposition* (Section VII) blended with narration of details. Paragraph 6 characterizes the new mayor as a saint and supports this *classification* (Section III) by several *examples* (Section IV). Paragraph 7 characterizes the mayor by the two symbols of the canaries and the crucifix (a species of comparison) and two direct *comparisons* (Section V) with St. Francis and St. Dominic. In paragraph 8 Mayor La Pira's regime is *contrasted* (Section V) with the communist regime. Paragraph 9 states the purposes of Mayor La Pira's regime. This is equivalent to telling *why* La Pira, the cause, intends to act. Hence it is a brief *analysis by cause* (Section VI). Paragraph 10 speculates on the current circumstances of Italian politics or the conditions which may affect the operation of the "four-point program" (relation of cause and condition, Section VI). The final paragraph, 11, restates the central theme.

Thus we see that Mrs. McCormick's analysis has *combined* all the basic forms of analysis studied in Part I: definition, Section II; classification and division, Section III; example, Section IV; contrast and comparison, Section V; cause and effect, Section VI; and process, Section VII. Moreover, she has used each of these forms of analysis only to the extent that they help her to achieve her main intention, the exposition of her central theme. The principal form of analysis is *contrast,* since a contrast is implied by the central theme—Mayor La Pira is a striking personification of *change* from communist rule to Christian democracy.

Mrs. McCormick's arrangement is equally effective. It is *clear,* with an orderly beginning (¶1-2), development (¶3-10), and end (¶11). It is *unified,* since each paragraph is directly related to the central theme, as we have indicated in the analysis above.

Analysis and Composition

1. Explain in detail why the brief history of Florence is necessary to introduce the author's main point. In your answer consider Mrs. McCormick's audience, the readers of the New York *Times.*
2. Show how the contrast between Mayor Fabiani and Mayor La Pira sets off the main characteristics of the latter.
3. Reread paragraphs 5-9. This sequence of paragraphs in the heart of the essay is narration harmonized with exposition. Show how the facts recounted about Mayor La Pira actually seem to illustrate the chief trait of his character, his resemblance to St. Francis.
4. How do the quotations in paragraphs 6, 7, and 9 help us to understand Mayor La Pira?
5. a. By consulting references in your library,* investigate the life of a prominent public person whom you admire.
   b. Choose several outstanding traits which sum up your reason for admiring him. Make sure these traits illustrate an important idea.
   c. Find three or more illustrations of these traits or this idea in his biography.
   d. Draw up a brief outline arranging these traits in the order you think will best communicate your admiration to a reader.
   e. Write an essay of about 500 words based on your outline. Include as many methods of analysis as you can.
6. How does Mrs. McCormick's style help to achieve coherence and emphasis in the whole composition? (Section VIII)

* Foerster, *38*; Hodges, *33b3*; Kierzek, pp. 176-86; Perrin, pp. 374-77; Wykoff, *48a–b.*

b. Let the subject of a character exposition explain himself by his own words and by his own actions.

Will Rogers

BY ALISTAIR COOKE

1 If a Russian or a Finn asked you today who was this Will Rogers, what did he do, you'd have a hard time answering him. A cowboy?—yes, that's how he started life, getting nowhere at school and running away and staking his horse outside some western town every night till he managed to get a job trailing herd from Oklahoma up to Kansas. A world traveler?—well, yes, I suppose so. He heard that the Argentine was good ranching country and hit the road for New Orleans to take a boat. No boats from here, they said, better go to New York. So—with that remarkable ease of roaming that poor American boys seemed to have in the days when they were restricted to a cow pony, a pair of bandy legs, and their wits—he rode and bummed his way to New York. Last boat for Buenos Aires just left, they said, why not go to England?—they appreciate South America, they have boats all the time. So he didn't think twice, but signed on as night-watchman to a shipload of sheep and landed up in London, where he sailed for Rio. And in the same casual way, but sweating it out along with the crew or the cattle all the way, he went to India and South Africa. He broke in horses for the British Army in the Boer War and it might well be one of the forgotten meetings of history that he broke

WILL ROGERS: reprinted from *One Man's America* (published in England by Rupert Hart-Davis Ltd. as *Letters from America*) by Alistair Cooke, by permission of Alfred A. Knopf, Inc. Copyright 1952 by Alistair Cooke.

in a charger for Winston Churchill. Then, in the same spirit, to Australia and New Zealand and back to America, all before he was twenty-five.

2 Still, a generation of cowboys with happy feet have done all this and died obscure. Was he a vaudeville actor?—yes, indeed. He got to showing off rope tricks at county fairs and one night found himself on a stage in Johannesburg roping a dashing horse and lassoing the trombone player. He got into Wild West shows and ended up in the Ziegfeld Follies, and at state banquets—the favorite performer of presidents and kings. Just standing there twirling a rope and saying whatever was on his mind that he'd read in the newspapers that day. This was an idea that came to him years after his talent was known as that of one of the best ropers alive. He felt nervous once before his big trick—roping a steer with one hand and its rider with the other—and he happened to say, "If this thing comes off, it'll be quite a trick. If it doesn't, you better all go home." The house roared, and this simple and astonished cowboy, part Cherokee Indian, born on Indian territory, was urged by his pals to talk when he felt like it. He did this in New York, in Berlin, in London, in San Francisco, and there has never been an act like him.

3 Imagine him, small and wiry, hair like soft rope, a nose like a carrot, two quizzical blue eyes with pin-point pupils, two clefts in tanned cheeks, and a huge firm mouth, trembling somewhere between mischief and tears. Imagine him, standing in chaps and shirt before President Wilson or King George V, his right hand doing marvelous things, and drawling observations about taxes, submarines, the Russians, the wonders of Paris. Then he looks up with the calculated shyness that was his protection against humans in the raw, quiets his rope, and clears his throat. It's absurd, almost an insult to the whole idea of staged entertainment. A cowboy rambling on before half the hushed statesmen of Europe. "Your Majesty," he says, "you sure put on some great sights in London. But I wish you'd have been with me on Saturday nights in Claremore, Oklahoma. Saturday night was the real thing there. You'd have been crazy about it. Course, ropin' and ridin' and tent shows and circuses is nice stuff. But Saturdays we used to go down to the barber shop *and watch haircuts!*"

4 He went to the Test Match at Lord's and thought cricket was fine, but the lunch and tea intervals made him restless. Asked by the Prince of Wales if the game could ever take in America, he thought it might, with one improvement. And what was that? "Before the game starts,"

he said with a melancholy look, "I'd line the teams up and say, 'Now, listen, fellas, no food till you're through.'"

5 [1]He talked like this all the time, only the pin points of his eyes glinting in a homely, sad face. [2]His voice had the twanging, syncopated drawl of the Texas panhandle and Oklahoma. [3]He never went beyond the fourth grade at school. [4]And he was one of the few self-made men who truly regretted it. [5]Yet he had a God-given gift for sentences of pure running wit that made hard ideas look as smooth and beautiful as rocks under a trout stream:

"A holding company is the people you give your money to while you're being searched."

"One revolution is just like one cocktail, it just gets you organized for the next."

"A difference of opinion is what makes horse racing and missionaries."

"Russia is a country that buries its troubles. Your criticism is your epitaph. You simply say your say and then you are through."

6 Will Rogers was already a national institution when the New York *Times* had the brilliant idea of asking him to write a daily piece —two sentences or twenty—about the state of the nation. For many years he always appeared in a little box on the front page. And usually two or three sentences were enough, for though he honestly regarded himself as illiterate, his character and mind had long ago done all the work that more learned, but less wise, men have to do on paper before they can say what they would really like to mean.

7 Will Rogers enjoyed a license, which was given to no president, to bawl out the army, the taxpayer, the banks, the presidency itself. And when he said, "I never met a man I didn't like," his good nature or self-defense was getting the better of his memory. His great sweetness and unpretending face helped him put over on the American people more unpleasant home truths than they would have tolerated from a smart man, a handsome man, or a Congressman.

Comment

Note how closely this short character study approaches the classic pattern of analysis studied in Part I. Here Mr. Cooke

1. Traces Will Rogers' career from childhood to maturity (*process, Section VII*).

2. *Classifies* (Section III) him as a cowboy, world traveler, vaudeville actor, and homespun philosopher.
3. Gives numerous *examples* (Section IV) of all these activities, especially of the last.
4. *Contrasts* (Section V) Will Rogers with the more learned but less wise.
5. *Describes* Rogers' *effect* (Section VI) upon Americans and people in general.
6. *Defines* (Section II) or describes Rogers' personal appearance.

Although this essay is primarily an exposition, there is an element of narrative (especially in ¶1-2) and certain touches of description (¶3).

The *arrangement* supports the author's intention to explain Will Rogers' casual ways, genial nature, and unpretentious common sense. The essay itself gives the effect of being casual, genial, and unpretentious. Its order is mainly chronological, tracing Rogers' career from cowboy to philosopher, but it digresses briefly from this order to describe Will Rogers (¶3) and breaks the narrative flow to quote several samples of Rogers' wit (¶5).

Analysis and Composition

1. Determine which of the following sentences is the most nearly accurate statement of the main idea in paragraph 1. Give reasons for your choice.
   a. Will Rogers was both a cowboy and a world traveler.
   b. It is difficult to characterize Will Rogers.
   c. Will Rogers was more than a cowboy and world traveler.
2. State in as many ways as you can the main idea in paragraph 2. Choose that statement which seems the most accurate to you. Give reasons for your choice.
3. The arrangement of details in paragraph 3 is especially effective in arousing interest. Show by listing specific examples just how the following qualities present in the paragraph help to make it emphatic:
   a. Concrete details
   b. Words which portray or describe emotion
   c. Repetition
   d. Suspense
   e. Climax
   f. Deliberate bathos
4. How are the first four sentences of paragraph 5 connected with the main idea of the paragraph? The main idea is stated in sentence 5.
5. Give the gist of paragraph 6 in one sentence.
6. In a paragraph of not more than 100 words summarize Mr. Cooke's impression of Will Rogers.

7. The diction throughout this essay is colloquial rather than formal. Expressions like "getting nowhere," "trailing herd," "bummed his way," "sweating it out" are often criticized as slang. Can you justify this informality on the grounds of the author's purpose and subject? Consult handbooks * before writing out your opinion.

C. Make the various characteristics of your subject serve to present one *predominant* impression.

John Quincy Adams

BY GEORGE DANGERFIELD

1 John Quincy Adams also deserved well of the state, and was to attain an eminence that foreign birth denied to Gallatin. Yet the eminence, once reached, was a thorny one: there are few examples of political mismanagement more instructive than the presidency of John Quincy Adams, unless it be that of his father, John Adams.

2 ¹He [John Quincy Adams] spent his life in the public service, for which he was peculiarly fitted except in one respect—he was almost totally deficient in the art of getting on with other people. ²He was an independent man, but he wore his independence with a difference. ³It was like a *tunica molesta*—a shirt of fire—smeared with the inflammable materials of pride and suspicion, awkwardness and singularity, a chemical composition which burst into dull flame at the slightest contact with the outer world. ⁴"Of all the men," wrote a prejudiced Englishman who met him in 1812 when he was the American min-

* Foerster, pp. 93-94, 55; Hodges, pp. 193-98; Kierzek, pp. 15-23; Perrin, pp. 39-48.

ister to Russia, "whom it was ever my lot to accost and to waste civilities upon, [he] was the most doggedly and systematically repulsive. ⁵With a vinegar aspect, cotton in his leathern ears, and hatred to England in his heart, he sat in the frivolous assemblies of Petersburg like a bulldog among spaniels; and many were the times that I drew monosyllables and grim smiles from him and tried in vain to mitigate his venom." ⁶The writer little guessed at the self-mortifying processes perpetually at work behind that forbidding exterior. ⁷"I was not satisfied with myself this day," Adams wrote in his diary, after dining at Philadelphia with the president of the Bank of the United States, "having talked too much at dinner. . . . Nor can I always (I did not this day) altogether avoid a dogmatical and peremptory tone and manner, always disgusting and especially offensive in persons to whose age or situation others consider some deference due." ⁸Once, after speaking too harshly to a religious maniac called Jenkins, who called on him with some printed sheets of scriptural texts against dueling, he confided to his diary: ⁹"I am a man of reserved, cold, austere, and forbidding manners; my political adversaries say, a gloomy misanthropist, and my personal enemies, an unsocial savage." ¹⁰And he confessed to himself that he had not the pliability to reform this "defect."

3 ¹A bull-dog among spaniels! ²The tribute is an unconscious one, but it is a tribute none the less. ³If he could not fawn, he could fight. ⁴In the intensity of his self-scourgings one can detect a certain pride. ⁵The very lack of pliability that so perplexed him in his moments of self-abasement was also a source of pleasure. ⁶"I think I touched them up," he would often say, after some particularly angry scene of his own contriving. ⁷He had—he could not help it—the instinct for the jugular. ⁸His printed assault upon Jonathan Russell—who had been so ill-advised as to cast doubts upon the patriotism of Adams' conduct at Ghent—was so deadly that for many years afterwards the vocabulary of America was increased, though not enriched, by the transitive verb "to Jonathan-Russell," meaning to pulverize an opponent.

4 He fought persistently, splenetically—sometimes expending his energies upon the meanest objects, sometimes putting them to the service of purely personal ambitions, but more often dedicating them to what he believed to be the cause of justice and of virtue. For he was, above all things, a moral man; it is, indeed, the clue to his character. And though one hesitates to apply the extinguishing substantive "puritan" to so complex a personality, there were certain aspects of Adams' character which no other word seems to fit. He was a puritan in his

distrust of political expedients; a puritan in his hatred of himself; a puritan in his belief—nowhere expressed but everywhere apparent—that this hatred was evidence of an innate superiority; a puritan in his anxious welcome of personal disaster and in his conviction that every great success must be followed by a compensatory failure; a puritan in his individualism; and a puritan in his virulence.

5 It is perhaps unnecessary to say that a man of this kind would not make a good party politician. In 1808, John Quincy Adams was forced to resign from the Senate, of which he was a Federalist member from Massachusetts, because of a rebellious tendency to support Republican policies. The tendency was a sound one: he deserted the Federalists because he thought that they were degenerating into a treasonable faction; but, somehow or other, this did not turn him into an acceptable Republican. Ostracized in State Street, he was by no means *persona grata* in Virginia. There are few charitable references to him in Jefferson's correspondence. When Madison suddenly offered him, in 1809, the post of Minister to Russia, the fathers of the democratic church were gravely perturbed. "That both the Adams' are monarchists," said John Taylor of Caroline, "I never doubted. Whether monarchists, like pagans, can be converted by benefices, is a problem the solution of which I always feared Mr. Madison would attempt."

6 ¹But John Quincy Adams was no monarchist. ²He was a scientific republican, who hoped to advance his country's fortunes in a regular series of rationally planned steps, and who, when at length he became President, ruined what little chances of success he had by actually outlining some such scheme in his first annual message. ³It is typical of the man and of his destiny that he should have dreamed of planned economies long before the time was ripe for them; that he should have taken the American people into his confidence; and that the American people, with a sure instinct, should have hurled him from the seats of power. ⁴He himself declared that he had much more confidence in the calm and deliberate judgment of the people than President Monroe had, but one might qualify this statement by adding that he would have had little confidence in the people's judgment, however calm and deliberate, if it did not accord with his own. ⁵If to be a Federalist meant distrusting the people and loving strong government, and to be a Republican meant loving the people and distrusting strong government, then John Quincy Adams was always more a Federalist than a Republican. ⁶But let us admit that he wore his Federalism, like his independence, with a difference.

7 That he became, after his labors at Ghent and London were over, one of the greatest of Secretaries of State, has rarely been denied. And here he would not have become great if he had not been gifted with imagination. He longed to put this gift to other uses than those of the public service. It would have been the summit of his ambition, he wrote, "by some great work of literature to have done honor to my age and country, and to have lived in the gratitude of future ages." He tried his hand at poetry—he is one of the very few translators of Horace who has been able to recast that subtle Roman into the likeness of Messrs. Moody and Sankey; at belles lettres; at contemporary history. He confidently believed that his *Report on Weights and Measures* would be his most important literary labor, and the *Report*—a superb example of a gift for generalization working but not lost among the minutiae of scientific research—did, in fact, survive him. But it was not the *Report,* it was his diary which became his monument—his diary which, he thought, if only his intellectual powers had been greater, might have become "next to the Holy Scriptures, the most precious and valuable book ever written by human hands." There was nothing modest about his modesty.

8 The diary, that vast repository of priceless historical information, has its failings too. Strictly trustworthy as to fact, it is slightly less so when it approaches the interpretation of fact. And when it deals with his fellow Americans, it is not trustworthy at all. It projects us into a scorched and gloomy world where almost everyone is sooner or later engaged in a conspiracy to retard or ruin the career of Mr. Adams. Though it is filled with valuable sketches, and illuminated by flashes of intuition, it has to be read with extreme caution. *Incedo super ignes* —I walk over fires—he wrote at one of the critical moments in his career. Did he realize that the fires, for the most part, shot up from the abyss of his own nature? Perhaps he did. The diary is a testament to his queer, inverted honesty: it proves that at one time or another he successfully misinterpreted almost every character but his own.

9 For these voluminous pages reveal him with a singular fidelity— his lofty intelligence, his capability, his wide and curious learning, his generous ambitions, his corroding meannesses and more corroding fears. As one reads them one realizes that his spirit was never resigned to the shackles of practical affairs or the mean diet of official routine; that it was always straining at its bonds; that sometimes—not very often, just occasionally—it soared clean away. At such times the ap-

pearance was the appearance of a crow or a raven, but the flight was the flight of an eagle.

Comment

Few expositions of character are more carefully composed or more pungently written than Mr. Dangerfield's brief analysis of John Quincy Adams. His introduction (¶1) announces his subject, John Quincy Adams, and the main point he wishes to make about his subject, his "thorny" eminence. Mr. Dangerfield aims, as we recognize more clearly later on, to define John Quincy as a complex character. This complexity he establishes in the main part of his exposition (¶2-8) by *definition* (Section II), *classification* (Section III), *examples* (Section IV), *cause* (Section VI), and *comparison* (Section V). The author sums up his main point and his attitude toward his subject in the concluding paragraph, 9.

Note: This exposition partly depends on documentation. Adams is quoted several times, as are John Taylor (¶5) and W. H. Lyttleton (¶2). In a narrow sense quotation is not a means of analysis because it offers the views of someone other than the author on the subject explained. Quotation is an external support to the author's reasoning. It helps to establish a fact as a witness would or to give weight to an opinion in the manner of an authority.

However, a quotation from a witness as to a fact, or a quotation from an authority for an opinion may be assimilated into the author's own analysis. In this sense quotation becomes a part of the author's own analysis and may be classified under the various forms of analysis. Thus we may classify the quotations in this essay as specific examples of the main topic of the paragraphs. For example, Lyttleton's comment in sentences 4 and 5, paragraph 2, is a specific example of Adams' irritating independence.

Analysis and Composition

1. In paragraph 2 John Adams is classified as an independent man, but independent with a difference. In other words, Adams was independent in his own peculiar way. This idea is
   a. Analyzed by a comparison in sentence 3, and
   b. Supported by
     (1) The testimony of an Englishman (Ss 4 and 5)
     (2) Quotations from Adams' diary (Ss 7-10)
   Show how the analysis of the idea in the comparison and the quotations differentiates Adams' quality of independence from the general characteristic of independence.

2. Paragraph 3 classifies Adams as a fighter. This classification is developed by a comparison (Ss1-7) with the bulldog whose instinct is for the jugular, by a specific example (S6) of Adams' fighting quality, and by another kind of analysis in sentence 8. Analyze sentence 8 to discover which method of analysis (Sections II-VII) Mr. Dangerfield employs.

3. Paragraph 4 characterizes Adams as a moral man and a puritan. Analyze this paragraph carefully and then decide which of the three statements is the most nearly accurate summary of the author's thought. Give reasons for your answer.

   a. Mr. Dangerfield suggests that a moral man and a puritan are equivalent terms.

   b. Mr. Dangerfield means to say that Adams belonged to the class of moral men and the subclass puritan. Thus he *defines* Adams' character.

   c. Mr. Dangerfield means to say that a moral man and a puritan are contradictory terms. Thus he is showing the *contrast* or complexity in Adams' character.

4. In paragraph 4 Mr. Dangerfield lists the following characteristics of the puritan:

   a. Distrust of political expedients

   b. Self-hatred

   c. A sense of innate superiority

   d. Acceptance of personal disaster

   e. Belief in the cycle of success and failure

   f. Individualism

   g. Virulence

   This list constitutes an informal definition of the puritan. Decide whether this informal definition is

   a. Accurate and objective, or

   b. Merely descriptive of the sense in which the author uses the term. Give reasons for your answer.

5. What method of analysis does the author use to show that John Adams was not a good party politician (¶5)?

6. The main idea in paragraph 6 is stated in sentence 2, where the author says Adams "was a scientific republican." Define the exact meaning of this expression in its context. Be sure to look up the various meanings of the word *republican*. Note the different usage of the word in sentence 2 and in sentence 5.

7. Pick out those ideas in paragraph 6 which explain why Adams should be classed as a republican.

8. Pick out those ideas in paragraph 6 which explain why his republicanism was scientific.

9. Does sentence 5 contribute to the unity of paragraph 6? Explain.

10. In what sense is the word *imagination* used in paragraph 7? Give rea-

sons for saying that Mr. Adams' imagination is the key idea in paragraph 7.

11. In paragraph 8 Mr. Adams' diary is cited as evidence of its author's "queer, inverted honesty." By a careful analysis of this paragraph show exactly what the author means by the terms *queer, inverted,* and *honesty* in this context.

12. Paragraph 9, the conclusion, does not summarize the key ideas in paragraphs 2-8, which are

¶2: Adams could not get along with people.

¶3: He was a fighter.

¶4: He was moral.

¶5: He was not a good party man.

¶6: He was a scientific republican.

¶7: He had the gift of imagination.

¶8: He showed a queer, inverted honesty.

However, does it sum up the main *impression* we have received of Adams? Give reasons for your answer.

13. Write a summary of this essay by linking the key ideas in paragraphs 2-8.

14. Write a character exposition on one of the subjects listed below. Draw up an outline by listing the key ideas. Then devote one paragraph to each key idea in a manner similar to that of Mr. Dangerfield.

<table>
<tr><td>Theodore Roosevelt</td><td>John L. Lewis</td></tr>
<tr><td>Woodrow Wilson</td><td>Dean Acheson</td></tr>
<tr><td>Winston Churchill</td><td>Robert A. Taft</td></tr>
<tr><td>Walter Reuther</td><td>Douglas MacArthur</td></tr>
<tr><td>Harry S. Truman</td><td>Dwight D. Eisenhower</td></tr>
<tr><td>Franklin D. Roosevelt</td><td></td></tr>
</table>

15. Exposition of character is the basis of much fictional writing. True, as we shall see in Sections XII-XIV, fiction is chiefly narrative with some elements of description. Still, much character portrayal in fiction is at least partly expository. In approximately 500 words attempt to write a fictitious character exposition illustrating one of the following themes, or a theme of your own choice.

a. Mr. Crump was a man of a queer, inverted integrity; he was eternally faithful to false ideals.

b. Jessie made the great error of confusing bluntness with honesty.

c. Malone wanted perfection; he wanted to live with a perfect wife in a perfect suburb surrounded by perfect neighbors.

d. Account for any major change in the order of arrangement (1) by announcing the change and (2) by explaining briefly the necessity for the change.

Robert E. Lee: The Pattern of a Life

BY DOUGLAS SOUTHALL FREEMAN

1 The first reference to Robert E. Lee in an extant letter is the significant statement of his father that "Robert was always good and will be confirmed in his happy turn of mind by his ever-watchful and affectionate mother. Does he strengthen his native tendency?" Penned when the boy was ten, this language registered the impression the absent father had formed when Robert was not more than seven years of age. The stamp of character must, then, have been upon him from childhood. When he emerges dimly as a personality, in the later days of his cadetship at West Point, many of his essential qualities are apparent. Thereafter, from the time he appears clearly at Cockspur Island and at Fort Monroe, he exhibits every characteristic that later distinguished him. Subsequent change in his character was negligible and is simply the development of the man by challenging circumstance. Of this there can be no question. So consistent is the description of the young lieutenant of engineers, in the early 1830's, alike by those who became his foes and by those who remained his friends, that one need not fear the picture is touched up with the later remembrance of qualities the grizzled general displayed when he had endured the hard ordeal of the War Between the States.

ROBERT E. LEE: THE PATTERN OF A LIFE: reprinted from *R. E. Lee*, Volume IV by Douglas Southall Freeman; copyright 1935, 1936 by Charles Scribner's Sons; used by permission of the publishers.

2 This early development of character, like everything else that relates to Lee as an individual, is easily understood. Despite the ill health of the mother and her unhappiness during her pregnancy, he had a strong and normal nervous system that was invigorated by a simple outdoor life. Although there is no evidence that Mrs. Ann Lee had any secret dread that her son would develop the recklessness of his father, there is abundant proof that, with tactful wisdom, she inculcated in him from childhood the principles of self-control. From earliest adolescence he had upon him the care of his mother. George Washington, the embodiment of character, was his hero, made real and personal in the environment of Alexandria. At West Point his ambition to excel in his class led Lee to subject himself willingly and with a whole heart to a discipline that confirmed every excellence he had acquired at home. Physically more developed than most of the cadets, he had from the outset a better appreciation of what the training of the academy was intended to accomplish. All his early assignments to engineering duty were of a sort to impose responsibility. These circumstances did not destroy his sunny exuberance of spirit, but they set his character so early and so definitely that it did not change with years or woes.

3 Whether it was at the Des Moines Rapids, or during his superintendency of West Point, or in the president's house at Washington College—wherever he was in full four decades when the burden of battle was not on him—an old acquaintance would have observed little difference in his daily outlook, his nature, or his manners. Only in four particulars was the man who went to that last vestry meeting at the Episcopal church in Lexington unlike the lieutenant who bantered the "Beautiful Talcott" at Old Point in the moments he was not watching the contractors who might circumvent the government. His buoyant bearing had given place to a calmer cheerfulness, which might have been the case with any man who has bridged the chasm that divides the twenties of life from the sixties, even though no river of blood has flowed through the chasm. Again, the natural dignity of his person had settled into a more formal reserve, not because he had become less simple in heart or less approachable in manner, but because his conception of his duty to promote peace and national unity compelled him to put a wall between him and those who might have stirred unhappy memories and would certainly have kept open the old wounds of fratricidal war had he permitted them to talk of war. Even then it is quite likely that some of those who knew him after the

war mistook their reverence for his reserve. He was changed, also, in that, after 1865, he put out of his heart the military career that long had fascinated him. All the misgivings he had felt before the war regarding the pursuit of arms were confirmed by five years at Lexington. He spoke his conviction, as always, when he told young Professor Humphreys that the great mistake of his life had been in pursuing the education of a soldier, and he was not jesting in his encomium to General Ewell on the delights of a civil life. It was not by chance that he failed to keep step with the superintendent of V.M.I. when the two walked together at the head of the column of cadets.

4 These things apart, anyone who had worked with him on the wharf at St. Louis would have felt at home in his office in Lexington and would have found him the same man in the habits of life, in the steady routine, and in the simplicity of spirit that were his very ego. He rose early and cheerfully and had his private devotions. If he was away from home, he would write his domestic letters before breakfast. At the meal hour he would appear promptly, with greetings to all and with gentle, bantering reproaches for his always tardy wife. Were his food the sumptuous fare of bountiful Arlington, he would enjoy and praise each dish, eating with heartiness; but, when he sat down to the plain diet of the first hard days at Lexington, he showed the same relish and made no complaint.

5 Family worship over, he would go to work immediately, neatly dressed and with the whitest of linens, but never ostentatiously appareled. In his labor he was swift and diligent, prompt and accurate, always systematic and instinctively thrifty. His ambition was in his labor, whatever its nature. He did not covet praise. Blushing to receive it, he assumed that others would blush when he bestowed it, and he spared what he thought were their feelings, though no man was quicker to appreciate and, at the proper time, to acknowledge the achievement of others. Place and advancement never lured him, except as promotion held out the hope of larger opportunity and better provision for his family. Even then he was meticulous regarding the methods he would employ to further himself financially, and he would never capitalize his name or draw drafts on the good opinion of friends or public. Yet he had all his life the desire to excel at the task assigned him. That was the urge alike of conscience, of obligation, of his regard for detail, and of his devotion to thoroughness as the prime constituent of all labor. He never said so in plain words, but he desired everything that he did, whether it was to plan a battle or to

greet a visitor, to be as nearly perfect as he could make it. No man was more critical of his own performance because none demanded more of himself. The engineer's impulse in him was most gratified if something was to be created or organized, but, if it concerned another's happiness or had a place in the large design of worth-while things, he considered the smallest task proper to perform. Only the useless was irksome.

6 He endured interruption of his work without vexation. Rarely was he embarrassed in his dealings with men. He met every visitor, every fellow worker, with a smile and a bow, no matter what the other's station in life. Always he seemed to keep others at a judicious distance and did not invite their confidences, but he sought as a gentleman to make every right-minded person comfortable in his presence. With a tact so delicate that others scarcely noticed it, when he was busy he kept conversation to the question at issue, and he sought to make his interviews brief; but, even so, his consideration for the sensibilities of others cost him many a precious hour. Wrangles he avoided, and disagreeable persons he usually treated with a cold and freezing courtesy. Should his self-control be overborne by stupidity or ill-temper, his eyes would flash and his neck would redden. His rebuke would be swift and terse, and it might be two hours or more before he was completely master of himself. Whoever visited him meantime would perhaps find him irascible, though sure to make amends. Exacting of his subordinates, he still reconciled himself often to working with clumsy human tools. Resentments he never cherished. When he found men unworthy of his confidence, he made it his practice to see them as little as possible and to talk to them not at all. Silence was one of his strongest weapons. During the war he summarized his code when he wrote these words on a scrap of paper that nobody saw until after his death:

"The forbearing use of power does not only form a touchstone, but the manner in which an individual enjoys certain advantages over others is a test of a true gentleman.

"The power which the strong have over the weak, the employer over the employed, the educated over the unlettered, the experienced over the confiding, even the clever over the silly—the forbearing or inoffensive use of all this power or authority, or a total abstinence from it when the case admits it, will show the gentleman in a plain light. The gentleman does not needlessly and unnecessarily remind an offender of a wrong he may have committed against him. He cannot only forgive, he can forget; and he strives for that nobleness of self and mildness of character which impart sufficient strength to let the past be but the past. A true man of honor feels humbled himself when he cannot help humbling others."

7 Lee sought to conclude his work by early afternoon, even if that compelled him to set a late hour for the meal. When dinner was done, he was glad of a brief period of relaxation and sometimes of a little sleep, usually upright in his chair. Then he sought his daily exercise in a ride on his horse. He delighted to have a companion, and, if he had one, he talked of pleasant topics. Riding alone, which he often did, he would close his mind to the difficulties of the day and to the problems of the morrow and would soothe himself with the discovered beauties of the countryside. Nothing of a physical nature gave him the same thrill as a glowing sunset. Usually, on these rides, he paid his calls on the sick and on strangers, as diligently as if he had been the parson of the town. This he regarded as one of his social duties, and he discharged it not only with willingness but also with satisfaction. Whether his ride included social calls or simply carried him to a given objective, he was always on the alert for the children, and he never passed them without a greeting and, usually, a chat.

8 His return home, like all his other movements, was according to a precise schedule. Unless a sudden storm detained him, he would be at his door promptly at dusk, and would soon be ready for his light evening meal—"tea," as the family called it. The hours then belonged to Mrs. Lee, to his children, and to his guests. He would read to them or converse cheerfully until bedtime, which was usually after ten o'clock. When he retired to his own room, he had his evening prayers and was soon asleep. His quarters at Lexington were always as neat as if he were still a cadet at West Point, but the only suggestion of the soldier was the army pistol that hung in its holster by the head of his bed. After Mrs. Lee's invalidism afflicted her, he rarely went out to social affairs. Before that time he sometimes attended her to parties or to dinners, where he preferred the company of women to that of men, and that of the daughters to the mothers'. Always his address was dignified, but to the young girls it was often bantering. Nothing delighted him more than gently to tease some blushing young beauty. He had neither high wit nor quick repartee, though occasionally he essayed a pun; but his smile, his manners, and his quick understanding made him socially irresistible. His conversation, however, never turned to forbidden topics, nor was there in it anything suggestive or

of *double-entendre*. In all his letters, and there are several thousand of them, as in all his reported conversation, and there are countless anecdotes of him, no oath or vulgarism appears. He was clean-minded, though definitely and unfeignedly attracted to intelligent, handsome women.

9 Leaves and furloughs during his army service and vacations after the war found him ready to travel, not to distant lands but to the spas of Virginia or, better still, to the houses of congenial friends. Most of all did he relish a round of visits to his own kin, with whom he delighted to talk of the doings of their relatives. Chatter of this sort never bored him. Naturally sociable and devoted to his countless cousins, he sympathized with all their distresses and rejoiced in their little triumphs. Rarely was he too busy, when time allowed of his writing at all, to chronicle every wedding, every birth, every journey, every sickness, for the information of his family correspondents. At home, in his earlier periods of leisure, he shared in the sports of his sons, and to the end of his life he gave to each of his daughters a measure of courtly attention fitted to the temperament and age of each of them.

10 At intervals his habitual cheerfulness was marred by a sense of failure. This was most apt to overtake him when he was absent from home on long tours of military duty, for his simple nature made him dependent on his wife and children. Separated from them he often suffered loneliness and sometimes acute nostalgia. On occasion, and particularly during the difficult period when he was struggling to settle Mr. Custis' estate and to repair Arlington in 1857-59, this sense of frustration came upon him even at home. Then he would wonder why he did not advance more rapidly in the army and would puzzle himself to know how he could make adequate provision for his daughters, none of whom, in his heart of hearts, he wished to be married. These were the most unhappy times of his life, except perhaps those of his occasional illnesses. When sick, he would have few words even for his family, and was more than apt to lose his grip upon himself in dealing with others.

11 This was the pattern of his daily life. There is every reason to believe it was the mirror of his own soul. Those who look at him through the glamor of his victories or seek deep meaning in his silence will labor in vain to make him appear complicated. His language, his acts, and his personal life were simple for the unescapable reason that he was a simple gentleman.

12 Simple and spiritual—the two qualities which constitute the man

cannot be separated. The strongest religious impulse in his life was that given him by his mother. After that, in youth, he probably came most under the indirect influence of Reverend William Meade, later bishop, the clergyman who did more than anyone else to restore the Protestant Episcopal Church in Virginia from the ruin that had overtaken it during and after the American Revolution. Mr. Meade was rector in Alexandria for only eighteen months and then at a time when Robert was too young to heed his sermons; but he preached there often during Robert's youth, and his spirit dominated the Episcopal Church in Virginia. He was a picturesque personality, one of the prophets of his generation. Holding to the beautiful forms of his faith, Mr. Meade breathed into its worship an evangelism as ardent as that of the younger American denominations. In his eyes, religion concerned itself equally with acts and with beliefs. No reformer was ever more uncompromising in his denunciation of cards or more unyielding in opposition to the old habit the barons of the Northern Neck had of staging races and of backing their horses with their dollars. None excoriated the stage with warnings more sulphurous than did Mr. Meade. Had he been sent to idolatrous Israel, he could not more solemnly have proclaimed the day of the vengeance of the Lord or have portrayed more darkly the fearsome punishment visited on the sinner for his hardness of heart. Yet he spoke "comfortably to Jerusalem." He gave the promise of forgiveness to the repentant, pictured glowingly to the faithful the bliss of a hard-won heaven, and somehow planted in the hearts of the dominant class in that section of the Old Dominion a religion of simplicity, vigor, and sincerity.

13 It is a singular fact that young Robert Lee was not prompted by the exhortations of Mr. Meade or of like-minded clergymen to submit himself to confirmation. The reason cannot be surmised, unless it was that the theology of his youth had a vehemence and an emotionalism alien to his nature. He was content until he was past forty-five to hold to the code of a gentleman rather than to the formal creed of a church. The experiences of the Mexican War, the gentle piety of the Fitzhughs at Ravensworth, the example and death of Mrs. Custis, the simple faith of Mrs. Lee, and, more immediately, the purpose of his daughters to enter into the full fellowship of the church induced Lee in 1853 to renew his vows. After that time, first his sense of dependence on God for the uprearing of his boys during his long absences from home, and then the developing tragedy of the war, deepened every religious impulse of his soul.

14 And what did religion imply for him . . . ? To answer that question is to employ the terms of a theology that now seems to some outworn and perhaps archaic. It was, however, the credo of a man who met the supreme tests of life in that he accepted fame without vanity and defeat without repining. To understand the faith of Robert E. Lee is to fill out the picture of him as a gentleman of simple soul. For him as for his grandfather, Charles Carter, religion blended with the code of *noblesse oblige* to which he had been reared. Together, these two forces resolved every problem of his life into right and wrong. The clear light of conscience and of social obligation left no zone of gray in his heart: everything was black or white. There cannot be said to have been a "secret" of his life, but this assuredly was the great, transparent truth, and this it was, primarily, that gave to his career its consistency and decision. Over his movements as a soldier he hesitated often, but over his acts as a man, never. There was but one question ever: What was his duty as a Christian and a gentleman? That he answered by the sure criterion of right and wrong, and, having answered, acted. Everywhere the two obligations went together; he never sought to expiate as a Christian for what he had failed to do as a gentleman, or to atone as a gentleman for what he had neglected as a Christian. He could not have conceived of a Christian who was not a gentleman.

15 Kindness was the first implication of religion in his mind—not the deliberate kindness of "good works" to pacify exacting Deity, but the instinctive kindness of a heart that had been schooled to regard others. His was not a nature to waste time in the perplexities of self-analysis; but, if those about him at headquarters had understood him better, they might often have asked themselves whether, when he brought a refreshing drink to a dusty lieutenant who called with dispatches, he was discharging the social duty of a host or was giving a "cup of cold water" in his Master's name. His manner in either case would have been precisely the same.

16 Equally was his religion expressed in his unquestioning response to duty. In his clear creed, right was duty and must be discharged. "There is," he wrote down privately for his own guidance, "a true glory and a true honor: the glory of duty done—the honor of the integrity of principle." He probably never summed up this aspect of his religion more completely than in that self-revealing hour before he started to meet General Grant, when he answered all the appeals of his lieutenants with the simple statement: "The question is, is it right

to surrender this army? If it is right, then I will take all the responsibility." It was a high creed—right at all times and at all costs—but daily self-discipline and a clear sense of justice made him able to adhere to it.

17 Humility was another major implication of his religion. So lofty was his conception of man's duty to his Maker and to his neighbors, so completely did his ambition extend, all unconsciously, into the realm of the spirit, that he was never satisfied with what he was. Those who stood with him on the red field of Appomattox thought that his composure was due to his belief that he had discharged his full duty, and in this they were partially correct; but he always felt, with a sincerity no man can challenge, that he had fallen immeasurably short of his ideal of a servant of God. "So humble was he as a Christian," wrote Mrs. Lee on the day of his death, "that he said not long ago to me he wished he felt sure of his acceptance. I said all who love and trust in the Savior need not fear. He did not reply, but a more upright and conscientious Christian never lived."

18 Born of this humility, this sense of unworthiness in the sight of God, was the submission to the Divine will that has so often been cited in these pages to explain his calmness in hours that would have wrecked the self-control of lesser men. There was nothing of blind fatalism in his faith. Resignation is scarcely the name for it. Believing that God was Infinite Wisdom and Eternal Love, he subjected himself to seeming ill fortune in the confidence that God's will would work out for man's good. If it was a battle that had been won, to "Almighty God" he gave the glory; if it was a death that had brought grief to the family, he reminded his wife that their "Heavenly Father" knew better than they, and that there was eternal peace and sure reunion after life. Nothing of his serenity during the war or of his silent labor in defeat can be understood unless one realizes that he submitted himself in all things faithfully to the will of a Divinity which, in his simple faith, was directing wisely the fate of nations and the daily life of His children. This, and not the mere physical courage that defies danger, sustained him in battle; and this, at least equally with his sense of duty done, made him accept the results of the war without even a single gesture of complaint.

19 ¹Of humility and submission was born a spirit of self-denial that prepared him for the hardships of the war and, still more, for the dark destitution that followed it. ²This self-denial was, in some sense, the spiritual counterpart of the social self-control his mother had incul-

cated in his boyhood days, and it grew in power throughout his life.
³He loved the luxury that wealth commanded. ⁴Had he been as rich
as his grandfather Carter, he would have lived in a style as hospitable.
⁵Fine horses and handsome clothes and lavish entertainments would
have been his; Arlington would have been adorned; and his daughters
would have enjoyed travel and the richest comfort. ⁶But Arlington
was confiscated; its treasures were scattered; each stage of his sacrifice
for the South brought him lower and lower in fortune until he was
living in a borrowed tenant house and his wife was husbanding the
scraps from a pair of trousers a farmer's wife had made for him. ⁷His
own misfortunes typified the fate of the Confederacy and of its adher-
ents. ⁸Through it all, his spirit of self-denial met every demand upon
it, and, even after he went to Washington College and had an income
on which he could live easily, he continued to deny himself as an
example to his people. ⁹Had his life been epitomized in one sentence
of the book he read so often, it would have been in the words, "If any
man will come after me, let him deny himself, and take up his cross
daily, and follow me." ¹⁰And if one, only one, of all the myriad incidents of his stirring life had to be selected to typify his message, as a
man, to the young Americans who stood in hushed awe that rainy
October morning as their parents wept at the passing of the Southern
Arthur, who would hesitate in selecting that incident? ¹¹It occurred
in northern Virginia, probably on his last visit there. ¹²A young mother
brought her baby to him to be blessed. ¹³He took the infant in his
arms and looked at it and then at her and slowly said, "Teach him
he must deny himself."

20 That is all. There is no mystery in the coffin there in front of the
windows that look to the sunrise.

Comment

The central theme of this essay is that Robert E. Lee was a gentleman
whose life was characterized by the spirit of simplicity (¶4-11) and the
spirit of religion (¶11-20).

As in all extended expositions, this essay *combines* the various forms of
analysis. The essential elements of the central theme, that is, the terms *gentleman, spirit of simplicity,* and *spirit of religion* are all *defined* (Section
II) (see ¶4, 5, 6, and 14). Analysis by *classification* (Section III) is apparent
in paragraph 1 (Lee was a "good" boy) and in paragraphs 15-19, where
the spirit of his religion is classified as kindness, duty, humility, submission

to Providence, and self-denial. *Examples* (Section IV) are manifold, often mixed with other forms of analysis. They are used effectively in paragraphs 8, 16, and 19. Short *comparisons and contrasts* (Section V) occur frequently but are not a prominent method of analysis. *Causal analysis* (Section VI) appears in paragraph 2, where his mother's influence is mentioned, and in paragraphs 12-13, which discuss the effect of religion on General Lee. *Cause* combines with *classification* and *example* in paragraphs 18-19. Paragraphs 4-11 contain a long *process analysis* (Section VII) of the typical pattern of Lee's day.

The arrangement in this essay is not uniform. It begins with a chronological order.* Paragraph 1 deals with Lee's childhood; paragraph 2 is concerned with Lee's youth. In paragraph 3 the chronology of four decades is foreshortened, and we are brought up to the last days of Lee's life, at Lexington, where he was president of Washington College.

Paragraphs 4-11 tell of a typical day in Lee's later life. The order is chronological, in that it proceeds from morning to evening, but the chronological scale is different from that of paragraphs 1-3. The earlier paragraphs were concerned with years, the later paragraphs with typical hours in the day.

The chronology returns to the larger scale in paragraphs 12 and 13, which cover the years from Lee's youth to his old age. But in paragraphs 14-19 the chronological order is abandoned. As we have noted above, Mr. Freeman here gives the characteristic qualities of Lee's spirit of religion and offers illustrations of these qualities. There is very little concern for chronological sequence in paragraphs 14-19. Does this constitute a fault against unity and coherence in the whole composition? (See Section VIII.)

Now the test of a good arrangement is not mere consistency, or the following of a single order, but adequacy to the main intention. And part of Mr. Freeman's main intention is to show that Lee's character was all of a piece. To do this he had to show, very briefly, that Lee's essential traits were the same throughout his life. "Subsequent change in his character was negligible and is simply the development of the man by challenging circumstance" (¶1). Hence Freeman's two excursions (¶1-3 and 12-13) into large-scale chronological order.

But how to explain the difference between the small-scale chronological order in paragraphs 4-11 and the logical order in paragraphs 14-19? † First it should be observed that, while Lee's simplicity of character can be shown

---

* See handbooks: Foerster, p. 79; Hodges, *32e2*; Kierzek, pp. 91, 470; Perrin, pp. 210-16; Wykoff, *46a* (p. 255), *56b*.

† For logical order see handbooks: Foerster, p. 79; Hodges, *32e2*; Kierzek, pp. 91, 469-70; Perrin, pp. 220-24; Wykoff, *56a-b*.

by his activities on a typical day, his spirit of religion requires more careful expository analysis. Simplicity is defined as an absence of complexity or essential conflict. This characteristic is readily displayed by Lee's cheerful endurance of routine tasks, his systematic, diligent, prompt, and accurate habits of work, his acceptance of his family and his society. Indeed, this phase of his character is more evident in routine activities than in extraordinary situations. But the spirit of religion is a characteristic of the soul of man. It is a matter of hidden motives. It cannot be explained by observing routine. As a subject, it offers peculiar difficulties. Furthermore, Mr. Freeman has in mind not only the difficulty inherent in the subject, but the religious inexperience of some of his readers. "And what did religion imply for him?" he asks (¶14). "To answer that question is to employ the terms of a theology that now seems to some outworn and perhaps archaic." This sentence accounts for the necessity of shifting from a chronological order to the logical order in paragraphs 14-19. The author lists five characteristics of Lee's spirit of religion and exemplifies these characteristics by citing events in General Lee's life, because *he cannot assume* that his audience possesses a common understanding of the spirit of religion.

Thus the difference in the order of arrangement in this essay may be traced to the main intention, the problems inherent in certain phases of the subject, and the attitude of some of the prospective readers.

Analysis and Composition

1. Test the clarity of paragraph 2 by studying the relation of the sentences to the topic sentence. The first sentence is the topic sentence. (See Section VIII on clarity in paragraphs.)
2. Locate the topic sentence in paragraph 3. Test the paragraph for clarity by studying the relation of the sentences to the topic sentence.
3. Test the coherence of paragraph 5 in the following ways:
   a. Point out the number of times Mr. Freeman mentions the key idea. (The key idea here is Lee's attitude towards work. Note especially the many synonyms for work.)
   b. Point out all the sentences which are connected with previous sentences by means of pronouns referring to antecedents in the previous sentences.*
   c. Point out transitions expressive of
      1. Addition (besides, in addition)
      2. Contrast (but, yet)

* See handbooks: Foerster, p. 65; Hodges, *31b2*; Kierzek, p. 92.

   3. Comparison (similarly, in like manner, such as, more so)
   4. Purpose (in order to, for the purpose)
   5. Result (therefore, hence, so that)

4. Study the sentences of paragraph 6 for variety (see Section VIII) by classifying under the following heads:
  a. The length of each of the sentences
  b. The kinds of sentences (simple, complex, compound)
  c. The ways in which the sentences begin (whether with subject, object, verb, adverb, adjective, clause, phrase, or conjunction)
  d. The proportion of loose and periodic sentences

5. Analyze the sentences of paragraph 19 by the same procedures as in Exercises 2, 3, and 4 above.

6. Test paragraph 19 for vigor (see Section VIII) in the following ways:
  a. Point out three instances of examples that arouse a feeling of admiration for General Lee.
  b. Indicate an order of climax in this paragraph.
  c. Indicate an order of climax in one of the sentences of this paragraph.
  d. Point out expressions which directly solicit our pity for General Lee.

7. The diction throughout this essay is formal, at times grandiloquent, as in sentences 3, 4, 5, and 10 of paragraph 19. List a dozen examples of this kind of diction from the selection. Can you justify the author's diction on the grounds that it fits his purpose, his subject, and his audience? Give reasons for your answer.

8. Compare this essay with that of George Dangerfield in Example C of this section, by examining the tone, that is, the attitude of the two authors toward their subject matter and their audience. You may examine their respective attitudes by answering the following questions:
  a. Does the author approach his subject impersonally, or does he have feelings for or against his subject? How is his approach to the subject manifested in his language?
  b. Does the author intend only to explain his point of view, or does he also desire to convince and to persuade his reader to think and to feel as he does? How are these intentions manifested in his style?
  c. Does the author write primarily for a special audience—for scholars, for example, or for Americans—or is he addressing the general community of educated men? How is this purpose manifested in his style? (See Section VIII.)

GENERAL EXERCISES

A

Most students enjoy writing a character exposition of one of their friends, associates, or teachers. Such an exposition may easily be prepared without a great deal of research, but it does require sharp observation and intelligent interviewing. Observe one of your friends for a week or so; make notes on his or her predominant traits. When you have completed the study of your friend, prepare an outline. Then write a character exposition of 750 to 1000 words.

The generalized outline below may help you form one of your own.

Occasion and purpose: A character exposition of 1000 words.

Central theme: Mary O'Brien is a rare coed; she is personally attractive but mildly unsocial, intellectually ambitious but unconventional.

I. First acquaintance with Mary O'Brien
   a. Where
   b. When
   c. How

II. Her attractive personality, the first trait of which I was aware
   a. Appearance
   b. Voice
   c. Conversation
   d. Accomplishments

III. Her unsocial side, the second trait encountered
   a. Dislike of fraternities and sororities
   b. Contempt for football games
   c. Her preference for the quiet room in the library

IV. Her intellectual ambitions, the third trait
   a. Her admiration for English poets
   b. Her own experiments in verse
   c. Her willingness to work hard to achieve her ambition to write good poetry

V. Her unconventional character, the fourth trait
   a. Her amusement with freshman English
   b. Her avoidance of cosmetics
   c. Her curious liking for baseball

VI. Final estimate of Mary O'Brien

B

Most of the authors of the selections in this book are appropriate sub-jects for a biographical sketch or essay. For the convenience of the student a few authors already studied have been listed below. The biographies of each of these authors are readily available in libraries. Select one author and write a character exposition as directed by your instructor.

1. Subjects for an appreciative sketch of 500 words similar to Mrs. Mc-Cormick's "The Mayor of Florence":
   Charles Malik, a democratic leader in the United Nations
   Alan Devoe, a literary naturalist
   George Orwell, enemy of sham
   Paul Horgan, chronicler of the American Southwest
2. Subjects for a sketch of 500 words in the manner of Alistair Cooke:
   Clifton Fadiman, apostle of culture to the masses
   F. P. Adams, American humorist
   Mark Twain, chief of the redskins (see Example III C3 and IV D)
3. Subjects for an essay of 800 words similar in structure and tone to George Dangerfield's study of John Quincy Adams:
   Charles A. Beard, champion of economic history
   Arnold Bennett, author, socialite, businessman
   Lewis Mumford, critic of society and its arts
   Arnold Toynbee, historian of the universe
4. Subjects for an essay of about 1000 words similar in tone to D. S. Free-man's study of Robert E. Lee. The student should not attempt an essay of the scope of Mr. Freeman's monumental work. He may, however, attempt to write about a venerable figure with an attitude of admiration:
   Plato
   J. H. Newman
   Abraham Lincoln

A. Whenever possible, state your key ideas in a topic paragraph at the beginning of your essay. Make each key idea the topic of one of the succeeding paragraphs.

HENRY STEELE COMMAGER:
The Civil War and American Tradition

B. Where effective, develop a complex event by combining exposition with narration, description, and persuasion as well as by combining the various methods of analysis.

JACQUETTA HAWKES:
The Industrial Revolution in Great Britain

C. Develop a complex idea by a sustained contrast with an opposing idea; make your contrast effective by combining argument with exposition.

BARBARA WARD: *Faith for Freedom*

D. In an investigative paper of an historical nature coordinate or fuse the chronological order of events and the logical order of ideas to achieve clarity and emphasis.

HENRY NASH SMITH:
The Dime Novel Heroine

REVIEW EXERCISES FOR SECTIONS VIII-X

Exposition of Facts and Ideas

IN SECTION IX we learned that exposition is a form of discourse that aims primarily to explain a subject. Exposition, we discovered, is divided into two main types: exposition of character, which attempts to explain the meaning of persons, and exposition of facts and ideas, which attempts to explain the meaning of physical realities, or happenings, and of mental realities, or ideas. (See the introduction to Section III for an extended treatment of the distinction between physical and mental realities.)

Both types of exposition apply the general principles of rhetoric to their special problems. Both of them employ the various methods of development (Sections II-VII) singly and in combination; both follow the principles of good arrangement, namely unity, coherence, and emphasis; and both attempt to express ideas with clarity, vigor, and interest (Section VIII).

From our study of character exposition in Section IX we learned how

1. To select as a subject a character with definite traits.
2. To develop an exposition of character by letting the subject explain himself in his own words and actions.
3. To maintain unity and coherence in explaining a complex character by making the various traits of the subject serve one predominant impression.
4. To vary the order of our arrangement to meet the particular needs of a subject.

To sum up, we saw how the principles of analysis, arrangement, and style were adapted to the special needs of a particular subject, occasion, and purpose.

EXPOSITION OF FACTS AND IDEAS

In studying the exposition of facts and ideas we encounter a more complex set of problems. This type of exposition is concerned not with a single person, like Robert E. Lee, but with a large event like the Civil War; not with a complex individual, like John Quincy Adams, but with a complex social development like the Industrial Revolution, which requires the use of narrative, descriptive, and persuasive elements in the exposition. Exposition of this type deals with ideas such as communism, which must be explained by a sustained contrast with the opposing idea, democracy. Frequently the exposition is concerned with the orderly presentation of facts and with the interpretation of those facts—a double intention which calls for a parallel arrangement of the physical events and of the sequence of ideas.

Since exposition of facts and ideas deals with such a wide range of subjects, each of which lends itself to special treatment, it is impossible to list any set of rules or principles that will cover every case. Again we must repeat the general rule: Apply prudently the principles of analysis, arrangement, and style in meeting the needs of your subject, purpose, and occasion.

In this section you will find four examples of exposition of facts and ideas. Taken together they illustrate the main problems of exposition that you will meet in your college career and in your future professional life. Taken separately each one solves a special problem by appropriately combining the various methods of analysis, by effectively arranging ideas, by harmonizing exposition with various other forms of discourse, and by using a prose style in consonance with its basic purpose.

THE FIRST PROBLEM: HOW TO EXPLAIN A LARGE BODY OF FACTS

We encounter the first problem, how to explain a large body of facts, in Henry Steele Commager's "The Civil War and American Tradition." Here is a subject of great magnitude, the Civil War.

The author wants to explain, within the limits of an essay of several thousand words, the impact of that war on the mind of the American people. Obviously he cannot give a detailed account of the various battles. He cannot quote at length from diaries and memoirs. Nor can he select a splinter of the subject, since his purpose is to explain the impact of the Civil War *as a whole* on the American people.

Hence he is committed to developing a central theme that asserts several characteristics of the subject: of all the wars fought by Americans, the Civil War has left the strongest impression on our minds, our imagination, and our hearts. The Civil War, the subject, is explained by eleven key ideas, all of which bear, but not necessarily in serial order, on the areas of mind, imagination, and heart. These eleven key ideas (all are analyzed below in the comment following the selection) are summed up in an introductory paragraph, which scans or previews the ideas in a manner that may be compared to the announcement of a theme and its principal movements in the opening bars of an orchestral composition. It thus becomes the topic paragraph of the essay, bearing the same relation to the other paragraphs of the composition that a topic sentence bears to the other sentences of a paragraph.

Each of these eleven characteristics or key ideas then becomes the topic of one of the succeeding paragraphs. Thus the essay is arranged according to the following scheme:

¶1: The Civil War is characterized by the following traits: *a, b, c, d, e, f, g, h, i, j, k*.

¶2: Trait *a* is . . .

¶3: Trait *b* is . . .

Obviously it is not always desirable to begin with such a long paragraph. Not every writer has Mr. Commager's ability to fuse a great many ideas in one splendid cluster. Moreover, not every subject lends itself to such a neat pattern of arrangement. But this is, nevertheless, an ideal pattern for developing an exposition of events on a large scale. Study it and use it whenever you can. You will remember Mr. Commager's practice best as an adaptation of the general principle of *unity* in arrangement—an adaptation that may be summed up thus: *Whenever possible, state your key ideas in a topic paragraph at the beginning of your essay. Make each key idea the topic of one of the succeeding paragraphs.*

THE SECOND PROBLEM: HOW TO COMBINE NARRATION,
DESCRIPTION, AND PERSUASION IN AN EXPOSITION

We meet the second problem in "The Industrial Revolution in Great Britain" by Jacquetta Hawkes. Here the problem is not only how best to combine methods of development to achieve unity, but more importantly, how to blend narrative, descriptive, and persuasive elements with exposition. (We have already pointed out the close relationship of exposition to the other forms of discourse in the introduction to Section IX. See pp. 311-12.)

The subject—the Industrial Revolution in Great Britain—and the author's point of view on the subject create peculiar difficulties. First of all, the subject, the Industrial Revolution, is a continuing historical process. It had a definite beginning in the eighteenth century and is still developing. Hence any explanation of the Industrial Revolution must be narrative as well as expository in character. Thus the author refers accurately to her piece as "a chronicle." Furthermore, the Industrial Revolution not only is a continuing historical process but also involves a causal development. It has had a direct, immediate, and necessary effect on the lives of the British people. It has affected their housing, their habits of work, their thinking and feeling. These effects may of course be stated generally, but they are best *described* in vivid detail.

Furthermore, this essay, which frequently crosses into the area of poetic prose, is indirectly persuasive in its intention. The author not only attempts to tell us what the Industrial Revolution is, why it started, and how it works—which are the aims of expository discourse; she not only blends this exposition with a narration of events and a description of the effects of the Industrial Revolution—she also pleads for a restoration of creative human life. She aims, and succeeds brilliantly, in stirring her readers to oppose the brutalizing effects of certain features of the Industrial Revolution.

Thus Miss Hawkes's subject, and her particular purpose, require a combination of several methods of development, as well as a blending of several forms of discourse. From her practice we find an answer to our second problem, that is: *Where effective, develop a complex event by combining exposition with narration, description, and persuasion as well as by combining the various methods of analysis.*

THE THIRD PROBLEM: HOW TO BLEND EXPOSITION AND ARGUMENT IN EXPLAINING AN IDEA BY CONTRAST

The third problem may be stated thus—to explain fully a complex idea such as freedom or democracy, we must explain the contrary idea. And if we explain an idea in this way we are unavoidably involved in argument, that is, in affirming the truth of our idea as against the truth of the contrary idea.

The solution to this problem appears in Barbara Ward's penetrating essay, "Faith for Freedom." Here a contrast is used, not as a mere method of development but as the unifying theme of the whole essay. Here Western civilization and communism continuously illustrate and explain each other, even in those passages that are not formally developed by the method of comparison and contrast. The two opposing ideas are as intimately related as up is to down, as sunrise to sunset, as ebb to flow. Even the historical section of the essay (see B1-5 in the outline) is intimately linked to the contrast between communism and Western civilization. The similarity between the Jews and the Greeks and the West on the one hand, and between the primitive omnipotent state and communism on the other, supports the contrast by analogies.

The two sides of the contrast are linked again by the paradox, or the absurdity, of communism's assumption of the Western faith in spiritual ideas and of the West's assumption of the communist belief in economic determinism. Thus contrast here is not merely a method of development but a unifying point of view which animates every part of the essay and imparts to it a remarkable cogency.

This use of contrast on a large scale also points out how exposition is combined with argument. Thus in proving her central theme—that the ideas and aspirations of Western man are still the most startling thing that has ever happened to the human race—Miss Ward is directly contradicting the communist thesis. Obviously she is attempting to win assent to her belief that economic determinism and the denial of freedom and moral responsibility, the main tenets of communism, are wrong. In her final paragraphs there is also a note of persuasion, that is, an attempt to stimulate her reader to some kind of action. Here (paragraphs 21-24) Miss Ward calls upon the Western world to renew its creative spirit and to oppose a free, responsible, democratic faith to communist statism and fatalism.

Thus, as we shall see, Miss Ward solves the third problem in a manner we may summarize best in this statement: *Develop a complex idea by a sustained contrast with an opposing idea; make your contrast effective by combining argument with exposition.*

THE FOURTH PROBLEM: HOW TO COMBINE AN EXPOSITION OF EVENTS WITH AN EXPOSITION OF IDEAS

The fourth problem concerns the investigative paper of an historical nature. Such a paper necessarily has a twofold function: (a) to present facts in a definite historical order and (b) to evaluate, that is, to draw a logical inference from these facts. Hence the arrangement must coordinate two orders, not, as in D. S. Freeman's essay on Robert E. Lee, by a warranted transfer from one order to another, but by the use of parallelism.

Henry Nash Smith arranges his research paper on "The Dime Novel Heroine" in this manner: First, there is a chronological order set forth in a series of steps (process analysis) tracing the decline of the genteel heroine of 1850 to the mindless moll of the present-day Wild West story. But paralleling this order is the logical order of induction from specific examples to a general truth, that is, from an examination of the typical examples of western heroines to the conclusion that the western novel as a class has progressively deteriorated and is now devoid of ethical and social meaning. The two orders are so perfectly fused that the logical inference is drawn as the author reaches the last step in his chronological process.

This parallel arrangement, or fusion, of two orders also shows the necessary combination of exposition with narrative. If Mr. Smith merely explained his logical point we would not be informed about the stages of the deterioration of the western novel; if he merely recounted the stages in the decline of the novel we would not be so keenly aware of its ethical and social meaning. The two types of discourse unite to give us a complete and compelling analysis of a popular literary genre.

Thus Mr. Smith solves the fourth problem of exposition by means of an arrangement that may be summed up as follows: *In an investigative paper of an historical nature coordinate or fuse the chronological order of events and the logical order of ideas to achieve clarity and emphasis.* (Note: Mr. Smith's research essay observes the appropriate formalities of this kind of writing. We shall mention these characteristics in the comment on "The Dime Novel Heroine.")

---

a. Whenever possible, state your key ideas in a topic paragraph at the beginning of your essay. Make each key idea the topic of one of the succeeding paragraphs.

The Civil War and American Tradition

BY HENRY STEELE COMMAGER

1 [1]We have fought five major wars in the last century or so, and three since Appomattox, but of them all it is the Civil War that has left the strongest impression on our minds, our imagination, and our hearts. [2]It is the Civil War songs that we sing—who does not know "Marching Through Georgia" or "Tramp, Tramp, Tramp" or "Dixie"? —and that war gave us the one great battle hymn of our literature. [3]It furnished our best war poetry, both at the time and since; no other war has produced anything as good as "Drum Taps" or the "Harvard Commemoration Ode," nor has any other been celebrated by an epic poem comparable to Stephen Benét's *John Brown's Body*. [4]It has inspired more, and better, novels than any other of our wars and it excites even Hollywood to rise above mediocrity. [5]It has furnished our standards of patriotism, of gallantry, and of fortitude; it has given us our most cherished military heroes—Lee and Jackson, Grant and Sherman, Sheridan and "Beauty" Stuart, and a host of others, and it has given us, too, our greatest national hero and our greatest sectional one,

THE CIVIL WAR AND AMERICAN TRADITION: from *The Blue and the Gray*, by Henry Steele Commager, copyright, 1950, used by permission of the publishers, The Bobbs-Merrill Company, Inc.

Lincoln and Lee. [6]*No other chapter in our history has contributed so much to our traditions and our folklore.* [7]The very words—whether they are Civil War or War Between the States—conjure up for us a hundred images: Jackson standing like a stone wall; U. S. Grant becoming Unconditional Surrender Grant; Lee astride Traveller, "It is well war is so terrible, or we should get too fond of it"; Barbara Frietchie waving her country's flag; A. P. Hill breaking through the wheat fields at Antietam; Thomas standing like a rock at Chickamauga; Pickett's men streaming up the long slope of Cemetery Ridge; Farragut lashed to the mast at Mobile Bay, "Damn the torpedoes, full steam ahead"; the Army of the Cumberland scrambling up the rugged heights of Missionary Ridge; Hood's Texans forcing Lee to the rear before they would close the gap at Spotsylvania; Sheridan dashing down the Winchester Pike; Lincoln pardoning the sleeping sentinels, reading Artemus Ward to his Cabinet, dedicating the battlefield of Gettysburg; Grant and Lee at Appomattox Court House.

2 [1]It was, in many respects, a curious war, one in which amenities were preserved. [2]It could not begin until high-ranking officers of the army and navy had been permitted to resign and help organize a rebellion. [3]Southerners tolerated outspoken Unionists, like Petigru or Botts; Northerners permitted Vallandigham to campaign openly against the war, and at the crisis of the conflict almost two million of them voted for a party that had formally pronounced the war a failure. [4]Journalists seemed to circulate at will, and Northern papers had correspondents in the South while Confederates got much of their information about Federal army movements from the Northern newspapers. [5]There was an immense amount of trading back and forth, some of it authorized or at least tolerated by the governments, and Sherman could say that Cincinnati furnished more supplies to the Confederacy than did Charleston. [6]Officers had been trained in the same schools and fought in the same armies, and most of them knew one another or knew of one another; Mrs. Pickett tells us that when her baby was born Grant's staff celebrated with bonfires. [7]There was a great deal of fraternization—a word which did not have the ugly connotations it achieved after World War II—both among soldiers and civilians. [8]Pickets exchanged tobacco, food, and news; if Yankee officers did not marry Southern beauties as often as novelists imagined, there was at least some basis for the literary emphasis on romance. [9]Confederates cheered Meagher's Irish Brigade as it charged up Marye's Heights, and the Yankees almost outdid the Confederates in

admiration for Jackson and Pelham. [10]There were plenty of atrocity stories, but few atrocities. [11]There was a good deal of pillaging and vandalism—as in all wars—but little of that systematic destruction we know from two world wars. [12]On the whole, civilians were safe; there were crimes against property but few against persons, and women everywhere were respected. [13]When Butler affronted the ladies of New Orleans he was transferred to another command, and Sherman engaged in a wordy correspondence with the mayor of Atlanta seeking to justify what he thought a military necessity. [14]Whether Sherman burned Columbia is still a matter of controversy; the interesting thing is that there should be a controversy at all. [15]Both peoples subscribed to the same moral values and observed the same standards of conduct. [16]Both displayed that "decent respect to the opinions of mankind" to which Jefferson had appealed three-quarters of a century earlier. [17]Both were convinced that the cause for which they fought was just—and their descendants still are.

3 [1]Nor did the war come to an end, psychologically or emotionally, with Appomattox. [2]Politicians nourished its issues; patriotic organizations cherished its memories; scholars refought its battles with unflagging enthusiasm. [3]No other war has started so many controversies and for no other do they flourish so vigorously. [4]Every step in the conflict, every major political decision, every campaign, almost every battle, has its own proud set of controversies, and of all the military figures only Lee stands above argument and debate. [5]Was the election of Lincoln a threat to the South, and was secession justified? [6]Was secession a revolutionary or a constitutional act, and was the war a rebellion or an international conflict? [7]Was the choice of Davis a mistake, and did Davis interfere improperly in military affairs? [8]Should the Confederacy have burned its cotton, or exported it? [9]Was the blockade a success, and if so at what point? [10]Should Britain have recognized the Confederacy, or did she go too far toward the assistance of the South as it was? [11]Who was responsible for the attack on Fort Sumter, Lincoln or Beauregard, and was the call for 75,000 men an act of aggression? [12]Was Jackson late at Seven Days? [13]Was Grant surprised at Shiloh? [14]Did the radicals sabotage McClellan's Peninsular campaign? [15]Who was responsible for the disaster of Second Bull Run and was Fitz-John Porter a marplot or a scapegoat? [16]Should Lee have persisted in his offensive of the autumn of 1862 even after the discovery of the Lost Order? [17]Should McClellan have renewed battle after Antietam? [18]Why did Pemberton fail to link up

with Johnston outside Vicksburg and why did Johnston fail to relieve Pemberton? [19]Would Gettysburg have been different had Jackson been there, or had Longstreet seized Little Round Top on the morning of the second day, or had Pickett been properly supported on the third? [20]Who was responsible for the Confederate failure at Stone River and who for the debacle of Missionary Ridge, and why did Davis keep Bragg in command so long? [21]Could Johnston have saved Atlanta, and did Hood lose it? [22]Was Hood's Tennessee campaign strategically sound but tactically mismanaged, or was it the other way around? [23]Was Lee deceived during those critical June days when Grant flung his army across the James? [24]And why did the Federals fail to break through the thin lines of Petersburg? [25]Who burned Columbia, and was Sherman's theory of war justified? [26]What really happened at Five Forks, and would the outcome have been different had Pickett been more alert? [27]What explains the failure to have supplies at Amelia Court House, and could Lee have made good his escape and linked up with Johnston had the supplies been there? [28]Could the Confederacy ever have won the war, or was defeat foredoomed; if defeat was not foredoomed what caused it? [29]These and a thousand other questions are still avidly debated by a generation that has already forgotten the controversies of the Spanish War and the First World War.

4 [1]Nor is it by chance that the cause lost on the battlefield should be celebrated in story and in history, or that the whole people, victors and vanquished alike, should exalt its heroism and cherish its leaders. [2]Lee is only less of a hero than Lincoln, and the Federal army boasts no figure so glamorous as Stonewall Jackson. [3]Novelists have been kinder to the Confederacy than to the Union, and so, too, in our own day, the moving pictures and the radio. [4]There is no literary monument to any Union general comparable to those erected to Lee and Jackson, and for a generation Northern historians found themselves apologizing for Appomattox. [5]Southerners everywhere accept the verdict of the war, and even are thankful for it, but there are none so lacking in filiopietism that they would change a line of history.

5 [1]From the point of view of the student of military history, too, the Civil War is inexhaustibly interesting, and it is no wonder that English, French, and German strategists and historians have assiduously studied its battles and campaigns. [2]It was, in a sense, the last of the old wars and the first of the new. [3]It had many of the characteristics of earlier wars—the chivalry that animated officers and

men, and the mutual esteem in which the combatants held each other, for example; the old-fashioned weapons and tactics such as sabers and cavalry charges; the woeful lack of discipline; the pitiful inadequacy of medical and hospital services, of what we would now call service of supply, of any provision for welfare and morale; the almost total absence of any proper intelligence service or adequate staff work, and the primitive state of maps; the casual and amateur air that pervaded it all. [4]But it was, too, in many and interesting respects, a modern war, one that anticipated the "total" wars of the twentieth century. [5]It was the first in which the whole nation was involved, and it is probable that a larger proportion of the population, North as well as South, was actually in uniform than in any previous war of modern history. [6]It was the first in which there was an even partial control of the economy—this largely in the South rather than in the more fortunate North. [7]It was the first in which a large-scale blockade was a really effective if not indeed a decisive weapon. [8]It was the first in which the railroad and the telegraph played a major role. [9]It involved almost every known form of warfare: large-scale battles, guerrilla fighting, trench warfare, sieges and investments, bold forays into enemy country and large-scale invasions, amphibious warfare along coastal and inland waters, blockade, privateering, surface and subsurface naval war, the war of propaganda and of nerves. [10]It produced in Lee one of the supreme military geniuses of history; in Farragut one of the great naval captains; in Grant a major strategist; in Sherman, Hancock, Jackson, A. P. Hill, and Joseph E. Johnston captains whose tactics are still worthy of study; in Thomas a master of artillery; in Forrest and Stuart, Buford, Sheridan, and Wilson, cavalry leaders whose exploits have rarely been surpassed.

6 [1]Every war dramatizes the ordinary and accentuates the characteristic; more than any other in which we have ever been engaged the Civil War brought out in sharp relief those qualities that we think of as distinctively American. [2]The American was practical, experimental, inventive, intelligent, self-reliant, opportunistic, energetic, careless, undisciplined, amateurish, equalitarian, sentimental, humorous, generous, and moral. [3]He believed that the civil was superior to the military even in war, and that privates were as good as officers, that it was wrong to begin a war or to fight in a cause that was not just, that a war should be fought according to rules, and that moral standards should obtain in war as in peace. [4]All these qualities and principles were carried over from the civil to the military arena.

7 [1]Thus the war discovered a people wholly unprepared, and never willing to prepare, either materially or psychologically. [2]Neither side ever really organized for war; neither ever used the whole of its resources—though the South came far closer to this than the North; neither accepted the iron discipline which modern war imposes. [3]The war required the subordination of the individual to the mass, of the particular to the general interest, and of the local to the central government; but both Federals and Confederates indulged their individualism in the army and out, rejected military standards and discipline, selected officers for almost any but military reasons, pursued local and state interest at the expense of the national. [4]The war required organization and efficiency, but both sides conducted the war with monumental inefficiency—witness the shambles of conscription, or of the procurement of ordnance or of finances. [5]The war required the husbanding of resources, but both sides wasted their resources, human and material—witness the medical services, or desertion, or the indulgence of business as usual, especially in the North.

8 [1]The Americans were an educated, informed, self-reliant, and resourceful people, and the Civil War armies undoubtedly boasted the highest level of intelligence of any armies in modern history up to that time. [2]It took foreigners to remark this quality, however; Americans themselves took it for granted. [3]Everyone, as both Dicey and Trollope remarked in wonder, read newspapers, followed political debates, and had opinions on the war, slavery, politics, and everything else; almost everyone—as an editor knows—kept a diary or a journal. [4]Resourcefulness was almost their most striking quality. [5]This resourcefulness appeared in Grant, who kept at it until he had found the road to Vicksburg; it appeared in Lee, who was able to adjust his plans to his shifting opponents, and to count on the understanding and cooperation of his lieutenants; it appeared in the engineers, who built dams and bridges, laid railroad tracks—or tore them up—solved problems of transport and supply that appeared insoluble; it appeared in the privates of both armies, who improvised breastworks or camp shelters, foraged for food and supplies, chose their own officers, voted in the field, provided their own newspapers, theatricals, and religious services, and often fought their own battles with such weapons as they could piece together. [6]It appeared, too, in civilians, especially in the South, who managed somehow to improvise most of the weapons of war and the essentials of domestic economy, to make do with such

labor and such materials as they had, and to hold society together through four years of strife and want.

9 [1]Thus the conduct of the war confounded both the critics and the prophets. [2]It was thought a people as unmilitary as the Americans could not fight a long war, or would not—but they did. [3]It was thought that an agricultural South could not produce the matériel of war, but no single Southern defeat could be ascribed to lack of arms or equipment. [4]It was supposed that neither side could finance a major war, but both managed somehow, and though Confederate finances were a shambles the North emerged from the conflict richer than she had entered it. [5]To blockade thousands of miles of coast line, to invade an area of continental dimensions—these had never been done successfully in modern times, but the Union did them. [6]Curiously, Europe was not convinced; the same basic errors of judgment that plagued England and France during the Civil War reappeared in Germany in 1917 and in Germany, Italy, and France in 1940.

10 [1]The Americans were a good-natured people, easygoing, careless, and kindly, and in a curious sense these qualities carried over even into war. [2]Lincoln set the tone here, for the North—Lincoln, who somehow managed to mitigate the wrath of war and his own melancholy with his humor, and who never referred to the Confederates as rebels; and Lee for the South, Lee, who always called the enemy "those people." [3]Relations between the two armies were, somehow, good-natured: the very names the combatants had for each other, Johnny Reb and Billy Yank, testified to this. [4]Only occasionally were relations between these enemies who so deeply respected each other exacerbated by official policy or by the prejudices of an officer. [5]The soldiers themselves—boys for the most part, for it was a boys' war—were high-spirited and amiable, and endured endless discomforts and privations with good humor. [6]Their good humor emerged in their songs—"Goober Peas," "Mister, Here's Your Mule," "Grafted into the Army," "We Are the Boys of Potomac's Ranks"—their stories, their campfire jokes, so naïve and innocent for the most part; it spilled over into their letters home and into the diaries and journals they so assiduously kept. [7]There was bitterness enough in the war, especially for the South and for the women of the South, but probably no other great civil war was attended by so little bitterness and no other recorded so many acts of kindness and civility between enemies; certainly no other was so magnanimously concluded. [8]Read over, for example,

that moving account of the surrender at Appomattox by Joshua Chamberlain:

> Before us in proud humiliation stood the embodiment of manhood: men whom neither toils and sufferings, nor the fact of death, nor disaster, nor hopelessness could bend from their resolve; standing before us now, thin, worn, and famished, but erect, and with eyes looking level into ours, waking memories that bound us together as no other bond;—was not such manhood to be welcomed back into a Union so tested and assured? . . . How could we help falling on our knees, all of us together, and praying God to pity and forgive us all!

11 [1]The Americans were a moral people and carried their ordinary moral standards over into the conduct of war. [2]They thought aggressive warfare wrong, and the war could not get under way until Beauregard had fired on Fort Sumter; Southerners insisted that the firing was self-defense against Yankee aggression. [3]Every war is barbarous, but—Sherman, Hunter, and Sheridan to the contrary notwithstanding—there was less barbarism in the Civil than in most other wars. [4]Both peoples, as Lincoln observed, read the same Bible and prayed to the same God; both armies were devout; leaders on both sides managed to convince themselves that they stood at Armageddon and battled for the Lord. [5]When the end came there was no vengeance and no bloodshed; this was probably the only instance in modern history where rebellion was crushed without punishing its leaders.

12 [1]Above all, the generation that fought the war had that quality which Emerson ascribed pre-eminently to the English—character. [2]It is an elusive word, as almost all great words are elusive—truth, beauty, courage, loyalty, honor—but we know well enough what it means and know it when we see it. [3]The men in blue and in gray who marched thirty miles a day through the blistering heat of the Bayou Teche, went without food for days on end, shivered through rain and snow in the mountains of Virginia and Tennessee, braved the terrors of hospital and prison, charged to almost certain death on the crest of Cemetery Ridge, closed the gap at the Bloody Angle, ran the batteries of Vicksburg and braved the torpedoes of Mobile Bay, threw away their lives on the hills outside Franklin for a cause they held dear—these men had character. [4]They knew what they were fighting for, as well as men ever know this, and they fought with a tenacity and a courage rarely equaled in history. [5]So, too, their leaders, civil and military. [6]It is, in last analysis, grandeur of character that assures immortality to Lincoln as to Lee, and it is character, too, we

admire in Grant and Jackson, Sherman and Longstreet, the brave Reynolds and the gallant Pelham, and a thousand others. [7]Winston Churchill tells us, in his account of Pearl Harbor, that there were some in England who feared the consequences of that fateful blow and doubted the ability of Americans to stand up to the test of modern war. [8]"But I had studied the American Civil War," he says, "fought out to the last desperate inch," and "I went to bed and slept the sleep of the saved and thankful."

13 [1]But it is a veteran of the war itself who paid the finest tribute to his comrades in blue and in gray. [2]"Through our great good fortune," said Justice Oliver Wendell Holmes—and he spoke for his whole generation—

> in our youth our hearts were touched with fire. [3]It was given us to learn at the outset that life is a profound and passionate thing. [4]While we are permitted to scorn nothing but indifference, and do not pretend to undervalue the worldly rewards of ambition, we have seen with our own eyes, beyond and above the gold fields, the snowy heights of honor, and it is for us to bear the report to those who come after us.

Summary

Introduction: Statement of the central theme

¶1: Of all the wars fought by Americans, the Civil War has left the strongest impression on our minds, our imagination, and our hearts.

Development (¶2-12)

¶2: The Civil War was a war in which amenities were preserved.

¶3: It has furnished unending motives for the discussion of political and military issues and for cherishing heroic memories.

¶4: The Civil War gave many examples of heroism on both sides.

¶5: It is inexhaustibly interesting to military strategists.

¶6: It dramatized the typical American characteristics.

¶7: It revealed, for example, the essentially civilian mentality of the American people in their unwillingness to organize for war.

¶8: It revealed the American people as informed and resourceful.

¶9: It confounded the critics of the American people.

¶10: It revealed the good nature of the American people.

¶11: It revealed the special morality of the American people.

¶12: It revealed the moral grandeur of the American people.

Conclusion: Restatement of the central theme

¶13: The Civil War touched our hearts with fire.

Comment

The main purpose of this essay is to show how the Civil War made a deep impression on the American mind, imagination, and heart; that is the Civil War, by making Americans understand the meaning of war, made them picture it vividly and respond to it emotionally.

The summary above clearly reveals the *unity* of the essay. The central theme—that the Civil War deeply impressed the mind, imagination, and heart of the American people—is stated in paragraph 1. Paragraph 1 also contains an informal listing of the key ideas and thus serves as a topic paragraph to which paragraphs 2-12 contribute. Each of the eleven key ideas developed in paragraphs 2-12, illustrates the central theme. Each paragraph in turn develops one key idea.

Coherence is achieved by clearly marked transitions, balanced sentences, repetitions of key words, short summaries, and concrete language. *Emphasis* is achieved by presenting the key ideas in an order of increasing importance. Paragraphs 2-4 present the vivid but less important details of the war; paragraphs 5-12 deal with the essential traits of the American people culminating in the trait of moral courage or grandeur (implied by the word *character*). The concluding paragraph, with its eloquent quotation from Oliver Wendell Holmes, marks the emotional climax of the essay.

The style, or arrangement, of the sentences and words is clear, vigorous, and interesting. *Clarity* is achieved here chiefly by sentence and paragraph unity. *Vigor* is attained by the use of dramatic details, questions, direct appeals to patriotic emotions, apt quotations, figurative language, and a tone of excitement admirably sustained up to the concluding paragraph. *Interest* is achieved by occasional epigrams and slogans, a careful variation of the sentence structure, and a rich assemblage of familiar historical details. All these qualities will be illustrated in the following exercises.

Analysis and Composition

1. Note that the topic sentence of paragraph 1 is first stated in sentence 1 "The Civil War . . . has left the strongest impression on our minds, our imagination, and our hearts." The key idea stated in the topic sentence is repeated in sentence 6. Test the unity of this paragraph by showing how each sentence refers directly to the key idea stated in the topic sentence.

2. Show how the parallel structure in paragraph 1, sentences 2-5, is an aid to unity.

   It is the Civil War songs that . . .

It furnished. . . .

It has inspired. . . .

It has furnished. . . .

3. Comment on the emotional force of the details listed in sentence 7, paragraph 1.

4. How do the quotations from Lee and Farragut in sentence 7, paragraph 1, contribute to interest?

5. Diagram sentence 7, paragraph 1.* Explain briefly how Commager's use of parallel structure within the sentence achieves unity.

6. How does the arrangement of the participial expressions in sentence 7 arouse interest? † Give reasons for your answer.

7. In the light of the whole essay show how paragraph 1 stands in the same relationship to the several paragraphs of the essay as a topic sentence stands in relation to the several sentences of a paragraph.

8. Sentence 1 of paragraph 2 is the topic sentence of that paragraph. Show how all the other sentences in this paragraph develop the topic sentence.

9. Comment on the persuasive force of the examples given by Commager in sentences 6, 8, 9, 13 of paragraph 2.

10. The key idea of paragraph 3 is stated several times in slightly different ways. Locate these several statements of the key idea.

11. Commager illustrates his key idea in paragraph 3 by a series of examples stated in question form. Comment on the vigor and interest attained by the use of questions in sentences 5 to 28.

12. Paragraph 4 is considerably shorter than the other paragraphs in this essay. Examine the following reasons for the brevity of the passage and determine which is acceptable:

   a. The author rightly assumes that his readers are familiar with Civil War heroes.

   b. The author decided to write a short paragraph because the preceding paragraph was unduly long.

   c. The author had already developed the key idea of this paragraph in paragraph 1, and thus did not need to elaborate the same idea here.

13. Paragraph 5 develops its key idea—that the Civil War is inexhaustibly interesting to the student of military history—by listing the chief characteristics of the Civil War in sentences 3-9. Under what two main headings does Commager group these characteristics?

14. Sentence 10 of paragraph 5 is clearly related to the key idea stated in the topic sentence, but it is developed by a different method of analysis from that used in the rest of the paragraph. In sentences 3-9 there is an analysis by classification (Section III). What method of analysis (Sections II-VII) is used in sentence 10?

* See handbooks: Hodges, *1*; Kierzek, pp. 37-49; Wykoff, Appendix B.

† See handbooks: Foerster, *76*; Hodges, *26*; Kierzek, pp. 59-62; Perrin, pp. 282-83; Wykoff, *74*.

15. Paragraph 6 states the typical characteristics of the American. Particular illustrations of some of these characteristics appear in paragraphs 7-13. In what sentence does the author point ahead to the illustrations?

16. Sentence 2 of paragraph 6 lists fifteen characteristics of the American. Would the author have been better advised to abbreviate his list of characteristics to three or four? Give reasons for your answer.

17. Which of the characteristics listed in sentence 2, paragraph 6, are illustrated in paragraph 7?

18. Sentence 1 of paragraph 8 states that Americans were educated, informed, self-reliant, and resourceful. Sentence 3 illustrates the first two qualities. Sentences 4-6 illustrate the second two qualities. Why does the author spend twice as much space in illustrating self-reliance and resourcefulness as he does in illustrating the other characteristics?

19. Were the critics and prophets who allegedly maintained (¶9) that Americans could not fight a long war reasoning from false cause? Before framing your answer review Section VI.

20. Paragraph 10 is especially notable for its excellent style. The key idea in the topic sentence (S1) is illustrated by effective examples. These examples mount to a climax in the fervent quotation from Chamberlain in sentence 8. Commager clearly communicates his own interpretation of the Civil War. But does he forestall the question, "If Americans were a good-natured, easy-going, careless, and kindly people, how did they sanction war in the first place?"

    This question suggests that Commager's reasoning is faulty on two counts:

    a. It fails to consider an important fact (fallacy of omission).

    b. It classifies Americans on the basis of only those facts favorable to the author's purpose.

    Do you consider that these criticisms are justified? In forming your answer consider the author's main intention.

21. What definition of "morality" is implied in paragraph 11? Does this definition meet the requirements of a logical definition set forth in Section II? Give reasons for your answer.

22. Examine the definition of character in paragraph 12. Does this definition meet the requirements of a logical definition set forth in Section II? Give reasons for your answer.

23. Show how paragraph 13 sums up the meaning of the Civil War and its emotional effect upon the reader.

24. In the manner indicated in Section VIII write a brief style analysis of:

    a. Clarity, vigor, and interest in paragraph 5.

    b. Clarity, vigor, and interest in the sentences of paragraph 8.

    c. Clarity, vigor, and interest in the diction of paragraphs 12, sentences 3 and 4; paragraph 13, sentences 2 and 3.

25. This essay is an excellent model for an historical paper. The student will find Commager's use of the topic paragraph (see summary, comment, and Exercise 7 above) and a clear topic sentence for each paragraph an excellent device for managing otherwise cumbersome historical details. In an essay not exceeding 1000 words, develop one or more of the following central themes (or another of your own choice) by a method similar to that employed by Commager.

a. World War II made many Americans aware of international affairs.
b. The automobile changed modern life.
c. The opening of the frontier stimulated American growth.
d. The submarine revolutionized naval warfare.
e. Television has made a great impression on the American family.
f. The communist policy of aggression has united the free nations of the West.
g. Cinerama has opened new fields for the motion picture industry.
h. Advertising has revolutionized retail selling.

---

b. Where effective, develop a complex event by combining exposition with narration, description, and persuasion as well as by combining the various methods of analysis.

The Industrial Revolution in Great Britain

BY JACQUETTA HAWKES

1 The Industrial Revolution appears not as a mark on a continuous road, but an abrupt turning point. For an incalculably great length of time men had been relating themselves more and more closely and

effectively to the land. For the past four or five thousand years they had laboured as farmers, clearing the forests, reclaiming waste and swamp, hedging and ditching. The struggle of two hundred generations of cultivators had its culmination in the high farming of the eighteenth and early nineteenth centuries. Now those thousands of years of wooing fertility under the sun and rain were to be half forgotten in a third way of living which resembles the first, that of the hunters, in its predatory dependence on the natural resources of the country.

2 From this time the pattern of settlement was no longer to be decided by the character of the soil, the surface features of the land and the climate, but by the distribution of the deposits which time had left far below the surface. Huge numbers left farms and villages and swarmed to the places where coal and metal ores lay hidden; once there they showed an extraordinary fecundity. The population doubled and doubled again. By the middle of the nineteenth century half the people of Britain were living in towns, a situation new in the history of great nations.

3 Those town dwellers, cut off from the soil and from food production, soon lost all those arts and skills which had always been the possession if not of every man, then of every small community. The sons and daughters of the first generation of town dwellers were not taught how to use eye and hand in the traditional skills, and, a loss of absolute finality, they could not inherit all the traditional forms, the shape for an axe handle, a yoke, for a pair of tongs; the proportions of cottage doors and windows, the designs for smocking, lace making, embroidery. Some of these forms, because they had achieved fitness for their purpose as complete as the unchanging bodies of the insects, had remained constant for centuries or millennia; others were always evolving yet maintained their continuity. Now all of them, or almost all, were to fade from the common imagination, to become extinct. I know of only one traditional form for an everyday tool which has been adapted without loss to machine production; this is the exquisitely curved and modulated handle of the woodcutter's axe.

4 With the extinction of ancient arts and skills there went also countless local rites, customs, legends and histories. All these, whether or no they had been adapted to Christianity, were survivals of a paganism that helped to unite country people with nature and their own ancestors. Stories and names for fields and lanes recalled men and women who had worked the land before them; legends still com-

memorated local deities who had lived in wood, water, and stone; many customs recognized and assisted in the main crises of individual lives; rites helped to harmonize these individual rhythms with the greater rhythms of nature—they celebrated the return of the sun, the resurrection of the corn, harvest, and the return of death.

5 Without these immemorial ties, personal and universal, relating men to their surroundings in time and space, the isolation of human consciousness by urban life was a most violent challenge. It gave opportunity for the heightening of consciousness and the sharpening of intellect, but human weakness and material circumstances made it impossible for any but the few gifted or fortunate to respond. The urban masses having lost all the traditions I have just named which together make up the inheritance which may be called culture, tended to become, as individuals, cultureless. The women were in better case, for all except the most downtrodden could rear children, clean, launder, sew, and cook after a fashion, though all their work was dulled and robbed of distinction by the standardization and poor quality of their materials. (It is one of the more bizarre results of industrialism that the rich will now pay great sums to obtain goods that were once taken for granted by quite humble people. Such things as real honey, fresh butter and eggs, hand needlework, tiles made of real stone, reed thatch.) For the men it was far worse. Usually they could do only one thing, and that without direct relation to their own lives; when they returned from the set hours of "work" there was nothing for hand or imagination to do. So, when at last leisure was won for them, it proved to be a barren gift.

6 I do not wish to suggest that there was any lessening of man's dependence on the land, of his struggle to extract a living from it; that is the stuff of existence and cannot be reduced. It is not true either that industry is lacking in its own bold regional variations; the collieries with hoists and slag heaps, the steel furnaces, the clustering chimneys of the brick kilns, the potteries, all create their own landscape. But the individual life, the individual culture, was not sensitively adjusted to locality, and the nature of the relationship was profoundly changed. It ceased to be creative, a patient and increasingly skilful lovemaking that had persuaded the land to flourish, and became destructive, a grabbing of material for man to destroy or to refashion to his own design. The intrusion of machines between hand and material completed the estrangement.

7 By this new rapacious treatment of the land man certainly made himself abundantly productive of material goods. But he cannot be sure of getting what he wants from the great cauldron of production. Meanwhile the land, *with which he must always continue to live,* shows in its ravaged face that husbandry has been succeeded by exploitation—an exploitation designed to satisfy man's vanity, his greed and possessiveness, his wish for domination.

8 As a starting point for the Revolution I shall choose the time about two hundred years ago, when men began to smelt iron with coke. Earlier attempts to use coal instead of wood had failed, but now, largely through the efforts of generations of one family, the Darbys of Shropshire, the new process was mastered and the coal-and-iron age of Victorian England was already within sight. It is, of course, possible to say that the real revolution, the tipping of the balance from agriculture to manufacture, took place later than this. Equally, or indeed with more justification, it can be claimed that it began much earlier with Tudor commerce and the scientific ferment of the seventeenth century. I would agree, I would even willingly push it back to the depths of the Carboniferous forests; there is never a beginning. But I prefer to select the mating of coal and iron, for with the thought of it the weight and grime of the Black Country, the bustle and energy of material activity, at once take shape in the imagination. Besides, it was a time when the intellect, sharpened by the new scientific, analytical modes of thought, was achieving many other of the devices that made industrialism possible. In one year, 1769, Arkwright gave the water frame to the cotton industry and Watt patented the steam engine. Within another ten years the gorge of the Severn which had been cut in the Ice Age by the overflowing waters of Lake Lapworth was spanned by the first iron bridge to be built in the world. Together these closely consecutive events well represent the new forces of the Revolution: coal and iron, mechanical power, mechanization, and the corresponding development of transport.

9 The Industrial Revolution was certainly in part brought about by the scientific mode of thought that had grown from the Renaissance intellect. Yet it was not itself a rational episode. To me it seems an upsurge of instinctive forces comparable to the barbarian invasions, a surge that destroyed eighteenth-century civilization much as the Anglo-Saxons destroyed that of Roman Britain. No one planned it, no one foresaw more than a tittle of the consequences, very few people said that they wanted it, but once begun the impetus was irresistible; more

and more individual lives became helplessly involved, drawn into the vortex. It went forward as irresistibly as the evolution of the dinosaurs and in it was included the roaring of *Tyrannosaurus*. It seems indeed that *Tyrannosaurus* and Apollo of the Intellect worked together for the Revolution and no combination could be more powerful or more dangerous.

10 It lent to its instruments an astonishing strength. It enabled this chip of the earth's surface, the small fund of human mind, will and energy that it supported, momentarily to dominate the whole surface of the planet and in so doing, like a gigantic, slow explosion, to disperse fragments of itself all over that surface. It seems possible that had there not been this association of coal and iron, growing population and intellectual ferment within the bounds of a temperate island, the industrialization that in two centuries has totally changed human life might never have assumed its present forms.

11 They were there, and the new way of life developed with a speed that is almost unbelievable when it is compared with any other experience of human history. In south Wales, south Yorkshire, and Tyneside, all those regions where past events had left iron and coal in close proximity, there sprang up foundries whose crimson glare by night repeats something of the volcanic furies of other ages. With them there grew to colossal stature the manufacture of metal goods, a manufacture centred on Birmingham in a region that had remained longer than almost any other under the peaceful covering of the forests. On the moist western side of the Pennines the cotton industry, the first to be wholly dependent on material produced outside the island, grew up in obscene relationship with the trade in African slaves. The little mills once turned by the Pennine streams, family cottage manufacture, were soon abandoned for the factories of Manchester and the neighbouring towns that were growing round it. Away on the east of the central mountains, the ancient conservatism of the wool trade long resisted the new methods; in time, however, first spinning and then weaving left the rural valleys and moved to towns like Bradford, where the foamy white wool is combed and spun in mills of blackened rock, and to Leeds and Huddersfield, where it is woven on looms whose descent from those of the Bronze Age it is hard to credit. The salt that the evaporation of the Triassic lakes and lagoons had left under the Cheshire plain became the source of a chemical industry, a thing new even among so much innovation. One other industry there was which I will mention because it shows how, exceptionally, a few

individuals may impose themselves on the land, creating something from their own wills that is not dictated by circumstances. There was no material reason beyond a supply of coal for his furnaces why Josiah Wedgwood and his family should have built up the pottery business in Staffordshire. Much of his material was dug in Cornwall (where the glistening white heaps of kaolin look so alien, so improbable among the soft, warmly coloured granite moorlands), and his kilns were inconveniently far from the coast for the carriage of both the raw clay and the finished china. However, Wedgwood lived there and started his work there and so the existence of the Five Towns was determined. The craft that even in Britain had a history of four and a half millennia now went into mass production largely through the inspiration of one man. It was appropriate that for a time his name was identified with that of the clay he manipulated—that "common Wedgwood" should become the accepted term for the people's crockery. Because of their history, the Potteries have remained more patriarchal in organization, more personal in feeling than other industries, just as from its nature the work itself remains exceptionally individual and unmechanized. I will not leave the Potteries without commenting on the extraordinary forethought that nature seems to me to have shown in the formation of kaolin; nearly two hundred million years after its deposition, it has proved that this substance can be used for making china, for fulling cloth, for keeping the shine from women's faces, for paper-making, and as a cure for diarrhoea.

12 Transport was of course one of the keys of industrialism. Upon it depended a state of affairs in which men no longer made things for local use and in which a locality no longer provided the food for its people. By the eighteenth century Britain was more closely unified by roads than it had been since Roman times and soon this was reinforced by the canals, a quiet, deliberate form of carriage that came to have its own nomadic population. Then down the ringing grooves of change came the railway engine begotten by Watt and Stephenson on the iron-and-coal age. Gangs of navvies were moved about the country embanking, cutting, tunnelling, bridge-building; thousands of tons of metal were laid across our meadows, along our valleys, round our coasts. The incidental result of this activity in stimulating consciousness in its search for its origins has already been demonstrated in the life of William Smith, the Father of Stratigraphy.

13 The shift in population was the fourth and infinitely the greatest that had taken place since Mesolithic times. The north of England

and southern Wales, formerly rather thinly settled, soon had the bulk of a sharply rising population. As mills, factories, foundries, and kilns multiplied, the little streets of the workers' houses spread their lines over hills that belonged to wild birds and mountain sheep, and up valleys where there was nothing busier than a rushing beck. Without intention or understanding the greater part of the people of Britain found themselves living in towns, uprooted, and in a strange, unstable environment. The growths of brick and stone, later of concrete, whose ragged outer edges were always creeping further, might coalesce one with another in urban areas so large that it was difficult for the inhabitants to set foot on grass or naked earth. The results were grim, but sometimes and particularly in the Pennine towns they had their own grandeur. Where houses and factories are still built from the local rocks and where straight streets climb uncompromisingly up hillsides, their roofs stepping up and up against the sky, they have a geometric beauty that is harsh but true, while the texture of smoke-blackened lime- or sandstone can be curiously soft and rich, like the wings of some of our sombre night-flying moths. Nor do such cities ever quite lose the modelling of their natural foundations. On my first visit to the industrial north I rode on the top of a tram all the way from Leeds to Batley and all the way I rode through urban streets. In the last daylight it seemed a melancholy and formless jumble of brick and stone, but as darkness closed and a few smoky stars soothed and extended my thoughts, the lamps going up in innumerable little houses restored the contours of hill and dale in shimmering lines of light.

14 At least much of this nineteenth-century building showed the force, the ruthless purpose of its age. The railways, too, served to concentrate it and to keep it truly urban. Far more pitiful are the housing estates, the ribbon development, and all the flimsy scattered new building that our own century has added as a result of the internal-combustion engine. The railways took far too many people to certain places, the motor-car takes rather too many people everywhere. The dormitory housing estates on the outskirts of cities are a limbo created by the combination of meanness with theoretical good intentions. The little gardens that man's incurable love of earth has obliged the council or the speculative builder to provide, soon make a ragged wilderness of broken fences and sheds. The streets wander aimlessly about, representing either simple chaos or the whimsy notions of a planning officer. Nothing has grown; nothing is inevitable. All over England the houses are the same; for they are built of materials that are not

local but cheap. A house at Bradford, a house at Dagenham, will show the same silly stucco, the same paltry composition roof. Since 1945 there has been an improvement, and the sight of these better houses, flats, schools, is the most hopeful thing to be seen in Britain, more convincing than ten million optimistic words. It is the only thing that suggests that new roots are going down and new sources of vitality being found.

15 [1]Perhaps what is worst in the effects of motor transport and of the partial shift of the balance of population back to the south and the southern Midlands, has been the wreckage left in its wake. [2]When the uplands so thickly peopled in prehistoric times were deserted, the scars that human activity had left upon them were so slight, so readily healed, that soon they melted back into the scene and enriched it. [3]The gentle knolls of chieftains' graves adorn the horizon, fortress walls become grass banks for lovers' meetings. [4]But once men had taken to using chemical change on an immense scale to convert the natural substances of the land for their own purposes, this natural healing could hardly again take place. [5]Iron and concrete are not readily softened. [6]A robin may nest in a rusty kettle, but that is about the largest scale on which adaptation is possible. [7]The present derelict parts of industrial Britain assume a degraded ugliness never before known. [8]Who can ever express the desolation of these forlorn scenes? [9]The grey slag heap, the acres of land littered with rusted fragments of machinery, splintered glass, tin cans, sagging festoons of barbed wire; vile buildings, more vile in ruin; grimy stretches of cement floors, shapeless heaps of broken concrete. [10]The air about them still so foul that nothing more than a few nettles and tattered thistles will grow there; not even rosebay and ragwort can hide them with a brief midsummer promise. [11]This is the worst that has happened to the land.

16 One curious result of the Industrial Revolution can claim a special place in this chronicle of the relationship between men and their land. For the medieval peasant eight weeks in the year were holy days, days when a service in the parish church was followed by freedom for rest and celebration. Each chosen black- and red-letter day, each Church festival, was a part of the wheel of the year and served for rites so much more ancient than Christianity as to be almost as old as the consciousness of man. No countryman could have celebrated them away from his own cottage, fields, and animals, his neighbours, and his church, for they were important threads in the fabric of life where all these things were woven together in a single design.

17 Now the sharp division of work from play and the natural from the supernatural has turned holy days into holidays, and the compelling restlessness and ugliness of towns has made holidays an occasion for escape from home. So there is this new form of mass migration—no longer to pursue game animals or pasture domestic ones, no longer for fishing or fowling or the visiting of shrines. Instead a flight from a man-made world too hard, dirty, and hideous to allow its inhabitants to rest, to lie down on the ground or to dance upon it, to turn back to their surroundings for refreshment. Three hundred years ago how impossible it would have seemed that England should be cumbered with towns built as an escape from towns, that half its south and east coasts should be encrusted with red bricks, walled behind concrete, the sea itself grasped after with iron piers. If the migrations have largely defeated their purpose by spreading more hardness and a new ugliness, at least the resorts are clean, and human beings can find just room enough to stretch their bodies on the sand.

18 Elsewhere in the country, as has already appeared, crowds make for wide views, for wild country, for unusually dynamic manifestations of nature or ancient manifestation of man, feeding themselves while they may on something which they most urgently need, some nourishment quite lacking in urban existence.

Comment

This essay is notable for two kinds of combination: (a) the combination of various methods of development (Sections II-VII) and (b) the combination of several types of discourse.

The combination of the methods of development may be seen in a brief paragraph summary:

· The central theme—the Industrial Revolution is an abrupt turning point in the relationship of the English people with their land—is introduced and explained in paragraph 1. The six succeeding paragraphs contain specific examples (Section IV) of the change introduced by the Industrial Revolution:

¶2: The population shifted from the land to industrial towns and twice doubled itself.
¶3: The town dwellers lost their traditional arts and skills.
¶4: The town dwellers lost their memory of local rites, customs, and legends, derived from their association with the land.

¶5: Town dwellers became an urban mass that had lost its creative culture.

¶6: Individual life became sterile.

¶7: The land, as well as the people, was impoverished.

Thus in paragraphs 2-7 we are given specific examples of the fact of abrupt change brought on by the Industrial Revolution.

Paragraphs 8-12 combine process analysis (Section VII) and causal analysis (Section VI) to show how the Industrial Revolution developed and why it happened.

Paragraph 8 locates the beginning of the Industrial Revolution in the middle of the eighteenth century when conditions favorable to the Industrial Revolution were discovered (process analysis).

Paragraphs 9 and 10 state the *causes* of the Industrial Revolution as (a) scientific thought, which was direct and immediate, and (b) historical forces, which cannot be directly analyzed.

Paragraph 11 resumes a process analysis by tracing the rapid growth of industrialism in the coal and iron regions.

Paragraph 12 continues the process analysis by showing how real transportation, itself a product of the Industrial Revolution, accelerated the revolution already underway.

Paragraphs 13-18 are concerned with the continuing effects of the Industrial Revolution:

¶13: The greater part of the British population shifted to new and inhospitable urban areas.

¶14: The new suburban areas were depressingly uniform.

¶15: The countryside was visited with a blight.

¶16-18: The Industrial Revolution affected the soul of man.

This essay not only combines the various methods of development but also harmonizes exposition with narration, description, and persuasion in developing its central theme. These various forms of discourse are blended throughout the essay. However, each form has a predominant role in those sections of the essay where it is particularly appropriate to the method of development being used.

Thus in the first seven paragraphs, where the author exemplifies her central theme, the form of discourse is chiefly *expository* with a narrative blend. Paragraphs 8-12, developed by process analysis, are chiefly *narrative* blended with exposition. Paragraphs 13-18, developed by effects, employ *description* with narration and exposition. A *persuasive* note also appears in paragraphs 13-14, where the author indirectly appeals for some corrective measures to stop the evil effects of certain phases of the Industrial Revolution.

Yet, so harmoniously are these forms of discourse blended, that the reader is aware only of a splendid unity in the whole essay.

Analysis and Composition

1. Show how paragraph 1 effectively introduces the subject of this essay, the Industrial Revolution in England,
   a. By stating the central theme of the essay clearly
   b. By indicating the general method of development
   c. By expressing the author's own emotional response to the subject
2. Paragraphs 2-7 constitute a series of examples of "abrupt change." Paragraphs 8-12 show how the change happened. Paragraphs 13-18 show the effects of the change. A close reading of the essay reveals that the first group of paragraphs (1-7) covers much the same ground as the third group of paragraphs (13-18). Can you justify this repetition by showing how it aids in achieving unity, coherence, or emphasis?
3. Show how Miss Hawkes uses each of the following methods of analysis to develop an idea in a paragraph. (Note that some paragraphs contain several methods of analysis.)
   a. Definition: of the Industrial Revolution (¶8-9)
   b. Classification: of the urban masses (¶5)
   c. Examples
      (1) Of the loss of arts and skills (¶3)
      (2) Of the results of the shift in population (¶13)
      (3) Of the ruthless purpose of the age (¶14)
      (4) Of the wreckage of the land (¶15)
   d. Comparison and contrast
      (1) Of the English countryside before and after the Industrial Revolution (¶15)
      (2) Of the peasants and townsmen (¶16-17)
   e. Causal analysis: of the Industrial Revolution (¶16)
   f. Process analysis: of the development of the Industrial Revolution (¶8-12)
4. This essay combines certain narrative and descriptive methods with exposition. For example, in the process analysis (¶8-12) a time order is observed in the account of the Industrial Revolution; in paragraphs 13-15, which explain the results of the Industrial Revolution, the author *describes* the physical details she observed during her visits to industrial areas. Decide whether these and other elements of narration and description
   a. Destroy the unity of the exposition, or
   b. Are properly subordinated to the exposition of the main ideas and thus contribute to the unity of the exposition.
   Give reasons for your answer.

5. This essay demonstrates clearly that the social scientist need not write jargon and need not shy away from metaphorical language. The diction is always clear, frequently vivid, and at times profoundly sensitive. Study the connotations of the following italicized expressions in the context of the sentence and paragraph in which they appear and explain how they evoke a picture in your imagination or stir up an emotional response. In other words, what do they make you see? How do they make you feel?

    a. "Legends still *commemorated local deities*" (¶4).

    b. "Leisure . . . proved to be a *barren gift*" (¶5).

    c. "The collieries . . . , the steel furnaces, the clustering chimneys . . . , all *create their own landscape*" (¶6).

    d. "The land . . . shows . . . its *ravaged* face" (¶7).

    e. "It seems indeed that *Tyrannosaurus* and *Apollo of the Intellect* worked together for the Revolution" (¶9).

    f. "Like a gigantic, *slow explosion,* to *disperse fragments* of itself all over that surface" (¶10).

    g. "Crimson *glare by night* repeats something of *the volcanic furies* of other ages" (¶11).

    h. "In *obscene* relationship with the trade in African slaves" (¶11).

    i. "Where the *foamy white wool* is combed and spun in mills of *blackened rock*" (¶11).

    j. "The canals, a *quiet deliberate form of carriage* that came to have its own *nomadic* population" (¶12).

    k. "The little streets of the workers' houses *spread their lines* over hills" (¶13).

    l. "Like the wings of some of our *sombre night-flying moths*" (¶13).

    m. "A few *smoky stars soothed* and *extended* my thoughts" (¶13).

    n. "Soon make *a ragged wilderness* of broken fences and sheds" (¶14).

    o. "The streets *wander aimlessly* about" (¶14).

    p. "A robin may nest in *a rusty kettle*" (¶15).

    q. "*Sagging festoons* of barbed wire" (¶15).

    r. "The sea itself *grasped after* with iron piers" (¶17).

6. Paragraph 15 is one of the most effective paragraphs in the entire essay.

    a. It has unity. The main idea is stated in sentence 1. It is repeated in sentences 7 and 11. Show how each of the other sentences contributes to the main idea.

    b. It has emphasis. Show how the emotional effect in this paragraph increases in intensity, reaching a climax in sentences 9 and 10.

    c. It has excellent variety in sentence structure. Classify the sentences in this paragraph under the following headings:

        (1) Simple, complex, compound *

---

* See handbooks: Foerster, pp. 9-17; Hodges, pp. 29, 463-64; Kierzek, pp. 39-45; Perrin, pp. 247-59; Wykoff, *4a.*

(2) Loose and periodic *
(3) Balanced and unbalanced †

d. How is emphasis achieved in sentences 5, 8, and 10?

e. What is the effect of the contrast between the uplands before the Industrial Revolution (Ss 2 and 3) and the same areas after the Industrial Revolution (Ss 4-10)?

f. The parts of this paragraph are logically related to the key idea of the paragraph and are arranged in climactic order. Show how the paragraph itself is the climax of the whole composition.

7. As we have indicated in the preceding comment and analysis, the effectiveness of this essay depends in great part on the author's own emotional response to the subject reflected in her choice of details and her charged language. Construct an emotional chart or graph of the essay by indicating the relative emotional intensity of the individual paragraphs.

8. Select one of the following subjects for a composition of about 1000 words modeled on "The Industrial Revolution in Great Britain." Strive to emulate the vigor and interest of Miss Hawkes's style.

a. Pittsburgh (or any other industrial region) before and after the introduction of industry

b. The effect of the railroad on the western United States

c. Germany after World War II

d. Television and its effect on the American home

e. The effect of aviation upon Alaska

f. The social consequences of the New Deal

g. What created the Dust Bowl

h. The effect of progressive education upon the schools

i. Some results of the Point Four policy

j. The draft law and its effect upon the careers of young men and women

* See handbooks: Foerster, pp. 27-28, 75; Hodges, 29*b*; Kierzek, 61; Perrin, pp. 280-82; Wykoff, 4*c*.

† See handbooks: Foerster, pp. 28-29, 77; Hodges, 29*g*; Kierzek, 63; Perrin, p. 283; Wykoff, pp. 54, 117-18.

C. Develop a complex idea by a sustained contrast with an opposing idea; make your contrast effective by combining argument with exposition.

Faith for Freedom

BY BARBARA WARD

1 [1]Any human enterprise, even the smallest, needs a measure of faith. [2]Men must believe that what they have undertaken can be carried through. [3]They must believe that their partners will work with them loyally. [4]How much more is faith needed when the enterprise is the building of a free and peaceful world and the partners include all the races of the earth. [5]One of the greatest obstacles to an effective Western policy today is men's uncertainty whether peace can in fact be maintained. [6]Particularly among young people, a future apparently dominated by atomic war cuts off at the roots the rising sap of hope and confidence. [7]Yet the essence of containment is the belief that war is not inevitable and that a combination of strength and patience in the West will deter the Soviets from further aggression and persuade them either to negotiate or at least to live as they did in the twenties and thirties, primarily concerned with their own affairs.

2 [1]An almost equal obstacle to successful containment is distrust among the different partners—the tendency of each to pick out and concentrate on the worst aspects of the others' policy, to rub the sore spots, to put salt in old wounds. [2]Out of a million small reactions of unfamiliarity and misunderstanding, national moods grow up, critical,

FAITH FOR FREEDOM: reprinted from *Policy for the West* by Barbara Ward. By permission of W. W. Norton & Company, Inc., and Barbara Ward Jackson. Copyright 1951 by W. W. Norton & Company, Inc.

carping and envenomed. [3]Yet what do the free peoples expect? [4]That their neighbors should be exactly like themselves? [5]That they should escape altogether from the fatality of human weakness and error? [6]That they should be incapable of stupidity or tactlessness or self-interest?

3 [1]No private undertaking, no human enterprise of any sort could be run on such expectations. [2]The Western allies have to be patient with one another and keep the larger unity of their common purposes alive in their minds to defeat all the day-to-day inconveniences of close alliance. [3]The essence of faith is that it does not depend upon a perpetual renewal of absolute proof. [4]No ally in the West is likely to give its neighbors a daily exhibition of all the virtues necessary for a great undertaking. [5]Let the others therefore give the tolerance they expect. [6]If the concept of American greed, of British duplicity or French cowardice or Italian irresponsibility is brought in over and over again to interpret policies and explain reactions, no common enterprise can possibly succeed. [7]It should be as easy to think the best as to think the worst of an ally, but apparently this is not so, and only an effort of faith, constantly renewed, can counter the tendency of men and nations to misunderstand, to recriminate, to grow suspicious, and at last permit their alliances to fall apart.

4 [1]Faith in the enterprise itself and faith in one's partners is, however, no more than the minimum—the least with which free men can hope to survive. [2]The weakness of the phrase "containment" is its negative and defensive ring. [3]The Communists do not make the mistake of thinking that they are simply defending themselves against "Western encirclement." [4]This may be the jargon they use to explain to their own people why they have remained armed and alert. [5]But the essence of their drive, of their propaganda, of their picture of themselves is that they must remake the world according to their own gospel, the single unalterable Marxist-Leninist gospel of salvation.

5 [1]It is curious that we in the West should tend so uniformly to underestimate or misunderstand the passion that drives communism on. [2]Western critics are never tired of pointing out that it is based upon materialism, that there is no room in the communist system for mankind's highest aspirations or deepest hopes, that all the power and poetry and inspiration of humanity are banished by communism's fundamental tenet—that the economic structure of society determines all the rest. [3]It may be that, in theory, there is no room in communism for these things, but it is vital to remember that, in practical reality,

the Communists hardly give economics a thought. [4]They do not condemn Western society because it is inefficient. [5]On the contrary, they are immensely impressed with the technical achievements of the West. [6]They blame it because it is immoral. [7]They do not extol their own system because it is materially more satisfactory. [8]They extol it because it is a new heaven and a new earth, a transfiguration of the conditions of human existence, the raising up of men's lives to new levels of creativeness and joy. [9]When the tanks pour through the streets of Moscow in a gigantic military parade the radio commentators burst into verse:

> Spring has come. It has come here, it has come in China, in the new streets of Warsaw, in Prague, in the gardens of Bucharest, in the villages of Bulgaria. The banner of victory flies over us. The spring of humanity is with us. It is nearing the workers' suburbs of Paris; it is marching like a master upon the piazzas of Rome. In Calcutta, Karachi, and Bombay, it sings of freedom. Our Stalin, whose hand guides the spring of humanity, is leading us to victory.

6 [1]When a new program of irrigation and public works is announced, the newspapers grow lyrical:

> For centuries the peoples of the East have dreamed of crystal-clear rivers, of fertile gardens in the desert, of a fairyland of happiness. Songs passed down from one generation to the next told of these yearnings. The people were confident that the time would come when clear, transparent rivers and streams would cut through the heart of the desert, when birds would sing in the once-silent stretches of dead sands, when blossoming gardens would flourish under a deep blue sky, when beautiful palaces would appear and crowds of gay people assemble to acclaim with gratitude the conquerors of the desert. Today the Soviet peoples praise in all their tongues the courageous conquerors of the desert—the Bolsheviks; and they glorify the Bolshevik Party and the beloved Comrade Stalin, whose genius has opened the path to fulfillment of these age-old aspirations.

The first aspect to strike eyewitnesses of communist rule in China is the attempt to instill "new thoughts" and "self-criticism" in the unconverted Chinese. Police officers confess on the wall-sheets pinned up in their offices that they have stayed awake until four in the morning wondering in agony of spirit whether their self-criticism has been sufficiently honest and far-reaching; and, lest the cynic should dismiss these wrestlings, it should be said that foreign observers also notice a marked increase in their capacity to recover lost or stolen goods without resorting to bribery.

7 ¹Long before the technician and the economist and the social engineer begin expounding the economics of communism, the poet and the moralist have fired men's minds with the picture of a moral and inspiring way of life. ²Whatever the shams of communism—and they are immense—they come clothed in the language of poetry and hope. ³The dream that has haunted the world from its infancy—of a golden age from which it has been banished and a golden age to which it can return—is repeated in the myth of a primitive communism destroyed by the evil of private property and restored triumphantly in the latter days by the return to communism. ⁴The anger and outrage of the prophets of old, denouncing social injustice and considering "the evils that are done under the sun," the promise of the Magnificat, "He hath . . . exalted them of low degree," the exquisite and heartbreaking hope of the Apocalypse "and there shall be no more death, nor sorrow nor crying, neither shall there be any more pain; for the former things are passed away"—all these echoes and intimations which lie deepest in men's hearts are evoked by these so-called materialists, by these men who are supposed to think only in terms of economics and from whose lips the appeal of faith and righteous wrath and world-conquering hope is almost never absent.

8 ¹It must be admitted that, in comparison with this apocalyptic vision of the world's warring between communist good and capitalist evil, Western policy seems, remarkably and inexplicably, to have lost sight of its own vision of the good society or at least to have lost confidence in its powers of explaining what that vision really is. ²If a visitor from Mars had arrived on earth during 1949 and examined the published statements of East and West, it is not likely that he would have found the "materialists" in the Communist half. ³The constant preoccupation with economics, the careful calculation of what could and could not be afforded, the ceaseless discussion of the limits of taxation, budgetary equilibrium, and the perils of inflation would have met him in almost every capital—until he came to the Iron Curtain. ⁴Beyond he would have found himself in a world dominated not by a certain view of economics but by a new—and terrible—view of life. ⁵This contrast is all the more extraordinary when one reflects that, on any standard of comparison, the really radical and revolutionary way of life does not lie in the East at all, but in the West. ⁶The ideas and aspirations of Western man are still the most startling thing that has ever happened to the human race. ⁷Stalin's views of man and society are, by comparison, mortally static and archaic. ⁸In fact the world today

presents the astonishing spectacle of Western man sleeping unaware on the powder keg of his own revolutionary philosophy and the Stalinists leaping up and down proclaiming as a new revolution a view of man and society which was old when the Pyramids were built.

9 [1]We know something of the civilizations that have risen and fallen in the long history of mankind. [2]Through all of them two themes of human belief and organization appear to run—the first that man and society are molded by the immense impersonal forces of destiny and circumstance, the second that the state—whether spiritual or temporal—is omnipotent and the source of all meaning. [3]Subjects were no more than shadows of shadows. [4]Reality rested with king and priest and temple. [5]And humankind together, king and peasant, priest and servant, were bound to the "melancholy wheel" of fate, the impersonal and unchanging order of times and seasons, the infinite fatality of history. [6]For thousands upon thousands of years, the great civilizations rose and fell, the people in servitude to the state, state and people alike in servitude to destiny. [7]Behavior, ritual, thought itself were determined collectively. [8]Men and women lived out their lives within the closed circle of omnipotent government and omnipotent fate.

10 [1]Into this static world with its slow rhythm of rise and fall, exhaustion and renewal, there broke a new force of ideas and vitality which wrought probably the most radical transformation of the human scene since man became recognizably man. [2]Two peoples brought about this transformation, each small in number and vast in energy and fertility—the Jews and the Greeks. [3]It is interesting to speculate what an orthodox Marxist historian would have prophesied for mankind had he lived a few thousand years before Christ and had seen Egypt in its static power, the Hittites building a civilization in Asia Minor, Crete crumbling, the Sumerians a memory, and Babylon at its zenith. [4]Which empire would he have chosen as the source of future power and influence? [5]Which ideas would he have foreseen dominating and molding the next age? [6]The guess is permissible that he would have overlooked altogether a pastoral people of Judea who, owing to their curiously indigestible national characteristics, were now sitting in exile by the waters of Babylon and refusing to forget their native land. [7]Nor would this same historian, studying all the barbarian peoples who broke through the barriers of mountain and steppe from the north to settle by the Mediterranean, have recognized in the rude Acheans the predecessors of Aristotle and Socrates. [8]There is, in history, a recurring refusal to be bound by the predictors and the analysts. [9]History mocks the men who claim, like Marx, to have mastered its secrets, and

this infinite unpredictability should be the perennial hope of anyone who believes in the resources of freedom.

11 ¹With the advent of these two societies—Jewish and Greek—the whole character of human development changed, and there entered into history something which we may reasonably call "the Western spirit." ²The measure of its revolutionary power was that it completely contradicted and annihilated the two dominant themes of the archaic world—the fatality of environment and the omnipotence of the state. ³There is no space here to set down all that Western man owes to his Jewish and Christian heritage on the one hand and to Greece and Rome on the other. ⁴It is a commonplace that our society is grounded to its deepest foundations in classical and Christian antiquity. ⁵But of all the riches and diversity, these two entirely revolutionary facts must be remembered, for they are the key to the understanding of our own society and to its fundamental divergence from communism. ⁶It is only in their light that the radical newness of Western thought and the fundamentally reactionary character of communist thinking can be fully grasped.

12 ¹The Greeks and the Jews shared with the older civilizations the idea of a divine order of society, but whereas before this order seemed on the whole to have been made up of the sum of circumstances—the seasons, the days, the cycle of agriculture, the chances of flood and storm, the social order as it existed—in Greek and Jewish thought a gulf opened between the divine order as it existed in the mind of God, and the very human order as it existed on earth. ²The idea that the sum of things could by human will and action be transformed and remade in the image of the divine took hold of men's imaginations. ³The static idea of social order began to give way to the revolutionary, to the ideas of a possible perfect society which could be achieved, provided men overcame the irrational and immoral aspects of their own lives and their own institutions. ⁴The desire to transform, the desire to create, the desire to seize on material circumstances and change and mold them as an artist transforms the material he works with, this was the immense energy injected into the Western world by the rational vision of the Greeks and the moral vision of the Jews. ⁵The divine order ceased to be the sum of things that are and began to become the sum of things as they should be. ⁶Try as he would—and to return to the static is always a temptation—Western man could never again drive the fever of creation and transformation and progress out of his blood.

13 ¹The two streams of thought were equally potent in sweeping away the other principle of ancient society—the acceptance of the omnipotent state. ²The Greek saw the reflection of the Logos in the rational nature of man. ³As a creature endowed with reason he acquired inalienable social and political rights, among them the right to self-government. ⁴For the Jew, it was the divine image in man that created in him moral responsibility. ⁵From the first question of Cain, "Am I my brother's keeper?" flowed out the doctrine of personal responsibility. ⁶In the Christian tradition the Greek concept of reason and the Hebrew belief in man's accountability met in the idea of the "free and lawful man," which, in medieval Europe, was the basis of the great constitutional experiment of placing government itself under the law and, in the centuries that followed, developed into the full doctrine of representative government and political freedom.

14 ¹No one will pretend that the progress of these two transforming ideals—of justice and liberty—was regular or complete. ²The Greek insight into the irrationality of much in man's nature and the institutions he set up has been more than justified. ³The Hebrew and Christian concept of sin—the pride of the mind and the lust of the heart—has darkened every page of Western history. ⁴Yet underneath failure and collapse and defeat, the Western spirit has constantly renewed itself and, in the darkest ages, the voice of the saint and the prophet and the reformer was raised to denounce the things that were and point once again to the things that ought to be. ⁵The whole social order could never again be entirely accepted. ⁶The state could never again maintain an unquestioned omnipotence. ⁷Angry, restless, adventuring, protesting, the reformer fought his way through the thickets of ignorance and prejudice. ⁸Pitying, loving, rebuking, and consoling, the saint and the mystic sought entrance to the darkest hearts and most wayward lives. ⁹Under these pressures, Western society became the most restlessly dynamic and explosive social order the world had ever seen. ¹⁰There could be no rest once these ideals of progress and perfection had been let loose in the mind of Western man.

15 ¹It is the tragedy of Marxist communism that it restores the old fetters of fatality and tyranny. ²Because it borrows the terminology of the West and speaks of true freedom and true democracy and true science, men often overlook the profoundly and terrifyingly reactionary character of its doctrine. ³The free and morally responsible human being with rights and duties and aspirations which transcend any given social order vanishes. ⁴Why? ⁵Because there is nothing beyond the

social order. ⁶Every act of human life, every thought of human minds is entirely conditioned by the general state of material events at that time. ⁷History becomes once more the arbiter of all destiny. ⁸It is no longer an arena in which men struggle in freedom to remold recalcitrant matter and fashion it to their ideals. ⁹Their freedom is an illusion, and recalcitrant matter is itself responsible for their ideals. ¹⁰The world of freedom closes. ¹¹In its place returns the stifling world of necessity in which the childhood of the race was spent. ¹²Once again men are bound to the melancholy wheel of their social conditioning. ¹³Once again, events mold them, not they events. ¹⁴The collective crust forms once again over the experiment of human freedom. ¹⁵The Western vision fades, and in the darkness there are glimpses of Moloch and Baal and the terrible gods of state and circumstance reasserting their ancient sway.

16 ¹In such a world, the return to omnipotent government is inevitable. ²If man is no more than a unit in a social calculation, to what rights and pretensions can he lay claim? ³It is the total social process, society, the environment as a whole that has significance, just as thousands of years ago the apparatus of the state—city or temple—was reality and men no more than its component parts. ⁴No one doubts the omnipotent claims of the Soviet state today, but some are inclined to overlook the even more omnipotent claims inherent in the prophecy that eventually "the state will wither away." ⁵In any conceivable society where variety of claims and interests is admitted, some government must remain as arbiter. ⁶The only highly complex societies that can dispense with government are those in which social conditioning has produced such perfect adaptation to circumstance and work that no conflicts are conceivable—and no change and no progress either. ⁷We know of such societies. ⁸The bees and the ants have reached just such a degree of adaptation to environment. ⁹(And if environment is fatality, is reality, is God itself, what greater purpose for humanity can there be than to adapt itself?) ¹⁰Behind the concept of the withering away of the state lies not only the loss of freedom, but the loss of rationality and humanity itself.

17 ¹These are not idle fears. ²We know from man's long history that the Western experiment of freedom and responsibility is a flash in the pan, a spark in the longest night, an experiment bounded in space and time and preceded by aeons of collective servitude. ³To step back into an older environment, to regress, to abandon an experiment at once so testing and so abnormal must be a temptation at the very

roots of our being. [4]Communism presents it in a form in which language and propaganda are borrowed from the liberal experiment but fundamental thought and direction lead back into the anonymous tyrannies of antiquity and of primitive mankind. [5]Environment as destiny, the state as omnipotence—these are the principles under whose mastery mankind has spent by far the longest part of its conscious span. [6]The Western phase is a tremendous, a breath-taking experiment. [7]It is not yet certain that it can stay the course.

18 [1]Yet if the Western experiment is really the most audacious and exhilarating that mankind has ever made, how is it that today the audacity and the creativeness and the revolutionary zeal so often seem to be on the other side? [2]There is a tremendous paradox here. [3]The crusaders for freedom and progress, for man's ever-renewed struggle to build a just and holy society appear to be on the defensive before those who seek to eliminate human freedom and restore the twin tyrannies of fate and government. [4]The real revolutionaries cede ground to the pseudo-revolutionaries. [5]The radicals retreat before the reactionaries, the idealists before the materialists. [6]Indeed, the idealists seem to have turned themselves into materialists and to fight their war of words in calculations and statistics while their adversaries sing of deserts blossoming and spring returning to a resurrected humanity. [7]How have we in the West contrived so to dim our vision that we appear to have lost it? [8]How have we come to do remarkable things in such a totally unremarkable way? [9]When was the initiative lost? [10]How is it that we have yet to recapture it?

19 [1]There can be only one answer. [2]We have not lost it because the Marxist vision is more potent than ours or because communism offers a more attractive version of society. [3]Indeed, it would be difficult to find anything more unattractive than, say, contemporary Bulgaria, and even if we prefer our communism in idealized form, one searches Marx's pages in vain for a concrete description of what communist society would be like. [4]No, his strength lay in what he attacked, not in what he promised. [5]And it is still true of communism today that wherever it is not imposed by force, it owes its strength not so much to its own attractiveness as to the weakening of the Western way of life. [6]In the last hundred years, we have seen our grip slacken on those two revolutionary principles upon which the Western experiment has been based. [7]The classical and Christian tradition has grown weaker. [8]In its place, even in the West, the concept of fatality and of almighty circumstance has crept back. [9]The men who founded the Industrial

Revolution and believed in unchanging and unaltering economic laws were introducing a god of economic determinism into one sector of their society. [10]It was a savage but appropriate justice that led Marx to turn economic determinism against them in their own industrial stronghold. [11]Workers had been sacrificed to misery and degradation in the name of the "iron laws" of demand and supply. [12]Very well, their employers would now be sacrificed in their turn in the name of economic determinism and dialectical materialism. [13]If matter was to be master, Marx had as good a version of the future to offer as Richard Cobden and John Bright and a much more attractive version from the standpoint of the masses.

20 [1]Nor was the Manchester School's confidence in the beneficence of *laissez faire* the only entry point for fatalism and historical materialism. [2]The present reality of God and of an ideal world of law and justice which men should struggle to observe and create even if circumstance drag them the other way, began to fade and the great fatalities—environment, conditioning, heredity, evolution—sapped and weakened the concept of freedom, moral responsibility, and will. [3]Unconsciously at first, but with steadily increasing realization and indifference, a vast mass of Western men and women sloughed off their society's traditional idealism and became in practice, if not in belief, materialists as convinced as any on the other side of the Iron Curtain —but with this difference. [4]The materialism preached by communists was a religion of materialism, materialism raised to a total explanation of life, guide of conduct, and spur to action. [5]The materialism of the West was all too often no more than an attitude of "eat, drink, and be merry, for tomorrow we die." [6]In a conflict between religious materialism and practical materialism, it seems certain that the religious variety will have the strength to prevail. [7]An idea has never yet in human history been defeated by no idea at all.

21 [1]Yet, although it is true that communism has gained strength by the West's own weaknesses, it may yet be true that the West will learn from the Communists how to recapture its own freedom-loving, transforming, and creative spirit. [2]In the first place, men and women in the West can see in Soviet society some of the possible results of their own betrayal of the Western ideal. [3]They see what a society can become which is systematically materialist, godless, and "scientific." [4]They see how speedily the safeguards of freedom vanish once the idea of law independent of race or class fades and in its place is put

the convenience of the community. [5]They see how terribly human compassion can be maimed if there is no appeal to a higher authority than that of government. [6]They see that science itself, on which the regime is supposedly based, can be perverted if the search for truth gives way to the acceptance of the politically expedient. [7]And reflecting on these things, they are perhaps more ready to reconsider the old safeguards of independence and pity, of justice, and of truth. [8]They look perhaps with new interest at an earlier belief—that liberty itself is grounded in the fact that God's authority overrules all others and that, in St. Thomas More's words, a man can be the state's "good servant, but God's first."

22 [1]But communism does more than provide the Western world with a species of rake's progress of some of its own ideas and assumptions. [2]It is, in a real sense, the conscience of the West. [3]Every pretension, every false claim, every complacency of our Western society is relentlessly exposed by Communist propaganda, and all too often our dislike of the critics is rendered a thousand times more bitter by our inner knowledge that their gibes are true. [4]It is infuriating, it is exasperating, it is exhausting for the West to know that every weakness is spied on, every social failure capitalized, every injustice trumpeted abroad, every lack of charity and understanding blown up into a major social crime. [5]But is it certain that without these enraging critics we in the West would be so aware of where we fail ourselves? [6]Might we not drift on in indifference beyond the point at which this weakened institution or that false situation could be repaired? [7]In many ways, we today are paying for the complacency of our grandfathers and great-grandfathers. [8]It was not only the injustice, it was also the appalling smugness of the Victorian possessing classes which put the real vitriol into Marx's pen. [9]Today, at least, no false complacency can hold us back from seeing where are the weaknesses and the shams. [10]Bitterly as a man may resent the shooting pain that warns him of some internal disorder, would he see to curing himself in time without that pain?

23 [1]Communists today leave us in no doubt where our weaknesses lie. [2]They await in a fever of tension and expectation the coming of another disastrous depression. [3]They seek to exacerbate by every means the gulf between East and West, between Asia and the Atlantic, between developed and backward areas, between rich and poor, slave and free. [4]They search for every chink in the armor of Western unity.

[5]They batten on every national prejudice and try to poison every potential conflict between the allies of the West. [6]Above all, they preach the decadence and decline of Western ideals, the false pretensions of Western society, the myth of Western religion, the hypocrisy of Western freedom, and the certainty of Western collapse. [7]We need therefore have no doubts about the necessary means of Western survival—to be stable, reliable, and prosperous ourselves, to share with others our prosperity, to rebuild our defenses, to be patient allies and good friends, to restore our vision and moral purpose, to drive out the gods of fatalism, to restore the "glorious liberty of the sons of God," and, in this spirit, to confront our adversaries with a calm fortitude that allays both their fears and their ambitions—these are the main themes for a common policy in the West. [8]Nothing in them is beyond the competence of the Western Powers. [9]Never, indeed, have the material means of fulfilling them been so assured. [10]If there is a doubt at all, it can only be a doubt of the necessary vision and will.

24 [1]This surely is the crux. [2]In all that they say of the Western world, the Communists are proclaiming the fatal laws of historical necessity. [3]Capitalist society must collapse. [4]The United States must practice selfish imperialism. [5]The Western states must exploit their workers, fight for markets in the world at large, trample down their Asiatic helots, and plunge the world into wars of aggression. [6]It follows that every policy of the West that contradicts these fears—every Marshall Plan, every extension of economic aid to backward areas, every increase in social and economic opportunity, every act of justice and reconciliation breaks with the Communists' fundamental gospel—the fatality of history—and restores, triumphantly and creatively, the freedom of the West. [7]We are not bound by collective selfishness. [8]No iron law of economics holds us down. [9]The Western world is a world of freedom, and in it the Western Powers can freely choose and freely act.

Summary

Central Theme (stated in ¶8 and ¶18): The ideas and aspirations of Western man are still truly revolutionary.

Introduction (¶1-8)
A. In contrast to communism the West appears effete and materialistic.

1. A great obstacle to effective Western policy is uncertainty (¶1).
2. A second great obstacle is the distrust between nations (¶2).
3. There is a necessity for faith to preserve freedom among the Western nations (¶3).
4. The Communists have a faith in the Marxist-Leninist doctrine in contrast to the Western doubt and mistrust (¶4).
5. Paradoxically the Communists advance their doctrine with power and poetry, as is evident in their lyrical reports on military parades (¶5),
6. in their excitement about irrigation projects, and in their agonized self-criticism (¶6).
7. The Communists speak with the anger and outrage of the poets and prophets of old (¶7).
8. In contrast to Communists, the Western nations appear effete and materialistic (¶8, Ss 1-4).

Development (¶8-20)

B. Actually, the ideas and aspirations of Western man are still the most startling thing that has ever happened to the human race (¶8, Ss 5-8). (Central theme.)
  1. Throughout history men have been oppressed by two dominant ideas: the omnipotent state and omnipotent fate (¶9).
  2. The power of these two ideas was broken by the wisdom of the Jews and the Greeks (¶10-11).
  3. The Jews and the Greeks believed that human will and action could transform the social order to the image of a divine order, and thus they rescued humanity from its bondage to destiny (¶12).
  4. The Jews and the Greeks freed men's minds from bondage to the idea of the omnipotent state by stressing man's rational nature and moral responsibility (¶13).
  5. Western society derived its inspiration for progress from the Jewish and Greek concepts of man (¶14).
  6. Marxist communism, in denying the free and morally responsible human being, returns to the primitive concepts of the omnipotence of the state and the omnipotence of fate (¶15).
  7. Behind the communist concept there lies the loss of freedom, rationality, and humanity itself (¶16).
  8. Communism leads to the anonymous tyrannies of antiquity; Western civilization points ahead to experiment in freedom and rationality (¶17).
C. The real revolutionaries (the Western nations) have ceded the ground to the pseudo-revolutionaries, the communists (¶18)
  1. Because the West yielded to economic determinism during the Industrial Revolution (¶19).

2. Because the West weakened the concept of freedom, moral responsibility, and will by yielding to the fatalistic doctrines of environment, conditioning, heredity (¶20).

Conclusion (¶21-24)

D. The West may renew its transforming creative spirit
1. By observing the evil effects of materialistic principles at work in the Communist world (¶21).
2. By regarding communism as a conscience which warns against Western weakness and complacency (¶22-23).
3. By opposing a free, responsible, democratic faith to Communist statism and fatalism (¶24).

Comment

The summary suggests that the organization of this essay is much more complex than that of the two preceding essays of this section and that in this sequence we have been proceeding from the less difficult to the more difficult. The first essay, by Mr. Commager, explained an historical event; the second essay explained the effects of the Industrial Revolution, a social development of greater complexity than the Civil War. Miss Ward's paper involves history of events, social development, and ideas. Hence her elaborate introduction (Summary A), explaining the background of her central idea in a series of paragraphs culminating in paragraph 8, rather than in a single paragraph, as in Example A. The development (Summary B and C) is proportionately long. The conclusion (Summary D) draws a necessary inference from her preceding remarks and applies this meaning to the future of Western policy.

"Faith for Freedom" is noteworthy for its logical order, or *unity*. This unity is achieved chiefly by the sustained contrast, noted in the introduction to this section and made apparent in the preceding summary.

The contrast also contributes to the emphatic arrangement of the essay, since it develops a tension between the ideas of Western civilization and communism that reaches a climax in the concluding paragraphs.

Note too the combination of argument with exposition in this essay. The attempt to win assent to a belief, rather than merely to explain an idea, appears in paragraph 15. Here communism is seen as a return to primitive concepts of man and the state. The argumentative element increases in the succeeding paragraphs. There is no doubt here that the author intends to convince her readers of (1) the value of Western democracy and (2) the aggressive force of communism. Moreover, a subordinate persuasive intention to stimulate the Western nations to renew their creative spirit and to restore certainty and trust in their dealings with each other is clearly evident in paragraphs 21-24. Here Miss Ward brings the whole force of her exposition and argument to bear on the future actions of the free nations of the West.

Analysis and Composition

1. Miss Ward, a one-time spokesman of the British Labor party, is a brilliant economist and political philosopher. She uses many terms in the course of her essay that, while simple for experts, require careful definition for students. An up-to-date unabridged dictionary will help to explain many of these terms. For others you may have to consult special reference books, such as the *Encyclopaedia of the Social Sciences*. Use whatever resources are available to find out Miss Ward's meaning of the terms below. For the convenience of the student, who should study these terms in their several contexts, we give their location in the essay.

Containment (¶1, S7)	Moral vision (¶12, S4)
Essence (¶3, S3)	Logos (¶13, S2)
Marxist-Leninist gospel (¶4, S5)	Inalienable rights (¶13, S3)
Transfiguration (¶5, S7)	Dynamic ... social order (¶14, S9)
Magnificat (¶7, S4)	Recalcitrant matter (¶15, S8)
Apocalypse (¶7, S4)	Liberal experiment (¶17, S4)
Budgetary equilibrium (¶8, S3)	Economic determinism (¶19, S9)
Melancholy wheel of fate (¶9, S5)	Manchester School (¶20, S1)
Infinite fatality (¶9, S5)	*Laissez faire* (¶20, S1)
Divine order (¶12, S1)	Materialism (¶20, Ss 4, 5)
Rational vision (¶12, S4)	Marshall Plan (¶24, S6)

2. Show how Miss Ward uses the following methods of analysis to develop the main idea of the paragraphs in which they occur.
   a. Definition
      (1) Of containment (¶1)
      (2) Of faith (¶3)
      (3) Of the Western spirit (¶11)
      (4) Of materialism (¶20)
   b. Classification
      (1) Of civilizations (¶9)
      (2) Of the civilization of the Jews and Greeks (¶11)
      (3) Of real and pseudo-revolutionaries (¶18)
   c. Examples
      (1) Of Soviet "enthusiasm" (¶5-6)
      (2) Of empires (¶10)
      (3) Of Soviet aims (¶23)

    d. Comparison and contrast
- (1) Of Communists with Western nations (¶4, 5, 8, 18, 24)
- (2) Of Communists with poets and prophets (¶7)
- (3) Of communism with a shooting pain (¶22)

    e. Causal analysis
- (1) Why communism is reactionary (¶15-17)
- (2) Why the Western nations ceded leadership to communism (¶19-20)

    f. Process analysis: How the Western nations developed the ideas of freedom and responsibility (¶9-14)

3. Analyze paragraphs 7, 15, and 21 according to the following outline:
   a. Locate the topic sentence.
   b. Decide whether the various sentences in the paragraph develop the topic sentence.
   c. Indicate the transitional sentences and expressions.

4. Analyze the following expressions in their context to determine how they appeal to the imagination and the emotions:
   a. "The rising sap of hope and confidence" (¶1, S6).
   b. "History mocks the men who claim" (¶10, S9).
   c. "Bound to the melancholy wheel" (¶15, S12).
   d. "The bees and the ants have reached" (¶16, S8).
   e. "An idea has never yet . . . been defeated by no idea at all" (¶20, S7).
   f. "No iron law of economics holds us down" (¶24, S8).

5. Paragraphs 3, 14, 23, and 24 illustrate many principles of good style. Study these paragraphs closely. Choose the best illustrations you can find of each of the following points of style. Give reasons for your choice. (See Section VIII and handbooks.)
   a. Parallel structure *
   b. Periodic sentences †
   c. Climactic arrangement within the sentence ‡
   d. Climactic arrangement within the paragraph §
   e. Repetition for the sake of emphasis ||
   f. The use of epigrams or slogans
   g. Variety of sentences within the paragraph ¶

---

* Foerster, pp. 17-20, 76; Hodges, 26, 31b5; Kierzek, pp. 59-62; Perrin, pp. 282-83; Wykoff, 74.

† Foerster, pp. 25-28, 75; Hodges, 29b; Kierzek, 61; Perrin, pp. 280-82; Wykoff, 4c, 79d.

‡ Foerster, 76; Hodges, 29c; Kierzek, 64; Perrin, pp. 293-95; Wykoff, 79e.

§ Foerster, p. 59; Hodges, 31b1; Kierzek, 71; Perrin, pp. 222-24; Wykoff, 56c.

|| Foerster, pp. 29-31, 78; Hodges, 29e; Kierzek, pp. 92-100, 62a; Perrin, pp. 291-92; Wykoff, 44d.

¶ Foerster, pp. 39-41, 81; Hodges, 30; Kierzek, pp. 53-59, 67; pp. 278-80; Wykoff, 80.

h. Direct emotional appeal

i. Euphony through alliteration or assonance *

6. Summarize in your own words the author's reasoning in paragraphs 9-14. (See Section VII C1, for methods of reasoning.)

7. How does Miss Hawkes's exposition of the Industrial Revolution in paragraphs 16-18 of Example B support the ideas set forth in paragraphs 19-20 of "Faith for Freedom"?

8. Miss Ward's essay was directed to informed readers of considerable maturity. Her subject and her ideas, however, are of great interest to the beginning college student. Draw up an outline for a 1000-word article on the subject "Faith for Freedom" calculated to appeal to your fellow classmates. Determine in advance an order of development and a style that is appropriate to your audience. Then write the article. Combine a few paragraphs of argument with your exposition.

* Kierzek, pp. 62-66, *44*; Perrin, pp. 295, 427, 444-45.

---

d. In an investigative paper of an historical nature coordinate or fuse the chronological order of events and the logical order of ideas to achieve clarity and emphasis.

The Dime Novel Heroine

BY HENRY NASH SMITH

1 The evolution of the Beadle Wild Western heroine illustrates impressively the increase of sensationalism in the dime novel toward the end of the century.

THE DIME NOVEL HEROINE: reprinted by permission of the publisher from Henry Nash Smith, *Virgin Land: The American West as Symbol and Myth*. Cambridge, Mass.: Harvard University Press. Copyright, 1950, by The President and Fellows of Harvard College.

2 Everyone is aware of the awe-inspiring gentility of Cooper's heroines.[1] Lowell's remark that they were flat as a prairie and sappy as maples[2] does less than justice to the address and energy which some of them could display on occasion, but it is nevertheless true that no lady in Cooper was capable of the remotest approach to indelicacy of thought, speech, or action. The escape of the Western story from the canons of gentility had greater consequences for the women characters than for the men, because the genteel female had been the primary source of refinement in the traditional novel. One method of transforming the heroine from the merely passive sexual object she had tended to be in the Leatherstocking Tales was to introduce a supposed Indian girl able to ride and shoot who later proves to be an upper-class white girl captured long ago by the Indians. But this device, like that of disguising the genteel hero as a hunter, did not involve a fundamental change in the heroine's character. Beneath the savage costume she was almost as genteel as ever.

3 A much more promising means of effecting a real development in the heroine was the ancient device of introducing a woman disguised as a man, or wearing male attire. Maturin M. Ballou's Fanny Campbell, who appeared in 1845, was a female pirate captain;[3] and Charles E. Averill caused the two Eastern heroines of his *Life in California* to disguise themselves as boys.[4] The earliest Western heroine wearing men's clothing seems to be Eulalie Moreau in Frederick Whittaker's *The Mustang-Hunters; or, The Beautiful Amazon of the Hidden Valley,* apparently published in the late 1860's.[5] Eulalie is pos-

---

[1] Even William Dean Howells agreed that Cooper's upper-class females exhibited "such an extremely conventional and ladylike deportment in all circumstances that you wished to kill them" (*Heroines of Fiction*, New York, 1901, 2 vols., vol. i, p. iii). Cf. Bret Harte's burlesque of Cooper's Leatherstocking tales, "Muck-a-Muck. A Modern Indian Novel. After Cooper" (*The Complete Works of Bret Harte*, London, 1880-81, 5 vols., vol. v, pp. 339-46). Genevra Tompkins, in this tale, is a caricature of Cooper's painfully refined heroines, such as Alice Munro in *The Last of the Mohicans* and Sarah and Frances Wharton in *The Spy*. The literary tradition to which Cooper's heroines belong is described in Herbert R. Brown, *The Sentimental Novel in America, 1789-1860*, Durham, N. C., 1940, *passim.*

[2] *A Fable for Critics*, New York, 1848, p. 47.

[3] Ralph Admari, "Ballou, the Father of the Dime Novel," *American Book Collector*, vol. iv, September-October 1933, p. 128.

[4] *Life in California; or, The Treasure Seekers' Expedition. A Sequel to Kit Carson, the Prince of the Gold Hunters*, Boston, 1850, pp. 12, 26.

[5] Beadle's Pocket Novels, No. 222, p. 87. The copyright date of this story reads "1862," but it refers to events of the Civil War and to the collapse of the Confederacy; the date must be an error.

sibly derived from Emilie in Charles W. Webber's *Old Hicks, The Guide,* who is likewise French and inhabits a hidden valley in the far Southwest. If this surmise is correct, it would suggest that Webber's experiment in cultural primitivism [6] exerted some influence on the creation of the ferocious women who came finally to people the Beadle stories. Whittaker, like Webber, may have felt that violation of propriety was less shocking in a French girl than in an American one.

4 Eulalie, for that matter, is virtuous enough. She does not invariably wear male attire, but pays obeisance to her literary ancestors by appearing on occasion in the costume of an Indian princess. She lives with her father, an exiled "Red Republican" of 1848,[7] in a luxurious establishment three weeks' journey northwest of Austin, Texas. With the "marvelous mixture of feminine gentleness and masculine firmness that marked her character" she easily tames the splendid black mustang stallion that the elegant hero Frank Weston has succeeded in lassoing on the plains. There is more than enough bloodshed of a somewhat sadistic flavor in this story, but Eulalie does not take part in it. At the end she is married to the hero and they go to live in New Orleans. The hunter Pete Wilkins, an authentic Leatherstocking type,[8] continues a faithful friend of the family and this somehow makes the whole thing seem more domestic and respectable.

5 The first heroine who commits an act of violence is most likely Dove-Eye, alias Kate Robinette, half-breed daughter of the Indian trader Silas Wormley in Edward Willett's *Silver-spur; or, The Mountain Heroine. A Tale of the Arapaho Country.* Supposed at first to be a full-blooded Indian maiden, Dove-Eye rides astride and carries a

---

6 Cultural primitivism is the belief that a relatively simple social environment is more conducive to man's virtue and happiness than a complex urban environment. The idea is embodied in the familiar phrase, "Back to Nature."

7 The year 1848 was marked by political disturbances in several European countries, especially France and the various German states. A considerable number of radicals migrated to the United States when the revolutionary uprisings failed. Cf. Marcus L. Hansen, *The Atlantic Migration, 1607-1860,* Cambridge, Mass., 1940, pp. 272-76.

8 "Leatherstocking" is a pseudonym given by Cooper to Nathaniel Bumppo, an important character in five novels which are for this reason called the Leatherstocking tales. The titles and dates of publication are as follows: *The Pioneers* (1823), *The Last of the Mohicans* (1826), *The Prairie* (1827), *The Pathfinder* (1840), *The Deerslayer* (1841). Although in *The Pathfinder* and *The Deerslayer* Bumppo is represented as a young man, he is usually remembered as he appears in *The Pioneers* and *The Prairie.* In these novels he is an elderly hunter who lives alone, or with occasional virtuous companions, in the wilderness beyond the frontier. He is distinguished by his deerskin costume, his unerring

battle axe, which she throws at the hero Fred Wilder.[9] This initial misunderstanding is soon overcome and the two are betrothed; but Fred's father Colonel Wilder opposes the match as unsuitable. Dove-Eye thereupon rescues the Colonel from a buffalo and from hostile Indians, wielding her battle axe to great effect. Thus mollified, the old gentleman consents to the marriage. But Dove-Eye has to be revised somewhat before she can become a full-fledged heroine. She is given a large fortune by opportune inheritance from her father. Colonel Wilder then suggests the standard treatment of a few years in a young ladies' seminary. Fred, however, begins the full enfranchisement of the nongenteel heroine by rejecting this plan:

Do you think I could allow the ducks and turkeys of the settlements to laugh at my wild bird? Do you think I could be separated from her a few years, or a few months? She is sufficiently polished, and no one can educate her better than her husband.

The author assures us that Kate's "brains and will soon made amends for the deficiencies of her education," and when she arrived at St. Louis "no one who was not acquainted with her story would have supposed that the greater part of her life had been spent among savages."

6 The earliest available case of aggressiveness on the part of a Beadle female is that of the beautiful white girl Aneola who, like Dove-Eye, has been reared by the Indians and who has acquired a perfect command of English against what must have been very great odds. When the hero Uriah Barham is captured by the Indians and given the traditional choice of death or an Indian wife, Aneola offers herself as a solution, confessing her passionate love for him. On this occasion she has the decency to blush. But he loves another, and refuses her. Despite the blush, she threatens him with death, but relents, helps him escape, and then leaps from a cliff.[10] Badger's Mountain Kate, the daughter of a white outlaw in the northern Rockies, has a better fate. She is a master of the pistol. When the traitorous companions of the hero attack him, she turns fiercely on the miscreants, killing three and wound-

---

marksmanship, his skill in following trails, his untutored wisdom, and his impeccable virtue.

[9] Beadle's Pocket Novels, No. 127. First published in 1870.

[10] Joseph E. Badger, *The Forest Princess; or, The Kickapoo Captives. A Romance of the Illinois.* Beadle's New Dime Novels, n.s., No. 133; o.s., No. 454, p. 102. First published in 1871.

ing one: "The stately thumb and forefinger worked like magic." But since she has not been guilty of overt aggressiveness she does not have to die. Instead, she marries the hero and achieves a home and children in St. Louis.[11]

7 Frederick Whittaker, creator of Eulalie Moreau, ventured a more pronounced Amazon a few years later in *The Jaguar Queen; or, The Outlaws of the Sierra Madre*.[12] As in the earlier story, the action concerns a secret valley in the far Southwest, but the coloring is noticeably more lurid. A certain Count Montriche who, like Webber's Count Albert, has become an Apache chief, maintains an imposing harem in a remote part of northern Mexico. The Amazon in this story is the Wagnerian Katrina Hartstein, six feet tall, who is accompanied by seven trained jaguars. Because she loves the previously committed Gerald Leigh, Katrina must also die, and is accordingly killed in the course of an assault on Count Montriche's establishment for the rescue of the fortunate heroine Blanche Hayward.

8 Toward the end of the 1870's the Amazons and heroines in male attire took a distinct turn for the worse, no doubt corrupted by the general increase of sensationalism. One can even think of fixing the date 1880 as a critical point in the transformation of the genteel heroine. Philip S. Warne's *A Hard Crowd; or, Gentleman Sam's Sister,* a tale laid in Omaha, "the 'hardest place' east of Denver," and devoted to what the author describes as the scum and dregs of society in the low groggeries and gambling hells of this railroad town,[13] has two women characters wearing men's clothing, expert in firearms, and fully at home amid the violence and bloodshed which surround them. Pepita, who sometimes appears in the guise of Nebraska Larry, is motivated by an insatiable desire for vengeance against the man who has wronged her. The vengeance motive was a favorite way of accounting for the ferocious behavior of characters, especially of women. It has the advantage of affording a rationale of violence less cumbersome than the older method of staging a war between Indians and whites. But the narrowing of the frame of ethical reference involves a marked loss of social significance. Characters bent on private vengeance may owe something to the monomaniac Indian haters who had long peo-

---

[11] *Mountain Kate; or, Love in the Trapping Grounds. A Tale of the Powder River Country.* Beadle's Pocket Novels, No. 143, 1872, pp. 94, 102.

[12] Beadle's New Dime Novels, No. 389. First published in 1872.

[13] Beadle's Dime Library, No. 1, 1878, p. 2. First published in 1877.

pled Western fiction,[14] but their motivation seems more closely related to the melodramatic stage.

9 The character of Iola, Gentleman Sam's sister in Warne's story, who is "quite an Amazon," capable of shooting down instantly a man who accosted her on the street,[15] marks a drastic weakening of the long-prevalent taboos against sexual passion in women. The hero of the story has been wounded and is being nursed by Iola. One day, when his convalescence has set in, he slips an arm about her waist as she straightens the pillows on his bed.

> Unconsciously she yielded to the persuasive clasp of his arms, until she rested, almost fainting, on his breast, and felt the throbbing of his heart, and his warm breath on her cheek.
>
> Their love sought no expression in words. But the woman, whose free heart had been little curbed by the conventionalities of artificial society, let her arms glide about his neck, as was most natural that she should, and clasped him closer and closer until their lips met.
>
> Thus lip to lip they drank in the first incense of mutual love. . . .[16]

Not all writers who exploited the sensational possibilities of the woman desperado were inclined to take precisely this advantage of the decline of gentility, but there is certainly a more perceptible awareness of sex as a physical fact in the stories published after 1880 than in those published during the 1860's.

10 The transference of the skills and functions of the Wild Western hero to a woman, the use of the theme of revenge to motivate violence, and the promotion of the Amazon to full status as a heroine are all exemplified in Edward L. Wheeler's Hurricane Nell, who appeared in 1878 almost simultaneously with the first appearance of Deadwood Dick. At the opening of the story Nell is the conventional distressed female, victim of the ruffian Bob Woolf's cruelty in firing her house and hastening the death of her parents. She swears the customary oath of vengeance and reappears after a time in the Pikes Peak mining towns wearing men's clothing, a mistress of all the accomplishments of the Wild West. She can "out-run, out-ride, out-shoot, out-lasso, and out-yell" any man in town.[17] When the hero, a handsome Philadelphia

[14] A good example is Hugh Bradley in James McHenry's *The Spectre of the Forest*, New York, 1823, 2 vols. Cf. especially vol. i, p. 92. Bradley has taken three hundred Indian scalps (*ibid.*, vol. i, p. 96).

[15] Beadle's Dime Library, No. 1, p. 4.

[16] Beadle's Dime Library, No. 1, p. 16.

[17] *Bob Woolf, the Border Ruffian; or, The Girl Dead-Shot*. Beadle's Half Dime Library, No. 32, 1878, p. 3.

lawyer, hires her as a guide, she lassoes a mustang for him and rescues him from the Indians in a scene that reverses a vast tradition. As the hero's horse tires, Hurricane Nell seizes the man about the waist, raises him high overhead "by the power of her wonderful arms," and deposits him on the back of the wild stallion. She also kills three men with three shots from her rifle.[18] The heroine's assumption of the functions of the Leatherstocking type is complete when the hero bets a thousand dollars on her skill in a shooting match and she wins:[19] at the very beginning of Leatherstocking's career in literature, in *The Pioneers,* Elizabeth Temple had backed him in a turkey shoot.

11 The tendency to make the Amazon athletic might seem likely to detract from her feminine charms, but Wheeler does not mean to surrender this source of interest. He takes pains to make Hurricane Nell overwhelmingly beautiful, gives to her lustrous eyes a soft, dreamy, wistful expectancy when she looks at the hero, and indulges in a touch of sadism by having her dangled over a fire by her torturers.[20] Wheeler's Wild Edna, leader of a band of highwaymen in *Old Avalanche, The Great Annihilator; or, Wild Edna, the Girl Brigand,* is likewise but a wistful ingenue beneath her formidable exterior. There is "a vacant spot in her pure virgin heart" of which she becomes painfully aware when she meets the dashing titled English hero.[21]

12 Wheeler's celebrated creation, Calamity Jane, the feminine counterpart of Deadwood Dick, has much in common with these preliminary studies of the softhearted Amazon. Like much of the inner structure of the Deadwood saga, the relations between Deadwood Dick and Calamity Jane are hard to make out. For one thing, the date of publication of the stories seems to bear little relation to the supposed order of events in the hero's career. In *Blonde Bill; or, Deadwood Dick's Home Base. A Romance of the "Silent Tongues,"* Calamity Jane, "the girl sport," "nobbily attired in male garb," is represented as being hopelessly in love with Deadwood Dick, who has a wife named Edith. Edith is killed in the course of the story.[22] When Dick tells Calamity Jane of this event, she turns away "lest the yearning, hungry look in

18 *Ibid.,* p. 8.
19 *Ibid.,* p. 11.
20 *Ibid.,* pp. 6, 16.
21 *Old Avalanche, the Great Annihilator; or, Wild Edna, the Girl Brigand.* Beadle's Half Dime Library, No. 45; thirteenth edition, 1878, p. 17.
22 Beadle's Half Dime Library, No. 138, 1880, pp. 2, 6.

her wildly beautiful eyes should pain him," [23] and matters stand more or less at this point when the story ends. In the earlier part of *Deadwood Dick of Deadwood; or, The Picked Party. A Romance of Skeleton Bend,* Jane is jealous of Deadwood Dick, but at the end of the story they are to be married.[24] Calamity Jane does not appear in No. 195 of this series, but Dick is involved with no less than three girls in men's attire, each of whom proposes marriage to him.[25] One of these young ladies, Phantom Moll, the Girl Footpad, is the first Beadle female character within my acquaintance who lights a cigarette. In trying to persuade Dick to join her band and marry her, she exclaims, " 'Tis a jolly life we outlawed sinners lead. . . ." [26] 'Shian Sal, developed at greater length than the other women characters, speaks dialect, and despite the fact that she is only eighteen or so, is proprietress of the Eureka Saloon. She confesses that she smokes, gambles, swears, drinks, "and sometimes I pop over a rough, jest to keep my hand in and let 'em know Sal is old bizness." She is also good with her fists; she knocks down one of the men with a single blow.[27]

13 Calamity Jane is studied most fully in Wheeler's *Deadwood Dick on Deck; or, Calamity Jane, The Heroine of Whoop-Up. A Story of Dakota.* Colonel Joe Tubbs's description of Jane makes it clear that she belongs to the group of heroines whom great wrongs have transformed into ruthless Amazons. Deserted by her lover, she has become "the most reckless buchario in ther Hills. Kin drink whisky, shute, play keerds, or sw'ar, ef et comes ter et." But, "Ther gal's got honor left wi' her grit, out o' ther wreck o' a young life." [28]

14 The most convincing evidence that Calamity Jane was once a lady is the fact that she can drop her dialect at will and speak a correct English.[29] Her tough appearance and manner are, in other words, a voluntarily assumed mask like that of Seth Jones. Yet a woman cannot shed such a *persona* as easily as a man. Jane's beautiful face is lined with dissipation and hard usage. It is true that even in her buckskin trousers, beaded leggings, and boiled shirt she retains visible evidences of her former appearance—her feet are clad in dainty slip-

[23] *Ibid.,* p. 12.
[24] Beadle's Half Dime Library, No. 156, 1880, pp. 13, 15.
[25] *Deadwood Dick's Dream; or, The Rivals of the Road. A Mining Tale of "Tombstone."* Beadle's Half Dime Library, No. 195, 1881, pp. 5, 6, 10.
[26] *Ibid.,* pp. 4-5.
[27] *Ibid.,* pp. 6, 8.
[28] Beadle's Pocket Library, No. 57, 1885, p. 2. First published in 1878.
[29] *Ibid.,* p. 16.

pers and her shirt opens to reveal a throat "of alabaster purity." But her behavior is extremely boisterous. She first appears dashing through the streets erect in the saddle, leaping sluices and other obstructions, "lighting a cigar at full motion," and uttering "a ringing whoop, which was creditable in imitation if not in volume and force to that of a full-blown Comanche warrior." [30] Jane realizes what such conduct must mean to a young lady's reputation. Concerning another girl she remarks with a delicate sense of propriety, "Life here in the Hills has—well, has ruined her prospects, one might say, for she has grown reckless in act and rough in language." [31]

15 In this story Deadwood Dick has a wife named Leone, although she does not figure prominently in the plot. Calamity Jane loves Sandy, a handsome young Easterner who, deceived by villains into believing himself guilty of forgery, has come West to the mines. But the author says she will probably never marry. Her prospects, too, have suffered sadly from her neglect of appearances. [32]

16 By 1877, when Wheeler began his Deadwood Dick series, the Wild Western hero had been transformed from a Leatherstocking with an infallible sense of right and wrong and feelings which "appeared to possess the freshness and nature of the forest" [33] into a man who had once been a bandit, and who even after his reformation could not easily be distinguished from the criminals opposing him. Cut loose first from the code of gentility that had commanded Cooper's unswerving loyalty, and then from the communion with God through nature that had made Leatherstocking a saint of the forest, the Western hero had become a self-reliant two-gun man who behaved in almost exactly the same fashion whether he were outlaw or peace officer. Eventually he was transformed into a detective and ceased in any significant sense to be Western. The heroine, undergoing an even more drastic evolution when she was freed from the trammels of gentility, developed at last into an Amazon who was distinguished from the hero solely by the physical fact of her sex.

17 These changes in the characters reveal a progressive deterioration in the Western story as a genre. It is true that the abandonment of the artificial code of gentility was a necessary step in the develop-

---

[30] *Ibid.,* p. 4.
[31] *Ibid.,* p. 13.
[32] *Ibid.,* p. 31.
[33] *The Pathfinder; or, The Inland Sea,* Philadelphia, 1840, 2 vols., vol. i, p. 139.

ment of American literature. But when a frontiersman in the Leather-stocking tradition replaced the genteel heroine as the pivotal center of plot construction, the Western story lost whatever chance it might once have had to develop social significance. For Leatherstocking was a child of the wilderness to whom society and civilization meant only the dread sound of the backwoodsman's axe laying waste the virgin forest. A genre built about such a character could not establish any real contact with society.

18 On the other hand, the theme of communion with nature in the West proved too flimsy to sustain a primitivistic literature of any magnitude. The spiritual meaning which a former generation had believed it found in nature became more and more inaccessible after the middle of the century. The static ideas of virtue and happiness and peace drawn from the bosom of the virgin wilderness—the ideas symbolized in Charles W. Webber's Peaceful Valley [34]—proved quite irrelevant for a society committed to the ideas of civilization and progress, and to an industrial revolution. Devoid alike of ethical and social meaning, the Western story could develop in no direction save that of a straining and exaggeration of its formulas. It abandoned all effort to be serious, and by 1889, when Erastus Beadle retired from the firm of Beadle & Adams, it had sunk to the near-juvenile level it was to occupy with virtually no change down to our own day. The Street & Smith enterprises like the Buffalo Bill stories, the Log Cabin Library, the Jesse James stories, the *Tip-Top Weekly,* and the Red, White, and Blue Library, together with Frank Tousey publications like the Boy's Story Library, *Frank Manley's Weekly,* the New York Detective Library, the Pluck and Luck stories, and the *Wild West Weekly*—the cheap series widening downward from the 1890's into the twentieth century almost baffle enumeration—lead in a straight line from the Beadle publications to the Westerns of the present day.[35] The movies and the radio have tidied up the morals, or at least the manners, of the genre, but plot construction and characterization follow an apparently unbreakable pattern.

[34] Cf. *supra,* note 2. Webber's Indians in the valley bear a strong resemblance to many earlier Noble Savages in English and American literature (cf. Hoxie N. Fairchild, *The Noble Savage. A Study in Romantic Naturalism,* New York, 1928; Gregory L. Paine, "The Indians of the Leather-Stocking Tales," *Studies in Philology,* vol. xxiii, January 1926, pp. 16-39.

[35] Literary depiction of the cowboy in the twentieth century is traced in Douglas Branch, *The Cowboy and His Interpreters,* New York, 1926, pp. 185-91, 210-35.

A SHORT SELECTED BIBLIOGRAPHY

History of the American West

Frederick Jackson Turner, *The Frontier in American History*, New York, 1920.

Cardinal Goodwin, *The Trans-Mississippi West (1803-1853)*, New York, 1922.

Ray A. Billington, *Westward Expansion*, New York, 1950.

Primitivism

Arthur O. Lovejoy, Gilbert Chinard, George Boas, and Ronald S. Crane, eds., *A Documentary History of Primitivism and Related Ideas*, vol. i, *Primitivism and Related Ideas in Antiquity*, Baltimore, 1935.

George Boas, *Essays on Primitivism and Related Ideas in the Middle Ages*, Baltimore, 1948.

Hoxie N. Fairchild, *The Noble Savage. A Study in Romantic Naturalism*, New York, 1928.

Lois Whitney, *Primitivism and the Idea of Progress in English Popular Literature of the Eighteenth Century*, Baltimore, 1934.

Roy H. Pearce, "The Leatherstocking Tales Re-examined," *South Atlantic Quarterly*, vol. xlvi, October 1947, pp. 524-36.

Dime Novels

Albert Johannsen, *The House of Beadle and Adams and Its Dime and Nickel Novels. The Story of a Vanished Literature*, Norman, Okla., 2 vols., 1950.

Edmund Pearson, *Dime Novels; or, Following an Old Trail in Popular Literature*, Boston, 1929.

Richard J. Walsh (in collaboration with Milton S. Salsbury), *The Making of Buffalo Bill. A Study in Heroics*, Indianapolis, 1938.

Merle Curti, "Dime Novels and the American Tradition," *Yale Review*, n.s., vol. xxvi, June 1937, pp. 761-78.

Summary

Central theme: The evolution of the Beadle Wild West heroine [from 1850 to the present] illustrates impressively the increase of sensationalism and the progressive deterioration of the Western story as an literary genre (¶1, 17)

Step 1: Cooper's genteel heroine was transformed by disguising the heroine as a man (¶2-4).

Step 2: The heroine (Dove-Eye) commits acts of violence (¶5).

Step 3: The heroine (Aneola; Mountain Kate) becomes romantically aggressive (¶6).

Step 4: The heroine (Katrina Hartstein, the Jaguar Queen) meets a violent end (¶7).

Step 5: The heroine (Pepita) commits acts of ferocious violence (¶8).

Step 6: The heroine (Iola) exhibits passion (¶9).

Step 7: The heroine (Hurricane Nell) is transformed into the Wild West hero with a full measure of violence, revenge, and masculine skills (¶10) but not without feminine charm (¶11).

Step 8: The heroine (Calamity Jane; Phantom Moll; 'Shian Sal) degenerates into reckless vice (¶12-15).

Step 9: The decline of the heroine from the ideal of the Leatherstocking Tales was even more drastic than the decline of the hero (¶16).

Step 10: These changes in the characters represent a progressive deterioration in the Western story; the Western story lost its chance to develop social significance (¶17).

Conclusion: The Western story in its final stage is devoid of ethical and social meaning (¶18).

Comment

"The Dime Novel Heroine" is simultaneously (a) an excellent example of an exposition and (b) a fine model of the research paper.

As an exposition it deals with a subject and purpose that require (a) the proof of the general conclusion by a sufficient number of apt examples and (b) a chronological order that accounts for each step in the deterioration of the Western story. As we have shown in the introduction, the subject and purpose of this essay require the coordination or fusion of two orders. How well Mr. Smith has succeeded in this coordination may be judged by the preceding outline.

As a research paper, "The Dime Novel Heroine" is a model of good sense and good form. The author displays good sense

a. By selecting a subject that is important, timely, and relevant to other pressing problems, such as the artistic and ethical standards of the radio, television, movies, and comics

b. By studying the subject in original sources

c. By treating the subject fully, if not exhaustively

d. By handling the subject with originality, maturity, and wit

e. By drawing a conclusion from his analysis of the subject instead of merely compiling facts about the subject

Good form is evident in the paper

a. In the accurate quotation from and allusion to original sources
b. In the use of footnotes to indicate source material and to supply parenthetical information that is not completely evident in the text or readily available to the reader
c. In the inclusion of a selected bibliography that will help the reader expand his knowledge of the subject
d. In the adherence to a recognized form of footnoting and bibliographic reference. (Note: The mechanical arrangement of this paper is that recommended by the *Harbrace College Handbook*. Other standard arrangements are equally acceptable.)

Analysis and Composition

1. How does the author achieve unity in this essay? (See Section VIII.)
2. What means does the author use to achieve coherence? (See Section VIII.)
3. What means does the author use to achieve emphasis? (See Section VIII.)
4. What is the principal characteristic of the author's style? Show how this characteristic is consonant with the subject, purpose, and occasion of his essay.
5. The subject in paragraph 2 is Cooper's heroines. Show how each sentence in the paragraph in some way explains the subject.
6. Pick out several examples of the author's ironic treatment of his material in paragraphs 6-8.
7. Select in paragraphs 9-12 those expressions which indicate the ethical standards by which the author judges the heroines of the dime novel.
8. In about 500 words argue for or against the idea that the movies and the radio of today follow the same pattern as present-day Western novels.
9. The basic steps in writing an investigative paper (also called a term paper or a research paper) are four in number:
   a. Choosing a subject
   b. Reading, note taking, and analyzing the subject
   c. Working up an outline
   d. Preparing the paper with due attention to annotation and bibliography.*

With this procedure as a guide choose one of the topics listed below and prepare an investigative paper of approximately 1500 words. Be careful to limit the topic to an appropriate subject, in the manner described in

---

* See handbooks: Foerster, *39*; Hodges, *33*; Kierzek, pp. 186-215; Wykoff, *50*.

Section I. Use the form of footnoting and bibliography recommended by your instructor.

Suggested Topics for a Research Paper

Literature

1. Regional fiction (New England, southern, western, midwestern)
2. The literary reputation of Edgar Allan Poe
3. The naturalistic movement in American literature
4. The New England transcendentalists
5. Witchcraft in the novels of Hawthorne
6. Emigré European novelists in the United States
7. The imagist theory of poetry
8. The poetic drama in the twentieth century
9. The southern agrarian movement
10. The Great Books tradition in contemporary America

History

1. The rise of the universities in the Middle Ages
2. The development of the university in the United States
3. The liberal arts college in the twentieth century
4. Attempts at world federation from the League of Nations to the United Nations
5. The medieval walled city
6. The rise of the French monarchy
7. The Spanish colonial empire in North America
8. The development of English parliamentary government
9. The development of unions in the United States since World War I
10. The committee system in the United States Congress

General Topics

1. The miracle drugs—sulfa, penicillin, aureomycin, and others
2. The use of Community Chests
3. The Seeing Eye dog
4. American music from jazz to bebop
5. Radar in industry—aeronautics, merchant shipping, and so forth
6. The Missouri Valley Authority
7. The Pan-American Highway
8. Intercollegiate basketball (or baseball or football)
9. The place of foreign languages in a college curriculum
10. Divorce and juvenile delinquency

REVIEW EXERCISES
FOR SECTIONS VIII-X

A

1. Compare the selection by Malik in Section VIII with the selection by Commager in Section X with reference to coherence in the whole composition.
2. Compare the selections by Hawkes and Ward in Section X with reference to emphasis in the whole composition.
3. Which selection in Sections VIII-X has the clearest style? the most vigorous style? the most interesting style? Justify your choices by referring to the standards of effective style set forth in Section VIII.
4. Which selection or selections in Sections VIII-X would you choose as a model for each of the following assignments in expository writing? Give reasons for your answer.
   a. A general statement of the reasons for the Spanish-American War
   b. A 3000-word essay on "The Decline of Reading"
   c. A newspaper sketch on a new member of the President's cabinet
   d. A survey of popular movie stars of the last three decades
   e. An explanation of the meaning of the United Nations
   f. An analysis of the basic aims of the United States' foreign policy
   g. A biographical study of Mussolini
   h. A survey of America's natural resources
   i. A satirical study of manners on the campus
   j. A popular magazine story about Jimmy Durante

B

1. Read three expository articles in *Harper's*, *The Atlantic Monthly*, *Fortune*, or a magazine assigned by your instructor. Make a paragraph analysis of each article. Then decide whether each article achieves unity, coherence, and emphasis.

2. Use the principles studied in Sections VIII-X in preparing a detailed outline for an expository essay of approximately 1000 words on one of the topics listed below:

The meaning of politics
Morals in international relations
Science—master or servant
The nationalization of railways
The influence of veterans' organizations
The President's cabinet
Floor leaders in Congress
The migratory laborer
The federal security system
Why foreigners like (or dislike) Americans
The menace (or blessing) of football in American education
The effects of motor transport on America
Portrait of a class president
The decline of the triple-threat halfback
(See also the topics listed in Exercise A4.)

3. Write an expository essay according to the outline prepared in answer to Exercise B2. Follow the check list provided in Exercise H in the review exercises for Sections I-VII.

A. In argument arrange the basic proofs under deduction, induction, or analogy. Refute directly by denial, distinction, and retort. Refute indirectly (1) by attacking the competence of the speaker or writer; (2) by attacking his method of arguing; (3) by exposing his fallacies.

General Exercises on Argument

B. In persuasion (1) emphasize the action you wish your audience to take; (2) make the proofs serve as motives for action; and (3) pay particular attention to the vigor and vividness of your style.

SECTION
XI

Argument and Persuasion

ARGUMENT is that form of discourse which attempts to win assent to a belief or opinion.

Persuasion is that form of discourse which presents arguments as motives for some proposed action.

It is clear from these two definitions that the discussion of argument must precede the discussion of persuasion.

ARGUMENT

Argument is closely allied to, and often blended with, exposition, as we have seen in Section X, notably in Example C. Like exposition, a good argument presents its evidence in a unified, coherent, and emphatic arrangement and in a clear, vigorous, and interesting style (Section VIII). Thus good argument embodies the same general principles of the whole composition that apply to exposition and other forms of discourse.

There are, however, certain special characteristics of argument that distinguish it from exposition. These characteristics are (a) the proposition, (b) the point at issue, (c) proof. In addition many extended arguments include (d) a refutation. Each of these characteristics stems from the specific aim of argumentative discourse, namely the attempt to win assent to a belief or opinion.

THE PROPOSITION—THE FIRST CHARACTERISTIC OF ARGUMENT

We may best understand what the proposition in argument means by a brief comparison of the aims of exposition and argument. Whereas the main intention or aim of exposition is to explain, the main intention of argument is to convince. In an argument a writer does not merely state and clarify; he also reasons. He proves one statement by another statement. In exposition he merely explains what *A* is; in argument he reasons that *A* is *C* because *A* is *B* and *B* is *C*. (See Example VII C, "The Method of Scientific Investigation" by T. H. Huxley for an explanation of reasoning by deduction and induction.)

Exposition unravels a *subject;* argument reasons about a connected series of statements on a subject. Another important difference between exposition and argument is that in argument the central theme (traditionally called in argument the *proposition*) is disputed. Thus in exposition the writer can explain rain by telling what rain is, why it is, how it falls. But he cannot argue about rain as such. The mere subject, rain, is not a disputable proposition. On the other hand, the writer *can* argue on the question, "Is rainy weather good for business?" because this is a disputed proposition phrased as a question.

Similarly you, as writer, may explain but not argue about true and evident facts, laws, and processes. You may explain the income tax law. You *cannot* argue about the evident fact that the income tax law exists. But you may argue whether the tax laws are fair, or whether they apply to a given person, or whether they should be changed. Thus the first essential characteristic of an argument is a proposition, that is, a statement of a central theme about which there is some dispute.

Each of the examples in this section contains a proposition—a statement of central theme that is arguable. Thus the proposition in "Suburbia: Of Thee I Sing" is: The suburbanite enjoys a freer and fuller life than the city dweller or the country dweller. Messrs. Lloyd and Barzun in their debate on language take opposite sides on the question of whether there is a correct standard of written English Viscount Bryce and Peter Drucker argue for and against the proposition that America is uniform in character.

Moreover, the proposition in each example appears in various ways

(a) It is often implied in the title.
(b) It is stated in the introduction as the belief proposed for acceptance.
(c) It is repeated in various ways in connection with the presentation of the evidence that supports it.
(d) It is repeated at the end as the conclusion established by the proof.

The first characteristic of argument, then, is a proposition argued to a conclusion.

All the other elements of argumentative discourse stem from the writer's intention to prove the proposition. The proposition, for instance, leads to the consideration of the point at issue, the second essential of argument.

THE POINT AT ISSUE—THE SECOND CHARACTERISTIC OF ARGUMENT *

To prove the proposition you must state the issue, that is, the precise phase of the proposition which you are attempting to prove. Sometimes, as we shall observe, there is more than one point at issue. Even the simplest proposition is difficult to prove without restricting its meaning. Thus in attempting to prove a proposition that few will dispute—for example, that General Lee was a great military leader in the Civil War—you must limit the proposition. General Lee was not a great military leader in every possible sense of the term. He was not an expert in logistics, for instance, nor was he an active cavalry leader, nor an expert in general staff management (see General Exercise, Section IV).

If it is necessary to limit propositions that few people are inclined to dispute, it is even more necessary to limit propositions that involve sharp differences of opinion. Hence Miss McGinley defines her very arguable proposition—that the suburbanite enjoys a freer and fuller life than the town dweller and the country dweller—by explaining the exact sense in which she means the terms "freer" and "fuller" life.

Mr. Drucker's proposition in "The Myth of American Uniformity"

---

* The relation between the proposition and the point at issue (argument) is the same as that between the central theme and the key ideas in exposition (see Section VIII and Example A of Section IX). The subordinate elements in each case, that is, the point at issue and the key ideas, limit and define the central theme or proposition.

is that the American character is diversified. This general statement is first limited to several main points at issue. The American character is said to be diversified (a) in the material aspects of life, (b) in the intellectual aspects of life, and (c) in business. Each of these main issues is further limited by more specific subordinate issues, as the outline on pp. 484-85 indicates.

The issue (the precise sense in which you define your proposition) * is thus equivalent to the heading under which you will marshal your proofs. Thus Miss McGinley does not prove her proposition in all the possible senses of the two terms "freer" and "fuller." There are some senses in which the country dweller is freer than the suburbanite. (He is freer from zoning regulations, for instance.) There are also some senses in which the country dweller may be said to live a fuller life. (He can farm, hunt, ranch.) But Miss McGinley is not concerned with these other issues. For her the points at issue are those specific aspects of the proposition with which she is directly concerned. They define the sense in which she intends to argue the proposition.

PROOF—THE THIRD CHARACTERISTIC OF ARGUMENT

Just as the proposition leads us to consider the points at issue, so the points at issue lead us to consider the proof. In argument the basic forms of analysis (Sections II-VII) are grouped under one or more of the three methods of proof: deduction, induction, and analogy.† Deduction is an argument which proceeds from the general to the particular, from the whole to one of its parts. In deduction the argument is from a general truth, such as that nations which betray a marked diversity in their material, intellectual, and business aspects cannot be accused of uniformity, to the particular conclusion, such as that America cannot be accused of uniformity in virtue of her marked diversity in the material, intellectual, and business aspects of life. Deductive argument appears prominently in Mr. Lloyd's "Snobs, Slobs, and the English Language," as well as in Peter Drucker's "Myth of American Uniformity."

---

* In a debate the point at issue is not only the precise sense in which a writer or speaker defines his proposition; it is also the sense in which his opponent denies the proposition. If two opponents do not define the proposition in the same way, there can be no clash of issues and hence no debate.

† Deduction, induction, and analogy have already been explained in connection with other problems. For deduction see pp. 69-70, 257-60; for induction see pp. 69-70, 146-47, 257-60; for analogy see p. 158. See also index.

Induction is an argument in which a general conclusion is drawn from particular instances. Such an argument proceeds from the parts to the whole. Thus, by examining the particular lives of her neighbors' wives, husbands, and children, Miss McGinley concludes that suburbanites (the whole) live a fuller life. Induction is also a principal feature of Mark Twain's essay in Example IV D.

Analogy is an argument that draws an inference not from the part to the whole (induction) or from the whole to the part (deduction) but from part to part. An analogy is called "strict" when the two parts compared belong to the same class. An example of strict analogy occurs in "The Uniformity of American Life," in which Viscount Bryce compares the character of Americans with the character of Europeans. An analogy is called "relative" when the two parts compared belong to two different classes. Thus the analogy between the average American and the Aldrich family in "Perennial Adolescence" (Section VIII) is a relative analogy because the Aldriches are fictitious and the average American is real.

Extended arguments normally employ all three forms of proof. Thus in "The Myth of American Uniformity" Mr. Drucker first proves by a series of specific examples (induction) that Europeans accept the myth of American uniformity. A second induction (Part II of the essay) supports his generalization that the American character is diversified. In Part III he argues deductively in refuting a false generalization. In Part V he uses an analogy to show that the European myth of American uniformity is as fallacious as the American myth of the immobility of European society.

REFUTATION—THE FOURTH CHARACTERISTIC OF ARGUMENT

Refutation is the fourth characteristic of argument. Refutation is a formal reply to arguments urged against the proposition. All the essays in this section contain some elements of refutation; several are markedly refutational in character. In some, as in Miss McGinley's essay, the refutation attacks a general attitude rather than an actual objection. In others, as in the Lloyd-Barzun debate, the refutation is a direct and formal answer to specific objections.

Direct, formal refutation consists of the denial, distinction, or retort of the opponent's proposition or proofs.*

---

* A more specific or detailed discussion of refutation and fallacies will be found in the comment and in Exercises 3-5 of Example A2, pp. 452-57 ff., and in the comment and exercise on "The Myth of American Uniformity," Example A5.

Denial is counterassertion and proof. Thus a denial of the objection that Smith is a liar is simply that Smith is not a liar. Distinction points out that the statement of an opponent has more than one meaning, and that the meaning he accepts does not have the force of proof. Thus we may distinguish the objection that Krivitsky was a traitor because he deserted from Stalin by saying (a) Krivitsky is a traitor in the sense that he broke his pledge to Stalin, but (b) he is not a traitor in that he obeyed his conscience. But (b) is the relevant meaning rather than (a) because it is better to obey one's conscience than to obey Stalin. Retort is the use of an opponent's argument in one's own favor. General de Gaulle used a retort when, taking up the French collaborationist charge that he was a traitor for disobeying General Petain, he charged the collaborationists with treason for obeying General Petain rather than the government of Free France. Denial, distinction, and retort must be proved, just as the proposition must be proved, by arguments from deduction, induction, and analogy. The mere statements given above are illustrations, not proofs.

Indirect refutation consists in the familiar *argumentum ad hominem* (attack on the man rather than on his argument) and *reductio ad absurdum* (reduction to absurdity), which shows that an argument is contradictory, inconsistent, or inconsequential.

Another common device of refutation is the exposure of the fallacies in an opponent's argument. A fallacy is an erroneous process of reasoning or analysis. Thus one may err by a faulty deduction, induction, or analogy.

Special Types of Argument. Like exposition and other forms of discourse, argument must be adapted to the needs of the subject and the conventions of debate. Some types of argumentative discourse are subject to strict rules of procedure. In legal argument, for example, the writer cannot define his proposition at random. The general issues are always the same—guilty or not guilty, justified or not justified. Legislative argument (often called deliberative argument) is usually centered on the same kind of proposition—to pass X law, to reject Y law. Political argument asks the reader to support or reject A or B. The conventions of formal debate often demand reference to permanent issues (sometimes called stock questions), such as the importance of the topic, the necessity of a course of action, the expediency of a given undertaking. Legal arguments in particular are sharply regulated by rules of evidence and a thousand years of precedent.

The average student, however, rarely encounters these special problems of argument. But he does find the general forms of argument a continuing necessity in his social life, in his intellectual life at college, in his activity as a citizen in his community. Arguments on matters of opinion, such as Miss McGinley's defense of the suburbs, or the nature of language, or the character of American life occur daily. The student must know how to analyze these arguments and how to present arguments of his own. Next to exposition, argument is the most important form of discourse in a student's career.

THE LINK BETWEEN ARGUMENT AND PERSUASION

Argument and persuasion are so closely linked that they are almost always considered together. This may easily be seen by a close inspection of the definition of persuasion.

Persuasion is a form of discourse which presents arguments *as motives for some proposed action.*

Note that the unitalicized part of this definition puts persuasion in the same genus as argument. Like argument, a persuasion attempts to win assent to a belief or opinion. But the difference is that in persuasion the proofs (that is, the evidence derived from the analysis of facts, of general principles or ideas, or of the statement of authorities grouped under deduction, induction, and analogy) are directly related to a proposed action. Just as one may explain a subject (exposition) without proving a proposition (argument), so too one may prove a proposition (argument) without using it *as a motive for action* (persuasion). Thus a similar subject may be adapted in different ways to the three methods of discourse. Let us illustrate this by showing how the same subject, the need for European unity, is handled in exposition, in argument, and in persuasion.

I. EXPOSITION

After World War II the European nations faced the seemingly impossible task of reviving the culture and prosperity that had been shattered by the war. Europe had lost unity that was needed for her very existence. Central Europe and the Baltic states were cut from Europe's bleeding body. Britain, France, and Italy were agitated by profound political and social struggles. The ruins of Germany were divided between Russia and the West. This disunity became evident in the

United Nations, where European influence vis-à-vis the United States and Russia declined sharply. Moreover, violent antagonisms thwarted all efforts at union. The victors hated and feared Germany, despised and ignored Italy. Spain and Portugal were pariah nations. France felt that Great Britain was shirking her responsibility on the Continent, and Great Britain was repelled by De Gaulle's chauvinism. These problems were aggravated still further by the immediate restoration of economic nationalism and tariff barriers and by competition for Marshall Plan aid. When cooperation for prosperity was most essential, Europe was most divided.

This lack of unity left Europe unprepared to withstand the shocks that threatened to topple her shaky economic structure. Faced with the disappearance of great trading areas in Asia and Africa, Europe had to look to inter-European trade for her own revival. But there were no agencies to promote such trade. England strove to mend her contacts with her colonies and to cultivate the American market rather than to join in a common effort at European revival. France too looked outward—toward North Africa—for a new source of economic strength. Germany doggedly set about her task of providing reparations. Gradually, however, the need for European unity forced itself upon the minds of the bewildered and distracted people. When China fell into the arms of Russia, when India and Indonesia became independent, when the Iron Curtain countries appeared to be irretrievably lost, when Arab nationalism threatened to destroy the last remaining European investments in the Middle East and in North Africa, when the end of Marshall Plan aid was in sight, Europe began to look to herself for help.

The leading statesmen of free Europe called for European unity. Schuman in France, Adenauer in Germany, Paul Spaak in Belgium, Churchill in England, De Gasperi in Italy rose above the prejudices of nationalism to demand a united Europe. They pleaded for a customs union, economic cooperation, joint political action to pool resources, and regional federation within the United Nations. No one can accuse the top leadership of ignoring the basic fact of Europeon disunity. But the need for European unity still remains.

Note that in this exposition the purpose is merely to explain the need for European unity. The exposition here is blended with narrative. First, the lack of unity is set forth in paragraph 1. Secondly, the effects of disunity are described in paragraph 2. Finally, the need for unity is recognized by European statesmen in paragraph 3.

The author does not argue about the need for European unity. He merely states what the facts imply. In the next example you will note that the first sentence announces a proposition: European unity is essential; and the point at issue: it is essential in the sense that it is the necessary condition for peace, for prosperity, for survival.

2. ARGUMENT

European unity is essential in the sense that it is a necessary condition for peace, for prosperity, for survival. That some form of unity is necessary for peace is an evident fact in international politics. Today peace cannot be had for the wishing. Strength alone guarantees peace. Strength alone prevents aggression. Obviously Germany, France, and Italy cannot individually resist Russian aggression. Expert military opinion agrees that Russia could swallow up these countries piecemeal in ninety days. But taken together, in union with England and the United States, these European nations, according to General Eisenhower and his staff, can successfully defend themselves. A European army, united under one head, believing in a common principle of freedom, could support a formidable military unit. The mere threat of such an army has already tempered the Soviet attitude toward western Germany and Austria. The actuality of such a force might well defer aggression permanently.

Prosperity, we know, is a necessary condition of military strength. An army is the product of many causes. It needs an *esprit de corps,* it needs leaders, it needs intelligent and willing soldiers. But an army must be supplied and equipped. Hence the need for economic prosperity. But no European nation is economically self-sufficient. France lacks coal, iron, and petroleum; Germany lacks food; Italy has an immense endowment of skilled workers but little else. No one European nation can prosper by itself. But Europe as a whole can prosper. A united Europe may well become self-sufficient. Furthermore, as a regional federation of the United Nations, trading with other nations and groups in the free world, Europe can prosper beyond all its dreams.

Hitherto a fanatical nationalism has inspired the several European states to cling to the outmoded ideal of national self-sufficiency. The head is not more native to the heart, the hand more instrumental to the mouth than is united Europe to the prosperity of the member nations. Europe must recognize this fact if she wants to be strong and peaceful. Economic unity is even more important than political unity.

Conceivably a desperate and divided Europe might prefer to stay desperate and divided rather than to be peaceful, prosperous, and united. Some Frenchmen hate Germany so intensely that they cannot imagine a political or economic union in which their old enemy has a rightful place. In the nineteenth century such an attitude might not have had disastrous results. But ultranationalism is now an unmitigated evil. In the age of airplanes, submarines, radar, rockets, and atomic energy no nation can avoid cooperation with its neighbors. Unity is necessary for survival. If European nations nurse their ancient grudges they will fall one by one, as Czechoslovakia fell, as Hungary and Rumania fell. Moreover, the hatred that divides nation from nation will eventually divide the nations themselves. The Frenchman who hates Germans eventually hates other Frenchmen. This creeping paralysis of hate is already under way. Consider, for example, the poisonous hatred of the French communist for the De Gaulliste, of the socialists for MRP.

How Europe can be united, what steps should be taken, no American can say. It is distinctly a European problem, just as the FEPC is an American problem. We cannot force unity on Europe, and we should not try to. But I am convinced that unity is essential to European peace, prosperity, and survival.

We Americans know how thirteen small and helpless colonies found independence in unity, strength in unity, peace in unity, prosperity in unity. Our national motto is *e pluribus unum*—one out of many. We learned too that unity is not uniformity, but agreement. A united Europe does not mean the abolition of nations any more than our federal union means an abolition of states. Man is big enough to be two things at once—a good Frenchman and a good European. If European nations realize unity can mean for them what it has meant for us, the peace of the world will be much more secure.

Note here that the argument stops short of persuasion. The author clearly aims to convince his readers that European unity is essential, but he does not ask them to take any immediate steps to bring that unity about. Below Winston Churchill cites the reasons why European unity is necessary, but he stimulates his British audience to a definite action, that is, the founding of an organization in Great Britain to promote the cause of united Europe. This selection is part of a larger speech reproduced in full in this section.

3. PERSUASION

Are the states of Europe to continue forever to squander the first fruits of their toil upon the erection of new barriers, military fortifications, tariff walls, and passport networks against one another?

Are we Europeans to become incapable, with all our tropical and colonial dependencies, with all our long-created trading connections, with all that modern production and transportation can do, of even averting famine from the mass of our peoples? Are we all, through our poverty and our quarrels, forever to be a burden and a danger to the rest of the world? Do we imagine that we can be carried forward indefinitely upon the shoulders—broad though they be—of the United States?

The time has come when these questions must be answered. This is the hour of choice, and surely the choice is plain. If the peoples of Europe resolve to come together and work together for mutual advantage, to exchange blessings instead of curses, they still have it in their power to sweep away the horrors and miseries which surround them and to allow the streams of freedom, happiness, and abundance to begin again their healing flow.

This is the supreme opportunity, and, if it be cast away, no one can predict that it will ever return or what the resulting catastrophe will be.

In my experience of large enterprises, it is often a mistake to try to settle everything at once. Far off, on the skyline, we can see the peaks of the Delectable Mountains. But we cannot tell what lies between us and them.

We know where we want to go, but we cannot foresee all the stages of the journey or plan our marches as in a military operation. We are not acting in the field of forces, but in the domain of opinion. We cannot give orders. We can only persuade.

We must go forward step by step.

I will therefore explain in general terms where we are and what are the first things we have to do. We have now at once to set on foot an organization in Great Britain to promote the cause of united Europe and to give this idea the prominence and vitality necessary for it to lay hold of the minds of our fellow countrymen to such an extent that it will affect their actions and influence the course of national policy.

—Winston S. Churchill *

CHARACTERISTICS OF PERSUASION

A close reading of these three examples shows that each one illustrates the special characteristics of the several kinds of discourse. Example 1 merely explains the need for unity in Europe after World War II. It does not attempt to argue or dispute a proposition explicitly. True, a perceptive reader can discover in Example 1 an "expository argument," that is, an explanation which implicitly supports a proposition; but Example 1 is not formally or explicitly argumentative. (See comment on A4 below for additional notes on expository argument.)

On the other hand, the second example clearly intends to prove that European unity is necessary for peace, prosperity, and survival. It expresses a belief and offers reasons for the belief. But it does not ask the audience to do anything more than accept the author's conviction. Similarly, Miss McGinley in "Suburbia" aims to convince you that the suburbs provide a freer and fuller life for its residents, but she does not urge you to move to the suburbs. Viscount Bryce tries to prove that the American character is uniform, but he does not urge any action on the part of his readers. Argument then aims only to establish a conviction.

Persuasion adds the note of action. In the third example, the need for European unity is proved argumentatively. But these proofs are also *motives for action*. Here Churchill appeals to pride, shame, honor, and other feelings—to the psychological and moral springs of action—in order to stimulate a resolution to unite. He is not satisfied with mere conviction. Indeed his proofs were self-evident to Europeans in 1947. The obstacle to his purpose was the possible refusal of his audience to act in accordance with the evidence. The real obstacle was not the intellect of his audience but its will. Its spiritual resources spent during four bitter years, its ideals blurred by the spectacle of postwar squabbling, the audience needed a fresh charge of moral force. Hence too the appeal to pride in Europe's past, pity and shame for her present. Hence the stinging reminder of her dependence on the United States.

* From *Europe Unite*, 1950, by Winston S. Churchill. Reprinted by permission of The Houghton Mifflin Company, publishers.

Because persuasion aims to stimulate action it emphasizes certain characteristics that are either not present at all in exposition and argument or, when present, are not given a prominent place. These characteristic elements are (a) action, (b) the fusion of proof and motive, and (c) a heightened style.

ACTION

The first of these elements, action, is the emphasis on what the audience is to *do*. A good persuasion keeps reminding the audience about a specific action. Thus Churchill in his "Save Europe by Uniting Europe" speech * never lets his English audience forget what they are to do. He wants them not only to resolve to support a united Europe but to work actively through the British association to promote European unity. He lays down a specific program for such an organization. He stipulates the order according to which the organization should work. He bends all arguments in the direction of action. We must help Germany, we must persuade, we must act now—are his constant refrain.

FUSION OF PROOF AND MOTIVE

Thus this fusion of proof and motive, this linking of argument to action, this joint appeal to the intellect and to the will of the audience is the second element of persuasion. In persuasion this literary economy is essential. The same argument must at once be clear as proof and stimulating as motive. So too the arrangement of proof convinces and moves at the same time. Notice how each step in Churchill's development, each proof used in Hutchins' analysis of American educational problems (Example B2) stimulates to action. Churchill does not say merely that Germany is a problem; he says we must solve the German problem. Hutchins does not merely prove that the American educational policy is deficient; he urges his audience to help remove the defects by demanding the kind of education they need. Furthermore, he defines the kind of education they need, labels it, and shows them where they can get it. In addition, both speakers have arranged their arguments in the sequence that is best calculated to make the audience act.

* The reference here is to the whole speech reproduced as **Example B1**, rather than to the excerpt given above.

HEIGHTENED STYLE

Along with the emphasis on action and the fusion of proof and motive, the third characteristic element stressed in persuasion is the emotional and imaginative appeal of the style. An old axiom states that you cannot move another person to laughter or to tears unless you first laugh or weep yourself. If you wish to excite an audience you must be excited yourself. If you wish to interest them you must be interesting. A plain unemotional style befits an exposition of facts, such as the workings of a gasoline engine. But, when you are attempting to stir your audience to perform difficult tasks that require moral ardor and severe thought, you, the writer, must practice what you preach.

Imagine for instance a speaker urging you to read Shakespeare because Shakespeare will inspire you with lofty thoughts and profound emotions. Suppose the speaker started by saying, "The facts about Shakespeare are few, and these few are not very revealing. Nevertheless, scholarship compels us to inspect these facts before we attempt to read the plays." Suppose he continued in this vein. Unconsciously, perhaps, you would conclude that if the study of Shakespeare can make a man that dull it may be well to avoid it. The hypothetical speaker has defeated his own purpose. He should have announced his intention to explain rather than to persuade.

Churchill and Hutchins prove the opposite truth—that a vigorous and vivid style has much to do with effective persuasion. In different ways both men charge their language with feeling and imagination. When Churchill speaks of Europe's grandeur, he manifests that grandeur in the splendor of his language. When he asks his audience to picture the devastation of Europe, he paints that picture in vivid sentences. Similarly, in arguing for an education that trains the mind, Huchins displays in his logical development the precision, coherence, and balance which are the marks of a trained mind.

ETHICAL APPEAL IN PERSUASION

Persuasion, then, is notable for its emphasis on action, the coherence of proof and motive, and a heightened emotional and imaginative style. These are the three essential elements; they point to other important characteristics. Because a persuasion often aims at a specific audience it is a more personal and direct form of discourse than exposition and argument. A persuasive writer speaks not only from mind to mind but from heart to heart. In the final analysis an audience is won over not only by the speaker's arguments and explanations but by the speaker's whole personality. "Your actions speak so loudly I cannot hear what you say" is a proverb that may, with certain adjustments, be applied to persuasion. Confucius' sense of the word *actions* in this quotation was meant to apply to personal morals. We do not judge a persuasion by the morals of the writer, but we do judge the moral meaning of the speech. This means simply that we respond to ideas that appeal to our sense of honor, justice, and integrity, especially when those ideas are uttered in a manner that is appropriate to the importance of the subject, the dignity of the occasion, and the respect that a speaker owes to the opinions of mankind. At bottom we submit to a legitimate ethical appeal, the morality of mind, in the persuasive effort.

No trick of style, no demagogic cleverness, no learning however wide can impart moral character to a persuasion. This moral character stems from the writer's own reasoned conviction and passionate belief. Thus when Churchill holds up the ideal of European culture, and when Hutchins wrathfully contrasts true and false ideals of education, we are as much impressed by the force of their belief as we are by the power of their reasoning. The true source of persuasion, then, flows from conviction and belief finding utterance in language.

The student is not called upon to persuade as often as he is to explain or to argue. Nevertheless, persuasion is a most important form of discourse. It is the means by which many men are prompted to do the best they can, a channel through which you too can express those reasoned convictions and passionate beliefs that are the marks of a liberally educated person.

The seven examples selected for study in this section will help you to master the basic principles of argument and persuasion. Individually these essays include most of the main characteristics of argumentative and persuasive discourse. The pairing of the Lloyd-Barzun essays and the Bryce-Drucker essays are lively debates that will interest and excite as well as help to instruct the average student. You should be forewarned, however, that argument and persuasion require even more attention and study than exposition.

Remember: The writer who argues with you or attempts to persuade you is asking for your assent. Your assent is the collaboration of your mind and will. Watch him. Make him prove his point. Do not yield until you are fully convinced.

---

a. In argument arrange the basic proofs under deduction, induction, or analogy. Refute directly by denial, distinction, and retort. Refute indirectly (1) by attacking the competence of the speaker or writer; (2) by attacking his method of arguing; (3) by exposing his fallacies.

Proposition and Issues: The suburbanite enjoys a freer and fuller life than the town dweller and the country dweller
Because:
The suburbanite conforms less to convention
Men, women, and children who reside in the suburbs live a fuller and more creative life

1. Suburbia: Of Thee I Sing

BY PHYLLIS MC GINLEY

1 Twenty miles east of New York City as the New Haven Railroad flies sits a village I shall call Spruce Manor. The Boston Post Road, there, for the length of two blocks, becomes Main Street, and on one

side of that thundering thoroughfare are the grocery stores and the drug stores and the Village Spa where teen-agers gather of an afternoon to drink their cokes and speak their curious confidences. There one finds the shoe repairers and the dry cleaners and the second-hand stores which sell "antiques" and the stationery stores which dispense comic books to ten-year-olds and greeting cards and lending library masterpieces to their mothers. On the opposite side stand the bank, the fire house, the public library. The rest of this town of perhaps four or five thousand people lies to the south and is bounded largely by Long Island Sound, curving protectively on three borders. The movie theater (dedicated to the showing of second-run, single-feature pictures) and the grade schools lie north, beyond the Post Road, and that is a source of worry to Spruce Manorites. They are always a little uneasy about the children, crossing, perhaps, before the lights are safely green. However, two excellent policemen—Mr. Crowley and Mr. Lang —station themselves at the intersections four times a day, and so far there have been no accidents.

2 Spruce Manor in the spring and summer and fall is a pretty town, full of gardens and old elms. (There are few spruces, but the village Council is considering planting a few on the station plaza, out of sheer patriotism.) In the winter, the houses reveal themselves as comfortable, well-kept, architecturally insignificant. Then one can see the town for what it is and has been since it left off being farm and woodland some sixty years ago—the epitome of Suburbia, not the country and certainly not the city. It is a commuter's town, the living center of a web which unrolls each morning as the men swing aboard the locals, and contracts again in the evening when they return. By day, with even the children pent in schools, it is a village of women. They trundle mobile baskets at the A & P, they sit under driers at the hairdressers, they sweep their porches and set out bulbs and stitch up slip covers. Only on weekends does it become heterogeneous and lively, the parking places difficult to find.

3 Spruce Manor has no country club of its own, though devoted golfers have their choice of two or three not far away. It does have a small yacht club and a beach which can be used by anyone who rents or owns a house here. The village supports a little park with playground equipment and a counselor, where children, unattended by parents, can spend summer days if they have no more pressing engagements.

4 It is a town not wholly without traditions. Residents will point out the two-hundred-year-old manor house, now a minor museum; and in the autumn they line the streets on a scheduled evening to watch the Volunteer Firemen parade. That is a fine occasion, with so many heads of households marching in their red blouses and white gloves, some with flaming helmets, some swinging lanterns, most of them genially out of step. There is a bigger parade on Memorial Day with more marchers than watchers and with the Catholic priest, the rabbi, and the Protestant ministers each delivering a short prayer when the paraders gather near the War Memorial. On the whole, however, outside of contributing generously to the Community Chest, Manorites are not addicted to municipal get-togethers.

5 No one is very poor here and not many families rich enough to be awesome. In fact, there is not much to distinguish Spruce Manor from any other of a thousand suburbs outside of New York City or San Francisco or Detroit or Chicago or even Stockholm, for that matter. Except for one thing. For some reason, Spruce Manor has become a sort of symbol to writers and reporters familiar only with its name or trivial aspects. It has become a symbol of all that is middle-class in the worst sense, of settled-downness or rootlessness, according to what the writer is trying to prove; of smug and prosperous mediocrity—or even, in more lurid novels, of lechery at the country club and Sunday morning hangovers.

6 To condemn Suburbia has long been a literary cliché, anyhow. I have yet to read a book in which the suburban life was pictured as the good life or the commuter as a sympathetic figure. He is nearly as much a stock character as the old stage Irishman: the man who "spends his life riding to and from his wife," the eternal Babbitt who knows all about Buicks and nothing about Picasso, whose sanctuary is the club locker room, whose ideas spring ready-made from the illiberal newspapers. His wife plays politics at the P.T.A. and keeps up with the Joneses. Or—if the scene is more gilded and less respectable—the commuter is the high-powered advertising executive with a station wagon and an eye for the ladies, his wife a restless baggage given to too many cocktails in the afternoon.

7 These clichés I challenge. I have lived in the country, I have lived in the city. I have lived in an average Middle Western small town. But for the best eleven years of my life I have lived in Suburbia and I like it.

8 "Compromise!" cried our friends when we came here from an expensive, inconvenient, moderately fashionable tenement in Manhattan. It was the period in our lives when everyone was moving somewhere. Farther uptown, farther downtown, across town to Sutton Place, to a half-dozen rural acres in Connecticut or New Jersey or even Vermont. But no one in our rather rarefied little group was thinking of moving to the suburbs except us. They were aghast that we could find anything appealing in the thought of a middle-class house on a middle-class street in a middle-class village full of middle-class people. That we were tired of town and hoped for children, that we couldn't afford both a city apartment and a farm, they put down as feeble excuses. To this day they cannot understand us. You see, they read the books. They even write them.

9 ¹Compromise? ²Of course we compromise. ³But compromise, if not the spice of life, is its solidity. ⁴It is what makes nations great and marriages happy and Spruce Manor the pleasant place it is. ⁵As for its being middle-class, what is wrong with acknowledging one's roots? ⁶And how free we are! ⁷Free of the city's noise, of its ubiquitous doormen, of the soot on the windowsill and the radio in the next apartment. ⁸We have released ourselves from the seasonal hegira to the mountains or the seashore. ⁹We have only one address, one house to keep supplied with paring knives and blankets. ¹⁰We are free from the snows that block the countryman's roads in winter and his electricity which always goes off in a thunderstorm. ¹¹I do not insist that we are typical. ¹²There is nothing really typical about any of our friends and neighbors here, and therein lies my point. ¹³The true suburbanite needs to conform less than anyone else; much less than the gentleman farmer with his remodeled salt-box or than the determined cliff dweller with his necessity for living at the right address. ¹⁴In Spruce Manor all addresses are right. ¹⁵And since we are fairly numerous here, we need not fall back on the people nearest us for total companionship. ¹⁶There is not here, as in a small city away from truly urban centers, some particular family whose codes must be ours. ¹⁷And we could not keep up with the Joneses even if we wanted to, for we know many Joneses and they are all quite different people leading the most various lives.

10 The Albert Joneses spend their weekends sailing, the Bertram Joneses cultivate their delphinium, the Clarence Joneses—Clarence being a handy man with a cello—are enthusiastic about amateur chamber music. The David Joneses dote on bridge, but neither of the Ernest

Joneses understands it, and they prefer staying home of an evening so that Ernest Jones can carve his witty caricatures out of pieces of old fruit wood. We admire each other's gardens, applaud each other's sailing records; we are too busy to compete. So long as our clapboards are painted and our hedges decently trimmed, we have fulfilled our community obligations. We can live as anonymously as in a city or we can call half the village by their first names.

11 On our half-acre or three-quarters, we can raise enough tomatoes for our salads and assassinate enough beetles to satisfy the gardening urge. Or we can buy our vegetables at the store and put the whole place to lawn without feeling that we are neglecting our property. We can have privacy and shade and the changing of the seasons and also the Joneses next door from whom to borrow a cup of sugar or a stepladder. Despite the novelists, the shadow of the country club rests lightly on us. Half of us wouldn't be found dead with a golf stick in our hands, and loathe Saturday dances. Few of us expect to be deliriously wealthy or world-famous or divorced. What we do expect is to pay off the mortgage and send our healthy children to good colleges.

12 For when I refer to life here, I think, of course, of living with children. Spruce Manor without children would be a paradox. The summer waters are full of them, gamboling like dolphins. The lanes are alive with them, the yards overflow with them, they possess the tennis courts and the skating pond and the vacant lots. Their roller skates wear down the asphalt, and their bicycles make necessary the twenty-five mile speed limit. They converse interminably on the telephones and make rich the dentist and the pediatrician. Who claims that a child and a half is the American middle-class average? A nice medium Spruce Manor family runs to four or five, and we count proudly, but not with amazement, the many solid households running to six, seven, eight, nine, even up to twelve. Our houses here are big and not new, most of them, and there is a temptation to fill them up, let the décor fall where it may.

13 Besides, Spruce Manor seems designed by providence and town planning for the happiness of children. Better designed than the city, better, I say defiantly, than the country. Country mothers must be constantly arranging and contriving for their children's leisure time. There is no neighbor child next door for playmate, no school within walking distance. The ponds are dangerous to young swimmers, the woods full of poison ivy, the romantic dirt roads unsuitable for bicycles. An extra

acre or two gives a fine sense of possession to an adult; it does not compensate children for the give-and-take of our village, where there is always a contemporary to help swing the skipping rope or put on the catcher's mitt. Where in the country is the Friday evening dancing class or the Saturday morning movie (approved by the P.T.A.)? It is the greatest fallacy of all time that children love the country as a year-around plan. Children would take a dusty corner of Washington Square or a city sidewalk, even, in preference to the lonely sermons in stones and books in running brooks which their contemporaries cannot share.

14 As for the horrors of bringing up progeny in the city, for all its museums and other cultural advantages (so perfectly within reach of suburban families if they feel strongly about it), they were summed up for me one day last winter. The harried mother of one, speaking to me on the telephone just after Christmas, sighed and said, "It's been a really wonderful time for me, as vacations go. Barbara has had an engagement with a child in our apartment house every afternoon this week. I have had to take her almost nowhere." Barbara is eleven. For six of those eleven years, I realized, her mother must have dreaded Christmas vacation, not to mention spring, as a time when Barbara had to be entertained. I thought thankfully of my own daughters whom I had scarcely seen since school closed, out with their skis and their sleds and their friends, sliding down the roped-off hill half a block away, coming in hungrily for lunch and disappearing again, hearty, amused, and safe—at least as safe as any sled-borne child can be.

15 Spruce Manor is not Eden, of course. Our taxes are higher than we like, and there is always that eight-eleven in the morning to be caught, and we sometimes resent the necessity of rushing from a theater to a train on a weekday evening. But the taxes pay for our really excellent schools and for our garbage collections (so that the pails of orange peels need not stand in the halls overnight as ours did in the city) and for our water supply which does not give out every dry summer as it frequently does in the country. As for the theaters—they are twenty miles away and we don't get to them more than twice a month. But neither, I think, do many of our friends in town. The eight-eleven is rather a pleasant train, too, say the husbands; it gets them to work in thirty-four minutes and they read the papers restfully on the way.

16 "But the suburban mind!" cry our die-hard friends in Manhattan and Connecticut. "The suburban conversation! The monotony!" They imply that they and I must scintillate or we perish. Let me anatomize

Spruce Manor, for them and for the others who envision Suburbia as a congregation of mindless housewives and amoral go-getters.

17 From my window, now, on a June morning, I have a view. It contains neither solitary hills nor dramatic skyscrapers. But I can see my roses in bloom, and my foxglove, and an arch of trees over the lane. I think comfortably of my friends whose houses line this and other streets rather like it. Not one of them is, so far as I know, doing any of the things that suburban ladies are popularly supposed to be doing. One of them, I happen to know, has gone bowling for her health and figure, but she has already tidied up her house and arranged to be home before the boys return from school. Some, undoubtedly, are ferociously busy in the garden. One lady is on her way to Ellis Island, bearing comfort and gifts to a Polish boy—a seventeen-year-old stowaway who did slave labor in Germany and was liberated by a cousin of hers during the war—who is being held for attempting to attain the land of which her cousin told him. The boy has been on the Island for three months. Twice a week she takes this tedious journey, meanwhile besieging courts and immigration authorities on his behalf. This lady has a large house, a part-time maid, and five children.

18 My friend around the corner is finishing her third novel. She writes daily from nine-thirty until two. After that her son comes back from school and she plunges into maternity; at six, she combs her pretty hair, refreshes her lipstick, and is charming to her doctor husband. The village dancing school is run by another neighbor, as it has been for twenty years. She has sent a number of ballerinas on to the theatrical world as well as having shepherded for many a successful season the white-gloved little boys and full-skirted little girls through their first social tasks.

19 Some of the ladies are no doubt painting their kitchens or a nursery; one of them is painting the portrait, on assignment, of a very distinguished personage. Some of them are nurses' aides and Red Cross workers and supporters of good causes. But all find time to be friends with their families and to meet the 5:32 five nights a week. They read something besides the newest historical novel, Braque is not unidentifiable to most of them, and their conversation is for the most part as agreeable as the tables they set. The tireless bridge players, the gossips, the women bored by their husbands live perhaps in our suburb, too. Let them. Our orbits need not cross.

20 And what of the husbands, industriously selling bonds or practicing law or editing magazines or looking through microscopes or

managing offices in the city? Do they spend their evenings and their weekends in the gaudy bars of Fifty-second Street? Or are they the perennial householders, their lives a dreary round of taking down screens and mending drains? Well, screens they have always with them, and a man who is good around the house can spend happy hours with the plumbing even on a South Sea island. Some of them cut their own lawns and some of them try to break par and some of them sail their little boats all summer with their families for crew. Some of them are village trustees for nothing a year and some listen to symphonies and some think Milton Berle ought to be President. There is a scientist who plays wonderful bebop, and an insurance salesman who has bought a big old house nearby and with his own hands is gradually tearing it apart and reshaping it nearer to his heart's desire. Some of them are passionate hedge-clippers and some read Plutarch for fun. But I do not know many—though there may be such—who either kiss their neighbors' wives behind doors or whose idea of sprightly talk is to tell you the plot of an old movie.

21 It is June, now, as I have said. This afternoon my daughters will come home from school with a crowd of their peers at their heels. They will eat up the cookies and drink up the ginger ale and go down for a swim at the beach if the water is warm enough, that beach which is only three blocks away and open to all Spruce Manor. They will go unattended by me, since they have been swimming since they were four, and besides there are lifeguards and no big waves. (Even our piece of ocean is a compromise.) Presently it will be time for us to climb into our very old Studebaker—we are not car-proud in Spruce Manor—and meet the 5:32. That evening expedition is not vitally necessary, for a bus runs straight down our principal avenue from the station to the shore, and it meets all trains. But it is an event we enjoy. There is something delightfully ritualistic about the moment when the train pulls in and the men swing off, with the less sophisticated children running squealing to meet them. The women move over from the driver's seat, surrender the keys, and receive an absent-minded kiss. It is the sort of picture that wakes John Marquand screaming from his sleep. But, deluded people that we are, we do not realize how mediocre it all seems. We will eat our undistinguished meal, probably without even a cocktail to enliven it. We will drink our coffee at the table, not carry it into the living room; if a husband changes for dinner here it is into old and spotty trousers and more comfortable shoes. The children will then go through the regular childhood routine—com-

plain about their homework, grumble about going to bed, and finally accomplish both ordeals. Perhaps later the Gerard Joneses will drop in. We will talk a great deal of unimportant chatter and compare notes on food prices; we will also discuss the headlines and disagree. (Some of us in the Manor are Republicans, some are Democrats, a few lean plainly leftward. There are probably anti-Semites and anti-Catholics and even anti-Americans. Most of us are merely anti-antis.) We will all have one highball, and the Joneses will leave early. Tomorrow and tomorrow and tomorrow the pattern will be repeated. This is Suburbia.

22 But I think that some day people will look back on our little interval here, on our Spruce Manor way of life, as we now look back on the Currier and Ives kind of living, with nostalgia and respect. In a world of terrible extremes, it will stand out as the safe, important medium.

Suburbia, of thee I sing!

Comment

Miss McGinley's purpose here is clearly implied in her title. She wishes to convince her readers that the suburbanite enjoys a freer and fuller life than the country dweller or the town dweller (central theme or proposition). Thus, after an exposition of suburban life (¶1-5), she challenges two opinions commonly held by writers and reporters (¶6). These opinions are (1) that suburban living is a bad compromise between country and town (¶8-15) and (2) that the suburbs are populated by mindless housewives and amoral go-getters (¶16-20). Paragraphs 21-22 summarize the argument and restate the proposition.

This essay combines various forms of analysis (Sections II-VII) to explain and to prove the central theme.

Thus, in the introduction (¶1-7) the suburb, Spruce Manor, is *defined* in several ways. Paragraph 1 defines Spruce Manor by listing its various parts. In paragraphs 2-3, Spruce Manor is *classified* as the epitome of Suburbia, "not the country and certainly not the city." *Essentially* it is a commuter's town. Paragraph 4 continues the definition of Spruce Manor by offering several *examples* of local traditions which set apart the suburban village from city and country. In paragraphs 5 and 6 Miss McGinley defines a false opinion held by others about suburbs in general and about Spruce Manor in particular. Paragraph 7 states her own opinion about Spruce Manor (proposition or central theme).

Paragraph 8 defines the charge that suburban living is a shabby compromise, and begins the development of the essay. Paragraph 9 answers the charge of shabby compromise by offering a more accurate *definition* of compromise. Note too that this is a refutation by retort. In paragraph 9 the true suburbanite is defined as one who "needs to conform less than anyone else" (the first point at issue). Paragraphs 10-15 illustrate the freedom of Suburbia by giving a large number of *specific examples* of "quite different people leading the most various lives" in *contrast* to the country dwellers (¶13) and the city dwellers (¶13-14).

Paragraph 16 states the second charge against Suburbia. This is refuted by a denial supported by a series of examples showing how the wives, the husbands, and the children live free and full lives (¶16-20) (the second point at issue).

The conclusion (¶21-22) gives a résumé of the proof in vivid descriptive form and restates the proposition. Miss McGinley has used several forms of analysis to refute the charges against Suburbia and to convince her audience that suburban life is a freer and fuller life than that in the city and the country. These methods of analysis are grouped under the predominant principle of induction, that is, the proof of a general truth by specific examples.

Analysis and Composition

1. Construct a topical outline of this essay according to the model for "On Weekend Guests" by Russell Lynes, III C2.*
2. Show how Miss McGinley's essay is basically an attempt at refutation. Point out the principal methods of refutation used.
3. A good introduction usually accomplishes the following:
   a. It leads up to the central theme by explaining the author's purpose and subject.
   b. It disposes the reader to accept the author's interpretation of the subject.
   c. It creates interest by its selection of important details and by the quality of the style.
   Show how the introduction of this essay (¶1-7) does or does not accomplish these results.
4. Paragraph 7 contains an explicit statement of the proposition or central theme. Other statements of the proposition occur in paragraph 22 and throughout the essay. Construct your own statement of the central theme in a single sentence.
5. How does the device of challenging literary clichés (¶6-7) arouse interest? Explain.

* See handbooks: Foerster, *36, 36a*; Hodges, *32c2*; Kierzek, pp. 142-44; Perrin, p. 671; Wykoff, *36, 36a.*

6. Paragraph 9 is a good example, on a small scale, of the author's use of combined forms of analysis. The predominant method of this analysis is definition: definition of compromise in sentences 1-4, of freedom in sentences 6-10, and of the true suburbanite in sentence 13. What other methods of analysis can you find in this paragraph?

7. How do the examples cited in paragraphs 10-12 support the author's contention that the suburban life is freer than urban or country life?

8. Locate the topic sentence in paragraph 13. Justify your choice by showing how the other sentences are related to the topic sentence you have selected.

9. How does the contrast in paragraph 14 support the author's main contention?

10. Paragraphs 17-19 cite several suburban housewives as proof that this class of women is intelligent and active. Granted that these examples illustrate the author's point of view, are they also convincing demonstrations of proof? Give reasons for your answer.

11. An example is forceful if the author makes it actual, local, personal, and fresh. To what extent can you apply these qualities to the examples cited in paragraphs 20 and 21?

12. A good conclusion sums up the proposition and reinforces a predominant emotional impression. Does paragraph 22 achieve these results? Explain your answer.

13. Much of the charm of this essay may be traced to its refreshing candor of thought and originality of expression. Cite several examples of this candor and originality.

14. Show how the following expressions, in their several contexts, help to stimulate interest in the reader:
   a. "Speak their curious confidences" (¶1)
   b. "Smug and prosperous mediocrity" ¶5)
   c. "Assassinate enough beetles" (¶11)
   d. "The summer waters are full of them, gamboling like dolphins" (¶12)
   e. "There is something delightfully ritualistic about the moment when" (¶21)

15. In both the second and third divisions of Miss McGinley's essay (¶8-15 and 16-21) the author emphasizes the value of the suburbs for children. Analyze the order in which she presents her ideas and determine whether the paragraphs on children are given emphasis by their place in this order.

16. Draw up a topical outline for an argument designed to challenge the following stereotyped expressions of opinion:
   a. A studious girl makes a bad wife.
   b. Gentlemen prefer blondes.

c. American cities lack cultural interests.

d. A humorous man lacks stability of character.

e. Familiarity breeds contempt.

f. Home cooking is best.

g. Let's return to the good old times.

h. Things were different in Grandmother's day.

i. You can't judge by appearances.

17. Write an informal argument on one of the themes outlined in Exercise 15.

Proposition: There is no correct standard of English speech and writing.

2. *Affirmative:* Mr. Lloyd, "Snobs, Slobs, and the English Language"

3. *Negative:*   Mr. Barzun, "The Retort Circumstantial"

2. Snobs, Slobs, and the English Language

BY DONALD J. LLOYD

There is at large among us today an unholy number of people who make it their business to correct the speech and writing of others. When Winston Churchill says, "It's me," in a radio address, their lips purse and murmur firmly, "It is I," and they sit down and write bitter letters to the New York *Times* about What Is Happening to the English Language. Reading "I only had five dollars," they circle *only* and move it to the right of *had,* producing "I had only five dollars" with a sense of virtue that is beyond the measure of man. They are implacable enemies of *different than,* of *loan* and *contact* used as verbs, and of dozens of other common expressions. They put triumphant exclamation marks in the margins of library books. They are ready to tangle the thread of any discussion by pouncing on a point of grammar.

2 If these people were all retired teachers of high school English, their weight in the community would be negligible; but unfortunately they are not. They are authors, scholars, business men, librarians—indeed, they are to be found wherever educated people read and write

SNOBS, SLOBS, AND THE ENGLISH LANGUAGE: from *The American Scholar,* Spring 1951. Reprinted with the permission of *The American Scholar* and the author.

English. And they are moved by a genuine concern for the language. They have brought us, it is true, to a state in which almost anybody, no matter what his education or the clarity of his expression, is likely to find himself attacked for some locution which he has used. Yet their intentions are of the best. It is only that their earnest minds are in the grip of two curious misconceptions. One is that there is a "correct" standard English which is uniform and definite and has been reduced to rule. The other is that this "correct" standard can only be maintained by the vigilant attention of everybody concerned with language—indeed, by the whole body of educated men and women.

3 The enemy these self-appointed linguistic sentries see lurking in every expression which stirs the correcter's instinct in them is something they call illiteracy—which is not a simple state of being unlettered, but something more. This illiteracy is a willful and obstinate disregard for the standards of civilized expression. It stirs anger in them when they think they see it, because it seems to them a voluntary ignorance, compounded out of carelessness and sloth. When they think they find it in men who hold responsible positions in the community, they feel it to be a summation of all the decline of the graces of culture, the last reaches of a great wave of vulgarity which is eroding the educated and literate classes. It seems to them to be a surge of crude populism; they hear in each solecism the faint, far-off cries of the rising mob. It is really a sort of ringing in their ears.

4 In view of the general agreement among the literate that a "correct" standard English exists, and in view of the vituperation directed at anyone suspected of corrupting it, one would expect some kind of agreement about what is correct. There is little to be found; the easy utterance of one educated man is the bane of another. "For all the fussiness about *which* and *that,*" remarks Jacques Barzun in the *Nation,* "the combined editorial brass of the country have feebly allowed the word *disinterested* to be absolutely lost in its original sense. One finds as careful a writer as Aldous Huxley using it to mean uninterested, so that by now a 'disinterested judge' is one that goes to sleep on the bench." And on the subject of what surely is a harmless word, *whom,* Kyle Crichton, associate editor of *Collier's,* is quoted in *Harper's:* "The most loathsome word (to me at least) in the English language is *whom.* You can always tell a half-educated buffoon by the care he takes in working the word in. When he starts it, I know I am faced with a pompous illiterate who is not going to have me long as company."

5 Probably only a cynic would conclude from the abundance of such comments that those who demand correct English do not know it when they meet it; but some students of language must have been led to wonder, for they have made up lists of disputed locutions and polled the literate on them. So far, the only agreement they have reached has to be expressed in statistical terms.

6 The latest of these surveys, a questionnaire containing nineteen disputed expressions, was reported by Norman Lewis in *Harper's Magazine* for March 1949. Lewis sent his list to 750 members of certain groups chosen mainly for their professional interest in the English language: lexicographers, high school and college teachers of English, authors, editors, journalists, radio commentators, and "a random sampling of *Harper's* subscribers."

7 If we count out two groups on the basis of extremely special knowledge and interest—the college professors of English and the lexicographers—we find all the others accepting about half the expressions. The authors and editors (book and magazine) were highest with about 56 per cent, and the editors of women's magazines lowest with about 45. (The expression which was least favored was *less* in the sense of *fewer*—"I encountered *less* difficulties than I had expected"—but even that received an affirmative vote of 23 per cent.) The distinguished electors seem individually to have played hop, skip, and jump down the column, each finding among the nineteen expressions about ten he could approve of. If any two fell on the same ten, it was merely a coincidence.

8 A person innocent in the ways of this controversy, but reasonably well informed about the English language, noticing that the disputants ignore the massive conformity of most writers in most of their language practices, in order to quibble about fringe matters, might assume that they would welcome the cold light of linguistic science. This is a naïve assumption. In response to an attempt of mine to correct some of the misapprehensions I found in Mr. Barzun's article—among them his curious notion that *detached* and not *uninterested* was the original meaning of *disinterested*—he replied by letter that I represented a misplaced and breezy scientism, and that what I said struck him as "the raw material of 'populism' and willful resistance to Mind. . . . All dictionaries to the contrary notwithstanding, the word disinterested is now prevailingly used in the meaning I deprecated. . . . The fact that an illiterate mistake may become the correct form . . . is no reason for not combating it in its beginnings. . . ." This rejection both of the

professional student of language and of the dictionary, when they disagree with the opinions of the writer, has the effect of making each man his own uninhibited authority on language and usage—an effect which I do not believe was exactly what Mr. Barzun had in mind.

9 What he did have in mind he stated clearly in one distinguished paragraph:

> A living culture in one nation (not to speak of one world) must insist on a standard of usage. And usage, as I need not tell you, has important social implications apart from elegance and expressiveness in literature. The work of communication in law, politics and diplomacy, in medicine, technology, and moral speculation depends on the maintenance of a medium of exchange whose values must be kept fixed, as far as possible, like those of any other reliable currency. To prevent debasement and fraud requires vigilance, and it implies the right to blame. It is not snobbery that is involved but literacy on its highest plane, and that literacy has to be protected from ignorance and sloth.

10 [1]It is a pity that these sentiments, so deserving of approval, should receive it from almost all educated people except those who really know something about how language works. [2]One feels like an uncultivated slob when he dissents—one of the low, inelegant, illiterate unthinking mob. [3]Yet as a statement about the English language, or about standard English, it is not merely partly true and partly false but by the consensus of most professional students of language, totally false. [4]It is one of those monstrous errors which gain their original currency by being especially plausible at a suitable time, and maintain themselves long after the circumstances which give rise to them have vanished. [5]Mr. Barzun's remarks are an echo from the eighteenth century; they reek with an odor mustier than the lavender of Grandmother's sachet. [6]They have little relevance to the use of the English language in America in our day.

11 In actual fact, the standard English used by literate Americans is no pale flower being overgrown by the weeds of vulgar usage: it is a strong, flourishing growth. Nor is it a simple, easily describable entity. Indeed, it can scarcely be called an entity at all, except in the loose sense in which we call the whole vast sum of all the dialects of English spoken and written throughout the world a single language. In this sense, standard American English is the sum of the language habits of the millions of educated people in this country. It is rooted in the intellectual life of this great and varied people. Its forms ex-

press what its users wish to express; its words mean what its users think they mean; it is correctly written when it is written by those who write it, and correctly spoken by those who speak it. No prim and self-conscious hoarding of the dead fashions of a superior class gives it its power, but its negligent use by minds intent on stubborn and important problems. There is no point in a tiresome carping about usage; the best thing to do is relax and enjoy it.

12 There are five simple facts about language in general which we must grasp before we can understand a specific language or pass judgment on a particular usage. It is a pity that they are not more widely known in place of the nonsense which now circulates, for they would relieve the native-born speaker of English of his present uncertainty, and give him a proper authority and confidence in his spontaneous employment of his mother tongue. They arise from a common-sense analysis of the nature of language and the conditions of its use.

13 In the first place, language is basically speech. Speech comes first in the life of the individual and of the race. It begins in infancy and continues throughout our lives; we produce and attend to a spoken wordage much greater than the written. Even the mass of writing which floods in upon us today is only the froth on an ocean of speech. In history, also, speech comes first. English has been written for only about fifteen hundred years; before this, it is of incalculable antiquity. In speech its grammar was developed; from changes in the sounds of speech, changes in its grammar come. The educated are inclined to feel that the most important aspect of language is the written form of it, and that the spoken language must and should take its standards from this. Actually, the great flow of influence is from speech to writing. Writing does influence speech somewhat, but its influence is like the interest a bank pays on the principal entrusted to it. No principal, no interest.

14 In the second place, language is personal. It is an experience and a pattern of habits of a very intimate kind. In the home, the family, the school, and the neighborhood we learn the speechways of our community, learning to talk as those close to us talk in the give and take of daily life. We are at one with our nation in our easy command of the pitch, tune, and phrase of our own home town. Language is personal, also, in that our grasp of it is no greater than our individual experience with it. The English we know is not that vast agglomeration of verbal signs which fills and yet escapes the largest lexicons and grammars, but what we have personally heard and spoken, read

and written. The best-read man knows of his native language only a limited number of forms in a limited number of combinations. Outside of these, the wealth which a copious tongue has as its potential is out of his world, and out of everybody's, for no dictionary is so complete or grammar so compendious as to capture it.

15 The third fact about language is that it changes. It changes in its sounds, its meanings, and its syntax. The transmission of sounds, words, and meanings from generation to generation is always in some respects imprecise. Minute differences add up in time to perceptible changes, and changes to noticeable drifts. Difference in changes and in rates of change make local speech sounds, pitches, tones, and vocabularies draw subtly and persistently away from one another. And all it takes to produce an identifiable dialect is sufficient segregation over a sufficient length of time.

16 The fourth great fact about language, then, is that its users are, in one way or another, isolated. Each has with only a few others the sort of familiar relationships which join them in one language community. Yet there are upward of two hundred million native speakers of English in the world. Obviously they cannot all be in close touch with one another. They congeal in nuclei—some stable, some transitory—which by a kind of double action draw them together and enforce isolation of many more or less shifting kinds: the isolation of distance, of education, of economic levels, of occupation, age, and sex, of hobbies and political boundaries. Any one of these will be reflected in language habits; any two or three will bring about, in one community, speech differences as great as those caused by oceans and mountain ranges.

17 The fifth great fact about language is that it is a historical growth of a specific kind. The nature of English is one of the absolutes of our world, like air, water, and gravity. Its patterns are not subject to judgment; they simply are. Yet they have not always been what they are; like the physical world, they have changed with time, but always in terms of what they have been. "Boy loves girl" means something different from "girl loves boy." It is futile for us to prefer another way of conveying these meanings; that is the English way, and we must live with it. Yet students of the language see in this simple pattern the result of a cataclysmic change, great and slow like the geologic upheavals that have brought old salt beds to the very tops of mountain ranges, and as simple. Each is what it is because of what it has been before.

18 Language as a social instrument reflects all the tides which sweep society, reacting in a local or surface way easily and quickly—as a beach changes its contours to suit the waves—but it offers everywhere a stubborn rock core that only time and massive pressures can move. The whim of a girl can change its vocabulary, but no will of man can touch its essential structure; this is work for the long attrition of generations of human use. Ever lagging a little behind human needs, it offers a multitude of terms for the things men no longer care about, but keeps them improvising to say what has not been said before.

19 Spoken English is, then, by its own nature and the nature of man, a welter of divergences. The divergences of class and place are sharpest in Britain, where the same dialects have been spoken in the same shires and villages for more than a thousand years. Although these can be heard in America by any traveler, no matter how dull his ear, they are relatively slight, for our language is essentially and repeatedly a colonial speech. Each of the American colonies drew settlers from various parts of Britain; each worked out a common speech based mainly on the dialect of its most influential group of immigrants (which differed from colony to colony); each remained in relative isolation from the others for about a hundred years. Then many colonists began to move to the interior: wave after wave of settlers traveled along rather distinct lines of advance until the continent was covered. Everywhere there was a mingling of dialects, with a composite speech arising, based mainly on the speech of the dominant local group. And so we have a northern speech fanning out from the northeastern states, a midland speech fanning out from the Mid-Atlantic states, and a southern speech in the land of cotton raisers, all crossing and merging as the pioneers moved west. Local differences are greatest along the Atlantic coast.

20 Wherever our people settled, they worked out local ways of talking about the things of common experience, and found their own verbal symbols of class distinctions. Here and there are areas where foreign-speaking groups clung together and developed special exotically flavored dialects, but otherwise most speech patterns in America can be traced back to the dialects of Britain. Everywhere there is a common speech used by the multitude which works with its hands, and a slightly different dialect spoken by the professional and leisure classes.

21 The standard English written by Americans is not, however, the written form of educated speech, which shows great local variation. Its spellings have only a rough equivalence to the sounds we make; its

grammatical system, which has nationwide and even worldwide currency, had its origin in the educated speech of the northeastern states, and before that in the dialect of London, England. The concentration of schools, colleges, publishing houses, and print shops in early New England and New York had the same effect in this country as the concentration in England, for centuries, of political power, commercial activity, and intellectual life in London: it established a written standard, native only to those who grew up near the Hudson River or east of it. Elsewhere in America this written standard has been a learned class dialect—learned in the schools as the property and distinguishing mark of an educated class. Like many of its spellings, it is itself a relic of the past, an heirloom handed down from the days when the whole nation looked to the schoolmasters of New England for its book learning.

22 The present controversy about usage is simply a sign that times have changed. The several vast and populous regions of this country have grown self-sufficient and self-conscious, and have taken the education of their youth into their own hands. Where the young once had to travel to the East for a respectable education, they receive it now in local public systems of rapid growth and great size. From local schools they may go to local universities of fifteen to fifty thousand students, where they can proceed to the highest degrees. Yale University is overcrowded with some six thousand students; in the community colleges alone of California more than one hundred fifty thousand are enrolled. Most of these young people take their diplomas and go to work among their own people. They form a literate class greater in numbers and in proportion to the total population than the world has ever seen before. Speaking the speech of their region, they mingle naturally and easily with its people. When they write, they write the language they know, and they print it, for the most part, in presses close at hand. Everywhere they speak a standard literate English—but with differences: a regional speech derived from the usages of the early settlers.

23 Standard written English is, after all, an abstraction—a group of forms rather arbitrarily selected from the multitude offered by the language as a whole—an abstraction which serves the peculiar needs of the intellect. It achieves its wide currency because the interests of its users are the common interests of the educated, which transcend frontiers and negate distances—law, literature, science, industry, and commerce. It is the tool of intelligence. Any thinking person must

use it, because only this form of the language provides the instruments of delicate intellectual discrimination. And it is not static. As the needs of the intellect change, standard English changes. Change is its life, as anyone can see who picks up a book written only a little time ago, or examines almost any old newspaper.

24 The common speech of the uneducated, on the other hand, is comparatively static. Though it varies greatly from place to place, it is everywhere conservative; far from corrupting the standard language, it follows slowly after, preserving old forms long ago given up by literate speakers. "Them things" was once standard, and so were "he don't," "giv," and "clumb" and "riz." Its patterns are archaic, its forms homely and local. Only its vocabulary is rich and daring in metaphor (but the best of this is quickly swiped by writers of standard English). Seldom written because its speakers seldom write, it is yet capable of great literary beauties, uncomplicated force, compact suggestion, and moving sentiment. But it will not bear the burden of heavy thinking, and anyhow, heavy thinkers have a better tool to use. It is about as much danger to the standard language as an old house cat.

25 I have often wondered at the fear of common English and its speakers which the cultural aristocracy display, at their curious definition of illiteracy, and at the intemperance of their terms, which verges on the pathological. A Freudian should have a picnic with them. They use such epithets as *illiteracies, crudities, barbarisms, ignorance, carelessness,* and *sloth.* But who is not negligent in language, as in the mechanics of driving a car? They mutter darkly about "inchoate mob feelings." They confess themselves snobs by denying that their attitudes are snobbish. The stridency of their self-assurance puzzles the mind.

26 We might better adjust our minds to the divergences of usage in standard written English, for time, space, and the normal drift of culture have put them there. We need not raise our eyebrows at a different twist of phrase, but enjoy it as an echo of a way of life somewhat different from our own, but just as good. We could do more than enjoy these things; we could recognize that the fixed forms of the language which do not come to our attention were developed in the past. We have come too late for the show. It is the changing forms that evidence the life in our language and in our society; we could learn much about our people and their ways by simply and objectively observing them.

27 If there is one thing which is of the essence of language, it is its drive to adapt. In an expanding culture like ours, which is invading whole new realms of thought and experience, the inherited language is not wholly suited to what we have to say. We need more exact and expressive modes of utterance than we have; we are working toward finer tolerances. The fabric of our language is flexible, and it can meet our needs. Indeed, we cannot stop it from doing so. Therefore it would be well and wholesome for us to see, in the locutions of the educated which bring us up sharply as we read, not evidences of a rising tide of illiteracy (which they are not), but marks of a grand shift in modes of expression, a self-reliant regionalism, and a persistent groping toward finer distinctions and a more precise utterance.

3. The Retort Circumstantial

BY JACQUES BARZUN

1 Mr. Lloyd's article is the culmination of a lively correspondence between him and me, in the course of which I feel sure that I repeatedly cut the ground from under his feet. Since from the outset he hadn't a leg to stand on, my efforts were bound to be useless, but we were both having such a good time that neither of us noticed his plight. At my suggestion he has consented to display his miraculous position in public, and I must therefore return to the charge. The public will judge.

2 It seems clear in the first place that by preaching the attitude of the mere recorder, the *registrar* of linguistic fact, Mr. Lloyd disqualifies himself for remonstrating with me or anybody else. I, as a writer, am his source, his document, his *raison d'être* [reason for being], and he can no more logically quarrel with me than he can with a piece of papyrus. Nevertheless, I am willing to concede his human (and very modern) right to inveigh against my moralism in the tones of an outraged moralist.

3 What then does his objection come to? That in seeking to criticize certain tendencies in current literary English, I am usurping an authority I do not possess, and interfering with the natural evolution of the language. This is the prime fallacy in his case, which rests on

THE RETORT CIRCUMSTANTIAL: from *The American Scholar,* Spring 1951. Reprinted with the permission of *The American Scholar* and the author.

a chain of reasoning somewhat as follows: English has greatly changed through the ages; many of these changes were resisted by purists; but the evolution was irresistible, and the result is something we now consider correct and natural. Hence Mr. Barzun's attitude is *contra naturam* [against nature]; he is an old fogey, a snob, and an ignoramus who thinks he can set his face against the future only because he is blind to the past.

4 The truth is, of course, that one does not obtain "nature" by merely removing opposition, wise or unwise. Nor can we know what is inevitable until we have tried good and hard to stop it. The whole analogy with nature is false because language is an artificial product of social life, all of whose manifestations, even when regular, bear only a remote likeness to the course of nature. Being a social product, language is everybody's football, and that is precisely what gives me, as well as Mr. Lloyd, the right to push it this way or that by argument.

5 And here it is important to remember that resistance to change is by no means futile. The history of the language is not what the gallant liberals make out—a struggle between the dauntless Genius of English and a few misguided conservatives. It is a free-for-all. At this point it is usual for the advocates of the "hands off" policy to trot out the word *mob,* which Swift attacked with several other curtailed forms, and pretend that it was ridiculous of the Dean to boggle at it, "in the light of what came after." Well, what came after is that we deodorized *mob,* and abandoned altogether the other vulgarities he was deprecating: we no longer use *rep, pozz, phiz, hipps,* or *plenipo.* The future, in short, belonged as much to Dean Swift as to his opponents—and rather more if we count the hits and misses.

6 So much for the pseudo-naturalism of the linguistic registrars. Their vow not to judge among words and usages is a fine thing as long as it expresses a becoming sense of incapacity, but it must not turn into a union rule enforceable on those who have taken precisely opposite vows—namely to exploit, preserve, and possibly enrich the language. This is the duty of the writer, it calls for judgment, and it brings us to that blessed word *disinterested,* which seems to have acted on Mr. Lloyd like a whiff of mustard to the nose.

7 My simple and meritorious deed as regards *disinterested* was to draw attention to its widespread misuse as a duplicate of *un*interested. Examples abound, and the fight against the plague may already be lost without the confusion being anything like over. Every piece of printed matter exhibits it, and nearly every conversation. Just the other day

I heard this sentence, spoken to identify a stranger: "He is an impresario, but when it comes to art, he's completely disinterested." Did the speaker mean X has no interest in art? Or: he is so much interested in it that money is no object? According to current usage this is impossible to determine without questioning the speaker. Not even his presumed degree of education will settle the matter, for the wrong use has affected all ranks.

8 At the phrase "wrong use," Mr. Lloyd twitched his nonexistent leg, and with his hands made the motions of a man taking to earth in a dictionary. A few American, and especially collegiate, dictionaries do give the meaning "uninterested" as a second choice—which is a sufficient reason for me to view with a lackluster eye Mr. Lloyd's naïve faith in lexicographers. The one work that seems relevant to the argument is the *O.E.D.* [*Oxford English Dictionary*], which gives us the history of the word. It tells us that the meaning *un*interested is obsolete, and it lists five separate earlier forms, going back to the French of Montaigne, all connected with the idea of "removing the self interest of a person in a thing." As an English adjective, examples are given from 1659 to Dr. Livingstone in 1865, with the meaning: "not influenced by interest, impartial, unbiased, unprejudiced." My original remark was to the effect that nowadays the "disinterested judge" is probably taken to mean one who sleeps on the bench. My final remark is: As a writer concerned with the precision and flexibility of the language I use, I cannot regard the return to an obsolete and ambiguous form as useful or in any other way justified.

9 I now carry the war into the enemy's camp. If instead of complacently taking notes on the growing confusion, and protecting under pretext of "science" the vagaries of modern usage, Mr. Lloyd and his compeers would reflect upon their data, they might be able to safeguard the complex instrument of our speech by telling us when and why these deplorable losses occur, and how they might be repaired— loss of clarity and exactness at large, absolute loss of meaning in a word such as *disinterested* and in another such as *connive.* Everyone has seen this last used as a synonym for *conspire* and *contrive;* I have heard it in the intransitive sense of *manage* about some trivial business: "How did you connive?" Hitherto, when you escaped from the concentration camp because the guard deliberately looked the other way, it was he who *connived* at your escape, no one else. Can it be that the action is obsolete and we no longer need the word?

10 These instances are not isolated, and I shall accept statistical refu-

tation only from someone who can show that he reads each year more
written matter than I, and hears a greater variety of local uses from
a larger body of students.

11 Meantime, the generality which I hazarded, and which Mr.
Lloyd assails as undemocratic and tainted with ethical feeling, is that
with the rapid extension of educational opportunities, many persons
of otherwise simple hearts are snatching at words half understood in
order to bedeck their thoughts. Only the other day I read in a "literary" review about a distinguished American critic who was so full
of insight that he could be called a *voyeur* [a peeping Tom]. The
writer meant *voyant* [a see-er], if anything, but he could certainly be
sued for slander before an educated court.

12 Foreign words are always treacherous, but what of the newspaper
editorial which states that Mr. So-and-so's election is "highly fortuitous" (meaning "fortunate"), or the college dean who tells parents
that his institution gives the students "a fulsome education"? Then
there are those who believe that "to a degree" means "to a certain extent," instead of just the opposite. Have not the oil and drug companies been forced to change their labels to "flammable" because
many users of their products took *"in*flammable" to mean *noncom-
bustible?* At that stage, the issue ceases to be comic or inconsequential.
With the tremendous output of verbiage by air and print to which
we are all subjected, the corruption of meaning is rapid and extensive.
We are at the mercy of anyone who thinks the sense of a word is discoverable by inspection, and whose misuse consequently liberates an
echoing error in the minds of his peers.

13 To put it differently, the danger to English today is not from bad
grammar, dialect, vulgar forms, or native crudity, but from misused
ornaments three syllables long. The enemy is not illiteracy but incomplete literacy—and since this implies pretension it justifies reproof.
There is no defense against the depredations of the brash except vigilance and no quarter given. I am certain that in this regard Mr.
Lloyd, who writes with so much felicity and force, does exactly this
in his capacity as a college teacher of English. Why then does he not
square his precepts with his practice? I cannot answer for him, but
to help his amputated philosophy to its feet, I want by way of conclusion to quote from a writer who, being anonymous and attached to
both journalism and business, can hardly be suspected of flaunting
pedantry and preciosity. The extract is from *Fortune* for November
1950:

"Language is not something we can disembody; it is an ethical as well as a mechanical entity, inextricably bound up in ourselves, our positions, and our relations with those about us."

Comment

The point at issue in this entertaining dispute is whether or not current literary usage is the inevitable product of historical change (Mr. Lloyd's position) or the temporary victory of semiliterates pretending to intelligence (Mr. Barzun's position).

'Mr. Lloyd for his part attempts to win our assent to his belief that there is no correct standard English. Deductively he argues: All written English is based on speech; but speech is personal, changing, divergent, and ever growing by the determination of its own laws. Therefore written English must also be personal, changing, divergent, and subject to these same laws.

Opponents of this necessary change in usage are characterized as "snobs" who follow outworn theories. Mr. Lloyd attacks Mr. Barzun's general position (¶9 and 10) and his specific interpretation of the meaning of *disinterested* (¶4 and 8) as evidences of monstrous error. Furthermore, he maintains that the snobs cannot agree even among themselves as to what is correct usage (indirect refutation). Their intemperance, Mr. Lloyd maintains, is almost pathological. Actually, current literary usage is seen as the essential drive of language to adapt to the needs of society. "Therefore it would be well and wholesome for us to see, in the locutions of the educated which bring us up sharply as we read, not evidences of a rising tide of illiteracy (which they are not), but marks of a grand shift in modes of expression, a self-reliant regionalism, and a persistent groping toward finer distinctions and more precise utterance."

Mr. Barzun, on the other hand, accuses Mr. Lloyd of inconsistency and fallacious reasoning. The inconsistency flows from the fact that, by virtue of his opponent's own theory of the rules of language, Mr. Lloyd must accept Mr. Barzun's attitude as one of the necessary features of social and therefore verbal change. If we are all bound by iron rules, the argument goes, then Mr. Barzun is bound by them, too, and Mr. Lloyd cannot logically object to Mr. Barzun. A further inconsistency is seen in Mr. Lloyd's intemperate denunciation of the snobs' intemperance, and the clash between Mr. Lloyd's practice and precept.

Mr. Barzun then points out that Mr. Lloyd's argument is based on a false analogy. Language, an artificial product of man's mind, cannot be compared with nature, whose processes develop without man's wish, consent, or cooperation. The two things are not in the same class (see Section V B).

Mr. Barzun argues further that resistance to change is not futile. Linguistic convention is established by a struggle between vulgarity and good sense, as history has repeatedly shown.

Mr. Barzun then restates his own general standard—the direct contrary of Mr. Lloyd's—namely that there is a correct standard of speech and writing and that it is the duty of the writer "to exploit, preserve, and possibly to enrich the language" by judging among words and usages. Arguing deductively from this general standard, he offers proof that current usage indicates sloppy thinking by analyzing Mr. Lloyd's sense of the word *disinterested*. Confused use of the word *connive*, the mistaken use of *voyeur* for *voyant*, *fortuitous* for *fortunate*, and of *inflammable* for a nonexistent *unflammable* are further illustrations of sloppy thinking. The position of the "slobs" is described not as illiteracy (as Mr. Lloyd defined it in paragraph 3 of his essay), but as incomplete literacy, which, since it implies pretension, justifies reproof. Thus both men are arguing from two different general truths.

One important question for the reader to decide is which standard is right. If both standards are right then there is no debate. This you will be asked to decide after a careful analysis of both sides of the question. A specific question on this point is asked in Exercise 5i below.

Analysis and Composition

1. Decide, in a paragraph of 300 words, whether Mr. Lloyd has stated Mr. Barzun's position fairly.
2. Decide, in a paragraph of 300 words, whether Mr. Barzun has stated Mr. Lloyd's view fairly.
3. Direct refutation answers an opponent's objection
   a. By denying it and *proving* the opposite
   b. By distinguishing several meanings in the statement and showing that the true meaning does not support the opponent's case
   c. By retorting the argument, that is, by using an opponent's argument to support your own statement

Brief examples * of these methods are:
a. Denial
   (1) of fact:
   > *Statement:* Lincoln was President in 1866.
   > *Refutation:* He was not President in 1866 because the **record** shows he died in 1865.

* Note: These examples merely state. Effective denial, distinction, and retort are accompanied by proof, as we have demonstrated in Example A1 of this section.

(2) of proof:

    Statement: Literature isn't worthy of study because it doesn't help you get a job.

    Refutation: The proof is not convincing. The study of literature may help you get a certain kind of job. Furthermore, even if it were convincing, the proof would be irrelevant because the study of literature is not a vocational subject but a liberal one.

(3) of inference:

    Statement: The United Nations is not a guarantee of peace because it has not succeeded in restraining Russia. Therefore we should withdraw from the United Nations.

    Refutation: The statement and proof are correct, but the inference does not follow. Rather we should try to strengthen the United Nations.

b. *Distinction*

    Statement: We should not attempt to win over the nations behind the Iron Curtain because we would thereby interfere with the rights of nations to do as they please.

    Refutation (distinction): A nation has the right to do as it pleases provided it acts according to the principles of justice and liberty, not if it chooses to disregard justice and liberty. The nations behind the Iron Curtain have disregarded justice and liberty.

c. *Retort*

    Statement: The United States by interfering in Korea has provoked war (argument urged by a Russian).

    Refutation: The communists by interfering in Korea have provoked war (retort urged by an American).

In the light of these definitions answer the following questions in an expository essay of about 600 words.

a. Show how Mr. Lloyd uses the methods of denial in his refutation of Mr. Barzun. (See especially ¶10, Ss 3-4.)

b. Show how Mr. Lloyd uses the method of distinction in his refutation of Mr. Barzun. (See especially ¶21.)

c. Show how Mr. Barzun uses denial and a retort in his refutation of Mr. Lloyd. (Note Mr. Barzun's title. See especially ¶9.)

4. Indirect refutation consists of

a. An attack upon the opponent rather than upon his objection. An example of this first type of indirect refutation is, "Do not believe *A*'s attack upon our school system because *A* is a professional anti-progressive." (Note: Abuse of this device may lead to the fallacy of ignoring the question. See Exercise 5 below.)

b. An attack upon an opponent's faulty method of argument, such as an exaggeration or an inconsistency, rather than upon the substance of the argument. An example of this second type of indirect refutation is, "Do not believe *A*'s attack upon our school system because *A*'s arguments are contradictory; in one place he says the state has a right to direct education, in another that the state has no right to legislate what the local school boards can do."

Find several examples of each type of indirect refutation in the two essays under discussion. Decide whether these refutations are effective in winning your assent to the writer's belief.

5. A common device of refutation is to point out the fallacies in an opponent's argument. A fallacy is a statement or series of statements that have the form but not the substance of truth. A fallacy is a faulty method of analysis or inference. For every correct method of exposition or reasoning there is a corresponding fallacy. Thus the basic methods of analysis—definition, classification, examples, comparison, causal analysis, and process analysis—are subject to misuse or manipulation, as we have shown in the exercises in Sections II-VII.

Hence we have the false definition as opposed to the true definition, as in the following shifting use of the word *environment:* "I am against strikes because it is a psychological law that we must adjust to our environment. Why can't the strikers adjust themselves to their environment?"

In the first sentence *environment* refers to conditions of nature, in the second to man-made conditions.

So too are there false classifications or generalizations (see pp. 85-86, 108-09), inexact examples (see pp. 152-53), false causes (see pp. 199, 234-35), false comparisons or analogies (see pp. 156-57, 168-69, 190-91), and a faulty process of induction or deduction (see pp. 258-60).

Other fallacies are

1. Begging the question
2. Ignoring the question

To beg the question is to confuse statement with proof. Thus to say that James Jones is a great author because he possesses all the elements of great writing is to beg the question by stating as proof what remains to be proved. The questions to be proved are

1. What are the qualities of great writing?
2. Does James Jones have these qualities?

You must *prove* what the elements of great writing are and then show that James Jones possesses them.

The fallacy of begging the question also includes the false assumption, that is, the use of a mere supposition as a fact. Thus if you say, "He is an officer and therefore a gentleman," or "He is a scholar and therefore removed from reality," you are assuming that an officer is always a gentleman and that a scholar is always removed from reality. Both assumptions are quite unprovable. Another form of this fallacy is the "many questions" error. A question like, "When will you cease your criminal activities?" contains several elements:

1. The assumption that the person addressed has engaged in criminal activities
2. That he is currently engaged in these activities

To ignore the question (also called dodging the issue) is to introduce arguments which are not directly relevant to the question. For example, suppose you are attempting to answer Viscount Bryce's argument that American uniformity is unpleasant (Example A4). If instead of answering Viscount Bryce's arguments you said, "Oh, well, what can you expect of an English aristocrat?" or "Let us talk about American vigor and fair play," you would be ignoring the question. In a sense, ignoring the question is an offense against the basic rule of unity because it introduces an argument that has no direct relevance to the central theme or proposition.

Both Mr. Lloyd and Mr. Barzun develop their arguments by attempting to point out the fallacies in their opponent's arguments, as well as by presenting direct and indirect proof. Examine the following comments carefully and state whether you agree or disagree with each comment. Give reasons for your answer. Comments a–e apply to Mr. Lloyd's essay:

a. In paragraph 2 of "Snobs, Slobs, and the English Language" Mr. Lloyd accuses the precisionists of maintaining false assumptions.

b. In paragraph 3 Mr. Lloyd accuses his opponents of dodging the real issue by talking of illiteracy instead of talking about change.

c. In paragraphs 4-7 Mr. Lloyd accuses his opponents of the fallacy of faulty exemplification; i.e., of advancing facts that do not prove the case, or facts that are inconsistent.

d. In paragraph 10 Mr. Lloyd again accuses Mr. Barzun of dodging the question and of bringing up irrelevant issues.

e. In paragraph 11 Mr. Lloyd implies that his opponents have incorrectly *classified* standard English.

Comments f–j apply to Mr. Barzun's essay:

f. In paragraphs 3, 4, and 5 Mr. Barzun accuses his opponent of using a false analogy.

g. In paragraph 6 Mr. Barzun accuses his opponent of raising a false issue, or dodging the question.

h. In paragraphs 7 and 8 Mr. Barzun accuses his opponent of an error of fact.

i. In paragraph 9 Mr. Barzun accuses his opponent of dodging the main question by proving that language has grown confused instead of showing when and why language has grown confused.

j. In paragraph 13 Mr. Barzun accuses his opponent of the fallacy of false cause; i.e., he asserts that his opponent ascribes illiteracy to a linguistic law rather than to the ignorance of the speakers and writers.

6. Mr. Barzun appeals to the public to judge the merits of his dispute with Mr. Lloyd. Render your verdict in this case by deciding for or against Mr. Barzun in an essay of approximately 1000 words. In forming your opinion consider the following questions.

a. Which writer has more precisely stated the issue under dispute?

b. Which writer has convinced you by the logic of his demonstration?

c. Which writer has successfully refuted the other?

d. Which writer has the clearer, more vigorous, and more pleasing style?

7. The following excerpts contain at least one of the fallacies discussed in Exercise 5. Select one of these excerpts as the basis for a short refutation of about 500 words. Be sure to name the fallacy.

a. Mr. Belcanto has been accused of failing to pay a debt of $1000 to Herr Vogelsong, his music teacher. As his attorney I protest this indictment. Who charges him with this crime? The very man whose ability as a teacher is under dispute. I claim that Herr Vogelsong is a fraud and an impostor. Furthermore, it is heartless to expect Mr. Belcanto, who has been unemployed, to pay $1000 at this time.

b. The development of higher education in this country is a mixed blessing, perhaps not a blessing at all. It has destroyed the incentive to real learning by satisfying the intellectual appetite with mere information. Washington never went to college, and neither did Jackson nor Lincoln. Ben Franklin, Thomas Edison, Henry Ford never went to college. Yet these men, and thousands of other self-made men, made America great. More than colleges and universities we need men with brains and ambition.

c. If democracy is a good thing in politics, surely it is a good thing in the classroom. In the Middle Ages students of Bologna frequently elected their own professors—and fired them when they didn't teach effectively. In Paris teachers had the same status as medical doctors have today. They had licenses to teach. They hung out their shingles and waited for students. If they were good the students flocked to their lectures. If not, the teachers moved away, to become masters in boys' schools or tutors in rich families. Students today should return to this democratic way of life, from grammar school on up to the university.

d. Our country depends upon the two-party system. If we don't have strong parties we won't have a strong government. Therefore I appeal to all good Democrats to vote the straight Democratic ticket. Be a good party man and help make democracy live.

e. What has happened before will happen again. Every time this nation has opened its gates to foreigners we have been flooded with strange un-American ideas. Immigration causes higher taxes, overpopulation, entanglement in foreign affairs, crime, social instability, and the total ruin of the American way of life. And by the American way of life I mean the way honest God-fearing Americans have always lived, a life of peace, progress, and prosperity unmatched in any nation in the world.

Proposition: The American character is marked by an unpleasant uniformity.

4. *Affirmative:* Viscount Bryce, "The Uniformity of American Life"

5. *Negative:* Peter Drucker, "The Myth of American Uniformity"

4. The Uniformity of American Life

BY JAMES BRYCE

1 To the pleasantness of American life there is one, and only one, serious drawback—its uniformity. Those who have been struck by the size of America, and by what they have heard of its restless excitement, may be surprised at the word. They would have guessed that an unquiet changefulness and turmoil were the disagreeables to be feared. But uniformity, which the European visitor begins to note when he has travelled for a month or two, is the feature of the country which Englishmen who have lived long there, and Americans who are familiar with Europe, most frequently revert to when asked to say what is the "crook in their lot."

2 It is felt in many ways. I will name a few.

3 It is felt in the aspects of Nature. All the natural features of the United States are on a larger scale than those of Europe. The four

great mountain chains are each of them longer than the Alps. Of the gigantic rivers and of those inland seas we call the Great Lakes one need not speak. The center of the continent is occupied by a plain larger than the western half of Europe. In the Mississippi valley, from the Gulf of Mexico to Lake Superior, there is nothing deserving to be called a hill, though, as one moves westward from the great river, long soft undulations in the great prairie begin to appear. Through vast stretches of country one finds the same physical character maintained with little change—the same strata, the same vegetation, a generally similar climate. From the point where you leave the Alleghenies at Pittsburgh, until, after crossing the Missouri, you approach the still untilled prairie of the West, a railway run of some thousand miles, there is a uniformity of landscape greater than could be found along any one hundred miles of railway run in western Europe. Everywhere the same nearly flat country, over which you cannot see far, because you are little raised above it, the same fields and crops, the same rough wooden fences, the same thickets of the same bushes along the stream edges, with here and there a bit of old forest; the same solitary farmhouses and straggling wood-built villages. And when one has passed beyond the fields and farmhouses, there is an even more unvaried stretch of slightly rolling prairie, smooth and bare, till after five hundred miles the blue line of the Rocky Mountains rises upon the western horizon.

4 There are some extraordinary natural phenomena, such as Niagara, the Yellowstone geysers, and the great canyon of the Colorado River, which Europe cannot equal. But taking the country as a whole, and remembering that it is a continent, it is not more rich in picturesque beauty than the much smaller western half of Europe. There is a good deal of pretty scenery and a few really romantic spots in the long Allegheny range, but hardly anything so charming as the best bits of Scotland or southern Ireland, or the English lakes. The Rocky Mountains are pierced by some splendid gorges, such as the famous canyon of the Arkansas River above South Pueblo, and show some very grand prospects, such as that over the Great Salt Lake from the Mormon capital. But neither the Rocky Mountains, with their dependent ranges, nor the Sierra Nevada can be compared for variety of grandeur and beauty with the Alps; for although each chain nearly equals the Alps in height, and covers a greater area, they have little snow, no glaciers, and a singular uniformity of character. One finds, I think, less variety in the whole chain of the Rockies than in the comparatively

short Pyrenees. There are indeed in the whole United States very few quite first-rate pieces of mountain scenery rivalling the best of the Old World. The most impressive are, I think, two or three of the deep valleys of the Sierra Nevada (of which the Yosemite is the best known), and the superb line of extinct volcanoes, bearing snowfields and glaciers, which one sees, rising out of vast and somber forests, from the banks of the Columbia River and the shores of Puget Sound. So the Atlantic coast, though there are pretty bits between Newport and the New Brunswick frontier, cannot vie with the coasts of Scotland, Ireland, or Norway; while southward from New York to Florida it is everywhere flat and generally dreary. In the United States people take journeys proportionate to the size of the country. A family thinks nothing of going twelve hundred miles, from St. Louis to Cape May (near Philadelphia), for a seaside holiday. But even journeys of twelve hundred miles do not give an American so much change of scene and variety of surroundings as a Parisian has when he goes to Nice, or a Berliner to Berchtesgaden. The man who lives in the section of America which seems destined to contain the largest population, I mean the states on the upper Mississippi, lives in the midst of a plain wider than the plains of Russia, and must travel hundreds of miles to escape from its monotony.

5 When we turn from the aspects of Nature to the cities of men, the uniformity is even more remarkable. With five or six exceptions to be mentioned presently, American cities differ from one another only herein that some of them are built more with brick than with wood, and others more with wood than with brick. In all else they are alike, both great and small. In all the same wide streets, crossing at right angles, ill-paved, but planted along the sidewalks with maple trees whose autumnal scarlet surpasses the brilliance of any European foliage. In all the same shops, arranged on the same plan, the same Chinese laundries, with Li Kow visible through the window, the same ice cream stores, the same large hotels with seedy men hovering about in the dreary entrance hall, the same streetcars passing to and fro with passengers clinging to the doorstep, the same locomotives ringing their great bells as they clank slowly down the middle of the street. I admit that in external aspect there is a sad monotony in the larger towns of England also. Compare English cities with Italian cities, and most of the former seem like one another, incapable of being, so to speak, individualized as you individualize a man with a definite character and aspect unlike that of other men. Take the Lan-

cashire towns, for instance, large and prosperous places. You cannot individualize Bolton or Wigan, Oldham or Bury, except by trying to remember that Bury is slightly less rough than Oldham, and Wigan a thought more grimy than Bolton. But in Italy every city has its character, its memories, its life and achievements wrought into the pillars of its churches and the towers that stand along its ramparts. Siena is not like Perugia, nor Perugia like Orvieto; Ravenna, Rimini, Pesaro, Fano, Ancona, Osimo, standing along the same coast within seventy miles of one another, have each of them a character, a sentiment, what one may call an idiosyncrasy, which comes vividly back to us at the mention of its name. Now, what English towns are to Italian, that American towns are to English. They are in some ways pleasanter; they are cleaner; there is less poverty, less squalor, less darkness. But their monotony haunts one like a nightmare. Even the irksomeness of finding the streets named by numbers becomes insufferable. It is doubtless convenient to know by the number how far up the city the particular street is. But you cannot give any sort of character to Twenty-ninth Street, for the name refuses to lend itself to any association. There is something wearisomely hard and bare in such a system.

6 I return joyfully to the exceptions. Boston has a character of her own, with her beautiful Common, her smooth environing waters, her Beacon Hill crowned by the gilded dome of the State House, and Bunker Hill, bearing the monument of the famous fight. New York, besides a magnificent position, has in the grandeur of the buildings and the tremendous rush of men and vehicles along the streets as much the air of a great capital as London itself. Chicago, with her enormous size and the splendid warehouses that line her endless thoroughfares, leaves a strong though not wholly agreeable impression. Richmond has a quaint old-world look which dwells in the memory: few cities have a sea front equal in beauty to the lake front of Cleveland. Washington, with its wide and beautifully graded avenues, and the glittering white of the stately Capitol, has become within the last twenty years a singularly handsome city. And New Orleans—or rather the Creole quarter of New Orleans, for the rest of the city is commonplace—is delicious, suggesting old France and Spain, yet a France and Spain strangely transmuted in this new clime. I have seen nothing in America more picturesque than the Rue Royale, with its houses of all heights, often built round a courtyard, where a magnolia or an orange tree stands in the middle, and wooden external staircases lead

up to wooden galleries, the house fronts painted of all colors, and carrying double rows of balconies decorated with pretty ironwork, the whole standing languid and still in the warm soft air, and touched with the subtle fragrance of decay. Here in New Orleans the streets and public buildings, and specially the old City Hall, with the arms of Spain still upon it, speak of history. One feels, in stepping across Canal Street from the Creole quarter to the business parts of the town, that one steps from an old nationality to a new one, that this city must have had vicissitudes, that it represents something, and that something one of the great events of history, the surrender of the northern half of the New World by the Romano-Celtic races to the Teutonic. Quebec, and to a less degree Montreal, fifteen hundred miles away, tell the same tale: Santa Fé in New Mexico repeats it.

7 It is the absence in nearly all the American cities of anything that speaks of the past that makes their external aspect so unsuggestive. In pacing their busy streets and admiring their handsome city halls and churches, one's heart sinks at the feeling that nothing historically interesting ever has happened here, perhaps ever will happen. In many an English town, however ugly with its smoke and its new suburbs, one sees at least an ancient church, one can discover some fragments of a castle or a city wall. Even Wigan and Northampton have ancient churches, though Northampton lately allowed the North-Western Railway to destroy the last traces of the castle where Henry II issued his assize. But in America hardly any public building is associated with anything more interesting than a big party convention; and nowadays even the big conventions are held in temporary structures, whose materials are sold when the politicians have dispersed. Nowhere, perhaps, does this sense of the absolute novelty of all things strike one so strongly as in San Francisco. Few cities in the world can vie with her either in the beauty or in the natural advantages of her situation; indeed, there are only two places in Europe—Constantinople and Gibraltar—that combine an equally perfect landscape with what may be called an equally imperial position. Before you there is the magnificent bay, with its far-stretching arms and rocky isles, and beyond it the faint line of the Sierra Nevada, cutting the clear air like mother-of-pearl; behind there is the roll of the ocean; to the left, the majestic gateway between mountains through which ships bear in commerce from the farthest shores of the Pacific; to the right, valleys rich with corn and wine, sweeping away to the southern horizon. The city itself is full of bold hills, rising steeply from the

deep water. The air is keen, dry, and bright, like the air of Greece, and the waters not less blue. Perhaps it is this air and light, recalling the cities of the Mediterranean, that make one involuntarily look up to the top of these hills for the feudal castle, or the ruins of the Acropolis, which one thinks must crown them. I found myself so looking all the time I remained in the city. But on none of these heights is there anything more interesting, anything more vocal to the student of the past, than the sumptuous villas of the magnates of the Central Pacific Railway, who have chosen a hilltop to display their wealth to the city, but have erected houses like all other houses, only larger. San Francisco has had a good deal of history in her forty years of life; but this history does not, like that of Greece or Italy, write itself in stone, or even in wood. . . .

8 Everywhere the same system of state governments, everywhere the same municipal governments, and almost uniformly bad or good in proportion to the greater or smaller population of the city; the same party machinery organized on the same methods, "run" by the same wirepullers and "workers." In rural local government there are some diversities in the names, areas, and functions of the different bodies, yet differences slight in comparison with the points of likeness. The schools are practically identical in organization, in the subjects taught, in the methods of teaching, though the administration of them is as completely decentralized as can be imagined, even the state commissioner having no right to do more than suggest or report. So it is with the charitable institutions, with the libraries, the lecture courses, the public amusements. All these are more abundant and better of their kind in the richer and more cultivated parts of the country, generally better in the north Atlantic than in the inland states, and in the West than in the South. But they are the same in type everywhere. It is the same with social habits and usages. There are still some differences between the South and the North; and in the eastern cities the upper class is more Europeanized in its code of etiquette and its ways of daily life. But even these variations tend to disappear. Eastern customs begin to permeate the West, beginning with the richer families; the South is more like the North than it was before the war. Travel where you will, you feel that what you have found in one place that you will find in another. The thing which hath been, will be; you can no more escape from it than you can quit the land to live in the sea.

9 Last of all we come to man himself—to man and to woman, not less important than man. The ideas of men and women, their funda-

mental beliefs and their superficial tastes, their methods of thinking and their fashions of talking, are what most concern their fellow men; and, if there be variety and freshness in these, the uniformity of nature and the monotony of cities signify but little. If I observe that in these respects also the similarity of type over the country is surprising, I shall be asked whether I am not making the old mistake of the man who fancied all Chinese were like one another, because, noticing the dress and the pigtail, he did not notice minor differences of feature. A scholar is apt to think that all business men write the same hand, and a business man thinks the same of all scholars. Perhaps Americans think all Englishmen alike. And I may also be asked with whom I am comparing the Americans. With Europe as a whole? If so, is it not absurd to expect that the differences between different sections in one people should be as marked as those between different peoples? The United States are larger than Europe, but Europe has many races and many languages, among whom contrasts far broader must be expected than between one people, even if it stretches over a continent.

10 It is most clearly not with Europe, but with each of the leading European peoples that we must compare the people of America. So comparing them with the people of Britain, France, Germany, Italy, Spain, one discovers more varieties between individuals in these European peoples than one finds in America. Scotchmen and Irishmen are more unlike Englishmen, the native of Normandy more unlike the native of Provence, the Pomeranian more unlike the Württemberger, the Piedmontese more unlike the Neapolitan, the Basque more unlike the Andalusian, than the American from any part of the country is unlike the American from any other. Differences of course there are between the human type as developed in different regions of the country—differences moral and intellectual as well as physical. You can generally tell a Southerner by his look as well as by his speech. A native of Maine will probably differ from a native of Kentucky, a Georgian from an Oregonian. But these differences strike even an American observer, much as the difference between a Yorkshireman and a Lancastrian strikes the English, and is slighter than the contrast between a middle-class southern Englishman and a middle-class Scotchman, slighter than the differences between a peasant from Northumberland and a peasant from Dorsetshire. Or, to take another way of putting it: If at some great gathering at a political party from all parts of the United Kingdom you were to go round and talk to, say, one hundred, taken at random, of the persons present, you would

be struck by more diversity between the notions and the tastes and mental habits of the individuals comprising that one hundred than if you tried the same experiment with a hundred Americans of the same education and position, similarly gathered in a convention from every state in the Union.

11 I do not in the least mean that people are more commonplace in America than in England, or that the Americans are less ideal than the English. Neither of these statements would be true. On the contrary, the average American is more alive to new ideas, more easily touched through his imagination or his emotions, than the average Englishman or Frenchman. I mean only that the native-born Americans appear to vary less, in fundamentals, from what may be called the dominant American type than Englishmen, Germans, Frenchmen, Spaniards, or Italians do from any type which could be taken as the dominant type in any of those nations. Or, to put the same thing differently, it is rather more difficult to take any assemblage of attributes in any of these European countries and call it the national type than it is to do the like in the United States.

12 These are not given as the impressions of a traveller. Such impressions, being necessarily hasty, and founded on a comparatively narrow observation, would deserve little confidence. They sum up the conclusions of Europeans long resident in America, and familiar with different parts of the country. They are, I think, admitted by the most acute Americans themselves. I have often heard the latter dilate on what seems to them the one crowning merit of life in Europe—the variety it affords, the opportunities it gives of easy and complete changes of scene and environment. The pleasure which an American finds in crossing the Atlantic, a pleasure more intense than any which the European enjoys, is that of passing from a land of happy monotony into regions where everything is redolent with memories of the past, and derives from the past no less than from the present a wealth and a subtle complexity of interest which no new country can possess.

13 Life in America is in most ways pleasanter, easier, simpler than in Europe; it floats in a sense of happiness like that of a radiant summer morning. But life in any of the great European centers is capable of an intensity, a richness blended of many elements, which has not yet been reached in America. There are more problems in Europe calling for solution; there is more passion in the struggles that rage round them; the past more frequently kindles the present with a glow of imaginative light. In whichever country of Europe one dwells,

one feels that the other countries are near, that the fortunes of their peoples are bound up with the fortunes of one's own, that ideas are shooting to and fro between them. The web of history woven day by day all over Europe is vast and of many colors: it is fateful to every European. But in America it is only the philosopher who can feel that it will ultimately be fateful to Americans also; to the ordinary man the Old World seems far off, severed by a dissociating ocean, its mighty burden with little meaning for him.

14 Those who have observed the uniformity I have been attempting to describe have commonly set it down, as Europeans do most American phenomena, to what they call democracy. Democratic government has in reality not much to do with it, except insofar as such a government helps to induce that deference of individuals to the mass which strengthens a dominant type, whether of ideas, of institutions, or of manners. More must be ascribed to the equality of material conditions, still more general than in Europe, to the fact that nearly everyone is engaged either in agriculture, or in commerce, or in some handicraft, to the extraordinary mobility of the population, which in migrating from one part of the country to another brings the characteristics of each part into the others, to the diffusion of education, to the cheapness of literature and the universal habit of reading, which enable everyone to know what everyone else is thinking, but above all to the newness of the country, and the fact that four-fifths of it has been made all at a stroke, and therefore all of a piece, as compared with the slow growth by which European countries have developed. Newness is the cause of uniformity, not merely in the external aspect of cities, villages, farmhouses, but in other things also, for the institutions and social habits which belonged a century ago to a group of small communities on the Atlantic coast have been suddenly extended over an immense area, each band of settlers naturally seeking to retain its customs, and to plant in the new soil shoots from which trees like those of the old home might spring up. The variety of European countries is due not only to the fact that their race elements have not yet become thoroughly commingled, but also that many old institutions have survived among the new ones; as in a city that grows but slowly, old buildings are not cleared away to make room for others more suited to modern commerce, but are allowed to stand, sometimes empty and unused, sometimes half adapted to new purposes. This scarcely happens in America. Doubtless many American institutions are old, and were old before they were carried across the Atlantic.

But they have generally received a new dress, which, in adapting them to the needs of today, conceals their ancient character; and the form in which they have been diffused or reproduced in the different states of the Union is in all those states practically identical.

15 In each of the great European countries the diversity of primeval and medieval times, when endless varieties of race, speech, and faith existed within the space of a few hundred miles, has been more or less preserved by segregative influences. In America a small race, of the same speech and faith, has spread itself out over an immense area, and has been strong enough to impose its own type, not only on the Dutch and other early settlers of the middle states, but on the immigrant masses which the last forty years have brought.

16 May one, then, expect that, when novelty has worn off, and America counts her life by centuries instead of decades, variety will develop itself, and such complexities, or diversities, or incongruities (whichever one is to call them) as European countries present be deeper and more numerous?

17 As regards the outside of things this seems unlikely. Many of the small towns of today will grow into large towns, a few of the large towns into great cities, but as they grow they will not become less like one another. There will be larger theatres and hotels, more churches (in spite of secularist lecturers) and handsomer ones; but what is to make the theatres and churches of one city differ from those of another? Fashion and the immense facilities of intercourse tend to wear down even such diversities in the style of building or furnishing, or in modes of locomotion, or in amusements and forms of social intercourse, as now exist.

18 As regards ideas and the inner life of men, the question is a more difficult one. At present there are only two parts of the country where one looks to meet with the well-marked individualities I refer to. One of these is New England, where the spirit of Puritanism, expressed in new literary forms by Emerson and his associates, did produce a peculiar type of thinking and discoursing, which has now, however, almost died out; and where one still meets, especially among the cultivated classes, a larger number than elsewhere of persons who have thought and studied for themselves, and are unlike their fellows. The other part of the country is the Far West, where the wild life led by pioneers in exploration, or ranching, or gold mining has produced a number of striking figures, men of extraordinary self-reliance, with a curious mixture of geniality and reckless hardihood, no less indif-

ferent to their own lives than to the lives of others. Of preserving this latter type there is, alas, little hope; the swift march of civilization will have expunged it in thirty years more.

19 When one sees millions of people thinking the same thoughts and reading the same books, and perceives that, as the multitude grows, its influence becomes always stronger, it is hard to imagine how new points of repulsion and contrast are to arise, new diversities of sentiment and doctrine to be developed. Nevertheless, I am inclined to believe that, as the intellectual proficiency and speculative play of mind which are now confined to a comparatively small class become more generally diffused, as the pressure of effort toward material success is relaxed, as the number of men devoted to science, art, and learning increases, so will the dominance of what may be called the business mind decline, and, with a richer variety of knowledge, tastes, and pursuits, there will come also a larger crop of marked individualities, and of divergent intellectual types.

20 Time will take away some of the monotony which comes from the absence of historical associations: for even if, as is to be hoped, there comes no war to make battlefields famous like those of twenty-five years ago, yet literature and the lives of famous men cannot but attach to many spots associations to which the blue of distance will at last give a romantic interest. No people could be more ready than are the Americans to cherish such associations. Their country has a short past, but they willingly revere and preserve all the memories the past has bequeathed to them.

Summary

Introduction: American uniformity is the one serious drawback to the pleasantness of American life (¶1).

Development

A. This uniformity appears in several ways (¶2).

    1. It appears in nature (¶3-4).

    2. It appears in cities (¶5).

        a. There are certain cities which are exceptions to the rule (¶6).

        b. In general the uniformity of cities is due to an absence of anything that speaks of the past (¶7).

    3. This uniformity appears in government, in schools, in institutions, in social customs (¶8).

    4. This uniformity appears in the ideas of men and women (¶9).

B. This uniformity appears in the comparison of the average American with the peoples of Europe (¶10-11) (argument from analogy).

    1. European residents of America and Americans themselves attest to American uniformity (¶12) and European variety (¶13).

    2. The basic cause of American uniformity is "newness" (¶14) in contrast to the survival of old institutions and customs in Europe (¶14-15).

C. This uniformity may give way in time to variety (¶16).

    1. It is unlikely that the appearance of cities will change (¶17).

    2. The tendency towards uniformity destroys individuality in ideas and the inner life of man (¶18).

    3. But the diffusion of knowledge may result in marked individualities and divergent intellectual types (¶19).

Conclusion: At present American life is unpleasantly uniform in character, but time may remove this monotony and uniformity (¶20).

Comment

The proposition of this essay is that American life is uniform (in contrast to the variety of European life). Thus the proposition states a disputable question. The author attempts to prove his proposition by advancing a series of points at issue. American life is uniform because (a) its natural surroundings are uniform, (b) its cities are uniform, (c) its government and social structures are uniform, (d) the ideas held by Americans are uniform, and (e) the Americans as a people are less varied than the peoples of Europe.

Although this example is technically argumentative, since it advances a disputable proposition and attempts to convince the reader of its truth, its method of development more closely resembles exposition. For this reason many books refer to essays of this type as expository arguments.

This example is notable for its gradual development. First, as the outline suggests, Bryce shows that, at the time he wrote the essay, about 1891, American life was marked by uniformity (¶2-9). The second section of the essay contrasts the uniformity of the average American with the diversified character of the peoples of Europe (¶10-15). The third part of the essay speculates as to the possible development of variety in the American character (¶16-20).

Unity in the essay is clearly marked by a brief introduction (¶1); clear statements of the main divisions (¶2, 10, and 16); and a conclusion (¶20).

Both unity and coherence are apparent in the orderly development of the three main divisions. The first division (see summary, A) attempts to prove that the uniformity of the American character is a reality by giving specific examples and contrasts of this uniformity in nature, cities, government, schools, institutions, social habits, and in the ideas of men and women. In the second main division (see summary, B) the uniformity of the American character is compared to the diversity of the European character. The reason for this difference is traced to history by the method of process analysis. The third main division (see summary, C) speculates upon the future development of the American character. These speculations are developed by examining the possible results of the diffusion of knowledge.

Thus the logical unity and coherence of the essay may be traced to a development of three main divisions by the method of example (Section IV), by the method of comparison and contrast (Section V), by process analysis (Section VII), and by causal analysis (Section VI). The chief method of proof is analogy.

Emphasis is achieved by an arrangement of the ideas so as to provoke the greatest interest in the reader. Final speculation on the development of the American character is the point of highest interest in the essay.

The style is clear, especially in the logical arrangement of the sentences within each of the paragraphs. The aptness of the author's examples and his specific references to American localities and cities also make the essay forceful. The many effective comparisons and contrasts, together with the challenging character of his subject matter, contribute to the interest.

Exercises

1. In paragraphs 3 and 4 Viscount Bryce gives examples to show that the natural features of the United States convey the impression of uniformity. Yet his list of these natural features indicates that they exhibit a considerable variety. Define the precise sense in which he uses the term *uniformity* when writing of the aspects of nature in the United States. Do you agree with his definition? Give reasons for your answer.

2. Paragraph 5 contains a threefold comparison or analogy among English, Italian, and American towns. Does this comparison between English towns and Italian towns and between English towns and American towns help Viscount Bryce to *prove* the main point or merely to illustrate it? That is, does he compel your assent or merely make his own position clear? Give reasons for your answer.

3. In paragraph 6 Viscount Bryce states that Boston, New York, and Chicago, Richmond, New Orleans, and Santa Fé have distinct characteristics. The monotony of most American cities, on the other hand, makes "one's heart sink at the feeling that nothing historically interesting ever has happened here, perhaps ever will happen" (¶7). State whether you

agree or disagree with this impression of American cities. Give reasons for your answer.

4. In paragraphs 9 and 10 why does Viscount Bryce compare the American people not with Europe as a whole but with the European nations?

5. In paragraph 14 Viscount Bryce says that "newness" is the cause of uniformity. In the context of this paragraph and of the entire essay what is the precise meaning of "newness"?

6. Pick out the topic sentence in paragraph 17. By what method of analysis is this topic sentence developed?

7. Comment on the accuracy of Viscount Bryce's prediction in sentence 2, paragraph 19, in the light of subsequent developments in the United States.

Note: For additional questions on this essay see Exercise 10 following Example A5, "The Myth of American Uniformity" by Peter Drucker.

5. The Myth of American Uniformity

BY PETER F. DRUCKER

I

1 "How can you Americans stand all this uniformity?" Every one of the dozens of visitors from all over Europe who, during these past few years, have discussed their American impressions with me, has asked this question in one form or another. Yet what makes every single one—business man, clergyman, or scientist; teacher, lawyer, or journalist; labor leader or civil servant—come to me for information is bewilderment, if not shock, at the incomprehensible and boundless diversity of this country.

2 "But *somebody* must lay out the standard curriculum for the liberal arts college. If the federal or the state governments do not do it, who does?"

3 "In what grade does the American high-school student start Latin? How many hours a week are given to it? And what works of Shakespeare are normally read in the American high schools?"

4 "It can't really be true that there is no one labor union policy on industrial engineering. I am told that some unions actually insist on a time and motion study of each job, some unions acquiesce in it, and others refuse to allow any industrial engineers. But surely no union

THE MYTH OF AMERICAN UNIFORMITY: from *Harper's Magazine*, May, 1952. Reprinted with the permission of the author.

movement could possibly operate, pulling in opposite directions on a matter as important as this?"

5 "Please explain to us what American managements mean when they talk of 'decentralization.' Wouldn't this mean that different units of a company would do things differently, adopt different policies, follow different ideas? And how could any management allow that and still keep its authority and control?"

6 The going gets really rough when the talk turns to political institutions or to the churches. That it makes all the difference in the world what congressional committee a pending bill is assigned to, will upset even the urbane visitor—if indeed he believes it. And among the most frustrating hours of my life was the evening I spent with a Belgian Jesuit who insisted that there must be one simple principle that decides when and where agencies of the Catholic Church in this country work together with other faiths, and when not. The only comfort was that he obviously had got no more satisfaction from his American brethren in the order than from me.

7 Yet it is quite clearly not in diversity that the visitors see the essence of America. They are baffled by it, shocked by it, sometimes frightened by it. But they don't really believe in it. Their real convictions about this country come out in the inevitable question: "But don't you find it trying to live in so uniform a country?"

8 It is not only the casual visitor, spending a few weeks here, who believes in "American uniformity" despite all he sees and hears. The belief survives extended exposure to the realities of American life.

9 A few months ago a well-known English anthropologist, reviewing an exhibition of American paintings for a most respectable London Sunday paper, explained the "mediocrity of American painting" by a reference to "the uniformity of the American landscape—all prairie and desert." One might remind the reviewer that nothing is more startling to the immigrant who comes to America to live than the tremendous variety of the landscape and the violence of contrasts in the American climate, soils, geology, fauna, and flora. Or one might reduce the argument to its full absurdity by asking which of these sons of Kansas, for example, is the typically uniform prairie product—William Allen White, Earl Browder, or General Eisenhower? But the essential fact is not that the argument is nonsense. It is that Geoffrey Gorer, the anthropologist, knows this country well, and that the newspaper that printed his nonsense is unusually knowledgeable about things American on the whole. Yet though they know

all about New England or Virginia or Minnesota or Oregon, though they probably also know about the artists who paint in the desert of Cape Cod—or is it a prairie?—they immediately think of "uniformity" when something American needs explanation.

10 Or take the case of the young Danish lawyer who came to see me just before sailing back home. He was going to stay just a few minutes, as he had only one question to ask. In the end he stayed almost the whole day—yet left with it still unanswered. His question? In one plant of the American company where he worked for seven months as a trainee, he found that output standards for the workers were set by a joint management-union committee. In another plant of the same company, located just a few miles away and organized by the same local of the same union, output standards, he found, were considered strictly a "management prerogative," with union action confined to formal protests against management decisions. He was sure he must have been mistaken in his observation; at the least, management and union must both be eager to have a uniform policy, whereas both seemed perfectly happy with the existing "disorder." I could not convince him that this was a fairly common situation all over the country. He left, certain that our labor relations must be uniform, if not for the whole country then at least for an industry, let alone for one company or one union.

11 And the "productivity teams" that have come over from Europe to study American methods these past few years insist in their reports that one of the basic reasons for the greater productivity of American industry is the "standardization" of the individual manufacturer on a very small number of models or lines. Yet most of the productivity reports themselves contain figures which show the exact opposite to be true: the typical American automobile manufacturer (even the smaller one), the typical shoe manufacturer, or the typical founder turns out more models than his European counterpart. The people who write these reports seem quite unconscious of the contradiction.

12 Clearly, "American uniformity" is an axiom for the European, before and beyond any experience. It is indeed the one thing the European *knows* he knows about this country. There are today plenty of people in Europe who know that not all Americans are millionaires —though there are still far too few who know from firsthand experience how high the standard of living of the American worker really is. There are even some Europeans who have come to suspect that race relations in this country are quite a bit more complex than in the books

of Richard Wright. But it is a very rare European indeed—if he exists
at all—who does not *know* that America is "uniform."

II

13 How is this dogma to be explained? The standard answer is
that there is an outward sameness, a uniformity to all things material
in this country. I have been skeptical of this answer ever since, a few
years back, a magnificently accoutered cowboy, complete from white
ten-gallon hat to woolly chaps and silver spurs, complained to me
bitterly about the "uniformity" of the American costume, and contrasted it with the picturesque leather pants, white knee stockings,
and green suspenders of the Austrian students among whom he had
spent a few months before the war. The "cowboy" was an earnest
young social worker riding the range in the great cow center of
Chicago. And he delivered himself of his plaint on the way from a
lecture on psychology to one on urban community problems during
a YMCA conference. His excuse for his dress—had he felt the need
for any—would have been that he went folk and square dancing both
in the morning, before the day's lectures, and in the evening. But the
Austrian students—I did not have the heart to tell him—wear their
leather pants because they possess at best one good suit and have to
go easy on it.

14 Altogether there is as little diversity in Europe's outward material
appearance as there is in this country. People all through Europe, right
through the Iron Curtain, dress pretty much alike. And when they
don't—surely even the quaintest Sunday costume of a Slovak maiden
can hardly rival the colors of a Californian going out on the golf
course, or the ties a Midwestern salesman wears on his rounds.

15 Our towns and cities, ugly maybe, are not as much uniform as
they are nineteenth- and twentieth-century towns and cities. Even in
Europe it is primarily the old cities which look different. At least I
know nothing in this country to rival the bleak monotony of sooty
brick and broken chimney pots on the railroad ride into London, or
the pea-in-the-pod uniformity of the famous Dutch housing developments, with their endless rows of identically neat bungalows. And
even the sun-drenched limbo—frowzy palms and peeling stucco—of
the middle-class sections of Los Angeles offers occasional variety and
architectural surprise compared to the numbing grayness through

which one drives from the airport into the city that to most Americans stands as the symbol of European diversity: Paris.

16 When it comes to manufactured goods there is actually more diversity in this country than Europe has ever known. The variety of goods carried by our stores is the first thing that impresses any visitor from abroad. Nor is this a postwar phenomenon. As far back as 1938 one of the leading department store chains in England studied the Sears, Roebuck catalogue. It concluded that in every single category of goods the American mail-order business, for all its "standardization," offered a wider range of goods in far more models than any European retailer could obtain from European manufacturers, let alone afford to carry.

17 But, you may say, when the European talks about "American uniformity" he is not thinking of the material and outward aspects of American life, but of American culture and society. And here the dogma of American uniformity becomes totally incomprehensible. For it is in the nonmaterial realms—in religion, political institutions, education, business life, even in entertainment—that the diversity of this country most deeply confuses the visitor from the other side.

18 Well-informed Europeans have heard that this country's political life is founded on pluralism and that our religious organization knows no rules—though they seldom seem to realize that these facts alone deny the legend of American uniformity. Most of them, however, believe that this country has uniformity in education. A hand-picked team of British educators, scientists, and industrialists who recently studied the relationship between industry and the universities in this country, obviously took uniformity for granted—though every single fact in their own report contradicted the assumption. Actually the diversity in politics and religion here is as nothing compared to the riot that prevails in education—the matrix of society.

19 There are colleges which look with distrust upon any book written later than 1300, are pained if they have to teach anything that is at all tainted with "usefulness," and occasionally even dream of going back to teaching in Latin. There are other colleges—giving the same B.A. and enjoying the same acceptance by the general public—in which a student can earn a degree through courses in night-club etiquette, horseback riding, and fashion drawing. And in at least one southwestern university you can now get a Ph.D. in square and folk dancing; last summer I was shown with great pride the first accepted

doctor's thesis, a formidable tome of 652 pages, mostly footnotes, on "The Left-Turn Hopsa Step in Lithuanian Polkas." Greater still is the diversity among different kinds and types of colleges, and among private schools, church schools, and state schools, let alone such phenomena, totally incomprehensible to any visitor from abroad, as the half-private, half-state university, or the church-supported but non-sectarian college. Some of the larger "liberal arts" colleges have flourishing engineering schools of their own, and one large engineering school, Carnegie Tech in Pittsburgh, also runs a first-rate art and music school. And how can one explain to a European, accustomed to a Ministry of Education, the role of the private foundations, such as Rockefeller or Carnegie, and their power?

20 It is scarcely possible to talk about trends in American higher education, so mixed are the currents. Many engineering schools for instance have lately broadened their curricula to include more and more of the arts and humanities; but Columbia University—itself preponderantly dedicated to the liberal arts—has just announced plans for the most highly specialized Engineering Center. The University of Chicago has for some years now been admitting freshmen after only two years of high school, with the avowed aim of making the undergraduate college an intermediate rather than a "higher" institution, whereas other well-known schools, in order to make "higher education" really "high," increasingly prefer men in their early twenties who have spent a few years at work after leaving high school.

21 Nor is the situation any more uniform in secondary schools. Within thirty miles of New York City there are public schools so progressive as to live up to the caricatures in the funny papers of the twenties, and others so conservative as to justify every word of the progressives' indictment of the traditional schools. I have taught college freshmen from public schools who had learned more mathematics than most college curricula offer, and others who had come from schools with an equal reputation where mathematics, beyond long division, was an "elective" and was taken only by children planning a career in science or medicine. There was one proper Bostonian who could remember only one American President, Benjamin Franklin; the main educational dish served at his very proper Bostonian school had been a rich stew called "civics" which contained odd pieces of almost anything except the history of his own country. And I have

taught other freshmen to whom school had given a sound knowledge of historical facts and even the thrill of history. Yet every one of these high schools is unmistakably and characteristically "American."

22 Even less compatible with the myth of American uniformity is the reality of American literature—and if education is the matrix of society, literature is its truest reflection. How "uniform" for instance are the American writers who emerged in the literary explosion of the 1920's: Sinclair Lewis, Hemingway, Willa Cather, John Dos Passos, Wolfe, Faulkner, T. S. Eliot, Robert Frost, Carl Sandburg? A more diverse lot, in style, mood, and subject matter, could hardly be imagined; and the diversity becomes the greater the more names are added: Sherwood Anderson, for instance, or Ellen Glasgow, Dashiell Hammett or H. L. Mencken, Scott Fitzgerald, Ezra Pound, Eugene O'Neill, or e.e. cummings. And just how "uniform" are the three magazine successes of the same decade, the *Reader's Digest, Time,* and the *New Yorker?* The educated European knows American literature and avidly reads our magazines; a good many American writers may indeed be better known in Europe than here. Yet if there is one thing he is sure of it is the "standardization" of the American mind.

23 Writers and journalists, it may be said, are nonconformists to begin with. Well, what about entertainment in America? Our radio stands perhaps first among the targets of the European critics of "American uniformity." If everything they are saying about it were true, it still would not account for the twenty-five to thirty-five stations—one in almost every major city—which offer "serious" music eight to twelve hours a day. None of the "serious" or "high-brow" programs of European radio systems draws enough of an audience to exist without heavy subsidies. But a great many of the two or three dozen "serious" radio stations in this country manage to operate at a profit, though they are supported only by advertisers who are unlikely to be interested in anything but a listening audience large enough to justify the investment.

24 One station, WABF in New York, is even running an entire Sunday of music without any advertising, financed solely by voluntary contributions from its listening audience.

25 And how is one to explain that young people weaned on "Good Night, Irene," the "Hit Parade," and the "Lone Ranger" rush headlong into chamber music, as listeners and, increasingly, as players, as

soon as they reach college? Walking across the campus on a fine spring evening one hears "long-haired" music, from Buxtehude to Bartok, streaming out of every other open window. Symphony orchestras are appearing in small towns as well as in large cities. And instead of being subsidized, these American orchestras are supported, as they are formed, by voluntary community action; the *Wall Street Journal* reports that more money is spent on symphonies than on basketball.

26 But what should completely destroy the European's concept of American uniformity is the diversity existing in industry. The fact that in this country business and industry are part of the country's culture is to the European the most remarkable thing about the United States—to the point where he greatly overstates the extent to which America has become a "business society." The European business men and labor leaders who have been touring this country under the auspices of ECA these last four years all report as their central finding the experiments in new techniques, new products or processes, in accounting or in labor relations, in organization structure or in foreman training, carried on in almost every company they visit. No two, they find, do the same things. In the words of one of these teams, "Every American company feels that it has to do something different to stay in the race." Many teams feel that American competition is too "extreme"; and when pressed to explain why they use this term, they talk about the demands on managerial imagination and worker adaptability made by the need always to do something different and something new. The same sort of variety is found in our labor relations. In Europe relations between management and union tend to be rigidly and uniformly molded by a central association of industries negotiating with a central federation of trade unions; the individual employer or the individual union local pays dues but is otherwise inert. Not so here.

27 Some of the members of these teams even feel that we carry diversity too far to be efficient. "I have seen a dozen plans for management development in as many companies," one of the senior men in British industry told me. "Every one—Standard Oil, Ford, Johnson & Johnson, Du Pont, General Electric, the Telephone Company—has a plan of its own, a staff of its own, a philosophy of its own. That just makes no sense. Why don't you fellows get together, appoint a committee, and have them work out the *one best plan* which every-

body could use and which could be run centrally by a few top-flight people?"

28 It is not even true that within the American plant there is more "standardization" than elsewhere, as we have all come to believe. The figures tell a different story. In this country of mass production a larger proportion of the workers in manufacturing industries are what the census calls "skilled workers and foremen" than in any other country on which we have data. And we have an even greater number of men, proportionately, in executive, technical, and managerial positions. In other words American productive strength lies in higher capital investment per worker and better management; better planning, better layout, better scheduling, better personnel relations, better marketing—all of which means more skilled and more trained people rather than more unskilled repetitive work.

III

29 I am not discussing here the *quality* of American culture, whether it be crude, shallow, vulgar, commercialized, materialist, or, as the Marxists maintain, full of "bourgeois idealism." My concern here is solely with the prevailing European conviction of American uniformity. And that conviction is an obvious absurdity. Nor could it be anything else considering the pragmatic bent of the American people and their deeply engrained habit of voluntary and local community action and community organization.

30 Indeed any serious student of America has to raise the question whether there is not *too much* diversity in this country. There is the danger that diversity will degenerate into aimless multiplicity—difference for difference's sake. Jefferson, de Tocqueville, and Henry Adams, as well as recent critics of American education such as Robert Hutchins, have seen in this the major danger facing American society and culture.

31 There is actually more uniformity in European countries, both materially and culturally, than in the United States. It may no longer be true that the French Minister of Education knows at every hour exactly what line of what page of what book is being read in every French school. But still, in education, in religious life, in political life, in business as well as in its cultural ideals, European countries tend to have at most a few "types," a few molds in which everything

is formed. What then can the European possibly mean when he talks
of the "uniformity of America"?

32 He himself, as a visitor, unconsciously furnishes the answer in
the way he sorts out his American experiences, in the questions he
asks, in the answers he understands and those he doesn't. When he
thinks of "diversity" he tends to think of the contrast between the
ways in which social and economic classes live. He is used to seeing
a definite and clear-cut upper-class civilization and culture dominating. And that indeed he does not find in this country. Therefore the
bewildering differences in American life appear to him meaningless—
mere oddities.

33 I still remember how the sage of our neighborhood in suburban
Vienna, the wife of the market gardener across the street, explained
the "Great War," the war of 1914-18, when I was a small boy of ten
or eleven: "The war had to come because you couldn't tell maids from
their ladies by their dress any more." Frau Kiner's explanation of history differed from that offered during the 1920's by Europe's learned
sociologists, whether of the Right or of the Marxist persuasion, mainly
by being brief and simple. They all assumed that there must be a
distinct upper-class way of life, an upper-class architecture, upper-class
dress, upper-class goods in an upper-class market—and contrasted with
it the "folk culture" of the peasantry or the equally distinct ways of life
of the middle class and working class. Indeed that eminently sane,
that notoriously Americophile magazine, the London *Economist,*
echoed Frau Kiner only a few months ago when it reported with apparent amazement that "to the best of their ability—and their ability
is great—the [American] manufacturers make clothes for the lower-
income groups that look just as smart as those they make for the more
fortunate"—and explained this perverse attempt to make maids look
like their ladies as the result of the "egalitarian obsession" of this
country.

34 The class-given differentiation in Europe is even more pronounced in the nonmaterial, the cultural spheres. One example is the
tremendous importance of the "right speech" in practically every European country; for the "right speech" is upper-class speech. Another
example is the extent to which European educational systems are
based on the education of a ruling class. The Renaissance Courtier, the
Educated Man of the Humanists, the Christian Gentleman of nineteenth-century England—the ideal types which embodied the three

basic educational concepts of modern Europe—were all in origin and intent ruling-class types. The rising middle class not only did not over-throw the class concept of education, it emphasized it as a symbol of its own emergence into the ruling group. Similarly, in Occupied Germany the working-class leaders—to the chagrin as well as the com-plete bewilderment of American educational advisers—have shown no enthusiasm for the plan to convert the traditional *Gymnasium* into an American high school. To deprive these schools of their ruling-class character would actually deprive them of social meaning for working-class children.

35 Europe has even succeeded in turning diversities and differences that were not social in their origin into class distinctions. One of the best examples of this is the way in which the "gentry" and its retainers became identified with the Church of England, while the "tradesman" went to "chapel"—a distinction that held till very recent times and is not quite gone yet.

36 Thus the European myth of American uniformity tells us less about America than about Europe. For it is based, in the last analysis, on Frau Kiner's belief that a class structure of society is the only genu-ine moral order.

37 That today the theme of "American uniformity" is played on above all by communist propaganda is thus no accident. For the "pro-letariat" of communist ideology is indeed a "master class." It is a re-affirmation of the European ruling-class concept and of its ruling-class way of life in an extreme form—only turned upside down. On this rests to a considerable extent the attraction of communism for Euro-pean intellectuals. There is an old Slav peasant proverb: "There will always be barons for there must always be peasants." All Vishinsky would have to do to change it into an orthodox Soviet proverb would be to change "barons" to "proletarian commissars." And Frau Kiner's philosophy of history he would not have to change at all.

IV

38 But Frau Kiner's statement could never have been made in this country, not even by a sociology professor in a three-volume tome. Whether the United States really has no ruling class—and therefore no classes at all—or whether, as the Marxists assert, the classes are only camouflaged in this country, one thing is certain: this country knows

no distinct upper-class or lower-class "way of life." It knows only different ways of making a living.

39 Indeed there has been only one genuine ruling-class way of life in this country since its beginning: that of the plantation aristocracy in the Old South between 1760 and 1860. When the *nouveaux riches* in the period between the Civil War and the first World War made the attempt to set themselves up as "society" they failed miserably. They could not even develop an upper-class American architecture—and of all the arts architecture is the mirror of the way of life. The tycoons had to be contented with imitation French châteaux, Italian Renaissance palaces, and Tudor manors—the white elephants which their servantless grandchildren are now frantically turning over to monasteries, hospitals, or schools. (It is not entirely an accident, perhaps, that the people most eager to live today in the baronial halls of yesterday's capitalists seem to be Soviet delegates.) To find an upper-class way of life the tycoons had to gatecrash the Scottish grouse moors, the Cowes Regatta, or the Kaiser's maneuvers in Kiel. In this country it was difficult indeed to lead a ruling-class life.

40 The closest we come today in this country to anything that might be called an "upper-class way of life" is to be found in the top hierarchy of the big business corporations. The way people in some of these companies talk about the "twelfth floor" or the "front office" faintly echoes Frau Kiner's concept of the "ladies." At work the big business executive has indeed some of the trappings of a distinct style of living in the ceremonial of receptionist, secretary, and big office, in his expense account, in the autographed picture of the "big boss" on the wall, the unlisted telephone, and so forth. But only at work. As soon as he leaves the office the "big shot" becomes simply another business man, anonymous and indistinguishable from millions of others. And he is quite likely to live, like the president of our largest corporation, in an eight-room house in a pleasant and comfortable but not particularly swank suburb.

41 In fact, it does not even make too much sense to talk of this country as a "middle-class" society. A middle class has to have a class on either side to be in the middle. There is more than a grain of truth in the remark made jokingly by one of my European visitors, an Italian student of American literature: "If there were such a thing as a working-class literature, *Babbitt* and *Arrowsmith* would be its models."

V

42 Any European who has perchance read thus far will growl that, if Europe's mental picture of "American uniformity" is absurd, America's mental picture of "European class society" is absurder. And he is right. In fact, the one myth is the reverse of the other. To the American, for instance, "class society" means a society without social mobility. But Frau Kiner was anything but respectable lower-middle class knowing its place. She was a successful social climber who had fought her way up from a sharecropper's shanty and a job as scullery maid at fourteen—and had pushed her man up with herself. And in those years after the first World War she was capping her social triumph by marrying off her beautiful and well-dowered daughters to "gentlemen"—elderly and moth-eaten, but undeniably "gentlemen."

43 Nor is a society in which an Eliza Doolittle can jump from slum waif to "great lady" just by learning upper-class speech a society without social mobility. (Indeed there is no better sign of America's failure to understand Europe's "class society" than our tendency to play *Pygmalion* as a farce and as a take-off on upper-class snobbery— whereas it is as much crusading pamphlet as comedy of manners, the only snobs in it being the class-conscious Cockneys.) Altogether there has been tremendous social mobility in any western or central European country whenever there was great economic expansion: in Britain between the Napoleonic Wars and 1860, in Germany a generation later, in Bohemia—perhaps the most startling example—between 1870 and 1900. The central difference between America and Europe may well be in the *meaning* rather than in the *extent* of social mobility. When the boss's son is made a vice president in this country the publicity release is likely to stress that his first job was pushing a broom. But when a former broompusher, born in the Glasgow slums, gets to be managing director in a British company the official announcement is likely to hint gently at descent from Robert Bruce.

44 I must break off here. Another European visitor has just come in for a chat, a young French philosopher, fresh from a six-month tour of American universities. I anticipate a pleasant and informative afternoon; the letter with which he introduced himself was interesting and intelligent. "The thing that impressed me most," he wrote, "is that no university I visited tries to develop a 'school of philosophy.' On the contrary each tries to stress different views and different schools

in its faculty—the exact opposite from what we would normally do." Yet I know that sooner or later in the course of the afternoon he will ask me, "Mr. Drucker, don't you find it very trying to live in so mechanically uniform a country?"

Summary

A. *Part I. Introduction* (¶1-12). The European is unalterably convinced that America is "uniform" despite direct evidence of America's diversity (¶1). Particular examples of this general attitude are:
1. The casual visitors (¶2-6), such as those
   a. Who assume American schools are standardized (¶2-3).
   b. Who assume American union policy is standardized (¶4).
   c. Who assume American business management is standardized (¶5).
   d. Who assume American political and religious policy is standardized (¶6).
   All these Europeans are shocked by America's diversity but will not believe it (¶7).
2. Other examples of European refusal to accept American diversity are furnished by those who have been here for some time (¶8), such as
   a. Geoffrey Gorer, the anthropologist, who knows America well (¶9) but reports inaccurately about her scenic uniformity.
   b. The Danish lawyer who persists in denying the facts of his own experience (¶10).
   c. The "productivity teams" whose economic reports contradict their stated impressions of American uniformity (¶11).
3. But the American character is diversified rather than uniform—*central theme or proposition* (¶12).
B. *Part II. Development* (¶13-28)
1. That the American character is diversified rather than uniform in material or outward aspects of life is evident in
   a. America's diversity of dress in comparison with European dress (¶13-14).
   b. The diversity of America's towns and cities in comparison with Europe's towns and cities (¶15).
   c. The diversity of America's manufactured goods in comparison with those of Europe (¶16).
2. That the American character is diversified rather than uniform in the nonmaterial realms (¶17) is evident in

a. The variety of American ideas in religion and politics (¶18).
b. The variety of American higher education (¶19-20).
c. The variety of American secondary education (¶21).
d. The variety of American literature (¶22).
e. The variety of American entertainment (¶23-25).

3. That the American character is diversified rather than uniform is especially evident in the conduct of business and industry (¶26-28).

C. *Part III. Development continued* (refutation) (¶29-37). The charge that the American character is uniform is absurd.

1. The European myth of American uniformity is absurd (¶29) in view of
   a. The excessive diversity of the American character (¶30).
   b. The greater uniformity present in Europe (retort) (¶31).
2. The European myth is the result of judging America by European standards of class (¶32 and 36). This European class consciousness is evident in
   a. The attitudes in Austria at the time of World War II and in present-day England (¶33).
   b. The class distinction of European education (¶34).
   c. The class distinctions in European religions (¶35).
   d. The class distinctions inherent in the communist ideology (¶37).

D. *Part IV. Development continued* (¶38-41). The European myth of American uniformity is based on the false assumption that America has a class system that is the same as Europe's. That America has no distinct class system (¶38) is evident in

1. The failure of "society" to become a ruling class (¶39).
2. The failure of big business executives to exercise leadership outside the business office (¶40).
3. The absurdity of a "middle" class with no class on the top or bottom (¶41).

E. *Part V. Conclusion* (¶42-44).

1. The European myth of American uniformity is matched by the American myth that the European class system lacks social mobility.
   a. The European class system does allow for mobility, as is evident in the case of
      (1) Frau Kiner and her family (¶42).
      (2) Eliza Doolittle (¶43).
      (3) The social revolutions during the nineteenth century (¶43).
2. The meaning of the term *social mobility* differs in America and Europe—*summation* (¶43).
3. The American character is diversified rather than uniform. The European, however, is convinced otherwise (¶44).

Comment

Of all the essays in Section XI Mr. Drucker's essay is the most extended example of argument. It illustrates more fully than the others the functions of the introduction, development, and conclusion; it presents more issues; it answers more objections.

You will have noticed in the outline the elaborate introduction (Part I). Here Mr. Drucker states and restates his central theme or proposition: the American character is diverse (¶1, 7, and 12).

This proposition is defined in its present context by showing how the European, despite evidence to the contrary, insists on regarding America as uniform.

Thus the author not only challenges our attention by an interesting contrast of two attitudes, but he also shows that his essay can make an important contribution to international understanding.

He develops the proposition that the American character is diversified rather than uniform by proving three main points at issue in Part II:

1. The diversity in American external life.
2. The diversity in American mental life.
3. The diversity in American business life.

The arrangement here is partly dictated by the needs of the audience. Note that the first two points at issue include the third point. But this third point is listed separately for the sake of emphasis; Europeans, to whom the author directs many of his remarks, are most conscious of American business as a symbol of the American character.

Each of these main points at issue is developed in turn by subordinate proofs. American diversity in external life is proved by a comparison of American and European dress, cities, and manufactured goods. The diversity of American mental life is proved by specific examples of American pluralistic practices in the several fields of education, literature, entertainment, and so on. The diversity of American business practice is proved by the testimony of Europeans themselves.

Part III *refutes* the opposite thesis by characterizing the charge as absurd. That is, Drucker accuses his opponents of making a false generalization about America. He supports this charge by pointing to a list of famous authorities who have complained about the excessive diversity of American life. A second proof of his refutation is his retort that there is more uniformity in Europe than in America.

Drucker reveals the basic fallacy of the European myth of American uniformity as a false assumption—the assumption that America and Europe have the same social structure. The European class system is defined and contrasted with the American lack of class system to prove that there is no real basis for a comparison between Europe and America.

In the conclusion, Part V, the European myth of American uniformity is shown to be as foolish as the American myth that the European social system lacks mobility. The meaning of the whole argument is thus summarized in terms of the essential difference between European and American standards of uniformity and variety. In short, European critics are guilty of a fallacious analogy.

"The Myth of American Uniformity" thus reveals many of the traits of a good argument.

A. It is clear and coherent.

    1. It states an arguable or disputed proposition and proves it directly by developing three points at issue according to well-defined methods of analysis. The chief method of reasoning in Part II is *induction*.

    2. It refutes the opposite view by giving proofs and reasons. The chief method of reasoning in Part III is *analogy*.

B. It is complete, i.e., fully developed.

    1. It has an introduction which states the subject and purpose, challenges the reader's interest, explains the background of the argument.

    2. It has a proper development composed of positive proof and refutation supported by consistent methods of analysis.

    3. It has a conclusion which sums up the main argument.

C. It is emphatic in its arrangement. This is made evident

    1. By the order of the three proofs in Part II. In this order the last proof—the diversity in American business life—is by far the strongest, since it retorts the opponent's strongest argument and prepares for the refutation.

    2. By the order of the refutation. European myth is ultimately traced to a false assumption in a series of steps which mount in interest.

    3. By the order of the individual parts, as for example Part III, paragraphs 33-36, where the proofs of European class consciousness advance from personal observation of Frau Kiner to the analysis of the communist mentality.

Analysis and Composition

1. Explain the method of analysis Drucker uses to prove that Europeans believe in American uniformity (Part I).

2. What is the chief method of analysis used to develop the following paragraphs in Part II: ¶13-16, 18-24, and 26-28?

3. In Part III, paragraph 30, the author cites three authorities to prove that there is too much diversity in America. Would he have made his argument more effective by quoting these authors? Give reasons for your answer.

4. Show how the definitions of uniformity and diversity are developed in Part III, paragraphs 31-33.

5. Determine whether paragraph 34 is developed by the method of examples or process analysis or both. Give reasons for your answer.

6. In Part III, paragraph 35, the author gives as an example of social distinction the distinction between members of the Church of England and those who went to "chapel."

   a. Has he the right to assume that this example is clear without further explanation?

   b. Does this example illustrate the practice of continental European countries as well as that of England?

7. Do you believe that Mr. Drucker has proved the failure of "society" to become a ruling class in Part IV, paragraph 39? If you feel he has proved it, show how he does so. If you feel he has not proved it, indicate what methods of development he might have used to prove his point.

8. In Part IV, paragraph 41, Mr. Drucker proves that we have no middle class because "A middle class has to have a class on either side to be in the middle." Is this proof or mere clever phrasing? Give reasons for your answer.

9. The device of concluding with a story (the device used in Part V, paragraph 44) is known as a fiction, i.e., an imaginary situation or dialogue which dramatizes a point. Show how this fiction sums up the main point of the essay.

10. Reread Viscount Bryce's essay on the uniformity of American life. Although this essay was written some 60 years ago it may still be read with profit in connection with Mr. Drucker's essay. Viscount Bryce's is a short essay and naturally does not reflect the many changes in American life since the time of its composition. Taken together, however, these two essays constitute a stimulating informal debate; Viscount Bryce upholds the affirmative of the proposition that the American character is uniform and that this trait is unpleasant, Mr. Drucker the negative.

You may see this clearly when you put their respective arguments side by side. Note that, although both men are arguing on the same proposition, they do not interpret it in the same way. In other words, they have chosen to develop separate points at issue. Thus in estimating the argument as a whole you must not only consider the cogency of the proof but you must also determine which issue is the more important.

Proposition: The American Character Is Uniform

Affirmative: Viscount Bryce	Negative: Peter Drucker
A. This uniformity exists, as is evident in	A. This uniformity does not exist, as is evident in
1. Nature (¶3)	1. Nature (¶9)
2. Cities (¶5); exceptions (¶6)	2. Cities (¶15)
3. Government (¶8)	3. Government (¶6 and 18)
4. Schools (¶8)	4. Schools (¶2-3 and 19-21) (retort, ¶31 and 34)
5. Social habits (¶8)	5. Society (¶13-14 and 33-36) (retort, ¶39-41)
6. Individual men and women (¶9-12)	6. Individuals (¶9 and 25) (retort, ¶29-30)
7. Ideas and inner life of men (¶18)	7. Ideas (¶22-24)
B. The cause of American uniformity is America's newness.	B. The cause of American diversity is its lack of a class system.

Naturally there are many points at issue on which these two men do not meet at all. Still there is a clash on the basic proposition. Decide which of the two authors is in your opinion more convincing. Give reasons for your answer in an essay of approximately 1000 words.

GENERAL EXERCISES ON ARGUMENT

Argue for or against one of the propositions listed below in an essay designed to convince a specific audience of your own choice. Let your procedure be as follows:

1. Decide on the audience you intend to address.
2. Choose the particular points at issue that you wish to develop. Thus, for example, if you were discussing the proposition, "Churchill is one of the great political leaders of our time," you would choose that aspect of his greatness which is most convincing. Your choice would be among his activities as a parliamentarian, as a cabinet minister in the capacities of Chancellor of the Exchequer, Home Minister, First Lord of the Admiralty, Prime Minister, and so on.
3. When you have decided on the precise phases of the proposition you

wish to develop, draw up a preliminary plan or outline. (The plan or outline of an argument is often called a brief. The brief differs from the ordinary outline only in its greater fullness. A brief is a complete outline or a summary which may be understood even by a reader who has not seen the argument itself. Examples of this kind of outline may be found on pp. 275-76 [Malik] and pp. 484-85 [Drucker]. A legal brief or a debater's brief is often so detailed that it is approximately one-third the length of the actual argument. For most purposes such detail is not desirable.)

Your outline should include an introduction, development, and conclusion. In an outline of an argument the introduction should be considerably more expanded than in other forms of discourse. You must give the background or history of the case and the particular circumstances of the discussion. Above all, you must define all the important terms you intend to use. The outline of the development itself should show the logical connection between the parts. If necessary a refutation of the opposite view should also be included.

The conclusion should summarize the proofs and relate the proofs to the issues and the proposition.

4. Write a composition of about 1000 words based on your preliminary outline. Do not hesitate to depart from your outline if you think of better proofs in the course of writing.

Suggested Propositions for an Argumentative Essay

Propositions with reference to college: .

1. The elective system in college should be abolished.
2. Every college student should be a member of the ROTC.
3. The fraternity system should be forbidden.
4. Big-time athletics are a detriment to the American university.
5. The honor system should be adopted in all American colleges.
6. Students should be permitted to elect teachers as well as courses.
7. Scholarships should be granted on the basis of merit rather than of need.
8. Honorary academic fraternities promote academic snobbery.

Propositions with reference to politics:

1. The federal government should increase its efforts to conserve the soil.
2. The rights to tideland oil should belong to the states.
3. The federal government should subsidize the college education of superior students.
4. Public utilities should be owned and operated by the individual states.
5. The federal government should reduce the number of its employees.

6. County government should be abolished in the interest of efficiency and economy.
7. The direct control of elementary education should be in the hands of state officials rather than of city or local officials.
8. Social security benefits should be increased.

Propositions with reference to taste and opinion:

1. The stage is a more important cultural phenomenon than motion pictures.
2. Ernest Hemingway is a better writer than John Steinbeck.
3. You can learn more in a library than in a classroom.
4. A great humorist like Will Rogers is a better representative of his country than a politician is.
5. A career in small business is more rewarding than a career in big business.
6. The midwesterner is more typical of America than a man from any other region.
7. Modern painting is less pleasing than classical painting.
8. An appreciation of music is essential for the enjoyment of life.

Propositions with reference to subjects discussed throughout this book:

1. The study of literature should be required for all college students. (See Examples II I1 by Faulkner, VI A3 by Morison, and VI C1 by Montague.)
2. The liberal arts college should emphasize a general rather than a specialized education. (See General Exercise F in Section VI and Example XI B2 by Hutchins.)
3. Every student should be acquainted with the study of semantics. (See General Exercise A in Section VI by Walpole.)
4. Every English student should know the basic rules of the syllogism. (See Example VII C by T. H. Huxley.)
5. Every student should question the authority of his professor. (See Example V D2 by Plato.)
6. American universities should transform the perennial adolescent into a mature adult. (See example by Bell in Section VIII.)
7. America should cultivate spiritual wisdom. (See example by Malik in Section VIII, and Example X C by Barbara Ward.)
8. The college student should repudiate mawkish literature. (See Example X D by Smith.)
9. Laws should be framed to avert the dehumanizing effects of industrialism. (See Example X B by Hawkes.)
10. Americans should support European efforts to achieve political and economic unity. (See Example XI B1 by Churchill.)

b. In persuasion (1) emphasize the action you wish your audience to take; (2) make the proofs serve as motives for action; and (3) pay particular attention to the vigor and vividness of your style.

Proposition: We must set on foot an organization to promote the cause of a united Europe.

Motives for action: Europe is worth saving.

Europe is in ruins.

Europeans must save Europe.

European unity will help preserve world peace.

To strive for such a cause is its own reward.

1. Save Europe by Uniting Europe

BY WINSTON S. CHURCHILL

1 All the greatest things are simple, and many can be expressed in a single word. Freedom; justice; honor; duty; mercy; hope. We who have come together here today, representing almost all the political parties of our British national life and nearly all the creeds and churches of the Western world—this large audience filling a famous hall—we also can express our purpose in a single word: Europe.

SAVE EUROPE BY UNITING EUROPE: by W. S. Churchill. Reprinted from *Europe Unite,* 1950, by permission of the Houghton Mifflin Company, publishers.

2 At school we learned, from the maps hung on the walls, that there is a continent called Europe. I remember quite well being taught this as a child, and, after living a long time, I still believe it is true. However, professional geographers now tell us that the continent of Europe is really only on the peninsula of the Asiatic land mass. I must tell you that I feel that this would be an arid and uninspiring conclusion and, for myself, I distinctly prefer what I was taught when I was a boy.

3 It has been finely said by a young English writer, Mr. Sewell, that the real demarcation between Europe and Asia is no chain of mountains, no natural frontier, but a system of beliefs and ideas which we call Western civilization.

4 In the rich pattern of this culture, says Mr. Sewell, there are many strands: the Hebrew belief in God; the Christian message of compassion and redemption; the Greek love of truth, beauty, and goodness; the Roman genius for law. Europe is a spiritual conception. But if men cease to hold that conception in their minds, cease to feel its worth in their hearts, it will die.

5 These are not my words, but they are my faith; and we are here to proclaim our resolve that the spiritual conception of Europe shall not die. We declare, on the contrary, that it shall live and shine, and cast its redeeming illumination upon a world of confusion and woe.

6 That is what has brought us all together here this evening, and that is what is going to keep us all together—however sharply or even deeply we may be divided on many other matters—until our goal is reached and our hopes are realized.

7 In our task of reviving the glories and happiness of Europe, her culture and her prosperity, it can certainly be said that we start at the bottom of her fortunes.

8 There is the fairest, most temperate, most fertile area of the globe. The influence and the power of Europe and of Christendom have for centuries shaped and dominated the course of history. The sons and daughters of Europe have gone forth and carried their message to every part of the world. Religion, law, learning, art, science, industry throughout the world all bear in so many lands, under every sky and in every clime, the stamp of European origin and traces of European influence.

9 But what is Europe now? It is a rubble heap, a charnel house, a breeding ground of pestilence and hate. Ancient nationalistic feuds

and modern ideological factions distract and infuriate the unhappy, hungry populations.

10 Evil teachers urge the paying off of old scores with mathematical precision, and false guides point to unsparing retribution as the path to prosperity.

11 Is there then to be no respite? Has Europe's mission come to an end? Has she nothing to give to the world but the contagion of the Black Death? Are her peoples to go on harrying and tormenting one another by war and vengeance until all that invests human life with dignity and comfort has been obliterated?

12 Are the states of Europe to continue forever to squander the first fruits of their toil upon the erection of new barriers, military fortifications, and tariff walls and passport networks against one another?

13 Are we Europeans to become incapable, with all our tropical and colonial dependencies, with all our long-created trading connections, with all that modern production and transportation can do, of even averting famine from the mass of our peoples? Are we all, through our poverty and our quarrels, forever to be a burden and a danger to the rest of the world? Do we imagine that we can be carried forward indefinitely upon the shoulders—broad though they be—of the United States?

14 The time has come when these questions must be answered. This is the hour of choice, and surely the choice is plain. If the peoples of Europe resolve to come together and work together for mutual advantage, to exchange blessings instead of curses, they still have it in their power to sweep away the horrors and miseries which surround them and to allow the streams of freedom, happiness, and abundance to begin again their healing flow.

15 This is the supreme opportunity, and, if it be cast away, no one can predict that it will ever return or what the resulting catastrophe will be.

16 In my experience of large enterprises, it is often a mistake to try to settle everything at once. Far off, on the skyline, we can see the peaks of the Delectable Mountains. But we cannot tell what lies between us and them.

17 We know where we want to go, but we cannot foresee all the stages of the journey or plan our marches as in a military operation. We are not acting in the field of forces, but in the domain of opinion. We cannot give orders. We can only persuade.

18 We must go forward step by step.

19 I will therefore explain in general terms where we are and what are the first things we have to do. We have now at once to set on foot an organization in Great Britain to promote the cause of united Europe and to give this idea the prominence and vitality necessary for it to lay hold of the minds of our fellow countrymen to such an extent that it will affect their actions and influence the course of national policy.

20 We accept, without question, the world supremacy of the United Nations organization. In the constitution agreed on at San Francisco, direct provision is made for regional organizations to be formed. United Europe will form one major regional entity.

21 There is the United States, with all its dependencies; there is the Soviet Union; there is the British Empire and Commonwealth; and there is Europe, with which Great Britain is profoundly blended. Here are the four main pillars of the world temple of peace. Let us make sure that they will all bear the weight which will be reposed upon them.

22 It is not for us at this stage to attempt to define or prescribe the structure of constitutions. We ourselves are content to present the idea of united Europe, in which our country will play a decisive part, as a moral, cultural, and spiritual conception, to which all can rally without divergence about structure.

23 It is for the responsible statesmen who have the conduct of affairs in their hands and the power of executive action to shape and fashion the structure. It is for us to lay the foundation, to create the atmosphere, and to give the driving impulsion.

24 First I turn to France. For forty years I have marched with France. I have shared her joys and sufferings. I rejoice in her reviving national strength. Certainly I will not abandon this long comradeship now.

25 But we have a proposal to make to France which will give all Frenchmen a cause for serious thought and valiant decision. If European unity is to be made an effective reality before it is too late, the wholehearted efforts, both of France and Britain, will be needed from the outset. They must go forward hand in hand. They must in fact be founder-partners in this movement.

26 The central and almost the most serious problem which glares upon the Europe of today is the future of Germany. Without a solu-

tion of this problem, there can be no united Europe. Except within the framework and against the background of a united Europe, this problem is incapable of solution.

27 In a continent of divided national states, Germany and her hard-working people will not find means or scope to employ their energies. Economic suffocation will inevitably turn their thoughts to revolt and revenge. Germany will once again become a menace to her neighbors and to the whole world; and the fruits of victory and liberation will be cast away.

28 But, on the wider stage of a united Europe, German industry and German genius would be able to find constructive and peaceful outlets. Instead of being a center of poverty and a source of danger, the German people would be enabled to bring back prosperity in no small measure, not only to themselves but to the whole continent.

29 Germany today lies prostrate, famishing among ruins. Obviously no initiative can be expected from her. It is for France and Britain to take the lead. Together they must, in a friendly manner, bring the German race back into the European circle.

30 No one can say, and we need not attempt to forecast, what will be the future constitution of Germany. Various individual German states are at present being recreated. There are the old states and principalities of the Germany of former days to which the culture of the world owes so much.

31 Without prejudice to any future question of German federation, these individual states might well be invited to take their place in the council of Europe. Thus, in looking back to happier days, we should hope to mark the end of that long trail of hatred and retaliation which has already led us all, victors and vanquished alike, into the pit of squalor, slaughter, and ruin.

32 The prime duty and opportunity of bringing about this essential reunion belongs to us and to our French friends across the Channel. Strong bonds of affection, mutual confidence, common interest, and similar outlook link France and Britain together.

33 The treaty of alliance that has lately been signed merely gives formal expression to the community of sentiment that already exists as an indisputable and indestructible fact.

34 It is true that this task of reconciliation requires on the part of France, who has suffered so cruelly, an act of faith, sublime in char-

acter; but it is by this act of faith and by this act of faith alone that France will regain her historic position in the leadership of Europe.

35 There is also another leading member of our ancient family of nations to be held in mind. There is Italy. Everything that I have said about the imperative need of reaching a reconciliation with the German race and the ending of the fearful quarrels that have ruined them, and almost ruined us, applies in a less difficult degree to the Italian people, who wish to dwell happily and industriously within their beautiful country and who were hurled by a dictator into the hideous struggles of the north.

36 I am told that this idea of a united Europe makes an intense appeal to Italians who look back across the centuries of confusion and disorder to the glories of the classic age, when a dozen legions were sufficient to preserve peace and law through vast territories and when free men could travel freely under the sanction of a common citizenship.

37 We hope to reach again a Europe purged of the slavery of the ancient times in which men will be as proud to say, "I am a European," as once they were to say, *"Civis Romanus sum."* We hope to see a Europe where men of every country will think so much of being a European as of belonging to their native land, and wherever they go in this wide domain will truly feel, "Here I am at home." How simple it would all be, and how crowned with glory, if that were to arrive.

38 It will next of course be asked, "What are the political and physical boundaries of the united Europe you are trying to create? Which countries will be in and which out?"

39 It is not our task or wish to draw frontier lines, but rather to smooth them away. Our aim is to bring about the unity of all nations of all Europe.

40 We seek to exclude no state whose territory lies in Europe and which assures to its people those fundamental human and personal rights and liberties on which our democratic civilization has been created.

41 Some countries will feel able to come into our circle sooner, and others later, according to the circumstances in which they are placed. They can all be sure that, whenever they are to join, a place and a welcome will be waiting for them at the European council table.

42 When I first began writing about the United States of Europe some fifteen years ago, I wondered whether the United States of America would regard such a development as antagonistic to their interest, or even contrary to their safety.

43 But all that has passed away. The whole movement of American opinion is favorable to the revival and recreation of Europe. This is surely not unnatural when we remember how the manhood of the United States has twice in a lifetime been forced to recross the Atlantic Ocean and pour out their treasure as the result of wars originating from ancient European feuds.

44 One cannot be surprised that they would like to see a peaceful and united Europe taking its place in the foundations of the world organization to which they are devoted. I have no doubt that, far from encountering any opposition or prejudice from the great republic of the New World, our movement will have their blessing and their aid.

45 We here in Great Britain have our own self-governing dominions —Canada, Australia, New Zealand, South Africa. We are joined together by ties of free will which have stood unyielding against all the ups and downs of fortune.

46 We are the center and summit of a world-wide commonwealth of nations. It is necessary that any policy this island may adopt towards Europe should enjoy the full sympathy and approval of the peoples of the Dominions. Why should we suppose that they will not be with us in this cause? They feel with us that Britain is geographically and historically a part of Europe and that they also have their inheritance in Europe.

47 If Europe united is to be a living force, Britain will have to play her full part as a member of the European family.

48 The Dominions also know that their youth, like that of the United States, have twice in living memory traversed the immense ocean spaces to fight and die in wars brought about by European discord in the prevention of which they have been powerless.

49 We may be sure that the cause of united Europe, in which the mother country must be a prime mover, will in no way be contrary to the sentiments which join us all together with our Dominions in the circle of the British crown.

50 It is, of course, alleged that all advocacy of the ideal of united Europe is nothing but a maneuver in the game of power politics, and that it is a sinister plot against Soviet Russia. There is no truth in this.

51 The whole purpose of a united democratic Europe is to give decisive guarantees against aggression. Looking out from the ruins of some of their most famous cities and from amid the cruel devastation of their fairest lands, the Russian people should surely realize how much they stand to gain by the elimination of the causes of war and the fear of war on the European continent.

52 The creation of a healthy and contented Europe is the first and truest interest of the Soviet Union. We had therefore hoped that all sincere efforts to promote European agreement and stability would receive, as they deserve, the sympathy and support of Russia. Instead, all this beneficent design has been denounced and viewed with suspicion by the Soviet press and radio. We have made no retort, and I do not propose to do so tonight.

53 But neither could we accept the claim that the veto of a single power, however respected, should bar and prevent a movement necessary to the peace, amity, and well-being of so many hundreds of millions of toiling and striving men and women.

54 We see before our eyes hundreds of millions of humble homes in Europe and islands outside which would be affected by war. Are they never to have a chance to thrive and flourish? Is the honest, faithful breadwinner never to be able to reap the fruits of his labor? Can he never bring up his children in health and joy and with the hopes of better days?

55 Can he never be free from the fear of foreign invasion, the crash of the bomb or the shell, the tramp of the hostile patrol, or what is even worse, the knock upon his door of the secret political police to take away the loved one far from the protection of law and justice; when all the time, by one spontaneous effort of his will, he could wake from all these nightmare horrors and stand forth in his manhood, free in the broad light of day?

56 The conception of European unity already commands strong sympathy among the leading statesmen in almost all countries. Europe must federate or perish, said the present Prime Minister, Mr. Attlee, before the late terrible war; and I have no reason to suppose that he will abandon that prescient declaration at a time when the vindication of his words is at hand.

57 Of course, we understand that, until public opinion expresses itself more definitely, governments hesitate to take positive action. It

is for us to provide the proof of solid popular support, both here and abroad, which will give to the governments of Europe a confidence to go forward and give practical effect to their beliefs.

58 We cannot say how long it will be before this stage is reached. We ask, however, that in the meantime His Majesty's government, together with other governments, should approach the various pressing continental problems from a European rather than from a restricted national angle.

59 In the discussions on the German and Austrian peace settlements, and indeed throughout the whole diplomatic field, the ultimate ideal should be held in view. Every new arrangement that is made should be designed in such a manner as to be capable of later being fitted into the pattern of a united Europe.

60 I must end where I began: namely, by placing this immense design of Europe within and subordinate to the United Nations organization. Unless some effective world supergovernment, for the purposes of preventing war, can be set up and begin its reign, the prospects for peace and human progress are dark and doubtful.

61 But let there be no mistake upon one point. Without a united Europe there is no prospect of world government. It is the urgent and indispensable step towards the realization of that ideal.

62 After the first Great War the League of Nations tried to build, without the aid of the United States, an international order upon a weak, divided Europe. Its failure cost us dear.

63 Today, after the second World War, Europe is far weaker and still more distracted. One of the four pillars of the temple of peace lies before us in shattered fragments. It must be assembled and reconstructed before there can be any real progress in building a spacious superstructure of our desires.

64 If, during the next five years, it is found possible to build a world organization of irresistible force and inviolable authority for the purpose of securing peace, there are no limits to the blessings which all men may enjoy and share. Nothing will help forward the building of that world organization so much as unity and stability in a Europe that is conscious of her collective personality and resolved to assume her rightful part in guiding the unfolding destinies of man.

65 In the ordinary day-to-day affairs of life, men and women expect rewards for successful exertion, and this is often right and reasonable.

But those who serve causes as majestic and high as ours need no reward; nor are our aims limited by the span of human life.

66 If success comes to us soon, we shall be happy. If our purpose is delayed, if we are confronted by obstacles and inertia, we may still be of good cheer, because in a cause, the righteousness of which will be proclaimed by the march of future events and the judgment of happier ages, we shall have done our duty and done our best.

Summary

2. It is for us to provide proof of popular support (¶57) and thus encourage the governments of Europe to think of broadly European rather than narrowly national problems (¶58-59).
3. *Summation*
   a. European unity is necessary to help the United Nations prevent war (¶60-63).
   b. European unity will help achieve peace and a better life within a world organization (¶64-65).
   c. To strive for such a cause is its own reward (¶66).

Comment

Mr. Churchill's oration contains some excellent illustrations of effective persuasive speech. First, its aim is clearly to present motives for action. The action desired is the restoration of Europe. This is stated repeatedly in paragraphs 1 to 18. It is implied in paragraph 1, where the speaker says that his purpose can be expressed in one word, "Europe." It is stated more vigorously in paragraph 5, where he says, "Europe shall not die." In paragraph 6 he repeats the same purpose when he says that his listeners must resolve to stay with the task until the goal is realized. Paragraph 7 also refers to the task of reviving the glories and happiness of Europe. This same purpose is repeated negatively or in terms of opposites in a series of vivid questions, beginning in paragraph 11, "Has Europe's mission come to an end?" and extending through paragraph 13. In paragraph 19 the purpose is incorporated in the proposition. The main point the author wishes to prove, the conclusion towards which his whole proof is directed, is: It is necessary for us "to promote the cause of united Europe and to give this idea the prominence and vitality necessary for it to lay hold of the minds of our fellow countrymen to such an extent that it will affect their actions and influence the course of national policy." Moreover, the proofs of the proposition are intimately united to the purpose. Each of the proofs stated in paragraphs 20-37 directs the audience to the main action, namely, the restoration of Europe. Paragraphs 56-66 in the conclusion repeat the purpose.

Secondly, this speech is clearly and effectively arranged. It contains an introduction, a clear development of the central theme, refutations of the outstanding objections to this theme, and an effective conclusion. The introduction makes the purpose clear and disposes the audience emotionally to assent to the speaker's ideas. It is challenging in its statements and exceptionally vigorous in its style. The development (¶20-37) explains the purpose and the necessity of an organization to promote the cause of united Europe. This purpose is defined in terms of the already existing United Nations organization in general and in the regional framework set up under that organization. It is further defined in terms of the structure of the national states (¶22-23) and of the particular problems relating to France, Germany, and Italy (¶24-37). The four objections to the formation of an organization to restore Europe are answered briefly but cogently. The first objection (¶38-41) is answered by means of an implied distinction between states which respect fundamental human and personal rights and those which do not. The second objection (¶42-44) is answered by a denial and by a proof that American opinion towards such a union would be favorable. The third objection (¶45-49) is also answered by a denial. The fourth objection is also denied and the denial is supported by an emotional appeal (¶50-55).

Effective persuasion is also evident in the concluding paragraphs, 56-66. Here an argument citing Mr. Attlee's support throws the might of authority behind the reasoning of the speech as a whole. A repetition of the purpose (¶57-59) and a recapitulation of the main proofs (¶60-66) reinforce the motives for action which the speaker desires. Note particularly the force of the final argument in paragraph 64. Here the basic reasoning of the speech finally appears in an enthymeme or an abridged syllogism (see Example VII C and analysis), which may be summed up as follows: If we can build a world organization with the force and authority to secure peace, limitless blessings will ensue. But we can help build such an organization by restoring European unity, stability, and leadership.

The third characteristic of a good persuasion, its emotional and imaginative appeal, is also evident throughout this speech. Mr. Churchill's own strong feeling about his subject is clear in the introductory paragraphs. He appeals to a lofty sense of pride (¶13), honor and faith (¶34), and duty (¶66). The contrast between Europe in her glory (¶2-8) and Europe in ruins (¶9-13) is calculated to excite the emotions of his audience. Frequent questions, all designed to arouse feelings of grief for Europe's distress and hope for her restoration, appear in paragraphs 11-13 and 54-55. Occasional metaphors, such as "a rubble heap, a charnel house, a breeding ground of pestilence and hate" (¶9), "the peaks of the Delectable Mountains" (¶16), and the "pillars of the temple of peace . . . in shattered fragments" (¶63) contribute to the imaginative excitement of the speech. Perhaps the most effective emotional appeal of all is the spirit that animates the entire persuasion. Throughout his speech Mr. Churchill manifests his disinterested love of European civilization, a spirit of generosity towards the vanquished, and of genuine friendship towards the victorious allies—qualities that cannot fail to win the confidence of his listeners.

Analysis and Composition

1. State as precisely as you can the emotional effect achieved in paragraph 1.
2. How is the emotional effect in paragraph 1 enhanced by the contrasted definitions of Europe in paragraphs 2-4?
3. Trace the increasing intensity of the emotion expressed in paragraphs 5-13. Show how the concluding sentence in paragraph 13 is calculated to win the audience to Churchill's own views on the restoration of Europe.
4. Many speakers place the emotional appeal at the end of the speech in order to assure a climactic arrangement. Churchill's most dramatic expression comes first. In your opinion, which of the following reasons best explains why Churchill used such a powerful appeal to the emotions at the beginning of his speech?

   a. Churchill was overcome by his own emotional response to Europe.
   b. Churchill knew that his war-weary English audience needed an extraordinary stimulus to action as well as convincing arguments.
   c. Churchill had no arguments to prove his main point; hence his reliance on emotions.

5. The proposition or central theme of this persuasion may be stated in various ways:

   a. We must go forward step by step to restore Europe.
   b. We must set on foot an organization to promote the cause of united Europe.
   c. We must save Europe by uniting Europe.
   d. Europe is worth saving.

   Which of the above statements is the best statement of the proposition?

   Base your choice upon the following principles:
   a. A proposition should be simple; i.e., it should not be too difficult to understand.
   b. A proposition should be arguable; i.e., it should be a statement that may be disputed.
   c. In persuasion a proposition should be definite; i.e., it should point to some immediate, concrete action to be decided upon by the audience.

6. A good persuasion is accurate in its facts and logical in its development. In addition it is also tactful; i.e., it takes into account national, partisan, and personal feelings. This speech shows several fine examples of tact. One example is the way in which Mr. Churchill avoids the suggestion

that an English organization for European unity might trespass on the authority of the United Nations or offend the sovereignty of the various national states. Another example of tact is his reference (¶56) to Mr. Attlee's support of the ideal of a united Europe. Decide whether similar examples of tactfulness appear in paragraphs 13, 24, 34, 51.

7. Contrast is a favorite method of development in this speech. Contrasts have already been pointed out in paragraphs 2-4, 8, and 9. Point out three other examples of contrast in this speech. Show how they contribute to the over-all aim of the speech.

8. In the outline of this essay the development of the proposition is phrased in a series of five sentences beginning, "We must . . ." This suggests Churchill's dependence upon the stock issue of necessity. Do you agree or disagree that the reasoning of the speech centers on the issue of necessity? Give reasons for your answer.

9. Why does Churchill say (¶25) that his proposal for a united Europe will give Frenchmen "a cause for serious thought and valiant decision"? In forming your answer consult paragraph 34.

10. In your opinion do the sentiments expressed in paragraph 37 argue to a lack of patriotic feeling on Churchill's part? Give reasons for your answer.

11. Discuss the following comment with reference to paragraphs 38-41: "Churchill's statement of the objection and his answer to the objection are deliberately vague. He wishes to avoid any direct reference to the status of the iron curtain nations."

12. On several occasions, notably in paragraphs 24, 36, 42, Churchill makes personal references to his own experience. Do these references help or hinder his purpose? Give reasons for your answer.

13. Although this address is directed to an English audience, it seems also to take into account the reactions of the peoples of Europe, America, and Russia, as well as the members of the British Commonwealth. Explain how the general circumstances of the speech justify this attitude on the part of the speaker.

14. What reasons does Churchill give for his statement in paragraph 61 that "without a united Europe there is no prospect of world government"?

15. Draw up an outline and write a persuasive speech of approximately 1000 words proving or disproving one of the following propositions:
    a. We must restore the Good Neighbor policy in the Western hemisphere.
    b. We should form local citizens committees to promote interest in good government.
    c. Americans should support the extension of the Fulbright Bill to promote international understanding.

d. We should support federal laws controlling automobile traffic on national highways.

e. American citizens should unite to support federal scholarships for advanced education.

Proposition: The American people should make an effort to get the kind of education they need.

2. Where Do We Go from Here in Education?

BY ROBERT M.. HUTCHINS

1 Now, in the twenty-five years, and more, that I have been in American education, I have noticed that it has certain permanent and abiding problems. They are caused by various paradoxes or contradictions in our educational system, and in our attitude toward it. It is about these problems, paradoxes, and contradictions that I wish briefly to speak.

2 The first paradox appears in our national behavior in the support of education. It is often said that American education is the American substitute for a national religion. But many countries have been able to reconcile support of religious establishment with disregard of its principles, and American support of education often appears to be of this kind. The devotion seems to be to the symbol, rather than to the activity, and is rather rhetorical than real.

3 Popular education is a splendid subject for a Fourth of July address; yet 350,000 teachers have been driven from the profession by the pitiful salaries now offered.

4 In some parts of this country, a teacher may count herself fortunate if she receives $500 a year, and we can be certain, I think, that if there is another depression the experience of the last one will be repeated. The expenditures on the schools will be the first cut and the last restored.

5 I have come to Detroit directly from the plane that brought me

WHERE DO WE GO FROM HERE IN EDUCATION? a speech delivered before the Detroit Economic Club, May 12, 1947. Used with the permission of the author.

home from a month in England. There is a country in which there is a shortage of all goods; a country whose empire, if not dissolving, is at least changing its shape; a country which has neither manpower, building materials, books, nor paper.

6 What is it doing?

7 It is putting into effect the provisions of the Education Act of 1944, the main result of which is an extension of the period of compulsory education from 14 to 15 years of age. I do not say that this is a wise decision, or that a mere increase in the school-leaving age produces necessarily sound educational results. I do say that this action which, under the circumstances, is so courageous as to be almost reckless, shows that the British really mean what we say about education.

8 They mean that education is important; it is more important than food, tobacco, or even beer; more important than capital equipment, military equipment, or houses. They mean that man does not live by bread alone, and that an intelligent nation is more likely to succeed economically and militarily than one which has great material resources but does not know what to do with them.

9 It is true that our own country is now committed, in the GI Bill of Rights, to the greatest educational expenditure in the history of the race. The appropriations for educational purposes under the GI Bill of Rights will run between ten and fourteen billion dollars. This legislation originated, not in the desire to educate veterans, but in the forebodings of the economist that there would be six to eight million unemployed within six months after the war.

10 The genesis of the National Youth Administration during the depression was the same. It did not result from the conviction that young people must be educated even if the stock market falls, but from a desire to keep young people off the labor market.

11 I applaud the expenditure and the consequences of the National Youth Administration and the GI Bill of Rights, although I must say it will be a little unfortunate if the young men now studying under the GI Bill of Rights come to the end of their grants and the end of their studies in a period of unemployment.

12 I am concerned here, not with what such measures accomplish, but with what they reveal of the American attitude toward education. They do not require any revision of my thesis that the American people, whatever their professions, do not take education very seriously. And, in the past there has been no particular reason why they should.

13 This country was impregnable to enemies from without, and apparently indestructible. It could not be destroyed even by the hysterical waste and mass stupidity of the people and its government. Foreign policy, for example, could be the blundering ground of nice old southern lawyers, and education could be regarded as a means of keeping children off the street; the schools kept young people out of worse places until we were willing to have them go to work.

14 Now, when the Russians have the atomic bomb—which, I am happy to say, was not solely the product of the University of Chicago— and the Russians certainly will have it within five years; Langmuir's prediction is about a year and a half—when the Russians have the atomic bomb, the position of the United States automatically undergoes a dramatic change. The position of the United States, then, is very little beyond that of Czechoslovakia before the war—one false step in foreign policy can mean the end, not only of our institutions, but also of civilization. In a war in which both sides have atomic bombs, the cities of both sides will be destroyed.

15 And we cannot place our hope on those agreements for the control of atomic energy, which are just around the corner in the sense in which Mr. Hoover remarked, in 1932, that prosperity was just around the corner. These agreements are absolutely imperative; but they will simply guarantee, if they are effective, that the next war will end with atomic bombs instead of beginning with them. And, if these agreements are ineffective, they will simply increase the element of surprise which the atomic bomb has added to the arsenal of the aggressor. And, if it becomes possible, as it theoretically is, to manufacture atomic bombs out of helium and hydrogen, all plans for control based on the control of uranium must fail.

16 We have now reached the point where we cannot have war and civilization, too!

17 Last week in Paris, I met with a staff of the United Nations Educational, Scientific, and Cultural Organizations. There is a group operating, by the way, on an annual budget which is about 25 per cent of the amount which the United States government spent every year during the war at the University of Chicago alone for the production of new weapons. And this group is dedicated to the proposition that, since war begins in the minds of men, and since education is supposed to have some effect on the human mind, the way to prevent war is to do something about education.

18 I put it to you that this proposition is sound; that education, as the British have decided, is the most urgent business before us, and that we must show, by our actions rather than by our speeches, that we regard it in this light.

19 Now, while we are about it, we might attack another paradox in American education, which is that a system, nominally democratic, operates in an oligarchical way. An oligarchy, I need not remind you, was a form of government based on wealth.

20 American education is founded on the belief that democracy is served if its schools, colleges, and universities charge low fees, or none; and if, at the same time, there is no discrimination among students in terms of their intellectual ability.

21 We have democratic education, then, if we do not charge for it, and if we make clear that every citizen is entitled, as a matter of right, to as much free education as every other citizen.

22 This assumption is false in all its parts.

23 Actually, the important cost of education is not fees. It is the cost of the pupil's subsistence if he lives away from home, and the loss of his earning power. In this country, however, scholarships given by private foundations rarely cover more than fees.

24 The educational institutions managed by local and state governments feel they have performed their full duty if they charge low fees or none. The books of the University of Chicago will show an expenditure on student aid of more than $600,000 a year, but the figure is meaningless, for almost every cent of this money is paid back to the University in the form of fees by the students who receive it.

25 Universal education in America has, therefore, meant that all those who could afford to continue in school have been able to, and those who have not had the money have not.

26 Hence the paradox, that in a country which provides free education for all, the length of a young person's education varies directly with his capacity to pay; and since, at these age levels, at least, and probably at all age levels, there is no relation between intellectual ability and capacity to pay, the educational system has been overwhelmed with students who are not qualified for the work they are supposed to be doing, and whose presence inevitably dilutes and trivializes the whole program.

27 Every study that has been made in this country shows that there are more good high school graduates out of college than in. The reason is that the ones who go to college are the ones who have the money

to go, and it would be undemocratic to say they were not bright enough to go. And those who are bright enough to go cannot go unless they have the money to go, because we have no adequate system of financial aid to those who are bright but impoverished.

28 Here I think it is safe to say that we fall behind every country in the Western world.

29 Until the National Youth Administration and the GI Bill of Rights, nothing was ever done by anybody to recognize the cost of living as an element in the cost of education.

30 Before the war, we used to boast that a student could go to the University of Illinois for $75 a year. He could. That is, he could if, in addition, he could command not less than $750 a year to live on, and if his family could do without his earnings.

31 By contrast, every European country has long since made provision that those who show themselves qualified through a rigorous system of competition to receive aid in their education shall receive aid which enables them to live as well as to study.

32 As a self-supporting student, who tried to live first and study afterwards, I can testify that the combination is possible only because the American university demands so little study.

33 If we had in this country real intellectual competition in our universities, it would at once become apparent that it is not possible for a boy to work eight hours a day in a factory, as I did, and get an education at the same time. Under those circumstances it must be clear that I did not get an education; I simply graduated from college, which is quite a different thing.

34 What we need is an adequate system of financial aid for those who deserve it, a national system of competitive scholarships—scholarships which are large enough to enable the student to study as well as live.

35 We also need a system by which those students who are not qualified for university work may be effectually excluded from the university. The basic task of education for citizenship should be performed outside the universities. The universities should be devoted to advanced study, professional training, research, and the education of leaders. Therefore, the university must be limited, if it proposes to succeed in any of these tasks, to those who have demonstrated their qualifications for advanced study, professional training, research, or leadership.

36 The notion that any American, merely because he is one, has the privilege of proceeding to the highest university degree must be abandoned. A six-year elementary school, a three- or four-year high school, a three- or four-year college, locally organized, would give us a system which would take care of the fundamentals of education, and would relieve the university of the necessity of doing so. Students graduating from this system would come to the end of it between the ages of 18 and 20, and only those who had demonstrated their qualifications to go on should be permitted to do so—at least at the cost of the taxpayer.

37 In order to induce the others not to go on, I should be perfectly prepared to have them receive the bachelor's degree at the age of 18 or 20.

38 I have, in fact, a good deal of sympathy for the proposal of Barrett Wendell of Harvard, that every American citizen should receive the bachelor's degree at birth.

39 With a six-year elementary school, a three- or four-year high school, and a three- or four-year college from which only carefully selected graduates should be permitted to proceed to the university, we might have a truly democratic system of education, democratic in the purest Jeffersonian sense.

40 Jefferson's proposals for the University of Virginia contemplated a rigorous selection of students, the like of which has never been seen in this hemisphere.

41 There is nothing undemocratic about saying that those who are to receive education at public expense should show they are qualified for it. On the contrary, it is most undemocratic to say that anybody can go as far as he likes in education, when what it actually means is he can actually have all the education he can pay for.

42 The creation of local colleges as the culmination of the six-four-four, or six-three-three system of education would give us a chance to develop institutions devoted to liberal education, free from the domination of the university, and would give us a chance to develop universities free from the domination of collegiate interests.

43 We should then have an intelligently organized educational system, democratically operated, and equipped to play its part in the new world that is struggling to be born; but, when all this is done, we should be left confronting a third paradox; namely, the paradox presented by what the people expect of education.

44 Our country, in which the rapidity of technical change is more dramatically presented than anywhere else in the world, has an educational program which largely ignores the rapidity and inevitability of such change.

45 Now, vocational training assumes that the machinery on which the boy is trained will be in use when he goes to work. Actually, the machines and the methods are likely to be so different that his training will be a positive handicap to him.

46 As our experience in wartime shows, the place to train hands for industry is in industry. The aircraft companies produced better mechanics in a few weeks than the schools could produce in years. And it must be obvious that education on a democratic basis cannot supply social standing, as Gilbert and Sullivan pointed out, when "Everybody is somebody and nobody is anybody."

47 Moreover, those who seek education for financial success are doomed to disappointment. Direct training for the purpose of producing financial success, like a course in how to make money, is obviously a fraud, and the number of occupations, I regret to tell you, in which what are known as college conditions are more of a help than a hindrance is certainly limited. Yet, the belief that education can in some way contribute to vocational and social success has done more than most things to disrupt American education.

48 What education can do, and about all it can do, is to produce a trained mind.

49 Now, getting a trained mind is hard work. As Aristotle remarked, "Learning is accompanied by pain." Those who are seeking something which education cannot supply are not likely to be enthusiastic about the pain which what it can supply must cause; and, since our false sense of democracy requires us to admit them to education anyway, then something must be done with them when they get into it, and it must, of course, be something which is not painful. Therefore, it must be something which interests them.

50 The vocationalism of our schools results, in part, from the difficulty of interesting many boys and girls in what are known as academic subjects, and the whole apparatus of football, fraternities, and fun is a means by which education is made palatable to those who have no business to be in it.

51 The fact is that the best practical education is the most theoretical one. This is, probably, the first time in human history in which change on every front is so rapid that what one generation has learned

of practical affairs, in politics, business, and technology, is of little use to the next, just as what the father has learned of the facts of life is almost useless to his son. It is principles—everlasting principles—which are of practical value today; not data, not methods, not facts, not helpful hints, but principles are what the rising generation requires if it is to find its way through the mazes of tomorrow. No man among us can tell what tomorrow will be like; all we know with certainty is that it will be different from today.

52 We can also see that it is principles which the adults of May 12, 1947, must understand if they are to be ready for May 13. The notion that education is something concerned with preparation for a vocational and social success, that it is composed of helpful hints to housewives and bond salesmen, has permeated the education of adults in the United States.

53 Adult education, in general, is aimed at making third-rate bookkeepers into second-rate bookkeepers by giving them classes by night, and in the general population this process has not aroused much enthusiasm because we have thought of education as something for children, anyway; we have thought of it as something like the measles—having had education once, one need not—in fact, one cannot—have it again.

54 Apart from mathematics, metaphysics, logic, astronomy, and similar theoretical studies, it is clear that comprehension comes only with experience. A learned Greek remarked that young men should not listen to lectures on moral philosophy, and he was right. Moral philosophy, history, political economics, and literature can convey their full meaning only in maturity.

55 Take *Macbeth,* for example. When I taught *Macbeth* to boys in preparatory school, it was a blood-and-thunder story—a very good blood-and-thunder story, one well worth reading, but a blood-and-thunder story still. *Macbeth* can mean what it meant to Shakespeare only when the reader has had sufficient experience, vicarious or otherwise, of marriage and ambition to understand the issues and their implications.

56 It happens that the kind of things we need most to understand today are those which only adults can fully grasp. A boy may be a brilliant mathematician, or a musician—and I have known several astronomers who contributed to the international journals at the age of 13—but, I never knew a child of that age who had much that was useful to say about the ends of human life, the purpose of organized

society, and the means of reconciling freedom and order. But, it is subjects like these about which we are most confused, and about which we must obtain some clarification if our civilization is to survive.

57 The survival of civilization, if the Russians are to have the atomic bomb in five years, depends on those who are adults today. We cannot wait for the rising generation to rise. Even if we succeeded in giving them a perfect education, it would be too late.

58 Therefore it is imperative that we enter upon a program of mass adult education such as we have never contemplated before. The beginnings of this program are already under way. They can be seen here in Detroit, in the efforts which your library and universities are making to force the consideration of fundamental issues through the study of the Great Books of the Western world. At the rate at which this program is now expanding, I expect to see fifteen million people in it within five years.

59 I do not suffer from the illusion that, if fifteen million Americans are studying the Great Books of the Western world within five years, we shall avert the next war. Education alone cannot avert war; it may increase the chances of averting it. Nor do I deny that, if by reading the Great Books, or otherwise, the hearts of the Americans are changed, and the hearts of the Russians remain unchanged, we shall merely have the satisfaction of being blown up with changed hearts rather than unchanged ones. I do not expect the American audience to have enough faith in the immortality of the soul to regard this as more dubious consolation. But, if we do not avert war by this kind of education, we can at least provide ourselves, in the time that is left to us, with some suitable alternative to liquor, the movies, and—if I may say so in Detroit—running around the country in secondhand cars, and catching glimpses of the countryside between the billboards.

60 At the age of 48 I can testify that all forms of recreation eventually lose their charm. I mean all!!! Partly as the result of the universal recognition of the great truth that eventually all forms of recreation lose their charm—partly in recognition of this great truth, the Great Books discussion classes have now begun to sweep the country from New York to Seattle.

61 Another explanation of their success is that the people are beginning to realize the shortcomings of their own education. They see now that the books they never read in school or college, the issues they never discussed, the ideas they never heard of, are the books, discussions, and issues that are directly relevant here and now. It may be

that this generation of parents will see to it that the shortcomings of their children are overcome so that the American of the future may not have to get all his education after he becomes an adult.

62 The final paradox of American education which I wish to mention will become apparent when you look at what the world requires, and what American education has to offer.

63 American education excels in every technological activity, every applied sphere, and it excels as well in pure science. The British, French, or German physician or engineer who had a chance to study in the United States would be a fool to decline the opportunity; but he should be educated first and not count on the possibility of getting an education afterward. In every technological, applied, scientific field, the United States is, without question, pre-eminent today.

64 We know, therefore, one thing with certainty about the American university—it can produce weapons of war. Any time that you would like to have weapons of war produced, the American universities will undertake to supply them, and they will be bigger, better, and more deadly than ever.

65 On the other hand, another great segment of the American university, the modern medical school, has done almost as much to lengthen life as the schools of engineering and physics have done to shorten it.

66 In short, wherever the material conditions of existence are in question, the American university can deliver the goods. If you want better bombs, better poison gases, better medicine, better crops, better automobiles, you will find the American university able—and usually willing—to help you.

67 Where the American university cannot help you is where you need help most. Because of the paradoxes I have listed, because of our indifference to the real purposes of education, and because of our preoccupation with the trivial, frivolous, and immediately impractical, the American university is gradually losing its power to save the world. It has developed the power to destroy it; it is ill equipped to save it.

68 What is honored in a country will be cultivated there. A means of cultivating it is the educational system. The American educational system mirrors the chaos of the modern world. While science and technology, which deal only with goods in the material order, are flourishing as never before, liberal education, philosophy, and theology, through which we might learn to guide our lives, are undergoing a slow but inevitable decay.

69 It is not enough to say, then, "Let us have lots of education," or even, "Let us have lots of expensive education." We must have universal education—let it cost what it may—of the right kind, and this is the kind through which we may hope to raise ourselves by our bootstraps into a different spiritual world; that is the kind which places a sound character and a trained intelligence above all other aims, and which gives the citizen a scale of values by which he can learn to live. Only by such a scale of values, rationally established and firmly held, can a democratic individual hope to be more than a transitory phenomenon lost in the confusion of a darkening world.

70 In a democratic country there is a sense in which there is never anything wrong with education. A democratic country gets the kind of education it wants. I have no doubt that, if the people of the United States understand the urgency of education today, and understand the kind of education they must have, they can get it. I hope they will make the effort to get it before it is too late.

Comment

This persuasion may be summarized by the following questions and answers.

What *action* does the speaker want his audience to take?

He wants the American people to help reform American education; specifically, to get the kind of education they need.

What *proof* does he offer to justify this action on the part of his audience?

He argues the *proposition* that American education is in need of reform. How does he prove the proposition?

He proves the proposition by advancing four disputed points at issue, for each of which he offers further proof. These points at issue are:

1. American education is supported symbolically rather than actively, that is, financially.
2. American education is not an intelligently organized educational system, is not democratically operated, is not equipped to play its part in the new world.
3. American education squanders its resources on vocational, social, and financial success instead of aiming to teach students how to master enduring principles or to comprehend experience.
4. American education answers our material needs but fails to meet our spiritual needs, that is, sound character and trained intelligence.

What is Mr. Hutchins' method of proof?

He argues deductively in a syllogism * that may be summarized as follows:

Major premise: An educational system that is not given adequate financial support, not intelligently organized, democratically operated or equipped to play its part in contemporary society, that does not aim at the mastery of principles and the comprehension of experience, that fails to foster the development of sound character and trained intelligence—such an education is in need of reform.

Minor premise: But American education is not supported . . . not intelligently organized . . . squanders its resources . . . fails to meet our spiritual needs. . . . (Note that the points at issue are minor premises of the syllogism.)

Conclusion: Therefore American education is in need of reform. (Note that the proposition is the conclusion of the syllogism.)

Thus we see the logical organization of "Where Do We Go from Here in Education?" In the actual presentation, however, this logical organization is less formal and less formidable. Each issue is introduced by a brief explanation or history. There are frequent summaries and repetitions. Mr. Hutchins' logical skeleton is covered with the firm flesh of facts, and the flesh has the colors of deep feeling.

In the more detailed paragraph outline below we shall see how Mr. Hutchins has arranged the proofs we have just summarized.

Paragraph Summary

I. *Introduction*

Subject: The paradoxes in American education (¶1).

II. *Development*

A. First paradox: American support of education is symbolic rather than real (¶2).

1. Popular education is venerated as a symbol, but 350,000 teachers have been driven from the profession because of low salaries (¶3).

2. If there is a depression the expenditures on the schools will be first cut and last restored (¶4).

3. In contrast to America, England's support of education is real, for England, despite her poverty (¶5),

a. Put into effect the provisions of the Education Act of 1944 (¶7),

* The syllogism was discussed at length in Section VII, Example C.

b. And by this action testified to the importance of education (¶8).

4. In contrast to England, American expenditure for education in the GI Bill of Rights and the National Youth Administration was not voted primarily to aid education but to prevent unemployment (¶9-10).

5. The results of the GI Bill and the NYA were good (¶11) but do not prove that American support of education is real rather than symbolic (¶12).

6. In the past serious attention to education was not as necessary as it is today because

   a. In the past America was impregnable to the force of foreign enemies and to the waste and stupidity of its own people (¶13), whereas

   b. Today, with the atom bomb (¶14-16), the only way to prevent war is by education (¶17).

7. Hence education is our most urgent business, and we must support education actively rather than symbolically (¶18).

B. Second paradox: American education is nominally democratic, but it operates in an oligarchical way (¶19).

   1. The assumption that American education is democratic if it is free and undiscriminating (¶20-21) is false in all its parts (¶22).

   2. This assumption is false in *fact* because

      a. Scholarships given by private foundations rarely cover more than fees, and do not cover subsistence or the loss of the student's earning power by his family (¶23).

      b. Public institutions do no more than provide free or low tuition, without regard to other expenses; student aid usually helps to pay bills to the university, not to pay for the student's subsistence (¶24).

      c. Hence our nominally democratic education is not free; in reality, it discriminates against the student who cannot afford to pay in favor of the student who can afford to pay (¶25-26).

      d. As a result, more good high school graduates are out of college than in (¶27).

   3. American failure to aid the bright student compares unfavorably with European countries (¶28-31) and fosters a system wherein the working student does little studying (¶32-33).

   4. Adequate student aid, fostered by national competitive scholarships, would allow qualified students to attend the university (¶34-35), while

   5. Unqualified students could attend a college (¶36-38).

6. Such a system is truly democratic in the Jeffersonian sense of demanding that students be qualified for advanced study (¶39-41).

7. Such a system could easily be created (¶42) and would contribute directly to an intelligently organized educational system, democratically operated (i.e., free to qualified students) and equipped to play its part in the new world (¶43).

C. Third paradox: The American people expect the wrong things from education (¶43-44). They expect that

1. American education will provide vocational success (¶44-46), social success (¶46), and financial success (¶47), rather than the trained mind (¶48).

2. The real aim of education is not to "interest" an unwilling student in an education which is made more palatable by vocationalism, football, fraternities, and fun (¶49-50), but to teach everlasting principles (¶51); not to impart helpful hints (¶52-53) but to foster theoretical studies and the mature comprehension (¶54) of an experience like that represented in *Macbeth* (¶55).

3. This mature comprehension of experience is urgent today (¶56-57) especially for adults; hence the need for a mass adult education program (¶58) such as the Great Books program.

4. The Great Books program will help to deepen and mature experience (¶59-60) and will make up for the shortcomings of early education (¶61).

D. Fourth paradox: American education offers what the world does not require (¶62)—that is, education for material things rather than spiritual things—in the sense that

1. It surpasses all other kinds of education in technology and applied science (¶63), in producing weapons of war (¶64), in medical science (¶65)—in summary, in dealing with the material conditions of life (¶66).

2. But the American university fails to supply the more important needs of the spirit because of its indifference to real education and its preoccupation with the trivial, frivolous, and immediately impractical (¶67).

3. The American educational system mirrors the chaos of the modern world in its neglect of liberal education, philosophy, and theology, which are the means of spiritual enlightenment (¶68).

4. The great need today is for an education that will produce a sound character and a trained intelligence capable of living by a scale of rational values (¶69).

III. Conclusion: Plea for action: People should make the effort to get the kind of education they need (¶70).

Hutchins' Persuasive Style

As the outline of this speech suggests, "Where Do We Go from Here in Education?" differs in some respects from Mr. Churchill's oration. First, it is primarily intellectual in its subject matter and tone, whereas the Churchill oration is primarily emotional in its attitude. Second, the subject of Mr. Hutchins' speech is more extensive, since he considers four separate aspects of American education. Mr. Churchill's argument is simple in the sense that all the proofs and demonstrations are united in a single purpose. Mr. Hutchins' argument on the other hand is multiple. Although all his proofs serve a main proposition, namely that American education is in need of reform, he urges a number of subordinate propositions, such as more financial support of education, stricter supervision of education, a redefinition of aims, the extension of the Great Books program, and the revival of liberal education, philosophy, and theology. A difference in style may also be observed. Churchill appeals directly to his audience's sense of pity and honor, while Mr. Hutchins uses the indirect methods of irony and understatement to motivate his appeal for reform.

Nevertheless, Mr. Hutchins' speech, in relation to his purpose, is an equally effective example of persuasion. Like Mr. Churchill, Mr. Hutchins continually stresses motives for action. He does not discuss the problems, paradoxes, and contradictions of American education merely to inform or entertain his audience. He wishes the audience to act, to make an effort to get the kind of education he feels they need. This preoccupation with action colors the entire speech. As early as the third paragraph we observe scornful references to the pitiful salaries paid to teachers in the United States. This indirect appeal for greater public assistance to education is fortified by a stinging comparison of American support of schools with the sacrifices the British people have made for education. The first part of the speech concludes with a forthright challenge (¶12-13) for a change in attitude. The need for action is stressed further when Mr. Hutchins argues with the trenchancy of an advocate that the atomic bomb and all that it implies present a challenge which can only be met by the most active support of real education.

Similarly, in the discussion of the second paradox (beginning in ¶19), the financial hardships that American students are required to endure remind the audience of its own responsibility to do something about education. To drive this point home Mr. Hutchins briefly outlines (¶34-43) a system of education that would accomplish the purpose he is urging upon his audience.

In like manner the reasoning on the third paradox is pointed to a practical end, namely the extension of the Great Books program. The fourth paradox concludes with a direct appeal to the American people to support that kind of education which produces a sound character and a trained intelligence, both absolutely essential for surviving in the present age. Note how each action Mr. Hutchins suggests—financial assistance, reform in the structure of the colleges and universities, change in emphasis from the vocational to the liberal—all serve the general purpose, namely the total reform of American education.

Mr. Hutchins' arrangement of his arguments deserves the most careful attention. At first glance it appears that he has scanted his introduction and conclusion. Closer inspection, however, reveals that the explanatory material which is usually developed in a tidy introductory section is here revealed bit by bit as the argument progresses. Mr. Hutchins' arrangement is similar to that of the skillful storyteller whose exposition is integrated with the narrative. Thus, for example, instead of a long preliminary résumé of the present state of American education—which might well have seemed tedious to his audience, the Economic Club of Detroit—he furnishes the background materials in short preliminary expositions to each of the four main parts of his address. Similarly, instead of summing up all of his conclusions in an elaborate final statement, he gives partial summaries at the end of each of the four sections. Furthermore, since each paradox blends with the one which succeeds it, the last section is in itself a summary of the three previous parts.

Note too the climactic order of Mr. Hutchins' arguments. The first of the four parts of his development asks for financial support. The second part of his development asks for financial support *and* reform in the structure of education. The third of the four parts asks for a new orientation of educational mentality. The fourth and concluding part solicits support for the spiritual aims of education. In a sense the argument ascends like a pyramid from the broad base of active financial support, the material means of education, and the external organization of the schools, to the narrower point of intellectual discipline, and finally to the apex of spiritual enlightenment. Thus the arrangement of his arguments not only achieves his purpose but satisfies the reader's sense of logic and esthetic proportion.

In contrast to Mr. Churchill's style, Mr. Hutchins' style does not appear to be emotional or imaginative. Actually this appearance is deceiving. Mr. Hutchins does not appeal directly to emotions, but he does so indirectly. Irony, paradox, open ridicule are powerful weapons in this speech. Note some of these characteristic remarks in the context in which they appear: "It [education] is more important than food, tobacco, or even beer" (¶8). The National Youth Administration is the result of "a desire to keep young people off the labor market" (¶10). "The educational system has been overwhelmed with students who are not qualified for the work they are supposed to be doing, and whose presence inevitably dilutes and trivializes the whole program" (¶26). "Every American citizen should receive the bachelor's degree at birth" (¶38). "The whole apparatus of football, fraternities, and fun is a means by which education is made palatable to those who have no business to be in it" (¶50). "Adult education, in general, is aimed at making third-rate bookkeepers into second-rate bookkeepers by giving them classes by night" (¶53). "Any time that you would like to have weapons of war produced, the American universities will undertake to supply them, and they will be bigger, better, and more deadly than ever" (¶64).

Phrases such as these are not glittering decorations. They are, rather, the expression of a disciplined wrath calculated to stir similar feelings in the minds of an audience.

Analysis and Composition

1. Are the words "problems, paradoxes, and contradictions" (¶1) to be taken as synonyms? Give reasons for your answer.
2. The style in paragraph 2 is an excellent match to the thought. The basic thought is a contrast between professed ideals and actual practice. The style in sentences 3 and 4 is antithetical or "contrasted" in its grammatical structure. These antitheses are also emphasized by a repetition of the *r* and *s* sounds. Show this match between style and thought by diagramming the sentences * and by underscoring the *r* and *s* sounds. †
3. In paragraph 5 Mr. Hutchins introduces a proof by referring to his own personal authority as a witness. What is the force of this argument from authority in its present context?
4. Paragraph 6, like paragraphs 16, 22, and several others, consists of a single sentence. How do these single-sentence paragraphs contribute to the clarity and interest of the speech?
5. Mr. Hutchins' use of sarcasm (a species of irony) in paragraph 13 is a daring device to stir his audience. Determine whether in your opinion this paragraph might antagonize his audience.
6. In paragraph 14 Mr. Hutchins compares the position of the United States with that of Czechoslovakia before the war. Reread the introduction to Section V of this book and determine whether there is a real basis for this comparison. Give reasons for your answer.
7. Examine the reasoning in sentence 3 of paragraph 17. Do you regard this reasoning as an effective proof or the unfinished outline of a proof? Defend your position.

* See handbooks: Hodges, *1*; Kierzek, pp. 37-49; Wykoff, Appendix B.
† See handbooks: Hodges, *19h*; Kierzek, pp. 62-66, *44*; Perrin, pp. 295, 427, 444-45.

8. Do you regard Hutchins' definition of oligarchy in paragraph 19 as a satisfactory one in view of the interpretation he gives to the word and its opposite, democracy, in the immediately succeeding paragraphs?

9. Paragraph 26 concludes that universal education in America is possible only for the moneyed class. What specific examples in the preceding paragraphs are used to justify this conclusion? Are you satisfied with the number and force of these examples? If not, explain.

10. In paragraph 28 Mr. Hutchins contrasts America unfavorably with every country in the Western world. What is the basis of this contrast? What are the proofs? Are these proofs adequate? Give reasons for your answer.

11. Analyze carefully the reasoning employed in paragraph 35. First define as accurately as you can "education for citizenship," "advanced study," "professional training," "research," and "the education of leaders." When you have defined these words decide whether the definitions include the idea of "training for citizenship." Explain your decision in a paragraph of approximately 300 words.

12. In paragraph 36 Mr. Hutchins indicates that there is a distinction between a college education and a university education. In paragraph 42 he again refers to colleges as free from the domination of the university. Thus he implies that there is a real distinction between colleges and universities. What in your opinion is the difference between a college and a university? Does Mr. Hutchins make this difference clear? If not, does this lack of clarity constitute a real defect in his basic argument?

13. In developing the third paradox (¶43-61), Mr. Hutchins necessarily is involved in paradoxes himself. Thus he speaks of *theoretical* education as being *practical* and of *practical* training as being a *positive handicap*. In what sense is he employing the italicized words in this section of his essay?

14. In paragraph 52 Mr. Hutchins shifts from collegiate and university education to adult education. How does his discussion of adult education tie in with the previous discussions? Note particularly his remarks in paragraphs 58-61.

15. In paragraphs 58-66 Mr. Hutchins refers to the Great Books of the Western world and to study clubs that have swept the country from New York to Seattle. Should he have assumed that his audience understood this reference to the Great Books program without exposition on his part? (Note: For a favorable description of the Great Books program see *Time*, March 17, 1952, pp. 76-84. For a critical approach see "The Great Books" by Jacques Barzun, *The Atlantic*, December, 1952, pp. 79-84.)

16. Do you agree or disagree with Mr. Hutchins' criticism of the spiritual

and intellectual defects of the American university stated in paragraphs 62-70? State your position in a proposition supported by several specific examples.

17. Mr. Hutchins' discussion of American education has stated with clearness, force, and originality a distinctly arguable point of view. You may not choose to contest his idea that Americans do not support higher education financially or that good students are frequently barred from higher education for financial reasons. You may, however, find grounds for disputing some of Mr. Hutchins' ideas expressed in the third or fourth parts of his speech. Some of the disputed issues are among those stated below. Take sides for or against one of these questions and write a persuasive speech of approximately 1000 words. (Before writing your essay reread the instructions for preparing General Exercise A on argument in this section. See pp. 489-90.)

    a. American higher education in general aims at financial and social success rather than intellectual excellence.

    b. A theoretical education is a better preparation for our changing world than one based upon a practical knowledge of changing techniques.

    c. Courses in business administration have a rightful place in a college curriculum.

    d. Courses in physical training should not be accredited in American universities.

    e. Every college graduate should be acquainted with a fair sampling of the Great Books of the Western world.

    f. The man who cannot discriminate among spiritual values is an imperfectly educated man.

SECTION XII

A. Give unity to description by selecting and organizing details to create a single dominant impression.

SECTION XII

B. Give coherence to your description by maintaining a point of view that is consistent with the physical position and mental attitude of the observer.

C. Give emphasis to your description by using vivid details, figurative language, and climactic order.

D. Blend description with narration to achieve realistic effects.

General Exercises

Description

DESCRIPTION is that form of discourse which aims (1) to present an object as it appears to the senses (scientific description) or (2) to create an imaginative impression of a real or fictitious object (artistic or impressionistic description). Both types of description are concerned with the report of, and the appeal to, the senses—the five external senses of sight, hearing, touch, taste, and smell, and that internal sense, ·often called awareness or consciousness, which reports sensations, or subjective impressions.

EXPOSITORY OR SCIENTIFIC DESCRIPTION

Scientific description states or reproduces (as does a photograph) the characteristics of an object, without personal coloring or imaginative suggestion. Police reports or real estate notices are descriptions of this kind. Thus the two examples below give us only the "objective" facts:

WANTED BY THE UNITED STATES MARSHAL

John Didymus, escaped from Lestertown prison, white, male, aged 23, brown hair, blue eyes, cleft chin, brownish birthmark on right cheek, two false front teeth, height 6 feet, weight 150-165 pounds, walks with short, hopping step because of ankle injury. May answer to nickname Hutch. $1000 reward for information leading to his arrest.

FOR SALE

Ranch-type house, 7 rooms, 4 bedrooms, living room 15' by 25', large den with brick fireplace, modern G.E. kitchen, 2 baths, 2-car garage,

corner plot 100' by 150', junction of Main and Huguenot Streets. Large
lawn in front with 6' privet hedge. Two blocks from public school, one
block First Calvinist Church. Oil heat, Johns-Manville insulation, stone
cellar. Excellent residence for professional man. Price $35,000.

Clearly these descriptions report the "objective" facts. That is, they
do not go beyond the identification, classification, and division of the
essential physical parts or characteristics of a wanted man and a suburban house. Similarly in strictly scientific writing, such as a botanist's
description of an acacia, an engineer's description of a diesel engine,
a social scientist's description of a broken home, a geographer's description of Lapland, a psychologist's analysis of a dream, the aim is merely
to report sense perceptions as exactly and as impersonally as possible.
An example of this type of scientific description may be found in T. H.
Huxley's "The Herring."

> The herring's body, tapering to each end, is covered with thin, flexible
> scales, which are very easily rubbed off. The taper head, with its under-
> hung jaw, is smooth and scaleless on the top; the large eye is partly
> covered by two folds of transparent skin, like eyelids—only immovable
> and with the slit between them vertical instead of horizontal; the cleft
> behind the gill cover is very wide, and, when the cover is raised, the large
> red gills which lie beneath it are freely exposed. The rounded back bears
> the single moderately long dorsal fin about its middle. The tail fin is
> deeply cleft, and on careful inspection small scales are seen to be con-
> tinued from the body, onto both its upper and its lower lobes, but there
> is no longitudinal scaly fold on either of these. The belly comes to an
> edge, covered by a series of sharply keeled bony shields between the
> throat and the vent; and behind the last is the anal fin, which is of the
> same length as the dorsal fin. There is a pair of forelimbs, or pectoral
> fins, just behind the head; and a pair of hindlimbs, or ventral fins, are
> situated beneath the dorsal fin, a little behind a vertical line drawn from
> its front edge, and a long way in front of the vent. These fins have bony
> supports or rays, all of which are soft and jointed.

This example shows how closely scientific description follows the
pattern of careful observation. In other words, this kind of description
is literal, factual, reproductive, photographic. Success in writing this
type of description depends upon a mastery of simple expository techniques (see Examples VII B1 and B2 and C, and Kroeber in General

Exercise B, Section VII) and a detailed and scientific knowledge of the subject matter of the description.

ARTISTIC OR IMPRESSIONISTIC DESCRIPTION

The second type of description, and the one with which rhetoric is specifically concerned, is artistic or impressionistic description. Contrary to scientific description, which we have compared to a photograph, this type of description aims to re-present, in the manner of a painting, the impression made by a real object or to create an imaginative impression of a fictitious one. Writers who employ artistic description attempt to make the reader as intensely aware of an object, real or imagined, as they can. In Joseph Conrad's phrase, they intend "by the power of the written word, to make you hear, to make you feel . . . to make you *see*."

To achieve this intention, it is necessary for a writer to do more than appeal to the senses. Thus we find in a child's reader sentences like these:

See the red pony. Hear the clip-clop of his hooves as he trots around the park. The skin on the pony's nose is as soft as velvet. The pony likes to munch sweet-smelling clover. It reminds him of the time when, as a very little pony, he trotted by his mother's side in Farmer Jones's meadow.

Here we have reference to the five external senses and an impression of the little pony's internal (that is, horse) sense. But this example merely catalogues sense impressions. It does not stir the feelings; it does not discriminate among the various shades of sense experience. To be effective it would need the active collaboration of a child's naturally poetic mind.

Nor does artistic description aim merely to supply vivid details. Details, however vivid, do not of themselves result in a dominant, meaningful impression. For instance, even those details expressed in forceful metaphor, such as Taine's "Man is a wild beast . . . delighting in blood" or Henry James's "The prince became flame to refute her" derive their meaningful force from the organization of details of which each metaphor is the tip or point. Details must be selected and organized to create a single dominant impression. Thus, in her 125-word description of Ethan Frome, Edith Wharton selects and arranges the details to produce a single unforgettable impression, namely that a bleak, unapproachable, *ruin* of a man was *the most striking figure in Starkfield*.

It was there that, several years ago, I saw him for the first time; and the sight pulled me up sharp. Even then he was the most striking figure in Starkfield, though he was but the ruin of a man. It was not so much his great height that marked him, for the "natives" were easily singled out by their lank longitude from the stockier foreign breed: it was the careless powerful look he had, in spite of a lameness checking each step like the jerk of a chain. There was something bleak and unapproachable in his face, and he was so stiffened and grizzled that I took him for an old man and was surprised to hear that he was not more than fifty-two.

This dominant impression (the most striking figure) is the result of unity, that is, the concentration of details to bring out the main impression of Ethan Frome.

UNITY IN DESCRIPTIVE WRITING EQUALS DOMINANT IMPRESSION

At bottom the principles of descriptive discourse are exactly the same as those which govern all good writing, namely the principles of unity, coherence, and emphasis (see Section VIII). But, as with exposition, argument, and persuasion, these principles must be applied to the particular aims of descriptive discourse. Thus unity in descriptive writing centers on the selection and organization of details to produce a dominant impression. We might even say that in artistic description unity *is* dominant impression.

In Example A1 below, Thomas Hardy presents the outward features of Eustacia Vye in such a way that her inner character, smoldering rebelliousness, is unmistakably conveyed. Example A2, "A Creole Courtyard," offers a selection and arrangement of detail calculated to produce an impression of tranquillity and quiet happiness. In presenting his collective descriptions of three great personalities in A3, Ellery Sedgwick stresses a single predominant trait of Pope Leo XIII, Rabindranath Tagore, and Madame Duse. In Example A4, Dickens organizes all the details of the Peggotty house to give an effect of romantic charm. This is especially evident in Dickens' concentration

From *Ethan Frome* by Edith Wharton. By permission of Charles Scribner's Sons, publishers.

in the concluding paragraph on the diminutive, shiny quaintness of the bedroom.

Taken together, these four examples illustrate various means of achieving a dominant impression. Thomas Hardy blends the exterior description of Eustacia's person with an interpretation of her inner character. Lafcadio Hearn stresses a contrast between the tranquil Creole patio and the hurly-burly of the street outside. Ellery Sedgwick, depending largely upon the impressions that his subjects made upon him, *suggests* the predominant trait of their respective characters. Charles Dickens creates an impression of over-all charm by describing the external setting as well as the interior of the Peggotty houseboat. In all four examples, however, unity is assured by the selection and organization of details to achieve a single predominant impression.

COHERENCE IN DESCRIPTIVE WRITING

A description is coherent when the various details are systematically arranged. In description systematic arrangement is achieved by maintaining a point of view consistent with the physical position and mental attitude of the observer who is describing an object.

Physical Point of View. In describing physical objects a writer has two options: (a) that of the fixed or stationary observer and (b) that of the moving or shifting observer.

The fixed point of view is illustrated in Examples B1 and B2. In B1, J. B. Priestley describes a scene as it appears to a fixed observer looking out from a study window. From this position the writer can describe only those objects within his range of vision. Moreover, these objects are visible only in a certain spatial order. From Priestley's angle of observation the tiny church that peeps out beyond the woods cannot, without confusing a reader, be described as the formidable building it might appear to be to a child standing directly under its walls. Another illustration of the fixed point of view is "Yosemite Falls" by John Muir. From his stationary place on Fern Ledge, Muir gives us a close-up description that would not be possible either at the top or at the foot of Yosemite. (Example C1 also illustrates a fixed point of view.)

On the other hand, Examples B3 and B4 illustrate the use of a *moving or shifting point of view.* In B3 Rio de Janeiro is described by an observer aboard a ship entering the harbor at sunset. The perspective of the scene changes, as do the color and shape of the city and its surrounding hills. The moving observer changes his post of observation and thus moves in space as well as in time. Hence he necessarily sees different things, and sees the same things differently, than does the fixed or stationary observer.

This difference between the two kinds of observer is also demonstrated in James Michener's "A Japanese Home" (B4). Here the author is attempting to describe a scene that could not possibly be described by a fixed observer. To achieve his purpose Michener must tell us what the house looks like outside and in, how the family conducts itself in the various living rooms. He must cross the threshold, move from room to room, pause for conversation, dine, stay overnight, and make his departure. Indeed, Michener's description requires not only a constantly shifting point of view but also a framework of narrative. The narrative element, as we shall see, far from complicating the description, is essential to indicate the shift from one point of view to another. (Note: The point of view of a moving observer is also demonstrated in Examples C2, C3, and D.)

Occasionally, especially in introductory passages, a writer will employ a metaphor to establish the point of view in the description of a large and complicated scene. Thus in Example C2 Robert Louis Stevenson describes the Bay of Monterey by reference to the image of the bent fishhook. This image frames the picture for his reader, reduces the whole scene to a familiar pattern, and enables him to foreshorten an introductory passage that might otherwise have required a lengthy geographical description. (Note: A consistent point of view does not necessarily mean that the writer is obliged to maintain a single point of view throughout his description. Occasionally, as in Example B4, where description is incorporated into a narrative frame, the moving observer pauses or rests, and thus, temporarily at least, becomes a fixed observer. Consistency merely demands that the point of view not be confusing to the reader. Careful transition can justify a change from a fixed to a moving point of view or the reverse.)

Mental Point of View. By mental point of view we mean the mood or subjective condition according to which the observer describes an object. It is a fact that an observer not only perceives an object at a certain distance, or in a certain spatial order, or according to a definite, chronological sequence, but, more importantly, he perceives an object and describes it according to his mental attitude or frame of mind. Thus, for example, T. H. Huxley's description of the herring is that of the deliberately impersonal scientific observer. The herring must appear very different indeed to a small boy catching his first fish, or to a tired canning-factory girl who scales herring for a living, or to a starving old man who is given a herring by a compassionate fisherman. Moreover, the same observer may have a different point of view, depending on time and other conditions. Mr. Huxley, at a cheerful breakfast, might describe a herring in terms of its savor; Mr. Huxley, somewhat out of sorts, might find the herring totally repulsive for his supper.

If a well-defined mental point of view is necessary in ordinary descriptive discourse, it is even more necessary in fiction. Here the writer must describe sense perceptions, not only as they appear to him directly but also as they affect an imaginary beholder. He must be constantly aware of the mentality of the various characters and shift his mental point of view with each character, as, for example, Smollett demonstrates in those celebrated passages in *Humphrey Clinker,* where Bath is described from the sharply different points of view of Bramble, Milford, Lydia, Wyn Jenkins, and Tabitha.

The examples in this section, nonfiction as well as fiction, illustrate a sharply focused mental point of view. In no selection is the attitude of the author or the imaginary observer left undefined. Thus in Example A1 Hardy describes Eustacia Vye from the mental attitude of an objective but sympathetic observer of Eustacia's forthcoming tragedy. Lafcadio Hearn describes the Creole courtyard in Example A2 from the mentality of an admirer of an old way of life. Ellery Sedgwick's tone of veneration suffuses his description of "Three Unforgettable Faces" (A3). In Example A4 Dickens communicates David Copperfield's mood of delight, excited by the romantic charm of the Peggotty house.

In these and in other examples the mental point of view harmonizes with the physical point of view to produce the dominant impression. Thus in Example B1 Priestley's description of the view from his window is *physically* that of a fixed observer, *mentally* that of inner delight. In Example C3 the mental attitude of the writer is just as important in bringing the details into focus as is the careful observance of the requirements of physical point of view. For Laurence (C3) is describing not only the physical appearance of the atomic explosion but also his own attitude towards it.

In summary, mental point of view is the attitude of mind according to which the observer, real or imagined, reports an impression made upon the senses.

EMPHASIS IN DESCRIPTIVE WRITING

Emphasis in description is achieved by using vivid details, figurative language, and climactic order.

A detail is *vivid* when it excites the reader and thus prompts him to see, feel, hear, or otherwise *experience* a scene as if he were present himself. Striking details, such as the flaming jungle at war with the tropical storm in Example C1, or the ducks, sea gulls, sandpipers, and the vast green curving waves with their changing color and modulated thunder in Example C2, make the reader feel the immediacy of the object, the moment, the sensation. Example C3, which describes the atomic bomb bursting over Nagasaki, from the first blue-green flash to the disappearing fleecy ruff of smoke, also supplies vivid details with awful and horrifying clarity.

Figurative language (see Section VIII) is particularly effective in description. Comparisons, whether metaphors or similes, appeal not only to the imagination by reason of their vividness and novelty, but also to the emotions. They convey to us the author's feelings as well as his perceptions. Thus, when Stevenson describes "the whispering rumble, . . . the thundering surges, . . . the distant circling rumour" of the ocean, his metaphorical expressions help us to distinguish between the different sounds and, at the same time, convey his feeling of the haunting presence of the sea. So too, when Peter Fleming in Example C1 describes the coming storm in the lines, "Massed black cohorts of clouds assembled in the west and came up across the sky under streaming pennons. The wind rose till its voice was a scream . . . ," we are in imagination at once in the very midst of the scene and struck by its emotional impact. Nor can we read without visual excitement and a chill of horror W. L. Laurence's simile (in Example C3) which likens the atomic bomb cloud to a decapitated monster growing a new head.

Figurative language, in which all the examples in this section abound, is, then, an especially effective device in artistic description.

Climactic order refers to the increasing intensity in the description of the dominant impression. In each of the examples in Section C the mood is gradually intensified. Thus in Example C1 Fleming builds up his description to an extraordinary pitch of excitement. The storm becomes a deluge, the fire whips up to an inferno. The climax of both storm and fire occur at the same time. At the height of this double fury the very "fabric of the universe" seems to crack. Stevenson's climax in Example C2 is less spectacular, but no less effective. Here we become more and more aware of the *sound* of the sea. The sea surrounds and besieges us until we are filled with its "thundering surges." In similar fashion W. L. Laurence in Example C3 intensifies our amazement and horror by his progressive insinuations that the atom bomb is a menacing prehistoric monster.

Note: Be careful to distinguish between direct and indirect emphasis. An author uses direct emphasis when he stimulates in his reader the exact imaginative and emotional response he himself has experienced He makes use of indirect emphasis when he describes a scene from a point of view that is not necessarily his own. Thus in Chapter 16 of *Pride and Prejudice* Jane Austen has Mr. Collins describe Lady Catherine's drawing rooms as models of grandeur. However, Miss Austen expects her readers to laugh at Mr. Collins' inordinate affectation. Thus the character's emphasis on grandeur indirectly stimulates the reader to humor.

NARRATIVE IN DESCRIPTION

Narration, which recounts events, and description, which presents objects as they appear to the senses, are frequently commingled. This union is born of necessity as well as convenience. In commenting on the moving point of view in Example B4 above, we have already shown how a narrative framework facilitates description from the point of view of a moving observer. A moving observer must have time to shift his point of view. But movement and time both imply narration. Thus narration is a necessity in any descriptive discourse that involves either the passage of time or a shift in point of view.

Without narration, much description would be unrealistic—at best a mere exercise in word painting, at worst still-life photography. In Example D we shall see how the descriptive passages are blended with narration to the mutual advantage of each form of discourse.

a. Give unity to description by selecting and organizing details to create a single dominant impression.

1. Eustacia Vye

BY THOMAS HARDY

1 Eustacia Vye was the raw material of a divinity. On Olympus she would have done well with a little preparation. She had the passions and instincts which make a model goddess, that is, those which make not quite a model woman. Had it been possible for the earth and mankind to be entirely in her grasp for a while, had she handled the distaff, the spindle, and the shears at her own free will, few in the world would have noticed the change of government.* There would have been the same inequality of lot, the same heaping up of favours here, of contumely there, the same generosity before justice, the same perpetual dilemmas, the same captious alteration of caresses and blows that we endure now.

2 She was in person full-limbed and somewhat heavy; without ruddiness, as without pallor; and soft to the touch as a cloud. To see her hair was to fancy that a whole winter did not contain darkness enough to form its shadow: it closed over her forehead like nightfall extinguishing the western glow.

3 Her nerves extended into those tresses, and her temper could always be softened by stroking them down. When her hair was

* [This sentence refers in fancy to Eustacia's acting the part of the Three Fates in classical myth. Clotho spins the thread of life; Lachesis measures its length; Atropos cuts it off.—Editor.]

brushed she would instantly sink into stillness and look like the Sphinx. If, in passing under one of the Egdon banks, any of its thick skeins were caught, as they sometimes were, by a prickly tuft of the large *Ulex europaeus*—which will act as a sort of hairbrush—she would go back a few steps, and pass against it a second time.

4 She had pagan eyes, full of nocturnal mysteries, and their light, as it came and went, and came again, was partially hampered by their oppressive lids and lashes; and of these the under lid was much fuller than it usually is with English women. This enabled her to indulge in reverie without seeming to do so: she might have been believed capable of sleeping without closing them up. Assuming that the souls of men and women were visible essences, you could fancy the colour of Eustacia's soul to be flame-like. The sparks from it that rose into her dark pupils gave the same impression.

5 The mouth seemed formed less to speak than to quiver, less to quiver than to kiss. Some might have added, less to kiss than to curl. Viewed sideways, the closing line of her lips formed, with almost geometric precision, the curve so well known in the arts of design as the cyma-recta, or ogee. The sight of such a flexible bend as that on grim Egdon was quite an apparition. It was felt at once that that mouth did not come over from Slesvig with a band of Saxon pirates whose lips met like the two halves of a muffin. One had fancied that such lip curves were mostly lurking underground in the South as fragments of forgotten marbles. So fine were the lines of her lips that, though full, each corner of her mouth was as clearly cut as the point of a spear. This keenness of corner was only blunted when she was given over to sudden fits of gloom, one of the phases of the night side of sentiment which she knew too well for her years.

6 Her presence brought memories of such things as Bourbon roses, rubies, and tropical midnights; her moods recalled lotus eaters and the march in *Athalie;* her motions, the ebb and flow of the sea; her voice, the viola. In a dim light, and with a slight rearrangement of her hair, her general figure might have stood for that of either of the higher female deities. The new moon behind her head, an old helmet upon it, a diadem of accidental dewdrops round her brow, would have been adjuncts sufficient to strike the note of Artemis, Athena, or Hera, respectively, with as close an approximation to the antique as that which passes muster on many respected canvases.

7 But celestial imperiousness, love, wrath, and fervour had proved to be somewhat thrown away on netherward Egdon. Her power was

limited, and the consciousness of this limitation had biassed her development. Egdon was her Hades, and since coming there she had imbibed much of what was dark in its tone, though inwardly and eternally unreconciled thereto. Her appearance accorded well with this smouldering rebelliousness, and the shady splendour of her beauty was the real surface of the sad and stifled warmth within her. A true Tartarean dignity sat upon her brow, and not factitiously or with marks of constraint, for it had grown in her with years.

Comment

The dominant impression—Eustacia Vye's passionate, rebellious pride—is achieved by presenting (1) the outward features of a majestically beautiful woman and (2) the inner character that is revealed in those outward features. The inner nature and the external characteristics of Eustacia Vye are all of one piece. Inwardly she is passionate, proud, rebellious. "Her appearance accorded well with this smouldering rebelliousness, and the shady splendour of her beauty was the real surface of the sad and stifled warmth within her." Thus the dominant impression here is of a total human personality, of the character's appearance merged with her inward meaning.

Note in paragraph 1 how Hardy classifies Eustacia as the raw material of divinity, a person of heroic mold, with a capacity for the tragic action in which she is later involved. Paragraph 2 describes her general appearance and introduces her most prominent characteristic, her dark hair, which is also treated in paragraph 3. Paragraph 4 describes Eustacia's eyes. Here too Hardy relates a physical characteristic to its spiritual counterpart when he says, "Assuming that the souls of men and women were visible essences, you could fancy the colour of Eustacia's soul to be flame-like." Paragraph 5 describes Eustacia's mouth, and paragraph 6 the effect of her whole personality. Paragraph 7 continues this general characterization of Eustacia as the raw material for a divinity, but a Tartarean or underworld divinity—one whose dark appearance marks her for a dark end.

Analysis and Composition

1. Eustacia's rebelliousness is symbolized by the note of darkness. List all those details referring to darkness which pertain to Eustacia and show how these expressions, taken together, create a mood of tragic expectancy.
2. Closely related to Eustacia's rebelliousness is her sullenness. Pick out the physical details that objectify this inner trait.

3. Hardy constantly compares Eustacia with figures of classical myth. In paragraph 1 she is compared with the three Fates; in paragraph 6 she is compared with Artemis or Diana, the goddess of chastity, with Athena, the goddess of Wisdom, with Hera or Juno, the queen of the gods and the patron of women and marriage; and in paragraph 7, with the goddesses of the underworld. Note that these comparisons have only one point in common, dignity and heroic stature. What other means does Hardy use to create an impression of dignity and heroic stature?

4. Do you consider the comparison of Eustacia's lips to an ogee arch (¶5) effective? Give reasons for your answer.

5. Hardy creates a vivid sense impression (a) by concrete, specific description of Eustacia's appearance, (b) by comparisons and metaphors, (c) by showing the effect Eustacia has on the beholder. In your opinion which of these methods does he use most successfully?

6. To what impression do the following details directly contribute:
   a. "Soft to touch as a cloud" (¶2)
   b. "Closed over her forehead like nightfall" (¶2)
   c. "Lips . . . like the two halves of a muffin" (¶5)
   d. "Egdon was her Hades" (¶7)

7. Choose some real or imaginary character suitable for description. Decide in advance upon a dominant impression you wish to create. Select those physical characteristics that betray inner characteristics. Then write a descriptive sketch of approximately 350 words. (Note: Students who have access to art museums, or who can acquire good reproductions, may find it helpful to use as their subjects the characters of famous paintings.)

2. A Creole Courtyard

BY LAFCADIO HEARN

¹An atmosphere of tranquillity and quiet happiness seemed to envelop the old house, which had formerly belonged to a rich planter. ²Like many of the Creole houses, the façade presented a commonplace and unattractive aspect. ³The great green doors of the arched entrance were closed; and the green shutters of the balconied windows were half shut, like sleepy eyes lazily gazing upon the busy street below or the cottony patches of light clouds which floated slowly, slowly across the deep blue of the sky above. ⁴But beyond the gates lay a little Paradise. ⁵The great court, deep and broad, was framed in tropical green;

A CREOLE COURTYARD: from *Creole Sketches,* Boston, Houghton Mifflin Company, 1922. Reprinted by permission of the publishers.

vines embraced the white pillars of the piazza, and creeping plants climbed up the tinted walls to peer into the upper windows with their flower eyes of flaming scarlet. [6]Banana trees nodded sleepily their plumes of emerald green at the farther end of the garden; vines smothered the windows of the dining room, and formed a bower of cool green about the hospitable door; an aged fig tree, whose gnarled arms trembled under the weight of honeyed fruit, shadowed the square of bright lawn which formed a natural carpet in the midst; and at intervals were stationed along the walks in large porcelain vases—like barbaric sentinels in sentry boxes—gorgeous broad-leaved things, with leaves fantastic and barbed and flowers brilliant as hummingbirds. [7]A fountain murmured faintly near the entrance of the western piazza; and there came from the shadows of the fig tree the sweet and plaintive cooing of amorous doves. [8]Without, cotton floats might rumble, and streetcars vulgarly jingle their bells; but these were mere echoes of the harsh outer world which disturbed not the delicious quiet within— where sat, in old-fashioned chairs, good old-fashioned people who spoke the tongue of other times, and observed many quaint and knightly courtesies forgotten in this material era. [9]Without, roared the Iron Age, the angry waves of American traffic; within, one heard only the murmur of the languid fountain, the sound of deeply musical voices conversing in the languages of Paris and Madrid, the playful chatter of dark-haired children lisping in sweet and many-voweled Creole, and, through it all, the soft, caressing coo of doves. [10]Without, it was the year 1879; within, it was the epoch of the Spanish domination. [11]A guitar lay upon the rustic bench near the fountain, where it had evidently been forgotten, and a silk fan beside it; a European periodical, with graceful etchings, hung upon the back of a rocking chair at the door, through which one caught glimpses of a snowy table bearing bottles of good Bordeaux, and inhaled the odor of rich West India tobacco. [12]And yet some people wonder that some other people never care to cross Canal Street.

Comment

The dominant impression is that of tranquillity and quiet happiness; the Creole courtyard is a little paradise. This impression is as carefully prepared as Dickens' impression of romantic charm in example A4.

First we see the Creole dwelling from the outside (Ss1-3), then from within the court (Ss4-7), and finally in contrast with the busy outside world (Ss8-12). Virtually all the details contribute to the impression of tranquillity and quiet happiness. The closed doors, the half-shut balcony windows seem to shut out the noise and unhappiness of the city. The court within is framed in soothing tropical green. The bright lawn, the faintly murmuring fountain, the cooing doves also convey impressions of serenity. The harsh metallic clatter of the traffic without sharpens the contrast with the courtyard within. In sentences 8-12 the description includes the people as well as the place, and such significant details as the guitar, the silk fan, the snowy table, the fragrance of tobacco, all of which add to the impression of tranquillity and quiet happiness. Several impressions clash slightly with this mood. The plants that stand like barbaric sentinels, the scarlet creepers, and the nameless flowers as brilliant as hummingbirds rescue the passage from monotonous passivity by a small and gentle stirring of the senses.

Especially notable is the variety of the sensory appeal. Images appealing to the eye are the most prominent, but there are many references to sound (the fountain, the cooing doves, the angry waves of traffic, the chatter of children), to taste (the Bordeaux wine), to smell (the tobacco), and indirectly to touch (the silk fan and the guitar).

Analysis and Composition

1. Comment on the exactness (see Section VIII) of the following italicized expressions in the context of the sentences in which they appear:
   a. "Like *sleepy* eyes" (S3)
   b. "Creeping plants *climbed* . . . to *peer* . . . with their *flower eyes* of flaming scarlet" (S5)
   c. "Banana trees *nodded*" (S6)
   d. "An aged fig tree, whose gnarled arms *trembled*" (S6)
   e. "Streetcars *vulgarly jingle* their bells" (S8)
   f. "The *angry waves* of American traffic" (S9)
   g. "Dark-haired children *lisping*" (S9)
   h. "The *soft, caressing coo* of doves" (S9)
2. Sentences 8-12 develop a contrast between old-world atmosphere and American hurly-burly. (a) Decide whether or not this contrast supports the main idea announced in sentence 1, or whether it introduces another impression. Give reasons for your answer. (b) What effect is created by the repetition of "without" and "within" in sentences 8-10?
3. Certain expressions in this passage are vague. The "gorgeous broad-leaved *things*" in sentence 6 could be more exactly identified. "Old-fashioned

chairs" and "good old-fashioned people" are very indefinite expressions. Moreover, the exact proportions of the courtyard are not clear. What is the western piazza? Is it part of the courtyard? Are we also to imagine an eastern piazza? Are the people described as speaking Creole talking simultaneously in French and Spanish, or in a mixture of both? Decide (a) whether these questions point to disunity in the passage and (b) whether they point to carelessness on the part of the author.

4. List the many sensory perceptions (sight, sound, smell, taste, touch) that you have observed about some place on the campus, such as the chapel, the library, the stadium, a classroom, a dormitory. Then select the dominant impression the place has made upon you. Write a description of about 300 words. Be sure to state the dominant impression. If possible make your description appeal to each of the five senses.

3. Unforgettable Faces

BY ELLERY SEDGWICK

1 Across more than sixty years I see a face like none other. I was a child in Rome. My parents promised to take me with them to their audience with Leo XIII, the Supreme Pope of modern times. All winter long my French governess perfected me in my address, *"Votre bénédiction, Saint Père"* *—again and again I was taught to say it— but as, clasping my mother's hand, I walked through those stately antechambers, the Swiss guard in Michelangelo's red and yellow at the door, the Guardia Nobile grouped about, gentlemen in black silk smallclothes and long gold chains showing the way, my ten-year-old trepidation shook me in my shoes. I felt I must be approaching the presence of the Eternal. Clearly as I saw him then, I see him now: that erect and stately figure dressed in purest white, the only color the immense violet stone on the middle finger. His face, cut like a cameo under a skin of palest parchment, seemed to shine from within. In my childish mind there rose the picture of an alabaster lamp diffusing its shaded light, for by a curious illusion the classical features seemed translucent. Such a link between earth and heaven I had not seen. My

* Your blessing, Holy Father.

UNFORGETTABLE FACES: from *The Happy Profession* by Ellery Sedgwick, by permission of Little, Brown & Company and the Atlantic Monthly Press. Copyright 1946 by Little, Brown & Company.

tongue stuck fast. The toil of months was gone. As I kissed the ring
I bumbled over my *"bénédiction,"* and His Holiness, smiling at my
mother, gently boxed my ears and blessed her child.

2 Another face that will not leave my remembrance is that of
Rabindranath Tagore. I had talked with him once or twice and cor-
responded with him much, and one evening Professor Royce took me
with him to the house of the professor of Indic literature at Harvard,
where a group of philosophers gathered to discuss the immortalities.
The slow and earnest talk flowed over me. I was fathoms deep beneath
immensity, but not for two hours did I take my eyes from the poet's
face. It looked the symbol of eternal contrast with the philosophies of
the West. The delicate olive of his cheek, the high-bridged, aquiline
nose, the sensitive mouth, were purely Oriental. Across my mind flut-
tered remembrances of Saladin, the glorious Moor, and I remembered
that other contrast when the sword of the Lion Heart, which hacked
a steel bar in twain, was powerless against the silken pillow, parted at
a single stroke of Saladin's scimitar. But the memorable feature of
Tagore's face was his eye—the eye of a hawk without its cruelty. The
lids were like a bird's. The poet often closed them in meditation and,
as the eyes slowly opened, the lids rolled up not in curves but like
horizontal curtains. Then his penetrating glance would shoot out, escaping like a beam of imprisoned light. The pupils were dark, the
whites a pale gray. To me, fancifully enough, those eyes seemed not
like man's but Nature's. I see them still.

3 Actors' faces belong not to themselves but to their parts. To me
the face of all stage faces was Madame Duse's. It was not its beauty
that held me, but its exquisite mobility and the look of the eternal
feminine which poets have praised from Lilith to the Blessed Damozel.
Duse's voice had not the range and power of Bernhardt's. Hers was
not a dynamic art, startling you from your seat, but her charm was
infinite. When she smiled, the radiance of it purled and rippled over
the footlights. A thousand shared it, but you felt it yours alone. When
Bernhardt played *La Dame aux Camélias,* she *was* the heroine of that
slightly grubby drama. She was everything that Dumas *fils* wrote into
it. Madame Duse lifted the part to another sphere. Melodrama became
tragedy. All the suffering of woman was in her face when, turning
from her lover, she cried in a voice that pierced to the heart's core:
"Armando, Armando!" In the middle of the night I would start from
sleep, "Armando, Armando!" sounding in my ears.

Comment

This description is a remarkably economic presentation of three person-alities, each of whom is effectively described by one predominant trait. Leo XIII is the symbol of spirituality; Rabindranath Tagore, the symbol of the eternal contrast between the East and the West; Madame Eleonora Duse, the symbol of the eternal feminine. In each case all the details serve to por-tray the one predominant trait.

Leo XIII is gradually revealed as a luminous spirit. First we observe the setting in the Vatican Palace, and then we are led to the Pope's presence. The Pope's physical features are barely mentioned. We are aware that he was erect and stately, that he wore a white robe and a ring with a violet stone. We know that he smiled and blessed the author. But it is the emo-tions stirred in the author by the Pope's presence that convey to the reader the impression of Leo's personality.

On the other hand, Sedgwick describes Tagore by presenting him directly to the reader and also by describing his effect upon the beholder. The poet's complexion, his nose, his mouth, and his eyes are clearly described. But, more importantly, Tagore is associated in the writer's mind with the great men of the East.

Madame Duse is described almost entirely by the effect of her femininity upon the beholder. We know only that the radiance of her face "purled and rippled over the footlights." She moved her audience by the exquisite mo-bility of her countenance and by the thrilling power of her elocution.

Thus each person is described in terms of one predominant impression.

Analysis and Composition

1. Show how the following expressions are employed in their several con-texts to achieve the dominant impression the author aimed to create:
   a. "My ten-year-old trepidation" (¶1)
   b. "Cut like a cameo under a skin of palest parchment" (¶1)
   c. "My tongue stuck fast" (¶1)
   d. "Talk flowed over me" (¶2)
   e. "Like horizontal curtains" (¶2)
   f. "Melodrama became tragedy" (¶3)
2. In your opinion which of the three characters is described most effec-tively? Give reasons for your answer.

3. In a manner similar to that of this example write a description of three persons who have made a deep impression on you. Vary your method of description, but be sure to create a dominant impression of each person.

4. Peggotty's House

BY CHARLES DICKENS

"Yon's our house, Mas'r Davy!"

I looked in all directions, as far as I could stare over the wilderness, and away at the sea, and away at the river, but no house could *I* make out. There was a black barge, or some other kind of superannuated boat, not far off, high and dry on the ground, with an iron funnel sticking out of it for a chimney and smoking very cosily; but nothing else in the way of a habitation that was visible to *me*.

"That's not it," said I—"that ship-looking thing?"

"That's it, Mas'r Davy," returned Ham.

If it had been Aladdin's palace, roc's egg and all, I suppose I could not have been more charmed with the romantic idea of living in it. There was a delightful door cut in the side, and it was roofed in, and there were little windows in it; but the wonderful charm of it was, that it was a real boat, which had no doubt been upon the water hundreds of times, and which had never been intended to be lived in, on dry land. That was the captivation of it to me. If it had ever been meant to be lived in, I might have thought it small, or inconvenient, or lonely; but never having been designed for any such use, it became a perfect abode.

It was beautifully clean inside, and as tidy as possible. There was a table, and a Dutch clock, and a chest of drawers, and on the chest of drawers there was a tea tray with a painting on it of a lady with a parasol, taking a walk with a military-looking child who was trundling a hoop. The tray was kept from tumbling down by a Bible; and the tray, if it had tumbled down, would have smashed a quantity of cups and saucers and a teapot that were grouped around the book. On the walls there were some common coloured pictures, framed and glazed, of Scripture subjects; such as I have never seen since in the hands of pedlars, without seeing the whole interior of Peggotty's brother's house again, at one view. Abraham in red going to sacrifice Isaac in blue, and Daniel in yellow cast into a den of green lions, were the most prominent of these. Over the little mantelshelf was a picture of the *Sarah Jane* lugger, built at Sunderland, with a real little wooden stern stuck on to it—a work of art, combining composition with carpentry, which I considered to be one of the most enviable possessions that the world could afford. There were some hooks in the beams of the ceiling, the use of which I did not divine then; and some lockers and boxes and conveniences of that sort, which served for seats and eked out the chairs.

All this, I saw in the first glance after I crossed the threshold—childlike, according to my theory—and then Peggotty opened a little door and showed me my bedroom. It was the completest and most desirable bedroom ever seen—in the stern of the vessel; with a little window, where the rudder used to go through; a little lookingglass, just the right height for me, nailed against the wall, and framed with oyster shells; a little bed, which there was just room enough to get into; and a nosegay of seaweed in a blue mug on the table. The walls were whitewashed as white as milk, and the patchwork counterpane made my eyes quite ache with its brightness. One thing I particularly noticed in this delightful house was the smell of fish, which was so searching that, when I took out my pocket handkerchief to wipe my nose, I found it smelt exactly as if it had wrapped up a lobster. On my imparting this discovery in confidence to Peggotty, she informed me that her brother dealt in lobsters, crabs, and crawfish; and I afterwards found that a heap of these creatures, in a state of wonderful conglomeration with one another, and never leaving off pinching whatever they laid hold of, were usually to be found in a little wooden outhouse where the pots and kettles were kept.

Comment

Note here the careful organization of this descriptive passage from *David Copperfield*. The reader's attention is caught first by Ham Peggotty's pointer, "Yon's our house!" At a *distance* David makes out a black barge with an iron funnel sticking out. On nearer view it strikes David as wonderfully *charming* and *romantic,* an impression enhanced by the comparison with Aladdin's palace. This dominant impression is fortified (a) by the description of the interior as seen from the threshold and (b) by the description of the bedroom. The objects described are chiefly visual, but the concluding paragraph also contains a pungent impression of the sense of smell.

Analysis and Composition

1. What elements in the description justify the statement that the Peggotty house-boat was a perfect abode?
2. Show how the selection of detail in the description of the interior as seen from the threshold warrants David's romantic enthusiasm. Remember that David Copperfield, the narrator, is a young boy.
3. How do the qualities of littleness and brightness contribute to the desirability of the bedroom?
4. How does Dickens introduce the description of the shellfish in the outhouse without changing David's place of observation?
5. Show how each of the following expressions contributes to the dominant effect of the passage:
   a. "Smoking very cosily"
   b. "Daniel in yellow cast into a den of green lions"
   c. "Nosegay of seaweed"
   d. "Wonderful conglomeration"
6. Write a 400-word description on one of the topics listed below. Describe your subject (a) from a distant perspective and (b) on closer view. Be sure to state and support *one* dominant impression.

An old mansion   A watchman's shanty
The cleanest house in town   A lighthouse
A student lounge   The Dean's office
A houseboat in the river

b. Give coherence to your description by maintaining a point of view that is consistent with
the physical position and mental attitude of
the observer.

1. The Delighted Eye

BY J. B. PRIESTLEY

The view [from my study] is very special. I might have put it together myself, like the scenery of our dreams. There is in this view
nearly everything I love in the English scene. Down below on the right
are downlands and heath, green slopes and gorse in bloom. Lower
and nearer the center are cultivated fields; then, toward the left, some
woods; and beyond, just in the picture, a glimpse of a tiny church,
some cottages, and the ruin of a large manor house. Further off, but
dominating the scene, is the long chalk cliff that ends in the Needles,
which have been to so many travelers the first sign of England. And
full in the middle panes of my window is that flashing mirror, that
blue diamond or that infinite haze, that window for the mind, which
is the sea. I hold this tenure of the delighted eye in the most precarious
world since the Ice Age. My security is as brittle as the teeth I am
fast losing. But I have arrived at my high window; I have already
lolled at the broad seat; I have looked down by the hour upon the
gorse, the woods, the cliffs, the sea; and the glory my eyes have seen—
praise the Lord! cannot be robbed of its yesterdays. . . .

THE DELIGHTED EYE: from *Delight* by J. B. Priestley. By permission of A. D. Peters,
London.

Comment

The dominant impression here is that of joy in a beautiful view. It is the scenery of the writer's dreams, a view that comprises all that he loves in the English countryside.

The point of view is that of the fixed observer. From his high window, the author observes things in what may be called a space order. His delighted eye moves from right, to center, to left; from the near to the far.

Note that, although the space order is clearly marked and gives coherence to the whole piece, it is not meticulously exact. There is no effort here to report a scene as a military observer would report it.

Analysis and Composition

1. Point out the expressions that mark the transitions from one object to another.
2. Show how the physical objects listed below provide delight (a) considered in themselves and (b) considered in their position in the scene described:
   a. The downlands and heath, green slopes and gorse in bloom
   b. Cultivated fields
   c. The woods in the foreground, the church, cottages and ruined manor
   d. The long chalk cliff
   e. The sea
3. Show how the phrases listed below contribute to the dominant impression of delight:
   a. "That blue diamond"
   b. "That window for the mind"
   c. "This tenure of the delighted eye"
   d. "My security is as brittle as the teeth I am fast losing"
4. Select some favorable place of observation near your home or on the campus, such as a rooftop, a hill, a window that commands a view. Spend some time observing the view from this place of observation. Discover and name the special characteristic of this scene or view. Then write a paragraph of description in the manner of the example above. Do not attempt to describe objects that cannot be seen from the fixed point of observation. Maintain order by describing the view in a clearly marked space order—for example, from left to right, from near to far.

2. Yosemite Falls

BY JOHN MUIR

1 [1]During the time of the spring floods the best near view of the fall
is obtained from Fern Ledge on the east side above the blinding spray
at a height of about 400 feet above the base of the fall. [2]A climb of
about 1400 feet from the Valley has to be made, and there is no trail,
but to any one fond of climbing this will make the ascent all the more
delightful. [3]A narrow part of the ledge extends to the side of the fall
and back of it, enabling us to approach it as closely as we wish. [4]When
the afternoon sunshine is streaming through the throng of comets,
ever wasting, ever renewed, the marvelous fineness, firmness and variety of their forms are beautifully revealed.

2 [1]At the top of the fall they seem to burst forth in irregular spurts
from some grand, throbbing mountain heart. [2]Now and then one
mighty throb sends forth a mass of solid water into the free air far
beyond the others, which rushes alone to the bottom of the fall with
long streaming tail, like combed silk, while the others, descending in
clusters, gradually mingle and lose their identity. [3]But they all rush
past us with amazing velocity and display of power, though apparently drowsy and deliberate in their movements when observed from
a distance of a mile or two. [4]The heads of these comet-like masses are
composed of nearly solid water, and are dense white in color like
pressed snow, from the friction they suffer in rushing through the air,
the portion worn off forming the tail, between the white lustrous
threads and films of which faint, grayish pencilings appear, while the
outer, finer sprays of water-dust, whirling in sunny eddies, are pearly
gray throughout.

3 [1]At the bottom of the fall there is but little distinction of form
visible. [2]It is mostly a hissing, flashing, seething, upwhirling mass of
scud and spray, through which the light sifts in gray and purple tones,
while at times, when the sun strikes at the required angle, the whole
wild and apparently lawless, stormy, striving mass is changed to brilliant rainbow hues, manifesting finest harmony.

4 [1]The middle portion of the fall is the most openly beautiful; lower, the various forms into which the waters are wrought are more closely and voluminously veiled, while higher, towards the head, the current is comparatively simple and undivided. [2]But even at the bottom, in the boiling clouds of spray, there is no confusion, while the rainbow light makes all divine, adding glorious beauty and peace to glorious power.

5 [1]This noble fall has far the richest, as well as the most powerful, voice of all the falls of the Valley, its tones varying from the sharp hiss and rustle of the wind in the glossy leaves of the live oaks and the soft, sifting, hushing tones of the pines, to the loudest rush and roar of storm winds and thunder among the crags of the summit peaks. [2]The low bass, booming, reverberating tones, heard under favorable circumstances five or six miles away, are formed by the dashing and exploding of heavy masses mixed with air upon two projecting ledges on the face of the cliff, the one on which we are standing and another about 200 feet above it. [3]The torrent of massive comets is continuous at time of high water, while the explosive, booming notes are wildly intermittent, because, unless influenced by the wind, most of the heavier masses shoot out from the face of the precipice, and pass the ledges upon which at other times they are exploded.

6 Occasionally the whole fall is swayed away from the front of the cliff, then suddenly dashed flat against it, or vibrated from side to side like a pendulum, giving rise to endless variety of forms and sounds.

Comment

The dominant impression is that of grandeur or awe—an emotion created (a) by the magnitude of the falls, (b) by the form or shape of the falls, and (c) by the sound of the falls. Yosemite adds "glorious beauty and peace to glorious power."

In paragraph 1 the point of view is fixed at Fern Ledge, 400 feet above the base, on the east side.

The order of observation, as in Example B1, is space order. The author proceeds to describe visually the top or head of the falls (¶2), then the bottom (¶3), then the middle portion in contrast to the top and bottom of the falls (¶4). Note that this space order is slightly irregular. The middle portion of the falls is described last because it is the most beautiful part and hence deserves the climactic position. In paragraph 5 Muir describes the sound of the falls. Paragraph 6 sums up the general impression of both the sight and the sound of Yosemite.

In addition to maintaining a clear order marked by clear transitions, this passage is interconnected by a sustained metaphor. Yosemite Falls are likened to comets. This image is introduced in sentence 4, paragraph 1. It appears again in the phrase "long streaming tail" in sentence 2, paragraph 2, and in sentence 4 of the same paragraph. The comet metaphor is repeated in sentence 3, paragraph 5.

Analysis and Composition

1. In addition to the comet metaphor described above, Muir uses other metaphorical expressions with good effect. What impressions are created by the following comparisons?
   a. "Grand, throbbing mountain heart" (S1, ¶2)
   b. "Like combed silk" (S2, ¶2)
   c. "Like pressed snow" (S4, ¶2)
   d. "Faint, grayish pencilings appear" (S4, ¶2)
   e. "Vibrated from side to side like a pendulum" (¶6)
2. Kinetic imagery, that is, words connoting movement or action, contribute greatly to the vividness of this passage. Some examples are

   burst forth   *rushes* alone
   irregular *spurts*   *streaming* tail
   throbbing mountain heart

   Pick out twenty additional vivid motion words in paragraph 2. Explain briefly what impression each word conveys.
3. In sentence 4, paragraph 1, Muir mentions (a) the fineness, (b) the firmness, and (c) the variety of forms to be observed in the falls. In what sentences does he show each of these qualities? Give reasons for your answers.
4. How many sounds does Muir list in paragraph 5? Are all these sounds distinct, that is, differentiated one from the other?
5. Analyze the following sentences for vigor and interest (see Section VIII): S2, ¶2; S2, ¶3; S1, ¶5; S3, ¶5.
6. Compare this passage with Example A2 from the point of view of the clarity, vigor, and interest of the diction and sentences (see Section VIII).
7. In a manner similar to that employed in the Muir passage write a description of one of the following subjects. Be sure to create a dominant impression and to maintain a consistent point of view.
   a. A river in flood   d. A gorge or canyon
   b. A hurricane   e. A mountain lake
   c. A dust storm

3. Rio de Janeiro

BY PETER FLEMING

1 [1]We came into Rio at sunset. [2]This must surely be the best time to do it.

2 [1]For some hours Brazil had been in sight, a dark green, formidable outline, a coast (as far as we could see) almost unscathed by man. [2]The huge cliffs slanted a little backwards, as if the land had been reined in sharply on the brink of salt perdition. [3]The charging jungle stopped short only at the sea. [4]I got the impression of a subcontinent with imperfect self-control.

3 [1]We were passing a little island in the harbour's mouth. [2]Against a tawny sunset the hills behind the city stood up fiercely. [3]On their crests the tiny black silhouettes of trees showed with more than their share of detail and prominence. [4]Some frigate birds went out past us to the darkening sea, flying low. [5]The water front, still some way ahead of us, flaunted a solitary skyscraper. [6]All skyscrapers look foolish and unnatural when isolated from their kind. [7]It is only in the mass, huddled and strenuously craning, that they achieve a sort of quaint, crude dignity. [8]Alone, cut off from their native background of competition and emergency, they appear gauche and rather forlorn. [9]With this one it was particularly so. [10]Ridiculously at variance with all that we could see, hopelessly irrelevant to all that we imagined, it had the pathos of the boor. [11]It domineered without conviction, the totem of another tribe. [12]It knew itself for a mistake, an oversight, an intrusion. [13]It was like a bag of tools left behind, when the curtain rises, on a stage set for romance.

4 [1]Later I was told that during the last revolution they threw a full-sized billiard table out of a window on its fourteenth floor. [2]Then I forgave it. [3]Where that sort of thing can happen to them, there is a place for skyscrapers.

5 [1]As we came closer the city evaded us. [2]The hills drew in with the darkness, and Rio merged into her bodyguard. [3]Between their shoulders we saw under a furled bank of cloud a strip of lemon-coloured sky, level and straight-edged like a wainscot. [4]A little covey of

rockets went up from somewhere in the town. [5]They burst in a chorus of inoffensive plopping noises and left surprised balls of smoke hanging in the air. [6]There are always rockets in Brazil. [7]The birth of a saint or the death of a patriot, the outbreak or suppression of revolt, the rise or fall of a government—if there is none of these things to commemorate today, there was yesterday. [8]There are sure to be some fireworks left over. [9]Rockets are to the Brazilian calendar what exclamation marks are to the correspondence of a debutante.

6 [1]In the twilight—yes, in the swift tropical twilight of which you have all read—the political exiles, no longer able to control their emotion, pointed out to us again and again the Sugarloaf and Corcovado, those astonishing peaks. [2]We duly marvelled. [3]Our aesthetic susceptibilities were on their mettle. [4]Two people were heard to say that the scene, if reproduced on canvas, would fail to command belief. [5]The ship buzzed with ecstasy.

Comment

The predominant impression here is the special character of Rio revealed in (a) its physical setting and (b) its appearance at dusk.

The point of view is that of the *moving* observer aboard a ship entering the harbor. The first point of observation (¶2) is from some distance out. Here Rio is not identifiable, but the coast appears to be "a charging jungle," "a subcontinent with imperfect self-control." The second point of observation (¶3) is at the harbor mouth, where the author can discern the hills surrounding the city and a solitary skyscraper. The third point of observation is within the harbor itself (¶5 and 6), where the city disappears in darkness and the observer sees only the rockets and the twin peaks.

Note the importance here of the time element. The description begins at sunset and ends at dusk. The quickly growing darkness explains in great part the prominence given to the hills, the skyscraper, and the rockets in this passage.

The great vitality of the description may be traced in large part to its figurative language. The implied comparison of the Brazilian coast with a charger reined in at the brink of salt perdition (¶2), the personification of the skyscrapers (¶3) and of the city and the hills (¶5) dramatize this description of Rio. The humorous comment on the skyscraper (¶4) and on the rockets (S9, ¶5), as well as the ridicule of esthetic sentimentality (S4, ¶6), contributes to the sprightliness of the selection.

Analysis and Composition

1. Does the author's description of Rio justify his statement (¶1) that sunset is the best time to approach that city? Give reasons for your answer.
2. How is the impression that the coastline is a subcontinent "with imperfect self-control" (¶2) a natural result of the observations made in the three previous sentences?
3. Sentences 6-13 of paragraph 3, and paragraph 4, appear to digress from the descriptive intent of the passage. Can you justify this digression? Give reasons for your answer.
4. Sentences 6-8 of paragraph 5 are expository rather than descriptive. Decide whether the author's explanation of the fireworks is pertinent or not.
5. This passage contains a large number of image-making words that leave clearly defined emotional impressions. Some sense of the author's success in descriptive technique may be gained by answering the following questions:
   a. Show how the word *unscathed* (S1, ¶2) reinforces the impression created by "dark green, formidable outline."
   b. Show how the word *slanted* and the word *reined* are related to each other (S2, ¶2).
   c. Why would the hills behind the city stand up more *fiercely* in a *tawny* sunset? Show the connection between *fiercely* and *tawny* (S2, ¶3).
   d. Why are the *tiny black silhouettes* of the trees unusually prominent (S3, ¶3)?
   e. What are the connotations of the word *flaunted* in S5, ¶3?
   f. How do the words *huddled* and *strenuously craning* prepare for the impression of *quaint, crude dignity* (S7, ¶3)?
   g. In what sense may a skyscraper appear *gauche* and *rather forlorn* (S8, ¶3)?
   h. What is the exact implication of the phrase *pathos of the boor* (S10, ¶3)?
   i. Comment on the aptness and force of the simile in S13, ¶3.
   j. How does the word *evaded* convey the idea of approaching darkness and prepare for the author's concentration on rockets (S1, ¶5)?
   k. Show how the word *covey* (S4, ¶5), is linked with the words *burst in a chorus* (S5, ¶5).
   l. Why are the *plopping noises* (S5, ¶5) inoffensive?
   m. In what sense may the balls of smoke be called *surprised* (S5, ¶5)?
   n. What is the basis of the comparison between *rockets* and *exclamation marks* (S9, ¶5)? (See Section V for the basis of comparison.)

o. How does the author mean us to understand Ss2-5 in paragraph 6? Is he ridiculing the reaction he describes, or not? If he is, to what extent does he forfeit the dominant impression he intends to create, namely the special flavor of Rio at dusk?

6. In 500 words describe a city, town, or prominent locality of your own choice from the point of view of a moving observer. Imagine yourself approaching or leaving a locality by automobile or airplane or on foot. Clearly define each separate perspective.

4. A Japanese Home

BY JAMES A. MICHENER

1 Come with me on a visit to Takeo Sato, of Morioka. As you approach his home you will be disappointed. It is unpainted, weather-beaten, on a street dreary with similar unpainted, weather-beaten houses. For Japan likes to hide its inner beauty from the street, so that when you enter the quiet home the effect of tranquillity and art will be heightened.

2 At the doorway of the Sato home Mrs. Sato, a dainty little kimonoed woman of forty, kneels on the floor and bows till her head touches her knees. Her two quite beautiful daughters, seventeen-year-old Akira (beautiful sun) and eleven-year-old Yasuko (peace of mind)—adorned in gold and silver kimonos—also bow to the floor, then rise to take your wraps. Mr. Sato, a forty-seven-year-old professor, is dressed in Western clothes; he greets you with a sturdy handshake.

3 You kick off your shoes and step across the threshold—never on it, for that is dangerous luck—onto one of the finest floorings yet invented: *tatami* mats, six by three feet, made of a two-inch-thick rice-straw filler covered by an exquisite woven white reed of the I plant and edged with a one-inch maroon or blue cloth binder.

4 Above the doorway hangs a long length of rice-straw rope, which you will see constantly in Japan. From the rope hang strips of white paper cut in an ancient design somehow resembling Christmas tree decorations. This is the Satos' Shinto shrine and here reside the benevolent spirits of this house.

5 Mrs. Sato, bowing, leads you to your room. It's fourteen *tatami* large—room size is always indicated in this way—and is cut off from

the rest of the house by twelve sliding doors made of thin strips of wood to which have been pasted sheets of strong opaque rice paper. Your room contains no furniture. There is an alcove, where a picture hangs on a brocaded scroll over a vase with one flower. Across the room stands another vase, holding a large bouquet.

6 For your clothing the Sato girls bring in low shallow trays, which they place upon the floor. When your bags are unpacked, the girls whisk them away and you stand in the middle of a completely furnished Japanese room. Low lines predominate; the soft, natural wood blends with the beautiful *tatami* matting. There are no rooms like these anywhere else in the world, and they tell much about the Japanese character: controlled, art-conscious, unostentatious, everything in the place ordained for it by custom and law.

7 Now the family leads you to their quarters, and again there is no item of furniture to be seen. Thin cushions line the wall, and on one of these you sit. Many nations have the custom of sitting cross-legged on the floor, but the Japanese double their legs directly under them and sit upon their ankles. Mr. Sato says, "Don't you try it! In fact, it would probably be better for us if we didn't either." Like most successful Japanese, Mr. Sato speaks good English. He brings out a low armrest such as the ancient Romans used, and with little difficulty you find a comfortable position.

8 Just as you are beginning to feel cold, for although this is winter the Satos have no heat, Mrs. Sato leads you to the *kotatsu:* in the center of the floor is a deep hole five feet square, its edges lined with old bed quilts. At the bottom is a small iron brazier of burning charcoal. From the corners of the hole rise stout poles to which, eighteen inches above the floor, a table is fastened. From the edges of the table hang three thicknesses of heavy blanket. You wriggle under them, sit on the floor, dangle your feet against the brazier, and tuck the blankets around your middle. In a moment you are glowingly warm.

9 (I once sat with Mr. Sato and two of his professor friends for three days in the *kotatsu,* arguing about the economics of Japan, and although the weather was well below freezing and the sliding doors were kept open so we could appreciate the snow, we were quite warm.)

10 After you have been warmed Mrs. Sato leads you to another room, where she serves *sushi,* Japan's national dish. To a bowl of rice flavored with salt, sugar and vinegar she adds bits of fresh fish and

flakes of a remarkable dehydrated fish that looks like black petrified wood but which tastes better than any fish you've ever eaten. On the side there are soup, bits of vegetable, and condiments.

11 It is not only Mrs. Sato's excellent cooking which makes this meal unique. It is the ritual of serving food that you will never forget. Mrs. Sato, of course, does not eat with her guests. She approaches the dining room door with trays, drops to her knees, and crawls forward daintily with each dish.

12 Before you she places a small lacquered table of exquisite artistry. On it she arranges six or seven lacquered dishes, each a work of art that has been inherited through many generations. They are inky black with a hint of gold design. The chopsticks are ivory, the exquisite ceramic block on which they rest came from Korea centuries ago, and the sake cups are fragile china.

13 Each dish contains one item of food, arranged to emphasize its color, texture and design. The clear brown soup contains one piece of beet, one wedge of onion, and one shred of meat. Even the *sushi,* which you might expect to be thrown together in the Chinese style, has been carefully designed, with the bits of fish artistically arranged. Mrs. Sato has spent four hours preparing this meal.

14 After lunch you inspect the house. Like most Japanese houses it is on one floor, but unlike most it is large: fourteen rooms plus one each for the three servants. Mrs. Sato says it takes her all morning to clean the house; she keeps it spotless.

15 Mr. Sato says, "This house is a bother. Much too big for the way we live today. My grandparents had half a dozen servants and sixteen members of the family living here at once. I'd like to sell it, but I can't give up the gardens."

16 He takes you outside. If you prefer formal French gardens, you may not think much of Mr. Sato's, which seem more like casual bits of woodland enclosed by the walls of his house. Rocks, sand, trees and shrubs combine to make a rugged and handsome landscape, whose outstanding glory is a big pine tree some two hundred years old.

17 Generations of gardeners have studied this tree, trying to discover precisely which way each branch should grow to produce the finest artistic effect. Some branches were drawn toward the house; others were wired into lovely, fantastic shapes or were weighted down with stones to keep them hovering a few inches above the earth. Since

winter snows might damage such a tree, each autumn Mr. Sato sets a tall bamboo pillar up through the branches; from it he suspends strong ropes which hold each single branchlet in place through the winter. Today the old pine looks like an umbrella, and you can scarcely see the green branches through the white ropes.

18 Each tree and shrub in the Sato gardens is so protected every year. Each stem is studied to see whether it adds to the general beauty of the garden. The result is a natural setting symbolizing Japan: everything in its place, everything drawn up tight.

19 At dinner Mrs. Sato serves you *sukiyaki,* the second of Japan's national dishes, and by all odds the best. In the middle of the *kotatsu* table she places a large charcoal brazier on which rests a big, low-edged iron skillet. While it gets red-hot she brings in a very large china tray on which have been piled in perfect design green vegetable leaves, a silvery, slippery kind of noodle, mushrooms, white leeks, quartered onions, little chunks of bean curd, squares of suet—all topped by long thin slices of very red meat.

20 Mrs. Sato draws in her breath as the guests compliment her on the attractiveness of the ingredients; then she pops the suet into the skillet. As it sizzles she pours in soy sauce and sake wine. When the broth seems right, she takes long chopsticks and places the vegetables in one by one with strips of meat on top. As the dish sizzles and its aroma rises, Mrs. Sato throws in many spoonfuls of sugar, some salt and large pinches of *aji,* a remarkable condiment which enhances all true flavors.

21 While this has been going on you have been whipping a raw egg in your individual bowl. Mr. Sato says, "*Sukiyaki* always presents a nice philosophical problem. You get so hungry waiting that as soon as it's ready you start to eat. But if you're wise you wait until well toward the end, when all the juices have begun to blend."

22 You can't wait. You dive your chopsticks into the skillet and come forth with some meat, a bit of onion, and a chunk of bean curd. These go into the egg sauce for cooling and then into your mouth. *Sukiyaki* is an especially admirable dish because its sociable manner of preparation, its pervading aroma, and the fellowship of pitching into the common pot for what you like best all add gusto to the excellence of the food.

23 After dinner Mrs. Sato and her daughters—who would not, of course, eat with guests—climb into the *kotatsu;* conversation becomes animated. You ask what a brilliant kimono like the one Akira is wear-

ing costs, and Mr. Sato winces. His wife says, "For the outer kimono, $35. For the inner one, $25. For the flowered coat, $35. And for the brocaded sash, $100."

24 Mr. Sato says, "There are other items, too."

25 Mrs. Sato laughs. "Counting all my kimonos for work I have about 100 major pieces of cloth which I can combine in various ways just as Western women combine blouses and skirts. You might say I have thirty-five kimonos."

26 Akira says, "What is important is to wear the right color at the right time."

27 Mr. Sato adds, "A Japanese can look at a kimono and say, 'That's for a nineteen-year-old girl,' or, 'That's for a woman of forty.'"

28 Akira says, "Most of us at school prefer Western clothes. The kimono is not at all satisfactory. Too difficult to take big steps."

29 It is now bedtime, and Mrs. Sato shows you to your room. In the middle of the floor a very thick bedroll has been spread. During the day it was stored away in a closet, as were all the other beds.

30 You leave some of the sliding doors open so that you can see the garden as the moon rises over Mr. Sato's priceless pine tree.

31 In the morning, when you leave this beautiful and simple home, Mrs. Sato is out front polishing your shoes, and her daughters are bowing low in respect to the parting guest. Then Mrs. Sato hurries in to help you on with your coat, Mr. Sato shakes hands vigorously, and you are back on the dark and ugly street. If you had never stepped into the Sato home you could not have had the slightest idea of what delicate beauty there is behind every street in Japan.

Comment

The dominant impression is that of tranquillity and delicate beauty. This impression is clearly stated in paragraphs 1 and 31 and supported by the details that appear in the intervening paragraphs. The point of view is that of the moving observer. The author first stands outside the house, then moves from room to room, remains overnight, and then departs. Each movement is clearly marked by an appropriate transitional expression so that the reader is prepared for the shift in point of view. (Note: Although there is a progressive shift in point of view, certain descriptions [¶30, for example] are those of a fixed observer.)

In this passage the author describes a variety of subjects: the house and its furnishings, the Sato family and its dress, the routine of the household.

Each part receives its own proper emphasis; all contribute to the dominant impression.

It will be noted that the point of view in this description is clarified by the observance of a time sequence. The descriptive elements are suspended on a slender thread of narrative incident. (The blend of narrative and description is explained in Example D of this section.)

The paragraph summary below is arranged to recall for the student (1) the particular subject described, (2) the quality in the particular subject that contributes to the dominant impression, and (3) the transitional expression that indicates the shift in point of view.

Particular Aspect of the Subject Described	*Quality That Contributes to the Dominant Impression*	*Words Expressing Transition or Indicating the Point of View*
1. Exterior of house	Dreary, weather-beaten [for sake of contrast]	"As you approach"
2. Sato family	Beauty of women's dress, beauty of the Sato daughters	"At the doorway"
3. The *tatami* mats	Exquisite weaving	"Step across the threshold"
4. Shinto shrine	Ancient design	"Above the doorway"
5-6. Guest room	Scroll and flowers, low lines, *tatami* matting	"Leads you to your room"
7-9. Family quarters, the *kotatsu*	Warmth and comfort	"Leads you to their quarters . . . leads you to the *kotatsu*"
10-13. Lunch	Excellence of meal, service, ritual	"Leads you to another room"
14-15. Inspection of house	Spotlessness	"After lunch"
16-18. The garden	Artistic effect	"He takes you outside"
19-22. The dinner	Excellence of food, sociability of atmosphere	"At dinner. . . . While this has been going on"
23-28. Kimonos	Variety and purpose of kimonos	"After dinner"
29-30. Bedroom	Simplicity of arrangement; view of the garden	"It is now bedtime"
31. The Sato family	Summary impression of courtesy, charm, and delicate beauty	"In the morning"

Analysis and Composition

1. In paragraph 1 the author emphasizes the dreariness of the exterior of the Sato house and promises a contrast within. Show how this contrast is made effective by the use of words expressing color in paragraphs 2-4.
2. This selection is literal in its exact reporting of details. Note that the author states the exact age of each member of the Sato family, translates the girls' names, gives the measurement of the *tatami* mats. List ten other observations that are equally exact. Decide whether precision of this sort is necessary or desirable in a descriptive passage.
3. Show how the verbs and verbals in paragraph 8 convey a sense of movement.
4. In paragraphs 10-13 pick out the expressions that appeal to the various senses. To which of the five senses does the author make his principal appeal?
5. Show how the author blends process exposition with description in paragraphs 17-18 and in paragraphs 19-20.
6. In paragraphs 23-28 the description of the kimonos is presented by way of dialogue. Read these paragraphs carefully and decide which details appearing in the dialogue are descriptive and which are narrative.
7. The author asserts that the Japanese character is "controlled, art-conscious, unostentatious" (¶6). Show how these qualities are evident (a) in the garden, (b) in the ritual of the evening meal, (c) in the manners displayed by Mrs. Sato.
8. Study the passages describing Mrs. Sato's appearance and activity. Decide whether or not the author has given a vivid picture of Mrs. Sato. Give reasons for your answer.
9. Decide whether the dialogue that appears in paragraphs 15 and 21 contributes directly to the main descriptive intention.
10. First construct a paragraph summary, similar to that given above, for a descriptive essay of 1000 words on an American home. Then write the essay.

C. Give emphasis to your description by using vivid details, figurative language, and climactic order.

1. Fire and Storm

BY PETER FLEMING

1 I wanted to have a look at the lie of the land; so while Queiroz was making a fire I stripped and tied a pair of trousers round my head and waded across. The water came up to my neck; the river was deeper here than we had known it since we had left São Domingo.

2 As usual, the open country on the other side was less open than it looked. The scattered trees and the tall grass made a screen which the eye could not penetrate to any great depth. About 400 yards inland there was a thickish belt of low scrub, and on the edge of it stood a tree with a broad but curiously twisted trunk. This I climbed.

3 I stayed up it for half an hour, and in that half-hour the world below me changed. A wind began to sing in the sparse leaves round my observation post. The sky darkened. Massed black cohorts of clouds assembled in the west and came up across the sky under streaming pennons. The wind rose till its voice was a scream; great weals appeared in the upstanding grass, and in the straining thickets the undersides of leaves showed pale and quivering in panic. My tree groaned and bent and trembled. The sky grew darker still.

4 The earth was ablaze. That fire which the Indians had lit raced forward under the trampling clouds, and, behind me, on the other side of the river, a long battle line of flames was leaping out across the

campo we had fired that morning. Huge clouds of smoke charged down the wind, twisting tormented plumes of yellow and black and grey. The air was full of fleeting shreds of burnt stuff. The fall of sparks threw out little skirmishing fires before the main body of the flames. A dead tree close beside me went up with a roar while the fire was still half a mile away.

5 There was something malevolent in its swift advance. The light thickened and grew yellow; the threatening sky was scorched and lurid. If there could be hell on earth, I thought, this is what it would look like.

6 There was indeed a kind of horrible beauty in the scene. A fury had fallen upon the world. All the sounds, all the colours, expressed daemonic anger. The ponderous and inky clouds, the flames stampeding wantonly, the ungovernable screaming of the wind, the murky yellow light—all these combined to create an atmosphere of monstrous, elemental crisis. The world would split, the sky would fall; things could never be the same after this.

7 The fire was almost on me now, but my retreat to the river was open and secure. Flames flattened and straining in the wind licked into the belt of scrub beside my tree; great gusts of heat came up from below and struck me. Little birds—why so tardily, I wondered—fled crying to the trees on the river bank. Two big kites warily quartered the frontiers of the fire, though I never saw either stoop. Presently one of them came and sat on a branch below me, so close that I could have hit him with a stick. He stayed there brooding majestically, with his proud eyes, over the work of desolation. Every now and then he shrugged himself and fluffed his feathers: for fear, I suppose, that he might entertain a spark unawares. I felt oddly friendly towards him, as one might to a coastguard in a storm; his imperturbability, his air of having seen a good deal of this sort of thing in his time, were comforting. But a spark stung my naked back, and I swore. The kite looked at me in a deprecating way and dropped downwind to the next tree.

8 Then the storm broke. It opened first a random fire of huge and icy drops. I saw that we were in for worse and scrambled down the tree: not without regret, for I had seen a fine and curious sight and would willingly have watched for longer, the cataclysmic evening having gone a little to my head. But shelter of a sort was essential, and I found the best available under the trees on the river bank.

9 On the opposite side Roger and Queiroz had bundled our belongings into a hole between the roots of a tree and were sitting on them, to keep them dry. It was a hopeless task, though. There began such rain as I had never seen before. It fell in sheets and with ferocity. It was ice-cold. It beat the placid river into a convulsive stew. The world darkened; thunder leapt and volleyed in the sky. From time to time lightning would drain the colour and the substance from our surroundings, leaving us to blink timidly at masses of vegetation which had been suddenly shown up as pale elaborate silhouettes, unearthly, ephemeral, and doomed. The rain beat land and water till they roared. The thunder made such noise in heaven as would shortly crack the fabric of the universe. The turmoil was almost too great to intimidate. It could not be with us that Nature had picked so grandiose a quarrel; her strife was internecine. Dwarfed into a safe irrelevance, dwarfed so that we seemed no longer to exist, we had no part in these upheavals. Roger and I smiled at each other across the loud waters with stiff and frozen faces.

Comment

The author describes not only the objective features of fire and storm but his own subjective impressions. The dominant impression is one of mingled beauty and horror. The point of view is principally that of the fixed observer.

This passage is notable for its splendid excitement. The vivid conjunction of fire and storm, the metaphorical language, the gradual intensification of the emotional impression, all combine to create a high-pitched Wagnerian effect.

The pattern of the passage may be charted as follows:

1. The observer takes his post in the branches of a tree.
2. He observes the beginning of the storm and describes what he sees, hears, and feels.
3. He turns his attention to the progress of the fire and watches its approach.
4. As the fire reaches the observation post the storm breaks.
5. He describes the storm as it appears to the senses and as it affects him subjectively.

Analysis and Composition

1. List the words and expressions that appeal to the several senses of sight, hearing, taste, touch, and smell. To which sense does the author appeal most frequently?

2. By reference to paragraphs 5, 6, and 9 show how the scene affected the observer subjectively.

3. What emotional effect is created by the appearance of the little birds and the two kites (¶7)?

4. Show how the figurative expressions below, when studied in their individual contexts, contribute directly to a specific emotional impression.
   a. "Massed black cohorts . . . under streaming pennons" (¶3)
   b. "The wind rose until its voice was a scream" (¶3)
   c. "Leaves showed pale and quivering in panic" (¶3)
   d. "My tree groaned and bent and trembled" (¶3)
   e. "The trampling clouds" (¶4)
   f. "A long battle line of flames" (¶4)
   g. "Tormented plumes" (¶4)
   h. "Little skirmishing fires" (¶4)
   i. "Daemonic anger" (¶6)
   j. "Flames stampeding wantonly, the ungovernable screaming of the wind" (¶6)
   k. "It beat the placid river into a convulsive stew" (¶9)
   l. "Thunder leapt and volleyed in the sky" (¶9)
   m. "Pale elaborate silhouettes" (¶9)

5. In a paragraph of 300 words show why the continued comparisons of the fire and storm with war or battle (some are indicated in the expressions listed in Exercise 4a, e, f, h, l) are appropriate in this example.

6. Show how Fleming achieves vigor or emphasis by arrangement of the words within the sentences in paragraphs 3 and 6. (See Section VIII.)*

7. Show how paragraph 9 achieves vigor by the arrangement of the sentences within the paragraph. (See Section VIII.)

8. Select the three details that you consider the most effective in this example. Give reasons for your answer.

9. Write a descriptive essay of approximately 500 words according to the following plan:
   a. Briefly explain who the observer is.
   b. Establish a fixed point of observation.
   c. Describe the physical impact of a tornado, a storm at sea, a forest fire, a lightning storm, or a similar phenomenon.
   d. Describe the emotional effect of the event on the observer.

* See handbooks: Foerster, pp. 25-27, *82*; Hodges, *29a*; Kierzek, *61-64*; Perrin, pp. 293-95.

2. Monterey

BY ROBERT LOUIS STEVENSON

1 [1]The bay of Monterey has been compared by no less a person than General Sherman to a bent fishhook; and the comparison, if less important than the march through Georgia, still shows the eye of a soldier for topography. [2]Santa Cruz sits exposed at the shank; the mouth of the Salinas River is at the middle of the bend; and Monterey itself is cosily ensconced beside the barb. [3]Thus the ancient capital of California faces across the bay, while the Pacific Ocean, though hidden by low hills and forests, bombards her left flank and rear with never-dying surf. [4]In front of the town, the long line of sea beach trends north and northwest, and then westward to enclose the bay. [5]The waves which lap so quietly about the jetties of Monterey grow louder and larger in the distance; you can see the breakers leaping high and white by day; at night, the outline of the shore is traced in transparent silver by the moonlight and the flying foam; and from all round, even in quiet weather, the low, distant, thrilling roar of the Pacific hangs over the coast and the adjacent country like smoke above a battle.

2 [1]These long beaches are enticing to the idle man. [2]It would be hard to find a walk more solitary and at the same time more exciting to the mind. [3]Crowds of ducks and sea gulls hover over the sea. [4]Sandpipers trot in and out by troops after the retiring waves, trilling together in a chorus of infinitesimal song. [5]Strange sea tangles, new to the European eye, the bones of whales, or sometimes a whole whale's carcase, white with carrion gulls and poisoning the wind, lie scattered here and there along the sands. [6]The waves come in slowly, vast and green, curve their translucent necks, and burst with a surprising uproar, that runs, waxing and waning, up and down the long keyboard of the beach. [7]The foam of these great ruins mounts in an instant to the ridge of the sand glacis, swiftly fleets back again, and is met and buried by the next breaker. [8]The interest is perpetually fresh. [9]On no other coast that I know shall you enjoy, in calm, sunny weather, such a spectacle of Ocean's greatness, such beauty of changing colour, or such degrees of thunder in the sound. [10]The very air is more than usually salt by this Homeric deep.

3 [1]Inshore, a tract of sand hills borders on the beach. [2]Here and there a lagoon, more or less brackish, attracts the birds and hunters. [3]A rough, spotty undergrowth partially conceals the sand. [4]The crouching, hardy, live oaks flourish singly or in thickets—the kind of wood for murderers to crawl among—and here and there the skirts of the forest extend downward from the hills with a floor of turf and long aisles of pine trees hung with Spaniard's beard. [5]Through this quaint desert the railway cars drew near to Monterey from the junction at Salinas City—though that and so many other things are now forever altered—and it was from here that you had the first view of the old township lying in the sands, its white windmills bickering in the chill, perpetual wind, and the first fogs of the evening drawing drearily around it from the sea.

4 [1]The one common note of all this country is the haunting presence of the ocean. [2]A great faint sound of breakers follows you high up into the inland canyons; the roar of water dwells in the clean, empty rooms of Monterey as in a shell upon the chimney; go where you will, you have but to pause and listen to hear the voice of the Pacific. [3]You pass out of the town to the southwest, and mount the hill among pine woods. [4]Glade, thicket, and grove surround you. [5]You follow winding sandy tracks that lead nowhither. [6]You see a deer; a multitude of quail arises. [7]But the sound of the sea still follows you as you advance, like that of wind among the trees, only harsher and stranger to the ear; and when at length you gain the summit, out breaks on every hand and with freshened vigour, that same unending, distant, whispering rumble of the ocean; for now you are on the top of Monterey peninsula, and the noise no longer only mounts to you from behind along the beach towards Santa Cruz, but from your right also, round by Chinatown and Pinos lighthouse, and from down before you to the mouth of the Carmello River. [8]The whole woodland is begirt with thundering surges. [9]The silence that immediately surrounds you where you stand is not so much broken as it is haunted by this distant, circling rumour. [10]It sets your senses upon edge; you strain your attention; you are clearly and unusually conscious of small sounds near at hand; you walk listening like an Indian hunter; and that voice of the Pacific is a sort of disquieting company to you in your walk.

Comment

The dominant impression in this passage is the haunting presence of the sea. (The Pacific Ocean is mentioned in nineteen of the thirty sentences.)

In paragraph 1 Stevenson gives a general impression of the Monterey Bay area by means of a frame image. (See introduction to this section.) The remaining paragraphs are progressive descriptions from a moving point of view.

Thus by the adroit combination of the two points of view Stevenson has presented to us (1) a panoramic impression of the Monterey Bay area, (2) the beaches of Monterey, (3) the inshore area, and (4) the Monterey peninsula.

Paragraph 1 demonstrates on a small scale the literary virtues of the whole passage. It is an objectively accurate description of the Monterey Bay area, as a topographical map will certify. The comparison of the Bay of Monterey with a bent fishhook frames the scene and thus helps to achieve a consistent point of view. This paragraph does not serve merely to describe the objective details. It describes also the feelings of the observer—his excitement at the scene and above all his consciousness of the sea.

Throughout the entire passage Stevenson emphasizes the haunting presence of the sea by his use of significant details. Some exciting sight, sound, or smell of the Pacific thrusts itself upon the imagination in each sentence. Moreover, these sense impressions are stated in figurative expressions, such as: the Pacific *bombards* the shore; sandpipers *trot* in like *troops* after the *retiring* waves; the waves *curve their translucent necks; the long keyboard of the beach;* the township's white windmills *bickering* in the chill, perpetual wind; the first fogs of evening *drawing drearily around it.*

The passage is also notable for the gradual intensification of feeling. Each succeeding paragraph builds up our awareness of the sea. This impression reaches its climax in the last four sentences of the selection, where Stevenson calls upon his splendid descriptive powers to fill our ears with the "whispering rumble, . . . thundering surges, . . . this distant circling rumour" of the ocean. Thus we are left with an objectively clear picture harmonized with a dominant subjective impression.

Analysis and Composition

1. In paragraph 1 pick out the expressions that appeal (a) to the sense of sight and (b) to the sense of hearing.

2. Underline the *l, n, r,* and *s* sounds in sentence 5 of paragraph 1. Does the combination of these sounds help you to feel the presence of the sea? Explain your answer.

3. In sentence 5 of paragraph 1 Stevenson says that the *"roar* of the Pacific hangs . . . *like smoke* above a battle." Is this metaphor exact? Give reasons for your answer.

4. To what senses do the following verbs and verbals (studied in the context of the sentences) appeal directly?

Paragraph 2

    hover (S3)   curve, burst (S6)

    trot, trilling (S4)   mounts, fleets, is met and buried (S7)

Paragraph 3

    bickering, drawing (S5)

Paragraph 4

    haunting (S1)   follows (S7)

    dwells (S2)   is begirt (S8)

    surround (S4)   strain (S10)

5. In a brief paragraph show how each of the following expressions, read in its context, conveys simultaneously (a) a sense impression and (b) an emotional impression:

"never-dying surf" (S3, ¶1)
"flying foam" (S5, ¶1)
"infinitesimal song" (S4, ¶2)
"strange sea tangles" (S5, ¶2)
"white with carrion gulls" (S5, ¶2)
"vast and green" (S6, ¶2)
"these great ruins" (S7, ¶2)
"degrees of thunder in the sound" (S9, ¶2)
"this Homeric deep" (S10, ¶2)
"quaint desert" (S5, ¶3)
"lying in the sands" (S5, ¶3)
"chill, perpetual wind" (S5, ¶3)
"great faint sound" (S2, ¶4)
"wind among the trees" (S7, ¶4)
"circling rumour" (S9, ¶4)

6. Comment on the climactic arrangement and the onomatopoeic quality of sentence 5, paragraph 2, and sentence 7, paragraph 4. (Onomatopoeia is the use of words whose sound is suggestive of the sense.)

7. Analyze paragraphs 2 and 4 (a) to determine the variety of sentences within the paragraphs and (b) to determine the variety in the structure of the individual sentences.
8. Write a short descriptive essay on one of the topics suggested below according to the following outline:
   A. In an introductory paragraph give a panoramic description of the whole scene. If possible create a unified impression by using a comparison of the same type as Stevenson's comparison of the Bay of Monterey to a bent fishhook.
   B. In two separate paragraphs describe the scene from two different places of observation.
   C. In a concluding paragraph state your dominant impression.

Suggested Topics

San Francisco Bay	The Chicago Lake Shore
New York Harbor	The Grand Canyon
Boston Harbor	The Mississippi at Natchez

(The student may substitute for these some other topographical feature with which he is more familiar.)

3. The Atom Bomb

BY WILLIAM L. LAURENCE

1 We flew southward down the channel and at 11:33 crossed the coastline and headed straight for Nagasaki, about one hundred miles to the west. Here again we circled until we found an opening in the clouds. It was 12:01, and the goal of our mission had arrived.

2 We heard the prearranged signal on our radio, put on our arc welder's glasses, and watched tensely the maneuverings of the strike ship about half a mile in front of us.

3 "There she goes!" someone said.

4 Out of the belly of *The Great Artiste* what looked like a black object went downward.

5 Captain Bock swung around to get out of range; but even though we were turning away in the opposite direction, and despite the fact

THE ATOM BOMB: reprinted with the permission of the New York *Times* and the author. This is part of the story of Atom Bomb III, which was dropped over Nagasaki.

that it was broad daylight in our cabin, all of us became aware of a giant flash that broke through the dark barrier of our arc welder's lenses and flooded our cabin with intense light.

6 We removed our glasses after the first flash, but the light still lingered on, a bluish green light that illuminated the entire sky all around. A tremendous blast wave struck our ship and made it tremble from nose to tail. This was followed by four more blasts in rapid succession, each resounding like the boom of cannon fire hitting our plane from all directions.

7 Observers in the tail of our ship saw a giant ball of fire rise as though from the bowels of the earth, belching forth enormous white smoke rings. Next they saw a giant pillar of purple fire, ten thousand feet high, shooting skyward with enormous speed.

8 By the time our ship had made another turn in the direction of the atomic explosion the pillar of purple fire had reached the level of our altitude. Only about forty-five seconds had passed. Awe-struck, we watched it shoot upward like a meteor coming from the earth instead of from outer space, becoming ever more alive as it climbed skyward through the white clouds. It was no longer smoke, or dust, or even a cloud of fire. It was a living thing, a new species of being, born right before our incredulous eyes.

9 At one stage of its evolution, covering millions of years in terms of seconds, the entity assumed the form of a giant square totem pole, with its base about three miles long, tapering off to about a mile at the top. Its bottom was brown, its center was amber, its top white. But it was a living totem pole, carved with many grotesque masks grimacing at the earth.

10 Then, just when it appeared as though the thing had settled down into a state of permanence, there came shooting out of the top a giant mushroom that increased the height of the pillar to a total of forty-five thousand feet. The mushroom top was even more alive than the pillar, seething and boiling in a white fury of creamy foam, sizzling upward and then descending earthward, a thousand Old Faithful geysers rolled into one.

11 It kept struggling in an elemental fury, like a creature in the act of breaking the bonds that held it down. In a few seconds it had freed itself from its gigantic stem and floated upward with tremendous speed, its momentum carrying it into the stratosphere to a height of about sixty thousand feet.

12 But no sooner did this happen when another mushroom, smaller in size than the first one, began emerging out of the pillar. It was as though the decapitated monster was growing a new head.

13 As the first mushroom floated off into the blue it changed its shape into a flowerlike form, its giant petals curving downward, creamy white outside, rose-colored inside. It still retained that shape when we last gazed at it from a distance of about two hundred miles. The boiling pillar of many colors could also be seen at that distance, a giant mountain of jumbled rainbows, in travail. Much living substance had gone into those rainbows. The quivering top of the pillar was protruding to a great height through the white clouds, giving the appearance of a monstrous prehistoric creature with a ruff around its neck, a fleecy ruff extending in all directions, as far as the eye could see.

Comment

The dominant impression is that of awe and horror. The point of view is that of the moving observer. The order is one of increasing intensity, beginning with the initial detonation and ending with the final comparison between the bomb cloud and a prehistoric monster.

Any description of an atomic bomb is likely to seem vivid because the contemporary reader immediately relates the words to pictures he has seen and to descriptions he has heard or read elsewhere. In one sense nothing is more emphatic than the bomb itself. Nevertheless, this passage does supply additional vigor by the force of its language. Figurative expressions like "the flash that broke through the dark barrier of our arc welder's lenses," "a living totem pole, carved with many grotesque masks," "a thousand Old Faithful geysers rolled into one," "a decapitated monster . . . growing a new head" make this description vivid and effective.

Analysis and Composition

1. Pick out five details that contribute directly to the impression of awe.
2. Show how in paragraphs 5-8 each paragraph introduces a shift in the point of view of the description of the explosion.
3. Note that many expressions underline the intensity of the effect upon the senses, such as "a *giant* flash that . . . *flooded* our cabin with *intense* light." Pick out five other expressions that also stress the intensity of the explosion.
4. In a paragraph of 100 words comment on the imaginative and emotional effect of each of the following metaphors and similes:
   "like the boom of cannon fire" (¶6)
   "belching forth enormous white smoke rings" (¶7)
   "like a meteor coming from the earth" (¶8)
   "a living totem pole" (¶9)
   "seething and boiling in a white fury of creamy foam" (¶10)
   "like a creature in the act of breaking the bonds" (¶11)
   "the decapitated monster was growing a new head" (¶12)
   "its giant petals curving downward" (¶13)
   "a giant mountain of jumbled rainbows, in travail" (¶13)
   "a monstrous prehistoric creature with a ruff around its neck" (¶13)
5. Show how the metaphors and similes listed in Exercise 4, as well as other significant details, combine to create an impression of horror as well as of awe.
6. Compare this selection with Example C1 with reference to the intensity of emotional expression.
7. Few students have had the opportunity of witnessing an event as spectacular or awesome as an atomic explosion or a volcano in eruption. But, thanks to visual communication by means of films and television, most students have witnessed similar phenomena on a smaller scale. This visual and auditory experience, together with an effort of the imagination, should help you to write a short descriptive essay on one of the subjects listed below. Adopt the point of view of an observer on a hill or a high building.
   a. Earthquake and fire strike San Francisco
   b. The blitzkrieg strikes London
   c. What would happen if New York (or some other large city) were bombed
   d. An artillery barrage in Korea
   e. Torpedo attack on an aircraft carrier

d. Blend description with narration to achieve realistic effects.

Flight over the Wilderness

BY LAURENS VAN DER POST

1 We all climbed into the aircraft, strapped ourselves to our seats, and took off straight into the sun, leaving a trail of red dust over the airdrome.

2 We circled the town, which was just coming to life. I remember in particular *how very golden some bunches of bananas looked on the heads of the native women carrying them to the market.*

3 We rose over *the hills just outside the town* and swung south on our true course. There was no sign of yesterday's storms, no hint of *cloud, wind, or dust in the sky.* We could see clearly and very far.

4 To the north the 17,000-foot mass of Mt. Kenya stood up *distinctly with a long feather of snow in the centre of its blue mitre.* Far to the southeast, Kilimanjaro was *humped and crouched along its 19,000-foot summit, under a far greater burden of snow.*

5 I thought what an artist Africa is in the way it displays its great mountains. The greatest of them are *never jumbled together* as they are in Switzerland, the Himalayas, or the Caucasus. They are set in great open spaces and *around them are immense plains, rolling uplands, and blue lakes like seas,* so that they can see and be seen and take their proper place in the tremendous physical drama of Africa.

6 For it is a drama of great and absorbing interest, this continent of

Africa, as we saw it that morning after the storm. It is a drama in the sense that the sea is one. I do not know of any country, except perhaps the far interior of Asia, which is, in terms of earth, of solid matter, so nearly the equivalent of the sea. There seems to be no end to it. One goes on for thousands of miles. One goes on until one's eyes and limbs ache with the sight and the bulk of it, *dazzled by this inexhaustible repetition of desert, lake, escarpment, plateau, plain, snow-capped mountain, plateau, plain, escarpment, lake, and again desert.* And one almost thinks and hopes that there will be no more of it. But in the morning, across the next blue horizon, there is more. And what is stranger still, it is there as the sea is there, in a right of its own that is indifferent if not unfriendly to man.

7 One cannot fly over Europe, as I had done only forty hours before, and fail to realize how close the earth and man are to each other, how much and how deeply in one another's confidence. This land below us did not as yet care much about human beings. It was, as D. H. Lawrence—with that strange intimate sense of his for the character, the personality almost, of inorganic matter—called it, "a continent of dark negation." The native, *whose brown huts, thorn and mud kraals tucked themselves discreetly with a kind of implied fear and trembling into the shelter of the hills and ridges there below,* may be closer to it than the European, but he too is not entirely at home. His spirit bows down before it, is overburdened and exhausted by it. The only living things which look as if they really belonged to it are the wild animals. Between the animals and Africa there is an understanding that the human beings have not yet earned.

8 Over the Serengetti plain the pilot, out of goodness of heart, a desire to please his passengers, and because it was such a beautiful morning, brought the aircraft down so low that we nearly touched the tops of the acacias.

9 "I wish he wouldn't do that," said the fat man, going quite pale. "I do get so sick."

10 As he spoke, the aircraft began to plunge and heave like a trawler off the Hebrides. We were indeed close to the earth. I realized suddenly that for a brief second I had looked almost straight into the antique eye of a large giraffe. It was staring at the plane over the top of an acacia tree with an expression composed equally of intense alarm and the immense curiosity of its species.

11 "That is why the bloody fool does it!" the fat man said with a groan, pointing to the giraffe and referring to the pilot.

12 Thousands of wild animals now came into view. *Hartebeest, eland, zebra, impala, gnu, thousands of gazelle threw up their startled heads and stopped grazing.* If they were far away they just stared at the plane; but if close, first they bunched tightly together and then, as the aircraft came steadily nearer, they started desperately running in circles.

13 I found myself thinking of an incident in the war with the Japanese. At Leweeuliang in Java, when our light machine guns on the left flank opened up on the Japanese infantry, they were completely taken by surprise. Instantly they had lost their heads and all conscious control. They had bunched just like those animals, and then started to run in circles *screaming with voices that sounded as if they came not from their throats but from their stomachs;* and all the while we continued to shoot them down.

14 When in doubt, it seems, when in fear, when taken by surprise, when lost in bush or desert and without a guide, the human, the animal, heart prescribes a circle. It turns on itself as the earth does and seeks refuge in the movement of the stars. That circle, that ballet danced down there by light, fantastic antelope feet was magic once. But what use is it now?

15 Further on a furious rhino came charging out of a clump of trees. No circles for him today, no instinctive nonsense; the evidence of the noise of the plane is sufficient for him, or for any right-minded animal. There is no room for doubt. There is danger about, and he will deal with it. We saw him disappear across the plain behind us, still charging the empty blue distances with undiminished rage, while his mate and her terrified young calf trotted energetically round and round a dark pool of water.

16 "That rhino," said the fat man, looking green, "reminds me of a bloke I knew in the army."

17 A short while later we saw a lion with a very dark mane. He got to his feet and casually looked upwards, then seemed to shrug his shoulders and to flop down again with an air of intense boredom. As far as one could see there was nothing but this plain with a few acacias spinning like tops in their own shadows, and the animals.

18 But soon we had to climb out of it. The sun grew hotter and the bumping increased, and so we were sent back into the cool, blue sky. The detailed earth fell away from us. It became more and more difficult to distinguish the herds of native cattle, the kraals, and the narrow red ribbons of winding footpaths and earth roads.

19 We flew over lakes that would be considered big anywhere except in Africa, *over streams and long savannahs and over dry river beds which were great gashes of red, yellow, and white in the earth.* Africa looked to me, as it always does, more eroded and scarred, drier and less friendly than it had looked the time before.

20 After about three hours' flying, we came down at Tabora in the centre of flat, featureless bush country infested with tsetse fly.

Comment

That narration and description go hand in hand has already been demonstrated in Example B4 and to a lesser extent in Example C3, where the narrative sequence of events facilitates the shifting point of view of the description.

The Van der Post selection provides a still more effective illustration of the commingling of description and narration.

The italicized parts of the text are those sections that are primarily descriptive. (Note: Not all descriptive passages are italicized.) Examination of the italicized sections reveals that the descriptive passages are framed, or set up, by the successive stages of the flight. Hence the descriptions do not appear as inert blocks of detail but as the natural results of an action under way. Thus the description flows from a natural, or realistic, situation.

For example, as the plane circles the town (¶2), the author observes the golden bananas on the heads of the native women. So, too (¶4), the mountain Kilimanjaro appears humped and crouched because of the position of the plane. Similarly, the impressionistic description of Africa in contrast to Europe (¶7) is the direct result of the author's flying experiences. Even the snatches of dialogue (¶9, 11, and 16) are both narrative and descriptive. Thus the paleness (description) of the fat man (¶9) is the result of the movement or action (narration) of the plane. As something happens (narration) something impresses the eye or the ear or some other sense organ. When the plane plunges downward (¶10) the observer notices the antique eye of the giraffe (description). When the plane rises (¶18-19) the observer notices the harsh, eroded contours of the terrain. A narrative pattern provides a context or a natural situation in which detailed and extended description can best achieve its effect, namely the representation of sensory experience.

Hence by blending narrative and description the author achieves his dominant impression, that is, the vastness of Africa, its tremendous, physical drama (see especially ¶5, 6). By blending narration with description the author also makes it easier to shift from the observation of objective detail to the report of subjective impressions, from observation at close range to observation at long range.

Just as narration is essential to some types of description, description is also necessary to narration. In Section XIII we shall see, from a slightly different point of view, how the blending of these forms of discourse is mutually advantageous and necessary.

Analysis and Composition

1. Underline descriptive elements that are not italicized in the text.
2. Underline or write out (as your instructor directs) the descriptive elements in Examples B4 and C3.
3. In two paragraphs of 100 words each, show how each of the following expressions are (a) clear and vigorous in their description of detail and (b) related to the dominant impression. Be sure to study the expressions listed below in the context of the paragraphs from which they are taken.
   a. "With a long feather of snow in the centre of its blue mitre" (¶4)
   b. "Kilimanjaro was humped and crouched . . . under a far greater burden of snow" (¶4)
   c. "Blue lakes like seas" (¶5)
   d. "Across the next blue horizon" (¶6)
   e. "Brown huts, thorn and mud kraals tucked themselves discreetly with a kind of implied fear and trembling into the shelter of the hills and ridges" (¶7)
   f. "Plunge and heave like a trawler off the Hebrides" (¶10)
   g. "Intense alarm and the immense curiosity" (¶10)
   h. "That ballet danced down there by light, fantastic antelope feet" (¶14)
   i. "Still charging the empty blue distances with undiminished rage" (¶15)
   j. "Great gashes of red, yellow, and white" (¶19)
4. One feature of this selection is the variety of the description. The details vary, the point of view varies.
   a. Indicate this variety in the passage by showing how, in different paragraphs, the author describes the scene from the following points of view:
      (1) Fixed observer of external events
      (2) Moving observer of external events
      (3) Reporter of subjective impressions
   b. Indicate the variety in the passage by classifying the objects described under the heading
      (1) The terrain

(2) Animal life

(3) Subjective impressions

5. Decide whether this example, or B4 or C3, is most successful in blending description with narration.

6. Write a composition of approximately 300 words developing one of the topic sentences listed below or a similar topic sentence of your own choice. Be sure to blend narration with description.

   a. From the air Minnesota displays its lakes and meadows like a jeweler spreading blue diamonds on a dark green cloth.

   b. California, the Cleopatra among the states, charms with an infinite variety of desert, mountain, fertile plain, and fascinating seashore.

   c. Main Street is a hodgepodge of stores, offices, and disintegrating dwelling places.

   d. A train ride through Industrial Valley is like a tour through a gigantic machine shop.

   e. Each year the great farmland of the Middle West stages the eternal drama of birth, maturity, and decay.

GENERAL EXERCISES

A

Reread Examples IX B and D. Show how the descriptive elements contribute to the exposition of character.

Write a composition on one or more of the topics listed below, or on a topic of your own choice.

Topic	Point of View	Dominant Impression
Sunday traffic	Moving observer	Frustration
An old man	Fixed observer	Resignation
An old man	Fixed observer	Resentment
A young woman	Fixed observer	Charm
A young woman	Subjective impression	Complexity of character
A mother	Moving observer	Multiple activity
A city apartment house	Elevator boy	Variety of tenants
A farm	Seen from a hill	Appreciation of nature's bounty
A river	Moving observer on excursion boat	Detachment from hurly-burly
Times Square	Bus driver	Boredom

Topic	Point of View	Dominant Impression
Times Square	Sailor on leave	Excitement
Rockefeller Center and St. Patrick's Cathedral	Subjective impression	Contrast
Lincoln Memorial	1. From outside	Awe
	2. From inside	
An airport	Panoramic	Movement
A speaker or preacher	Television spectator	Sincerity

In narration (1) maintain unity by arranging the incidents of a whole action in a beginning, middle, and end; (2) maintain coherence by a systematic presentation of the chronology, point of view, and setting; (3) maintain emphasis by the proper use of pace, proportion, and climax; (4) maintain a style appropriate to narration by stressing movement and by harmonizing diction with the narrator's point of view.

SECTION XIII

Narration

NARRATION is that form of discourse which aims to tell a story, that is, aims to recount a connected series of incidents that together make up a significant action. In the broadest sense of the term, narration embraces history, biography, autobiography, personal adventure, travel, news reports, and fiction. Thus any discourse that answers the question, "What happened?" by relating events in a definite order is narration.

In this section we shall be concerned with the principles of composition insofar as they apply to narrative discourse in general. In Section XIV we shall examine some of the special problems of one important type of narration, the short story.

There are four closely related principles of good narration:

1. The narration must be unified and complete; that is, it must have a beginning, middle, and end.
2. The narration must be coherent, that is, systematic in its presentation, with reference to time, to point of view, and to setting.
3. The narration must be emphatic; that is, it must have pace, proportion, and climax.
4. The narration must have an appropriate style and tone, that is, diction in harmony with the action and with the point of view of the narrator.

THE FIRST PRINCIPLE IN NARRATION: UNITY

We have already observed in Section VIII and in succeeding sections that unity is the principle which draws together the parts of a composition into a meaningful whole. In exposition (Sections IX-X) and in argument and persuasion (Section XI) this unity is achieved by relating the subordinate parts to an explicitly stated central theme. In narration, however, the central theme is usually implicit rather than explicit; the subordinate parts are incidents, the whole is a complete action. The incidents become united to form a complete action when they are properly arranged in a beginning, a middle, and an end.

Here it is important to realize that the rhetorical terms, *beginning, middle,* and *end,* are especially significant. They express a literary law with the same accuracy that the statement, "A complete man must have a head, a torso, and limbs," expresses a physical law. Without a good beginning, middle, and end narration would become a mere jumble of random incidents or pointless anecdotage; with a good beginning, middle, and end narration can achieve logical unity, organic wholeness, and an esthetically satisfactory form.

Beginning. Since action is essentially a movement of events in time and through space, it must begin at a certain moment and a certain place. But it must *begin,* not merely *start.* A beginning is a source of action, a point of origin, a dynamic situation, a coil of circumstance out of which incidents spring. Beginning necessarily implies a forward movement, and looks ahead to an ending. It is the seed of definite action and not an arbitrary starting point for indefinite activity.

A true beginning, then, is an initial situation that sets an action in movement. Thus in Example 1 Commander Beach begins, not merely by placing the U.S.S. *Trigger* in Tokyo Harbor on June 10, 1943, but by sighting the Japanese carrier *Hitaka* with her escorts. This coil of circumstance springs a question, "Will the *Trigger* sink the *Hitaka* and escape, or be sunk in the effort?" Similarly, in Example 2 Carl Carmer builds up the atmosphere of rivalry between the river boats *Armenia* and *Henry Clay* and the dangers of steamboat racing in the 1850's. When, contrary to the promise of their owners, the rival queens of the Hudson begin to race, we ask, "Who will win? Will there be an accident?" In "Flash Flood," Example 3, Mary-Carter Roberts is entangled in frustrations. No one can direct her to her destination. People warn her of difficulties. These circumstances, together with her obvious determination to reach the Apache reservation, set the narrative in motion. In Example 4, Francis Parkman also begins with a dynamic situation. A weak Huron settlement of apathetic and sodden tribesmen is suddenly faced by a thousand bloodthirsty Iroquois braves bent on exterminating their hated enemies. "Will the Iroquois succeed?" Again a good beginning thrusts the reader into the heart of the story.

As the above explanation suggests, the beginning contains the reason for the narrative. Hence it is often called the *exposition,* that is, the part of the narrative that sets forth all the facts necessary to understand the action. This function of the beginning is particularly evident in the first paragraph of "The *Graf Spee*" (General Exercise A), in which Winston Churchill explains the particular mission of Commodore Harwood's cruiser squadron in the South Atlantic. Paragraphs 1-5 in Hal Borland's "Lost Retreat" (General Exercise B) set forth the circumstances of earlier visits to Pagosa Springs, Colorado, and thus help the reader to understand impressions developed in the subsequent narrative. Thackeray also uses his beginning paragraphs in General Exercise D as an exposition preliminary to the action that follows, namely young Rawdon Crawley's attendance at Whitefriars.

Middle. The middle is the series of incidents that arise from the initial situation. Thus in Example 1, once the U.S.S. *Trigger* moves towards the *Hitaka,* the incidents advance with increasing tension until the *Trigger* escapes and surfaces. In Example 2 the race between the *Henry Clay* and the *Armenia* proceeds in clearly marked stages from Albany to Riverdale, New York, where the front-running *Henry Clay* explodes into flames. "Flash Flood" (Example 3) presents the sequence of events in the writer's progress from Phoenix to the Apache reservation. In the middle section of "The Massacre of the Hurons" Francis Parkman recounts the main incidents in the Iroquois massacre of their tribal enemies.

Just as the beginning fulfills the function of an exposition, so the middle contains the *complication.** The complication (a term borrowed from dramatic criticism) results from the conflict of men and events. Thus a complication arises from the struggle of the crew of the *Trigger* against the Japanese naval units, from the *Henry Clay's* rivalry with the *Armenia,* from Miss Roberts' difficulty with time, space, weather, and local custom, from the Hurons' ancient quarrel with the Iroquois. Each successive stage of the conflict or movement of events complicates the question posed in the beginning situation by

---

* Some atypical narratives develop the exposition progressively, that is, in the course of the narrative, instead of in the beginning sections.

making the action increasingly difficult until a turning point is reached and the question is finally resolved.

End. The end of the action is that part of the narrative in which the movement of the action comes to a natural conclusion. The end is a conclusion in another sense, in that it answers the question posed in the beginning situation and adds whatever else is necessary to give the action a full meaning. Thus the ending is a *resolution* of the complication.

The ending in *"Trigger,"* for example, is the escape of the submarine. The additional information about the extent of the damage done to the *Hitaka* completes the meaning of the action. In Example 2 the ending answers the initial question by telling of the destruction of the *Henry Clay* and the loss of many passengers. The aftermath of the action, namely the criminal charges against the owners and officers of the *Henry Clay* and the passage of a law preventing steamboat racing, interprets the social and historical significance of the whole action. Similarly, "Flash Flood" ends with the author's mission completed and a humorous explanation of Apache superstitions. "The Massacre of the Hurons" concludes with the Iroquois retreat after their destruction of the Huron settlement. We understand not only what happened, but the full import of the action, namely that the Hurons are a defeated nation and that the Jesuit missionary effort has met disappointment.

Note: In fictional narrative (treated in Section XIV) the pattern of beginning, middle, and end, frequently referred to as exposition, complication, and resolution, is called the plot, that is, an arrangement of fictional events in an order calculated to express the author's theme or central idea.

THE SECOND PRINCIPLE IN NARRATION: COHERENCE

A narration achieves coherence by a systematic presentation of the events that make up the whole action, that is, by limiting and clarifying the time sequence, by maintaining a suitable point of view, and by connecting the action with a given place or atmosphere.

Time. In recounting events time is an essential element. Events happen in time; time helps to fashion events.

In the examples in this section you will notice that the writers (1) have limited the time to manageable proportions and (2) have used each stage in the chronological process to mark the logical development of their theme. Thus the time span of the action in Example 1 is approximately twenty-four hours; in Example 2 it is approximately twelve hours; in Example 3 it is approximately twenty-four hours; in Example 4 it is approximately four days. This limitation of time reminds us that no writer should attempt the impossible task of crowding into a brief narrative the events of years or of centuries.

Each temporal stage marks a logical step in the process of the narrative. Thus in Example 1 the successive moments of time are also successive stages in a running battle; in Example 2 the frequent mention of time also records the progress of the race; in Example 3 time measures the difficulties of the writer in her journey to the reservation.

Normally the time sequence is strictly chronological, that is, an uninterrupted sequence of hours, days, and weeks. Occasionally, however, especially in complex narratives, the chronological sequence resembles a stop watch rather than a clock. Thus in Example 4 Parkman relates one incident in the action from beginning to end, turns the time back with a "meanwhile," and then records a second incident from beginning to end. This is a normal procedure in historical writing, where it is frequently necessary to employ a parallel time sequence.

Other exceptions to a simple chronological sequence are called the flashback and the *in medias res* beginning. The flashback consists in moving back and forth in time. Thus instead of narrating events in A-B-C-D order, the narrator, for reasons of dramatic emphasis or psychological interpretation, may present his incidents in B-A-D-C order. For example, in General Exercise B, Hal Borland shifts his narrative from the present to the 1920's, and then from the 1920's to the present, in response to his own reminiscent mood.

Another exception to conventional time order is to begin *in medias res,* that is, in the midst of the action. This device allows a writer to introduce his story at a critical moment and then, after engaging the reader's attention, to return to less exciting details that are necessary to explain the motives of a character or the meaning of an action.

The beginning writer is best advised to use both the flashback and the *in medias res* beginning with caution. The advantages these devices provide may, for the beginner, be outweighed by the disadvantages of a confused time order.

Point of View. Point of view in narration is very similar to point of view in description (see especially Section XII D). It plays an equally important role in establishing and in maintaining coherence. This may be seen by examining the three chief questions that are normally asked about a narration. These questions are:

1. Who is telling the story?
2. From what physical point of view, or angle of narration, is he telling the story?
3. From what mood, or mental point of view, is he telling the story?

The reader must know *who* is telling the story if he is to get a proper focus on the events themselves and on the meaning of the events. For instance, it is a matter of moment for us to know that Commander Beach is a U.S. naval officer actually participating in the *Trigger* action and not, as is Carl Carmer in Example 2, an historian of a past event. Churchill's personality and his position in the British government affect the reader's response to the narrative of the sinking of the *Graf Spee.* On the other hand, Thackeray's characters in General Exercise D are clearly imaginary. The narrator is a puppet master. The reader senses this and adjusts his own attitude accordingly.

But the identity of the narrator is perhaps less important than the point of view from which he tells the story, for the point of view offers us our immediate access to a story. Thus the writer may present his action

1. As an observer or as an observer-participant, in the first person, or
2. In the third person, with
   a. Limited knowledge, or
   b. Unlimited knowledge (the omniscient point of view).

Each of these points of view has its special advantages and disadvantages. The special advantage of the *first-person point of view* is its illusion of immediacy. Thus in Example 1 Commander Beach, the narrator, is an observer-participant. As narrator he succeeds in presenting the action directly as it affects one person. In Example 3 the intimacy of the first-person narrative allows the reader to share the feeling of hot sun and drenching rain. As in *"Trigger,"* the reader is made to participate in the action. But even when the writer is not a participant in the action but merely a sensitive observer of it, as in General Exercise C, the first-person point of view brings events to a sharp focus. Thus Saint-Exupéry's narrative of the evacuation of a French village is touched with a sensitive and poetic melancholy, a measure of poignancy that no impersonal narrative could convey.

The disadvantages of the first-person point of view are its limitation of range. Hence *"Trigger,"* for all its splendid vitality and color, cannot account for the action in the wider perspectives of naval strategy and tactics. For instance, the reader knows nothing about the movements of the Japanese naval units except as they are reported by one man. Furthermore, the feelings of other participants in the action are necessarily ignored. Had the movements of the Japanese navy and the feelings of the other participants been essential to his theme the author would have been obliged to use, or to shift to, a different point of view.

Third-person point of view does not provide such an immediate sense of illusion as first-person point of view, but it has the advantage of greater range. Thus in Example 2 Carl Carmer can avail himself of the artistic license of the omniscient historian and can move from the present to the past tense, from the mind of one spectator to that of another in telling of "The Fatal Hudson River Steamboat Race." And, although the selection in General Exercise A presents a limited third-person point of view (Churchill confines his report to information available in the Admiralty War Room), the narrative includes significant details, such as the position of the various vessels and the general strategic picture, which no firsthand observer or participant could be expected to know. Similarly, Francis Parkman (Example 4) and Thackeray (General Exercise D) exhibit many sides of an action by the use of the third-person point of view.

Coherence in narrative is largely a matter of establishing and of carefully maintaining a physical point of view in the first or the third person. But the *mental point of view* is equally important. Note, for example, how each of the narrators in this section adopts and maintains a single predominant tone or attitude toward his story. Commander Beach is the professional naval officer responding to the thrill of combat. Carl Carmer is the story teller, the vivid reporter of action for its own sake. Francis Parkman is the objective historian, Thackeray the satirist of human nature. It is not the physical point of view alone but the mental point of view or tone that also keeps a story in focus.

Setting and Atmosphere. Coherence in narrative is also achieved by the integration of setting with action. By setting we mean (1) the physical background of the action and (2) the emotional atmosphere or climate.

The need for a definite physical *setting* is largely supplied by integrating description and exposition with narration. (See Examples IX B and XII D.) Thus, for instance, in Example 1 of this section the submarine is the scene of the action. Remove the vivid description of the submarine—the sounds, smell, shape, and feel of the *Trigger*—and the action itself becomes abstract and vague. Similarly, the account of the steamboat race, without the background supplied by the river, the scenery, and the passengers (Example 2) would no longer be narration but rather a colorless insurance report. Scenery and topography are likewise essential to the action of "Flash Flood" (Example 3). In Example 4 the wilderness setting is an essential condition of the action. Only in a wilderness could such a massacre take place.

An action requires time and place in which to develop. Some actions also require *atmosphere*. By atmosphere we mean not merely the physical surroundings but a mental or moral climate, the pressure of circumstances such as Hal Borland describes in General Exercise B and Saint-Exupéry describes in General Exercise C. In the first the author defines the spirit of the 1920's and of the 1950's in addition to the physical details of his lost retreat. Mr. Borland's sentence, "Any retreat is a place in the mind and emotions as well as a place on the map," suggests what is meant by the term *atmosphere*. Similarly, in "Evacuation" Antoine de Saint-Exupéry adds to the physical setting an atmosphere of defeatism and disintegration. Thus it is evident that atmosphere is closely allied to mental point of view. That it is not exactly the same may be seen, for instance, in Example 4, where the wilderness atmosphere does not reflect the narrator's mental point of view.

THE THIRD PRINCIPLE IN NARRATION: EMPHASIS

Narration achieves emphasis by the proper use of pace, proportion, and climax.

By *pace* we mean the rate of movement of the action. Normally the more rapid the movement, the more exciting the narrative becomes. Rapidity is achieved (1) by the selection of incidents that suggest movement and (2) by economy of treatment, that is, by the minimum use of expository comment and description. Among the examples in this section *"Trigger"* is fast in pace, the selection from Thackeray slow in pace. Note how the incidents in *"Trigger"* are, of their nature, quickly moving actions. The *Trigger* dives, fires her torpedoes, evades her pursuers. The descriptive element is welded into the narrative. The whole action takes place in twenty-four hours. On the other hand, Thackeray's incidents are not physical actions but mainly the thoughts and decisions of several characters. Moreover, these incidents are presented in a reflective manner with a large amount of authorial comment. Furthermore, the action covers an indefinite period. Thackeray's slow, meditative gait is designed to encourage reflection, while Beach's sprinting pace is designed to emphasize the action. Pace is also accelerated by the use of the present tense, which, like the first-person point of view, gives the reader a sense of immediacy and participation. (See Example 1 and General Exercise C.)

By *proportion* we mean the relative amount of space given to the various parts of the narrative. The introductory parts are normally presented in small scale, that is, by a summary of the details. Thus in Example 2 Carl Carmer merely summarizes the events before the race. The more important incidents, however, are treated much more fully, that is, on a large scale. Hence, when Carmer reaches the incident of the explosion, he includes many more details, and treats these details more exhaustively, than he does the less important incidents that merely lead up to the main event. So too in Example 3 Miss Roberts elaborates the incident of the cloudburst and the flood but summarizes the less important occurrences of her journey.

By *climax* we mean the point of highest interest in a narrative. A climactic arrangement builds up tension and creates suspense. Tension increases with the rise in our emotional response to a narration, as in Example 4, where Parkman makes the reader more and more aware of the horror of the Iroquois attack. Tension mounts with suspense, which is a state of anxiety as to the outcome of an action, as in General Exercise A, where Churchill withholds the outcome of the battle until the last three paragraphs. Example 2 develops a climax both by tension and by suspense.

Note: Pace, proportion, and climax are all relative to the needs of a specific narrative. Thus a fast pace is fitting to "Trigger," a slow pace to "Lost Retreat." Three short paragraphs suffice as a beginning for "The Massacre of the Hurons," while Thackeray's introduction extends through two relatively long paragraphs. Examples 1, 2, 4, and General Exercise A reach rousing climaxes, while Example 3 and General Exercises B and C reach quieter and subtler climaxes. (Review Section I with special reference to the importance of purpose and occasion; review Section VIII for the interconnection of purpose and arrangement.)

THE FOURTH PRINCIPLE IN NARRATION: STYLE

Thus far we have been stressing the arrangement of narrative, that is, the unity, coherence, and emphasis of the whole action (see Section VIII). The fourth principle is concerned with style.

Narrative style, like good style in general, is clear, vigorous, and interesting. But these qualities, in a narrative context, have a special meaning.

Since a narrative aims to recount action, its style will necessarily evoke a sense of *movement*. A sense of movement is conveyed not only by the report of an action, such as, "Marlow walked across the street and bought a paper," but, more effectively, by image-making words that stimulate the reader's imagination to the point where he feels the action vicariously.

This element of narrative style we shall study in each of the examples of this section.

Since a narration is related from a definite point of view, the language also must be appropriate to the point of view of the real or imagined narrator. Hence each narrative will differ widely in *style*. Thus Commander Beach (Example 1) speaks in the character of a naval officer. His narrative and dialogue are crisp, colloquial, technical. On the other hand, Carl Carmer writes a standard literary prose, except when he uses dialogue; that is, when the characters speak the language appropriate to their time, their social status, and their personal character.* In Example 3 Miss Roberts' narrative style shifts from her own informal but literary diction to the colorful southwestern dialect of Jeff Miller and the cruder English of the Apache. In longer fictional narratives the style takes on the color and flavor of the character from whose point of view the particular part of the story is told.

Style also expresses the personality of the writer. This element we shall consider in Section XV.

---

* Dialogue is considered in greater detail in Section XIV.

> *In Narration* (1) maintain unity by arranging the incidents of a whole action in a beginning, middle, and end; (2) maintain coherence by a systematic presentation of the chronology, point of view, and setting; (3) maintain emphasis by the proper use of pace, proportion, and climax; (4) maintain a style appropriate to narration by stressing movement and by harmonizing diction with the narrator's point of view.

1. Trigger

BY COMMANDER EDWARD L. BEACH, U.S.N.

1 Time passed, and *Trigger* was a veteran. Her lean snout had explored the waters of the Pacific from the Aleutians to the Equator, and she had sunk ships wherever she went. We had also accumulated our share of depth charges, although none—for chills and thrills—the equal of our first working over.

2 On the tenth day of June, 1943, at about five o'clock in the afternoon, we were once again off Tokyo. We had been there for thirty days, and were due to start for Pearl Harbor at midnight. "Captain to the conning tower!" Benson dashed past me in the control room, leaped up the ladder to the conning tower where Lieutenant (j.g.) Willy Long had the periscope watch. "Smoke inside the harbor!" I heard Willy tell the skipper. "Looks like it's coming this way!"

3 You could feel *Trigger* draw a deep, hushed breath. Captain Benson ordered me to plane upward two feet, to allow him to raise the periscope that much higher out of the water and thus see a little farther. Then the 'scope came slithering down and the musical chimes of the general alarm, vibrant with danger, reverberated through the ship, and started our hearts beating faster and our blood racing as we ran to our battle stations.

4 A few swift observations, and the voice of the skipper: "Men, this is the jackpot. We've got the biggest aircraft carrier I've ever seen up here, plus two destroyers. We're going to shoot our whole wad at the carrier."

5 Men's jaws slackened. This was big-league stuff. Silence answered the captain's announcement.

6 The carrier's escorts were two of the biggest and most powerful Japanese destroyers. And they were certainly doing a bang-up job of patrolling for submarines. The carrier was coming out of Tokyo Bay at high speed, zigzagging radically, but the tin cans were working on a complex patrol plan of their own, and they were all over the lot. Long before we reached firing position we rigged *Trigger* for depth charging and silent running. We knew we were going to catch it—there was simply no way to avoid it if we did our job properly.

7 There was even a good chance, the way the escorts were covering the area, that we'd be detected before shooting. For after firing, when a long, thin fan of bubbles suddenly appeared in the unruffled water—well, at the apex of the fan you were pretty sure of finding the submarine responsible.

8 I can remember how the palms of my hands sweated, and how the flesh crawled around my knees, as we bored steadily into firing position. This way and that zigzagged the carrier, and that way and then the other went our rudder as we maneuvered to keep ourselves in position ahead of the task group.

9 "Make ready all tubes!" Captain Benson is taking no chances, plans to have all ten tubes ready to shoot from either end of the ship. "Stand by forward."

10 We maneuver for a shot. This boy is coming like hell, and no fooling! Twenty-one knots, we clock him. One destroyer on either bow, the whole trio zigzagging radically.

11 We twist first one way, then the other, as the carrier presents alternately starboard and port angles on the bow. Evidently we lie on his base course. What a break!

12 "Up periscope. Bearing—mark! Three five zero. Range—mark! Down periscope. Range, six one double oh. Angle on the bow five starboard. How long till he gets here? What's the distance to the track? Control, sixty-three feet. Right full rudder. New course, zero six zero."

13 I can hear snatches of the clipped conversation between Steve Mann and the skipper.

14 "He'll be here in eight and one-half minutes. Zigged three minutes ago, at thirteen minutes. Another zig due about three minutes from now, at nineteen minutes, probably to his right. Distance to the track, five double oh. Depth and speed, Captain?"

15 "Set all torpedoes depth twenty feet, speed high. Spread them two degrees. What's the time now?"

16 "Seventeen and one-half minutes."

17 "We'll wait a minute. Sound, what does he bear?"

18 "Three five one—sound."

19 "That checks, Captain. Better take a look around. The starboard screen is coming right for us."

20 "Up periscope. There he is—mark! Three five three. Range—mark! Four seven double oh. Looking around—bearing—mark! Three three seven—screen, down periscope! Angle on the bow seven and one-half starboard. Near screen angle on the bow zero. He will pass overhead. Sound, keep bearings coming on light high-speed screws bearing three three seven!"

21 "High-speed screws, three three seven, sir. Three three seven—three three seven—three three six-a-half—three three six-a-half—three three six—three three six—three three five—three three oh—three two oh—I've lost him, sir. He's all around the dial!"

22 The familiar *thum, thum, thum* sweeps unknowingly overhead. We heave a big sigh of relief. He's out of the way for a minute.

23 "Never mind him now! Sound, pick up heavy screws bearing about three five eight."

24 "Heavy screws zero zero one, sir, zero zero two—zero zero three."

25 "It's a zig to his left! Up periscope. Bearing—mark! Zero zero five. Range mark! Down periscope. Two two double oh. Angle on the bow thirty starboard. The son of a gun has zigged the wrong way, but it's better for us at that. Right full rudder. Port ahead full! Give me a course for a straight bow shot! Make ready bow tubes! Match gyros forward!"

26 "One two five, Captain, but we can't make it. Better shoot him on zero nine zero with a right twenty gyro."

27 "Steady on zero nine zero! All ahead one-third. How much time have I got?"

28 "Not any, sir. Torpedo run one one double oh yards. Range about one eight double oh, gyros fifteen right, increasing. Shoot any time." Good old Steve is right on top of the problem.

29 I shout for more speed, which we will need to control the depth while shooting. Each torpedo being some three hundred pounds heavier than the water it displaces, we stand to become 3000 pounds lighter all of a sudden.

30 "Up periscope—bearing—mark! Three three five! Set! Fire ONE! . . . Fire TWO! . . . Fire THREE! . . . Fire FOUR! . . . Fire FIVE! . . . Fire SIX! . . . All ahead two-thirds."

31 As we in the control room fight savagely to keep from broaching surface, I can feel the repeated jolts which signify the departure of the six torpedoes in the forward tubes. The sudden loss of about 1800 pounds forward makes *Trigger* light by the bow. The increase in speed comes too late, and inexorably she rises.

32 WHANG! WHANG! WHANG! WHANG! Four beautiful solid hits. The carrier's screws stop. He lists, and drifts, helpless. We have time to notice that he is brand-new, has no planes visible, and is of a huge new type not yet seen in action. Little men dressed in white run madly about his decks. His guns shoot wildly in all directions.

33 We spin the periscope around for a look at the destroyers. Oh, oh! Here they come, and pul-lenty mad! *Take her down!*

34 We are up to fifty-six feet when finally we start back down. Back to sixty feet, and now we can plainly hear that malignant *thum, thum, thum, thum* again. Down she plunges, seeking the protection that only the depths can give. THUM, THUM, THUM, THUM—WHAM! WHAM! WHAM! WHAM! WHAM! WHAM! WHAM! WHAM! WHAM! WHAM! WHAM! WHAM! and so on for forty-seven consecutive bull's-eyes, no clicks at all! It seems inconceivable that any machine, made of man, can withstand such a vicious pounding. The air inside the *Trigger* is filled with fine particles of paint, cork, and dust. Ventilation lines and pipe lines vibrate themselves out of sight and fill the confined spaces with the discordant hum of a hundred ill-matched tuning forks. Everyone is knocked off his feet, clutches gropingly at tables, ladders, pipes, or anything to help regain his footing. A big section of cork is bounced off the hull and lands on the deck alongside the auxiliaryman; as he stoops to pick it up and drop it in a trash can, he is knocked to his hands and knees,

and the trash can spills all over the cork. The lights go out, but the emergency lights give adequate illumination. The heavy steel pressure bulkheads squeeze inward with each blow and spring out again. Deck plates and gratings throughout the ship jump from their places and clatter around, adding missile hazard to our troubles. The whole hull rings and shudders, whips and shakes itself, bounces sideways, up and down.

35 Two hundred feet, and still the agony continues; the rain of depth charges, if anything, increases in fury. How can man, made of soft flesh and not steel, stand up under such merciless, excruciating pounding? But stand it we do, with dry lips and nervous eyes.

36 We are scared, but fear leaves our brains clear, our bodies quick and sure. As usual, the temperature soars, 120 degrees or better. We reach 300 feet but cannot stop sinking, for we are heavy. Forward torpedo room bilges are full of water taken in when we fire the torpedoes. Stern tube packing leaks at this depth, and motor room bilges are filling up. Pump room and engine rooms are taking water more slowly through tortured sea valves and fittings. Besides that, the compression of the hull due to the great depth decreases our buoyant volume. We are heavy by about three or four tons, and we dare not pump, because it would make too much noise, especially bucking sea pressure at this depth.

37 The depth charges cease, but we can hear the angry screws buzzing around overhead. Maybe they've temporarily lost us. If we can keep silent, creep away, we have a chance of evading. But we slink slowly, although we run with a fifteen-degree up angle. We dare not increase speed over the silent speed, and thus increase our chances of being heard. Absolute silence. The auxiliaryman and trim-manifold man have their tools laid on the deck instead of in their usual racks. Some men take off their shoes. The bucket brigade bails water silently from the motor room bilges. All hands talk in whispers. The bow and stern planes and steering have been put into hand operation instead of hydraulic, and brawny sailors sweat profusely as they turn the huge wheels. They must be relieved every five minutes, for they gasp for breath in the foul air.

38 We've been breathing this same air since early morning, and now it is night again. Eighty-five men use up a lot of oxygen, especially when doing hard physical work. We test the atmosphere—2½ per cent carbon dioxide. Three per cent is the danger line—can knock you out. Four per cent will kill you if you can't get out of it. So we

spread CO_2 absorbent, and release oxygen from our oxygen bottles. That helps. But the heat—nothing can be done about that. You simply sweat and eat salt tablets. Your clothes and shoes are soaked. The decks and bulkheads are slippery, and literally alive with water. The humidity is exactly 100 per cent. But you don't notice it.

39 Slowly *Trigger* sinks. Down, down, far below her safe tested depth. *Trigger,* if you are worthy of your heritage, if you can keep the faith of those who built you—who will never know—and of those who place their lives in yours—who will know, if only for an instant— keep it now! We have faith in you, else we'd not subject you to this test. Vindicate that faith, we pray you!

40 Far, far below where she was designed to go, *Trigger* struggles on. Sinking slowly, her hull creaking and groaning at the unaccustomed strain, her decks bulging in the center, light partition doors unable to close because of the distortion caused by the terrific compression, she finally brings us to the point where it is safe to speed up a little, enough to stop her descent. And so we creep away, finally surfacing to complete our escape.

41 It wasn't until more than a year later that our carrier was spotted and photographed by a reconnaissance plane. We had set him back a long time, at a critical period. Too bad he didn't sink, but the effect on the Japs of seeing the half-sunken wreck come dragging back on the end of a towline and settle ignominiously into the mud of Tokyo Bay after his brave departure the day before must have been considerable and significant. For we had tagged the uncompleted aircraft carrier *Hitaka* on his maiden trial trip, just as he poked his freshly painted nose outside the torpedo nets.

Summary

A. Beginning (¶1-7): the initial situation from which the action flows. The *Trigger* sights the Japanese aircraft carrier *Hitaka* and two destroyers. Captain Benson gives the order to attack. The initial situation poses this question: Will the *Trigger* accomplish her mission successfully?
B. Middle (¶8-40): the series of incidents that make up the main action.
   1. The *Trigger* moves into firing position.
   2. The *Trigger* takes range on the oncoming *Hitaka*.
   3. Sonar detects the *Hitaka* passing overhead.
   4. The *Trigger* again takes range on the *Hitaka*.

5. The *Trigger* fires six torpedoes.
6. Four torpedoes strike the *Hitaka*.
7. The two destroyers attack the *Trigger*.
8. The *Trigger* is struck by forty-seven depth charges.
9. The *Trigger* sinks to 200 feet and is still bombarded.
10. The *Trigger* sinks to 300 feet, where the attack ceases.
11. The *Trigger* continues to descend.

C. End (¶40-41): the final result of the action. The conclusion answers the question posed in the initial situation.
1. The *Trigger* escapes and surfaces.
2. Later the damage to the *Hitaka* is determined.

Comment

The purpose of this narrative is to communicate an experience of the author as the executive officer of the U.S.S. *Trigger*. Commander Beach recreates the battle of the U.S.S. *Trigger* with the Japanese aircraft carrier *Hitaka* and two destroyers off Tokyo Bay. In doing this he gives us a complete action, that is, the connected sequence of physical events and the feelings and sensations of one of the participants. The author tells the story from a participant's point of view.

Pace: The action moves at a high rate of speed. Note particularly the rapidity of the movement in paragraphs 9-33. The dialogue reported in these paragraphs increases the reader's sense of movement in time (one day) and through space.

Proportion: Note, too, how the author magnifies the importance of the critical moments (¶34-40) by treating fewer events in greater detail and by dwelling at greater length on these details.

Climax: The writer attains a climax

a. By presenting the incidents in an order of increasing interest
b. By maintaining suspense (he withholds the final answer until the end)
c. By describing the tension experienced by the main characters (see especially ¶3, 8, 35, 38)
d. By a sustained intensity of style

Analysis and Composition

1. Decide whether the author, who chose to relate the action
a. In the first person
b. In the present tense

c. As a participant

could have achieved the same effect by relating the action

a. In the third person

b. In the past tense

c. From the point of view of a nonparticipant

2. Approximately how much time elapses in the course of this narrative? In a paragraph of 300 words show how the limitation of time contributes to the dramatic intensity of the story.

3. The setting, i.e., the place in which the action occurs, is the submarine itself. Decide whether this limited setting adds to the excitement of the narrative.

4. Show how the dialogue recorded in paragraphs 2, 4, 9, 12, 14-21, 23-28, and 30 helps to

a. Advance the action

b. Increase the pace of the action

c. Supply some elements of the physical setting or atmosphere of the action

d. Characterize the speakers

5. In this example *movement* is achieved

a. By the arrangement of the incidents

b. By the use of *action* words—expressions which stimulate the imagination to reproduce moving pictures. List five action words from this narrative. In a sentence describe the action each word suggests.

6. Although this passage avoids bookish language, it contains a number of figurative expressions. Show how the figures listed below aid in achieving the writer's purpose.

a. Personification, or the transfer of human characteristics to inhuman objects. Examples: the *Trigger* is personified (1) as a fish with a lean snout (¶1), (2) as a living creature (¶39).

b. Simile, or an expressed comparison between two unlike things. Example: the vibrations compared to ill-matched tuning forks (¶34).

c. Onomatopoeia, or the use of words whose sound suggests the sense. Examples:

(1) "Slithering" (¶3)

(2) *"Thum, thum, thum"* (¶22, 34)

(3) "WHANG! WHANG!" (¶32)

(4) "WHAM WHAM" (¶34)

7. Some of the diction here is markedly colloquial. Examples:

a. "This is the jackpot. . . . We're going to shoot our whole wad" (¶4)

b. "This was big-league stuff" (¶5)

c. "Doing a bang-up job" (¶6)

d. "Coming like hell, and no fooling" (¶10)

e. "Pul-lenty mad" (¶33)

Is this diction in harmony
a. With the point of view of the narrator, and
b. With the tone of the whole example?
Give reasons for your answer.
8. Which of the following adjectives characterize the style of this example? Give reasons for your answer.

simple	technical	colorful
exciting	racy	colloquial
amateurish	homely	obscure
literary	descriptive	

9. This example combines some elements of exposition and description with the basic narrative.
   a. Point out the expository elements that pertain to the operation of a submarine.
   b. Point out the descriptive elements that present sense impressions of sight, sound, touch, smell.
   c. Decide whether the action in this example could have been as meaningful without these expository and descriptive passages.
10. In about 750 words tell the story of some personal adventure. Before writing your composition
    a. Determine a suitable point of view
    b. Limit your time
    c. Limit your setting
    d. Decide whether your style will be serious, light, literary, or colloquial
    Use the informal outline below as a guide.

Coming Home from the Big Game

1. Initial situation: At 8 P.M. I am in Detroit, 200 miles away from campus. My 1940 convertible is weak in the engine, I have $5 left, and I must check in at Midwestern at 12 P.M. or be suspended for a month. Will I make it?
2. Middle: main incidents
   a. Because of a traffic snarl in Detroit I do not get out of the city until 9 P.M.
   b. I break all records from Detroit to Centralia.
   c. Outside Centralia it begins to snow.
   d. At 10 P.M. I am in Bushing Forks, 100 miles away from campus.
   e. The engine begins to cough outside Marysville at 10:30, still 70 miles away.
   f. The engine wheezes and dies at Petting Bridge, 10:50, 60 miles away.
   g. A safe and sound driver gives me a lift to Egypt, 10 miles further, 25 minutes, 11:15 P.M. I have 50 miles to go in 45 minutes.

h. I hail a new car with a Midwestern sticker. The driver is a white-haired man with glasses.
i. I explain my problem. The driver reveals himself as Dean Budderidge.
3. Conclusion
   a. I arrive at Midwestern at 12:15.
   b. The dormitory prefect accepts my excuse.

Suggested Topics

a. The day I got lost
b. I took the wrong train
c. Meeting the stranger
d. Looking for a job
e. A brush with the law
f. Facing the music

g. Interview with the principal
h. How I earned a whipping
i. Outwitting adults
j. The affair of the practical joke
k. My first dance
l. The little hero, or my first gold star

2. The Fatal Hudson River Steamboat Race

BY CARL CARMER

1 There was an early hubbub along the Hudson wharves at Albany on July 28, 1852. Awakened sleepers in the houses on the lower slope of the hill city looked from their windows down to the water where the night mists were being swiftly burned away by hot sunlight. They saw two long slim steamers, side by side, glitter in white and gold. "Hurrah for Harry of the West! Take the *Henry Clay!*" men shouted along the docks, but their cries were answered by other runners: "Be in New York first. Take the *Armenia*. No decent American would board the *Henry Clay!*" Prices for the voyage had started at a half-dollar, but the competing runners cut them desperately, calling twenty-five cents a few minutes before sailing time.

2 Prim, maidenly Maria Hawthorne, sister of the distinguished novelist, much improved from taking the waters at Saratoga Spa, stepped in dignity up the gangplank of the *Henry Clay* on the arm of her uncle, old John Dike of Salem. She was returning home by way of New York so that she might see the scenic grandeur of the Hudson; even Europe was said to have nothing that surpassed it. Joseph Speed—genial Baltimore bachelor and boon companion of young Jerome Bonaparte in the days when Betsy Patterson, his shapely

THE FATAL HUDSON RIVER STEAMBOAT RACE: from *The Hudson.* Copyright 1939 by Carl Carmer, and reprinted by permission of Rinehart and Company, Inc., publishers.

mother, was still trying to marry him off to someone suitable for the son of a king—tripped aboard more swiftly. He was glad to be on his way home after a visit with his York State relatives in Tompkins County.

3 It was seven o'clock, and more than three hundred other passengers had come aboard when the *Henry Clay* moved out into the river, her white-coated black stewards in a knot at her bow, waving and cheering. Two hundred and six feet long, built less than two years before, she looked every inch the "new and swift steamer" she was advertised to be. She had cost $38,000 to construct and was designed to beat even the champion racer of the river, the great *Reindeer*. Thomas Collyer, proud builder and part owner of the big boat, was himself aboard. Collyer and his employees had built the *Armenia,* too, in his East River shipyard at the foot of Twenty-first Street, New York, and had sold her to Captain Isaac Smith only a few years before.

4 Prostrated by food poisoning, Captain John Tallman of the *Henry Clay* lay ill in his cabin, confident that Mr. Collyer with all his riverboat experience would be able to command the crew expertly on the daylong trip. Collyer and his partners had recently made a contract with Captain Smith not to race their boats, and agreed that the *Henry Clay* was to sail in advance of her rival.

5 The *Armenia* did not sail until the *Henry Clay* had cast off, but she was under way a moment afterward. Thick ribbons of smoke trailed out behind the two steamers, and live sparks flew from the tall stacks. The horizontal beams above the steeple engines moved up and down with swift regularity, and the big side wheels thrashed through the water, leaving long white wakes. It was evident that the *Armenia* was striving desperately to catch up with her rival. The run to Hudson seemed short, and the *Henry Clay* was well out ahead as she swung toward the landing. Sudden cries of consternation rose from her decks as the *Armenia,* failing to follow, steamed straight ahead down the Athens channel.

6 There was a great bustle on the Hudson wharf. Passengers who had bought tickets on the *Armenia* vociferously demanded their money back and more vociferously objected when the price of a passage on the *Henry Clay* rose immediately to a dollar, twice the advertised fare for the entire voyage from Albany to New York. The landing was desperately hurried. Baggage was thrown aboard, and distinguished elderly Stephen Allen, once mayor of New York City, was rushed up

the gangplank with less respect than his white hairs, wealth, and public achievement bespoke.

7 The *Armenia* was over a mile ahead when the *Henry Clay* once more hove into the channel. Lady passengers and some of the more timorous gentlemen felt relieved, assuming that the boat would not attempt to overcome so great a handicap. Too many lives had been lost already, they said, through accidents caused by the racing of steamers on the Hudson, and they spoke of the tragic fate of the *Swallow,* wrecked in her race with the *Rochester,* and the *Express* on the rocks of Noah's Brig in the Athens channel one April night in 1845 with the loss of scores of passengers.

8 Their previous fears were doubled when the shaking of the boat, under the increasing pressure, and a loud humming noise, given off by the blowers, plainly showed that Mr. Collyer and his crew had no intention of giving up the contest. A continuous blast of intolerably hot air came from the boilers amidships, making passage between fore and after decks practically impossible. Frantically some of the ladies pleaded with their escorts to ask the captain to stop the race. The indignant gentlemen were told by the crew that the captain was ill in his cabin and could see no one. A lady fainted, and the gentleman with her appealed to John Germaine, the chief engineer.

9 "Are you afraid?" asked that officer.

10 "No, but the ladies are."

11 "The lives of my fellow officers and of the men are as valuable as those of the ladies. There is nothing to be afraid of," said Mr. Germaine.

12 Slowly the *Henry Clay* began to overtake the *Armenia.* The mile dwindled to a half-mile, a quarter. As the *Armenia* swung in to the Catskill landing, the triumphant yells of her agents and runners on the wharf drowned the noise of her engines, but she was only three lengths ahead. Quickly she took on passengers and baggage and was away again, but not before the *Henry Clay* had landed and the two crews had cursed each other with loud and hearty sincerity. The *Armenia* had gained three-quarters of a mile before her rival was once more moving downriver. Again the *Henry Clay* began the long pursuit. Soot and fragments of unburned anthracite drifted down on her decks; the shaking was more violent, and the humming noise grew louder.

13 "If there is a single gentleman aboard," said a lady loudly, "he will go and compel the captain to stop racing."

14 Isaac MacDaniel of Rutland, Vermont, traveling with his wife and daughter, proposed to two gentlemen, one from Canada and one from Missouri, that they find the captain and threaten to throw him overboard if he did not order the racing stopped. Mr. MacDaniel appealed to James Jessup, clerk of the boat.

15 "There is no danger," said Mr. Jessup.

16 In the *Henry Clay's* barroom exhausted firemen, smutty with coal and sweating streams, lifted foam-crowned glasses to eager mouths, pledging success to the officers who drank with them and who excitedly urged them to go back to their fires and keep them blazing high.

17 Now the *Henry Clay* was gaining again. In deep channel she was faster, and the *Armenia* seemed sluggish as her swift enemy approached. The distance that separated the two became a matter of lengths, and the *Armenia* moved over toward the west bank as the *Henry Clay* bore down on her. Pilot Jim Elmendorf nosed her in close to the *Armenia* as she moved alongside. An officer called for fenders, and a man stood on the paddle box ready to throw them out along the starboard rails as the distance between the boats narrowed. Now the two prows, only a few feet apart, were even, and the long white boats swept on like giant twins, straining to the utmost as they passed Turkey Point, about five miles above Kingston. Then the *Henry Clay* shot out ahead a yard, two yards, and Jim Elmendorf in the pilot-house suddenly spun the wheel. There was a grinding roar, and the *Armenia's* woodwork just forward of the larboard wheelhouse splintered as the *Henry Clay* cut across her bow.

18 Above the shrieks of the ladies sounded the cries of the *Henry Clay's* crew: "All passengers to larboard." There was a rush away from the interlocked prows. The maneuver lifted her starboard guard above the larboard guard of the *Armenia,* and there it rested for more than five minutes as the *Henry Clay* relentlessly drove her helpless opponent toward the western bank, now within a stone's throw. The officers of the *Armenia* had to choose between throwing off her steam and being run aground. There were quick sharp orders, and she drifted clear as the *Henry Clay* steamed down the center of the channel, her crew shouting derisively.

19 The *Henry Clay* was not headed again, but she kept on trembling and humming. She had cleared Kingston before the *Armenia* landed and, since she still pressed on with the apparent intent of defeating her rival by as great a margin as possible, twenty indignant passengers

trooped down the gangplank at Poughkeepsie, protesting that they would not continue to endanger their lives in a racing steamer. At Newburgh the *Armenia* was just a small blurred white spot to the north, and her runners were asking only sixpence for passage to New York, while the exuberant agents for the winning boat, cheering "Harry of the West," charged a shilling and shouted, "Take the *Henry Clay*—the *Armenia* won't get here till night." A large number of passengers followed this advice, among them Andrew Jackson Downing, with his wife, his mother-in-law—Mrs. John Peter De Windt—two of Mrs. De Windt's children, Frank and Mary, and the romantically beautiful Mrs. Matilda Wadsworth of New Orleans, a widow at twenty-six. The long white-covered tables in the dining salon were crowded, and there were people waiting at the door for places as the hot July afternoon began. Miss Hawthorne might now gaze at the blue mist-shrouded highlands to her heart's content. The grim walls of Sing Sing prison, rising sheer from the green waters, could not fail to remind aged Stephen Allen that it was his report on the conditions of the old New York City prison that had caused them to be built. And Mr. Speed knew that with every turning of the big side wheels he was nearer to his beloved Baltimore home, to his prized portrait of the Duke of Wellington, strange present for a Bonaparte to give, and to all the amusing associations of his youth.

20 Steadily the *Henry Clay* clove to the middle of the channel, still at her top speed. The Palisades lifted above her now, dwarfing her and dulling the high, gilded eagle perched on her foremast. She had passed the town of Yonkers, lying in sunlight and making the shadowed west bank look lonely and cool. Still the rain of anthracite dust drifted down on the gay awnings of her top deck, still yellow sparks darted upward in the black smoke from her stacks. The ebb tide was running against a strong south wind, and the river was choppy, filled with curling white-capped waves. It was three o'clock, the midday dinner was over, the journey was almost ended. A few of the passengers were laughing at a frightened man, Harry Lawrence, who had stationed himself far forward on the bow and had piled his baggage up as a barricade between himself and the boilers.

21 When they later recalled the events of that afternoon, no one seemed to remember who first noticed the wisp of smoke drifting from the midship hatchway. Beneath the deck a fireman was desperately throwing buckets of water on the flaring canvas cover of the larboard boiler. Almost overcome with smoke, his clothes ablaze, he staggered

from the boiler room and made for the deck. As he reached it and jumped overboard, the whole midship section of the *Henry Clay* burst into flames. Jim Elmendorf, standing with his wife in the pilothouse, took one look at the leaping yellow streaks and spun the wheel over. Without diminishing her speed the *Henry Clay* swung sharply and started for the east bank. White-faced Jake Zimmerman, in the engine room already filled with smoke, put on full steam and fastened the control so that the engine would work at top speed until the boat was beached, before he leaped for the deck. Screaming passengers started forward, those on the afterdecks dashing through the flames. The bartender, suddenly assuming the duties of a ship's officer, urged them back, shouting orders for all passengers to go aft, possibly with the idea of lifting the prow as the boat ran ashore. Many returned. Helplessly they lined the rails as the *Henry Clay* raced for the bank. A gardener, working among the flower beds along the river edge of Assemblyman Russell Smith's Riverdale estate, looked up to see a blazing steamboat bearing down on him.

22 It was only a few minutes before the *Henry Clay* struck with terrific force, her bow sliding up the shelving bank twenty-five feet and nosing eight feet into the earth of a high railroad embankment. The shock knocked over one of the smokestacks and threw benches and tables about. Many passengers on the promenade deck were hurled to the deck below or into the water. A few far forward, including pilot Elmendorf and his wife and the foresighted Harry Lawrence, were thrown to safety on land. The jolt seemed to have stirred the fires, and the flames united into a solid sheet that began slowly moving aft, blown by the south wind. Now the fatal stupidity of the bartender's order was obvious. There was no going forward, and the stern was over deep water. It was burn or drown for the passengers who could not swim. A white boat with a green line about its gunwale suddenly appeared, its occupant rowing about aimlessly and picking up no one of the dozens already struggling in the water. A gentleman named Dunning seized upon a large wooden sign, a milliner's advertisement which stood on the deck, and leaped overboard with it. A gallant Mr. Edwards, standing upon the taffrail, saw a panic-stricken young lady in great danger of being burned and exclaimed (according to the report of the New York *Herald* for July 31, 1852), "Will you go with me into the water and run the risk of being drowned, or will you be burned to death?" The report concludes, "The female accepted the noble offer, and both were saved."

23 The flames were working aft swiftly now, and the frantic passengers began to drop into the deep water by scores. A large black boat with a red streak arrived from upriver, picked up seven, and made for shore, though it could easily have held fifteen. Mr. Downing, a strong swimmer, was very calm. He gave minute directions to all his charges, then went up on the promenade deck and threw many wooden chairs into the water. On two of these his tiny wife was able to float to shore. His children also escaped, but Mrs. De Windt was drowned. A Newburgh passenger, struggling in the water, saw that Mr. Downing was trying to keep Mrs. Wadsworth afloat and that the task was difficult. Neither of them was seen alive after that.

24 Mr. Collyer, already ashore, had begun breaking up a rail fence and shoving the pieces out into the water to struggling people. Captain Tallman, at last aroused from his sickbed, and already so exhausted that he could not speak, was in the water, helping passenger after passenger to shore. Mr. Thompson, of Perry Street in New York City, let down from the deck a wooden settee, jumped after it, and had just climbed upon it when someone grabbed him by the leg and pulled him off. At that moment he saw his wife, who could not swim, jump into the water. He succeeded in working along the side of the boat with her to the paddle wheel, which they grabbed. The weight caused the wheel to revolve, throwing them off and emptying flaming fragments on them. They finally floated to safety on fence boards.

25 The gardener, who had been the first to see the burning boat from shore, and Mr. Smith's coachman had just launched a small boat when they saw a sloop, occupied by four men who did not help with the rescue but were picking up floating valuables, robbing helpless, drowning victims. Bravely the two servants boarded the river pirates, threw them overboard, and used the sloop to save as many as it would hold. One gentleman, said to be from Newark, New Jersey, methodically saved his wife and each of his nine children. One at a time they jumped and were rushed ashore by the valiant father, who was hurried away "entirely senseless" by his grateful brood and their mother. A train puffed along the embankment and stopped, its men passengers scurrying from the coaches down to the river to help in the rescue work.

26 "A noble Newfoundland dog named Neptune (to quote again from the New York *Herald* of July 31) rushed into the water and seized a young child that was drowning by the dress near the shoulders and bore it safely to shore. He returned and approached a woman to

assist in the same way, but she was so frightened that the dog had to be called off, and he was thus deprived of the opportunity of extending that relief to the sufferers to which his noble nature prompted him."

27 All was over in about twenty minutes. The watch found in dead old Stephen Allen's pocket, along with a slip of paper reading "Keep good company or none," had stopped at 3:26. Along the shore for over a mile lay hats, shawls, dresses, an occasional body. The *Armenia* loitered out in the channel, its two small boats searching the waters for any sign of a living being, but the *Henry Clay* had raced on too far ahead of her. The train moved on, bearing a distressing load of the burned and drowned. Another train came down from the north and stopped. In the hot sunlight on the river men worked, slowly dragging for corpses, while the *Henry Clay* burned to the water. Isaac MacDaniel, searching among the bodies on the shore for his dead wife, came upon James Jessup, the clerk who had so smugly reassured him a few hours before.

28 "Is there any danger here?" said Isaac.

29 By five o'clock nothing was left except a fragment of the bow, some ten or twelve feet high, which burned slowly "like a warning beacon to light up the shapeless wreck of charred timbers and iron below." William Lawrence, coroner of Westchester County, wrote in his tent beside the water that night: "The last scenes of the day were singularly impressive and solemn. The night was remarkably clear, the full moon dimly lighting up the river and the hills; at one side of a gloomy arch over the railroad was the wreck, the bow still slowly burning; half revealed in its lurid light lay the bodies of two men; above the arch a group of some twenty persons were busy with newly discovered corpses, trying to identify them. . . . The surface of the stream, placid and silent as the grave, was broken only by the oars of a few men who were still dredging for bodies."

30 They covered the dead that moonlit evening with green boughs. The coroner and his jury had to draw guns and threaten a dark craft filled with plunderers, "sacrilegious harpies who hover about." All night long cannon boomed out over the Hudson as the workers ashore tried to dislodge bodies and bring them to the surface of the river.

31 And in the morning the details of the disaster reached New York. Stephen Allen was dead. Andrew Jackson Downing was dead, and so were his mother-in-law and the lovely, tragic Mrs. Wadsworth. Miss Hawthorne had been lost, and genial Mr. Speed. The number of dead

was reported as eighty, and Captain Tallman was already regretting his early statement to a passenger, "There were only ten or fifteen persons drowned, and they were common people." In the Astor House gentlemen's parlor an excited crowd of men, some of them with tear-stained faces, denounced Mr. Collyer, Captain Tallman and his crew, and the officers and crew of the *Armenia* for racing their steamers in complete disregard of the safety of passengers. Answering these accusations on the next day, the owners of the two boats made public announcement of their agreement that there would be no racing, and pilot Isaac Polhemus of the *Armenia* wrote a letter, which was immediately published, stating that the latter steamer had not attempted to beat the *Henry Clay* because racing had been forbidden by her captain and owner, Isaac P. Smith (who was not aboard on the day of the disaster). Charges of criminal murder against the owners and officers of the *Henry Clay* were set aside by Judge Edmonds in Westchester County, but he held the accused to bail for manslaughter in the jurisdiction of the United States district court.

32 In the meantime James Gordon Bennett, editor of the New York *Herald,* waged an editorial war against steamboat racing on the Hudson, a campaign made more bitter by complaining letters from passengers of the steamers *Frances Skiddy* and *Alida,* which frequently entered into competitions, and by the boiler explosion of the racing *Reindeer* at Bristol Landing in September of the same year. Mr. Bennett wrote: "How long are human hetacombs [sic] to be thus offered upon the altar of an avaricious speculation which sacrifices all things to itself?"

33 The trial of the defendants in the *Henry Clay* case ended in their acquittal on November 2, 1852. A few months later the New York State legislature passed a rigid Steamboat Inspection Act, which finally put an end to the racing of steamers on the Hudson.

Summary

A. Beginning (¶1-5): rivalry of the *Armenia* and the *Henry Clay*. Departure from Albany. The beginning of the race. The question posed by this situation is, "What will be the outcome of the race?"
B. Middle (¶6-26): the series of incidents that make up the main action.
　1. The *Henry Clay's* landing at the Hudson wharf.
　2. The *Armenia* goes a mile ahead of the *Henry Clay*.

3. The landing at Catskill wharf.
4. The *Henry Clay* passes the *Armenia* and crosses her bow.
5. The *Henry Clay* extends her advantage as she clears Kingston, Poughkeepsie, and Newburgh and passes the Palisades ahead of her rival.
6. Fire aboard the *Henry Clay*.
7. The *Henry Clay* is beached.
8. The destruction of the *Henry Clay*.

C. End (¶27-33): the final result of the action.
 1. The extent of the disaster.
 2. Criminal charges against the owners and officers of the *Henry Clay*.
 3. Law passed to prevent steamboat racing on the Hudson.

Comment

Pace: The movement in this example is somewhat slower than that in Example 1. More attention is paid to expository details, such as the description of the passengers and the reports of various witnesses. Nevertheless, the movement is swift.

Proportion and climax: The destruction of the *Henry Clay* receives extended treatment in five paragraphs (21-26) and thus receives a major proportion of the emphasis. This incident is also the climax of the narrative. Note how the climax is prepared by signposts that foreshadow the tragedy. The title suggests a catastrophe but leaves us in suspense. As early as paragraph 8 it is evident that the race is immediately dangerous to the passengers of the *Henry Clay*. In paragraph 13 a lady calls for someone to stop the race. In paragraph 20 a frightened passenger on the *Henry Clay* piles his baggage as a barricade between himself and a possible fire.

Analysis and Composition

1. How does the narrator's chosen point of view permit him to tell the story from the following different perspectives? Explain your answer.
 a. As an historian who is aware of the personal background of the various passengers and the newspaper comments of the day
 b. As a panoramic observer aboard the *Henry Clay*
 c. As a participant in the action
2. What advantages are gained by telling this story predominantly in the past rather than in the present tense?
3. Show how the various places and settings mentioned in this example,

that is, the river, the shore, the landings, and the boats themselves, contribute to the meaningfulness of the action.

4. Exposition and description are frequently employed in this example to
   interpret some phase of the action. Below are listed some expository and
   descriptive passages, together with an explanation of their tie-in with
   the narrative element. In a short paragraph give your reasons for accepting or rejecting each of these explanations.
   a. ¶1-3. The *description* of the pleasant scene at the Albany wharves
      sets up a contrast to the tragedy that follows.
   b. ¶5 and 6. The *description* of the activity of the two boats and of the
      bustle at the Hudson wharf suggests the intensity of the action itself.
   c. ¶29. The *description* of the coroner helps us to appreciate the horror
      of the action.

5. Decide whether paragraphs 21-22 are primarily narrative or descriptive.
   Give reasons for your answer.

6. In this story does the author stress principally
   a. The physical action
   b. The criminal avarice of the steamboat owners and their captains, or
   c. The fatal stupidity of the bartender?
   Give reasons for your answer.

7. In a brief comment show whether the following expressions convey a
   sense of movement.
   a. "Thick ribbons of smoke trailed out behind the two steamers, and
      live sparks flew from the tall stacks" (¶5)
   b. "The big side wheels thrashed through the water, leaving long white
      wakes" (¶5)
   c. "She kept on trembling and humming" (¶19)
   d. "Still the rain of anthracite dust drifted down" (¶20)

8. What emotional effect does the author intend to suggest by his references to
   a. The man in the white boat (¶22)
   b. The rapacity of the river pirates (¶25)
   c. The dog Neptune (¶26)
   d. The "sacrilegious harpies" (¶30)

9. Write a short essay comparing the narrative style of this example with
   that of Example 1 with reference to
   a. Clarity of diction
   b. Variety of sentence structure
   c. Length and coherence of paragraphs
   d. Use of dialogue

10. Consult newspaper files in your library for the details of a train wreck,
    an airplane disaster, or a shipwreck. In a manner similar to that em-
    ployed by Carl Carmer write a narrative of approximately 1500 words.

3. Flash Flood

BY MARY-CARTER ROBERTS

1 Some years ago, I was sent by the government bureau I worked for in Washington, D.C., on a trip to an Apache Indian reservation in Arizona. The Apaches were building some dams, and my office wanted a report on them. The Southwest was having a summer of appalling drought. I was told to fly out to Phoenix, take a quick look around, and then fly back. At such a distance from the scene, my assignment sounded routine to the point of being dull.

2 I left the plane at Phoenix and asked the airport's information clerk about getting to, as I put it, "the Indian reservation." He, in turn, asked me, with an indulgent smile, where the reservation was. That brought the interchange to a temporary halt. We looked at one another and began again. This time, we did better. He had thought, I discovered, that I wished to fly to some distant reservation, and was too femininely unprecise to give, or maybe even know, the name of it. He was waiting to help me out of this predicament. I exclaimed, Not at all! I had finished my flight and now wanted to know how to proceed, on the ground, to the Apaches.

3 "The Apaches!" he said incredulously.

4 "Yes," I said.

5 "The Apaches?" he repeated, full of doubt. "Have they a reservation?"

6 I told him firmly that they had, within fifty miles of Phoenix. He shook his head. He became nettled. His airline, he said, had Navajos, near Gallup, and Pueblos, near Albuquerque, and many other interesting tribes within easy distance of various airfields. Thousands of travelers visited these places annually. He could not, however, remember anybody's ever before seeking information about the Apaches. I realized that I had hurt his feelings by asking a question he could not answer. I thanked him and took a cab into Phoenix. En route, I asked my question of the driver. He advised me to give up my quest. "You might could get yourself murdered," he said.

7 "How?" I inquired.

8 "Them Apaches're gorillas, purely. They'd as soon murder a lady as anybody else. They don't care."

9 Neither of us spoke for a moment after this. Then he asked, "You going out there for a vacation?" I said I hoped that the trip would be a vacation in some respects. He said, "If I was a lady planning on a vacation, maybe after I'd worked hard to earn myself the dough, I wouldn't spend it with no Indians. I'd go where there was something doin'. Lights and boogie-woogie. Ain't it the truth now—we're only young once? Whyn't you give yourself a break?" He turned his head to give me an encouraging smile.

10 At the railroad station, I sought help from the ticket agent, a bald-headed, eyeshaded, shirt-sleeved man who was working at a ledger under a naked electric-light bulb. He said, without looking up, "Only transportation is by bus, ma'am. Terminal at ——," and gave me the street and number. I thanked him, and took another cab, but I asked no question on that ride.

11 The ticket agent at the bus terminal said, "We can take you to within twenty miles of it. That's thirty closer than you are right now." "What does the bus connect with?" I asked, and was told that it connected with nothing whatever. The little mountain town where the bus line ended was the last outpost. "Beyond which," the ticket agent cried, "there ain't nothing!"

12 "The reservation," I said doggedly.

13 "Hey, Al," he said, over his shoulder. A young man working at the next desk looked up. The ticket agent said, "Lady wants to know how to get to the Apache reservation."

14 Al flicked his eyes in my direction but did not appear to see me. "Go to the end of the line and sort of ask around," he said.

15 "Is there a road?" I demanded.

16 "There used to be," he said.

17 The loudspeaker announced that the bus was taking passengers. I thanked them both, and picked up my bag and hurried out.

18 I had to stand up the first half of the journey. We had left the desert and were climbing into the mountains before I had a chance to sit down, and then I was on the aisle. Consequently, I did not see much. There was usually a rock wall sliding by the windows on one side, and most of the time the engine groaned. It was late afternoon when we reached the outpost town. I got out on the main street, which looked like any main street except for one thing—it seemed to end at the brink of a precipice. The town stood on a lofty red plateau that to all

appearances stopped in midair. Beyond the edge of the precipice I could see, miles away, the yellow desert floor rising up and, farther still, the solidly blue sky. That was all.

19 I went into the drugstore, and an enthusiastically polite old man behind the prescription counter told me yes, indeedy, I could get somebody to take me to the reservation. I could get Jeff Miller.

20 "Has he a taxi?" I inquired.

21 "I wouldn't call it *just* that," the old man answered. "Jeff, though, he's got a Chevvy and he hauls passengers."

22 I found Jeff Miller—or, rather, he was pointed out to me—in front of a garage half a block away. He was lying on his back in the street, under the Chevvy. His feet, sticking out into the middle of the road, were all of him that was visible, so I spoke to them. I said, "Is Mr. Miller here?"

23 The feet gave a spasmodic wag and began to retract beneath the car. I deduced from this that their owner's head was emerging on the other side. I hastened around to the sidewalk. The head was in sight. The face was unshaven, oil-smudged, with one cheek rounded to accommodate tobacco, and endowed with periwinkle-blue eyes. Reclining so (the eyes sad and remote), Jeff Miller listened to my request. "Cost you sixteen dollars" was his answer.

24 I said, "Very well."

25 He remained motionless and silent for some seconds. Then he said, "O.K.?"

26 I revised my formula. I, too, said, "O.K."

27 The bargain consummated, Jeff Miller hitched himself fully into view. He was about forty, tall, lank, and melancholy. Nothing about him suggested that he ever hurried. He stood on the curb beside the Chevvy, and an air of broken-spirited patience spread out from him. He pointed to the car's dust-coated hood and remarked, "I *was* aimin' to give her a wash. But I see now it wouldn't signify. She'll get her wash." He transferred his gaze and the feminine pronoun to the sky. "She's gonna rain," he told me.

28 No words in the language could have surprised or stirred me more than those. Was the terrible drought about to end? That day? I looked at the sky. It was cloudless. I said, "It's going to rain?"

29 "It's gonna pepper," replied Jeff Miller. He opened the car door. "O.K.?" he said, with formality. I thanked him and got in the front seat.

30 Jeff Miller put my bag in the car and then, with his personal calm unflawed, drove down the main street, straight toward the precipice, at more than fifty miles an hour. We reached the edge and plunged over. I saw before me a bare, bulging, boulder-studded slope marked with a rudimentary dirt track. Jeff Miller did not slacken speed. The car accelerated in making the descent, and rocks burst from the earth beneath our passage. They pursued us, accompanied us, and passed us. We hoorahed down the hill.

31 As we whirled by one great, brutish clump of boulders, Jeff Miller remarked, "That shows you for sure she's gonna rain—if they's any kind of doubt about it." He even took a hand off the wheel to point.

32 I looked, and saw, or thought I saw, the outline of a horse among the rocks. By the time I could speak, we were beyond the spot. "What was it?" I asked.

33 " 'Pache. Makin' camp."

34 "Was there an Indian there?"

35 " 'Pache. Makin' camp," repeated Jeff Miller. "On his way back home from town. Seen she was gonna rain. Don't want to get wet none. Stopped to make camp till it's over. They'll do it ever' time."

36 "I didn't see a tent," I said.

37 Jeff Miller slewed the car around a murderously outthrust abutment and let it bounce across a sunken spot. After that, he explained. " 'Pache don't make no great use of them-there. This fellow's got a wagon. He's drove into the lee of them rocks. Comes the rain, now, they'll be like about one square foot under that wagon where it'll not be wet. Just so much. And right there on that spot, and not on no other, ol' John 'Pache'll be a-settin', huggin' his knees. Everything else on this mountain'll be soaked through. And ol' John, he'll be as dry as my hand."

38 This was interesting news about Apache customs, but I found the certainty of rain more impressive. I peered at the sky again. It was blue and empty.

39 We finished our crashing descent and came out on the desert floor in a series of lurching leaps. The road that "used to be" lay before us. It was a blacktop so pitted that I was dismayed, but Jeff Miller had a way of dealing with it. He tore along it where it had continuity enough to let him keep his speed, and where it did not, he simply left it and sent the Chevvy flying over the rough ground alongside.

40 I remarked, "With the road so bad, I can see why you're anxious to get to the reservation before it rains."

41 "There ain't a chance of that," he said. "What I'm aimin' at is to get across the river. That's all."

42 I hazarded politely, "Is the road better on the other side?"

43 He waited a moment before answering. Then he said, "I'll feel better when I'm on it."

44 Soon afterward, the great drought broke and the promised rain descended. The actual symptoms were not different from those of storms I had known elsewhere, but they were stepped up indecently in timing. The sky grew black as suddenly, it seemed to me, as if a light had been turned off, and the rain began with the volume and fury of a normal downpour at its height. A still blue aridity became a bellowing black drench with scarcely a transition. We drove along, amid thunder and lightning, as if we were at the bottom of a lake.

45 This lasted for perhaps twenty minutes. Then it was over; the sky was blue again, and the sun, by that time setting, turned the west into pure fairy gold. I said, "That was quite a rain."

46 "It wasn't no rain," Jeff Miller said. "It was a cloudburst."

47 A short while later, we arrived at the place he designated as the river—a steep-sided little gully, about forty feet across, with a flow of water about ten feet wide coiling among boulders at its bottom. There was no bridge; there was just a ford. Jeff Miller halted the car and stared down consideringly.

48 "I don't know as I'd ought to try goin' over," he said. "To be truthful, it ain't safe."

49 I knew what he meant. I had read of the rapid rising of streams after rains in this country. I could not see, however, that the danger was confronting us. We could cross that brook, I thought, in seconds. I said, "Let's try it."

50 "It ain't safe," Jeff Miller repeated. "She ain't here yet, but she's comin'."

51 Even as we talked, the water was rising, but it came up peaceably and spread out across the bottom of the gully. "We can still make it," I insisted.

52 "Well-l-l," Jeff Miller said, and started the car. He was reluctant, though, and halfway down the bank he stepped on his brakes and said once more, "She's comin'." Then he put the Chevvy in motion and drove into the stream. It was his last act of control over the ma-

chine. A wall of water three feet high came sweeping down the gully just when we were at the lowest point. It propelled a series of smaller waves ahead of it, and these stalled our engine. "Here she *is!*" Jeff Miller shouted, and flung open the door on the downstream side of the car, pushed me out, seized my bag, and scrambled after. We splashed forward and got beyond the Chevvy's radiator before the wall struck. It was lucky for us that we did. The poor Chevvy turned over on its side and bumped away among the boulders.

53 I lost my footing but was not overwhelmed. Instead, I was borne along as if I were much lighter than the water, and at once I realized that there were many other objects being similarly carried. These seemed to be mostly branches and twigs; I felt, indeed, more as if I were in a thicket than in a stream. One fellow piece of flotsam, however, was not vegetation. First the head and then the neck of a dead steer emerged from the foam and surged forward toward me, proceeding steadily and—whether from rigor mortis or the action of the flood, I cannot say—with rodlike stiffness, empty-eyed. I felt then that I was really quite far from everything.

54 The lifeless brute, having heaved its fore end up as if it were about to make a leap, fell flatly on one side and sank, its hoofs cutting toward the surface where its spine had been. Then I caught hold of some scrubby bushes on the bank of the gully and climbed out. I turned and saw Jeff Miller scrambling out of the water, not far from me. He still had my bag. He explained the apparition of the carcass. It was a casualty of the drought. Cattle had been dying of thirst everywhere.

55 We waited for help on the gully brim a long time. Night came. The flood subsided. Our clothes dried and we were not too cold, for the rain had made little change in the temperature; it was a long time notwithstanding. Jeff Miller, under the subduing influences of disaster and the dark, melted toward me. He confessed that he had had a date. He had been fixing to take a widow woman to the movies back in town. That was why he had been so anxious to cross the stream. He had wanted to avoid having to wait for the water to go down, so that he could return on time.

56 "But that way of doing don't pay off," he said.

57 I assured him that the widow would excuse him. "She'll understand," I said.

58 "I ain't personally fond of askin' no woman to do that for me," he replied. "I told her I'd be there."

59 Downstream, the Chevvy hung by its hind wheels over a projecting tree. "She ain't no money loss," Jeff Miller said. "I'm covered. But she was a good car. If you know what I mean."

60 Help came at last, though not by motor. We heard it in the distance, and its sound was the sound of hoofs. Its approach was slow. Its deliberate clopping in the desert's vastness implied that there was no such thing as hurry in the world. It descended the far side of the gully, crossed, and climbed up to us. Horse and vehicle took shape out of the dark. Jeff Miller sighed. It was the Apache who had stopped to make camp on the mountain.

61 I rode the rest of the way to the reservation sitting on the floor of the Indian wagon, a springless contraption made of loose planks. Before I got into it, however, I offered Jeff Miller his money. He refused. I besought him. "Take it and buy your friend a present," I said. "To make up for the movies. Please." A faint smile appeared on his lonely countenance. He took the bills. I thanked him and got into the wagon. How he got back to town I have never known.

62 I was not alone with my Apache on the drive. He had a small boy with him. The two sat on an elevated seat in front. They were shadowy silhouettes to me, exactly alike in style—broad-hatted, impossibly slim, hunched over but with a wiriness alien to stoop-shouldered white men. I had seen that both had long braids at the sides of their heads, but almost nothing of their physiognomies. The child had refused to look at me, not shyly but with a blazing, still, implacable rejection. I had had a brief glimpse of the man's regular, swarthy-bronze features and white teeth, under his wide hat. He was not without concern for me as a passenger. When the wagon struck the potholes, and the planks leaped from the jolt, he turned his head and shouted, "You, Missis?"

63 I shouted back, "I'm still here!"

64 With so much conversation, we crawled along.

65 It was after midnight when we reached the reservation, but the government office building was alight. My driver stopped before it. I climbed down and went to the wagon seat, and the Apache made a joke. He said, "You still here? Not any more. You *there* now!" He pointed at the building and laughed—quite freely and merrily laughed.

66 I asked, "What do I owe you?"

67 "No money, you," he replied, and gathered up the reins. He meant it.

68 It was the cloudburst, as I soon discovered, that had kept the government staff up so late. The waters had threatened the unfinished dams; crews were at work, reports were coming in. The superintendent, a competent-looking, fat white man, gave me a hasty greeting and sent a domestic to take me to a guest room. I washed off the debris of the flood and went to sleep.

69 The next day, I learned the—as it were—inside story of the storm. The superintendent said that an old Apache woman, weary of the drought, had led a group of her people up into the hills and organized a dance. For two hours it went on—and then the heavens exploded. "I don't know what I'll say to Washington," the official said, looking haggard as only a fat man can.

70 "But the dams held!" I exclaimed.

71 He was surprised at my ignorance. "It's not *them*," he said. "A rain dance is a superstition. And Washington's trying to root these superstitions out."

72 I met the cloud-compeller before I left. She was sitting on a bench in the yard of her bungalow home. She was about sixty—short, stout, unwrinkled, cotton-clad, and neat. She looked a good deal like my Quaker grandmother. She was fanning herself with a cardboard fan with a Corn Flakes advertisement on the back of it. A row of geraniums growing in tin cans stood against the bungalow's foundation.

73 She received me with a polite, comfortable little flutter, but I threw everything to the winds. I said, "I hear you made the rain."

74 She let me look into her face for a moment. It was there in her eyes—the Apache blaze, the fury, the desert glare. Then she dropped those eyes demurely. "I'm *so* sorry about you getting wet," she said. "If we'd just known you were coming, we would have waited." She hesitated. "I really didn't mean to make a *cloudburst*," she said with great sincerity.

Summary

A. Beginning (¶1-17): The author is directed to go to an Apache Indian reservation in Arizona to report on the progress of some dams. The indefiniteness of the assignment and the difficulty in finding transportation provokes the questions, "Will she get there? What will she find out about the dams?"

B. Middle (¶18-68): the series of incidents that make up the main action.
   1. The journey on the bus
   2. Procuring the taxi
   3. The journey to the river
   4. The first encounter with the Apache
   5. The cloudburst
   6. Crossing the river
   7. Second encounter with the Apache
   8. The ride in the Apache wagon
C. End
   1. Arrival at the reservation
   2. The dams hold
   3. Humorous aftermath—the Apaches' superstitious beliefs about rain making

Comment

"Flash Flood" is a notable example of informal narrative. This lively adventure begins with the false promise, "My assignment sounded routine to the point of being dull." The author's encounters with the airport information clerk, the taxi driver, the ticket agents at the railroad and bus station quickly reverse this first impression of the assignment. The routine trip begins to grow exciting. The sense of adventure increases when the author meets Jeff Miller. She is warned that a storm is brewing. The incident of the Apache's making camp is another indication of the approaching storm. Jeff Miller's remarks furnish a progressive exposition of Arizona weather and of Apache customs.

The journey itself is a series of bucks and leaps across the desert. The cloudburst and the crossing of the river represent the point of highest tension. Here narrative and description are blended with such skill that happening and sense impression are one. The narrator's subsequent ride with the Apache and the story of the woman rain-maker may be regarded as a humorous aftermath.

This example is especially successful in its rendering of the setting. The Arizona desert, characters like Jeff Miller, "John" Apache, and the woman rain-maker, the storm and flood, are thoroughly assimilated into the narrative. This integration is partly the result of combining description with narration, partly of diction, particularly the flavorsome dialect of Jeff Miller.

Analysis and Composition

1. Decide whether the anecdote contained in paragraphs 69-74 is
   a. A natural conclusion of the main action
   b. A self-contained sketch illustrating the superstitions of the Apaches but unrelated to the main action
   Give reasons for your answer.
2. Comment on the pace or rate of movement of the incidents in this example by comparing it to the pace in Examples 1 and 2.
3. To what extent does the author dwell on the storm and flood? Is the emphasis by proportion sufficient to justify the title of the example?
4. Do you agree or disagree with the statement that the climax, or point of highest interest, in this example is the flood (¶52-54)? Give reasons for your answer.
5. Account for the time element in this example
   a. By showing the total time that elapses (approximately)
   b. By showing the time of the principal incidents
6. Which of the following adjectives best describes the mental point of view of the narrator? Give reasons for your answer.

   a. Objective   d. Amused
   b. Humorous   e. Serious
   c. Satirical   f. Noncommittal

7. Show how the setting, that is, the region itself and the mentality of the inhabitants, accounts for several phases of the action.
8. The expressions listed below contribute directly to the movement, to the characterization of the narrator, or to the setting. In a short paragraph state precisely what each expression contributes.
   a. "It seemed to end at the brink of a precipice" (¶18)
   b. "The feet gave a spasmodic wag and began to retract beneath the car" (¶23)
   c. "They [the rocks] pursued us, accompanied us, and passed us" (¶30)
   d. "Jeff Miller slewed the car around a murderously outthrust abutment and let it bounce across a sunken spot" (¶37)
   e. "A still blue aridity became a bellowing black drench with scarcely a transition" (¶44)
   f. "Its deliberate clopping in the desert's vastness implied that there was no such thing as hurry in the world" (¶60)
   g. "With a blazing, still, implacable rejection" (¶62)
   h. "Looking haggard as only a fat man can" (¶69)

9. **To** what extent does the dialogue
   a. Moderate the pace of the story
   b. Increase its interest?
10. Show how the speech of each of the characters listed below differs in respect to
    a. Diction
    b. Rhythm
    c. Intellectual content

| the taxi driver | Jeff Miller | "John" Apache |
| the superintendent | the narrator | the Apache woman |

11. Write a 1000-word narrative in the first person of a tour in which you
    a. Encounter several characters representative of a given region
    b. Describe some prominent feature of the region such as a view, a storm, a festival
    Before writing your composition determine
    a. The area you wish to describe
    b. The length of time your narrative will cover
    c. The tone of your narrative, or the attitude of mind you wish to adopt
    d. The effect you wish to create in the minds of your readers
    Be sure that the dialogue fits the character who is speaking.

Suggested Topics

a. A day with the shrimp fishermen
b. Visiting Cape Cod
c. Fisherman's Wharf in San Francisco
d. An Indian reservation
e. Yellowstone (or another national park)
f. The Pennsylvania Dutch country

g. A tour of the mines
h. A modern factory
i. A visit to our state capitol
j. A day in court
k. A weekend in New York (or another large city)

4. The Massacre of the Hurons

BY FRANCIS PARKMAN

1 More than eight months had passed since the catastrophe of St. Joseph. The winter was over, and that dreariest of seasons had come, the churlish forerunner of spring. Around Ste. Marie the forests were gray and bare, and in the cornfields the oozy, half-thawed soil, studded

with the sodden stalks of the last autumn's harvest, showed itself in patches through the melting snow.

2 At nine o'clock on the morning of the sixteenth of March, the priests saw a heavy smoke rising over the naked forest towards the southeast, about three miles distant. They looked at each other in dismay. "The Iroquois! They are burning St. Louis!" Flames mingled with the smoke; and, as they stood gazing, two Christian Hurons came, breathless and aghast, from the burning town. Their worst fear was realized. The Iroquois were there; but where were the priests of the mission, Brébeuf and Lalemant?

3 Late in the autumn, a thousand Iroquois, chiefly Senecas and Mohawks, had taken the warpath for the Hurons. They had been all winter in the forests, hunting for subsistence, and moving at their leisure towards their prey. The destruction of the two towns of the mission of St. Joseph had left a wide gap, and in the middle of March they entered the heart of the Huron country, undiscovered. Common vigilance and common sense would have averted the calamities that followed; but the Hurons were like a doomed people, stupefied, sunk in dejection, fearing everything, yet taking no measures for defense. They could easily have met the invaders with double their force, but the besotted warriors lay idle in their towns, or hunted at leisure in distant forests; nor could the Jesuits, by counsel or exhortation, rouse them to face the danger.

4 Before daylight of the sixteenth, the invaders approached St. Ignace, which, with St. Louis and three other towns, formed the mission of the same name. They reconnoitered the place in the darkness. It was defended on three sides by a deep ravine, and further strengthened by palisades fifteen or sixteen feet high, planted under the direction of the Jesuits. On the fourth side it was protected by palisades alone; and these were left, as usual, unguarded. This was not from a sense of security; for the greater part of the population had abandoned the town, thinking it too much exposed to the enemy, and there remained only about four hundred, chiefly women, children, and old men, whose infatuated defenders were absent hunting, or on futile scalping parties against the Iroquois. It was just before dawn, when a yell, as of a legion of devils, startled the wretched inhabitants from their sleep; and the Iroquois, bursting in upon them, cut them down with knives and hatchets, killing many, and reserving the rest for a worse fate. They had entered by the weakest side; on the other sides there was no exit, and only three Hurons escaped. The whole was the

work of a few minutes. The Iroquois left a guard to hold the town, and secure the retreat of the main body in case of a reverse; then, smearing their faces with blood, after their ghastly custom, they rushed, in the dim light of the early dawn, towards St. Louis, about a league distant.

5 The three fugitives had fled, half naked, through the forest, for the same point, which they reached about sunrise, yelling the alarm. The number of inhabitants here was less, at this time, than seven hundred; and, of these, all who had strength to escape, excepting about eighty warriors, made in wild terror for a place of safety. Many of the old, sick, and decrepit were left perforce in the lodges. The warriors, ignorant of the strength of the assailants, sang their warsongs and resolved to hold the place to the last. It had not the natural strength of St. Ignace, but, like it, was surrounded by palisades.

6 Here were the two Jesuits, Brébeuf and Lalemant. Brébeuf's converts entreated him to escape with them; but the Norman zealot, bold scion of a warlike stock, had no thought of flight. His post was in the teeth of danger, to cheer on those who fought, and open heaven to those who fell. His colleague, slight of frame and frail of constitution, trembled despite himself; but deep enthusiasm mastered the weakness of Nature, and he, too, refused to fly.

7 Scarcely had the sun risen, and scarcely were the fugitives gone, when, like a troop of tigers, the Iroquois rushed to the assault. Yell echoed yell, and shot answered shot. The Hurons, brought to bay, fought with the utmost desperation, and with arrows, stones, and the few guns they had, killed thirty of their assailants and wounded many more. Twice the Iroquois recoiled, and twice renewed the attack with unabated ferocity. They swarmed at the foot of the palisades and hacked at them with their hatchets till they had cut them through at several different points. For a time there was a deadly fight at these breaches. Here were the two priests, promising heaven to those who died for their faith—one giving baptism, and the other absolution. At length the Iroquois broke in, and captured all the surviving defenders, the Jesuits among the rest. They set the town on fire; and the helpless wretches who had remained, unable to fly, were consumed in their burning dwellings. Next they fell upon Brébeuf and Lalemant, stripped them, bound them fast, and led them with the other prisoners back to St. Ignace, where all turned out to wreak their fury on the two priests, beating them savagely with sticks and clubs as they drove them

into the town. At present, there was no time for further torture, for there was work in hand.

8 The victors divided themselves into several bands, to burn the neighboring villages and hunt their flying inhabitants. In the flush of their triumph, they meditated a bolder enterprise; and, in the afternoon, their chiefs sent small parties to reconnoiter Ste. Marie, with a view to attacking it on the next day.

9 Meanwhile the fugitives of St. Louis, joined by other bands as terrified and as helpless as they, were struggling through the soft snow which clogged the forests towards Lake Huron, where the treacherous ice of spring was still unmelted. One fear expelled another. They ventured upon it, and pushed forward all that day and all the following night, shivering and famished, to find refuge in the towns of the Tobacco nation. Here, when they arrived, they spread a universal panic.

10 Ragueneau, Bressani, and their companions waited in suspense at Ste. Marie. On the one hand, they trembled for Brébeuf and Lalemant; on the other, they looked hourly for an attack; and, when at evening they saw the Iroquois scouts prowling along the edge of the bordering forest, their fears were confirmed. They had with them about forty Frenchmen, well armed; but their palisades and wooden buildings were not fireproof, and they had learned from fugitives the number and ferocity of the invaders. They stood guard all night, praying to the saints, and above all to their great patron, Saint Joseph, whose festival was close at hand.

11 In the morning they were somewhat relieved by the arrival of about three hundred Huron warriors, chiefly converts from La Conception and Ste. Madeleine, tolerably well armed, and full of fight. They were expecting others to join them; and meanwhile, dividing into several bands, they took post by the passes of the neighboring forest, hoping to waylay parties of the enemy. Their expectation was fulfilled; for, at this time, two hundred of the Iroquois were making their way from St. Ignace, in advance of the main body, to begin the attack on Ste. Marie. They fell in with a band of the Hurons, set upon them, killed many, drove the rest to headlong flight, and, as they plunged in terror through the snow, chased them within sight of Ste. Marie. The other Hurons, hearing the yells and firing, ran to the rescue, and attacked so fiercely, that the Iroquois in turn were routed, and ran for shelter to St. Louis, followed closely by the victors. The houses of the town had been burned, but the palisade around them

was still standing, though breached and broken. The Iroquois rushed in; but the Hurons were at their heels. Many of the fugitives were captured, the rest killed or put to utter rout, and the triumphant Hurons remained masters of the place.

12 The Iroquois who escaped fled to St. Ignace. Here, or on the way thither, they found the main body of the invaders; and, when they heard of the disaster, the whole swarm, beside themselves with rage, turned towards St. Louis to take their revenge. Now ensued one of the most furious Indian battles on record. The Hurons within the palisade did not much exceed a hundred and fifty; for many had been killed or disabled, and many, perhaps, had straggled away. Most of their enemies had guns, while they had but few. Their weapons were bows and arrows, warclubs, hatchets, and knives; and of these they made good use, sallying repeatedly, fighting like devils, and driving back their assailants again and again. There are times when the Indian warrior forgets his cautious maxims and throws himself into battle with a mad and reckless ferocity. The desperation of one party, and the fierce courage of both, kept up the fight after the day had closed; and the scout from Ste. Marie, as he bent listening under the gloom of the pines, heard, far into the night, the howl of battle rising from the darkened forest. The principal chief of the Iroquois was severely wounded, and nearly a hundred of their warriors were killed on the spot. When, at length, their numbers and persistent fury prevailed, their only prize was some twenty Huron warriors, spent with fatigue and faint with loss of blood. The rest lay dead around the shattered palisades which they had so valiantly defended. Fatuity, not cowardice, was the ruin of the Huron nation.

13 The lamps burned all night at Ste. Marie, and its defenders stood watching till daylight, musket in hand. The Jesuits prayed without ceasing, and Saint Joseph was besieged with invocations. "Those of us who were priests," writes Ragueneau, "each made a vow to say a mass in his honor every month, for the space of a year; and all the rest bound themselves by vows to divers penances." The expected onslaught did not take place. Not an Iroquois appeared. Their victory had been bought too dear, and they had no stomach for more fighting. All the next day, the eighteenth, a stillness, like the dead lull of a tempest, followed the turmoil of yesterday—as if, says the Father Superior, "the country were waiting, palsied with fright, for some new disaster."

14 On the following day—the journalist fails not to mention that it

was the festival of Saint Joseph—Indians came in with tidings that a panic had seized the Iroquois camp, that the chiefs could not control it, and that the whole body of invaders was retreating in disorder, possessed with a vague terror that the Hurons were upon them in force. They had found time, however, for an act of atrocious cruelty. They planted stakes in the bark houses of St. Ignace, and bound to them those of their prisoners whom they meant to sacrifice, male and female, from old age to infancy, husbands, mothers, and children, side by side. Then, as they retreated, they set the town on fire, and laughed with savage glee at the shrieks of anguish that rose from the blazing dwellings.

15 They loaded the rest of their prisoners with their baggage and plunder, and drove them through the forest southward, braining with their hatchets any who gave out on the march. An old woman, who had escaped out of the midst of the flames of St. Ignace, made her way to St. Michel, a large town not far from the desolate site of St. Joseph. Here she found about seven hundred Huron warriors, hastily mustered. She set them on the track of the retreating Iroquois, and they took up the chase—but evidently with no great eagerness to overtake their dangerous enemy, well armed as he was with Dutch guns, while they had little beside their bows and arrows. They found, as they advanced, the dead bodies of prisoners tomahawked on the march, and others bound fast to trees and half burned by the fagots piled hastily around them. The Iroquois pushed forward with such headlong speed that the pursuers could not, or would not, overtake them; and after two days they gave over the attempt.

Summary

Time sequence: from 9 A.M., March 16 to March 21.
Point of view: omniscient third-person.
A. Beginning: initial situation. The Iroquois appear. This situation poses the question, "Will the Hurons and the missionaries survive?"
B. Middle
   1. The Iroquois raid St. Ignace.
   2. The Iroquois raid St. Louis.
   3. The Iroquois raid Ste. Marie and are repulsed.
   4. The Iroquois make a second attack on St. Louis.
   5. The Iroquois massacre their prisoners at St. Ignace.

C. End

   1. The Iroquois retreat and escape the pursuing Hurons.
   2. The Huron nation is ruined.

Comment

This passage, taken from Francis Parkman's historical classic, *The Jesuits in North America,* is one of the samples of excellent historical narration praised by S. E. Morison in Example VI A3. The Parkman selection is particularly interesting as an example of narration, since it raises and solves several problems that are different from those presented by the other examples in this section.

While the action here is unified and complete, as the summary suggests, it is also very complex. Thus, for example, in paragraph 8 we read that the attacking Iroquois divide themselves into several bands. In paragraph 9 we must picture the little groups of terrified Huron refugees running through the forests and crossing the treacherous ice of Lake Huron. In paragraph 11 we hear that 300 Huron warriors arrive from the other villages. In paragraph 15 we are told of another 700 Huron warriors being hastily mustered. The scene shifts rapidly from one stockade to another. The objective historian presents the action now through the eyes of one group of people, and now through the eyes of another. But this omniscience of point of view with reference to the narrative does not of course extend to the historical situation itself.

The obscurity of the historical picture is not evidence that Parkman lacks literary skill. As an historian Parkman was obliged to follow the story revealed in his documentary sources. Thus, for example, the 700 Hurons in paragraph 15 are puzzling. Where did they come from? Are they a new war party? The reader wants them identified. Presumably the documents did not permit such certain identification.

The narrative is further complicated by the problem of *scale,* that is, the relative amount of detail that the author can afford to present in the light of his over-all purpose. Here Parkman is merely giving us a glimpse of *one* phase of the Jesuit missionary effort in North America. Therefore he foreshortens or summarizes the action instead of developing it in detail. Obviously, he could have, in the manner of a novelist, expanded each scene by characterizing the participants more specifically. Also he might have penetrated into the imaginations of the characters, and thereby have presented the emotions of the two priests (¶6), the anxiety of the group at Ste. Marie (¶10), and the terror of the old woman (¶15). A biographer would certainly have followed Brébeuf and Lalemant to their excruciating deaths. But if Parkman had done this he would have thrown his whole history out of proportion.

The nature of the subject also required Parkman to fuse some elements of exposition and description with his narrative. Thus, for example, paragraph 3 supplies some information about the Huron psychology, and the beginning sentences of paragraph 4 help us to understand the physical setting of St. Ignace. But in the main this example is the narrative of a whole action rendered by a summary treatment of the significant details.

Analysis and Composition

1. What is the mood suggested by the description of the country in paragraph 1? How does this mood tie in with the purpose of the passage as a whole?
2. Paragraph 2 contains three dramatic devices
   a. The sight of smoke
   b. The shocked exclamations
   c. The appearance of the messengers
   What effect do these devices have upon the reader?
3. Decide whether a full-scale rendering of the events in paragraph 2 would have increased the effectiveness of the narrative. Before answering this question attempt to expand this paragraph to twice its present length.
4. Show how the pace of paragraph 4 is faster than that of paragraph 3. What accounts for this change of pace?
5. List all the expressions that stress movement in paragraphs 4, 7, 11, 12. After studying these expressions carefully decide whether the action they portray may be summed up as
   a. Bloody
   b. Ferocious
   c. Hideous
6. Comment on the change of pace that occurs in paragraphs 12 and 13.
7. Which of the five main incidents outlined in the summary is emphasized by proportion, that is, given the greatest amount of space? Does this emphasis indicate the climax of the narrative? Give reasons for your answer.
8. Define the chronology of this narrative by assigning the day and the probable hour to each important event. Decide whether Parkman could have improved his narrative by indicating a more exact chronology.
9. The predominant point of view here is that of a third person. Yet from time to time the point of view of the participants is included in the

narrative. Do you find any incoherence in the point of view? Explain your answer.

10. Does the action of the Hurons throughout justify Parkman's statement in paragraph 3 that the Hurons were a doomed people?

11. In paragraphs 7 and 15 pick out the passages that explain the meaning of the action.

12. In 1000 words write a narrative on one of the following topics from the point of view of an objective observer. Whenever necessary consult your library for specific details.

a. A student riot
b. A police raid
c. A prison break
d. A commando attack
e. Custer's Last Stand

f. The Cherry Valley Massacre
g. The Black Hole of Calcutta
h. The Mau Mau guerillas of Kenya
i. The Thugs of India
j. Sir Francis Drake, pirate

GENERAL EXERCISES

A

Study the account of the sinking of the *Graf Spee* below and then answer as directed.

1. Indicate the beginning, middle, and end of this narrative. Is this example unified?

2. Draw up a chronology of the action by listing the principal events and the time of their occurrence.

3. What is the point of view of the narrator? Show how the point of view aids the author in making his narrative clear.

4. Point out several instances where Churchill uses exposition to interpret the action.

5. Mr. Churchill's narrative suggests that the engagement was a brilliant victory for the Royal Navy. Is this suggestion inherent in the incidents of the narrative or is it an interpretation advanced by the author for patriotic or other reasons? Explain your answer.

6. History abounds with celebrated naval engagements. Consult your library for details about one of the topics listed below, or another of your own choice. Prepare to write your narrative
a. By listing the principal events in chronological order
b. By determining the initial situation
c. By selecting an appropriate point of view
Then write a composition of about 1000 words.

Suggested Topics

a. The *Monitor* and the *Merrimac*
b. The sinking of the *Bismarck* in World War II
c. The loss of H.M.S. *Prince of Wales*
d. The loss of the U.S.S. *Hornet*

The Graf Spee

BY WINSTON S. CHURCHILL

1 From the beginning of the war, Commodore Harwood's special care and duty had been to cover British shipping off the River Plate and Rio de Janeiro. He was convinced that sooner or later the *Spee* would come towards the Plate, where the richest prizes were offered to her. He had carefully thought out the tactics which he would adopt in an encounter. Together, his eight-inch cruisers *Cumberland* and *Exeter* and his six-inch cruisers *Ajax* and *Achilles* could not only catch but kill. However, the needs of fuel and refit made it unlikely that all four would be present "on the day." If they were not, the issue was disputable. On hearing that the *Doric Star* had been sunk on December 2, Harwood guessed right. Although she was over three thousand miles away, he assumed that the *Spee* would come towards the Plate. He estimated with luck and wisdom that she might arrive by the thirteenth. He ordered all his available forces to concentrate there by December 12. Alas, the *Cumberland* was refitting at the Falklands, but on the morning of the thirteenth *Exeter, Ajax,* and *Achilles* were in company at the centre of the shipping routes off the mouth of the river. Sure enough, at 6:14 A.M. smoke was sighted to the east. The longed-for collision had come.

2 Harwood in the *Ajax,* disposing his forces so as to attack the pocket battleship from widely divergent quarters and thus confuse her fire, advanced at the utmost speed of his small squadron. Captain Langsdorff thought at the first glance that he had only to deal with one light cruiser and two destroyers, and he too went full speed ahead; but a few moments later he recognized the quality of his opponents, and knew that a mortal action impended. The two forces were now closing at nearly fifty miles an hour. Langsdorff had but a minute to make up his mind. His right course would have been to turn away immediately so as to keep his assailants as long as possible under the superior range and weight of his eleven-inch guns, to which the British could not at first have replied. He would thus

THE GRAF SPEE: from *The Gathering Storm* by Winston S. Churchill. Reprinted by permission of Houghton Mifflin Company, the publishers.

have gained for his undisturbed firing the difference between adding speeds and subtracting them. He might well have crippled one of his foes before any could fire at him. He decided, on the contrary, to hold on his course and make for the *Exeter*. The action, therefore, began almost simultaneously on both sides.

3 Commodore Harwood's tactics proved advantageous. The eight-inch salvos from the *Exeter* struck the *Spee* from the earliest stages of the fight. Meanwhile, the six-inch cruisers were also hitting hard and effectively. Soon the *Exeter* received a hit which, besides knocking out B turret, destroyed all the communications on the bridge, killed or wounded nearly all upon it, and put the ship temporarily out of control. By this time, however, the six-inch cruisers could no longer be neglected by the enemy, and the *Spee* shifted her main armament to them, thus giving respite to the *Exeter* at a critical moment. The German battleship, plastered from three directions, found the British attack too hot, and soon afterwards turned away under a smoke screen with the apparent intention of making for the River Plate. Langsdorff had better have done this earlier.

4 After this turn the *Spee* once more engaged the *Exeter,* hard hit by the eleven-inch shells. All her forward guns were out of action. She was burning fiercely amidships and had a heavy list. Captain Bell, unscathed by the explosion on the bridge, gathered two or three officers round him in the after control station and kept his ship in action with her sole remaining turret until at 7:30 failure of pressure put this, too, out of action. He could do no more. At 7:40 the *Exeter* turned away to effect repairs and took no further part in the fight.

5 The *Ajax* and *Achilles,* already in pursuit, continued the action in the most spirited manner. The *Spee* turned all her heavy guns upon them. By 7:25 the two after turrets in the *Ajax* had been knocked out, and the *Achilles* had also suffered damage. These two light cruisers were no match for the enemy in gunpower, and, finding that his ammunition was running low, Harwood in the *Ajax* decided to break off the fight till dark, when he would have better chances of using his lighter armament effectively, and perhaps his torpedoes. He therefore turned away under cover of smoke, and the enemy did not follow. This fierce action had lasted an hour and twenty minutes. During all the rest of the day the *Spee* made for Montevideo, the British cruisers hanging grimly on her heels with only occasional interchanges of fire. Shortly after midnight, the *Spee* entered Montevideo and lay there repairing damage, taking in stores, landing wounded, transshipping personnel to a German merchant ship, and reporting to the Fuehrer. *Ajax* and *Achilles* lay outside, determined to dog her to her doom should she venture forth. Meanwhile, on the night of the fourteenth, the *Cumberland,* which had been steaming at full speed from the Falklands, took the

place of the utterly crippled *Exeter*. The arrival of this eight-inch-gun cruiser restored to its narrow balance a doubtful situation.

6 It had been most exciting to follow the drama of this brilliant action from the Admiralty War Room, where I spent a large part of the thirteenth. Our anxieties did not end with the day. Mr. Chamberlain was at that time in France on a visit to the Army. On the seventeenth I wrote to him:

December 17, 1939

If the *Spee* breaks out, as she may do tonight, we hope to renew the action of the thirteenth with the *Cumberland,* an eight *eight*-inch-gun ship, in the place of the six-gun *Exeter*. The *Spee* knows now that *Renown* and *Ark Royal* are oiling at Rio, so this is her best chance. The *Dorsetshire* and *Shropshire,* who are coming across from the Cape, are still three and four days away, respectively. It is fortunate that the *Cumberland* was handy at the Falklands, as *Exeter* was heavily damaged. She was hit over a hundred times, one turret smashed, three guns knocked out, and sixty officers and men killed and twenty wounded. Indeed, the *Exeter* fought one of the finest and most resolute actions against superior range and metal on record. Every conceivable precaution has been taken to prevent the *Spee* slipping out unobserved, and I have told Harwood (who is now an admiral and a K.C.B.) that he is free to attack her anywhere outside the three-mile limit. We should prefer, however, that she should be interned, as this will be less creditable to the German navy than being sunk in action. Moreover, a battle of this kind is full of hazard, and needless bloodshed must never be sought. . . .

7 From the moment when we heard that action was joined, we instantly ordered powerful forces to concentrate off Montevideo, but our hunting groups were naturally widely dispersed and none was within two thousand miles of the scene. In the north, Force K, comprising the *Renown* and *Ark Royal,* was completing a sweep which had begun at Capetown ten days before and was now six hundred miles east of Pernambuco and twenty-five hundred miles from Montevideo. Farther north still, the cruiser *Neptune* with three destroyers had just parted company with the French Force X and was coming south to join Force K. All these were ordered to Montevideo; they had first to fuel at Rio. However, we succeeded in creating the impression that they had already left Rio and were approaching Montevideo at thirty knots.

8 On the other side of the Atlantic, Force H was returning to the Cape for fuel after an extended sweep up the African coast. Only the *Dorsetshire* was immediately available at Capetown and was ordered at once to join Admiral Harwood, but she had over four thousand miles to travel. She was followed later by the *Shropshire*. In addition, to guard against the possible escape of the *Spee* to the eastward, Force I, comprising the *Cornwall, Gloucester,* and the aircraft carrier *Eagle* from the East Indies station,

which at this time was at Durban, was placed at the disposal of the Commander-in-Chief, South Atlantic.

·   ·   ·   ·   ·   ·   ·

9 Meanwhile Captain Langsdorff telegraphed on December 16 to the German Admiralty as follows:

> Strategic position off Montevideo. Besides the cruisers and destroyers, *Ark Royal* and *Renown*. Close blockade at night; escape into open sea and break-through to home waters hopeless. . . . Request decision on whether the ship should be scuttled in spite of insufficient depth in the estuary of the Plate, or whether internment is to be preferred.

At a conference presided over by the Fuehrer, at which Raeder and Jodl were present, the following answer was decided on:

> Attempt by all means to extend the time in neutral waters. . . . Fight your way through to Buenos Aires if possible. No internment in Uruguay. Attempt effective destruction if ship is scuttled.

10 As the German envoy in Montevideo reported later that further attempts to extend the time limit of seventy-two hours were fruitless, these orders were confirmed by the German Supreme Command.

11 Accordingly, during the afternoon of the seventeenth the *Spee* transferred more than seven hundred men, with baggage and provisions, to the German merchant ship in the harbour. Shortly afterwards Admiral Harwood learnt that she was weighing anchor. At 6:15 P.M., watched by immense crowds, she left harbour and steamed slowly seaward, awaited hungrily by the British cruisers. At 8:54 P.M., as the sun sank, the *Ajax's* aircraft reported: "*Graf Spee* has blown herself up." The *Renown* and *Ark Royal* were still a thousand miles away.

12 Langsdorff was broken-hearted by the loss of his ship. In spite of the full authority he had received from his government, he wrote on December 19:

> I can now only prove by my death that the fighting services of the Third Reich are ready to die for the honour of the flag. I alone bear the responsibility for scuttling the pocket battleship *Admiral Graf Spee*. I am happy to pay with my life for any possible reflection on the honour of the flag. I shall face my fate with firm faith in the cause and the future of the nation and of my Fuehrer.

That night he shot himself.

13 Thus ended the first surface challenge to British trade on the oceans. No other raider appeared until the spring of 1940, when a new campaign opened, utilising disguised merchant ships. These could more easily avoid detection, but on the other hand could be mastered by lesser forces than those required to destroy a pocket battleship.

B

Read the passage below and then answer the following as directed.

1. What actually takes place in "Lost Retreat"? To what extent is the narrative element merely auxiliary to the exposition of the central theme, that is, "a retreat like Pagosa is impossible in our times"?

2. In your own words state your impressions of the following topics defined in the course of this example:
   a. The characteristics of the 1920's
   b. An ideal retreat
   c. The characteristics of the 1950's
   d. Nostalgia
   e. Isolationism
   f. The good life

3. What changes occurred in Pagosa Springs between the author's two visits? What changes occurred in the author's mental outlook during the same period? Is the mental point of view of this selection consistent?

4. In the manner illustrated in the comment on and analysis of Example XII D, pick out the descriptive expressions in paragraphs 4 to 9. In a short composition show how the description is or is not integrated with the narration.

5. In the context of this example show how the expressions listed below are (1) exact, (2) vigorous, (3) interesting, or (4) exact, vigorous, and interesting at the same time. (See Section VIII.)
   a. "When the complexities of the world were less insistent" (¶1)
   b. "I was full of high mountain air" (¶5)
   c. "The aspens sang and the pines whispered" (¶5)
   d. "The flash of coral trumpet flowers and Indian paintbrush" (¶6)
   e. "A well-sprung, mountain-bred automobile" (¶7)
   f. "I never acquired and never forgot" (¶16)
   g. "Like the mariposas, my dream of a retreat up here bloomed in its proper season and was now gone" (¶24)

6. Many autobiographical narratives are records of self-discovery. This example tells how the writer changed from a romantic idealist to a mature and realistic man. In a like manner write an autobiographical narrative of 1000 words. Use contrast to make your narrative effective.

Suggested Topics

a. On rereading my grammar school geography
b. The old neighborhood
c. Old movies
d. I used to think Uncle Jim was the greatest man in the world

e. The policeman doesn't scare me any more
f. The girl next door, at eight and eighteen
g. Dream house, revisited
h. I don't want to be a fireman any more
i. I used to think Shakespeare used big words
j. My religious beliefs
k. I revise my code of manners

Lost Retreat

BY HAL BORLAND

PAGOSA SPRINGS, COLO.

1 At one time or another, most of us have dreamed of a retreat, a quiet place where we could escape from the cares of the world and live the simple life. There was a time when such dreams were themselves simple, when the complexities of the world were less insistent than they are today; and if what I am about to set down seems naïve as well as Elysian, it should be read with a memory of that time. For I have just revisited the place that was to have been my retreat in those simpler days.

2 The time was the 1920's. The War was over, the World War, and few saw any insistent reason for thinking of it as World War I. We had helped set up the League of Nations to keep the peace, and, if we had squabbled ourselves out of the League before we were really in it, that was only a matter of politics. America was booming, with the debacle of 1929 still in the unforecast future. All things were possible, including retreats from the turmoil of speakeasies, jazz, and the stock market. A good many young Americans sought such a retreat in Europe. Some went to the fabulous South Sea islands. Some turned to lesser known parts of America, hoping to find there the roots of their own culture and inheritance. I came to Pagosa Springs.

3 I had known Pagosa briefly as a boy, when I came here with my father to fish for trout in the swift white waters of the upper San Juan River. I came back here in the 1920's to write a book about the legends and folklore of the Indians. Pagosa was, and still is, a small town set in a bowl of high mountains in southwestern Colorado. The San Juan, a branch of the Colorado, flows through town, and in a loop of the river is a small plateau where hot sulphurous springs bubble from the volcanic rock. Indians gave the place its name, which means Healing Water. Trappers came, then gold miners and lumbermen and ranchers. And at last a narrow-gauge railroad reached this valley. By the 1920's Pagosa had a population of about 800 people, including a handful of Ute Indians and Paiutes and Navajos.

4 I came here and wrote my book, and when it was completed I loaded a pack horse and went back into the mountains to fish. The fishing was good, and the mountains were wonderful with summer. I was returning from that trip when I found my retreat.

5 Any retreat is a place in the mind and emotions as well as a place on the map. I was flushed with the exhilaration of a job done. I was full of high mountain air and rainbow trout and thimbleberries and sourdough biscuits and youth. The aspens sang and the pines whispered, and the mariposa lilies were the most beautiful flowers that ever grew.

6 The trail I was following came up from a valley through the straight-bolled aspens, wound through a grove of virgin pine, and came out on a hilltop meadow. A brook flowed there, and the grass stood so tall I could touch its heads while sitting in the saddle. The brook was not over two feet wide, but I could see trout in it. Serviceberries grew beside the brook, and wild raspberries with fruit big as my finger end. In the soft earth beside the water were deer tracks, tracks of the big mule deer of the Rockies. On the open slope was a great bed of mountain lupine, and beyond it was the flash of coral trumpet flowers and Indian paintbrush.

7 I got off my horse and walked to the crest of that high meadow. From there I could see the rugged Weminuche country, with its fabulous trout streams. To the northeast rose Pagosa Peak, more than 14,000 feet high, with snow lingering in its upper valleys. A dozen other high peaks were in sight, including Squaretop, where grizzly bears still prowled, and Treasure Mountain, where the early Spaniards hid the gold they had stolen from the Indians. Down the far slope, on the shoulder of this rise, was the wagon road that led to Pagosa. The town was two hours away for a man on a horse, a fraction of that if one had a well-sprung, mountain-bred automobile.

8 I spent the afternoon there, planning. What better life could one ask than to live here in these mountains and fish and write books? I chose the site for my cabin, in the open but near enough to the pines that they would break the winter violence of the wind. The trees themselves were tall and slim and straight, ideal logs for building. By damming the brook a hundred yards upstream, I could pipe water to the cabin for summer use. In winter I would have to carry water from a spring.

9 There was stone for foundations and a fireplace. There was enough down timber close by to feed that fireplace longer than I should ever need. There was grass aplenty for horses, and a cow, or goats. With deer and trout at hand, one need not go hungry there. Dawns would come early, on that height, and sunsets would be late and wonderful over the mountains to the west. Summer nights would be cool, summer days would be full of hot sun.

10 I was practical. I sat in the grass and considered how isolated I might

be; for I had no notion of embracing the hermit life. By car, over gravel roads and through the mountains, one could reach Denver with its theaters, concerts, and libraries, in a long, hard day's drive. From Denver it was a scant two days by rail to New York, less than that to San Francisco or Los Angeles.

11 Here, surely, was the ideal retreat. One could live here in simplicity, work as one wished, be isolated when one wanted isolation, or go out from here into the busy, fretful world. One could see the horizon in all directions, and horizons can be, at will, either a comfort or a challenge.

12 Late that afternoon I went down the far slope to the wagon road and came back to Pagosa, with my heart singing. That evening I asked Fred Catchpole, the banker and a friend of my father, about that beautiful high ridge. Was it for sale? Fred looked at me and frowned. Yes, he knew the place. Some good timber on it. He thought it could be bought pretty reasonably. A hundred acres or so of timber and that high meadow would probably cost a man $1000 or $1200.

13 Perhaps it was the extra acreage of timber that stopped me. Or it may have been a letter in the mail awaiting me, a letter from a friend saying there was a job open back east that I could have. I hesitated, and Fred said that if I wanted a fishing cabin he knew a much better site, up on Ten-Mile Creek. That high ridge I was talking about, he said, might make a little ranch, but there wasn't much grass acreage and it was pretty high up. Lots of snow.

14 I didn't try to tell him why I wanted that ridge. His reasoning was sound, from his viewpoint. The idea of a retreat would be ridiculous, particularly for a young man who hadn't even a job to retreat from. A fishing cabin was understandable. A house on a hilltop, where one just wanted to live and think and find something to say, was hard to make plausible. I didn't even try.

15 I left Pagosa a few days later and went east and took the job, telling myself I would come back. But annual vacations were brief, and Pagosa was a long way off. Then there was a depression, and after the depression there was another war. Somehow I never came back here until now.

16 This time I came deliberately, not looking for a retreat but to see if I could find the retreat I never acquired and never forgot. From Denver I drove through and over the mountains to Del Norte, over splendid modern highways. I came over Wolf Creek Pass, close by Pagosa Peak, and down the lovely valley of the San Juan to Pagosa.

17 Pagosa itself is not a great deal changed. The hot springs are still only casually exploited. Gold mining has dwindled away; in its place is a measurable amount of uranium excitement. There is more ranching than there used to be, and some dude ranching. But Pagosa is essentially a quiet little town with a serve-yourself market, a drugstore selling sunglasses and cheap

curios for tourists, a modest hotel, a rustic motel, and the usual assortment of filling stations.

18 Today I drove out of Pagosa on the asphalt road toward Bayfield and Durango, looking for my hilltop. I found it with little trouble. A side road, unpaved but of well-graded gravel, leads off into the hills. I followed it, and parked my car, and walked a quarter of a mile, and there I was.

19 At first I was uncertain. The pines have been logged over, and the beautiful grove is a field of stumps with second-growth timber now rising among them. The brook is only a thread of water, and I am sure there are no trout in it; when the timber was cut, some of the springs which fed the brook were dried up. The berry bushes still grow where they were before, and the grass, though not so tall, still flourishes. And the mountains stand, majestic and unchanged.

20 It is still a beautiful place, or could be made so with a few years of care. And yet as I stood there I couldn't recapture the old remote feeling.

21 I looked west, and I knew that just over the hills lay the uranium mines along the Colorado-Utah border, and the concentration plants working the uranium ore. I looked south, and just beyond the horizon lay Santa Fe and Los Alamos, and just beyond them Albuquerque and Sandia Base and White Sands. I looked east, and I knew that there were Denver and Boulder and Colorado Springs, the Strategic Air Command and Lowry Field, and the foundations for new atomic energy installations, new radiation and electronics laboratories. Just over those mountains I had seen jet planes playing tag in practice games for more serious matters.

22 My hilltop was no longer remote. There is even air service to Denver from Durango, less than two hours to the west. You can fly to Denver, shop, have lunch, see a show, and fly back in time for dinner. You can get from here to London or Paris in less time than it used to take to get to Chicago.

23 But it is still wild country, from my hilltop. Rugged and picturesque, with the persistent flavor of the Old West. It is so colorful, in fact, that Hollywood now uses it as the natural setting for stagecoach epics. The movie people are making several pictures right now just west of here.

24 I thought of these things as I walked about that high meadow looking in vain for a mariposa lily. It was several minutes before I remembered that the mariposas, which are like a vivid, three-petaled tulip, must have finished blooming a month or more ago. Then I realized that I had been trying to recapture something that is gone forever. Like the mariposas, my dream of a retreat up here bloomed in its proper season and was now gone.

25 It wasn't the air bases or the uranium mines or atomic bombs or even Hollywood that killed the idea of such a retreat. It was the fact that it is no longer possible to retreat, as we once could, to a hilltop anywhere and live in simple isolation. I had not only lost my retreat of long ago; I had lost the whole reason for such a place. Not only I but those who went to

Europe seeking the simplicities and those who went to the South Seas in search of romantic reality. The days of those dreams are gone. As David Bradley said, in a somewhat more grim connotation, there is no place to hide. Even more to the point perhaps, we have at last grown beyond the stage of wanting to hide.

26 But we still look back, from time to time, with nostalgia, and we make the journey to see again our lost retreats. Once there, we see how completely we have lost them. Put them away, rather, the lost retreats and all the yearnings that went with them. Or almost all; for we still can't completely forget that there once was a less complex world, and perhaps a simpler life, if we enough desired it. We lost those things because we wanted to retreat, because we were young and willful and strangely blind.

27 I came back down here to Pagosa and bought a Navajo rug, a Two Gray Hills rug probably woven by a squaw who remembers when the first gold miners came into these mountains, and whose grandson may be buried on Okinawa. Tonight I shall feel the mountain coolness on my face like a breeze when the sun drops behind the mountains. And tomorrow I hope to go fishing. Perhaps up on Ten-Mile Creek, where a friend of mine has a cabin. But only for a day or two. I must be in Los Angeles by next weekend, and I should be back home, in Connecticut, by the end of the month.

C

Read the passage below and answer the following questions.

1. What is the action in this passage? Is this action, in the main, described or in the main narrated? Give reasons for your answer.
2. Explain whether the narrator is
   a. An observer of the action
   b. A participant in the action
   c. Both an observer and a participant
3. Is chronology important or irrelevant in this passage? Explain your answer.
4. Show how the narrator's speculations in paragraphs 3 and 52 help to explain the action.
5. What is the predominant mental point of view of this selection?
6. Decide whether the expressions listed below are in harmony with the emotional tone of the narrative.
   a. "That clinging viscous memory" (¶1)
   b. "Bedsheets sagging with hernias" (¶2)
   c. "Sheep who have taken things into their own hands" (¶24)
   d. "[Death] was the nip in the hock by which the shepherd dog hurried the flock along" (¶52)
   e. "How long would a swarm of locusts last in a field of asphalt?" (¶61)

7. To what extent do the dialogue and the short, fragmentary sentences contribute
   a. To the sense of movement
   b. To the emotional atmosphere of the scene?
8. In a manner similar to this example narrate and describe one of the following actions:
   a. A company of Marines on its way back from an outpost
   b. A defeated team straggling through a passageway to the dressing room
   c. A group of prisoners returning from field work
   d. Refugees crossing a border

Evacuation

BY ANTOINE DE SAINT-EXUPÉRY

1 The highways too were part of our experience. We were pilots, and there were days when in a single morning our sortie took us over Alsace, Belgium, Holland, and the sea itself. But our problems were most often of the north of France, and our horizon was very often limited to the dimensions of a traffic tangle at a crossroads. Thus, only three days earlier, I had seen the village in which we were billeted go to pieces. I do not expect ever to be free of that clinging, viscous memory.

2 It was six in the morning, and Dutertre and I, coming out of our billet, found ourselves in the midst of chaos. All the stables, all the sheds, all the barns and garages had vomited into the narrow streets a most extraordinary collection of contrivances. There were new motorcars, and there were ancient farm carts that for half a century had stood untouched under layers of dust. There were hay wains and lorries, carryalls and tumbrils. Had we seen a mail coach in this maze it would not have astonished us. Every box on wheels had been dug up and was now laden with the treasures of the home. From door to vehicle, wrapped in bedsheets sagging with hernias, the treasures were being piled in.

3 Together, these treasures had made up that greater treasure—a home. By itself, each was valueless; yet they were the objects of a private religion, a family's worship. Each filling its place, they had been made indispensable by habit and beautiful by memory, had been lent price by the sort of fatherland which, together, they constituted. But those who owned them thought each precious in itself and for itself. These treasures had been wrenched from their fireside, their table, their wall; and now that they were heaped up in disorder, they showed themselves to be the worn and torn stock of a

junkshop that they were. Fling sacred relics into a heap, and they can turn your stomach.

4 "What's going on here? Are you mad?"

5 The café owner's wife shrugged her shoulders.

6 "We're evacuating."

7 "But why, in God's name?"

8 "Nobody knows. Mayor's orders."

9 She was too busy to talk, and vanished up her staircase. Dutertre and I stood in the doorway and looked on. Every motorcar, every lorry, every cart and charabanc was piled high with children, mattresses, kitchen utensils.

10 Of all these objects the most pitiful were the old motorcars. A horse standing upright in the shafts of a farm cart gives off a sensation of solidity. A horse does not call for spare parts. A farm cart can be put into shape with three nails. But all these vestiges of the mechanical age! This assemblage of pistons, valves, magnetos, and gear wheels! How long would it run before it broke down?

11 "Please, captain. Could you give me a hand?"

12 "Of course. What is it?"

13 "I want to get my car out of the garage."

14 I looked at the woman in amazement.

15 "Are you sure you know how to drive?"

16 "Oh, it will be all right. The road is so jammed, it won't be hard."

17 There was herself, and her sister-in-law, and their children—seven children in all.

18 That road easy to drive? A road over which you made two or ten miles a day, stopping dead every two hundred yards? Braking, stopping, shifting gears, changing from low into second and back again every fifty yards in the confusion of an inextricable jam. Easy driving? The woman would break down before she had gone half a mile! And gas! And oil! And water, which she was sure to forget!

19 "Better watch your water. Your radiator is leaking like a sieve."

20 "Well, it's not a new car."

21 "You'll be on the road a week, you know. How are you going to make it?"

22 "I don't know."

23 She won't have gone three miles before running into half a dozen cars, stripping her gears, and blowing out her tires. Then she and her sister-in-law and the seven children will start to cry. And she and her sister-in-law and the seven children, faced by problems out of their ken, will give up. They will abandon the car, sit down by the side of the road, and wait for the coming of a shepherd.

24 But it is astonishing how few shepherds there are. Dutertre and I are

staring at sheep who have taken things into their own hands. And these sheep are off in an immense clatter of mechanical equipment. Three thousand pistons. Six thousand valves. The grate, the grind, the clank of this machinery. Water boiling up in a radiator already. And slowly, laboriously, this caravan of doom stirs into movement. This caravan without spare parts, without tires, without gasoline, without a mechanic. They are mad!

25 "Why don't you stay home?"

26 "God knows, we'd rather stay."

27 "Then why do you leave?"

28 "They said we had to."

29 "Who said so?"

30 "The mayor."

31 Always the mayor.

32 "Of course we'd all rather stay home."

33 It is a fact that these people are not panicky; they are people doing a blind chore. Dutertre and I tried to shake some of them out of it.

34 "Look here, why don't you unload and put that stuff back into your house? At least you'll have your pump water to drink."

35 "Of course that would be the best thing."

36 "But you are free to do it. Why don't you?"

37 Dutertre and I are winning. A cluster of villagers has collected around us. They listen to us. They nod their heads approvingly.

38 "He's right, he is, the captain."

39 Others come to our support. A roadmender, converted, is hotter about it than I am.

40 "Always said so. Get out on that road and there's nothing but asphalt to eat."

41 They argue. They agree. They will stay. Some go off to preach to others. And they come back discouraged.

42 "Won't do. Have to go."

43 "Why?"

44 "Baker's already left. Who will bake our bread?"

45 The village has already broken down. At one point or another it has burst; and through that hole its contents are running out. Hopeless.

46 Dutertre said what he thought about it:

47 "The tragedy is that men have been taught that war is an abnormal condition. In the past they would have stayed home. War and life were the same thing."

48 The café owner came down, dragging a sack.

49 "You can let us have a cup of coffee, I suppose? We are flying in half an hour."

50 "Ah, my poor lads!"

51 She wiped her eyes. It was not us she was weeping for. Nor herself.

Already she was crying with exhaustion. Already she felt herself suffocating in that caravan which was to go further to pieces with every mile of its journey.

52 Farther on, in the open country, the enemy fighters would be flying low and spitting forth their bursts of machine-gun fire upon this lamentable flock. But it was astonishing how on the whole the enemy refrained from total annihilation. Here and there stood a car in flames, but very few. And there were few dead. Death was a sort of luxury, something like a bit of advice. It was the nip in the hock by which the shepherd dog hurried the flock along. Though one wondered why the enemy action was so little insistent, so altogether sporadic and local. The enemy was at no pains whatever to blow the caravan to bits. True, the caravan had no need of the enemy to go to pieces. The machines took care of that. They went spontaneously out of order. The machine is conceived for a deliberate and peaceful society, a society master of its time. When man is not present to repair the machine, regulate it, polish it, it ages at a dizzying pace. Tonight all these machines will look a thousand years old. I seemed to be looking on at the death throes of the machine.

53 Here is a peasant whipping up his horse. Perched on his seat with the majesty of a king, he lords it over the whole caravan.

54 "You look very satisfied up there."

55 "Ah, it's the end of the world."

56 Suddenly I felt queasy. All these workers, these simple people, each with his place in the world, were to be transformed into parasites, vermin. They were going to spread over the countryside and devour it. The thought made me sick.

57 "Who is going to feed you?"

58 "Nobody knows."

59 How is one to feed millions of migrants shuffling over miles of road at the rate of two to ten miles a day? If food existed, it could not be brought up to them.

60 All this muddle of men and old iron lost on the asphalt of the highways made me think suddenly of my march through the Libyan desert. Prevot and I had crashed in a landscape glassy with black rocks and covered with a carpet of sun-grilled iron. This was not far different.

61 I stared at the refugees in despair. How long would a swarm of locusts last in a field of asphalt?

62 "Do you expect to drink rain water?"

63 "Nobody knows."

64 They knew nothing. For ten days they had seen an unbroken stream of refugees from the north flow through their village. For ten days they had watched this unending exodus. And their turn had come. They would take their place in the procession. But without confidence:

65 "If it was up to me, I'd rather die at home."

66 "We'd all rather die at home."

67 That was true. Their village might have collapsed over their heads, and still none would have chosen to leave.

D

Read the passage below and then answer as directed.

1. Who is telling the story? How does the narrator betray his own attitude toward the several characters?

2. The narrator here appears to be equally familiar
   a. With Lord Steyne's intentions
   b. With the school called Whitefriars
   c. With Mr. and Mrs. Rawdon Crawley's inner dispositions
   d. With young Rawdon's feelings
   e. With the various attitudes of the other characters
   Do you accept such an omniscient point of view? If so, why? If not, why not?

3. Much of the author's comment in this passage from *Vanity Fair* is ironical. Pick out one example of irony in each paragraph.

4. Some critics of Thackeray's fiction complain that he is too much the essayist in manner. Judging from this passage, would you agree with this criticism? Give reasons for your answer.

5. Admirers of Thackeray point out that, by using the omniscient point of view, the author succeeds
   a. In compassing much more material than do writers who use a limited point of view
   b. In giving us a more complete sense of the social background or setting
   Judging from this passage, would you agree with these observations? Give reasons for your answer.

6. Thackeray's narrative style is dense, that is, highly compressed. Sometimes his expression is thick with meaning, as in the phrase "benevolent discrimination," which means a power of discernment employed in the interest of charity. Sometimes it is allusive, that is, dependent upon the reader's knowledge of historical or literary background as in the reference to Henry VIII's title of Defender of the Faith. The italicized expressions in the passage below will reveal something about the range of Thackeray's literary skill. When necessary, consult an unabridged dictionary for the meaning of these terms, and then write a sentence showing how each italicized expression contributes to the author's purpose. Watch out for Thackeray's latent irony.

7. Writing as an omniscient observer, develop by narration one of the situations stated below.

a. A suitor meets his girl's father, mother, and two brothers at a family dinner
b. An actress visits her teen-age daughter at a convent school
c. A family friend tries to advise a doting mother that her son is in danger of becoming a mother's boy and that her daughter should be allowed to join the Waves
d. A satirical newspaper columnist tells the story of a newly rich soap manufacturer's purchase of an estate in the Cadillac belt of a suburban town
e. A doctor tells how the various members of a large family respond to the death of a rich bachelor relative

Young Rawdon Goes to Whitefriars

BY WILLIAM MAKEPEACE THACKERAY

1 When Lord Steyne was benevolently disposed, he did nothing by halves, and his kindness towards the Crawley family did the greatest honour to his benevolent discrimination. His lordship *extended* his good will to little Rawdon: he pointed out to the boy's parents the necessity of sending him to a public school; that he was of an age now when *emulation, the first principles of the Latin language, pugilistic exercises,* and the society of his fellow boys would be of the greatest benefit to the boy. His father objected that he was not rich enough to send the child to a good public school; his mother, that Briggs was a *capital mistress* for him, and had brought him on (as indeed was the fact) famously in English, *the Latin rudiments,* and in general learning: but all these objections disappeared before the *generous perseverance* of the Marquis of Steyne. His lordship was one of the governors of that famous old *collegiate institution* called the Whitefriars. It had been a *Cistercian convent* in old days, when the Smithfield, which is contiguous to it, was a tournament ground. Obstinate heretics used to be brought thither *convenient for burning* hard by. Harry VIII, the Defender of the Faith, seized upon the monastery and its possessions, and hanged and tortured some of the monks *who could not accommodate themselves to the pace of his reform.* Finally, a great merchant bought the house and land adjoining, in which, and with the help of other wealthy endowments of land and money, he established a famous *foundation hospital* for old men and children. An *extern school* grew round the old almost monastic foundation, which subsists still with its Middle Age costume and usages; and all Cistercians pray that it may long flourish.

2 Of this famous house, some of the greatest noblemen, prelates, and dignitaries in England are governors; and, as the boys are very comfortably lodged, fed, and educated, and subsequently *inducted to good scholarships* at the University and livings in the Church, many little gentlemen are de-

voted to the ecclesiastical profession from their tenderest years, and there is considerable emulation to procure nominations for the foundations. It was originally intended for the sons of *poor and deserving clerics and laics,* but many of the noble governors of the Institution, *with an enlarged and rather capricious benevolence,* selected all sorts of objects for their bounty. To get an education for nothing, and a future livelihood and profession assured, was so excellent a scheme *that some of the richest people did not disdain it;* and not only great men's relations, but great men themselves, sent their sons to profit by the chance—right reverend prelates sent their own kinsmen or the sons of their clergy, while, on the other hand, some great noblemen *did not disdain to patronize the children of their confidential servants* —so that a lad entering this establishment had every variety of youthful society wherewith to mingle.

3 Rawdon Crawley, though the only book which he studied was the *Racing Calendar,* and though *his chief recollections of polite learning were connected with the floggings which he received at Eton in his early youth,* had that decent and honest reverence for classical learning which all English gentlemen feel, and was glad to think that his son was to have *a provision for life,* perhaps, and a certain opportunity of becoming a scholar. And, although his boy was his chief solace and companion, and endeared to him by a thousand small ties, about which he did not care to speak to his wife, who had all along shown the utmost indifference to their son, yet Rawdon agreed at once to part with him, and to give up his own greatest comfort and benefit for the sake of the welfare of the little lad. He did not know how fond he was of the child until it became necessary to let him go away. When he was gone, he felt more sad and downcast than he cared to own—far sadder than the boy himself, who was happy enough to enter a new career and find companions of his own age. Becky burst out laughing once or twice, when the colonel, in his clumsy, incoherent way, tried to express his sentimental sorrows at the boy's departure. The poor fellow felt that his dearest pleasure and closest friend was taken from him. He looked often and wistfully at the little vacant bed in his dressing room, where the child used to sleep. He missed him sadly of mornings, and tried in vain to walk in the park without him. He did not know how solitary he was until little Rawdon was gone. He liked the people who were fond of him, and would go and sit for long hours with his good-natured sister, Lady Jane, and talk to her about the virtues and good looks and hundred good qualities of the child.

4 Young Rawdon's aunt, we have said, was very fond of him, as was her little girl, who wept copiously when the time for her cousin's departure came. The elder Rawdon was thankful for the fondness of mother and daughter. The very best and honestest feelings of the man came out in these *artless outpourings* of paternal feeling in which he *indulged* in their pres-

ence, and *encouraged* by their sympathy. He secured not only Lady Jane's kindness, but her sincere regard, by the feelings which he manifested, and which he could not show to his own wife. The two kinswomen met as seldom as possible. Becky laughed bitterly at Jane's feelings and softness; the other's kindly and gentle nature could not but revolt at her sister's callous behaviour.

5 It estranged Rawdon from his wife more than he knew or acknowledged to himself. She did not care for the estrangement. Indeed, she did not miss him or anybody. She looked upon him as her errand man and humble slave. He might be ever so depressed or sulky, and she did not mark his demeanour, or only treated it with a sneer. She was busy thinking about her position or her pleasures or her advancement in society; she ought to have held a great place in it, that is certain.

6 It was *honest* Briggs who made up the little kit for the boy which he was to take to school. Molly, the housemaid, blubbered in the passage when he went away—Molly kind and faithful in spite of a long arrear of unpaid wages. Mrs. Becky could not let her husband have the carriage to take the boy to school. Take the horses into the *City!*—such a thing was never heard of. Let a cab be brought. She did not offer to kiss him when he went; nor did the child propose to embrace her, but gave a kiss to old Briggs (whom, in general, he was very shy of caressing) and consoled her by pointing out that he was to come home on Saturdays, when she would have the benefit of seeing him. As the cab rolled towards the City, Becky's carriage rattled off to the Park. She was chattering and laughing with a score of young dandies by the *Serpentine* as the father and son entered at the old gates of the school—where Rawdon left the child, and came away with a sadder, purer feeling in his heart than perhaps that *poor battered fellow* had ever known since he himself came out of the nursery.

7 He walked all the way home very dismally, and dined alone with Briggs. He was very kind to her, and grateful for her love and watchfulness over the boy. His conscience smote him that he had borrowed Briggs's money and aided in deceiving her. They talked about little Rawdon a long time, for Becky only came home to dress and go out to dinner; and then he went off *uneasily* to drink tea with Lady Jane, and tell her of what had happened, and how little Rawdon went off *like a trump,* and how he was to wear a gown and little knee breeches, and how young Blackball, Jack Blackball's son, of the old regiment, had taken him in charge and promised to be kind to him.

8 In the course of a week, young Blackball had constituted little Rawdon his fag, shoeblack, and *breakfast toaster;* initiated him into the mysteries of the Latin grammar, and thrashed him three or four times; but not severely. The little chap's good-natured honest face won his way for him. He only got that degree of beating which was, no doubt, good for him; and as for

blacking shoes, toasting bread, and *fagging* in general, were these offices not deemed to be necessary parts of every young English gentleman's education?

9 Our business does not lie with the second generation and Master Rawdon's life at school; otherwise the present tale might be carried to any indefinite length. The colonel went to see his son a short time afterwards, and found the lad sufficiently well and happy, grinning and laughing in his little black gown and little breeches.

10 His father *sagaciously* tipped Blackball, his master, a sovereign, and secured that young gentleman's good will towards his fag. As a protégé of the great Lord Steyne, the nephew of a country member, and son of a colonel and C.B., whose name appeared in some of the most fashionable parties in the *Morning Post,* perhaps the school authorities were disposed not to look unkindly on the child. He had plenty of pocket money, which he spent in treating his comrades royally to raspberry tarts, and he was often allowed to come home on Saturdays to his father, who always made a jubilee of that day. When free, Rawdon would take him to the play, *or send him* thither with the footman; and on Sundays he went to church with Briggs and Lady Jane and his cousins. Rawdon marveled over his stories about school, and fights, and fagging. Before long he knew the names of all the masters and the principal boys as well as little Rawdon himself. He invited little Rawdon's crony from school, and made both the children sick with pastry, and oysters, and porter after the play. He tried to look knowing over the Latin grammar when little Rawdon showed him what part of that work he was "in." *"Stick to it, my boy,"* he said to him with much gravity, *"there's nothing like a good classical education! Nothing!"*

E

1. Examples 1 and 3 and the selections in General Exercises B and C are narrated in the first person. Examples 2 and 4 and the selections in General Exercises A and D are related in the third person. Classify these examples also under the following heads:
   a. Omniscient observer
   b. Limited point of view
   c. Told chiefly in the present tense
   d. Told chiefly in the past tense
2. Example 1 and the selection in General Exercise A both recount naval actions. Show how the narratives achieve different effects
   a. Because of the personal character of the narrator
   b. Because of the point of view from which the narrator chooses to tell the story
   c. Because of the attitude the writer takes towards his story
3. Example 4 and the selection in General Exercise D are both told in the

third person. Are both also told from an omniscient point of view? Give reasons for your answer.

4. Which example or which selection in General Exercises A-D is most successful in its use of setting or atmosphere? Give reasons for your answer.

F

1. Grade the examples and selections in this section according to their position (1 to 8) with reference to each of the following qualities:
   a. Speed of pace
   b. Intensity of climax

G

Scale the examples and selections in this section according to the proportion of pure narrative to other forms of discourse. Rank in the first place that passage which has the least amount of description or exposition, in the last place that which has the greatest mixture of description and exposition.

H

1. *Which* of the words below, describing prose style, may be applied to each of the particular examples in this section?

staccato	dignified	objective
jerky	playful	terse
smooth	cadenced	dry
indirect	learned	vehement
cliché	colloquial	playful
mellifluous	poetic	precise
ornate	flat	loose
classical	balanced	rigid
severe	metaphorical	cold
lucid	impressionistic	jargon

2. Compare the narratives of Churchill and Parkman with respect to movement.
3. Compare the narratives of Beach and Carmer with respect to climax.
4. Compare the narratives of Borland and Roberts with respect to the scale of treatment.
5. Contrast the narratives of Saint-Exupéry and Thackeray with respect to proportion.

In the short story (1) present a theme or basic idea (2) in terms of a meaningful situation (3) elaborated by plot and characterization (4) in a style appropriate to the action and characters (5) against a background adequate to sustain the illusion of reality.

SECTION
XIV

The Short Story

IN SECTION XIII narration was defined as that form of discourse which recounts a series of incidents that together make up a whole action. Narration embraces many different types of writing. It includes fiction, such as the novel, the short story, the sketch, the imaginary chronicle; and nonfiction, such as history, biography, adventure, travel stories, news reports, and so on. All these types of narrative follow the general principles of unity, coherence, emphasis, and style explained in Section XIII and elsewhere in this book. But each specific type of narration has its own characteristic conventions and devices derived from these general principles. In this section we shall be concerned with one important type of narration—the short story.*

The short story is not merely a short narrative, but rather a brief, dramatic fiction in narrative form that aims to produce a single effect. In this definition *brief* means that the short story is normally between 2000 and 12,000 words; that is, a short story is neither an anecdote nor a novel. *Dramatic* means that the short story is the representation of an action, not the explanation or description of an action. Drama is an acting out, not a summary or report. *Fiction* means that the short story is an imaginative creation, not the reproduction of actual events. *A single effect* means that the story develops *one theme* rather than a variety of themes such as we find in a long novel like *War and Peace,* where virtually every aspect of life is represented. The *theme* is the total

---

* This section is by no means an introduction to the literature of the short story but merely an extended discussion of the principles of narration studied in Section XIII. The short story as a form of literature has, in its long, rich history, developed many varieties. Only a few of these varieties appear in this section.

meaning of the story conveyed by the imaginative, emotional, and intellectual elements of which a story is composed.

A good short story, then, achieves its aim, that is, a single effect, by revealing a theme or basic idea. This theme, however, must be developed in the context of an action. Thus the theme arises from a *meaningful situation,* a conflict, or complication, that sets the story in motion. The theme is revealed further when incidents are raveled and unraveled in the course of the *plot.* The plot necessarily involves the development of *character* and a narrative technique or style, which also contribute to the theme. Finally, a theme is revealed by and through a background that harmonizes with the action and the characters.

THE MEANINGFUL SITUATION

Every writer of fiction must face up to the primitive question, "Why tell the story?" Unlike workaday exposition, argument, and persuasion, a fictitious narrative must fashion an imaginary world. To do this it must create the illusion of reality, a sense that the story really happened.

The first step in creating illusion is to secure the reader's attention, that is, to offer him a meaningful situation.

A situation is made meaningful and attention is secured in three ways:

1. By promising a pleasurable excitement that appeals to the reader's imagination
2. By enlisting the reader's sympathies in the fortunes of a character and thus appealing to the reader's emotions
3. By pointing to a truth about human nature in a way that will provoke the reader to think or to speculate about it.

Obviously, attention is best secured when the author can appeal to all these sources of interest at the same time. The examples in this section make such a threefold appeal, each in its own degree.

Thus in Example 1 Conrad immediately excites our interest in his story by creating an atmosphere of mystery and suspense. When we meet Arsat, the main figure in the story, we sympathize with his sorrow because of his wife's illness. Gradually we perceive an underlying intellectual element in the story. As the narrative unfolds Arsat's problem is posed as the eternal conflict between love and duty. Arsat's situation symbolizes a universal problem of mankind, that is, the need to face up to duty with courage, to avoid the cowardice of private retreats and illusory pleasures.

In Example 2 Sean O'Faolain snares our attention by the same threefold appeal. At first we are amused by what appears to be a typical spat between husband and wife on the subject of the wife's new fur coat. Within a few short lines we begin to sympathize with both the characters, but particularly with the wife, for whom the fur coat is a symbol of all the domestic decencies that she has given up during the course of a hard life. As this situation is unraveled we realize that the author has touched upon a profound psychological truth. The dispute about the fur coat has been merely the occasion for revealing the central truth about the Maguires' life.

In Example 3 our attention is arrested first by our sympathy for the little boy Cotton, who is overcome by the universal human impulse to reach the high lonesome place. As he begins his journey, we become interested in his keen boy's observations of the road runner, the battle of the terrapins, the fight between the wasp and the tarantula, and his discovery of the Indian spearhead. Before long we realize that this simple adventure is an artful restatement of the perennial and excruciatingly painful problem of growth. In growing up Cotton cannot avoid giving pain to his parents and thereby to himself.

Thus in each example the writer has answered the question, "Why tell the story?" by supplying an imaginative, emotional, and intellectual situation that challenges the attention of a mature reader.

THE PLOT

A plot—that is, the arrangement of incidents in an effective order—is the means by which the writer exploits a meaningful situation. A plot is nothing more than a plan, a unifying principle, a systematic handling of events to make the meaning clear and the incidents exciting, and to reveal the characters in the most effective light.

As we have explained in Section XIII, a plot consists of a good beginning, middle, and end. In the short story, however, it is customary to employ a slightly different terminology. Thus the beginning is called the exposition, the middle includes the complication, turning point, and climax, and the end contains the resolution.

An *exposition* in the short story is that part of the story which explains all that is necessary in order to understand the subsequent action. It describes the setting or place where the action occurs. It evokes the special atmosphere of the scene. It introduces the main characters and establishes the physical angle of narration and the mental point of view or tone of the one who tells the story. Finally, it presents the reader with the meaningful situation, that is, the problem to be solved, or the conflict to be endured.

Thus in Example 1 the long exposition (its proportion will be treated later) locates the scene in Malaya, describes the brooding atmosphere of the lagoon, introduces the white trader, Arsat, and his wife, and lays the ground for Arsat's confession. To summarize, Conrad prepares the way for his whole action and asks the question, "Did Arsat choose wisely in coming to the lagoon?"

The *complication* is that part of the plot in which the writer develops the problem or conflict implied in the initial situation. In "The Lagoon," for instance, the complication in Arsat's narrative may be expressed in a series of problems. Arsat falls in love with Diamelen, the servant of Inchi Midah. The Ruler refuses Arsat's request for her hand. Arsat continues to court Diamelen. Arsat's brother helps him to abduct Diamelen. They flee and are pursued. In the ensuing fight the brother is wounded. The complication ends at the turning point or crisis, expressed in the critical question, "Will Arsat stay behind and fight, as his code requires, or will he attempt to escape with Diamelen?" Retrospectively we know that Arsat's decision here has determined the answer to the main question mentioned above, "Did Arsat choose wisely?"

The *turning point* or *crisis* is that part of the story in which the action takes a decisive turn. Thus the turning point in a tragic action is that point at which the ascending fortunes of a hero begin to decline; in a comic action it is that point at which the hero's embarrassments begin to disappear or his ill-fortunes are reversed. The turning point foreshadows the resolution of the main question. Thus in "The Lagoon" the turning point is Arsat's decision to abandon his wounded brother to his enemies. From that point on Arsat's fortunes begin to decline.

The *climax* is the point of highest emotional intensity, the moment of greatest suspense, in the story. Normally, the climax occurs near the close of a story because it sums up all the tension and suspense accumulated throughout the narrative. (Occasionally the climax and turning point occur together.) Thus the climax in "The Lagoon" occurs in the passage beginning with Arsat's cry, "I wanted peace in my own heart."

The *resolution* is that part of the story where the author finally unravels the complication and thus provides an answer to the main question. In "The Lagoon" the resolution occurs immediately after the climax cited above. Arsat stands revealed in his unappeasable sorrow. His betrayed brother is dead; Diamelen, the fruit of betrayal, is dead; his own self-respect is dead. He stands alone, "in the searching sunshine," seeing only darkness in the light. Thus we are aware of the author's judgment, not moralistically delivered, that Arsat has chosen unwisely, that no man chooses wisely who builds his own happiness on the betrayal of his brother man. Normally, as here, the resolution of the short story emphasizes the dominant impression, or the author's total judgment of the action, and thus contains a revelation of the *theme*.

It must be noted at once that many stories do not contain a fully developed plot. Indeed, some modern stories, particularly those written in a subjective or lyrical mood, stress the gradual revelation of character or an intensified awareness of the theme rather than direct action. The movement in stories of this kind may be compared to progressive illumination in the theater, where a character is first seen in semi-darkness, and finally in brilliant light. Some writers of fiction deliberately avoid climax and resolution in their desire to make their stories resemble the everyday world, where great problems occur without fanfare and complications are frequently unresolved.

REVELATION OF CHARACTER

A short story normally reveals character, that is, the personal habits of mind and action, the temperament and appearance of a fictitious person, *in the course of the action*. Indeed, it is difficult to imagine a short story without some degree of characterization. For action, to be human, must be conscious and deliberate; and conscious and deliberate human action in some degree characterizes the man who acts as good or evil, ignorant or learned, prudent or imprudent, and so on.

Thus, far from being a mere by-product, characterization is an essential part of plot. Plot involves character, and character in turn generates plot. We can hardly speak of one without the other. We shall understand this more vividly when we examine the six ways of revealing a character.

A character is revealed:

1. By his actions
2. By his thoughts
3. By his speech
4. By his physical appearance
5. By what other people in the story think of him
6. By the author's explicit comment

Action—free, conscious, deliberate—is the chief index of a man's character. "By their fruits ye shall know them." Men express their souls in action. We remember the Spartans at Thermopylae, the Light Brigade in the Crimea, the Old Guard at Waterloo, the Texans in the Alamo, the Marines at Iwo Jima—these brave men, and cowards, too, we know by their conscious and deliberate actions. They need not be great and spectacular actions either. One of Henrik Ibsen's women is known for a slam of the door, as one of Sir James Barrie's is for her twelve-pound look. In "The Lagoon" Arsat stands naked to our sight in one gesture—the push of a boat. Mrs. Maguire's inner struggle in "The Fur Coat" is revealed in one significant sentence, "And she crashed out and banged the door after her and put the children to bed as if she were throwing sacks of turf into the cellar." Cotton is characterized in "High Lonesome Place" by his brave, bold gesture of pitching away his hoe and scooting to his tall blue mountain.

But some actions are impossible to understand without a scrutiny of a character's motives. Hence there are times when we must also know what the character *thinks* he is doing and why he acts. Thus Conrad reveals the character of Arsat by telling his inmost thoughts, in addition to revealing his significant actions. Some writers who favor this second method of characterization have extensively developed the "stream-of-consciousness" technique.

The third method of characterization is by *dialogue*. Speech is a kind of mental action. It expresses a man's attitude on life, his response to his particular situation, his general mentality, and his particular intelligence. Thus through dialogue we come to know Arsat's sad fatalism, Molly Maguire's sense of humor, Cotton's boyishness. Their speech is as telltale as a fingerprint. Note how the following speeches mark (1) the heartsickness of Arsat, (2) the humorous self-deception of Molly, and (3) the boyishness of Cotton:

1. "Therefore I shall speak to you of love. Speak in the night. Speak before both night and love are gone—and the eye of day looks upon my sorrow and my shame; upon my blackened face; upon my burnt-up heart."

2. "Look," she explained, "what I want is something I can wear any old time. I don't want a fur coat for grandeur. . . . I want to be able to throw it on and go off and be as well-dressed as anybody. You see, you can wear any old thing under a fur coat."

3. And out yonder on the rim of the world stood the round, flat-topped mountain, tall and blue in the distance, calling, "Come on, Cotton! Come on!"

In this section, Example 2 is developed almost wholly by the speech of the characters. Here dialogue is represented at its best. It is brief, consistent with the characters, in keeping with the setting and atmosphere of the story; and it serves also to advance the action.

Physical appearance is not always an index of character, but, as we have already observed in Section XII, Examples A1 and A3, the outer appearance often betrays a significant inner trait or experience. "You could see the years on her fingertips, too pink, too coarse, and in her diamond-bright eyes," O'Faolain says of Molly, and we realize that this description, far from being an ornamental detail, helps to characterize Mrs. Maguire. Similarly, the following description of Arsat contributes directly to our understanding of his ambiguous character, composed partly of violence, partly of sensitive melancholy: "He was a man young, powerful, with broad chest and muscular arms. He had nothing on but his sarong. His head was bare. His big, soft eyes stared eagerly at the white man. . . ."

The fifth way of revealing character is to present the *opinions of other characters* in the story. Thus in "The Lagoon" we come to know that Arsat is marked by fate from the opinions of the Malay boatmen who dislike him as a stranger and as one who has defied the local deities. We know him too by the white trader's feelings towards him: "He liked him—not so much perhaps as a man likes his favorite dog. . . ."

The sixth way of revealing character is by the author's explicit *comment*. In Section XIII, General Exercise D, Thackeray employs this method to explain Lord Steyne and Rawdon Crawley. A favorite device of Victorian novelists, this method has declined in favor and is now generally regarded as a device of exposition rather than of narration.

In extended stories a writer is likely to use most of these methods of characterization. By combining these methods he conveys his own sense of the fictitious character, not in a legal or moralistic decision, but by a judgment of sensibility, that is, by a decision which conveys his own emotional impression of the character.

AN EFFECTIVE STYLE

Style in fiction conforms to the principles already set forth in Sections VIII and XIII. In addition to being clear, vigorous, and interesting, fictional style chimes with the action of the story and harmonizes with the point of view of the narrator. The last point, namely the harmony of style and point of view, requires some elaboration in the context of this section.

That the style in which the story is told depends upon the narrator is readily apparent in a first-person narrative. Thus in Example 1 Arsat's impetuous language, his selection of details that betray his obsession with Diamelen, his brother, and battle, his rich oriental imagery, his apparent artlessness in recounting the incidents of his life are all in character, that is, consonant with a proud but sensitive member of a Malay warrior caste. In Example 3, on the other hand, Cotton speaks as a boy. True, he has been given some strikingly poetic lines to recite, but the impression of a precocious ten-year-old farm boy is unmistakably evident. The vocabulary, the grammar, the selection of details, the rhythm of the sentences are in a boy's style, not as a boy actually talks, but as a boy *seems* to speak. The author represents, he does not reproduce his character. Cotton's personality echoes in sentences like these:

I thought about those big careless weeds that needed cutting. I thought of the hiding Papa would give me when I got back. I'd pestered Papa about going to the mountain before, and he'd said I was too little. He'd said, "Cotton, you get to prowling way off from home like that and I'll set the seat of your britches to smoking!" And he'd do it, too; there wasn't any bluff to Papa.

In Example 2, however, Sean O'Faolain presents a dramatic story in which the author is completely effaced. The story is told entirely through the Maguires. The author's style is faithful to the point of view of the two characters. Their frugality and common sense, their tough patriotism and tender consciences are evident in their unspoken thoughts as well as in the words they speak. Moreover, the rhythm, the accent, the nuances of the dialogue in "The Fur Coat" are authentically of a certain time, place, and class. Racy, colloquial, realistic, O'Faolain's style is in harmony with the humorously realistic mood of his story, as Conrad's ornate style is the match of his poetic and tragic vision of life, and as Gipson's style conveys the mood of homespun lyricism in which "High Lonesome Place" is conceived.

ADEQUATE BACKGROUND

While a short story is necessarily limited and selective, it is not a mere abstraction. Rather it focuses our attention on one aspect of a larger field. But the field, the background, the enveloping spirit of time, place, and cultural climate must be present in the reader's consciousness if the author is to succeed in creating the illusion of reality.

The background of "The Lagoon" is the invincible, mysterious darkness of the tropics, "the darkness scented and poisonous of impenetrable forests" where mankind seems doomed. Conrad's enveloping atmosphere is at once a concrete setting and a symbolic atmosphere, a real place but one suggestive of evil forces, as he insinuates in his description of the twisted root of a tree. It seemed "black and dull, writhing and motionless, like an arrested snake."

O'Faolain's background is not merely the setting, the middle-class home of the Maguires, but twentieth-century Dublin in the early days of De Valera's regime. It is a period of peace following a long civil war, a period of adjustment to new ways of life. Fred Gipson's world is that of the exhilarating high plateau of the Rocky Mountains, to which Hal Borland paid tribute in "Lost Retreat" (Section XIII, General Exercise B). In each story the background, without distracting the reader's attention from the central imaginative vision, helps to sustain the illusion of reality.

SUMMARY

The foregoing discussion has shown that a short story

1. Presents a theme or basic idea
2. In terms of a meaningful situation
3. Elaborated by plot and characterization
4. In an effective style and
5. Against a background adequate to sustain the illusion of reality

The discussion suggests that we may test the qualities of a short story by asking a series of questions similar to those listed below.

Note: All the principles set forth in Section XIII may also be applied to the short story.

A. Theme
1. What is the writer's theme, that is, the total meaning of the story, its basic idea?
2. How is the plot related to the theme?
3. How are the characters related to the theme?
4. How is the style related to the theme?
5. How is the background related to the theme?

B. Plot
1. Does the exposition set forth a meaningful situation, that is, the main problem or conflict?
2. How is the situation complicated? State the main incidents of the complication.
3. Where is the turning point in the action?
4. At what point does the climax occur?
5. How is the complication resolved? Is the resolution credible?
6. If the story lacks a plot, decide whether it may be more properly classified as
    a. An expository sketch
    b. Pure narration
    c. A narrative essay

C. Character
1. Who tells the story? From what point of view is the story told?
2. Are the characters credible, that is, lifelike, consistent, provided with believable motives for acting as they do?
3. By what methods are the characters revealed?
    a. Action
    b. Thought
    c. Dialogue
    d. Description
    e. Judgments of other characters
    f. The author's comment
4. Are the characters clearly distinguished one from another? How?

D. Style
1. Is the style clear, vigorous, and interesting?

2. Does the diction harmonize with the pace of the action and the point of view of the characters?
3. Are transitions from incident to incident clearly marked?
4. Are shifts in point of view clearly marked?
5. To what extent does the author employ a descriptive and expository style?
6. Does the author employ figurative language or symbols to underline his theme or interpret a character?

E. Background
  1. What is the particular setting? Does it blend with the action and characters?
  2. What is the general background of the piece? How does it contribute to the mood or tone of the story as a whole?
  3. How does the author communicate the setting and the background?

In the Short Story (1) present a theme or basic idea (2) in terms of a meaningful situation (3) elaborated by plot and characterization (4) in a style appropriate to the action and characters (5) against a background adequate to sustain the illusion of reality.

---

1. The Lagoon

BY JOSEPH CONRAD

1 The white man, leaning with both arms over the roof of the little house in the stern of the boat, said to the steersman,
2 "We will pass the night in Arsat's clearing. It is late."

THE LAGOON: reprinted by permission of J. M. Dent & Sons, Ltd.

3 The Malay only grunted, and went on looking fixedly at the river. The white man rested his chin on his crossed arms and gazed at the wake of the boat. At the end of the straight avenue of forests cut by the intense glitter of the river, the sun appeared unclouded and dazzling, poised low over the water that shone smoothly like a band of metal. The forests, somber and dull, stood motionless and silent on each side of the broad stream. At the foot of big, towering trees, trunkless nipa palms rose from the mud of the bank, in bunches of leaves enormous and heavy, that hung unstirring over the brown swirl of eddies. In the stillness of the air every tree, every leaf, every bough, every tendril of creeper and every petal of minute blossoms seemed to have been bewitched into an immobility perfect and final. Nothing moved on the river but the eight paddles that rose flashing regularly, dipped together with a single splash; while the steersman swept right and left with a periodic and sudden flourish of his blade describing a glinting semicircle above his head. The churned-up water frothed alongside with a confused murmur. And the white man's canoe, advancing upstream in the short-lived disturbance of its own making, seemed to enter the portals of a land from which the very memory of motion had forever departed.

4 The white man, turning his back upon the setting sun, looked along the empty and broad expanse of the sea reach. For the last three miles of its course the wandering, hesitating river, as if enticed irresistibly by the freedom of an open horizon, flows straight into the sea, flows straight to the east—to the east that harbors both light and darkness. Astern of the boat the repeated call of some bird, a cry discordant and feeble, skipped along over the smooth water and lost itself, before it could reach the other shore, in the breathless silence of the world.

5 The steersman dug his paddle into the stream, and held hard with stiffened arms, his body thrown forward. The water gurgled aloud; and suddenly the long straight reach seemed to pivot on its center, the forests swung in a semicircle, and the slanting beams of sunset touched the broadside of the canoe with a fiery glow, throwing the slender and distorted shadows of its crew upon the streaked glitter of the river. The white man turned to look ahead. The course of the boat had been altered at right angles to the stream, and the carved dragon head of its prow was pointing now at a gap in the fringing bushes of the bank. It glided through, brushing the overhanging twigs, and disappeared from the river like some slim and amphibious creature leaving the water for its lair in the forests.

6 The narrow creek was like a ditch: tortuous, fabulously deep; filled with gloom under the thin strip of pure and shining blue of the heaven. Immense trees soared up, invisible behind the festooned draperies of creepers. Here and there, near the glistening blackness of the water, a twisted root of some tall tree showed amongst the tracery of small ferns, black and dull, writhing and motionless, like an arrested snake. The short words of the paddlers reverberated loudly between the thick and somber walls of vegetation. Darkness oozed out from between the trees, through the tangled maze of the creepers, from behind the great fantastic and unstirring leaves; the darkness, mysterious and invincible; the darkness scented and poisonous of impenetrable forests.

7 The men poled in the shoaling water. The creek broadened, opening out into a wide sweep of a stagnant lagoon. The forests receded from the marshy bank, leaving a level strip of bright green, reedy grass to frame the reflected blueness of the sky. A fleecy pink cloud drifted high above, trailing the delicate coloring of its image under the floating leaves and the silvery blossoms of the lotus. A little house, perched on high poles, appeared black in the distance. Near it, two tall nibong palms, that seemed to have come out of the forests in the background, leaned slightly over the ragged roof, with a suggestion of sad tenderness and care in the droop of their leafy and soaring heads.

8 The steersman, pointing with his paddle, said, "Arsat is there. I see his canoe fast between the piles."

9 The polers ran along the sides of the boat, glancing over their shoulders at the end of the day's journey. They would have preferred to spend the night somewhere else than on this lagoon of weird aspect and ghostly reputation. Moreover, they disliked Arsat, first as a stranger, and also because he who repairs a ruined house, and dwells in it, proclaims that he is not afraid to live amongst the spirits that haunt the places abandoned by mankind. Such a man can disturb the course of fate by glances or words, while his familiar ghosts are not easy to propitiate by casual wayfarers upon whom they long to wreak the malice of their human master. White men care not for such things, being unbelievers and in league with the Father of Evil, who leads them unharmed through the invisible dangers of this world. To the warnings of the righteous they oppose an offensive pretense of disbelief. What is there to be done?

10 So they thought, throwing their weight on the end of their long poles. The big canoe glided on swiftly, noiselessly, and smoothly,

towards Arsat's clearing, till, in a great rattling of poles thrown down, and the loud murmurs of "Allah be praised!" it came with a gentle knock against the crooked piles below the house.

11 The boatmen with uplifted faces shouted discordantly, "Arsat! O Arsat!" Nobody came. The white man began to climb the rude ladder giving access to the bamboo platform before the house. The juragan of the boat said sulkily, "We will cook in the sampan, and sleep on the water."

12 "Pass my blankets and the basket," said the white man, curtly.

13 He knelt on the edge of the platform to receive the bundle. Then the boat shoved off, and the white man, standing up, confronted Arsat, who had come out through the low door of his hut. He was a man young, powerful, with broad chest and muscular arms. He had nothing on but his sarong. His head was bare. His big, soft eyes stared eagerly at the white man, but his voice and demeanor were composed as he asked, without any words of greeting—

14 "Have you medicine, Tuan?"

15 "No," said the visitor in a startled tone. "No. Why? Is there sickness in the house?"

16 "Enter and see," replied Arsat, in the same calm manner, and turning short round, passed again through the small doorway. The white man, dropping his bundles, followed.

17 In the dim light of the dwelling he made out on a couch of bamboos a woman stretched on her back under a broad sheet of red cotton cloth. She lay still, as if dead; but her big eyes, wide open, glittered in the gloom, staring upwards at the slender rafters, motionless and unseeing. She was in a high fever, and evidently unconscious. Her cheeks were sunk slightly, her lips were partly open, and on the young face there was the ominous and fixed expression—the absorbed, contemplating expression of the unconscious who are going to die. The two men stood looking down at her in silence.

18 "Has she been long ill?" asked the traveler.

19 "I have not slept for five nights," answered the Malay, in a deliberate tone. "At first she heard voices calling her from the water and struggled against me who held her. But since the sun of today rose she hears nothing—she hears not me. She sees nothing. She sees not me—me!"

20 He remained silent for a minute, then asked softly—

21 "Tuan, will she die?"

22 "I fear so," said the white man, sorrowfully. He had known Arsat years ago, in a far country in times of trouble and danger, when no friendship is to be despised. And, since his Malay friend had come unexpectedly to dwell in the hut on the lagoon with a strange woman, he had slept many times there, in his journeys up and down the river. He liked the man who knew how to keep faith in council and how to fight without fear by the side of his white friend. He liked him—not so much perhaps as a man likes his favorite dog—but still he liked him well enough to help and ask no questions, to think sometimes vaguely and hazily in the midst of his own pursuits, about the lonely man and the long-haired woman with audacious face and triumphant eyes, who lived together hidden by the forests—alone and feared.

23 The white man came out of the hut in time to see the enormous conflagration of sunset put out by the swift and stealthy shadows that, rising like a black and impalpable vapor above the treetops, spread over the heaven, extinguishing the crimson glow of floating clouds and the red brilliance of departing daylight. In a few moments all the stars came out above the intense blackness of the earth, and the great lagoon gleaming suddenly with reflected lights resembled an oval patch of night sky flung down into the hopeless and abysmal night of the wilderness. The white man had some supper out of the basket, then, collecting a few sticks that lay about the platform, made up a small fire, not for warmth, but for the sake of the smoke, which would keep off the mosquitoes. He wrapped himself in the blankets and sat with his back against the reed wall of the house, smoking thoughtfully.

24 Arsat came through the doorway with noiseless steps and squatted down by the fire. The white man moved his outstretched legs a little.

25 "She breathes," said Arsat in a low voice, anticipating the expected question. "She breathes and burns as if with a great fire. She speaks not; she hears not—and burns!"

26 He paused for a moment, then asked in a quiet, incurious tone—

27 "Tuan, . . . will she die?"

28 The white man moved his shoulders uneasily and muttered in a hesitating manner—

29 "If such is her fate."

30 "No, Tuan," said Arsat, calmly. "If such is my fate. I hear, I see,

I wait. I remember . . . Tuan, do you remember the old days? Do you remember my brother?"

31 "Yes," said the white man. The Malay rose suddenly and went in. The other, sitting still outside, could hear the voice in the hut. Arsat said: "Hear me! Speak!" His words were succeeded by a complete silence. "O Diamelen!" he cried, suddenly. After that cry there was a deep sigh. Arsat came out and sank down again in his old place.

32 They sat in silence before the fire. There was no sound within the house, there was no sound near them; but far away on the lagoon they could hear the voices of the boatmen ringing fitful and distinct on the calm water. The fire in the bows of the sampan shone faintly in the distance with a hazy red glow. Then it died out. The voices ceased. The land and the water slept invisible, unstirring and mute. It was as though there had been nothing left in the world but the glitter of stars streaming, ceaseless and vain, through the black stillness of the night.

33 The white man gazed straight before him into the darkness with wide-open eyes. The fear and fascination, the inspiration and the wonder of death—of death near, unavoidable, and unseen, soothed the unrest of his race and stirred the most indistinct, the most intimate of his thoughts. The ever-ready suspicion of evil, the gnawing suspicion that lurks in our hearts, flowed out into the stillness round him—into the stillness profound and dumb, and made it appear untrustworthy and infamous, like the placid and impenetrable mask of an unjustifiable violence. In that fleeting and powerful disturbance of his being the earth enfolded in the starlight peace became a shadowy country of inhuman strife, a battlefield of phantoms terrible and charming, august or ignoble, struggling ardently for the possession of our helpless hearts. An unquiet and mysterious country of inextinguishable desires and fears.

34 A plaintive murmur rose in the night; a murmur saddening and startling, as if the great solitudes of surrounding woods had tried to whisper into his ear the wisdom of their immense and lofty indifference. Sounds hesitating and vague floated in the air round him, shaped themselves slowly into words; and at last flowed on gently in a murmuring stream of soft and monotonous sentences. He stirred like a man waking up and changed his position slightly. Arsat, motionless and shadowy, sitting with bowed head under the stars, was speaking in a low and dreamy tone—

35 ". . . for where can we lay down the heaviness of our trouble but in a friend's heart? A man must speak of war and of love. You, Tuan, know what war is, and you have seen me in time of danger seek death as other men seek life! A writing may be lost; a lie may be written; but what the eye has seen is truth and remains in the mind!"

36 "I remember," said the white man, quietly. Arsat went on with mournful composure—

37 "Therefore I shall speak to you of love. Speak in the night. Speak before both night and love are gone—and the eye of day looks upon my sorrow and my shame; upon my blackened face; upon my burnt-up heart."

38 A sigh, short and faint, marked an almost imperceptible pause, and then his words flowed on, without a stir, without a gesture.

39 "After the time of trouble and war was over and you went away from my country in the pursuit of your desires, which we, men of the islands, cannot understand, I and my brother became again, as we had been before, the sword bearers of the Ruler. You know we were men of family, belonging to a ruling race, and more fit than any to carry on our right shoulder the emblem of power. And in the time of prosperity Si Dendring showed us favor, as we, in time of sorrow, had showed to him the faithfulness of our courage. It was a time of peace. A time of deer hunts and cockfights; of idle talks and foolish squabbles between men whose bellies are full and weapons are rusty. But the sower watched the young rice shoots grow up without fear, and the traders came and went, departed lean and returned fat into the river of peace. They brought news, too. Brought lies and truth mixed together, so that no man knew when to rejoice and when to be sorry. We heard from them about you also. They had seen you here and had seen you there. And I was glad to hear, for I remembered the stirring times, and I always remembered you, Tuan, till the time came when my eyes could see nothing in the past, because they had looked upon the one who is dying there—in the house."

40 He stopped to exclaim in an intense whisper, "O Mara bahia! O Calamity!" then went on speaking a little louder:

41 "There's no worse enemy and no better friend than a brother, Tuan, for one brother knows another, and in perfect knowledge is strength for good or evil. I loved my brother. I went to him and told him that I could see nothing but one face, hear nothing but one voice.

He told me, 'Open your heart so that she can see what is in it—and wait. Patience is wisdom. Inchi Midah may die, or our Ruler may throw off his fear of a woman!' . . . I waited! . . . You remember the lady with the veiled face, Tuan, and the fear of our Ruler before her cunning and temper. And if she wanted her servant, what could I do? But I fed the hunger of my heart on short glances and stealthy words. I loitered on the path to the bath houses in the daytime, and when the sun had fallen behind the forest I crept along the jasmine hedges of the women's courtyard. Unseeing, we spoke to one another through the scent of flowers, through the veil of leaves, through the blades of long grass that stood still before our lips; so great was our prudence, so faint was the murmur of our great longing. The time passed swiftly . . . and there were whispers amongst women—and our enemies watched—my brother was gloomy, and I began to think of killing and of a fierce death. . . . We are of a people who take what they want—like you whites. There is a time when a man should forget loyalty and respect. Might and authority are given to rulers, but to all men is given love and strength and courage. My brother said, 'You shall take her from their midst. We are two who are like one.' And I answered, 'Let it be soon, for I find no warmth in sunlight that does not shine upon her.' Our time came when the Ruler and all the great people went to the mouth of the river to fish by torchlight. There were hundreds of boats, and on the white sand, between the water and the forests, dwellings of leaves were built for the households of the Rajahs. The smoke of cooking fires was like a blue mist of the evening, and many voices rang in it joyfully. While they were making the boats ready to beat up the fish, my brother came to me and said, 'Tonight!' I looked to my weapons, and when the time came our canoe took its place in the circle of boats carrying the torches. The lights blazed on the water, but behind the boats there was darkness. When the shouting began and the excitement made them like mad, we dropped out. The water swallowed our fire, and we floated back to the shore that was dark with only here and there the glimmer of embers. We could hear the talk of slave girls amongst the sheds. Then we found a place deserted and silent. We waited there. She came. She came running along the shore, rapid and leaving no trace, like a leaf driven by the wind into the sea. My brother said gloomily, 'Go and take her; carry her into our boat.' I lifted her in my arms. She panted. Her heart was beating against my breast. I said, 'I take you from those people. You came to the cry of my heart, but my arms take you into my boat against the will of the great!' 'It is right,' said my brother. 'We are men who take what we want and can hold it against many. We should have taken her in daylight.' I said, 'Let us be off'; for since she was in my boat I began to think of our Ruler's many men. 'Yes. Let us be off,' said my brother. 'We are cast out and this boat is our country now—and the sea is our refuge.' He lingered with his foot on the shore, and I entreated him to hasten, for I remembered the strokes of her heart against my breast and thought that two men cannot withstand a hundred. We left, paddling downstream close to the bank; and as we passed by the creek where they were fishing, the great shouting had ceased, but the murmur of voices was loud like the humming of insects flying at noonday. The boats floated, clustered together, in the red light of torches, under a black roof of smoke; and men talked of their sport. Men that boasted, and praised, and jeered—men that would have been our friends in the morning, but on that night were already our enemies. We paddled swiftly past. We had no more friends in the country of our birth. She sat in the middle of the canoe with covered face; silent as she is now; unseeing as she is now—and I had no regret at what I was leaving because I could hear her breathing close to me—as I can hear her now."

42 He paused, listened with his ear turned to the doorway, then shook his head and went on:

43 "My brother wanted to shout the cry of challenge—one cry only —to let the people know we were freeborn robbers who trusted our arms and the great sea. And again I begged him in the name of our love to be silent. Could I not hear her breathing close to me? I knew the pursuit would come quick enough. My brother loved me. He dipped his paddle without a splash. He only said, 'There is half a man in you now—the other half is in that woman. I can wait. When you are a whole man again, you will come back with me here to shout defiance. We are sons of the same mother.' I made no answer. All my strength and all my spirit were in my hands that held the paddle— for I longed to be with her in a safe place beyond the reach of men's anger and of women's spite. My love was so great, that I thought it could guide me to a country where death was unknown, if I could only escape from Inchi Midah's fury and from our Ruler's sword. We paddled with haste, breathing through our teeth. The blades bit deep into the smooth water. We passed out of the river; we flew in clear

channels amongst the shallows. We skirted the black coast; we skirted the sand beaches where the sea speaks in whispers to the land; and the gleam of white sand flashed back past our boat, so swiftly she ran upon the water. We spoke not. Only once I said, 'Sleep, Diamelen, for soon you may want all your strength.' I heard the sweetness of her voice, but I never turned my head. The sun rose and still we went on. Water fell from my face like rain from a cloud. We flew in the light and heat. I never looked back, but I knew that my brother's eyes, behind me, were looking steadily ahead, for the boat went as straight as a bushman's dart, when it leaves the end of the sumpitan. There was no better paddler, no better steersman than my brother. Many times, together, we had won races in that canoe. But we never had put out our strength as we did then—then, when for the last time we paddled together! There was no braver or stronger man in our country than my brother. I could not spare the strength to turn my head and look at him, but every moment I heard the hiss of his breath getting louder behind me. Still he did not speak. The sun was high. The heat clung to my back like a flame of fire. My ribs were ready to burst, but I could no longer get enough air into my chest. And then I felt I must cry out with my last breath, 'Let us rest!' . . . 'Good!' he answered; and his voice was firm. He was strong. He was brave. He knew not fear and no fatigue . . . My brother!"

44 A murmur powerful and gentle, a murmur vast and faint; the murmur of trembling leaves, of stirring boughs, ran through the tangled depths of the forests, ran over the starry smoothness of the lagoon, and the water between the piles lapped the slimy timber once with a sudden splash. A breath of warm air touched the two men's faces and passed on with a mournful sound—a breath loud and short like an uneasy sigh of the dreaming earth.

45 Arsat went on in an even, low voice.

46 "We ran our canoe on the white beach of a little bay close to a long tongue of land that seemed to bar our road; a long wooded cape going far into the sea. My brother knew that place. Beyond the cape a river has its entrance, and through the jungle of that land there is a narrow path. We made a fire and cooked rice. Then we lay down to sleep on the soft sand in the shade of our canoe, while she watched. No sooner had I closed my eyes than I heard her cry of alarm. We leaped up. The sun was halfway down the sky already, and coming in sight in the opening of the bay we saw a prau manned by many

paddlers. We knew it at once; it was one of our Rajah's praus. They were watching the shore, and saw us. They beat the gong, and turned the head of the prau into the bay. I felt my heart become weak within my breast. Diamelen sat on the sand and covered her face. There was no escape by sea. My brother laughed. He had the gun you had given him, Tuan, before you went away, but there was only a handful of powder. He spoke to me quickly: 'Run with her along the path. I shall keep them back, for they have no firearms, and landing in the face of a man with a gun is certain death for some. Run with her. On the other side of that wood there is a fisherman's house—and a canoe. When I have fired all the shots I will follow. I am a great runner, and before they can come up we shall be gone. I will hold out as long as I can, for she is but a woman—that can neither run nor fight, but she has your heart in her weak hands.' He dropped behind the canoe. The prau was coming. She and I ran, and as we rushed along the path I heard shots. My brother fired—once—twice—and the booming of the gong ceased. There was silence behind us. That neck of land is narrow. Before I heard my brother fire the third shot I saw the shelving shore, and I saw the water again; the mouth of a broad river. We crossed a grassy glade. We ran down to the water. I saw a low hut above the black mud, and a small canoe hauled up. I heard another shot behind me. I thought, 'That is his last charge.' We rushed down to the canoe; a man came running from the hut, but I leaped on him, and we rolled together in the mud. Then I got up, and he lay still at my feet. I don't know whether I had killed him or not. I and Diamelen pushed the canoe afloat. I heard yells behind me, and I saw my brother run across the glade. Many men were bounding after him. I took her in my arms and threw her into the boat, then leaped in myself. When I looked back I saw that my brother had fallen. He fell and was up again, but the men were closing round him. He shouted, 'I am coming!' The men were close to him. I looked. Many men. Then I looked at her. Tuan, I pushed the canoe! I pushed it into deep water. She was kneeling forward looking at me, and I said, 'Take your paddle,' while I struck the water with mine. Tuan, I heard him cry. I heard him cry my name twice; and I heard voices shouting, 'Kill! Strike!' I never turned back. I heard him calling my name again with a great shriek, as when life is going out together with the voice—and I never turned my head. My own name! . . . My brother! Three times he called—but I was not afraid of life. Was she not there in that canoe? And could I not with her find a country where death is forgotten—where death is unknown!"

47 The white man sat up. Arsat rose and stood, an indistinct and silent figure above the dying embers of the fire. Over the lagoon a mist drifting and low had crept, erasing slowly the glittering images of the stars. And now a great expanse of white vapor covered the land: it flowed cold and gray in the darkness, eddied in noiseless whirls round the tree trunks and about the platform of the house, which seemed to float upon a restless and impalpable illusion of a sea. Only far away the tops of the trees stood outlined on the twinkle of heaven, like a somber and forbidding shore—a coast deceptive, pitiless, and black.

48 Arsat's voice vibrated loudly in the profound peace. "I had her there! I had her! To get her I would have faced all mankind. But I had her—and—"

49 His words went out ringing into the empty distances. He paused, and seemed to listen to them dying away very far—beyond help and beyond recall. Then he said quietly—

50 "Tuan, I loved my brother."

51 A breath of wind made him shiver. High above his head, high above the silent sea of mist the drooping leaves of the palms rattled together with a mournful and expiring sound. The white man stretched his legs. His chin rested on his chest, and he murmured sadly without lifting his head—

52 "We all love our brothers."

53 Arsat burst out with an intense whispering violence—

54 "What did I care who died? I wanted peace in my own heart."

55 He seemed to hear a stir in the house—listened—then stepped in noiselessly. The white man stood up. A breeze was coming in fitful puffs. The stars shone paler as if they had retreated into the frozen depths of immense space. After a chill gust of wind there were a few seconds of perfect calm and absolute silence. Then from behind the black and wavy line of the forests a column of golden light shot up into the heavens and spread over the semicircle of the eastern horizon. The sun had risen. The mist lifted, broke into drifting patches, vanished into thin flying wreaths; and the unveiled lagoon lay, polished and black, in the heavy shadows at the foot of the wall of trees. A white eagle rose over it with a slanting and ponderous flight, reached the clear sunshine and appeared dazzlingly brilliant for a moment, then soaring higher, became a dark and motionless speck before it vanished

into the blue as if it had left the earth forever. The white man, standing gazing upwards before the doorway, heard in the hut a confused and broken murmur of distracted words ending with a loud groan. Suddenly Arsat stumbled out with outstretched hands, shivered, and stood still for some time with fixed eyes. Then he said—

56 "She burns no more."

57 Before his face the sun showed its edge above the treetops rising steadily. The breeze freshened; a great brilliance burst upon the lagoon, sparkled on the rippling water. The forests came out of the clear shadows of the morning, became distinct, as if they had rushed nearer—to stop short in a great stir of leaves, of nodding boughs, of swaying branches. In the merciless sunshine the whisper of unconscious life grew louder, speaking in an incomprehensible voice round the dumb darkness of that human sorrow. Arsat's eyes wandered slowly, then stared at the rising sun.

58 "I can see nothing," he said half aloud to himself.

59 "There is nothing," said the white man, moving to the edge of the platform and waving his hand to his boat. A shout came faintly over the lagoon, and the sampan began to glide towards the abode of the friend of ghosts.

60 "If you want to come with me, I will wait all the morning," said the white man, looking away upon the water.

61 "No, Tuan," said Arsat, softly. "I shall not eat or sleep in this house, but I must first see my road. Now I can see nothing—see nothing! There is no light and no peace in the world; but there is death—death for many. We are sons of the same mother—and I left him in the midst of enemies; but I am going back now."

62 He drew a long breath and went on in a dreamy tone:

63 "In a little while I shall see clear enough to strike—to strike. But she has died, and . . . now . . . darkness."

64 He flung his arms wide open, let them fall along his body, then stood still with unmoved face and stony eyes, staring at the sun. The white man got down into his canoe. The polers ran smartly along the sides of the boat, looking over their shoulders at the beginning of a weary journey. High in the stern, his head muffled up in white rags, the juragan sat moody, letting his paddle trail in the water. The white man, leaning with both arms over the grass roof of the little cabin, looked back at the shining ripple of the boat's wake. Before the sampan passed out of the lagoon into the creek he lifted his eyes.

Arsat had not moved. He stood lonely in the searching sunshine; and he looked beyond the great light of a cloudless day into the darkness of a world of illusions.

Comment

Since we have in the introduction already commented rather extensively on the principal features of "The Lagoon," it may be more profitable here to dwell on three special problems, (1) point of view, (2) proportion, and (3) symbolism.

The problem of point of view manifests itself in the double focus maintained throughout the story. At first, the story is told in the *third* person and focuses on the white trader. It is not until Arsat begins to tell his own story in the *first* person (¶35) that the white man's role of reflector, or observer, is finally established. An inattentive reader may find this shift in point of view—a shift that also involves a change in the time sequence—confusing. But close reading will discover the value of this double focus. The white man's trip to the lagoon permits Conrad to develop the setting, that is, the physical background, and the atmosphere, that is, the mental point of view or mood of tragic loneliness, so important to the ultimate meaning or theme of this short story. Arsat's isolation is further established by the fact that his only friend, the white trader, regards him with less real affection than the average man bestows upon a dog. The superstitious natives think of Arsat as one accursed, as one who has offended the gods.

The ambiguous relationship between Arsat and the white man makes Arsat's tale at once credible and pathetic; credible because the white man has known Arsat, his brother, and Diamelen, and is therefore a natural repository of Arsat's secret; pathetic because the white man is not a profoundly sympathetic witness. He cannot heal Arsat's wounded soul any more than his medicine could heal Diamelen. Thus the white man performs one of the functions of the chorus in the old Greek tragedy. He understands, reflects, interprets the action; he is an ironic witness to the judgment of fate. Through the white man the world is also witness to the events.

The second problem, that of proportion, is intimately linked to the first. Arsat's story occupies approximately one-half of the whole narrative. The exposition (¶1-34) appears to be overlong. But again, close reading shows how these unusual proportions serve Conrad's purpose. As a result of the elaborate exposition the reader is aware of Diamelen's approaching death. "The fear and fascination, the inspiration and the wonder of death" stir the reader as well as the white man. Arsat's tale, then, is recited at the same time his wife is dying. His tale ends just as his wife dies. The death of

Diamelen and the death of Arsat's hopes are revealed together, and the two strands of the story are intertwined. Thus the double focus results in a doubly effective conclusion. When Arsat stumbles out of his house crying, "She burns no more," he announces both his wife's death and his own defeat. It is at this point that we can appreciate the value of the seemingly overlong exposition, for the exposition had prepared us for the almost simultaneous conclusion of the events witnessed by the white man, and of the tale told by Arsat.

The third problem is that of symbolism. In a broad sense of the term, a symbol is a sign, such as a cross or a flag, which refers to something else. In a literary context a symbol is a concrete image which has its own independent meaning, but in addition suggests a further meaning. In "The Lagoon," for instance, the setting itself is symbolic. The forest suggests the darkness and the tangled web of human motives. The lagoon stands in part at least for Arsat's isolation from human society and for his avoidance of obligations. Diamelen's death agony takes place in the darkness of night, as does Arsat's recital—night here symbolizing the death of Arsat's hope. Arsat speaks as if dreaming, that is, as one whose ideals are illusions. When the day dawns, the sunshine (reality) does not penetrate Arsat's clouded mind. "He stood lonely in the searching sunshine; and he looked beyond the great light of a cloudless day into the darkness of a world of illusions." At the moment of Diamelen's death a white eagle, symbolic of the soul, rises into the clear dawn and vanishes "into the blue as if it had left the earth forever."

These symbols are more or less obvious and inescapable. The real problem here is whether or not the entire story is symbolic.

"I can see nothing," Arsat says (¶48).

"There is nothing," says the white man (¶49).

These and similar lines might suggest to some that the story aims to dramatize man's inexplicable fate—that man bears the eternal curse of Cain who slew his brother Abel. Yet there are other possible meanings embedded in the narrative. Conrad stresses the ideals of brotherly love, of loyalty, of courage in the face of death—ideals that Arsat recognizes but does not fulfill. However tragic Conrad's attitude may be in this particular story, it is not that of a misanthropist or a pessimist. Arsat has his weakness, but essentially he is not a contemptible man.

A symbolic story will always be somewhat obscure. It hints, half-reveals a meaning, not because the author wishes to keep his readers in the dark but because his own vision grows dim when he attempts to penetrate the profound mysteries at the core of human life. Not all clarities are superficial, but all superficialities are clear. Conrad's story is anything but superficial. As a result, its total meaning must be described in a general way, rather than fixed in a single, simple, and misleading sentence.

Analysis and Composition

1. Reread Section XII C. Show how Conrad (in ¶3-7) employs vivid details and figurative language to achieve emphasis in his description.
2. Show how paragraphs 1-34 fulfill the function of exposition in the story
3. List the main incidents in Arsat's story (¶35-46). Decide whether these incidents are
   a. In a clear time order
   b. In climactic order
4. Is Arsat's story (¶35-46) independent of the rest of the narrative or not? Give reasons for your answer.
5. Decide whether the interruptions in Arsat's narrative that occur in paragraphs 38, 42, and 44 add to or detract from the realistic effect of the narrative.
6. Are the white man and Diamelen "characterized" in this story? Answer this question by referring to the six methods of characterization explained in the introduction to this section.
7. Is Arsat's diction credible? Does it conform to his character, background, and general point of view? Give reasons for your answer.
8. In an essay of about 1000 words discuss the theme of this story in relation to the meaningful situation, the plot, and the characterization. One short statement of the theme might be: " 'The Lagoon' aims to present the spiritual turmoil of a man who has betrayed a loyal brother."

2. The Fur Coat

BY SEAN O'FAOLAIN

When Maguire became Parliamentary Secretary to the Minister for Roads and Railways, his wife wound her arms around his neck, lifted herself on her toes, gazed into his eyes and said, adoringly,

"Now, Paddy, I must have a fur coat."

"Of course, of course, me dear," Maguire cried, holding her out from him admiringly, for she was a handsome little woman still, in spite of the greying hair and the first hint of a stoop. "Get two fur coats! Switzer's will give us any amount of tick from now on."

THE FUR COAT: from *The Man Who Invented Sin* by Sean O'Faolain. Reprinted by permission of The Devin-Adair Company, publishers.

Molly sat back into her chair with her fingers clasped between her knees and said, chidingly,

"You think I'm extravagant!"

"Indeed then I do not. We've had some thin times together, and it's about time we had a bit of comfort in our old age. I'd like to see my wife in a fur coat. I'd love to see my wife take a shine out of some of those straps in Grafton Street—painted jades that never lifted a finger for God or man, not to as much as mention the word Ireland. By all means get a fur coat. Go down to Switzer's tomorrow morning," he cried with all the innocence of a warm-hearted, inexperienced man, "and order the best fur coat that money can buy."

Molly Maguire looked at him with affection and irritation. The years had polished her hard—politics, revolution, husband in and out of prison, children reared with the help of relatives and Prisoners' Dependents' Funds. You could see the years on her fingertips, too pink, too coarse, and in her diamond-bright eyes.

"Paddy, you big fool, do you know what you'd pay for a mink coat? Not to mention a sable? And not as much as to whisper the word broadtail?"

"Say a hundred quid," said Paddy, manfully. "What's a hundred quid? I'll be handling millions of public money from now on. I have to think big."

She replied in her warm Limerick singsong, sedately and proudly as befitted a woman who had often, in her father's country store, handled thousands of pound notes.

"Do you know, Paddy Maguire, what a really bang-up fur coat could cost you? It could cost you a thousand guineas, and more."

"One thousand guineas? For a coat? Sure, that's a whole year's salary."

"It is."

Paddy drew into himself. "And," he said, in a cautious voice, "is that the kind of coat you had in mind?"

She laughed, satisfied at having taken him off his perch.

"Yerrah, not at all. I thought I might pick up a nice little coat for, maybe, thirty or forty, or at the outside, fifty quid. Would that be too much?"

"Go down to Switzer's in the morning and bring it home on your back."

But, even there, she thought she detected a touch of the bravo, as if he was still feeling himself a great fellow. She let it pass. She said she might have a look around. There was no hurry. She did not bring up the matter again for quite fifteen minutes.

"Paddy! About that fur coat. I sincerely hope you don't think I'm being *vulgar?*"

"How could you be vulgar?"

"Oh, sort of *nouveau riche*. I don't want a fur coat for show-off." She leaned forward eagerly. "Do you know the reason why I want a fur coat?"

"To keep you warm. What else?"

"Oh, well, that, too, I suppose, yes," she agreed shortly. "But you must realise that from this on we'll be getting asked out to parties and receptions and so forth. And—well—I haven't a rag to wear!"

"I see," Paddy agreed; but she knew that he did not see.

"Look," she explained, "what I want is something I can wear any old time. I don't want a fur coat for grandeur." (This very scornfully.) "I want to be able to throw it on and go off and be as well-dressed as anybody. You see, you can wear any old thing under a fur coat."

"That sounds a good idea." He considered the matter as judiciously as if he were considering a memorandum for a projected by-pass. She leaned back, contented, with the air of a woman who has successfully laid her conscience to rest.

Then he spoiled it all by asking, "But, tell me, what do all the women do who haven't fur coats?"

"They dress."

"Dress? Don't ye all dress?"

"Paddy, don't be silly. They think of nothing else but dress. I have no time for dressing. I'm a busy housewife and, anyway, dressing costs a lot of money." (Here she caught a flicker in his eye which obviously meant that forty quid isn't to be sniffed at, either.) "I mean they have costumes that cost twenty-five pounds. Half a dozen of 'em. They spend a lot of time and thought over it. They live for it. If you were married to one of 'em you'd soon know what it means to dress. The beauty of a fur coat is that you can just throw it on and you're as good as the best of them."

"Well, that's fine! Get the ould coat."

He was evidently no longer enthusiastic. A fur coat, he had learned, is not a grand thing—it is just a useful thing. He drew his brief case towards him. There was that pier down in Kerry to be looked at.

"Mind you," he added, "it'd be nice and warm, too. Keep you from getting a cold."

"Oh, grand, yes, naturally, cosy, yes, all that, yes, yes!"

And she crashed out and banged the door after her and put the children to bed as if she were throwing sacks of turf into a cellar. When she came back he was poring over maps and specifications. She began to patch one of the boy's pyjamas. After a while she held it up and looked at it in despair. She let it sink into her lap and looked at the pile of mending beside her.

"I suppose when I'm dead and gone they'll invent plastic pyjamas that you can wash with a dishcloth and mend with a lump of glue."

She looked into the heart of the turf fire. A dozen pyjamas . . . underwear for the whole house. . . .

"Paddy!"

"Huh?"

"The last thing that I want anybody to start thinking is that I, by any possible chance, could be getting grand notions."

She watched him hopefully. He was lost in his plans.

"I can assure you, Paddy, that I loathe—I simply loathe all this modern show-off."

"That's right."

"Those wives that think they haven't climbed the social ladder until they've got a fur coat!"

He grunted at the map of the pier.

"Because I don't care what you or anybody else says, Paddy, there *is* something vulgar about a fur coat. There's no shape to them. Especially musquash. What I was thinking of was black Indian lamb. Of course, the real thing would be ocelot. But they're much too dear. The real ones. And I wouldn't be seen dead in an imitation ocelot."

He glanced sideways from the table. "You seem to know a lot about fur." He leaned back and smiled benevolently. "I never knew you were hankering all this time after a fur coat."

"Who said I'm hankering! I am *not*. What do you mean? Don't be silly. I just want something decent to wear when we go out to a show, or to wear over a dance frock, that's all. What do you mean—hankering?"

"Well, what's wrong with that thing you have with the fur on the sleeves? The shiny thing with the what-do-you-call-'ems—sequins is it?"

"*That!* Do you mean *that?* For Heaven's sake don't be talking about what you don't know anything about. I've had *that* for fourteen years. It's like something me grandmother wore at her own funeral."

He laughed. "You used to like it."

"Of course, I liked it when I got it. Honestly, Paddy Maguire, there are times when . . ."

"Sorry, sorry, sorry. I was only trying to be helpful. How much is an ocelot?"

"Eighty-five or ninety—at the least."

"Well, why not?"

"Paddy, tell me honestly. Honestly, now! Do you seriously think that I could put eighty-five pounds on my back?"

With his pencil Maguire frugally drew a line on the map, reducing the pier by five yards, and wondered would the County Surveyor let him get away with it.

"Well, the question is will you be satisfied with the Indian lamb? What colour did you say it is? Black? That's a very queer lamb."

Irritably he rubbed out the line. The wretched thing would be too shallow at low water if he cut five yards off it.

"It's dyed. You could get it brown, too," she cried. "You could get all sorts of lamb. Broadtail is the fur of unborn Persian lambs."

That woke him up: the good farmer stock in him was shocked.

"Unborn lambs," he cried; "do you mean to say that they . . ."

"Yes, isn't it awful? Honest to Heaven, Paddy, anyone that'd wear broadtail ought to be put in prison. Paddy, I've made up my mind. I just couldn't buy a fur coat. I just won't buy it. That's the end of it."

She picked up the pyjamas again and looked at them with moist eyes. He turned to devote his full attention to her problem.

"Molly, darling, I'm afraid I don't understand what you're after. I mean, do you or do you not want a fur coat? I mean, supposing you didn't buy a fur coat, what else could you do?"

"Just exactly what do you mean?"—very coldly.

"I mean, it isn't apparently necessary that you should buy a fur coat. I mean, not if you don't really want to. There must be some other way of dressing besides fur coats? If you have a scunner against fur coats, why not buy something else just as good? There's hundreds of millions of other women in the world and they all haven't fur coats."

"I've told you before that they dress! And I've no time to dress. I've explained all that to you."

Maguire got up. He put his back to the fire, his hands behind him, a judicial look on him. He addressed the room.

"All the other women in the world can't all have time to dress. There must be some way out of it. For example, next month there'll be a garden party up at the President's house. How many of all these women will be wearing fur coats?" He addressed the armchair. "Has Mrs. de Valera time to dress?" He turned and leaned over the turf basket. "Has Mrs. General Mulcahy time to dress? There's ways and means of doing everything." (He shot a quick glance at the map of the pier; you could always knock a couple of feet off the width of it.) "After all, you've told me yourself that you could purchase a black costume for twenty-five guineas. Is that or is that not a fact? Very well then," triumphantly, "why not buy a black costume for twenty-five guineas?"

"Because, you big fathead, I'd have to have shoes and a blouse and hat and gloves and a fur and a purse and everything to match it, and I'd spend far more in the heel of the hunt, and I haven't time for that sort of thing, and I'd have to have two or three costumes— Heaven above, I can't appear day after day in the same old rig, can I?"

"Good! Good! That's settled. Now, the question is: Shall we or shall we not purchase a fur coat? Now! What is to be said for a fur coat?" He marked off the points on his fingers. "Number one: it is warm. Number two: it will keep you from getting cold. Number three: . . ."

Molly jumped up, let a scream out of her and hurled the basket of mending at him.

"Stop it! I told you I don't want a fur coat! And you don't want me to get a fur coat! You're too mean, that's what it is! And like all the Irish, you have the peasant streak in you. You're all alike, every bloody wan of ye. Keep your rotten fur coat. I never wanted it. . . ."

And she ran from the room, sobbing with fury and disappointment.

"Mean?" gasped Maguire to himself. "To think that anybody could say that I . . . Mean!"

She burst open the door to sob,

"I'll go to the garden party in a mackintosh. And I hope that'll satisfy you!" and ran out again.

He sat miserably at his table, cold with anger. He murmured the hateful word over and over, and wondered could there be any truth in it. He added ten yards to the pier. He reduced the ten to five, and then, seeing what he had done, swept the whole thing off the table.

It took them three days to make it up. She had hit him below the belt, and they both knew it. On the fourth morning she found a cheque for a hundred and fifty pounds on her dressing table. For a moment her heart leaped. The next moment it died in her. She went down and put her arms about his neck and laid the cheque, torn in four, into his hand.

"I'm sorry, Paddy," she begged, crying like a kid. "You're not mean. You never were. It's me that's mean."

"You! Mean?" he said, fondly holding her in his arms.

"No, I'm not mean. It's not that. I just haven't the heart, Paddy. It was knocked out of me donkeys' years ago." He looked at her sadly. "You know what I'm trying to say?"

He nodded. But she saw that he didn't. She was not sure that she knew herself. He took a deep, resolving breath, held her out from him by the shoulders, and looked her straight in the eyes. "Molly. Tell me the truth. You want this coat?"

"I do. O, God, I do!"

"Then go out and buy it."

"I couldn't, Paddy. I just couldn't."

He looked at her for a long time. Then he asked,

"Why?"

She looked straight at him, and shaking her head sadly, she said in a little sobbing voice,

"I don't know."

Comment

Art conceals art effectively in this example. The opening situation is at once familiar and amusing. The wife of a rising politician asks her husband for a fur coat. The dialogue bounces back and forth, flashing with humor, wit, pathos, and the bitter wisdom of experience. Molly's "I must have a fur coat" is her beginning statement. At the end she refuses the money. She still wants the fur coat with all her heart, but she can't bring herself to buy it. "Why?" her husband asks. "I don't know," she responds.

Between the beginning and the end much happens to explain the change. If Molly doesn't know why she can't bring herself to buy the coat, the reader does. For she has revealed herself thoroughly in her own thoughts and speech. She has talked herself out of the coat.

Note the following sequence of statements:

1. "Now, Paddy, I must have a fur coat." Molly expresses her unexamined wish.
2. "You think I'm extravagant!" Molly's caution and hereditary frugality begin to assert themselves.
3. "Paddy! About that fur coat. I sincerely hope you don't think I'm being *vulgar?*" Molly's middle-class social background rises to join her deep-rooted prudence in opposing her own wish.
4. "The last thing that I want anybody to start thinking is that I, by any possible chance, could be getting grand notions." Molly begins to worry about other people's opinions.
5. "You don't want me to get a fur coat. . . . I'll go to the garden party in a mackintosh." Molly's frustration is the result of her feminine instinct at war with her common sense, of her wanting her husband to want her to get the coat.
6. "No, I'm not mean. It's not that. I just haven't the heart, Paddy. It was knocked out of me donkeys' years ago."

Thus Molly's common sense prevails, but not without one final gasp from the young girl that lies hidden within her.

"Molly. Tell me the truth. You want this coat?" Paddy plies her with his blundering good will.
"I do. O, God, I do!"

But the fur coat is as lost to Molly as her childhood.

Note too how O'Faolain maintains suspense throughout this story. At least a dozen times Molly changes her mind about the fur coat. The reader is kept waiting for the final decision until the last line.

Analysis and Composition

1. Write an expository essay on "The Fur Coat." In writing your essay use the outline at the end of the introduction to this section.
2. Compare the point of view used in this story with that used in "The Lagoon." Show how the point of view in each story is determined by the theme.
3. Decide whether this story is basically serious or comic in purpose. Give reasons for your answer.
4. Show in detail how the dialogue in this story advances the action as well as characterizes the speakers.
5. Decide whether the references to Ireland are sufficiently clear to a non-Irish reader.

3. High Lonesome Place

BY FRED GIPSON

1 It come to me that morning in the cornfield that this was the time to go. Before I'd hoed to the end of my first row I knowed I couldn't put it off no longer. I had to go to the mountain.

2 It was the kind of a day, I guess, a prowling sort of May morning that was fresh and alive with soft stirrings. Dewdrops hung like white beads from the tips of the corn blades; they fell in showers from the careless weeds I cut, wetting my bare feet and making them cool. Out on the prairies the blue quail called from the tall grass. In the sky big restless thunderheads milled, threatening rain.

3 And out yonder on the rim of the world stood the round, flat-topped mountain, tall and blue in the distance, calling, "Come on, Cotton! Come on!"

4 It was Saturday morning. At daylight Papa had hitched his work mules to the wagon and pulled out to town for provender. And while I finished breakfast Mama was getting set to spend the day inside, working up a bolt of dress goods she'd laid off a month ago. Nobody would miss me before dinnertime, anyhow.

5 I thought about those big careless weeds that needed cutting. I thought of the hiding Papa would give me when I got back. I'd pestered Papa about going to the mountain before, and he'd said I was too little. He'd said, "Cotton, you get to prowling way off from home like that and I'll set the seat of your britches to smoking!" And he'd do it, too; there wasn't any bluff to Papa.

6 These thoughts come to my mind and didn't no more dent it than the shadow of a buzzard's wing dents the prairie. From the time five years back when I'd climbed to the top of that sun-hard manure pile in the cow lot and got my first look at the mountain shivering in the heat waves, I'd knowed the time would come when I'd have to go prowl it. And now it was here. The weeds could take the corn and Papa could wear my tail end down to the bones, but I still had to go.

7 Time I finished out the row, I was cutting weeds almost in a run.

I was that anxious to get gone. I pitched my hoe down and scooted under the fence.

8 The prairie grass stood tall on the other side, almost up to the frazzled brim of my straw hat. I stood in it and looked back toward the house once, then took out along a cow trail that wound in and out of a cut-banked draw toward some water hole out on the prairie.

9 The trail dust was soft and powdery underfoot. It held the tracks of the wild things fine. A fox had been along there last night, and an old muddle-headed possum. And farther on I saw where a big old he-coon had followed this trail awhile, leaving tracks you couldn't have told from a year-old baby's. Come winter, I'd trap some of them scamps. Get me some Christmas money!

10 Off to the side of the trail stood a scrubby mesquite with a road runner sitting in the top of it. That old bird waited till I was close enough to suit him, then flew out and lit in the trail to run it ahead of me. I watched how smooth he ran and thought how ragged-looking he flew and wondered why that old lizard eater ever bothered to fly at all. Seemed like I'd be ashamed to fly at all, if I couldn't beat what he done.

11 His tracks in the dust looked just like the letter K in my school-book, only the right one was turned around backwards.

12 I slowed down to see if he wanted to play, and he did. About fifty steps ahead, he slowed down, too. I stopped, and he stopped. He cocked an eye over his back till I got set and made a run at him, then he lifted his wings a little and really toed the dust. But when I slowed to a trot he slowed up, too, keeping just about the same safe distance ahead.

13 He led me better than a mile. Then he came to a fork in the trail and stopped, trying to make up his mind which one I aimed to take. I kept coming, crowding him, and finally he headed up the trail to the left, the one that stayed with the draw. When I got to the fork I made like I aimed to follow, then cut to the right and ran, hollering and laughing. Sure had me a big joke on that old road runner.

14 Where this trail topped the next rise of the prairie I got side-tracked into the tall grass by a clicking, rustling sound. I didn't know what it was. I stalked it plenty careful, all set to duck for cover in case it was something scary. But it was just a couple of old dry-land ter-rapins fighting.

15 I guess they was fighting; I don't know for sure. They was just

going round and round in their heavy, slow way, each one trying to shove a horny head under the other. Best I could tell, what they had in mind was to turn each other upside down.

16 They didn't pay me no mind and I got closer and closer, and finally squatted down on my heels right over them, nearly. I wanted to see what come next, after one had finally put the other one on his back.

17 But I never did learn. The fight went on and on till I was tired and the sun got to burning my back and I recollected the mountain again. That jerked me to my feet, and the terrapins saw me. Both stopped and lifted their heads and stared at me and then set to sneaking back into their shells.

18 I was through with them, anyhow. I was looking toward the mountain. Seemed like it ought to be closer, now that I'd come so far. I looked back toward the house. I was a long ways off, all right. I guessed this mountain was just farther away than I figured. Better get to humping it if I aimed to make it there and back today.

19 I set a straight course and held it, walking steady. I kept my mind right on the mountain so I wouldn't hear or see nothing else and piddle off a lot of time. I didn't aim to stop again, but I did.

20 It was a big old tarantula. We met in a bend in the trail, and I come close to jumping out from under my hat, trying to keep from setting a foot on him. He fell back, too, a big old black-legged booger, all shaggy with yellow hair. He lifted up some front legs and waved them at me, daring me to come on. But I wouldn't take him up on it.

21 Ojeno Morales, the Macy outfit's sheepherder, he'd told me one time how a tarantula-bit Mexican swelled up and turned blue all over and died with the slobbering fits. I guessed that was a lie—Ojeno's yarns mostly were. But I wasn't taking no chances.

22 I backed up and got me a rock to bust him with, but I was too late. The biggest kind of a wasp-looking thing beat me to it. He had a black body and yellow wings, and he dipped down out of nowhere and lit in the middle of the tarantula and humped his back and socked a stinger right into the big spider.

23 That stinger must have been red hot, from the fits that tarantula started having. He jumped this way and that and tried to claw the air with every foot at the same time. But the big wasp had done turned him loose and was circling in the air above him. The tarantula kept

running in circles till the poison hit him good, then he stopped and had a chill and finally started drawing his shaking legs in close to his body.

24 Right there before my eyes that old tarantula just shriveled up to nearly nothing. And that's when the big wasp with the yellow wings come in and picked him up and flew off with him.

25 I'd never seen a sight like that before. I stood and watched till the wasp and his tarantula was nothing but a black speck in the air; then I went on, feeling good all over. I'd seen a thing today that grown folks would listen to the telling of.

26 That mountain, it was a sneaky thing, the way it kept moving off ahead of me. Worse than that old road runner. I walked and I walked, and I still couldn't tell for sure that I was any closer. Finally I played a trick on it, too. I'd set my course and start walking, looking in every direction but toward the mountain. That way, when I'd kept my eyes off it long enough and then looked, I could tell I was gaining.

27 The sun got hotter and hotter, and the sweat started running down back of my ears, and I got thirsty, and still the mountain was a long ways off. I knowed if I kept going I'd get there; so I kept going, but I sure didn't like to think about how far I was getting from that old cedar water bucket on the front gallery. And Mama's kitchen table. A chunk of corn bread crumbled into a glass of sweet milk would sure taste good right now.

28 The trail dust got so hot that I had to pick grass-shaded spots to step in or run fast where there wasn't any, and it was 'way past dinnertime when I finally come to the last long slant that led up to the foot of the mountain.

29 I stopped and looked up to the top of it and forgot how wore out and thirsty I was. I could feel my heart kicking hard against my ribs. Maybe it wasn't much of a mountain. Maybe it was nearer just being a hill. But it looked like a terrible big mountain to me. It was taller even than the cottonwood growing beside the pond at home. And I'd never seen anything before as tall as that old cottonwood.

30 Big old spread-topped live oaks ringed the foot of the mountain and leaned against it, like they was tired, and up out of the middle of this ring reared the ragged slopes, getting steeper and steeper till they were finally capped off by a solid layer of limestone rock thicker than I was tall.

31 Here and there big slabs of cap rock had broke off and tumbled part way down the slopes, where they'd lodged and made traps for dirt that scrub brush and wild flowers could grow in. There was sweet williams and bluebonnets and pale pink primroses, all blooming together. And where a bunch of tall grass had got a foothold it grew higher there than out on the prairies.

32 It was a wild and shaggy-looking place, but big and grand and pretty, too, so that, going up to it, I had the sort of quiet, scared feeling I get sometimes going into a big church.

33 I left the hot sun and went into a scooped-out place under the trees where the twisted limbs of the live oaks made a solid arched roof over a shallow pool of seep-spring water. I felt the shade laying cool on me and lifted off my sweaty hat—and then scare-jumped ten feet to one side at a sudden booming roar and the threshing of low tree limbs.

34 A big shadowy thing whipped through a thicket of blooming buckeye and another shot directly over my head, so low that I had to duck, and both of them were gone before it come to me that I'd jumped a couple of wild turkey hens.

35 They'd nearly scared me out of my britches, them old turkey hens had, and I sure felt silly for a little bit, trying to get my breath back and thinking how jumpy I'd been. Then I heard the leaves rustling and some low, faint cheepings and hurried around the pool to investigate. But I wasn't quick enough. Already them little old baby turkeys had melted out of sight under bits of tree bark and dry leaves and wisps of grass.

36 I wanted to look for them. I'd held baby chickens and baby quail, and I'd love to catch one of them little old bitty turkeys and feel the warm softness of him in my hands. But I turned and went back to the pool. If I got to poking around here now, I knowed what'd happen —I'd trample one of the little old boogers and kill it.

37 I bellied down at the pool and got me a long drink and washed my face, then sat on the bank and worked my hot feet down into the coolness of the red mud at the bottom. I told myself that I wouldn't stay long. I'd get up and move on pretty quick and give them old turkey hens a chance to come back and collect their broods.

38 But this was such a hidden, secrety sort of place that I hated to leave. I never had before felt so all by myself and still not lonesome

either. I stayed a long time, making like I was the only person that'd ever been here, that nobody but me and the wild things knew about this place.

39 When I finally left the shade and stood right at the foot of the tall ragged slopes lifting almost straight up to the cap rock above, I got that churchy feeling again. It made me about half-scared to climb up, and yet crazy wild to stand on top and see what it was like. I waited till my heart quit thumping so hard, then caught hold of the butt of a wild persimmon bush and started climbing.

40 It wasn't such a hard climb. I stuck with a backbone ridge, and there was always a bush or a rock or a clump of tall grass for hand and toe holds. But where I reached the cap rock it was overhanging a little, and I had to circle it a piece to find a break I could climb through. The slope was steeper there, and my feet started little land-slides of crumbling dirt and loose rocks. They slid and rattled down through the brush and got bigger and louder as they went, and once one of the big rock slabs just needed my weight on it to start it slipping.

41 I felt it give under me and jumped and grabbed a scrub cedar and held on for life while that big boulder picked up speed and went crashing and pitching end over end toward the bottom, where it snapped off big live-oak saplings before it slammed to a stop against a tree with a trunk the size of a sugar barrel.

42 That was sure a close one, and I had to sit there, holding to the cedar bush a long time before I could rake up the nerve to climb up through the break I'd picked out in the cap rock.

43 Then I was on top at last, and one look at how high I was and how big the world was around me took my breath away and made me want to grab something and hold to it to steady myself.

44 I heard a slithering sound on the rock underfoot and turned to look. It was a mountain boomer lizard. I'd scared him, and he was sure hotfooting it for a crack in the edge of the cap rock behind me. He slid to a stop right at the edge of the crack and lay there with his long tail curled and waving and the bright orange and green of his new spring coat shining against the gray of the stone. He studied me for a minute, didn't like my looks, and darted over the edge, clinking a loose stone as he went.

45 That's how I found the spear point. It lay right at the edge of

the crack, and that old mountain boomer had come within a hair of knocking it off into that crack with him.

46 I went to pick it up, half-scared to believe my eyes. But that's what it was, a real flint spear point that a real wild Indian had brought and lost on the mountain at some time too long back to think about. It was long as my hand, liver-colored, with chipped edges sharp as ever, and polished glass-smooth all over.

47 I held it and looked at it and rubbed its smooth sides between my hands. Here for once was something that was all mine, a finer thing than I'd ever hoped to own. It wasn't an old empty medicine bottle or a broken-bladed pocket knife or a short length of frazzled rope—stuff that grown people can't use any more and turn over to kids for playthings. It wasn't even a toy like you get for Christmas and get to wind up a few times before the spring breaks and it won't work again.

48 This was a thing that would last forever, and no man living now had ever seen it. For no telling how many hundred years it had been laying right up here on the edge of the cap rock, waiting for the time when I'd get born and come and find it. Up here on the mountain I'd found a treasure!

49 I stood and held my spear point and looked across the grassy prairies, reaching out to the sky line. Away to the south, toward home, a cloud broke, spilling out a lacy blue curtain of rain. Closer, a little two-bit cyclone dropped out of the air and exploded the prairie dust like a stick of dynamite under a mesquite stump. It whirled away, spouting skyward a mile-high column of brown dust and prairie litter. And all around, the heat waves shimmered and danced.

50 I stood and watched and a big aching hurt came and kept swelling inside me till it finally burst and I was as lightheaded and giddy as the time one of the Macy cow hands brought Papa a jug of agerita-berry wine and I sneaked it out to the barn and tasted too long. For a time there, I wasn't a ten-year-old farm boy with two-colored hair and a trail of freckles across my nose. I was a bold, proud Indian warrior with painted head feathers and gripping a long spear with a point of liver-colored flint.

51 It was long after dark when I got home, and I'd never have found it if it hadn't been for the yellow lamplight shining out of the cabin window. I was so hungry I was cramping and so tired I could

have dropped down and slept in my tracks. I went past the cow lot and stopped at the front-yard gate when I heard Papa outside in the dark.

52 "He'll be all right, Mag," I heard him tell Mama. "He'll be all right. We'll find him. I'll ride over and get the Macy hands to help."

53 I heard the slap of leather and the stamp of a hoof and knowed Papa was saddling up a horse. Mama come and stood in the lighted doorway, and I could see that she'd been crying.

54 "I know, Jess," she said. "He'll be all right."

55 But the way she said it made me think of the time when the hoppers got the crop and Papa'd gone out and tried for a job to buy winter rations with and hadn't got it and Mama'd said, "We'll make out all right, Jess!" Even when she knowed we couldn't unless something turned up.

56 That give me a cold, jumpy feeling in my stomach. I hadn't thought of this. I hadn't aimed to scare them. I'd figured on a whipping for running off, but I sure hadn't bargained on scaring them.

57 I stepped into a patch of lamplight in the yard and said, "Here I am, Papa."

58 I tried to say it like I'd just been out to the cow lot and back, but it didn't sound that way. I heard Papa grunt in the dark and then here come Mama, saying, "Oh, Cotton! Oh, Cotton!" Over and over she said it, even after she'd got her hands on me and was hurrying me inside the house. She was crying again.

59 Papa come and stood in the door and looked at me, and his face was all red and there was a set to his jaws that I'd seen before. He slapped a pair of bridle reins against his legs and said: "Where you been, boy?"

60 I pulled away from Mama and wiped her tears off the back of my neck and said, "I went to the mountain."

61 "To the mountain!" Papa said. "You mean you run off and went all the way to that mountain by yourself?"

62 "Yes, sir," I said. "I couldn't hold off no longer. I just had to go!"

63 He stared at me and his face got redder. "You know what you got coming to you?"

64 "Yes, sir." I walked to the door and out into the dark yard.

65 Behind me I heard Mama beg, "Oh, Jess!"

66 "Confound hit, Mag, you know I've got hit to do!" Papa said,

and come out and got hold of my shirt collar and went to work on me with the bridle reins.

67 It was sure bad. It was worse even than I'd thought it would be. But I did my best not to jump and holler and twist around, like I usually did, because I knew I had this one coming. I gripped my spear point tight and did my best to think of the trip to the mountain instead of the stinging lash of those bridle reins.

68 After a while it was over, and I sure felt better. It's a mighty heavy load on a body, waiting to take a whipping they know is coming.

69 I felt a lot better when we went into the house. I was paid off now. The price had been high, but that trip to the mountain had been worth a dozen whippings.

70 Then I looked up at Mama and didn't feel so good. She was sitting in a chair back of the kitchen table now, with her eyes red and raw from crying and her pretty mouth all twisted up and pulled out of shape. There was a sort of lost, hurt look in her eyes, too, that I'd never seen there before.

71 I sat down to the cold supper she had laid out for me. But I couldn't eat a bite. I'd been mighty hungry when I came in, but now that look in Mama's eyes took my appetite.

72 I couldn't understand it. I'd taken my whipping; everything ought to be all right now. Why did Mama keep looking at me that way?

73 While I piddled with my biscuits and bacon and syrup, it come to me gradually what was the matter. Mama had been scared sick— so scared about me that she couldn't get over it!

74 I hadn't bargained for that. I hadn't once thought what I might be doing to Mama. It looked like I was a long way from being paid off yet.

75 When I finally thought of it my stomach balled up into a hard knot. But I was still willing—if it'd make things right with Mama.

76 I got up and took my spear point out of my pocket. I laid it on the table in front of her. "Here, Mama," I said. "Here's something I brought you from the mountain."

77 Mama glanced at it and then away, as if it didn't amount to a thing. That look stayed in her eyes.

78 I couldn't believe it. I'd given her the finest thing I'd ever had, and it still wasn't enough!

79 Suddenly she put her head down on her arms and went to crying. "It's all right, Son," she said. "I'm just crying for—well, I guess

it's for the baby I've lost. Seems like you just went and growed up before it come to my notice."

80 I tried to figure it all out that night while I lay in the dark on my corn-shuck mattress. But I never did. I couldn't see why Mama was so hurt about everything. I sure hadn't meant to hurt her. It was just that—well, when the high lonesome places get to calling, seems like a body's nearly got to go.

Comment

This example is a borderline story. It resembles a simple autobiographical narrative, such as "Flash Flood" and "Lost Retreat" (Section XIII), rather than the other two examples in this section. But it differs from Miss Roberts' account of her trip to the Apache reservation and Hal Borland's narrative of his visit to another high lonesome place because it is primarily fictional. The author speaks not in his own person but in the person of a character that is at least in part created.

The central situation here is posed in the first five paragraphs. Cotton decides to visit the mountain despite his father's warning. What will he discover? This discovery is the theme of the story.

He finds a world of sights and sensations outside himself, things "that grown folks would listen to the telling of," and within, a few scares and a crazy wild feeling of adventure. He begins to realize that he has grown up.

Especially interesting in this story is the author's handling of point of view. The narrator, a young boy of ten, is only partly aware of what is happening to him. He does not fully appreciate his father's solicitude, his own sudden loss of exhilaration and appetite at the "lost, hurt look" in his mother's eyes. Yet the reader is thoroughly aware of all these things and more besides. This awareness is traceable to a unique handling of point of view. We see the story through Cotton's eyes, but the author too is subtly present. We recognize this in the style. Cotton's prose is sometimes a little too firm, too finely balanced, too keenly poised and tense to be accepted as the diction of a child. Again, although the story is told as if it had occurred in the immediate past, it has a retrospective flavor. It is the past recaptured, the memory of youth by an older man clinging to his beginnings without, it should be mentioned admiringly, becoming childish in the process.

This story derives much of its excitement from its *atmosphere* rather than from the plot. As in "Lost Retreat" (Section XIII), the high lonesome place is a refuge of the spirit as well as an actual place. It is the rim of the world, "a hidden, secrety sort of place," where a man senses intimations of immortality, or, in Cotton's homely phrase, "churchy" feelings.

Another compensation for this story's lack of a complicated plot is the excellence of the descriptions. Cotton's animated observations of the road runner, the fight of the dry-land terrapins, the contest between the wasp and the tarantula, the wild turkey hens and their brood, the mountain lizard, the "two-bit" cyclone sweeping the prairie—all blend into the narrative movement.

Analysis and Composition

1. Is the central situation of this story meaningful in the sense that this term was defined in the introduction? Give reasons for your answer.
2. Decide whether this story lacks tension and suspense. (See the introduction to Section XIII.)
3. In a paragraph of 300 words describe Cotton's character.
4. Do you have a clear picture of the character of Cotton's mother and father? What methods of characterization does the author use in developing them?
5. Does this story have (a) a turning point and (b) a climax? If it does, explain. If it does not, argue in an essay of 1000 words whether this story should be considered a short story in the light of the principles advanced in the introduction to this section.
6. This example contains numerous expressions which handbooks list as illiterate, dialectal, and colloquial.* List three expressions in each group. Decide whether the theme, point of view, and setting of the story justify the use of these expressions.
7. Show how the expressions listed below contribute to one or more of the following purposes: the characterization of Cotton; the atmosphere of the story; the dramatization of the action.
   a. "A prowling sort of May morning" (¶2)
   b. "Big restless thunderheads milled, threatening rain" (¶2)
   c. "That mountain, it was a sneaky thing" (¶26)
   d. "I felt the shade laying cool on me" (¶33)
   e. "This was a thing that would last forever, and no man living now had ever seen it" (¶48)
   f. "Spilling out a lacy blue curtain of rain" (¶49)
   g. "A little two-bit cyclone dropped out of the air and exploded the prairie dust" (¶49)
   h. "My stomach balled up into a hard knot" (¶75)
   i. "Here's something I brought you from the mountain" (¶76)
8. In 750 words compare the emotional effect of this example and that of "Lost Retreat" (Section XIII, General Exercise B).

* Foerster, pp. 91-94; 300-02; Hodges, pp. 193-201; Kierzek, *38*; Perrin, pp. 37-54; Wykoff, *82-88*.

GENERAL EXERCISES

A

Draw up a plot outline involving an exposition, complication, turning point, climax, and resolution based on the narrative *"Trigger"* (Section XIII, Example 1).

B

Outline a plot suitable for a short story, based on "The Fatal Hudson River Steamboat Race," from the firsthand point of view of an observer (Section XIII, Example 2).

C

Study Example 4 in Section XIII. In 2000 words attempt to tell one phase of the story of the Huron massacre from the point of view of one of the survivors.

D

Outline a short story, based on General Exercise B in Section XIII, as told in the third person from the point of view of an *ironic* or *cynical* observer.

E

Attempt to tell the story related by Thackeray in General Exercise D, Section XIII, in the first person from the point of view of Rawdon Crawley, Jr.

F

In about 2000 words retell the story of the *Graf Spee* (General Exercise A in Section XIII) in dialogue from the point of view of two sailors of Winston Churchill's personal guard.

G

As directed by your instructor, read an anthology of short stories or a volume of short stories by a single author. Report on three stories according to the outline in the introduction to this section.

H

Using Example 3 as a model, draw up a plan for an original personal adventure tale of 3500 words. Be careful to select for your initial situation one that involves action and emotional excitement on the part of your main character. The subject, theme, and background should reflect your own immediate experience.

I

Using Example 2 as a model, draw up a plan for an original story of approximately 3500 words to be told largely by dialogue. Be careful to provide for dialogue that will

1. Advance the action
2. Be consistent with the character
3. Be natural to the situation or occasion
4. Be as brief as possible

J

Using Example 1 as a model, draw up a plan for an original story of 3500 words combining a third-person point of view and a first-person point of view. Be careful to establish the connection between the two points of view.

K

Write a short story based on one of the outlines prepared in accordance with the directions given in Exercises A, B, D, H, I, and J. Before preparing your manuscript consult your handbook for the paragraphing of dialogue * and the use of quotation marks.

* Foerster, *28*; Hodges, p. 337; Kierzek, *24*; Perrin, pp. 722-23; Wykoff, *25, 52c*.

**SECTION
XV**

The Informal Essay:
Personality and Style

IN its broadest sense an essay is a brief prose composition that combines several forms of discourse to communicate the author's ideas and impressions. Hence one way to classify the essay is to describe it as expository, argumentative, persuasive, descriptive, or narrative, depending upon the principal aim of the writer. According to the above definition and classification, the complete examples from Section III to XI A are all essays, and the smaller selections in Sections II-VII are parts of essays.*

THE FORMAL AND INFORMAL ESSAY

Another way of classifying the essay is to determine its range and scale, that is, to place it between the treatise or scientific study on the

---

* A partial breakdown of the essays contained in this book is listed here for the convenience of the student.

A. Essays predominantly expository
   Section III: "On Weekend Guests" by Russell Lynes
             "Paleface and Redskin" by Philip Rahv
   Section V: "America and Europe" by Aldous Huxley
   Section VII: "The Method of Scientific Investigation" by T. H. Huxley
   Section VIII: "The Meaning of America in the World Today" by Charles Malik
   The nine examples in Sections IX and X
B. Essays predominantly argumentative and persuasive
   Section IV: "Fenimore Cooper's Literary Offenses" by Mark Twain

[Continued on page 702]

701

one hand and pure narrative and fiction on the other. At one end of
the scale, touching the field of the treatise or scientific study, is the
formal essay. At the other end, adjacent to first-person narrative, is the
informal or *personal* essay. Between the two are many shades of the
formal and personal essay. Some essays, for instance, are formal in
structure and informal in style, like Phyllis McGinley's "Suburbia:
Of Thee I Sing." Others, like E. B. White's "Book Learning," are predominantly informal, but are subtly harmonized with the principles
of logic.

A *formal* essay, like the oration from which it stems, tends to follow
the logical rules of discourse—to state and develop a central theme according to the principles of unity, coherence, and emphasis (see Sections VIII-XI). It aims to communicate an important idea through a
logical arrangement of the theme. Its diction tends to be literary rather
than colloquial, and its tone is usually serious. But its style is not wholly
impersonal. However objective the logical structure may be, the style
bears the unmistakable impression of the author's personality, as the
formal expository essays in Section X have demonstrated.

At the other end of the scale, the *informal* essay tends to adapt the
rules of logical discourse freely, that is, to suit the logical rules of discourse to the personal mood or feeling of the writer. An informal essay
does not lack distinctive form, by which is meant structure and style.
If it did it would be meaningless. But the "form" of the informal essay
tends to be organic, or psychological, rather than strictly logical. Since
it mirrors the fluent subjective attitudes of the writer's mind rather
than fixed definitions, propositions, and reasonings, its structure and
style are more flexible and resilient than those of the formal essay.
It is, writes Irwin Edman, "the relaxed meditation, the causerie with
edge, elegance, and beauty." Charles Lamb writing a chapter on ears,
Hazlitt reminiscing on a walking tour, Stevenson describing his travels
with a donkey do not set forth skeleton proofs of their impressions.

[Continued from page 701]
    Section VIII: "Perennial Adolescence" by B. I. Bell
    The five examples in XI A
C. Essays predominantly narrative or descriptive
    Section IV: "Book Learning" by E. B. White
    Section XII: "A Japanese Home" by James A. Michener
    Section XII: "Flight over the Wilderness" by Laurens Van der Post
    Section XIII, General Exercises: "Lost Retreat" by Hal Borland

The majority of the shorter selections in Sections II-VII are excerpts from essays. The
student may find it interesting to classify these shorter selections in the same manner
as the complete essays are classified above.

Rather do they let their observations, their moods, their experiences form a pattern of their own. These patterns may be as fanciful as the quilt of clouds on a summer day or as sinuous as the rhythmical drift of a conversation that starts out discussing pretzels and winds up expounding Kant.

Our own study in the previous sections has stressed the formal, expository, and argumentative essay rather than the personal, informal essay because we were primarily concerned with explaining the principles of logical expression, the basic rules of discourse that are needed in the everyday life of the college-trained individual.* In this section, however, we shall investigate several examples of the informal essay (1) to complete our study of this type of composition and (2) to show the important connection between a writer's personality and his style. For the informal essay, by its very nature, stresses the personal style of a writer and thus leads us to our summary discussion of style, the fourth and final element in rhetoric.

PERSONAL STYLE IN THE INFORMAL ESSAY

Both the formal and informal essay, as we have observed, are brief prose compositions that combine several forms of discourse to communicate the author's ideas and impressions. The informal essay differs from the formal essay by its greater freedom of structure and its greater emphasis on the personality of the author. The difference between them stems from their distinctive purposes, occasions, and subjects.

Thus a formal essay, such as Barbara Ward's "Faith for Freedom" (Section X), presents a complex subject, is serious in tone, logical in structure, literary in style. E. B. White's "Book Learning" (Section IV), on the other hand, presents a simple subject, is colloquial in tone, informal in structure, idiomatic in style.

But both types of essays—and all good writing except specifically scientific prose—personalize the subject and echo the voice of the author. Even in oratory of a formal kind, such as Churchill's "Save Europe by Uniting Europe" (Example XI B1), the personality of the author is unmistakable. Churchill's characteristic diction and imagery, the peculiar structure and rhythm of his sentences, the distinctive

---

* The student has tasted the flavor of the informal essay in the selections from Peter Fleming (Sections III and V), from Addison (Section III), and from J. B. Priestley (Section IV), as well as in the essays by E. B. White and F. P. Adams (Section IV), and other selections.

cadence and variety of his paragraphs distinguish his utterance from
that of others. The tone, that is, Churchill's attitude to his audience
and his own emotional sense of his subject, is also clearly defined.
Even when we read the speech without recalling Churchill's elocution,
an unmistakable Churchillian ring identifies the prose. The language
echoes a distinct personality, a mind alive and moving in its own
characteristic rhythm. So too, Plato and Lincoln and Dickens each
possesses an unmistakable "voice." If each of them wrote about some
neutral subject like the weather, we feel certain we could identify their
several utterances by some word or phrase or manner of expression.

The personal style evident in all writing is accentuated in the informal or personal essay. The student has already observed this in his
previous readings. We distinguish Addison's "What Is a Pedant?" (Section III) from a purely logical discussion of pedantry by Addison's
easy, familiar tone—the sound of his voice. We separate J. B. Priestley's
"The Delighted Eye" (Section XII) from routine travel description
by the personal note of delight. We set apart E. B. White's "Book
Learning" from the usual homespun anecdote by the personal accent
in his essay. We remember these informal essays chiefly because of the
personality of the writer, whereas we remember the more formal
essays chiefly because of the idea or argument they set forth. The informal essay amuses, entertains, stimulates by establishing a familiar
personal relationship with the reader.

The personality of the good informal essayist is necessarily full,
generous, and flexible. His ideas flow spontaneously from an abundant
well of knowledge, not into the set channels of routine communication
but in the direction hinted by a questing wit, a prowling sense of humor, or a sympathizing spirit. At one time the writer of the personal
essay is the gracious tutor introducing the reader to his familiar
thoughts, at another a dinner guest amusing his host with anecdote
and tattle; at one time he is a grim and ironical satirist, at another
time, a cheerful sentimentalist singing the praises of good wine and
good companions. But at all times he is wholly and unmistakably *present as a person*. He is *all* there, and not merely in the character of a
public speaker or a man of ideas or a purveyor of information.

Thus in "Not Looking at Pictures" (Example 1 of this section)
E. M. Forster begins with a cultivated amateur's reflections on great
paintings. The speculation recalls particular visits to the art gallery
and the eternal problem of seeing a picture as it is rather than as it

appears to be in the interfering light of the spectator's preconceptions. As memory quickens, Forster recalls his experiments in applying the rules of composition and color to Titian and Velasquez. The result of the essay? The theme? Merely this: "I am learning to get myself out of the way a little, and to be more receptive, and my appreciation of pictures does increase." The reader has not learned very much, but he has shared a personal experience with a man of taste, good sense, and simple charm.

Neither is the reader likely to be "improved" by consulting Stephen Potter's "Gamesmanship" (Example 2), an essay that parodies scholarly writing at the same time that it reverses the traditional British notions of sportsmanship. Its sly, unemphatic humor is delightful for its own sake. To say that the humor is delightful is to sum up the meaning of the essay. And yet one would be hard put to it to explain how the delight is communicated. We *know* that Potter has pinned the donkey's tail on *homo sapiens,* but he did it while we were happily suspended in the rhythm of his archly declarative sentences. The mystery is never wholly explained by analyzing the author's purpose, method of development, or clarity of diction. We may recognize his underhanded appeal to humanity's perverse dislike of tall, athletic young men who set out to win every game; we may observe his gambit with phrases like "beautifully accurate," a cliché, which, in Potter's hands, flares into a delicately ironical play with words; we may be aware of his amusement with his own puppet, the narrator in the essay; but all this insight into method and device does not explain to us why we like the essay. We like it (some few may not), not because of Potter's artfulness but because of Potter's sense of humor.

In Example 3 Belloc also demonstrates the importance of personality and style in the informal essay. Although this essay is written in the first person, the narrator is not the author himself. He is rather an author's dummy, a Colonel Blimp among professors, the eternal rationalizer of contemporary prejudice, an admirer of the Nordic man. Mr. Belloc's professor is the British equivalent of the American who yearns to resemble the ineffable man of distinction in the magazine advertisements. Through his mouthpiece Belloc manages to achieve a double focus: he explains what the Nordic man is, and he also explains the mentality that accepts the myth of the Nordic man.

We would miss the point of "Talking (and Singing) of the Nordic

Man," however, if we were to regard it as a serious comment on the subject of racism. True, it is a satire on a form of Anglo-Saxon superciliousness that is based on bad history, bad science, and bad morals. But Belloc is not seriously relating English upper-class snobbery to its monstrous mother, racism. Rather is he enjoying the spectacle of the Nordic man playing the Ass with Bottom's solemn self-assurance. The essay is the personal expression of Hilaire Belloc, the cosmopolitan European laughing at Anglo-Saxon provincialism, the conservative intellectual proclaiming standards based on excellence of mind and spirit, the merciless wit delighting in the countless ironies of his cephalogian's ignorant erudition and irrational logic.

Just as E. M. Forster reveals himself as the cultivated liberal mind gently proposing the value of looking at pictures, and as Stephen Potter reveals himself as a prankish don amused by the absurdities of sports, so Belloc stands forth as the satirist of social snobbery and the defender of conservative values.

1. Not Looking at Pictures

BY E. M. FORSTER

1 Pictures are not easy to look at. They generate private fantasies, they furnish material for jokes, they recall scraps of historical knowledge, they show landscapes where one would like to wander and human beings whom one would like to resemble or adore, but looking at them is another matter; yet they must have been painted to be looked at. They were intended to appeal to the eye, but almost as if it were gazing at the sun itself the eye often reacts by closing as soon as it catches sight of them. The mind takes charge instead and goes off on some alien vision. The mind has such a congenial time that it forgets what set it going. Van Gogh and Corot and Michelangelo are three different painters, but if the mind is indisciplined and uncontrolled by the eye, they may all three induce the same mood; we may take just the same course through dreamland or funland from them, each time, and never experience anything new.

2 I am bad at looking at pictures myself, and the late Roger Fry

NOT LOOKING AT PICTURES: from *Two Cheers for Democracy,* copyright, 1951, by E. M. Forster. Reprinted by permission of Harcourt, Brace and Company, Inc., and also by permission of Edward Arnold & Co., London.

enjoyed going to a gallery with me now and then, for this very reason. He found it an amusing change to be with someone who scarcely ever saw what the painter had painted. "Tell me, why do you like this, why do you prefer it to that?" he would ask, and listen agape for the ridiculous answer. One day we looked at a fifteenth-century Italian predella, where a St. George was engaged in spearing a dragon of the plesiosaurus type. I laughed. "Now, *what* is there funny in this?" pounced Fry. I readily explained. The fun was to be found in the expression upon the dragon's face. The spear had gone through its hooped-up neck once, and now startled it by arriving at a second thickness. "Oh, dear, here it comes again; I hoped that was all," it was thinking. Fry laughed too, but not at the misfortunes of the dragon. He was amazed that anyone could go so completely off the lines. There was no harm in it—but really, really! He was even more amazed when our enthusiasms coincided: "I fancy we are talking about different things," he would say, and we always were; I liked the mountain back because it reminded me of a peacock, he because it had some structural significance, though not as much as the sack of potatoes in the foreground.

3 Long years of wandering down miles of galleries have convinced me that there must be something rare in those coloured slabs called "pictures," something which I am incapable of detecting for myself, though glimpses of it are to be had through the eyes of others. How much am I missing? And what? And are other modern sight-seers in the same fix? Ours is an aural rather than a visual age; we do not get so lost in the concert hall, we seem able to hear music for ourselves, and to hear it as music, but in galleries so many of us go off at once into a laugh or a sigh or an amorous daydream. In vain does the picture recall us. "What have your obsessions got to do with me?" it complains. "I am neither a theatre of varieties nor a spring mattress, but paint. Look at my paint." Back we go—the picture kindly standing still meanwhile, and being to that extent more obliging than music—and resume the looking business. But something is sure to intervene—a tress of hair, the half-open door of a summerhouse, a Crivelli dessert, a Bosch fish-and-fiend salad—and to draw us away.

4 One of the things that helps us to keep looking is composition. For many years now I have associated composition with a diagonal line, and when I find such a line I imagine I have gutted the picture's secret. Giorgione's "Castelfranco Madonna" has such a line in the

lance of the warrior-saint, and Titian's "Entombment at Venice" has a very good one indeed. Five figures contribute to make up the diagonal; beginning high on the left with the statue of Moses, it passes through the heads of the Magdalene, Mary, and the dead Christ, and plunges through the body of Joseph of Arimathea into the ground. Making a right angle to it flits the winged Genius of Burial. And to the right, apart from it, and perpendicular, balancing the Moses, towers the statue of Faith. Titian's "Entombment" is one of my easiest pictures. I look at photographs of it intelligently, and encourage the diagonal and the pathos to reinforce one another. I see, with more than usual vividness, the grim alcove at the back and the sinister tusked pedestals upon which the two statues stand. Stone shuts in flesh; the whole picture is a tomb. I hear sounds of lamentation, though not to the extent of shattering the general scheme; that is held together by the emphatic diagonal which no emotion breaks. Titian was a very old man when he achieved this masterpiece; that too I realise, but not immoderately. Composition here really has been a help, and it is a composition which no one can miss: the diagonal slopes as obviously as the band on a threshing machine, and vibrates with power.

5 Unfortunately, having no natural esthetic aptitude, I look for diagonals everywhere, and if I cannot find one think the composition must be at fault. It is a word which I have learnt—a solitary word in a foreign language. For instance, I was completely baffled by Velasquez' "Las Meniñas." Wherever was the diagonal? Then the friend I was with—Charles Mauron, the friend who, after Roger Fry, has helped me with pictures most—set to work on my behalf, and cautiously underlined the themes. There is a wave. There is a half-wave. The wave starts up on the left, with the head of the painter, and curves down and up through the heads of the three girls. The half-wave starts with the head of Isabel de Velasco, and sinks out of the canvas through the dwarfs. Responding to these great curves, or inverting them, are smaller ones on the women's dresses or elsewhere. All these waves are not merely pattern; they are doing other work too—e.g., helping to bring out the effect of depth in the room, and the effect of air. Important too is the pushing forward of objects in the extreme left and right foregrounds, the easel of the painter in the one case, the paws of a placid dog in the other. From these, the composition curves back to the central figure, the lovely child-princess.

I put it more crudely than did Charles Mauron, nor do I suppose that his account would have been Velasquez', or that Velasquez would have given any account at all. But it is an example of the way in which pictures should be tackled for the benefit of us outsiders: coolly and patiently, as if they were designs, so that we are helped at last to the appreciation of something nonmathematical. Here again, as in the case of the "Entombment," the composition and the action reinforced one another. I viewed with increasing joy that adorable party, which had been surprised not only by myself but by the king and queen of Spain. There they were in the looking glass! "Las Meniñas" has a snapshot quality. The party might have been taken by Philip IV, if Philip IV had had a Kodak. It is all so casual—and yet it is all so elaborate and sophisticated, and I suppose those curves and the rest of it help to bring this out, and to evoke a vanished civilisation.

6 Besides composition there is colour. I look for that too, but with even less success. Colour is visible when thrown in my face—like the two cherries in the great grey Michael Sweertz group in the National Gallery. But as a rule it is only material for dream.

7 On the whole, I am improving, and after all these years. I am learning to get myself out of the way a little, and to be more receptive, and my appreciation of pictures does increase. If I can make any progress at all, the average outsider should do better still. A combination of courage and modesty is what he wants. It is so unenterprising to annihilate everything that's made to a green thought, even when the thought is an exquisite one. Not looking at art leads to one goal only. Looking at it leads to so many.

Comment

Note that the structure of this essay is clearly indicated by the paragraph organization. Paragraph 1 deals with the difficulty of regarding pictures objectively. Pictures "were intended to appeal to the eye," but "the mind takes charge instead and goes off on some alien vision." Paragraph 2 gives examples of this difficulty. Paragraph 3 speculates on the reasons why the amateur viewer is so often distracted. Paragraph 4 explains how an elementary knowledge of "composition" helps one understand Titian's "Entombment." Paragraph 5 takes up a more complicated kind of composition in Velasquez' "Las Meniñas"—one in which composition and action reinforce each other. Paragraph 6 merely mentions that, in painting, color is an element whose function the author does not comprehend. This inconclusive explanation, which would be a grave fault in formal exposition, is a natural, sincere remark perfectly acceptable in the personal essay. Paragraph 7 states that the author has learned the value of receptivity and that, with courage and modesty, the average man could do better on this score.

Analysis and Composition

1. What is the significance of the title? To what extent does the title contribute to interest and suspense?
2. How does the structure of this essay differ from the formal expositions included in Sections VIII and IX? In working out your answer consider the following points:
   a. Beginning, middle, end
   b. Emphasis
   c. Clarity of allusion
3. What differences do you observe in the structure and rhythm of the sentences in this essay in contrast to Example IX C? What reasons serve to explain these differences? (See Section VIII for definitions of sentence structure and rhythm.)
4. Compare the diction and figurative language of this example with Example X B. If you discover that Example X B is richer in diction and figurative language, explain whether or not Example X B should be called a personal rather than a formal essay.
5. If Forster's purpose in this essay were purely expository what necessary changes would be required in structure and in style? Give reasons for your answer.
6. What is the general tone, or attitude, of this essay? Does this tone clash with the expository passage in paragraph 5? Give reasons for your answer.
7. Decide whether this essay, for full understanding, requires reproductions of the paintings the author discusses.
8. Write an informal essay of approximately 750 words on one of the following topics. Attempt to achieve a familiar tone such as Forster maintains in this example.

Listening to music	Looking at monuments
Visiting art museums	Watching the sunrise
Reading poetry	Looking
Speaking French (or another foreign language)	Hearing

2. Gamesmanship

BY STEPHEN POTTER

1 What is gamesmanship? Most difficult of questions to answer briefly. "The art of winning games without actually cheating"—that is my personal "working definition." What is its object? There have been five hundred books written on the subject of games. Five hundred books on play and the tactics of play. Not one on the art of winning.

2 I well remember the gritty floor and the damp roller towels of the changing-room where the idea of writing this book came to me. Yet my approach to the thing had been gradual.

3 There had been much that had puzzled me—I am speaking now of 1928—in the tension of our games of ping-pong at the Meynells'. Before that there had been the ardours and endurances of friendly lawn tennis at the Farjeons' house near Forest Hill, where Farjeon had wrought such havoc among so many visitors, by his careful construction of a "home court," by the use he made of the net with the unilateral sag, or with a back line at the hawthorn end so nearly, yet not exactly, six inches wider than the back line at the sticky end. There had been a great deal of hard thinking on both sides during the wavering tide of battle, ending slightly in my favour, of the prolonged series of golf games between E. Lansbury and myself.

4 But it was in that changing-room after a certain game of lawn tennis in 1931 that the curtain was lifted, and I began to see. In those days I used to play lawn tennis for a small but progressive London college—Birkbeck, where I lectured. It happened that my partner at that time was C. Joad, the celebrated gamesman, who in his own sphere is known as metaphysician and educationist. Our opponents were usually young men from the larger colleges, competing against us not only with the advantage of age but also with a decisive advantage in style. They would throw the service ball very high in the modern manner: the backhands, instead of being played from the navel, were played, in fact, on the backhand, weight on right foot, in the exaggerated copybook style of the time—a method of play which

GAMESMANSHIP: from *Gamesmanship* by Stephen Potter. Reprinted by permission of Henry Holt and Company, Inc., and by permission of Rupert Hart-Davis, Ltd., London.

tends to reduce all games, as I believe, to a barrack-square drill by numbers; but, nevertheless, of acknowledged effectiveness.

5 In one match we found ourselves opposite a couple of particularly tall and athletic young men of this type from University College. We will call them Smith and Brown. The knockup showed that, so far as play was concerned, Joad and I, playing for Birkbeck, had no chance. U.C. won the toss. It was Smith's service, and he cracked down a cannon ball to Joad which moved so fast that Joad, while making some effort to suggest by his attitude that he had thought the ball was going to be a fault, nevertheless was unable to get near with his racket, which he did not even attempt to move. Score: fifteen-love. Service to me. I had had time to gauge the speed of this serve, and the next one did, in fact, graze the edge of my racket frame. Thirty-love. Now Smith was serving again to Joad—who this time, as the ball came straight towards him, was able, by grasping the racket firmly with both hands, to receive the ball on the strings, whereupon the ball shot back to the other side and volleyed into the stop netting near the ground behind Brown's feet.

6 Now here comes the moment on which not only this match, but so much of the future of British sport was to turn. Score: forty-love. Smith at S^1 is about to cross over to serve to me (at P). When Smith gets to a point (K) *not less than one foot and not more than two feet* beyond the centre of the court (I know now what I only felt then— that timing is everything in this gambit), Joad (standing at J^2) called across the net, in an even tone:

"Kindly say clearly, please, whether the ball was in or out."

7 Crude to our ears, perhaps. A Stone Age implement. But beautifully accurate gamesmanship for 1931. For the student must realise that these two young men were both in the highest degree charming, well-mannered young men, perfect in their sportsmanship and behaviour. Smith (at point K) stopped dead.

SMITH: I'm so sorry—I *thought* it was out. (*The ball had hit the back netting twelve feet behind him before touching the ground.*) But what did you think, Brown?

BROWN: I *thought* it was out—but do let's have it again.

JOAD: No, I don't want to have it again. I only want you to say clearly, if you will, whether the ball is in or out.

8 There is nothing more putting off to young university players than a slight suggestion that their etiquette or sportsmanship is in question. How well we know this fact, yet how often we forget to make use of it. Smith sent a double fault to me, and another double fault to Joad. He did not get in another ace service till halfway through the third set of a match, which incidentally we won.

9 That night I thought hard and long. Could not this simple gambit of Joad's be extended to include other aspects of the game—to include all games? For me, it was the birth of gamesmanship.

Comment

Mr. Potter's triumph is largely a matter of establishing the humorous tone. The author assumes that his reader is quite capable of seeing the joke. The first element in the joke is the pseudo-scholarly attitude of the author toward "Gamesmanship." Potter addresses himself to the subject with the exaggerated respect of a scientist writing an important process exposition. His story of how the idea came to him parodies the unduly serious literature commemorating scientific discovery. Intimacy with the audience is established by the casual mention of his friends, his occupation, and the game of tennis with Smith and Brown. The confession of fraud implicit in gamesmanship also invites the reader to connive with the games-men against high-minded young men whose will to win is ruined by the imputation of unsportsmanship conduct.

Analysis and Composition

1. Compare this essay with Example VI A2 with reference to:
   a. Purpose
   b. Structure
   c. Style
   d. Personality of the author
2. Compare the humor of this essay with that of the essay by Russell Lynes (Example III C2).
3. Compare the personality revealed in this essay with those revealed in "Book Learning" and in "Quirks" (Examples IV B1 and B2). In your opinion which essay is the most amusing? Give reasons for your answer.
4. To what extent is this essay British in its idiom? In your opinion does

this British flavor make it more or less attractive to an American audience?

5. Comedy has been defined as "painless incongruity." Analyze this definition and decide whether this essay fulfills the requirements of the definition.

6. Find five humorous expressions in this essay and comment on the suggestions each expression conveys.

7. Show how the reader must imagine the tone of voice in which the narrator is "speaking" in order to understand the meaning of the essay.

8. Reread the introduction to Section VII and then decide whether or not this essay combines the structure of an historical process exposition and the style and tone of an informal essay.

9. Write a personal essay of about 750 words on one of the topics listed below. Attempt to develop the topic in your own style.

Huckstership, or the art of advertising

Classmanship, or the art of attending class without being present

Junior promsmanship, or how to appear like a Man of the World

Borrowmanship, or how to acquire things without actually stealing

Fencemanship, or how to argue every side of the case without coming to a conclusion

Bookmanship, or how to refer to books without bothering to read them

Freshmanship, or the art of appearing too young to accept responsibility

Datesmanship, or how to spend a pleasant evening without expense

3. Talking (and Singing) of the Nordic Man

BY HILAIRE BELLOC

I

Behold, my child, the Nordic man,
And be as like him as you can;
His legs are long, his mind is slow,
His hair is lank and made of tow.

II

And here we have the Alpine Race:
Oh! What a broad and foolish face!
His skin is of a dirty yellow.
He is a most unpleasant fellow.

TALKING (AND SINGING) OF THE NORDIC MAN: by permission of A. D. Peters, London.

III

The most degraded of them all
Mediterranean we call.
His hair is crisp, and even curls,
And he is saucy with the girls.

1 This translation is my own. I offer it with diffidence, for I recognize that it does not reproduce the deep organ tones of the original. But it gives the substance of that fine poem, and it is only with the substance—I mean that description of The Race which it conveys—that I have here to deal.

2 I heard so much about the Nordic Man in these last few months that I was moved to collect recently a great mass of information upon him and to coordinate it. Upon the Alpine Man and the Mediterranean Man I am not so erudite; nor is it indeed to any great purpose that I should be—for they are clearly inferior. But the Nordic Man is worth anybody's trouble; and here is what I have found out about him.

3 He is the Conqueror and the Adventurer. He is the Lawgiver and the essentially Moral Man. He arranges the world as it should be arranged. He does everything for his own good and for the good of others. He is a natural Leader. Even those who hate him, fear him; all respect him. The Alpine Man sits sullenly at his feet awaiting his orders; the Mediterranean Man flies in terror from his face.

4 But it is not enough to learn these general characters in the Nordic Man, pleasing though they are. No sound biologist could be content until he knew something intimate of his origin and habits; where he may be found, what he does, and how to tell him at sight.

5 This, then, is what I have found about the Nordic Man. I have space only for the most salient points, but I hope to complete the picture in detail when I shall have leisure to write my book on the species. It will be fully illustrated and will have a very complete Index.

6 The Nordic Man is born either in the West End of London or in a pleasant country house, standing in its own parklike grounds. That is the general rule; he is, however, sometimes born in a parsonage and rather more frequently in a Deanery or a Bishop's Palace, or a Canon's house in a Close. Some of this type have been born in North Oxford; but none (that I can discover) in the provincial manufacturing towns, and certainly none east of Charing Cross or south of the river.

7 The Nordic Man has a nurse to look after him while he is a baby, and she has another domestic at her service. He has a night and a day nursery, and he is full of amusing little tricks which endear him to his parents as he grows through babyhood to childhood.

8 Towards the age of ten or eleven, the Nordic Man goes to a preparatory school, the headmaster of which is greatly trusted by the Nordic Man's parents, especially by the Nordic Man's mother. He early learns to Play the Game, and is also grounded in the elements of Good Form, possibly the Classics and even, exceptionally, some modern tongue. He plays football and cricket; usually, but not always, he is taught to swim.

9 Thence the Nordic Man proceeds to what is called a Public School, where he stays till he is about eighteen. He then goes either to Oxford or Cambridge, or into the Army. He does not stay long in the Army, while from the University he proceeds either to a profession (such as the Bar, or writing advertisements) or to residence upon his estate. This last he can only do if his father dies early.

10 The Nordic Man lives in comfort and even luxury through manhood; he shoots, he hunts, he visits the South of France, he plays bridge. He hates the use of scent; he changes for dinner into a special kind of clothes every day. He is extremely particular about shaving, and he wears his hair cut short and even bald. The Nordic does not bother much about Religion, so when he approaches death he has to distract himself with some hobby, often that of his health. He dies of all sorts of things, but more and more of the cancer; after his death his sons, nephews, or cousins take up the role of the Nordic Man and perpetuate the long and happy chain.

11 Such is the life story of the Nordic Man. I have only given it in its broadest lines, and have left out a great many subsections; but what I have said will be sufficient to indicate places in which he is to be surprised and the kind of things which you will there find him doing. As for his character, which lies at the root of all this great performance, that is less easily described, for one might as well attempt to describe a colour or a smell; but I can attempt some indications of it.

12 The Nordic Man dislikes all cruelty to animals, and is himself kind to them in the following scale: first the dog, then the horse, then the cat, then birds, and so on till you get to insects, after which he stops caring. Microbes, oddly enough, he detests. He will treat them in the most callous manner.

13 In the matter of wine the Nordic Man is divided; you cannot predicate of him that he will drink it, or that if he drinks it he will know what it is. But in the matter of whisky you may safely say that it is his standby, save for a certain subsection of him who dare not touch it. These stand apart and are savage to their fellows.

14 The Nordic Man is very reserved, save in the matter of speech-making. He hates to betray an emotion, but he hates still more the complete concealment of it. He has therefore established a number of conventions whereby it may be known when he is angry, pleased, or what not; but he has no convention for fear, for he is never afraid. This reminds me that the Nordic Man despises conflict with lethal weapons unless it be against the enemies of his country; but he delights in watching, and will sometimes himself practise, conflict conducted with stuffed gloves. As for fighting with his feet, he would not dream of it; nor does he ever bite.

15 The Nordic Man is generous and treats all men as his equals, especially those whom he feels to be somewhat inferior in rank and wealth. This is a very beautiful trait in the Nordic Man, and causes him to believe that he is everywhere beloved. On the other hand, the Nordic Man prefers to live with those richer than himself. The Nordic Man detests all ostentation in dress, and detests even more the wearing of cheap clothes. He loves it to be known that his clothes were costly. No Nordic Man wears a made-up tie.

16 The Nordic Man boasts that he is not addicted to the Arts, and here he is quite right; but he is an excellent collector of work done by the inferior Mediterranean race, and is justly proud of the rare successes of his own people in this field. In the same way the Nordic Man will tell you with emphasis that he cannot write. Herein he tells the truth. Yet, oddly enough, he is convinced that no one has ever been able to write except Nordic Men; and this article of faith he applies particularly to True Poetry, which (he conceives) can only be inspired in his own tongue.

17 The Nordic Man does everything better than anybody else does it, and himself proclaims this truth unceasingly; but where he particularly shines is in the administration of justice. For he will condemn a man to imprisonment or death with greater rapidity than will the member of any other race. In giving judgment he is, unlike the rest of the human species, unmoved by any bias of class or blood, let alone of personal interest. On this account his services as a magistrate are sought far and wide throughout the world, and his life is

never in danger save from disappointed suitors or those who have some imaginary grievance against him.

18 The Nordic Man is a great traveller. He climbs mountains; he faces with indifference tropical heat and arctic cold. He is a very fine fellow.

19 I must conclude by telling you all that I am not obtaining these details from any personal observations, as the part of the country in which I live has very few Nordic Men, and most of them are away during the greater part of the year staying either in the houses of other Nordic Men or in resorts of ritual pleasure upon the Continent. But I have had the whole thing described to me most carefully by a friend of mine who was for a long time himself a Nordic Man, until he had the misfortune to invest in British Dyes and crashed. He guarantees me the accuracy of his description.

. . . .

20 Immediately after I had written those few words you have just read about the Nordic Man, I received a great quantity of letters from—I was about to write "from all quarters of the world," when I suddenly remembered that there would not be time for that, and that the lie would stick out—a great quantity of letters, I say, from all sorts of people. It shows at once how widely I am read, and what interest my handling of this great subject aroused.

21 Some of these letters are abusive, some laudatory, some critical; all three categories are to me sacred when the writers have the courage to give name and address, and I would not divulge to the public the confidences they contain. But I think I may be allowed to answer here such correspondents as refused to give name and address. They will serve as examples to show how little the true doctrine of the Nordic Man has, so far, penetrated the masses.

22 Of course it will soak through at last, as all great scientific truths do—such as the doctrine of Natural Selection and the peculiar properties of the stuff called Ether, not to speak of Magna Charta, which even the poorest scavenger in the street today reveres as the origin of his freedom.

23 But so far this new discovery of the Nordic Man has not spread as it should have done.

24 Thus the first of my correspondents (who signs "Gallio" and gives no address but Brighton) is puzzled by the apparent aptitude of the Romans in their best period for administration and govern-

ment, and even, in a primitive fashion, for war. He admits that all this may be much exaggerated, and from what he has seen of the Romans (he was down among them lately) he cannot believe all he hears of their ancestors. But still (he supposes) there must be a solid kernel of truth in it; for after all, the name "Roman" was given to a great number of institutions—including the Empire itself—and he asks me—rather crudely—how this was possible if the Mediterranean Race were as vile as our greatest authorities have discovered it to be? It is odd that the simple answer to this difficulty has not occurred to the writer. It is that those who governed the Empire, and led the armies, called "Roman" were Nordic. This could be proved in several ways, but all of them might be open to objection save the unanswerable one that if these men had not been Nordic they could not have succeeded as they did. The Scipios, the Julian House, Hadrian—to cite at random—were manifestly and necessarily Nordic: for men do not act as they acted unless they are of purebred Nordic stock.

25 The same is true of other manifestations of intelligence and vigour in Mediterranean countries. Thus the Italians and even the Greeks have left a considerable body of remarkable literature both in prose and in verse, and in the case of Italy, we have even quite modern examples of literary excellence—at least, so I am assured by those who are acquainted with the idioms of the inferior races. But upon examination it will always be found that the authors, though using a base medium, were Nordic. The committee which we collectively call by the mythological term "Homer," and which drew up and passed certainly the *Iliad* and possibly the *Odyssey,* were clearly Nordic in composition. Catullus was as Nordic as he could be. The Nordic character of Aristotle is a commonplace. Dante was Nordic. So was Leopardi.

26 Take any outstanding Italian or other Mediterranean name and you will find upon close examination that the man to whom it is attached was of the Nordic type: Napoleon Buonaparte occurs at once to the mind.

27 Another correspondent has come upon the thing from a different angle. He knows enough of the great new discovery to understand the term "cephalic index," and he has had his own cephalic index taken by a cephalogian who practises in Ealing. He did so under the impression, of course, that he was of sound Nordic stock; but to his horror the measurements have come out an extreme form of Alpine! He asks me what he is to do about it? I can assure him (and, though I do not claim to be an expert in Moronovitalogy, I am fairly well

up in my elements) that his anxiety is groundless. Though, of course, skull measurement is the basis of the three great divisions, yet if a man have Nordic qualities clearly apparent in his birth and culture, these easily predominate over what might be the natural tendencies of brachycephalic humanity. It would be a fine state of things, indeed, if we had to rule out of the Nordic excellence all those great men of the English past who, so far as we can judge from their portraits, had something flat-headed about them.

28 A third correspondent—who signs her letter "Onyx"—is troubled about her children. There are five: three charming boys and two delightful girls. She has measured their heads with her husband's callipers (he is an architect in full employment), and she finds that her eldest and her youngest are quite unmistakably Mediterranean; her second eldest painfully Alpine, only her second youngest clearly Nordic; while the one in the middle, a boy (by name, she tells me, Ethelred), seems to be a strange mixture of all three.

29 I cannot reply personally to this correspondent, as she does not give an address; but I trust that these lines will meet her eye. I would have her note that in the first place the skulls of children are no index to the shape they will have when they fossilize in mature years; and next, that even if these varied types appear in her family, it is not remarkable, for all three types are present in England. Moreover, she may have travelled.

30 A fourth correspondent, a clergyman, I fancy, who signs "Scholasticus," writes me a long rigmarole (I cannot call it by any politer name), in which he calls the whole theory subversive of sound morals, and asks whether we are to believe that man "created in the image of his Maker, and responsible to his Creator," etc., etc., etc.

31 Really, to this kind of thing there is only one answer. Science does not clash with religion; it clashes with nothing except unreason and untruth. Science is simply organized knowledge, based upon experiment and accurate measurement over so wide a field as to be established with absolute certitude. Now Science clearly proves that these three races, the Nordic, the Alpine, and the Mediterranean, exist side by side in Europe, and affirms that the Nordic (to which all scientific men belong) possesses those qualities upon which alone men can pride themselves. Science demonstrates the defects and vices of the Alpine, and the baseness and degradation of the Mediterranean stock. If my reverend critic likes to knock his head against a stone

wall, I cannot help it. But it seems to me an extraordinary thing to find any man possessed of enough education to write consecutively, opposing (at this time of day) established scientific truths in the name of hypothetical principles, the figments of imagination and vanity. His "Creator," "image," "responsibility," are all of them mere words; not one of them has been established by accurate and repeated measurement, nor have they one single experiment conducted under scientific conditions to support them; while on the other side we have the unanimous agreement of Meyerbath, Karsowitz, Brahmsohn, Farrago, Cent-Six, Blauwvenfeld, Tabouche, Smith of Milwaukee (Hamilcar Q. Smith—perhaps the greatest authority of all), Van Houten, and his famous relative Klotz—but why should I prolong the list? My objector will look in vain through all the distinguished ranks of modern science to find a single name supporting his ridiculous assumptions of a "God," "Free Will," and what not. All agree that our characters and actions proceed from a cephalic index, and all are agreed upon the relative values of the three main races of Europe.

32 P.S. To my correspondent "Tiny," who has also given no address, I must reply in this brief postscript. No, the facial angle, as measured from the point of the chin tangentially, the parietal curve of the forehead, and from the cusp of the left nostril to the base of the corresponding earlobe, is no longer the criterion of character. I thought I had made that plain. Thirty-five years ago, when I was a boy, all scientists were agreed that the facial angle was the one certain and only test of moral attitude and intellectual power; but that opinion is now universally abandoned, and the facial angle is replaced by the cephalic index.

33 So put that in your pipe and smoke it.

Comment

The reader who is sensitive to point of view (see Sections XIII and XIV) will recognize at once that Belloc is presenting his essay in a double focus. The narrator—Belloc's dummy—is an imaginary pedant who has collected a vast amount of data on the Nordic man. His learning, tact, and ability to reason leave much to be desired. His misinterpretation of the poem (¶1) and his confession of prejudice against the lesser breeds of Alpine and Mediterranean man prepare us for a double point of view: The author intends us to grasp both the pedant's point of view and his own point of view on the pedant. This double impression is conveyed chiefly by the ironical tone of the recital. The pedant's facts about the Nordic man do not support his admiration for his subject, and his praise is damning. The unconscious irony of phrases like "nor does he ever bite" (¶14) and "Microbes, oddly enough, he detests" (¶12) convict the narrator of invincible ignorance.

Beginning with paragraph 20 Belloc introduces a number of fictitious letters. These letters offer admirable arguments against racist theory, and each objection is answered by an outrageous sophistry. Thus to the objection that the Romans were great, but not Nordic, the narrator replies, "If these men had not been Nordic they could not have succeeded as they did." The "Science clearly proves" sophistry in paragraph 31 parodies the language and tone of pseudoscientists, who were described with the same humorous contempt by Anthony Standen in Example II J.

The complexity in point of view is matched by a complexity of tone. At times Belloc is amused, at times he is satirical, at times he lets his sense of humor get the better of him, as in paragraph 31, where his catalogue of scientists appears to be mere self-indulgence in ridicule. But complexity is exactly what one would expect in the treatment of such a subject. The concept of the Nordic man is funny, vulgar, and potentially dangerous at the same time. In a man like Belloc it evokes mixed feelings of intellectual disgust and laughter. But in the end, as at the beginning, laughter prevails.

Analysis and Composition

1. Paragraph 1 contains several attacks on pretense. There is a thrust at mock humility in offering the supposed translation "with diffidence," and at ritualistic reverence for poetry in "the deep organ tones of the original." Point out several other objects of satire in paragraphs 2-10.

2. Reread Aldous Huxley's essay in Section V and decide to what extent the generalized picture of the Nordic man in paragraphs 2-10 of Belloc's essay is a caricature of the upper-class Englishman. Give reasons for your answer.

3. In a composition of 500 words decide whether the character of the Nordic man described in paragraphs 11-19 is purely fanciful.

4. Belloc develops his impressions chiefly by irony. While his fictitious writer seems to praise the Nordic man, the reader is aware of the author's amusement at and contempt for the Nordic man. Belloc seems to take over the story from his appointed spokesman. Decide whether this double focus (a) enriches the essay or (b) merely confuses the point of view.

5. Reread the comment on fallacies in Section XI and then decide what fallacies are presented by the fictitious writer in paragraphs 24-26.
6. Consult a standard reference on anthropology to discover whether the cephalic index—"skull measurement is the basis of the three great divisions [of race]"—is fanciful or scientifically acceptable. In what sense does Belloc intend his readers to regard the so-called "cephalic index"? Give reasons for your answer.
7. Analyze paragraphs 30-31 carefully to determine the tone of the passage. Then in separate paragraphs of 250 words each state
   a. What you feel the narrator thinks
   b. What you feel Belloc himself thinks about Scholasticus' objections
8. Paragraph 32 contains an important, but indirect, comment on paragraph 31. Thus in paragraph 32 the fictitious narrator says that scientific criteria change with the times. But in paragraph 31 the same narrator answers "Scholasticus" on the basis of the presumably unchangeable scientific accuracy of the cephalic index. Decide whether or not Belloc intends the reader to draw the conclusion that the fictitious writer is arguing fallaciously. If he has intended the reader to see a fallacy, what fallacy is he exposing?
9. In view of the extensive reasoning developed throughout this essay, would you classify it
   a. As an argumentative essay
   b. As a personal essay
   c. As an argumentative and a personal essay
   Give reasons for your answer.
10. In your own manner write a satirical essay on one of the following topics:

Topic	*Fictitious Narrator*
The advantages of Florida	A member of the Florida Chamber of Commerce
The rugged individualist	A self-made man
The profession of journalism	A gossip columnist
The collegian	A professor emeritus
The successful business man	A man who failed in business
The 100 per cent American	A Daughter of the American Revolution
The American on vacation	A waitress
The Texan	A Californian
The Californian	A Texan
The New Yorker	A farmer
The farmer	A salesman
A cosmopolitan	A provincial

STYLE—A SUMMARY

Our study of the informal essay has underlined the important connection between personality and style. Each of the three preceding essays serves to remind us that, at bottom, style is so intimately linked to the writer's personality that the words *style* and *personality* may be used almost interchangeably. We shall have more to say on this subject shortly. Before we do, however, it might be well to summarize here the various ways in which we have studied style throughout this book. (See the Index also.)

In Section I, style, the fourth element of rhetoric, was defined as the effective use of language in the composition as a whole. It was stated too that one measure of a good style was a realistic writing situation, that is, a particular purpose, occasion, and subject.

Throughout Sections II-VII the student was asked to analyze the diction, that is, the denotation and connotation of words in the contexts of the sentence and the paragraph.

The analysis and composition exercises also developed the significance of tone, metaphor, rhythm, sentence unity, variety, and emphasis. The importance of semantics in developing an exact style was treated in Section VI.

In Section VIII the principles of style, considered as an extension of arrangement, were explained in connection with "Perennial Adolescence." The general exercises in this section referred the student to style in the examples in Sections II-VII.

The principles of style explained in Section VIII were illustrated throughout Sections IX-XII. In Sections XII-XIV increasing emphasis was placed on the artistic features of style, that is, on tone, irony, rhythm, and figures of speech. Symbolism was discussed in Section XIV.

This treatment of style was designed to keep the student constantly aware of the mutual interdependence of the manner of expression and the writer's purpose, subject, and occasion, that is, the realistic writing situation. Style is an integral part of the whole business of composition, not a veneer the writer has added to a subject, a theme, and a method of development.

Thus when we say that a style is clear we mean that the diction, the sentences, the paragraphs contribute directly to the development of the writer's theme or purpose on a given occasion in a given context. When we say that the style is vigorous we mean that the diction, sentences, and paragraphs are not only clear and coherent but stimulating. When we say that a style is interesting we mean that the diction, sentences, and paragraphs appeal to the imagination as well as to the intellect and the emotions—again in the light of the purpose, subject, and occasion.

Clearness, vigor, and interest are the essential elements of style. Hence many other terms used throughout the comments and analyses of this book—terms like tone, rhythm, metaphor, and irony (and other figures of speech)—are meaningful only in relation to clarity, vigor, and interest.

Tone, for instance, refers to the attitude of the writer toward his material (serious, ironical, flippant) and toward his readers (magisterial, apologetic, familiar). Insofar as tone explains the author's understanding of his subject, it relates to the stylistic note of clarity; insofar as it establishes rapport between the writer and his audience, it relates to the notes of vigor and interest.

Rhythm is the pattern of stress and pause in sentences, and the cadence of paragraphs. It is a device which helps to secure clarity by suiting the sound to the sense, to secure vigor by stressing the climactic words, and to secure interest by producing a varied effect.

Metaphor, irony (a statement implying its opposite), and other figurative expressions are means of arousing feeling (vigor) and of exciting the imagination (interest). Their importance in these two regards has been continuously stressed, as the exercises will attest. (See especially Section XIII, General Exercises B2 and B3 and C1 and C2.)

Symbolism, a device of the imagination by which an action or setting is endowed with significance other than its literal meaning, contributes to vigor and interest and, indirectly, to clarity. (See comment on Section XIV, Example 1.)

It is evident from this summary that style is determined by the writer's purpose, subject, and occasion, and that it involves the right combination of words, sentences, and paragraphs in a whole composition designed to achieve the writer's purpose relative to a given subject and a given occasion.

PERSONALITY AND STYLE

Now it must be asked how style is related to personality.

The source of a composition is the author himself. He is its efficient cause, the man who composes his thoughts according to a plan, the man who selects the words and breathes life into a composition. The author (as cause) must somehow express his own personality in the composition (the effect). (See Section VI.) Hence when we say that a good style is clear, vigorous, and interesting, we are assuming that these qualities in a composition must also be found in the cause— the writer. If the writer does not possess clear ideas, vigorous feelings, and vivid images, these elements cannot appear in his composition. Ultimately it is the writer's personality that shapes the style of a composition.

Hence it is most important for the student to understand the connection between personality and style because (1) it brings him closer to the true cause of good writing and (2) it reveals the necessity not only of developing his technical skill with language but also of cultivating his own personality.

In establishing the connection between personality and style in writing we shall proceed to show (1) that a writer's personality is equivalent to his thought, (2) that his thought and style are one, and (3) that the ultimate basis of a good style is sincerity, self-knowledge, and continuous mental development.

PERSONALITY IN LITERATURE EQUALS THOUGHT

The first proposition—a writer's personality is equivalent to his thought—is clearly implied in the definition of personality and of thought. By *personality* we mean the totality of an individual's characteristics, summed up by the distinctive quality of "blood, brain, and spirit" that makes Newman, for instance, a gracious Christian humanist and Mark Twain a sophisticated midwestern rustic. By *thought* we mean the total mental activity of the writer, his sense perceptions, intuitions, feelings, and reasoning power.

The range of a writer's sense experience, the actual amount of things felt, seen, heard, are all parts of his *thought*. Hence Conrad's awareness of the sights and sounds of the jungle, O'Faolain's canny ear for dialogue, Churchill's sense of the rhythm of an English phrase contribute to the integrity or wholeness of the author's thought. So too intuition, the power to understand without being able to explain how one understands, is another phase of the general term *thought*. Thus Cotton's intuitive sense of adventure in "High Lonesome Place," Potter's intuitive sense of humor in "Gamesmanship," Saint-Exupéry's intuitive sense of disintegration in "Evacuation" are also most important elements of the writer's mental attitude or thought. Similarly feeling or emotion—the power to rage, to pity, to love, to fear—helps to form the totality of thought. How much a writer's emotions are part of his mental life may be realized by attempting to separate the thought of R. M. Hutchins from his reforming zeal, that of Churchill from his veneration of the European past, that of Lincoln from his laconic love of freedom. Sheer intelligence, which implies a vast stock of knowledge and the ability to use that knowledge, also has its important role in shaping the writer's total thought. The philosophical knowledge of Plato, Weigel, Samuel, and Malik; the ripe historical learning of Toynbee, Morison, Freeman, and Ward; the judicial wit of Learned Hand and Thomas Woodlock; the dialectical brilliance and scholarship of Aldous Huxley, A. N. Whitehead, and Jacques Barzun—all these mental qualities are unequivocally the thought of the men who possess them. Thus thought, understood as a mental attitude composed of sense perceptions, intuitions, emotions, rational capacity, is equivalent to the writer's literary personality. Thought taken in its full sense supplies that distinctive tone or resonance, that quality of "blood, brain, and spirit" which we have defined as personality.

THOUGHT EQUALS STYLE OR MANNER OF EXPRESSION

Today it is generally assumed that thought and expression are one in all prose save purely scientific or impersonal discourse, where the writer is merely a recorder rather than a thinker. "It is hardly necessary to adduce proof that the identity of style and meaning is today firmly established," writes W. K. Wimsatt in his study of *The Prose Style of Samuel Johnson*. Mr. Wimsatt's comment is amply supported not only in special studies of individual authors but also in general considerations of the problems of rhetoric. Thus Bonamy Dobrée in *Modern Prose Style* reminds us that the essence of a good book is the personality of the author. This personality, he says, is displayed by his tone—the sound of his voice.

> It is this voice which we roughly call style, and however much a writer may ignore his personality, even seek to conceal it, he cannot disguise his voice, his style, unless he is deliberately writing a parody. It is here that the truth will out: *Le style, c'est l'homme même* (Style is the man himself).

Elsewhere Dobrée insists that style is not an ornament but knowledge or thought. A style, he writes, is:

> the *sense of one's self,* the knowledge of what one wants to say and the saying of it in the most fitting words.

The same concept of style is the burden of Herbert Read's *English Prose Style*. In the concluding chapter Mr. Read points out that the ultimate perfection of prose style is "the sustained power of reason." Read's understanding of reason is similar to the definition of thought given above.

> . . . by reason I do not mean ratiocination or rationality, but . . . the widest evidence of the senses, and of all processes and instincts developed in the history of man. It is the sum total of awareness, ordained and ordered to some specific end or object of attention.

This power of reason is the unifying principle of great prose. Hence, he maintains, thought and style are not separable and distinct virtues

> but two aspects of one reality. The thought seems to mold and accentuate the style, the style reacts to mold and accentuate the thought. It is one process of creation, one art, one aim.

Similarly in *Modern Rhetoric* Brooks and Warren argue that, while we may *distinguish* mentally between content (thought) and expression (style), "content and form never *exist* in separation." By this is meant that ideally, before actual composition, we may think of thought and expression separately; but, really, that is, after a composition has been written, we know the content only in and through the form in which it is presented, and the form only in its relation to a given body of content.

Such modern views on the relationship of thought and expression, personality and style, are derived from a long tradition of literary theory. The theory was certainly known to the Greek philosophers, who used one word, *logos,* to denote both the thought itself and the word that expresses the thought. The idea has been powerfully reaffirmed in various situations by many critics. Two of the most eloquent and luminous expositions of the theory occur in essays by Cardinal Newman and Thomas De Quincey, both of whom were keenly aware of the dangers of dividing man into various compartments. Because the same tendency to compartmentalize man exists today the remarks of Newman and De Quincey are still relevant in argument, just as they are admirable for their own sake.

In the "Essay on Literature" included in *The Idea of a University* Newman wrote:

> Thought and speech are inseparable from each other. Matter and expression are parts of one; style is a thinking out into language. . . . When we can separate light and illumination, life and motion, the convex and concave of a curve, then will it be possible for thought to tread speech underfoot, and to hope to do without it—then will it be conceivable that the vigorous and fertile intellect should renounce its own double, its instrument of expression, and the channel of its speculations and emotions. . . .

The intimate connection between the writer's thought, his "blood, brain, and spirit," and his style receives even greater emphasis in an eloquent paragraph later in the same essay.

> [A great author] writes passionately, because he feels keenly; forcibly, because he conceives vividly; he sees too clearly to be vague; he is too serious to be otiose; he can analyze his subject, and therefore he is rich; he embraces it as a whole and in its parts, and therefore he is consistent; he has a firm hold of it, and therefore he is luminous. When his imagination wells up, it overflows in ornament; when his heart is touched, it thrills along his verse. He always has the right word for the right idea, and never a word too much. If he is brief, it is because few words suffice; when he is lavish of them, still each word has its mark, and aids, not embarrasses, the vigorous march of his elocution. He expresses what all feel, but all cannot say; and his sayings pass into proverbs among his people, and his phrases become household words and idioms of their daily speech, which is tessellated with the rich fragments of his language, as we see in foreign lands the marbles of Roman grandeur worked into the walls and pavements of modern palaces.

Similarly De Quincey, commenting on Wordsworth's phrase—"style is the incarnation of thoughts"—reminds us that:

> The truth [of this phrase] is apparent on consideration: for, if language were merely a dress, then you could separate the two; you could lay the thoughts on the left hand, the language on the right. But, generally speaking, you can no more deal thus with poetic thoughts than you can with soul and body. The union is too subtle, the intertexture too ineffable—each coexisting not merely *with* the other, but each *in* and *through* the other. An image, for instance, a single word, often enters

into a thought as a constituent part. In short, the two elements are not united as a body with a separate dress, but as a mysterious incarnation. And thus, in what proportion are the thoughts subjective, in that same proportion does the very essence [of the thought] become identical with the expression, and the style become confluent with the matter.

If the interconnections of personality and thought, and thought and style, may be seen in all literature that is of a subjective or personal nature, as the above quotations from Newman and De Quincey suggest, it follows that the writer, particularly the student writer, must strive to develop his personality and his thought. He may do this by striving for sincerity, for self-knowledge, and for self-development.

THE BASIS OF A GOOD STYLE

Sincerity in writing is both a moral and an intellectual quality. To be sincere means simply to be oneself. We are what we are; we cannot be someone else. No amount of pretense can disguise our given temperament, our native endowment of wit and imaginative power, or the present state of our knowledge. We cannot write with vigor and conviction what we half-heartedly believe or imperfectly comprehend. That is why reproductive imitation, mere parroting, is instinctively rejected by readers. Good writing, even when it is not profoundly individual, even when it leans for support on the example of others, is always tested and shaped in the writer's own soul.

Sincerity is based on self-knowledge. "Know thyself," Socrates' simple motto, sums up the work of a lifetime. But how do you know yourself? You know yourself by studying yourself with the same care that you study others, by examining your conscience, your tastes, your actions, your emotional responses. Norms or models are most important in this study. We are all inclined to make flattering judgments about ourselves. Many a sincere but deluded man has magnified his delusion by taking Sidney's advice to look into his heart and write, with the disastrous result that he looked, he wrote, and produced sincere nonsense.

No one is his own measuring rod. You need models of excellence to help estimate yourself objectively. Hence the paradox—you come to know yourself by knowing others. You should choose your masters and models wisely. If you measure yourself by the average man you will be satisfied with average results. If you measure yourself by the best men you may never achieve their eminence, but you will not be content with mediocrity. To be discontented with mediocrity is no mean achievement. Hence choose your masters and models wisely, not to imitate them but to imitate their ideals, their standards, their devotion to excellence and to style—that element of their intellectual life which Whitehead calls "the ultimate morality of mind." This is most important, for one grows intellectually into the shape of one's admirations.

To be oneself, to know oneself, it is still necessary to cultivate oneself. How is this done? All your studies, your environment, your friends may contribute to this effort. You cultivate your personality by increasing your knowledge, and knowledge is derived from reading, from thinking, from conversation, from the hard labor of writing, and from intelligent dispute. You cultivate your personality further by discriminating between the values that knowledge provides, and by choosing those values that represent the highest standards of conscience, intelligence, and taste. You cultivate yourself still further by harmonizing these values, and thus achieving integrity—that still loftier harmony of thought and action, feeling and imagination which is the achievement of the free and full personality.

For the student the most practical access to this world of freedom is the wide and discriminating reading of the best authors. Great books—the dialogues of Plato, the immortal *Don Quixote,* the plays of Shakespeare, the poems of Milton, the satires of Pope, the essays of Lamb, the stories of Conrad (the list is endless)—are models of style and personality. When you live in them, and they live in you, you will possess incentives to composition that no formal exercise can supply. For the mind that is rich with wisdom is a motionable mind. It expresses itself as a necessary consequence of its own continuous and endlessly satisfactory reach for and grasp of truth. Just as analysis, arrangement, and style are all necessary parts of composition, so reading, thinking, and writing are all necessary phases in the rhythm of mental *growth.* To cultivate oneself, therefore, is to coordinate these complementary activities. To read the best books, to think earnestly about the problems they propose, to formulate your own ideas on these problems—this activity pursued with order, with enthusiasm, and with perseverance—cannot fail to develop a personality and a style

GENERAL EXERCISES

A

1. Which examples in Sections II-X would you classify as informal essays? Give reasons for your answer.
2. Which examples in Sections II-X would you classify as partly informal and partly formal in style? Give reasons for your answer.
3. Show how R. M. Hutchins in Example XI B2 uses informal style to achieve contact with his audience.
4. In the light of the predominantly personal point of view of the examples in Sections XII and XIII, decide whether a good description or narration is ever formal in tone.
5. "High Lonesome Place" (Example XIV 3) was described as a border-line story, that is, a narrative that might be classified either as a story or as an informal autobiographical essay. After rereading the introduction to Section XIV and the comment on the informal essay in Section XV, decide how you would classify this example. Give reasons for your answer.
6. Decide whether "Lost Retreat" (Section XIII, General Exercise B) may be classified as an informal autobiographical essay as well as a narrative.
7. A number of examples in this book describe places such as Brazil (V A1; XII B3), England (X B), Suburbia (XI A1), New Orleans (XII A2), Yosemite (XII B2), Japan (XII B4), Monterey (XII C2), Africa (XII D), the Hudson River (XIII 2), Arizona (XIII 3), Canada (XIII 4), Colorado (XIII, General Exercise B, and XIV 3), France (XIII, General Exercise C), and the South Pacific (XIV 1). In the course of your study of these and other examples you may have formed a wish to visit one or another of these places. Reread the examples cited above and then write an informal essay of approximately 1000 words on the topic, "An Armchair Traveler."

B

After studying the use of metaphors in each of the essays listed below, write an informal essay of approximately 1000 words on the topic, "Metaphors, the Poetic Part of Composition."

"The Last Question of All" (VI C1)
"The Industrial Revolution in Great Britain" (X B)
"Monterey" (XII C2)
"The Lagoon" (XIV 1)

C

Irony consists in a statement that implies its opposite. Normally irony is conveyed by exaggeration or understatement. After rereading the examples listed below, write an informal essay of approximately 1000 words on the topic, "Irony, a Source of Interest in Composition."

"The Decline of Attention" (II G)
"What Is Science?" (II J)
"What Is a Pedant?" (III A2)
"My Brazilian Expedition" (III B3)
"Apology" (III C1)
"On the Intelligence of Dogs" (IV A2)
"Book Learning" (IV B1)
"Fenimore Cooper's Literary Offenses" (IV D)
"You Can't Hurry in Brazil" (V A1)
"Perennial Adolescence" (VIII)
"The Retort Circumstantial" (XI A3)
"Where Do We Go from Here in Education?" (XI B2)
"The Fur Coat" (XIV 2)
"Gamesmanship" (XV 2)
"Talking (and Singing) of the Nordic Man" (XV 3)

D

1. Reread the examples in Section IV and decide what personal traits are revealed in the style of each selection.
2. Describe the personality revealed in Example D of Section IV and show how this personality is reflected in the style.
3. Reread the examples in Section VII. Decide whether each of these examples, most of which are explicitly scientific in character, reveals the personality of the writer.
4. In an essay of 1000 words compare and contrast the personality and style of the essays by Malik and Bell in Section VIII.

E

In a short essay of approximately 500 words argue for or against each of the following statements:

1. S. E. Morison's style in II D3 and VI A3 reveals a vigorous, scholarly, and urbane personality.
2. Winston Churchill's style in VI C2, in XI B1, and in XIII, General Exercise A, reveals a sanguine, belligerent, and dominating personality.

3. B. I. Bell's style in Section VIII reveals a conservative, classical, and truculent personality.
4. D. S. Freeman's style in IX D reveals a sentimental, old-fashioned, tender personality.
5. H. S. Commager's style in X A reveals a deeply emotional yet scholarly personality.
6. Barbara Ward's style in X C reveals a profoundly intellectual personality, while Jacquetta Hawkes's style in X B reveals a personality with both a scientific and poetic orientation.
7. R. M. Hutchins' style in XI B is curt, challenging, and disciplined.
8. Carl Carmer's style in XIII 2 is vivid and enthusiastic.
9. Antoine de Saint-Exupéry's style in XIII, General Exercise C, indicates a sensitive and brooding personality.
10. Joseph Conrad's style in XIV 1 reveals a profoundly interior orientation, that is, a personality greatly concerned with deep-seated motives.

F

Review the examples you have studied in this book and then determine which writers may be classified under each of the styles listed below. Give reasons for your answer.

1. Humorous	4. Deeply emotional
2. Satirical	5. Intellectual
3. Sentimental	6. Scholarly

G

Which examples in this book seem to lack personality or style? Does this lack of personality render them ineffective?

H

First reread the paragraphs on style in Section VIII and Section XV. Then compile your own anthology of fifty sentences drawn from the examples in this book that best exemplify the principles of good style. Explain briefly your reason for choosing each sentence.

I

Compile your own anthology of the ten shorter selections (under 1500 words) in this book that best exemplify the principles of good style. In 100 words explain your reason for each selection.

J

List three longer selections (over 1500 words) drawn from this book that best exemplify the principles of good style. In 500 words explain your reason for each selection.

K

Use the principles of composition learned in this book to write a personal essay of approximately 3000 words on the theme, "Style Is an Infallible Index of Personality." Be careful to choose as examples of this theme authors with whom you are familiar.

L

Reread the debate on language (Examples XI A2 and A3) and decide, in an essay of approximately 1000 words, whether style is a product of the general language habits of an age and place, or of the individual writer, or of both forces taken together.

Topical Index to Longer Selections

A Rhetoric Case Book *contains 103 selections of which approximately 48 are full enough to be read for their topical interest as well as for the rhetorical principle or type of discourse that they illustrate. Of these 48 longer selections, 36 are "full-length," that is, either complete works (essays and short stories) or continuous and unabridged sections from longer works. These longer selections may be grouped under the following major topics.*

* "Full-length" pieces are indicated by asterisks.

PERSONAL ADVENTURES

FICTION

Author-Title Index

* Full-length selections are marked with asterisks. They are either complete essays and short stories or continuous and unabridged sections from longer works.

Subject Index

Note: Pages in which the chief discussion of a given topic appears are printed in **bold face**. An "ex." indicates either that the reference will be found among the exercises on the page, or that relevant drill exercises follow the reference. Titles of selections—regardless of length—are in *italics*. Subjects that appear in virtually all sections (diction and unity, for instance) are, of course, indexed only when the subject is specifically and particularly treated.

The Schematic Arrangement of A Rhetoric Case Book: PART TWO

	a	b	c	d
VIII THE WHOLE COMPOSITION	Arrangement: unity, coherence, and emphasis pp. 273-85		Style as the final step in arrangement pp. 285-307	Clarity, vigor, and interest in words, sentences, and paragraphs pp. 297-307
IX EXPOSITION OF CHARACTER	Choose a character with definite traits pp. 315, 316-20	Characterize by speech and action pp. 315, 321-25	Aim to present one predominant impression pp. 315, 325-31	Vary order of arrangement to suit the subject pp. 315-16, 332-44
X EXPOSITION OF FACTS AND IDEAS	Begin essay with topic paragraph stating key ideas pp. 350-51, 355-67	Develop complex event by combining forms of discourse pp. 352, 367-79	Develop complex idea by contrasting with opposing idea pp. 353-54, 380-96	In an historical paper coordinate chronological, logical order pp. 354-55, 396-409
XI ARGUMENT AND PERSUASION	In argument arrange proofs under deduction, induction, or analogy. Refute directly or indirectly. pp. 413-19, 428-91	In persuasion emphasize action desired; make proofs motives for action; strive for vigorous style pp. 424-28, 492-524		

OF DISCOURSE